The Collected Works of John Dewey, 1882–1953

D0912481

John Dewey

The Later Works, 1925–1953

Volume 6: 1931–1932

EDITED BY JO ANN BOYDSTON

TEXTUAL EDITOR, ANNE SHARPE

With an Introduction by Sidney Ratner

Southern Illinois University Press

Carbondale

Copyright © 1985, 2008 by the Board of Trustees,
Southern Illinois University
All rights reserved
Printed in the United States of America
Designed by Richard Hendel

The Collected Works of John Dewey

COMMITTEE ON
SCHOLARLY EDITIONS

AN APPROVED EDITION

MODERN LANGUAGE
ASSOCIATION OF AMERICA

Editorial expenses for this edition have been met in part by grants
from the Editions Program of the National Endowment for the
Humanities, an independent Federal agency, and from the John
Dewey Foundation. Publishing expenses have been met in part by
a grant from the John Dewey Foundation.

ISBN-10: 0-8093-1199-2 (cloth: alk. paper)
ISBN-13: 978-0-8093-1199-6 (cloth: alk. paper)
ISBN-10: 0-8093-2816-X (pbk.: alk. paper)
ISBN-13: 978-0-8093-2816-1 (pbk.: alk. paper)

The Library of Congress has cataloged the original issue of this book
as follows:
Dewey, John, 1859–1952.
The later works, 1925–1953.
Vol. 6 has introd. by Sidney Ratner.
Continues The middle works, 1899–1924.
Includes bibliographies and indexes.
CONTENTS: v. 1. 1925—v. 2. 1925–1927—[etc.]—v. 6. 1931–1932.
1. Philosophy—Collected works. I. Boydston, Jo Ann, 1924-. II. Title.
B945.D41 1981 191 80-27285
ISBN 0-8093-1199-2 (v. 6)

The paper used in this publication meets the minimum requirements
of American National Standard for Information Sciences—Perma-
nence of Paper for Printed Library Materials, ANSI Z39.48-1992. ∞

Contents

Introduction
By Sidney Ratner

John Dewey and the American people confronted a series of economic, political, and social crises in 1931–1932 flowing from the Great Depression of 1929 and the early 1930s. At the same time, cultural life (philosophy, the arts, and the sciences) moved on, in some cases relatively unchanged, in others altered in a revolutionary or counter-revolutionary manner. The many essays, book reviews, statements, and other miscellaneous items in this volume express Dewey's thoughts on a wide variety of subjects that he and many others thought important at that time. These pieces may be loosely grouped under several headings, e.g., philosophy (in a technical sense), psychology, economics, political science, sociology, and education. I shall single out only a few important subjects in each category for analysis.

Among the philosophical essays, *Context and Thought* stands out as a brilliant analysis of the importance of the background of beliefs, things, persons, and relations that are taken for granted in an adequate understanding of any set of words, symbols, and formulated thoughts on which a reader's or speaker's attention is focused. Dewey shows how errors of an oversimplified analytical philosophy and an unnecessary philosophical organic synthesis arise from their neglect of context. Here he anticipates one of Wittgenstein's most original insights in *Philosophical Investigations* (1953); the parallelism in some respects has only recently been discovered by Richard Rorty in *Consequences of Pragmatism: Essays, 1972–1980* (1982).

In the essay "George Herbert Mead as I Knew Him," and in two Miscellany statements, Dewey expresses deep affection and esteem for Mead as a "seminal mind of the very first order," a champion of pragmatism with his own original insights and developments, and as an intimate, highly prized friend for some forty years. Dewey acknowledged generously how much he owed to Mead's thinking on the nature of the social act, and on man's interpretation of both the social and physical world. Mead ranks with William James as a major influence in Dewey's transition from Hegelianism to experimental naturalism. After 1931 Albert Barnes, in aesthetics, Arthur F. Bentley and Charles Sanders Peirce, in logic and the theory of the knowing-known, stand out as important sources of inspiration to Dewey.

Much that Dewey derived from Mead came from personal conversations and contacts between them at the University of Michigan and the University of Chicago. Mead published a relatively small number of articles in his lifetime. After his death, some of his students published four major volumes based upon his own lecture drafts and students' notes on those lectures: *The Philosophy of the Present* (1932); *Mind, Self & Society* (1934); *Movements of Thought in the Nineteenth Century* (1936); and *The Philosophy of the Act* (1938). The historian should note, however, that Dewey's influence on Mead was at least as great as Mead's on Dewey.[1] Dewey did not meet Mead until they became colleagues at the University of Michigan in the fall of 1891. Yet, as Herbert W. Schneider has pointed out, Dewey's 1887 textbook, *Psychology* (*Early Works* 2), in its 1889 and 1891 revised printings already contained the basic insights of *How We Think* (1910) (*Middle Works* 6:177–356). The textbook presented criticism of the "reflex arc concept," a formulation of the psychology of interest and intelligent choice in the context of a growing self, and his newly developed theory of self-realization.[2] In the spring of 1891 Dewey published *Outlines of a Critical Theory of Ethics* (*Early Works* 3:236–388). Although this book had various shortcomings, it expressed some fundamental ideas of Dewey's later philosophy. George Herbert Mead himself acknowledged in a 1929 essay that in this book Dewey affirmed the "one moral reality—the full free play of human life," the "analysis of individuality into function including capacity and environ-

---

1. Cf. Neil Coughlan, *Young John Dewey* (Chicago: University of Chicago Press, 1975), pp. 113–34, 143–48.
2. John Dewey, *The Early Works of John Dewey, 1882–1898*, ed. Jo Ann Boydston (Carbondale and Edwardsville: Southern Illinois University Press, 1967), 2:xxv.

ment," and the "idea of desire as the ideal activity in contrast with actual possession." In this work we also find "the will, the idea, and the consequences all placed inside of the act, and the act itself placed only within the larger activity of the individual in society."[3]

My conclusion is that the champions of Mead's influence on Dewey are partly correct. Here we have Dewey's own words supporting part of their claim. In fact, Dewey went beyond anything so far published in writing a letter in 1946 to a would-be biographer that "the biologizing of my approach & its influence upon converting my Hegelianism into something empirical & experimental came from Mead more than anything else."[4] Yet the analyses I have made of Dewey's *Psychology* and *Outlines of a Critical Theory of Ethics* demonstrate that contrary to Dewey's own words, he had already advanced to a position which anticipated some of Mead's key ideas. Dewey's meeting with Mead helped to carry further his own development along these lines. Mead can be credited with bringing these ideas of Dewey's to fruition, but not of planting his own ideas into the otherwise unprepared mind of Dewey. Need for a critical approach to the relations between Dewey and Mead cannot be overemphasized in the light of the controversial generalizations about Mead and Dewey made by J. David Lewis and Richard L. Smith in *American Sociology and Pragmatism: Mead, Chicago Sociology, and Symbolic Interaction* (1981). For an interesting series of critical essays, see *Symbolic Interaction* 6 (1983): 128–74.

Charles Sanders Peirce (1839–1914) had been one of Dewey's notable teachers at Johns Hopkins in the early 1880s and had a great impact on William James and Josiah Royce as well as on mathematical logicians in Europe. For most of his life and for two decades after his death Peirce was unknown to the general public. Since the 1930s, his originality and brilliance have inspired many to a cult of reverence and exaltation. Although Dewey had cited Peirce only briefly in various essays in 1892, 1903, and 1904, he helped to establish Peirce's reputation as a

---

3. George Herbert Mead, *Selected Writings*, ed., with an introduction, by Andrew J. Reck (Indianapolis: Bobbs-Merrill Co., 1964), pp. 387–88. See also Dewey, *Early Works* 3 : xxxi, lxviii–lxxi.
4. Dewey to Joseph Ratner, 9 July 1946, Joseph Ratner/John Dewey Papers, Special Collections, Morris Library, Southern Illinois University at Carbondale.

major thinker first by an essay in 1916, "The Pragmatism of Peirce,"[5] and then by an important review essay in 1932 on the first volume of Peirce's *Collected Papers*, eight volumes of which were eventually published by Harvard University Press. In his 1932 review Dewey praised Peirce as the "most original philosophical mind this country has produced," "a philosopher's philosopher." Then Dewey singled out some ideas of Peirce's which he was later to use in his own *Logic: The Theory of Inquiry* (1938). Dewey was intrigued by Peirce's doctrine of fallibilism, with its implications for the principle of continuity in knowledge and nature; his formulation of logical realism as "the reality of a way, habit, disposition, of behavior"; and his view of philosophy as the form of commonsense that has become "critically aware of itself." This recognition by Dewey of Peirce's insights grew steadily as he read and studied the succeeding five volumes of Peirce's *Collected Papers* that were published by 1935. In 1938 Dewey acknowledged his great indebtedness to Peirce particularly for "the principle of the continuum of inquiry," whose importance, so far as Dewey was aware, "only Peirce had previously noted."[6] The only other two thinkers cited as major sources of inspiration were Arthur F. Bentley and George Herbert Mead (*Logic*, p. v).

An American philosopher who shared Dewey's enthusiasm for C. S. Peirce, civil liberties, and social reform, but who differed from Dewey sharply in his exaltation of formal logic and rationalistic naturalism, was Morris R. Cohen (1880–1947). Cohen in the 1920s, 1930s, and 1940s was regarded as an outstanding philosopher, scholar, and teacher, but his reputation for originality does not measure up to that of a Peirce, James, Dewey, or Mead.[7] Since Cohen was one of Dewey's most persistent and forcible critics over some thirty years, Dewey's critique in 1931 of Cohen's first and major work, *Reason and Nature*, is worthy of careful attention. Dewey, with scrupulous fairness, first praises Cohen for his insights into, and lucid exposition of, the major

5. John Dewey, *The Middle Works of John Dewey, 1899–1924*, ed. Jo Ann Boydston (Carbondale and Edwardsville: Southern Illinois University Press, 1980), 10:71–78.
6. John Dewey, *Logic: The Theory of Inquiry* (New York: Henry Holt and Co., 1938), p. iii.
7. Cf. David A. Hollinger, *Morris R. Cohen and the Scientific Ideal* (Cambridge: MIT Press, 1977); *Dictionary of American Biography*, supp. 4 (1946–1950), s.v., "Cohen, Morris Raphael."

characteristics of the natural and social sciences. Cohen's focus, he points out, is on the universals or invariant relations that constitute the nature of things; his strength is in his analysis of the subject matter and method of the exact sciences. But Cohen's weakness is in failing to define certain issues clearly, e.g., in identifying all empiricism with sensationalistic particularism.

Dewey commended Cohen's use of the principle of polarity, the strife and balance of opposites, but pointed out that Cohen did not examine closely enough the interplay of contingency and law. Nor does Cohen, in Dewey's judgment, do justice to those philosophers who would derive the invariant forms of mathematics and logic from the rules or formulas of procedure adopted by scientists. Although Cohen made a vigorous reply to Dewey, I believe that Dewey's evaluation of Cohen's work stands up very well, especially in view of the fact that Cohen's life-long, and Bertrand Russell's early, neo-Platonic view of mathematics and logic has come to be repudiated by many contemporary philosophers.[8] The historian should note that the most severe critique of Cohen's book was made, not by Dewey, but by Cohen's former pupil Sidney Hook.[9]

A philosophical theme that is central to Dewey's philosophy and related to his discussions of Peirce and Cohen is the idea of human nature. In 1932 Dewey wrote an essay, "Human Nature," that is a masterpiece of lucid, incisive exposition and analysis. He surveyed the varying meanings given to the term in the course of human history and showed how each interpretation was related to the institutional and intellectual characteristics of the time and place in which it prevailed. In the heated controversy between those who asserted the essential fixity of human nature and those who affirmed a great range of modifiability, Dewey came out strongly for the second alternative. He believed in the possibility of controlled social change that might alter the future of war and of competitive capitalism. These beliefs affected his position on the outlawry of war and on the economic measures

8. Cf. Susan Haack, *Philosophy of Logics* (New York: Cambridge University Press, 1978), pp. 221–42; George W. Roberts, ed., *Bertrand Russell Memorial Volume* (New York: Humanities Press, 1979), pp. 128–38, 414–21; Mark Steiner, *Mathematical Knowledge* (Ithaca, N.Y.: Cornell University Press, 1975), pp. 109–37.
9. Cf. Sidney Hook, "Reason and Nature: The Metaphysics of Scientific Method," *Journal of Philosophy* 29 (7 January 1932): 5–24.

of Herbert Hoover and Franklin D. Roosevelt during the Great Depression.

Although Dewey's 1922 volume, *Human Nature and Conduct* (*Middle Works* 14), is far more widely read than this 1932 essay, the latter still is a splendid example of philosophical analysis. It also indicates how much thought Dewey gave to the study of history and anthropology. His friendship and interchange with the historians James Harvey Robinson and Charles Beard and the anthropologist Franz Boas undoubtedly enriched his approach to social philosophy. In turn, Dewey's insights influenced these and other historians and anthropologists. Ruth Benedict, for example, once said that one of the sources of inspiration for her *Patterns of Culture* (1934) was Dewey's *Human Nature and Conduct*.[10]

The major points made by Dewey in "Human Nature" became the basis for developing three other important essays. In "Politics and Culture," he analyzed with great clarity the relations between the political-economic system in America and the intellectual and aesthetic life of the American people. Although he admitted that the general cultural level of the great majority of the people was lower than in Europe, he argued that this condition was probably not due to the low mental ability of the masses, but to the dominance of crass commercial interests and goals in the American economy and society. The theme of this essay Dewey later developed in more systematic form in *Liberalism and Social Action* in 1935.

The critical attitude towards American society displayed in Dewey's discussion of politics and culture was extended in "Science and Society" and "Social Science and Social Control." He praised the scientific revolution of the seventeenth century; he regretted, however, that no comparable scientific revolution had occurred in the twentieth century to enable people to control great depressions and prevent gross misuse of natural and human resources. Part of the solution of these problems, Dewey felt, lay in recognizing a radical difference between the social sciences and the physical sciences, namely that the social sciences have to deal with human purposes, desires, emotions, ideas, and ideals as part of their data whereas the physical sciences do not have to

10. Oral statement to Sidney Ratner by Ruth Benedict, ca. 1935.

do so. He contended that social controls and experiments are necessary if the social sciences are to develop as sciences. This position was approved by such liberals as Rexford Tugwell and radicals like Robert Lynd in his *Knowledge for What?* (1939), but laissez-faire champions like Frank Knight of the University of Chicago were highly critical of Dewey. Philosophers today agree with Dewey on the existence of some differences between the natural and the social sciences, but also point out more parallels than Dewey acknowledged.[11]

The positions taken by Dewey in "Social Science and Social Control" were the theoretical basis for the program of action Dewey undertook during the early 1930s after the great crash of 1929. In these depression years he served as national chairman of the League for Independent Political Action (LIPA), as a vice-president of the League for Industrial Democracy (LID), and as president of the People's Lobby. In September 1929 Paul Douglas of the University of Chicago and other liberals organized the LIPA as a means of building up a Progressive party movement through research and education. Dewey became its first president; its national committee consisted of liberals like Stuart Chase, Oswald Garrison Villard, and Morris Ernst, along with Socialists like Norman Thomas and Harry Laidler. Shortly after the election of 1930 Dewey invited Senator George W. Norris to head a new party committed to the principles of economic planning and control, but Norris refused. He explained in a letter to Dewey: "Experience has shown that the people will not respond to a demand for a new party except in case of a great emergency, when there is practically a political revolution."[12]

Dewey, however, disagreed with Norris's analysis of the situation and wrote powerful articles in the *New Republic* and other periodicals criticizing the two major parties as tools of big business and incapable of bringing about comprehensive economic reforms. In this position he had the strong support of Paul Douglas in his 1932 volume, *The Coming of a New Party*. Read-

---

11. Cf. Ernest Nagel, *The Structure of Science: Problems in the Logic of Scientific Explanation* (New York: Harcourt, Brace and World, 1961), pp. 447–502, and Sidney Ratner, "Facts and Values in History," *Teachers College Record* 56 (1955): 429–34.
12. Arthur M. Schlesinger, Jr., *The Crisis of the Old Order, 1919–1933* (Boston: Houghton Mifflin Co., 1957), pp. 198–99.

ing these essays today gives Americans born after the New Deal a sense of the despair of many liberals and intellectuals concerning the organization and policies of both the Democratic and Republican parties in the early 1930s. Political scientists today would say that Dewey and most avant-garde intellectuals underestimated the possibility that the great economic crisis of 1929 and the 1930s could bring about an internal revolution in at least one major party—the Democratic—given a president as open to new ideas and sensitive to different group pressures as Franklin D. Roosevelt. Frederic C. Howe (1867–1940), a noted urban reformer of the early 1900s, said in a radio debate with Dewey in 1932 that Roosevelt was the only statesman that he knew of in either party who "seemed to face the fact that something very fundamental and something quite new was necessary to save us from collapse." On this crucial point Howe, Raymond Moley, Rexford Tugwell, and Adolph Berle, Jr., were more realistic, in the opinion of most historians, than either Dewey or Paul Douglas. Those more sympathetic to socialism, like Sidney Hook, were convinced that Dewey was correct in his diagnosis in the early 1930s and throughout the entire New Deal period.[13]

On the economic front, Dewey wrote and spoke for the League for Industrial Democracy (LID), a liberal organization basically sympathetic to socialism, and for the People's Lobby, whose main driving force was Benjamin Clarke Marsh (1877–1952), an old-time supporter of Henry George's Single Tax program and an admirer of British Fabian socialism. Marsh persuaded Dewey to become the first president of the People's Lobby (1929–1936), an organization committed to working on behalf of the great majority of the American people, and not for any narrow group interest. Dewey contributed various articles to the *People's Lobby Bulletin* and issued public statements to the press. Perhaps the most important program he proposed was formulated in July 1931. He urged Congress to appropriate $3 billion for public works, $250 million for direct relief, and $250 million for subventions to state unemployment systems to expedite their adoption and furnish cheap credit for urban housing programs. The

13. Cf. Frank Freidel, *Franklin D. Roosevelt: Launching the New Deal* (Boston: Little, Brown and Co., 1973), pp. 66–82; Sidney Hook, *John Dewey: An Intellectual Portrait* (New York: John Day Co., 1939), p. 168.

revenue needed for this program was to be raised by increasing the surtaxes on large incomes and inheritances and by repealing the exemption of gifts from taxation. All these measures were in accord with policies later adopted by the New Deal. Dewey, Marsh, and the People's Lobby differed from other reform groups in being strongly opposed to such potentially inflationary tools as crop restriction and deficit financing.

Dewey never could reconcile himself to the halfway reform measures of the New Deal. In this position, he, Benjamin Marsh, and various Marxist groups persistently opposed the New Deal. In part they were correct; certain defects in the economic system were not eliminated; certain reforms developed abuses that are still with us. On the other hand, reforms were instituted under the New Deal that had long-term benefits for previously exploited or underprivileged groups. Dewey, the People's Lobby, and the Socialist party performed a useful function in setting up higher social welfare goals than FDR had originally envisaged, but which he came to appreciate and even in part tried to achieve as he became increasingly aware of how great the problems of social welfare and economic growth were. Undoubtedly, admirers of John Dewey like Felix Frankfurter, Rexford Tugwell, Adolph Berle, Jr., Jerome Frank, and Walton H. Hamilton, working within the New Deal and the Democratic party did more to realize Dewey's own social welfare goals than they would have been able to do if they had stayed outside the traditional political system.[14]

Different groups of professional economists would fault Dewey and the People's Lobby for different reasons: the Keynesians would claim that Keynes's deficit financing program should have been adopted during the 1930s on a scale comparable to that in World War II; the monetarists would criticize Dewey for not urging expansion of the monetary supply as the top priority recovery measure in the 1930s; supply-side economists would take issue with Dewey on his high tax program. The reader can easily see that Dewey and the People's Lobby were justified in propo-

14. Cf. Joseph Dorfman, *The Economic Mind in American Civilization*, 5 vols. (New York: Viking Press, 1946–59), 5:638–49, 658–77, 722–76; Benjamin C. Marsh, *Lobbyist for the People: A Record of Fifty Years* (Washington, D.C.: Public Affairs Press, 1953), pp. 89–102.

sing their relief-employment programs, but did not probe as deeply into basic problems as professional economists today would have them do. But hindsight is notoriously better than most cases of foresight. Dewey probably did no worse than the majority of economists in the early 1930s.[15]

Dewey's interest in international peace rivaled his interest in economic reform. After enthusiastically supporting the participation of the United States in World War I, Dewey, like Charles Beard and other Wilsonian admirers, became disillusioned with the Versailles peace treaty and opposed American entrance into the League of Nations. Dewey became attracted to a program called the Outlawry of War, initiated by a Chicago lawyer, Salmon O. Levinson, as early as March 1918, and threw much energy into championing this program before the public in a series of forceful essays in the *New Republic* and other periodicals during the 1920s. In 1928 and 1929 he supported the Kellogg-Briand Pact of 1928 which condemned war as an instrument of national policy. After the Japanese invasion of Manchuria in 1931 and their attack on Shanghai early in 1932, American public opinion against Japan was aroused and some publicists, such as Raymond Leslie Buell, urged international sanctions against Japan. Dewey, however, in two essays deplored the invocation of sanctions, economic or military, against Japan and argued (wrongly, in my opinion) that the renunciation of armed force or war by all nations was the only proper measure to be taken even in the case of such aggression as Japan's. Otherwise he feared that the system of war would be maintained under the guise of sanctions to punish violators of the League of Nations Covenant or the Pact of Paris.

After Japan attacked Pearl Harbor in December 1941, Dewey reversed himself and supported the use of force against the "aggressor" nations—Japan, Germany, and Italy. In so doing Dewey repudiated the outlawry of war doctrine he had previously supported. His pre-World War II idealism was admirable in its in-

15. Cf. Sidney Ratner, *Taxation and Democracy in America* (New York: Octagon Books, 1980), pp. 451–538; S. Ratner et al., *The Evolution of the American Economy: Growth, Welfare, and Decision Making* (New York: Basic Books, 1979), pp. 494–531.

tent, but not effective in a world where rampant nationalism, racism, conflicting economic systems, and power politics prevailed.[16]

Despite my negative verdict on Dewey's peace efforts, the non-violence movement led by Gandhi in India and by Martin Luther King in the United States demonstrated that the resort to force could be effectively renounced on domestic issues in countries where the ruling groups could be influenced by appeals to human rights and by democratic governmental processes. In totalitarian countries, however, such movements have so far not succeeded. Efforts to expand such non-violent techniques into international disputes so far have not been effective. The plasticity of human nature, in which Dewey had such faith, has not until now proved great enough to avoid international wars. The United Nations Charter, it should be pointed out, obliges its members to refrain in their international relations "from the threat or use of force against the territorial integrity or political independence of any state, or in any other manner inconsistent with the purposes of the United Nations." Although these provisions were put into effect by the UN in a small number of cases, failure in other cases has been more noticeable. Hence, Quincy Wright, a noted authority on war, has concluded that "history has made it clear that outlawry of war has not eliminated the possibility, or even the probability, of hostilities or of war."[17]

The philosophy of education was for Dewey a lifetime concern. During the 1930s the Great Depression imperiled all phases of education, from the elementary to the graduate. On at least ten occasions during the years 1931 and 1932 Dewey wrote or spoke on major problems in American education; on several other occasions he discussed related issues. Perhaps his most important essay was *The Way Out of Educational Confusion*, dealing with the relative roles of academic and vocational schools and courses. He counseled educators to avoid concentration on subjects as such, and instead to stress the relation between the-

---

16. Cf. Charles F. Howlett, *Troubled Philosopher: John Dewey and the Struggle for World Peace* (Port Washington, N.Y.: Kennikat Press, 1977), pp. 96–143; Robert J. Maddox, *William E. Borah and American Foreign Policy* (Baton Rouge: Louisiana State University Press, 1970), pp. 150–253; John E. Stoner, *S. O. Levinson and the Pact of Paris* (Chicago: University of Chicago Press, 1942), *passim*.
17. *International Encyclopedia of the Social Sciences*, s.v., "War."

ory and practice in each subject. He also advised developing the complex and enriching interrelations of diverse subjects, e.g., mathematics and physics; history, economics, and political science. Both teachers and students were called on to work out for themselves the social bearing and application of each subject.

In another essay, *American Education Past and Future*, Dewey presented an historical background to contemporary problems of education by portraying the way in which American education has changed as the American society developed from an agrarian-industrial setting, relatively simple in its social arrangements, to a highly complex urban-industrial setting. A new social and economic structure required a new education based on the present and future relations of students and teachers to the new technology and the massive corporate and capital structures that had replaced the smaller and simpler business and finance institutions. Dewey thought that the individualism of the past frontier society had to be replaced by a philosophy of cooperation among individuals "in a common struggle against poverty, disease, ignorance, credulity, low standards of appreciation and enjoyment." He hoped that individuals would retain the ability to think and judge for themselves while learning to act with and for others.

Contemporary Americans are very conscious of efforts by governments or different pressure groups to abridge the freedom of teachers and students in colleges and universities to think, write, and speak on controversial issues as they wish. Dewey was ahead of his time when he organized the American Association of University Professors as far back as 1915. In 1932 he published a strong attack on "Political Interference in Higher Education and Research." Long before the Martin Dies House Committee on Un-American Activities in the 1930s and 1940s and Senator Joseph McCarthy's inquest into communism in the early 1950s, Dewey pointed out the danger to a healthy higher education if political, economic, or religious pressures were brought to prevent freedom of writing, speech, thought and political activity of students and faculty. But Dewey also proposed a program of action by professors. He suggested that the AAUP and other scientific and professional organizations should set up lists of accredited colleges and universities which respected academic freedom. This procedure would motivate educational administrations to maintain such freedom.

The Great Depression of the 1930s presented a threat to the survival of every educational institution in America, or at least to its functioning on as high a level as it had before the Wall Street crash of October 1929. Dewey confronted this danger in an essay, "The Economic Situation: A Challenge to Education." He did not present a program for economic recovery as a professional economist might have done. Instead he dealt with the problem of the proper educational philosophy that educators and the public should adhere to in such an economic crisis. As he saw it, the primary social duty of educators was not to perpetuate the existing social order but to contribute to its betterment by encouraging students and faculty to work out programs for improving the existing social, economic, and political systems. He dared to suggest that the prevailing creed of economic individualism and the glorification of private property might be replaced by theories about increased governmental control of national resources in the interests of the general public. In his judgment the specific program or solution was not as important as the stimulation of students and teachers to fresh thinking on important public problems.

Essays

Context and Thought

In a supplementary essay in Ogden and Richards' *Meaning of Meaning*, Mr. Malinowski gives a striking example of the need for understanding context in connection with the use of language. The literal translation into English of an utterance of New Guinea natives runs as follows: "We run frontwards ourselves; we paddle in place; we turn, we see companion ours; he runs rearward behind their sea-arm Pilolu." As he says, the speech sounds like a meaningless jumble. If one is to understand it one must be informed about the situation in which the words were spoken and have them placed in their own context of culture. As a matter of fact, the utterance refers to a victory in an overseas trading expedition of the natives, in which several canoes have taken part in a competitive spirit. "This feature of rivalry (he adds) also explains the emotional nature of the utterance; it is not a mere statement of fact, but a boast, a piece of self-glorification, extremely characteristic of the Trobrianders' culture in general and of their ceremonial barter in particular."

After going into some detail of explanation, he remarks that in trying to give an adequate analysis of meaning "we are faced by a long and not altogether simple process of describing wide fields of custom, of social psychology, of tribal organisation, which correspond to one term or another. Linguistic analysis inevitably leads us into the study of all the subjects covered by Ethnographic field-work." Furthermore, as he points out, knowledge of ethnography will not remove all difficulties; even those of exclusively linguistic problems can, some of them, be solved only on the basis of psychological analysis. He sums up by saying that

[First published in University of California Publications in Philosophy, vol. 12, no. 3 (Berkeley: University of California Press, 1931), 203–24, from the George Holmes Howison Lecture for 1930, delivered at Berkeley on 14 January 1931.]

"in the reality of a spoken living language, the utterance has no meaning except in the context of a situation."

We should all, I suppose, admit this contention in the case of the speech of an alien and remote savage tribe. But it would be a great mistake to imagine that the principle is limited in application to such peoples. There is indeed a great contrast with our own modes of utterance. But the contrast is significant because it throws into relief familiar traits which very familiarity tends to conceal from us. We grasp the meaning of what is said in our own language not because appreciation of context is unnecessary but because context is so unescapably present. It is taken for granted; it is a matter of course, and accordingly is not explicitly specified. Habits of speech, including syntax and vocabulary, and modes of interpretation have been formed in the face of inclusive and defining situations of context. The latter are accordingly implicit in most of what is said and heard. We are not explicitly aware of the role of context just because our every utterance is so saturated with it that it forms the significance of what we say and hear.

The illustrative episode with which I began refers to language. But in it there is contained in germ all that I have to say for the indispensability of context for thinking, and therefore for a theory of logic and ultimately of philosophy itself. What is true of the meaning of words and sentences is true of all meaning. Such a statement need not, however, involve us in controversy about the relation of thought to language. If language is identified with speech, there is undoubtedly thought without speech. But if "language" is used to signify all kinds of signs and symbols, then assuredly there is no thought without language; while signs and symbols depend for their meaning upon the contextual situation in which they appear and are used.

For the meaning of symbols is not inherent but derived. This appears from the fact that they *are* symbols. It is true that when we talk and write the meaning of a particular verbal symbol is given us by the context of other symbols in which it occurs. It is also true that there are systems of symbols, notably in mathematics, where the system determines the meaning of any particular symbol. We cannot however infer from these facts that symbols are capable of supplying the ultimate context which provides meaning and understanding. Continued and systematic discourse enables us to determine the meaning of special symbols within the discourse only because it enables us to build up a non-verbal and non-symbolic context to which the whole refers. The mathematician does not stop to think of the ulterior context of existences, which gives his system of symbols import; long familiarity and a long tradition behind it have made the connection highly indirect and tenuous. He would not only have difficulty in making the connection, but he would perhaps be irritated, as at a useless interruption and distraction, at any suggestion that he attempt to make the connection. But expertness in treating symbols as if they were things does not alter their symbolic character. Multiplication of symbols and increase in their intricacy facilitates manipulation. But reference of one symbol to another cannot destroy their character as symbols.

Now thought lives, moves, and has its being in and through symbols, and, therefore, depends for meaning upon context as do the symbols. We think *about* things, but not *by* things. Or rather when we do think by and with things, we are not experiencing the things in their own full nature and content. Sounds, for example, and marks in printed books are themselves existential things. But they operate in thought only as they stand for something else; if we become absorbed in them as things, they lose their value for thinking. If a man thinks, as he may do, by means of blocks and stones, he is not, as far as he is thinking, engaged in complete and intimate realization of them in their own intrinsic qualities. If he does become concerned with them in this fashion, he indulges in something that is either more or less than thought; more, if it is an esthetic absorption, less if it relapse into dumb stupor. The concern of thinking is with things as they carry the mind beyond themselves; they are vehicles not terminal stations.

These remarks have themselves an implicit context. Negatively, this context is the habit of philosophers of neglecting the indispensability of context, both in particular and in general. I should venture to assert that the most pervasive fallacy of philosophic thinking goes back to neglect of context. In the face to face communications of everyday life, context may be safely ignored. For, as we have already noted, it is irrevocably there. It is taken for granted, not denied, when it is passed over without notice. It gives point to everything said. A man engaged in a business transaction does not, for example, need to remind himself specifically of that fact—unless he is falling asleep. Context is incorporated in what is said and forms the arbiter of the value of every utterance. The same ideas and words apart from context would be the extravagancies of a madman. But in philosophizing there is rarely an immediately urgent context which controls the course of thought. Neglect of specific acknowledgment of it is, then, too readily converted into a virtual denial.

Let us consider an instance or two of virtual denial of context in philosophy and its effect. Some philosophers have attacked the validity of analysis. They have held that while it is important in "science," that fact is itself evidence of the partial nature of science, of its abstraction from the "whole" with which philosophy is concerned. Other thinkers reach much the same conclusion when they assert that all valid analysis is attended by a synthetic act of thought which deliberately restores what is left out of account in the act of analysis. Now I do not see how a super-added act of synthesis can be other than arbitrary. But I can see how analysis falsifies when its results are interpreted as complete in themselves apart from any context. And it seems to me that the fault found with analysis would be more correctly as well as more simply directed against the ignoring of context. When a physician sets out to diagnose a disease he analyzes what is before him by the best technique at command. He does not at the end require another and further act of synthesis. The situation from the first has been one of disease and that situation provides the connection between the particular details analytically detected. One always identifies by discovering differences that are characteristic. This is true whether the identification be that of a criminal, of a plant or an animal, a metal, a disease, or a law. So far there is no defect in analysis and no demand for an added act of synthesis. But if the physician were to so forget the presence of a human being as a patient, if he were virtually to deny that context, he certainly would have a meaningless heap of atomic particulars on hand, and might be led to appeal to some transcendental synthesis to bring them to significant unity.

And so in philosophy. The trouble is not with analysis, but with the philosopher who ignores the context in which and for the sake of which the analysis occurs. In this sense, a characteristic defect of philosophy *is* connected with analysis. There are a multitude of ways of committing the analytic fallacy. It is found whenever the distinctions or elements that are discriminated are treated as if they were final and self-sufficient. The result is invariably some desiccation and atomizing of the world in which we live or of ourselves. The outcome has often been made the object of critical attack, as in the case of Locke and the Mills, and, indeed, in much of British thought. It has been rightly pointed out that the logical conclusion is denial of all connection and continuity, terminating in a doctrine of atomistic particularism. But unfortunately these same critics have not been content with the simple act of indicating neglect of context, but have assumed that the conclusion points to the necessity of some overarching act of organic synthesis on the part of thought or "reason"—a method which, as I shall hope to show later, is the same disease of ignoring context in another form.

It is possible to find fresher straw to thresh than that of the systems of the thinkers just mentioned. Let me take an illustration from a field sufficiently remote from technical philosophical questions as not to arouse at once controversial associations. I have in mind the case of laboratory experimentation in psychology, say with respect to the discrimination of the least distinguishable color or sound, the finest possible discrimination of some sensory quality. Such qualities, when discriminated under conditions of refined control, have been assumed not only to be elements (which they are by definition, an element being only the last product of analysis), but to be original constituents out of which all mental life is built. They have been treated, in other words, as self-sufficient, independent in their isolation, so that all mental life is the result of their compounding.

Any such interpretation illustrates that ignoring of context which is virtually a denial of context. In fact there is present much besides the terminal elements. There is the background of the experimenter. This includes the antecedent state of theory which has given rise to his problem. It takes in his purpose in arranging the apparatus, including the technical knowledge which makes a controlled experiment possible. On the other side, there are the habits and present disposition of the subject, his capacity to give attention and to make verbal responses, etc., etc. Without the phase of context found on the side of the experimenter, there would be no scientific result at all, but an acci-

dent without theoretical import. The phase of context supplied
from the side of the subject furnishes the causal factor determining the appearance of the quality discriminated. The latter, instead of being an isolated original unit out of which mental life is
constructed by external composition, is the last term, for the
time being, of an inclusive mental life. The immanent presence of
the contextual setting of a moving experience provides connection. It renders unnecessary appeal to synthetic acts of thought,
transcendental or otherwise, in order to supply connection.
What takes place because of its connections does not require an
act of thought to give it connection.

This remark brings me to what I called shortly ago the same
disease in another form. The counterpart fallacy to that of analysis (as wrongly interpreted because of denial of context) is that of
unlimited extension or universalization. When context is taken
into account, it is seen that every generalization occurs under
limiting conditions set by the contextual situation. When this
fact is passed over or thrown out of court, a principle valid under
specifiable conditions is perforce extended without limit. Any
genuine case of thinking starts, for example, with considerations
which as they stand are fragmentary and discrepant. Thinking
then has the task of effecting unification in a single coherent
whole. In this sense the goal of all thinking is the attaining of
unity. But this unity is unification of just those data and considerations which in that situation are confused and incoherent.
The fallacy of unlimited universalization is found when it is
asserted, without any such limiting conditions, that the goal
of thinking, particularly of philosophic thought, is to bring all
things whatsoever into a single coherent and all inclusive whole.
Then the idea of unity which has value and import under specifiable conditions is employed with such an unlimited extension
that it loses its meaning.

All statements about the universe as a whole, reality as an unconditioned unity, involve the same fallacy. There is genuine
meaning in the act of inquiring into the reality of a given situation. It is equivalent to an attempt to discover "the facts of the
case," what is actually there or is actually happening—the addition of the adjective "real" to the substantive, "facts," being only
for rhetorical emphasis. Within the limits of context found in
any valid inquiry, "reality" thus means the confirmed outcome,

actual or potential, of the inquiry that is undertaken. There is some specifiable confusion and dispersion which sets the inquiry going, and the latter terminates when the confusion is cleared away and definiteness accrues under conditions of suitable test. When "reality" is sought for at large, it is without intellectual import; at most the term carries the connotation of an agreeable emotional state. A like conclusion holds with reference to the "absolute," the "total," the "unconditioned," and many other terms held sacred on the lips of philosophers.

These statements do not however bring out *why* this fallacy of unlimited extension is the same ailment as that of unbridled analysis, in another form. We may have recourse to the instance already cited, that of mental life. Isolation from context of the distinctions found in a laboratory experiment induces the generalization that all varieties of mental life are compounds of independent units: whether the latter are called sensations, sensa, states of feeling or consciousness, or reflex arcs, or reactions to stimuli, or whatever is the prevailing fashion. This generalization into a sweeping theory is nothing but the logical statement of the conclusion which emerges when the context is suppressed. Given this suppression, elements become absolute, for they have no limiting conditions. Results of inquiry valid within specifiable limits of context are *ipso facto* converted into a sweeping metaphysical doctrine.

Further illustrations, if time permitted, would elucidate the nature of these two fallacies that tend to haunt philosophizing. I think, for example, that it could be shown that the predilections of many contemporaries for sensa and essences are products of neglect of context. I pass by, however, these possibilities to consider the use made in some aspects of contemporary philosophy of the concept of "events." That all existences are *also* events I do not doubt. For they are qualified by temporal transition. But that existences as such are *only* events strikes me as a proposition that can be maintained in no way except by a wholesale ignoring of context. For, in the first place, every occurrence is a *concurrence*. An event is not a self-enclosed, self-executing affair—or it is not save by arbitrary definition. One may easily slip down a hill, but the slipping is not a self-contained entity, even though the *concept* of slipping may be self-contained—a transposition which makes it an essence, not an existence. The actual slide depends upon an interaction of several things, very many in an adequate account. Yet, unless I am mistaken in my interpretation, there is evidence that some contemporary writers tend to treat every existence as if to *be* an existence were to be a slide or a slip. To escape the difficulty by implying that the context of an event is simply other events is suspiciously like assuming that by putting enough slides together you can make a hill.

There are some cases of interaction which, relatively speaking, are merely displacements: like that which happens when one billiard ball impinges on another. What happens is then—or at least may be so treated for most purposes—merely a rearrangement. There are other transactions in which something happens to which the name interception can be given. In the interaction the product retains as it were something of the qualities of the concurring things. In this case, the event, viewed even as an event, is not merely an event. Such interception and coalescence of qualities hitherto distinct characterize anything that may be called an emergent. Put in a slightly different way, an event is both eventful and an eventuation.

Since every event is also an interaction of different things, it is inherently characterized by something from which and to which. The slide that starts with the slipping of the foot is not the same as that of a propelled sled; and it makes considerable difference to the slide as an event whether it terminates on rocks, water, or a pile of grass. The "from which" and "to which" qualify the event and make it, concretely, the distinctive event which it is. We may, indeed, by legitimate abstraction (legitimate for certain purposes) neglect the characteristic difference and reach the notion of slide in general. But the generalized abstraction would be impossible were there not events having their own qualitative traits. In other words, a *merely* general concept of "event" is undistinguishable from that of ascent, or perpendicular fall, or indeed from the meaning of any other term whatever which is equally treated as indifferent to all qualitative determination.

In the next place, when an event, because of neglect of context, is treated merely as an event, or as self-enclosed instead of as a change which takes place when qualitatively tempered things interact, it at once becomes necessary to invoke essences of eternal objects or some form of static eternal object to give any particular event an assignable character. The statement that interaction is constant and that consequently any existence at every point of its career is also an event, or that an existence may be looked at as *also* a serial set of events, seems to be authorized by the evidence. But to treat this proposition as equivalent to the proposition that every existence (apart from the entrance of an essence) is *merely* a collection of events is an instance of that unlimited extension that is entailed by neglect of context. The appeal to eternal objects has the same root, logically, as the appeal to an act of synthesis when the results of analysis, combined with ignoring of contextual connections, are taken to be the ground for invoking a further act of synthesis. As an added point we may note that a world of self-enclosed events, even when characterized by the entrance of eternal objects, requires something else to hold them together into anything like the semblance of one world. The supplementation takes the form of a framework of space-time—for an event as self-contained can have no change within it. It *is* a beginning and an end but it *has* no beginning nor end, and so an outside space-time must be superimposed.

Up to this point the discussion is negative in tone. It is meant to illustrate, though it cannot pretend to prove, that neglect of context is the greatest single disaster which philosophic thinking can incur. If we turn to consideration of the content and scope of the context that philosophizing should take into the reckoning, we approach the positive side of the discussion. Context includes at least those matters which for brevity I shall call background and selective interest. By "background" I mean the whole environment of which philosophy must take account in all its enterprises. A background is implicit in some form and to some degree in all thinking, although as background it does not come into explicit purview; that is, it does not form a portion of the subject matter which is consciously attended to, thought of, examined, inspected, turned over. Background is both temporal and spatial.

When we think, there are some things which we are immediately thinking *of*, considerations that are before us, and that are reflected upon, pondered over, etc. They are that with which we are wrestling, trying to overcome its difficulties and to reduce to order. Surrounding, bathing, saturating, the things of which we are explicitly aware is some inclusive situation which does not enter into the direct material of reflection. It does not come into question; it is taken for granted with respect to the particular question that is occupying the field of thinking. Since it does not come into question, it is stable, settled. To think of it in the sense of making it an object of thought's examination and scrutiny is an irrelevant and confusing distraction. It, or rather some part of it, comes into question, or into the explicit material of reflection, only when we suspect that it exercises such a *differential* effect upon what is consciously thought of as to be responsible for some of the confusion and perplexity we are trying to clear up. Then, of course, it enters into the immediate matter of thinking. But this transfer never disturbs the whole contextual background; it does not all come into question at once. There is always that which continues to be taken for granted, which is tacit, being "understood." If everything were literally unsettled at once, there would be nothing to which to tie those factors that, being unsettled, are in process of discovery and determination.

It was said that this background in thought is both spatial and temporal. The direct material of every reflection proceeds out of some precedent state of affairs in reference to which the existing state is disturbed or problematic or to which it is an "answer" or solution. In the episode related by Malinowski, the particular utterance served to sum up and record a previous struggle which issued in victory for one side. In the instance of the psychological experiment, the temporal background is the prior state of experimenter and subject. Take away the temporal background of the first incident and there is no triumph, nor any other significant happening; take away that of the second, and there is no experiment but merely an incident signifying nothing.

The temporal background of thinking in any case is intellectual as well as existential. That is, in the first cited instance there is a background of culture; in the second, of theory. There is no thinking which does not present itself on a background of tradition, and tradition has an intellectual quality that differentiates it from blind custom. Traditions are ways of interpretation and of observation, of valuation, of everything explicitly thought of. They are the circumambient atmosphere which thought must breathe; no one ever had an idea except as he inhaled some of this atmosphere. Aristotelian physics and Ptolemaic astronomy

were for centuries the taken-for-granted background of all special inquiries in those fields. Then came the Newtonian background, for two centuries more imperious than any Tsar. So the
fixity of species was the background of biological sciences until
the time of Darwinism came; it then reigned so completely (I am
speaking of the scientific inquirer) that Mendel's work did not
cause even a ripple.

Meyerson has remarked that we can explain why medieval
thinkers thought as they did and believed as they did, because we
are outside their age. We cannot explain why we believe the
things which we most firmly hold to because those things are a
part of ourselves. We can no more completely escape them when
we try to examine into them than we can get outside our physical
skins so as to view them from without. Call these regulative traditions apperceptive organs or mental habits or whatever you
will, there is no thinking without them. I do not mean, that a
philosopher can take account of this context in the sense of making it a complete object of reflection. But he might realize the
existence of such a context, and in doing so he would learn hu-
mility and would be debarred from a too unlimited and dogmatic universalization of his conclusions. He would not freeze
the quotidian truths relevant to the problems that emerge in his
own background of culture into eternal truths inherent in the
very nature of things.

Spatial background covers all the contemporary setting within
which a course of thinking emerges. That which is looked into,
consciously scrutinized, has, like a picture, a foreground, middle
distance, and a background—and as in some paintings the latter
shades off into unlimited space. Demarcations so sharp that they
amount to isolations do not occur in nature; their presence in
thought is a sure sign that we, for some purpose, have taken a
certain attitude toward the objective scene. Specify the contextual
purpose and no harm arises. Forget it, and the fallacy of misinterpreted analysis ensues. This contextual setting is vague, but it
is no mere fringe. It has a solidity and stability not found in the
focal material of thinking. The latter denotes the part of the road
upon which the spot light is thrown. The spatial context is the
ground through which the road runs and for the sake of which
the road exists. It is this setting which gives import to the road

and to its consecutive illuminations. The path must be lighted if one is not to lose his way; the remoter territory may be safely left in the dark.

Another aspect of context is that which I have called "selective interest." Every particular case of thinking is what it is because of some attitude, some bias if you will; and no general theory can be framed which is not based upon what happens in particular cases. This attitude is no immediate part of what is consciously reflected upon, but it determines the selection of this rather than that subject-matter. The word "interest" may be questioned; it undoubtedly has connotations alien to the point I wish to make. But as to the fact which the word is used to denote that can hardly be in doubt. There is selectivity (and rejection) found in every operation of thought. There is care, concern, implicated in every act of thought. There is some one who has affection for some things over others; when he becomes a thinker he does not leave his characteristic affection behind. As a thinker, he is still differentially sensitive to some qualities, problems, themes. He may at times turn upon himself and inquire into and attempt to discount his individual attitudes. This operation will render some element in his attitude an object of thought. But it cannot eliminate all elements of selective concern; some deeper-lying ones will still operate. No regress will eliminate the attitude of interest that is as much involved in thinking about attitudes as it is in thinking about other things.

The aspect of context which I have called "interest" is known in philosophical terminology as the "subjective." The organism, self, ego, subject, give it whatever name you choose, is implicated in all thinking as in all eating, business, or play. Since it cannot in its entirety be made an explicit object of reflection and yet since it affects all matters thought of, it is legitimately called a phase of context. Subjectivism has a bad name, and as an 'ism it deserves its ill repute. But the subjective as determining attitude is not to be equated to this 'ism. It is not concern which is objectionable even when it takes the form of bias. It is certain kinds of bias that are obnoxious. Bias for impartiality is as much a bias as is partisan prejudice, though it is a radically different quality of bias. To be "objective" in thinking is to have a certain sort of selective interest operative. One can only see from a certain standpoint, but this fact does not make all standpoints of equal value. A standpoint which is nowhere in particular and from which things are not seen at a special angle is an absurdity. But one may have affection for a standpoint which gives a rich and ordered landscape rather than for one from which things are seen confusedly and meagerly.

Interest, as the subjective, is after all equivalent to individuality or uniqueness. There is no reason to limit its presence and operation to the organic and mental, although it is especially exemplified there. Everything which exists may be supposed to have its own unduplicated manner of acting and reacting, even atoms and electrons, although these individual traits are submerged in statistical statement. But in any event that which I have designated selective interest is a unique manner of entering into interaction with other things. It is not a part or constituent of subject-matter; but as a manner of action it selects subject-matter and leaves a qualitative impress upon it. One may call it genius or originality or give the more neutral and modest name of individuality. One realizes its nature best in thinking of genuine works of art. In the field of fine art, one never objects to that peculiar way of seeing, selecting, and arranging which defines the actual nature of the "subjective." One recognizes that its opposite is not the objective but the academic and mechanical, the merely repetitive. This quality is found in the subject-matter of all genuine thinking, for thinking is not the attribute of parrots. Newton may have supposed that he was thinking God's thoughts after him, but so far as he thought, he thought Newton's thoughts.

Such statements are easily misinterpreted both by those who make them and by those who deny them. They are sometimes taken to signify that the entire subject-matter of thought consists of states of consciousness or the material of a thinker's mind. The logical conclusion is then some form of solipsism. But individuality is not, as we have already said, subject-matter, but is a mode of selection that determines subject-matter. The subject-matter of science, physical and mathematical, may at first sight, seem to offer an insuperable objection to the statement that subjectivity, in the sense defined, is contextual in all the material of thinking. For in science there is elimination of connection with the mind of any one in particular. Science is science only as far as any especial tie to the mind of its authors can be left out of account. In the objection, however, there resides a confusion of the product of thought with its acceptance and further use. Newtonian conclusions reigned as science just because they were no longer taken as thought, but as given material to be employed in further investigations and interpretations.

One may find an exact enough analogy in the case of coins having an artistic design. The design in its origin bore the impress of individuality. But its further use, its status as legal tender, is not dependent upon that fact. The attitude controlling the selection and arrangement that forms the esthetic pattern is aside from the purposes of trade. Use in exchange is now the significant affair. In devotion to common social use, the design becomes a mere mechanical identifying sign, a mark of fitness to serve in exchange. If we apply the analogy to science we shall distinguish between science as a conclusion of reflective inquiry, and science as a ready-made body of organized subject-matter. In the first case, it and its status, its worth, reside in its connection with the quality of the inquiry of which it is the outcome and this quality bears the impress of an individual attitude. In the second case, its status and worth are dependent upon serviceability in the prosecution of further discovery and interpretation. From this standpoint, the impress of individuality is negligible because irrelevant; facility for repeated use is the important matter.

Even so, however, indispensability of reference to context still holds. It is easy and too usual to convert abstraction from *specific* context into abstraction from all context whatsoever: another instance of the fallacy of unlimited extension. The fallacy is indulged in whenever the formally logical traits of organized subject-matter are treated as if they were isolated from all material considerations. One of the necessary characters of subject-matter arranged for effective use is internal coherence and economy. When context is ignored this character is taken to be independent of existential material. But these formal characteristics have to do with conditions which must be fulfilled if the given scientific subject-matter is to secure the maximum of applicability in further inquiries and organizations. Only by a formulation in terms of equivalences can old subject-matter be rendered most effectively available in new intellectual undertakings. For only subject-matter stated in terms of reciprocal equivalences renders substitution and free translation possible in an efficient way. This context of use is ignored when formal traits are regarded as self-sufficient in their isolation.

It can hardly have escaped notice that my underlying intention in this discussion concerns a desire to make a contribution to the theme of philosophic method. Thinking takes place in a scale of degrees of distance from the urgencies of an immediate situation in which something has to be done. The greater the degree of remoteness, the greater is the danger that a temporary and legitimate failure of express reference to context will be converted into a virtual denial of its place and import. Thinking is always thinking, but philosophic thinking is, upon the whole, at the extreme end of the scale of distance from the active urgency of concrete situations. It is because of this fact that neglect of context is the besetting fallacy of philosophical thought.

I should like to take my first example of the harmful working of this fallacy of philosophic method from the history of thought. The context of historic philosophies is too often treated as if it were simply other philosophies, instead of its being the perplexities, the troubles, and the issues of the period in which a philosophy arises. And strangely enough the limited context which is used in interpreting historic philosophy is frequently one which developed after the philosophy in question. I have just read an essay in literary criticism in which the writer remarks that a cursory examination of chronology will show that Aristotle's theory of poetry and tragedy was written subsequent to the production of the great dramatists of Athens, and that it is not likely that they wrote in order to prepare the way for Aristotelian theory. I wonder if the remark does not convey a lesson to interpreters of the history of thought. It may, for example, be reasonably asserted that Locke, Berkeley, and Hume wrote with reference to the intellectual conditions of their own times and not in order to initiate a movement which should find its consummation in Kant.

The significant positive content of this suggestion is the need of study of philosophical writings in their own vital context. I know that there are many persons to whom it seems derogatory to link a body of philosophic ideas to the social life and culture of their epoch. They seem to accept a dogma of immaculate conception of philosophical systems. I cannot argue the point here, but I can at least point to this attitude as an example of what I mean by neglect of context. The only alternative to the doctrine of the virginal birth of philosophies is recourse to the marriage of thinking with a tradition and a culture that are not themselves philosophical in character.

There exists at any period a body of beliefs and of institutions and practices allied to them. In these beliefs there are implicit broad interpretations of life and the world. These interpretations have consequences, often profoundly important. In their actual currency, however, the implications of origin, nature, and consequences are not examined and formulated. The beliefs and their associated practices express attitudes and responses which have operated under conditions of direct and often accidental stress. They constitute, as it seems to me, the *immediate* primary material of philosophical reflection. The aim of the latter is to criticize this material, to clarify it, to organize it, to test its internal coherence, and to make explicit its consequences. At the time of origin of every significant philosophy, this cultural context of beliefs and allied institutions is irretrievably there; reference to it is taken for granted and not made explicit. (I remark in passing, however, that part of the perennial significance of Plato's writings is due to the fact that in his dialogues the implied reference shines through much more than in most philosophic writings.) There are indeed historic philosophies in which reference to such cultural context is hard to detect. But examination will show that they are engaged in filling in chinks in other and more significant systems, or are engaged in a formal reconstruction of the latter.

If one is willing to adopt, even as a hypothesis for the time being, the idea that the immediate subject-matter for philosophy is supplied by the body of beliefs, religious, political, scientific, that determines the culture of a people and age, there follow certain conclusions regarding the problem and method of philosophy. The beliefs have their own context of origin, function, and determining interests or attitudes. But they are likely to be potent in the very degree in which these contexts are passed over in silence. Those who are most devoted to them take them as final revelations of truth, as spiritual Melchizedeks, without empirical generation. Moreover they "work"; they have consequences. But *how* they work, the connection of subsequent events and values, with them *as* consequences, is not subjected to examination. It is hardly even noted. Positive values, whatever their source, are treated as proper effects, while failures, evils, are attributed to some external source, even though examination would reveal that they flow directly from accepted beliefs in their institutional operation.

Here is the opportunity for that type of reflection which I should call philosophical. Philosophy is criticism; criticism of the influential beliefs that underlie culture; a criticism which traces the beliefs to their generating conditions as far as may be, which tracks them to their results, which considers the mutual compatibility of the elements of the total structure of beliefs. Such an examination terminates, whether so intended or not, in a projection of them into a new perspective which leads to new surveys of possibilities. This phase of reconstruction through criticism is as marked in justifying and systematizing philosophies as in avowedly skeptical ones, in the work of St. Thomas as of Hume. The clearer and more organized vision of the content of beliefs may have as an immediate outcome an enhanced sense of their worth and greater loyalty to them. But nevertheless the set of beliefs undergoes more than a sea-change in the process. It is dangerous to reflect seriously upon the nature, origin, and consequences of beliefs. The latter are safest when they are taken for granted without reasoned examination. To give reasons, even justifying ones, is to start a train of thoughts—that is, of questionings.

I have referred to religious, political, and scientific beliefs as instances of things that permeate and almost constitute a culture in their institutional accompaniments and their effects. One final example of the indispensability of reference to context will be alluded to, one taken from the relation of philosophy to science. It is sometimes assumed that this relation is exhausted in either an analytic examination of the logical foundations of the sciences, or in a synthesis of their conclusions, or both together. I would not derogate from the importance of such enterprises. But they are at best preparatory. For science itself operates within a context which is, relative to science, raw, crude, and primitive, and yet is pervasive and determining. To work exclusively within the context provided by the sciences themselves is to ignore their vital context. The place of science in life, the place of its peculiar subject-matter in the wide scheme of materials we experience, is a more ultimate function of philosophy than is any self-contained reflection upon science as such.

I am, of course, in this brief space of time only setting forth a possible hypothesis for your consideration. But I am confident that those who are willing to let their imaginations tarry with the hypothesis and follow its implications will at least get light upon the importance which some of us attach to "experience." If the finally significant business of philosophy is the disclosure of the context of beliefs, then we cannot escape the conclusion that experience is the name for the last inclusive context. A philosophy does not, of course, veritably acknowledge the significance of context merely by terming itself empirical. Sensational and nominalistic empiricism is perhaps as striking an example as can be found of the fallacy of neglecting context. But its error lay not in insisting upon experience as the basis and the terminus of philosophy but in its inadequate conception of experience. To refute the principle of empiricism by exposing the errors and defects of particular forms that self-avowed empiricisms have assumed is like supposing that when attention has been called to the eccentricities of a planetary orbit, the existence of an orbit has been disproved.

The significance of "experience" for philosophic method is, after all, but the acknowledgment of the indispensability of context in thinking when that recognition is carried to its full term. Let me recur for a moment to the illustration borrowed at the outset from Malinowski. Examination discloses three deepening levels or three expanding spheres of context. The narrowest and most superficial is that of the immediate scene, the competitive race. The next deeper and wider one is that of the culture of the people in question. The widest and deepest is found in recourse to the need of general understanding of the workings of human nature. We may without undue forcing find here an apt symbol of the necessary course of philosophical thinking.

The first, if most limited consideration, is the range and vitality of the experience of the thinker himself, that is, his most direct personal experience—which, however, only systematic misunderstanding construes to be merely an experience *of* his own person. However widely it reaches out into the world of things and persons, it is as personal, curtailed, one-sided, distorted. The remedy, however, is not divorce of thought from the intimacies of the direct contacts and intercourses of life, but a supplementation of limitations and a correction of biases through acquaintance with the experience of others, contemporary and as recorded in the history of the race. Dogmatism, adherence to a school, partisanship, class-exclusiveness, desire to show off and to impress, are all of them manifestations of disrespect for experience: for that experience which one makes one's own through sympathetic intercommunication. They are, as it were, deliberate perpetuations of the restrictions and perversions of personal experience.

Hence, the next wide circle or deepened stratum of context resides in what I have referred to as culture—in the sense in which anthropologists use the word. Philosophy proclaims its devotion to the universal. But as the profession of cosmopolitan philanthropy which is not rooted in neighborly friendliness is suspect, so I distrust the universals that are not reached by way of profound respect for the significant features and outcomes of human experience as found in human institutions, traditions, impelling interests, and occupations. A universal which has its home exclusively or predominantly in philosophy is a sure sign of isolation and artificiality.

Finally, there is the context of the make-up of experience itself. It is dangerous to begin at this point. Philosophies that have designated themselves empirical are full of warning to this effect. But the boundless multiplicity of the concrete experiences of humanity when they are dealt with gently and humanely, will naturally terminate in some sense of the structure of any and all experience. Biology, psychology, including social psychology and psychiatry, anthropology, all afford indications as to the nature of this structure, and these indications were never so numerous and so waiting for use as now. Those who try to interpret these indications may run the risk of being regarded by some other philosophers as not philosophers at all. They may, however, console themselves with the reflection that they are concerning themselves with that inclusive and pervasive context of experience in which philosophical thinking must, for good or ill, take place, and without reference to which such thinking is in the end but a beating of wings in the void.

George Herbert Mead
as I Knew Him

It was some forty years ago in Ann Arbor that Alice
Dewey and myself made the acquaintance of Helen and George
Mead, an acquaintance which ripened rapidly in a friendship
which is one of the most precious possessions of my life—a possession which is so much more than a memory that not death
itself can dull its force nor dim its reality. We lived in neighboring
houses; we came to Chicago at the same time; we lived many
years in the same building; there was hardly a day we did not
exchange visits; we went through like struggles and joys; to my
own children as to such a host of young people to whom Helen
and George extended their generous natures they were Aunt
Helen and Uncle George. It is a quarter of a century since our
paths in life took different courses. But the fifteen years in which
we were together are clearer and closer in my experience than
most things in the intervening years.

If I do not speak of the more intimate things which throng in
my memory, of their genius for friendship, of their unwearied
and unremitting pouring forth of their generous natures, it is not
because of coldness to these things but because I do not trust myself to speak of them.

As I look back over the years of George Mead's life, and try to
sum up the impression which his personality left upon me, I seem
to find running through everything a sense of energy, of vigor, of
a vigor unified, outgoing and outgiving. Yet as I say this I am
aware that perhaps only those who knew him best have a similar
impression. For there was nothing about him of the bustle and
ado, the impatient hurry, we often associate with vigor. On the
contrary he was rather remarkably free from the usual external

[First published in *Journal of Philosophy* 28 (4 June 1931): 309–14, from
Dewey's eulogy at the memorial service for George Herbert Mead in Chicago on
30 April 1931.]

signs of busy activity. He was not one to rush about breathless with the conviction that he must somehow convince others of his activity. It was rather that he threw himself completely into whatever he had to do in all the circumstances and relations which life brought to him. He gave himself with a single heart to whatever the day and the moment brought. When anything needed to be done, there was no distinction in his life between the important and the unimportant; not that he was careless and undiscriminating, but that whatever really needed to be done, whatever made a demand upon him, was important enough to call out his full vigor. If he did not give the impression of bustling energy, it was precisely because in all that he did his energy was so completely engaged and so unified from within. He faced everything as it came along; incidents were opportunities for reflection to terminate in decision. One can fancy him perplexed temporarily in thought by the complexities of some issue; one cannot imagine him hesitant to meet the issue nor shillyshallying in meeting it. His consciousness never sicklied over the scene of decision and action; it completely and inwardly identified itself with it. It might be household duties, it might be the needs of a friend, or of the physical and mental needs of the many young persons Helen and George gathered about them; it might be his reading, his study, his reflection, his recreations, tramps and travels. In each occasion as it arose there was found the natural opportunity for the free and vital release of his powers.

For his vigor was unified from within, by and from the fullness of his own being. More, I think, than any man I have ever known, his original nature and what he acquired and learned, were one and the same thing. It is the tendency of philosophic study to create a separation between what is native, spontaneous and unconscious and the results of reading and reflection. That split never existed in George Mead. His study, his ideas, his never ceasing reflection and theory were the manifestation of his large and varied natural being. He was extraordinarily free from not only inner suppressions and the divisions they produce, but from all the artificialities of culture. Doubtless like the rest of us he had his inner doubts, perplexities and depressions. But the unconscious and spontaneous vigor of his personality consumed and assimilated these things in the buoyant and nevertheless tranquil outgivings of thought and action.

He experienced great difficulty in finding adequate verbal expression for his philosophical ideas. His philosophy often found utterance in technical form. In the early years especially it was often not easy to follow his thought; he gained clarity of verbal expression of his philosophy gradually and through constant effort. Yet this fact is evidence of the unity of his philosophy and his own native being. For him philosophy was less acquired from without, a more genuine development from within, than in the case of any thinker I have known. If he had borrowed his ideas from without, he could have borrowed his language from the same source, and in uttering ideas that were already current, saying with some different emphasis what was already in other persons' minds, he would easily have been understood. But his mind was deeply original,—in my contacts and my judgment the most original mind in philosophy in the America of the last generations. From some cause of which we have no knowledge concerning genuinely original minds, he had early in life an intuition, an insight in advance of his day. Of necessity, there was not ready and waiting for him any language in which to express it. Only as the thoughts of others gradually caught up with what he felt and saw could he articulate himself. Yet his native vigor was such that he never thought of ceasing the effort. He was of such a sociable nature that he must have been disappointed by the failure of others to understand him, but he never allowed it to discourage his efforts to make his ideas intelligible to others. And while in recent years his efforts were crowned with success, there was no period in which his mind was not so creative that any one in contact with it failed to get stimulation; there was a new outlook upon life and the world that continued to stir and bring forth fruit in one's own thought. His mind was germinative and seminal. One would have to go far to find a teacher of our own day who started in others so many fruitful lines of thought; I dislike to think what my own thinking might have been were it not for the seminal ideas which I derived from him. For his ideas were always genuinely original; they started one thinking in directions where it had never occurred to one that it was worth while even to look.

There was a certain diffidence which restrained George Mead from much publication. But even more than that there was the constant activity of his mind as it moved out into new fields;

there were always new phases of his own ideas germinating within him. More than any one I have known he maintained a continuity of ideas with constant development. In my earliest days of contact with him, as he returned from his studies in Berlin forty years ago, his mind was full of the problem which has always occupied him, the problem of individual mind and consciousness in relation to the world and society. His psychological and philosophical thinking during the intervening years never got far from the central push of his mind. But his mind was so rich and so fruitful that he was always discovering new phases and relations. He combined in a remarkable way traits usually separated—a central idea and unceasing growth. In consequence he was always dissatisfied with what he had done; always outgrowing his former expressions, and in consequence so reluctant to fix his ideas in the printed word that for many years it was his students and his immediate colleagues who were aware of the tremendous reach and force of his philosophic mind. His abounding vigor manifested itself in transcending his past self and in immediate communication with those about him. His mind was a forum of discussion with itself and of sharing discussion with those with whom he had personal contact. I cannot think of him without seeing him engaged in untired discussion with himself and others, turning over and over his ideas and uncovering their hitherto unsuspected aspects and relations. Unlike, however, most minds of intense vigor he had no interest in imposing his mind on others—it was discussion and discovery that interested, not the creation of his own mental image in others.

No reference to his abounding and outgoing energy would be anything like adequate that did not allude to the range and breadth of his intellectual interests. His grasp and learning were encyclopedic. When I first knew him he was reading and absorbing biological literature in its connection with mind and the self. If he had published more, his influence in giving a different turn to psychological theory would be universally recognized. I attribute to him the chief force in this country in turning psychology away from mere introspection and aligning it with biological and social facts and conceptions. Others drew freely upon his new insights and reaped the reward in reputation which he was too interested in subject-matter for its own sake to claim for himself. From biology he went on to sociology, history, the religious literature of the world, and physical science. General literature was always his companion. His learning without exaggeration may be termed encyclopedic. But perhaps only a few are aware of his intense love of poetry. It is only within the last few days that I became aware from members of his immediate family of not only his appreciation of poetry but his capacious retentive memory. He knew large parts of Milton by heart, and has been known to repeat it for two hours without flagging. Wordsworth and Keats and Shakespeare, especially the sonnets, were equally familiar to him. Those who have accompanied him on his walks through mountains, where his physical energy and courage never flagged have told me how naturally and spontaneously any turn of the landscape evoked from him a memory of English poetry that associated itself with what he saw and deeply felt in nature. An accurate and almost photographic memory is rarely associated with a mind that assimilates, digests and reconstructs; in this combination as in so many others, Mr. Mead was so rare that his personality does not lend itself to analysis and classification.

George Mead's generosity of mind was the embodiment of his generosity of character. Everything in the ordinary and extraordinary duties of life claimed him and he gave himself completely. I am sure it never occurred to him that he was sacrificing himself; the entire ethics of self-sacrifice was alien to his thought. He gave himself so spontaneously and so naturally that only those close to him could be aware that he was spending his energy so freely. So too, while he was extraordinarily tolerant and charitable in his judgments of persons and events, I am confident it never occurred to him that he was so. His tolerance was not a cultivated and self-conscious matter; it grew out of the abundant generosity of his nature. He had the liveliest interest in every social problem and issue of the day. If at times he tended to idealize, to find more meaning and better meaning in movements about him than less generous eyes could see, it was because of the same outgoing abundance of his nature. While his insight was keen and shrewd, one can not associate anything of the nature of cynicism with him. Henry Mead has told me that the phrase which he most associates with his father when any social problem was under discussion is, "It ought to be possible to do so and so"; having seen the vision of possibility his mind at once turned to considering how the possibility could be realized. His extraordinary faith in possibilities was the source of his idealism.

I shall not try to give any idea, even an inadequate one of his philosophical conceptions; this is not the time or place. But there are three phases of them which are so intimately associated with his own natural being, his instinctive response to the world about him, that I cannot forego mentioning them. Every one who knew him philosophically at all is aware of his interest in the immediate aspect of human experience—an interest not new in literature but new in the form which it took in his philosophy. I am sure I am not wrong in connecting this interest, so central in his whole philosophy, with his own immediate sensibility to all the scenes of nature and humanity. He wrote little, I believe, on esthetics, but in many ways the key to his thought seems to me to be his own intense and immediate appreciation of life and nature and literature—and if we do not call this appreciation esthetic, it is because it includes so much more than is contained in the conventional meaning that word has taken on.

All who have intellectual association with Mr. Mead, directly or indirectly, also know how central was his conception of the "complete act"—the source of whatever is sound in the behavioristic psychology and active philosophy of our day. In the integrated act there is found the union of doing, of thought, and of emotion which traditional psychologies and philosophies have sundered and set against one another. This renovating, this regenerating, idea also had its source in George Mead's own personality. There was no division in his philosophy between doing, reflection and feeling, because there was none in himself.

Again every one who knows anything about Mr. Mead knows of his vital interest in social psychology, and in a social interpretation of life and the world. It is perhaps here that his influence is already most widely felt; I know that his ideas on this subject worked a revolution in my own thinking though I was slow in grasping anything like its full implications. The individual mind, the conscious self, was to him the world of nature first taken up into social relations and then dissolved to form a new self which then went forth to recreate the world of nature and social institutions. He would never have felt this idea so deeply and so centrally if it had not been such a complete embodiment of the depth and fullness of his own personality in all its human and social relations to others. The integrity and the continuing development of George Mead's philosophy is the natural and unforced expression of his own native being.

One feels not only a sense of tragic personal loss in the death of George Mead, but a philosophical calamity in that he was not able to extend and fill out his recently delivered Carus lectures. But if the publication of his ideas is incomplete and cut short, one has no such sense in connection with George Mead's own life and personality. In all relationships, it stands forth as a complete, because integral thing. Would that he might have lived longer with his family, his friends, his students, his books and his studies. But no added length of years could have added to the completeness of his personal being; it could not have added even to the fullness with which he continues to live in the lives of those who knew him. His life continues within us who knew him. It shames us from sloth, from indifference and cynicism; it lives not only as a precious and sweet memory, but as an invocation to whatever is positive, generous and outgoing. May we share in some measure his constant and untired faith in the possibilities of life, and his devoted interest in all the ways in which these possibilities may be realized. It was in and through that religious conviction that he gave unweariedly of himself and as he gave, grew in stature of manhood.

Human Nature

The significance of the idea of human nature for the social sciences gathers about three questions: (1) Are contemporary political and economic institutions necessary products of
human nature? Or, more generally, does the very constitution of
human nature show that certain social arrangements are likely to
be successful while others are doomed to failure? Is war, for example, inevitable because of facts of human nature? Is self-interest
so ingrained in human nature that the attempt to base industry
on anything except a competitive struggle for private gain is sure
to fail? (2) How far is human nature modifiable by deliberate
effort? Or, in other words, which is more important, nature or
nurture? Or, in still another form, how are heredity and environment related to one another? Which is more potent in the determination of behavior? (3) How great and how fixed is the range
of variations in human nature between individuals and between
groups? Are some racial or social groups by nature definitely inferior to others because of causes which cannot be altered? The
same question is asked concerning individuals within each group.

These questions are bound up with controversies involving intense feeling. They largely condition the differences between
conservatives and liberals, between aristocrats and democrats,
between nationalists and internationalists. They are associated
with emotions of complacency, pride and egoism. It is therefore
extremely difficult to attain impartiality with respect to them,
and discussions are often apologetics for some position already
assumed on partisan grounds. There is, however, one incontro-
vertible fact about human nature—that the term has been used
in a variety of senses and that in the history of thought there has
been some correspondence between the interpretation of the

[First published in *Encyclopaedia of the Social Sciences* (New York: Macmillan Co., 1932), 7:531–37.]

concept and the general institutional and intellectual character of the time.

Four principal conceptions of the term may be mentioned: (1) The term is used to designate an alleged original and native constitution; that which is instinctive instead of acquired. There is a possible ambiguity here unless it is made clear whether the native constitution is taken to be common to all normal human beings or is one peculiar to particular individuals. (2) Human nature is defined in terms of alleged psychological powers or faculties, the "psychological" being placed in antithesis to both the physical and the social. Every normal human being is said to have certain powers, like perception, judgment, memory, desire. These powers are formal; they are to be distinguished from what is perceived, remembered, thought about, wanted. The material content is held to come from sources outside of human nature, from either physical nature or social life. This assumed dualism between human nature and other nature has been so widely prevalent that it often affects discussions without being avowed: to many persons it is a direct product of "common sense." It has behind it a long intellectual history: formulated by John Locke, it was taken up by the British liberal school and became the basis of a distinction, on one side, between intrinsic "natural" law and "natural" rights (which are fixed and universal in the formal structure of human nature) and, on the other side, between artificial civil and political rights, which vary with conditions. (3) Human nature is in itself empty and formless and is therefore capable of being molded by external influences. Locke himself had declared that the mind is a piece of blank paper as far as any particular ideas and beliefs are concerned, although he had endowed it with certain formal faculties or powers. His French successors, like Condillac and particularly Helvétius, thought they were rendering him logically consistent when they held that "faculties" also were impressed on the mind by experience, mind being nothing but susceptibility to impressions from without. In this view education and the influence of the environment are all powerful. If men are corrupt and prejudiced, seeking only their private power and profit, it is only because institutions have formed them in their own likeness. (4) Human nature cannot be properly conceived or defined in terms of the constitution of individuals either native or acquired.

Human nature can be known only through its great institutional products—language, religion, law and the state, the arts. As displayed in individuals it is merely potential; it develops into reality under the influence of cultural institutions, which form the content of objective mind and will. This theory drew some of its support from the teachings of Aristotle, especially in applying the distinction of "potential" and "actual" to human nature. But it was formulated especially by the school of institutional idealists headed by Hegel. Aside from any metaphysical formulation it influenced for a generation or more German students of comparative language, religion and law and was a great factor in producing the conception of a social mind which was made the basis of an entire school of social psychology.

It is obviously hopeless to look for agreement as to the modifiability of human nature or its relation to society, where the very content of the term is so variously conceived. The last named conception, for example, expressly denies that the facts of original, or native, structure and instinct which the first conception treats as constituting human nature are anything more than crude and undeveloped potentialities, so inchoate in themselves that we could not even give them names were it not for knowledge of what they are capable of becoming, a knowledge which is had only by noting the institutional forms of a mature culture. We have here an instance of the controversy as old as Aristotle as to whether "nature" is to be defined in terms of origin or of complete development, i.e. of "ends." At first sight it might seem as if the difference could be explained away as merely one in verbal definition, one school using the word for one set of facts and the other school for another. If this were all there might be disagreement about the application of a word and yet agreement about the things to which different names are applied. Such, however, is not the case. The supposition that there is such a thing as a purely native original constitution of man which can be distinguished from everything acquired and learned cannot be justified by appeal to the facts. It is a view which holds good only when a static cross section is taken; when, that is to say, growth is ignored. The theory takes, as it were, a snapshot of man at, for example, birth, ignoring past history in the uterus and future history when the supposedly fixed and ready made structures will change as they interact with surroundings. Biologically all growth is modification and all organs have to be treated and understood as developments out of something else and as pointing forward to still something else. The conception of a fixed and enumerable equipment of tendencies which constitutes human nature thus represents at the best but a convenient intellectual device, a bench mark useful for studying some particular period of development. Taking a long enough time span, it is fruitless to try to distinguish between the native and the acquired, the original and the derived. The acquired may moreover become so deeply ingrained as to be for all intents and purposes native, a fact recognized in the common saying that "habit is second nature." And, on the other hand, taking a long biological evolution into account, that which is now given and original is the outcome of long processes of past growth.

Practically, however, with reference to the possibility of control the distinction between the native and the acquired is important. Barring some future possible development of eugenics, our practical control of growth begins at birth; in controlling future developments we must start with what exists at that time. Existing organs, impulses, instinctive tendencies, form the resources and the capital on which future development must build. Included in this native stock is, however, the tendency to learn and to acquire. That the tendency to learn and hence to modify and be modified is itself part of the native (and hereditary) structure may appear too much of a truism to need statement. Nevertheless, this must be borne in mind, since it is decisive in showing how impossible it is to make any hard and fast distinction between the natural and the acquired, the native and cultural. The capacity for modification is part of the natural make up of every human tendency; it belongs to an unlearned equipment (as that is defined at a particular time) for learning, in which process it is itself changed. Recognition of this fact will save us from devoting energy to unreal questions and lead to concentration upon the important ones: What are the limits to modification through learning? How does the modification concretely proceed? How is it controllable?

On this question—in fact, on all issues concerned with human nature—men have entertained historically a variety of views. Classic Greek thought is based upon belief in the natural and inherent inequality of men. The most widely known expression of this point of view is Aristotle's statement that some men are slaves "by nature" and hence are to be ranked with tools and domestic cattle as means of production. The entire class of mechanics even if legally freemen belongs in this category, being by nature shut out from the truly free or liberal life, that of the mind. Retail shopkeepers are means also of serving material purposes and do not belong to the realm of ends. While this view was to some extent a rationalization of social prejudices which had been incorporated into the Athenian system it was also something more—a systematically thought out interpretation of human nature. In this interpretation the reason given for holding that some men are slaves by nature—even more important than the view itself—was that they possess an inherent deficiency in rational insight. Reason is the governing power in man; it is a condition of self-government and participation in civic government. Impulses and passions must be kept in subjection to rational aims unless there is to be social and moral chaos. Hence it is intrinsically proper that some persons should be the animate instruments of others. The mass of non-Athenians who were not citizens and also not slaves but classed as mechanics (i.e. tools) by nature were said to occupy a lower status morally than slaves, since the latter, living in a certain intimacy of communication with their masters in the household, attained a kind of reflected rationality. Women were also ranked as constitutionally inferior and hence as properly subject to fathers and husbands; so also were the barbarians as compared with the Greeks, although the northern races, in whom spirited impulses are strong, were ranked higher than Asiatics, in whom appetites for ease, possession and passive enjoyment were dominant.

After the decay of Athenian culture at the time when the stoics were the ruling school of thought it was assumed as axiomatic that men are equal by nature and that differences among them are differences of status due to convention, to political organization and to economic relations, which are instituted rather than natural. So complete a revolution in thought in a few centuries is difficult to account for, but among the influences may be discerned the fact that the cynic precursors of the stoics were drawn largely from a proletariat class having no citizenship. The decay of the city-state with its intimate organization of loyalties, the growth of the impersonal Roman Empire, the weakening of local ties and the development of cosmopolitan sentiment were among the objective forces at work.

The doctrine in its original form did not have radical implications regarding existing institutions. The conception that political and economic inequality was based not on nature but on institution carried with it no attack on the latter. The stoic idea was favorable to the spread of a moral sentiment of confraternity among individuals as individuals, but in general it called for loyal acceptance of one's status in the existing social order. When the Christian church proclaimed the same doctrine of natural equality, it was also interpreted in a religious and moral sense free from political implications. Doctrines, however, outlive their original context, and at later times the stoic and Christian idea of natural equality was given a revolutionary interpretation.

The blend of Greek thought and oriental culture known as Hellenistic and centering at Alexandria took another turn, adverse to attaching value to nature in any form, physical or human. Because of what Gilbert Murray has termed "failure of nerve" the age centered its intellectual and emotional interest on the supernatural and on the special means by which favorable relations with it were to be established. Little value was attached to social institutions of any kind in comparison with the method by which redemption of the soul was to be effected. The depreciatory view of nature which was instilled became associated with religion in the degree in which the latter lost the definite civic form it had in classic antiquity.

The main direction of thought in the mediaeval period represents a synthesis of ideas derived from different sources. There was the idea of the natural equality of men, an idea especially cherished during the earlier period in which the membership of the Christian churches was composed mainly of the disinherited. Morally speaking, a strongly democratic sentiment was inculcated. There was also, however, the tradition of the insignificant value of the natural in comparison with the spiritual interests represented by a superworldly kingdom. In fact, because of the corruption of nature due to the fall of man complete subjection of the natural man to the discipline and sacraments of the church was required, since the church was the divinely instituted and supported guardian of spiritual truth. The ascetic influences which prevailed in monastic circles accentuated the depreciatory view taken of the natural. At the same time, as the church became established as the supreme European institution and its doctrine took shape in scholastic philosophy, its official theory grew far from hostile to the conception of nature. On the contrary, under the influence of revived Aristotelianism it gave nature a place and validity of its own within definite limits; namely, as subordinate to revelation wherever the latter had spoken authoritatively. Moreover, as the struggle for authority between church and empire became acute, the doctrine of the conventional and instituted or positive character of political authority took a form distinctly hostile to the claims of the latter, so that the teachings of the church theorists helped to furnish later revolutionaries with weapons of attack upon the authority of autocratic governments.

It is a commonplace that what is called the modern period was marked by a new interest in and by a new respect for nature. This extended to human nature. There were explicit attempts to free moral and political theory from ecclesiastic and indeed from all institutional influence. The positive side of this movement found the authority needed for the new morals and politics in human nature. But a cleavage showed itself almost at once with respect to the constitution of human nature in a controversy as to what element is dominant "naturally" and must therefore according to the theory be considered the support of political theory and practise. One school foreshadowed by Grotius and developed by his continental successors in the natural law tradition emphasized "reason" as the important factor. This, however, had little but the name in common with the classic Greek conception, although somewhat more kinship with the stoic conception. Reason was the universal element; the universal was the common, and the common was the bond of union among all men. It was the social tie which holds all human beings together in society even apart from and prior to the formation of a political state. Its social nature is expressed in the natural, or moral, laws which underlie political organization, and to which the latter must conform if it is to be just. A series of jurists and philosophers deduced the state with its basic laws and its systems of civil rights from this element in human nature.

English thought took a different turn in the seventeenth century, in which it was followed upon the whole by influential

French thought in the eighteenth century. Continental thought was meant to justify law and authority by showing their accord with rationality as the reigning element in human nature. English thought was concerned to protect individuals from the encroachments of governmental action and, when necessary, to justify revolt. Psychologically it started from desire and emotion instead of reason and ended in a theory of rights instead of obligations. The writings of Thomas Hobbes, the real founder of British theory, are important in this connection even though outwardly he employed his doctrine to substantiate the claims of a powerful centralized state. In so doing he was actuated by hostility to the claims of churchmen—Presbyterians, Independents, Church of England adherents as well as Catholics—and he appealed directly to the affective side of human nature as primary. Moved by the civil wars and disintegration of his time, he appealed especially to fear and the need of security. English political thought after Hobbes consistently interpreted human nature in terms of the primacy of non-rational factors, pointing out that these employed reason as a means of obtaining satisfaction for themselves.

With the rise of the new industry and commerce, however, an important variation was introduced. The economists who set out to give intellectual expression to the rising industrialism started from the affective side of human nature in accordance with prevailing English doctrine. They developed, however, a much more systematic theory than had ever been developed of the nature and operation of wants, out of which came a new conception of natural law. Economic activity, on this view, is basic; from it are derived the natural, in the sense of non-artificial, laws of human conduct. Society is the product of the efforts of human beings to satisfy their wants, since division of labor, exchange and permanent property are involved in this satisfaction. Government and political action exist in a secondary way in order to give security to the free play of economic forces. In its early stage the theory was thoroughly optimistic in its anticipations of the future of society when freed from the artificial regulations of political action. The conception of natural harmony was implicit or explicit. The land and rent theory of Ricardo and the population theory of Malthus introduced factors of inevitable disharmony and conflict which later gave a pessimistic turn to the view entertained of the workings of human nature.

It would thus appear that during the greater part of the history of European thought conceptions of human nature have been framed not with scientific objectiveness but on the basis of what was needed to give intellectual formulation and support to practical social movements. There is a reason for this beyond the ordinary tendency to use ideas to further practical activities. A new social movement brings into play factors in human nature which were hitherto dormant or concealed; in thus evoking them into action it also presents them to the notice of organized thought. A striking example of this fact is the reversal by most recent theory of the place attributed to wants in classic Greek speculation. In Greek thought wants were a sign of defect; they were to be kept under strict control inasmuch as they were the chief causes of social and moral disorder. Since the industrial revolution theory has generally held that wants are the motors of social progress, the dynamic force in creation of initiative, invention, the production of wealth and new forms of satisfaction.

The factors which have of late operated to put the question of the constitution of human nature on a more objective basis are the rise of a psychology with biological foundations and the development of anthropology. The psychological factor has made it clear that if definitive results are to be reached regarding the native or original equipment of man they must be sought from physiological study correlated with structural studies of human behavior at various stages of growth, especially intra-uterine and immediately postnatal. The native equipment is, roughly speaking, identical with the biological equipment; recognition of this fact will in time take the theories of the matter out of the area of speculation into that of observable fact. Anthropology, on the other hand, has made it clear that the varieties of cultural and institutional forms which have existed are not to be traced to anything which can be called original unmodified human nature but are the products of interaction with the social environment; they are functions, in the mathematical sense, of institutional organization and cultural traditions as these operate to shape raw biological material into definitively human shape. If we except the extreme partisan stand, it may be regarded as now generally accepted that the immense diversities of culture which have existed and which still exist cannot possibly be derived directly from any stock of original powers and impulses; that the problem is one of explaining in its own terms the diversification of the culture milieus which act upon original human nature. As this fact gains recognition, the problem of modifiability is being placed upon the same level as the persistence of custom or tradition; it is wholly a matter of empirical determination, not of a priori theorizing. It cannot be doubted that there are some limits to modifiability of human nature and to institutional change, but these limits have to be arrived at by experimental observation. At present there are no adequate experimental data on which pronouncements may be based. Moreover when such limits are found it will be important to discover whether they are intrinsic and absolute or whether they are to some extent due to limitations of our technique for effecting change. Certainly some of the limits existing at any particular time will recede, exactly as have the earlier limits in control of the energies of physical nature, with increased knowledge of causal factors. At the present time, for example, we can predict to some extent on a statistical basis the effects of educational measures. But the effect of education upon the development of a particular individual is, as far as foresight is concerned, still largely a matter of guesswork. It would be hard to find a fact by which to illustrate more forcibly the limitations of our present technique in effecting modification of human nature. Although schools abound, education as a controlled process of modification of disposition is hardly even in its infancy.

The present controversies between those who assert the essential fixity of human nature and those who believe in a great measure of modifiability centre chiefly around the future of war and the future of a competitive economic system motivated by private profit. It is justifiable to say without dogmatism that both anthropology and history give support to those who wish to change these institutions. It is demonstrable that many of the obstacles to change which have been attributed to human nature are in fact due to the inertia of institutions and to the voluntary desire of powerful classes to maintain the existing status. With regard to the possibility of economic reconstruction history demonstrates the comparative youth of the present regime; and revolutionary societies may be regarded as social laboratories in which is being tested the possibility of securing economic advance by means of other incentives than those which operate in capitalistic countries. For the immediate present all that can reasonably be hoped for with reference to the general issue of human nature are: a willingness to substitute special concrete plans of modification for wholesale claims and denials; the growth of a scientific attitude which will weaken the force of ideas and battle cries coming from the past; willingness to see social experiments tried without interference by outside force; and the use of educational means that are regulated by intelligent foresight and planning instead of by routine and tradition.

See: MAN; INSTINCT; HABIT; CONTINUITY, SOCIAL; CHANGE, SOCIAL; CONTROL, SOCIAL; INSTITUTION; RACE; CULTURE; ENVIRONMENTALISM; HEREDITY; ECONOMIC INCENTIVES; ALTRUISM AND EGOISM; EQUALITY; SOCIAL REFORM.

Consult: Dewey, John, *Human Nature and Conduct* (New York 1922), and *Experience and Nature* (Chicago 1925); Cooley, C. H., *Human Nature and the Social Order* (rev. ed. New York 1922), especially introduction; Hocking, W. E., *Human Nature and Its Remaking* (2nd ed. New Haven 1923); Thorndike, E. L., *The Original Nature of Man* in his *Educational Psychology*, vol. i (New York 1913); Boas, Franz, *The Mind of Primitive Man* (New York 1911), and *Anthropology and Modern Life* (New York 1928); Wallas, Graham, *The Great Society* (London 1914), *Our Social Heritage* (New Haven 1921), and *Human Nature in Politics* (3rd ed. London 1914); Bernard, L. L., *Instinct, a Study in Social Psychology* (New York 1924), especially ch. x; Josey, C. C., *The Role of Instinct in Social Philosophy* (New York 1921); Ward, Lester F., "Mind as a Social Factor" in *Glimpses of the Cosmos*, 6 vols. (New York 1913–18) vol. iii, p. 361–77, and *Applied Sociology* (Boston 1906) ch. viii; Carlyle, R. W. and A. J., *A History of Mediaeval Political Theory in the West*, 5 vols. (Edinburgh 1903–28) vol. i; Park, Robert E., "Human Nature, Attitudes, and the Mores" in *Social Attitudes*, ed. by Kimball Young (New York 1931) ch. ii; Ogburn, W. F., *Social Change with Respect to Culture and Original Nature* (New York 1922), especially pt. i; Veblen, Thorstein B., *The Instinct of Workmanship* (New York 1914), and "The Preconceptions of Economic Science" in *The Place of Science in Modern Civilisation* (New York 1919) p. 82–179; Mitchell, Wesley C., "Human Behavior and Economics" in *Quarterly Journal of Economics*, vol. xxix (1914–15) 1–47; Tawney, R. H., *The Acquisitive Society* (New York 1920).

Politics and Culture

If I should try to go into the underlying philosophy that is implied in this problem, I would be raising one of the most difficult and disputed questions. I refer to the problem of the relationship between conditions, environment, and one's mental and aesthetic development. There are those who hold that politics is an external matter, and that ideas are capable of free development irrespective of outer environment. And similarly there are those who claim that it is also putting the cart before the horse to attempt any kind of political reform or modification of the economic system before having changed man's beliefs, man's desires and aspirations. They hold, in general, that if only you change people's faiths, their hopes, beliefs and desires, that social changes will then take care of themselves. Social changes in themselves they regard as external, as not really affecting the makeup of people's minds, thoughts, currents of feeling—what for short I call culture. The opposing view holds that the mind, thought and mental activity which we call culture is essentially, for the mass of the people, so conditioned by the social environment in which they live that it results in merely a futile appeal to something that does not exist when cultural development is separated from the environmental.

However, I am not going to discuss that problem in general, but rather to take up a specific and limited question.

It is obvious that there are two tests or measures which we can apply to any social system. One of them is the physical and material.

What does the given system do to and with people's lives with respect to ease, comfort, maintenance of a secure and decent standard of living? It does not need any argument at the present

[First published in *Modern Thinker* 1 (May 1932): 168–74, 238, from a lecture at the Rand School of Social Science, New York City, 14 March 1932.]

time to say that our existing social system does not stand up very well under the application of this particular test. The other measure is the relation of the social system to the development and maintenance of what I shall for the moment call culture.

One of the phases of culture is free, easy, ready effective distribution of knowledge and ideas. By this free circulation of knowledge and ideas, I mean something more than the mere absence of censors, mere absence of deliberate suppression of new ideas, and of forms of knowledge that are not in consonance with the beliefs of a particular group that has political control. Of course those barriers are very important. But there is something more included in free circulation of ideas than simply the absence of legal restrictions on their circulation. There are restrictions that are more insidious, more intangible, and in many ways, more effective. People may be shut out from free access to ideas simply because of preoccupation of their time and energy. So taken up are they with other things that they do not have intellectual strength, and energy and time left to give any time to "ideas."

There may be lack of free circulation simply because of class barriers, and because a limited minority group holds a virtual monopoly of whole ranges of ideas and of knowledge. Communication, in other words, is not something which takes place automatically merely by the removal of legal barriers of censorship and suppression. It requires a common background of common experiences and of common desires to bring about this free distribution of knowledge.

In all existing societies the members speak in more or less different languages. Everybody in the United States might conceivably speak what grammatically would be classified as the English language and yet there would be different languages spoken. A trained technician speaks a different language from the ordinary layman; the ecclesiastic, church-going citizen speaks a different language from those who have a different moral or religious tradition and background.

There is food for thought in this matter of the variety of languages spoken among people that are outwardly using the same tongue, since they form barriers to free circulation of ideas and knowledge of all kinds. One might perhaps point to literary criticism. The function of literature is to use a language which potentially is capable of being understood, and of being conveyed to great masses. Perhaps, starting from this point of view, we could draw conclusions as to some of the troubles and difficulties from which literature suffers in this country at the present time.

Another aspect of culture is the enjoyment of poetry, literature, drama, music, the arts in general: enlarged capacity for the enjoyment of natural beauties and such things as gardens, the furniture of our houses, the utensils that we use. We lose a great deal by identifying culture in its aesthetic phase only with the arts to which we prefix the word "fine." Aesthetic enjoyment is superficial when it is not based upon and is not drawn out of the environment. A multiplicity of smaller things are needed to peace and enjoyment constantly in the daily contacts of life. The third aspect of culture is the active side of the two forms which I have just mentioned. Genuine culture stimulates the creative powers of imagination, of mind and of thought. It includes not merely free access to things of mind and taste already in existence, but a positive production of them, so that the waters of knowledge and of ideas are kept really fresh and vital.

I have made this sketchy survey of the chief element of culture in order to raise a question: How does our own civilization, how does American life, our social system, stand the test of the application of this measure of value. Do we not come out here as badly as, perhaps even worse, than we do under the more direct physical and material tests?

That is a question upon which you get very supreme difference of opinion. There are those who seem professionally committed to glorify everything in this country; to shout that it is the most wonderful country, the most wonderful system, that ever existed anywhere. And there are others who think that pretty much everything is down or going down in this country.

I think no one can deny that in certain ways we have in this country provided the external means of a very general development of culture. We have our school systems from the kindergarten up to the university. We have our free libraries, our museums, books, periodicals and so on. There is a machinery for a very general wide circulation and distribution of knowledge. On the other hand, I suppose no one would claim that we take full advantage of this machinery, or that our schools fully realize all their possibilities. They are potential assets rather than actualized resources.

Most people will agree, in their honest moments, that we sacrifice quality to quantity, we tend to be satisfied when we have provided the physical plan and the administrative means, assuming that things are going to work themselves, irrespective of the human minds behind them. In the higher forms of culture, of science and art we have as yet not reached the level of some countries in Europe, even of countries that have few of our external facilities.

One answer to this criticism is that Americans have been too occupied making a conquest of new territory, bringing it under subjection to man, to have time to devote to higher things, and that we shall make culture when we shall be finished with the physical, material side of life.

Another reason given by some, is that culture, by its very nature, in its higher forms, is limited to a minority group, so that higher culture and aristocracy are practically inseparable things. It is asserted that the attempt to bring culture to everybody means a dilution, an attenuation to such a point that it loses everything that makes it most distinctive.

Historically there is a great deal to be said for this view. As a rule, small groups of people belonging to the ruling leisure class have been the patrons of the arts. This is true from the time of ancient Greece well into the eighteenth century—as the dedication even of the writings of the greater authors in English literature testify. The literary people were accustomed to look to some nobleman for patronage and recognition. This was the only way of securing themselves a livelihood.

In the days of the Czar, music, drama, and the novel in Russia represented the highest level of achievement of any country in Europe, in spite of the political backwardness of the country. This fact suggests the argument of those that democratic culture, in approaching universality, attains a level much lower than the high-water marks of aristocratic cultures of the past.

Now, I want to make an abrupt deviation to a consideration of the economic phase of the social order in respect to the development of culture along the three lines of which I have spoken. I wish to raise the question whether the limitations to widely distributed culture, are really due to limitations in human nature itself, limitations which weaken and dilute it in exact proportion as it spreads, so that the intensity of culture is in inverse ratio to the number of people that share it.

First, is it not possible that the commercialism of our economic system is a greater restricting force than the inherent mental or psychological deficiencies on the part of the mass of the population?

Adverse opinions as to the possibility of a general democratic culture are also based on the low standards, intellectually and aesthetically, of the radio, the movie and the popular theatre. Is there not a possibility that the standards of these things are low (I think we all agree that they are much lower than they ought to be) ultimately because of economic causes?

Those in control of the existing system, those, that is, who are in control of the marketing of these products, find that the shortest and easiest way to get the money that they are after is to maintain low standards. It may be said in reply that they could not make money out of them unless they gave the people what they wanted, so that the fact that they can make money by giving a low order of product, intellectually and aesthetically, is none the less a proof of the incapacity of the mass to appreciate what is good. The argument, I think, is like that of the newspapers to the effect that they give the people what they want. First they created an appetite for certain kinds of things, and after they have led people to want those things, then they give it to them on the ground that they are merely handing out to people the things they want. It is not the populace that finally makes the demand but the source of supply which fixes its level. The pecuniary motivation that controls so much of art has to be taken into account. We should hardly get the kind of thing on the level that exists were it not for the pecuniary profit involved.

I have never been a great believer in what some people call "pure" science, meaning by that science with no human application. But there are a good many different kinds of application. There is the application of physiology to the improvement of health and the removal of disease. There is the application of physics to making money. There is the application of chemistry in the production of poison gases and high explosives for use in war. Is the cause, then, of the comparative backwardness of the United States in the sciences, the mere fact of interest in practical application? Or is it the existence of an economic regime which places emphasis upon application for the sake of pecuniary profit? Is it not due to the deflection that is given intellectual activity by the enormous premium that our economic system puts not just on the application of science, but on dominance by commercial and pecuniary ends? Often, literary people criticize American culture and society without any reference to the underlying economic system. And hence to my mind they deal with effects rather than causes.

I want to discriminate definitely between application in general and application of the narrower commercial and money-making type. Just why a scientific man would the less be concerned with scientific discoveries because they can be put to human use in raising the level of human life, I have never been able to see. There are some people in whom the mere motive of research is so strong that they do not need to think of anything else. But many of these would not lose interest in truth and in discovery if they were also aware of beneficial applications of their discoveries.

I have never heard that Pasteur's researches, the beginning of the revolution of modern medicine, were any the less strictly scientific in character because Pasteur was also moved by consideration of human suffering which might be relieved by the execution of his scientific researches.

One more illustration: I do not see how any very high popular artistic standard can exist where a great many of the people are living in slums. Such persons cannot get artistic culture simply by going to free concerts or the Metropolitan Museum to look at pictures, or the public library to read books, as long as their immediate surroundings, or what they come into direct contact with, unconsciously habituates them to ugly, sordid things. A small number of people may come through with genuine aesthetic appreciation even under these circumstances. Even those who have, economically speaking, the most opportunities for higher culture, become insensitive to the ugliness that exists in our human environment. Architectural critics point out, for example, that there are slums on Park Avenue as well as in other quarters of the city. The packing box architecture, produced for the sake of profit, has its advantage over that of tenement houses, but it is hardly of a type to raise the aesthetic and artistic standards.

When there has been a high popular degree of aesthetic appreciation, as by the free men in Athens, it was because the entire environment acted upon the senses so as to render them appreciative of symmetry and beauty, acutely aware of any deviation from the best type of aesthetic achievement.

We pride ourselves, and with some good reason, on a free universal system of education. But, leaving out even all question of quality, our accomplishment is rather elementary from the standpoint of the population that it reaches. Of course, there are a great many more colleges now than there existed forty years ago. But still over half the school population leaves school at twelve, fourteen, fifteen years of age.

When we consider the complexity of modern life, the extent to which it depends upon the application of scientific knowledge, and then consider how much the average young person of fourteen or fifteen can carry away from school at that age, we can see how the mentality is limited, if it has no further opportunities. We are still very far from having realized the ideal of a universal education even from the quantitative point of view. While the question of the qualitative values raises altogether too large a point to go into here.

Are, then, criticisms which are made as to the possibility of a genuine democratic culture rightly directed when they are centered upon the supposed inherent incapacity of a large part of the population? The problem is not a settled one. It is conceivable that the best possible economic system would still leave a very considerable part of the population remaining on a low intellectual and artistic level because of intrinsic incapacity. I say it is possible. But I also say that while it is conceivable, we simply do not know; there is no more evidence for that view than there is for the contrary, and for a very simple reason. No systematic effort has ever been made as yet to find out what the real capacities of human nature in the mass are. The idea that in spite of our public school system, the intelligence quotient of a large part of the population ranges low, has no force as evidence on this point. Before it could have any weight as positive evidence, we should have to know all of the conditions out of schools as well as in schools, the social, economic, political, indirect influences of all kinds that played on those persons who do not show up well in tests.

Some old Greek philosophers held that it is necessary that there should be a large class, intellectually undeveloped, in order to support the few, and to give that minority the leisure that would enable them to have a free intellectual and highly developed life. Perhaps they were right, under the limited conditions of production in the ancient world. With the modern machine and modern inventiveness, with present command of raw material and technical skill, the reason for separation between culture of an aristocratic few and the absence of culture of the great mass, no longer holds.

There is the type of literary critic who is very much troubled about the machine and what the machine is doing to people who think that the machine is inherently brutalizing. They think it is a sign of hard, unaesthetic type of mind if one does not join them in their condemnation of the machine.

Well, I agree with those who hold that what has brutalized us is not the machine, but the owners of the machine who for money profit speed up the machine, work people too many hours, and under unhealthful conditions, and shut them out from all the intelligent phases of industry, such as management.

It is quite obvious, on reflection, that the machine might be a great liberator not merely of the human hand and muscle, but of the human mind, giving increase of time, of leisure, removing unnecessary expenditure of energy on mere physical labor, so that opportunity for cultural development would be increased.

One conclusion seems so obvious that nobody except the stoniest defender of the present economic order could question it. We never have tried the experiment of producing a widespread culture throughout the whole of society. Culture instead, has been the private possession of a small number of individuals. In order to try the experiment we shall have to modify the economic system so as to provide a secure basis for the free operation of mind, imagination and emotion. We shall have to remove all of the barriers that now prevent the free circulation of knowledge and ideas. We shall have to change the motivation of human energy so that it will not be diverted and deflected into channels of getting power over others to anything like the present extent.

The greatest part of mental ability, acuteness of thought, ingenuity, etc., in this country has gone into business. Some of it has gone into industry, but more of it into the business of manipulating the needs of others so that pecuniary profit can be made out of them. Many phases of cultural depression are the heavy shadows cast by economic depression and oppression. Our original democratic ideas must apply culturally as well as politically, and this end cannot be accomplished without economic transformation.

If we cannot produce a democratic culture, one growing natively out of our institutions, our democracy will be a failure. There is no question, not even that of bread and clothing, more important than this question of the possibility of executing our democratic ideals directly in the cultural life of the country.

Science and Society

[Address]

There is nothing new in the idea that the significant forms of present civilization in the western world, especially in the United States, are the result of that great revolution in the science of nature which was effected in the seventeenth century.

It is a commonplace that we live in an industrial age, where all human relations and all institutions are modified by new agencies of production, distribution and communication. It is equally a commonplace (though one not so often recognized) that the social changes produced by the industrial revolution are themselves the product of the application of the new science of nature.

It is well to remind ourselves that science itself is but a technique, an instrumentality, a refined and effective method of procedure. If we bear this fact in mind we shall be saved from both adulation of science as the source of enlightenment and progress and from the condemnation of science as the author of the social ills that are so obvious all about us. For we shall then realize that science like every other form of technique has to be applied by human beings in order to achieve results, and that the manner of its use goes back to the ideals and ideas which animate the human beings who employ the instrument. The essential technique of gunpowder is the same whether it is used to secure rocks from the quarry for building better human habitations, or to rain missiles of death upon a hapless population. And the technique of the machine is the same whether it is used to satisfy enduring human needs and create social happiness or to foster and satisfy the love of pecuniary gain and power over others.

[First published in *Lehigh Alumni Bulletin* 18 (July 1931): 6–7, from Dewey's commencement address at Lehigh University, Bethlehem, Pa., on 9 June 1931.]

The greatest problem facing civilization today, one might almost say the only ultimate problem, is the use which humanity is to make of the instrumentality of science and its related techniques—by far the most powerful instrument for good and for evil that mankind has ever known. In comparison with the hundreds of thousands of years that mankind has lived on earth, the instrument is an infant, even though the infant be a giant in stature.

The question arises as to what is to be done with that which has reached such a development that it no longer has to struggle for existence. These are the critical times, the periods of mutation. So it seems to be with natural science. It has reached a point where it cannot stand still, but neither can it go on just as it has been going. It has created a new external social environment which reacts upon all the activities of men; it now must face a new responsibility: The problem of direction and use for planned social results. Human beings are in possession of a perfected powerful tool, and must consider, unless they are to be overwhelmed by the accidental and unplanned operation of the tool, what they are going to do with it, what they are going to use it *for*.

In general, science has served as a tool for promoting interests and values that originated before it came. It has done little to change men's fundamental beliefs and attitudes in social matters. It has provided efficient means for realizing desires and purposes that hold over from a pre-scientific period; it has accomplished little in creating new aims and interests in accord with its own methods of operation. And so I return to the idea already suggested: This new instrument, science, offers to mankind the greatest moral challenge which humanity has ever had put to it.

We have had enough intelligence to create a new technique and instrument; we have not had enough to use what we have created deliberately and systematically for social purposes in control of the factors that shape the destinies of men. In an age when the forces of nature are assembled on a vast scale for production and physical distribution, in an age when individual human effort is conditioned by a vast impersonal system, we still mouth platitudes about individual effort and initiative which echo from the pre-scientific age.

The first lesson of scientific method is that its fruit is control within the region where the scientific technique operates. Our almost total lack of control in every sphere of social life, international and domestic, is, therefore, sufficient proof that we have not begun to operate scientifically in these fields. There is a great deal said in print and in personal conversation about the five year and ten year plan in Soviet Russia. But the fact that the plan is being tried by a country which has a political policy of which most of us disapprove tends to obscure the fundamental fact: namely that it is an organized plan of control—in other words an attempt to utilize the scientific technique of coordinated knowledge and intellectual skill, in order to achieve direction of physical forces for social ends. Either this attempt is intrinsically bound up with the communist system or it is not. If it is so bound up, there is an overt admission that scientific approach to social problems is possible only under a communist régime. If, as I believe, it is not so bound up, then there is a challenge and a warning to those of us who live under another political system to work out a method for thinking scientifically, effectively, about our social needs, problems, means and consequences, even though to do so we shall have to scrap outworn catchphrases and slogans and the sinister exhibitions of egoism which stand in the way. For the ultimate issue is not between individualism and socialism, capitalism and communism, but between undisciplined thinking and confused action, and scientific planning and action.

I return to the commonplace with which I set out. We are living in a world wherein change is unprecedented in scope and in rapidity of pace. But this statement is only half true. It holds of the outward applications of science. It does not hold of our intellectual and moral attitudes. About physical conditions and energies we think scientifically. At least some men do so, and all of us are affected at every point of our daily living by the consequences of their thinking. But we have hardly begun to think scientifically about our human relations. The entrenched institutions of centuries stand in the way of our making the attempt. When it concerns social issues, our mental habits are dominated by institutions of family, church, school, government and business that were built up before men had hit upon an effective technique of inquiry and verification, effective because eventuating in control. This is the contradiction in our living today. This contradiction, through our present, not some remote original disobedience, is the source of those mortal woes so much in evidence today.

We cannot continue the contradiction of a world in which outward effects are planned and controlled, while attitudes of mind which use these external consequences are left without scientific control, without heading for disaster. If it is true, as it is sometimes said, that our physical knowledge has far outrun our social or humane knowledge, it is true only because we fail to employ our physical knowledge and physical technologies for social ends. The idea that we can develop social science merely by collecting and ordering facts is as futile as was the older idea that natural science could be had without the experimental control of action. When we systematically use the knowledge and instrumentalities we already have to achieve the ends of a secure and abundant life which we know to be desirable, we shall begin to build up social science, just as men built up physical science when they actively used the technique of tools and numbers in physical discovery.

The greatest scientific revolution is therefore still to come. It will ensue when men collectively organize their knowledge for social application, and when they systematically use scientific procedures for the objective control of social relations. Great as have been the changes of the last century, those who are going forth from the colleges this year and next year will see changes with which those of the past are not to be compared, provided they go forth with faith in the possibility of dealing scientifically with social changes and with the stern and courageous determination to make that faith effective in works.

Science and Society

[*Philosophy and Civilization*]

The significant outward forms of the civilization of the western world are the product of the machine and its technology. Indirectly, they are the product of the scientific revolution which took place in the seventeenth century. In its effect upon men's external habits, dominant interests, the conditions under which they work and associate, whether in the family, the factory, the state, or internationally, science is by far the most potent social factor in the modern world. It operates, however, through its undesigned effects rather than as a transforming influence of men's thoughts and purposes. This contrast between outer and inner operation is the great contradiction in our lives. Habits of thought and desire remain in substance what they were before the rise of science, while the conditions under which they take effect have been radically altered by science.

When we look at the external social consequences of science, we find it impossible to apprehend the extent or gauge the rapidity of their occurrence. Alfred North Whitehead has recently called attention to the progressive shortening of the time-span of social change. That due to basic conditions seems to be of the order of half a million years; that due to lesser physical conditions, like alterations in climate, to be of the order of five thousand years. Until almost our own day the time-span of sporadic technological changes was of the order of five hundred years; according to him, no great technological changes took place between, say, 100 A.D. and 1400 A.D. With the introduction of steam-power, the fifty years from 1780 to 1830 were marked by more changes than are found in any previous thousand years.

[First published in *Philosophy and Civilization* (New York: Minton, Balch and Co., 1931), pp. 318–30.]

The advance of chemical techniques and in use of electricity and radio-energy in the last forty years makes even this last change seem slow and awkward.

Domestic life, political institutions, international relations and personal contacts are shifting with kaleidoscopic rapidity before our eyes. We cannot appreciate and weigh the changes; they occur too swiftly. We do not have time to take them in. No sooner do we begin to understand the meaning of one such change than another comes and displaces the former. Our minds are dulled by the sudden and repeated impacts. Externally, science through its applications is manufacturing the conditions of our institutions at such a speed that we are too bewildered to know what sort of civilization is in process of making.

Because of this confusion, we cannot even draw up a ledger account of social gains and losses due to the operation of science. But at least we know that the earlier optimism which thought that the advance of natural science was to dispel superstition, ignorance, and oppression, by placing reason on the throne, was unjustified. Some superstitions have given way, but the mechanical devices due to science have made it possible to spread new kinds of error and delusion among a larger multitude. The fact is that it is foolish to try to draw up a debit and credit account for science. To do so is to mythologize; it is to personify science and impute to it a will and an energy on its own account. In truth science is strictly impersonal; a method and a body of knowledge. It owes its operation and its consequences to the human beings who use it. It adapts itself passively to the purposes and desires which animate these human beings. It lends itself with equal impartiality to the kindly offices of medicine and hygiene and the destructive deeds of war. It elevates some through opening new horizons; it depresses others by making them slaves of machines operated for the pecuniary gain of owners.

The neutrality of science to the uses made of it renders it silly to talk about its bankruptcy, or to worship it as the usherer in of a new age. In the degree in which we realize this fact, we shall devote our attention to the human purposes and motives which control its application. Science is an instrument, a method, a body of technique. While it is an end for those inquirers who are engaged in its pursuit, in the large human sense it is a means, a tool. For what ends shall it be used? Shall it be used deliberately, systematically, for the promotion of social well-being, or shall it be employed primarily for private aggrandizement, leaving its larger social results to chance? Shall the scientific attitude be used to create new mental and moral attitudes, or shall it continue to be subordinated to service of desires, purposes and institutions which were formed before science came into existence? Can the attitudes which control the use of science be themselves so influenced by scientific technique that they will harmonize with its spirit?

The beginning of wisdom is, I repeat, the realization that science itself is an instrument which is indifferent to the external uses to which it is put. Steam and electricity remain natural forces when they operate through mechanisms; the only problem is the purposes for which men set the mechanisms to work. The essential technique of gunpowder is the same whether it be used to blast rocks from the quarry to build better human habitations, or to hurl death upon men at war with one another. The airplane binds men at a distance in closer bonds of intercourse and understanding, or it rains missiles of death upon hapless populations. We are forced to consider the relation of human ideas and ideals to the social consequences which are produced by science as an instrument.

The problem involved is the greatest which civilization has ever had to face. It is, without exaggeration, the most serious issue of contemporary life. Here is the instrumentality, the most powerful, for good and evil, the world has ever known. What are we going to do with it? Shall we leave our underlying aims unaffected by it, treating it merely as a means by which uncooperative individuals may advance their own fortunes? Shall we try to improve the hearts of men without regard to the new methods which science puts at our disposal? There are those, men in high position in church and state, who urge this course. They trust to a transforming influence of a morals and religion which have not been affected by science to change human desire and purpose, so that they will employ science and machine technology for beneficent social ends. The recent Encyclical of the Pope is a classic document in expression of a point of view which would rely wholly upon inner regeneration to protect society from the injurious uses to which science may be put. Quite apart from any ecclesiastical connection, there are many "intellectuals" who appeal to inner "spiritual" concepts, totally divorced from scientific intelligence, to effect the needed work. But there is another alternative: to take the method of science home into our own controlling attitudes and dispositions, to employ the new techniques as means of directing our thoughts and efforts to a planned control of social forces.

Science and machine technology are young from the standpoint of human history. Though vast in stature, they are infants in age. Three hundred years are but a moment in comparison with thousands of centuries man has lived on the earth. In view of the inertia of institutions and of the mental habits they breed, it is not surprising that the new technique of apparatus and calculation, which is the essence of science, has made so little impression on underlying human attitudes. The momentum of traditions and purposes that preceded its rise took possession of the new instrument and turned it to their ends. Moreover, science had to struggle for existence. It had powerful enemies in church and state. It needed friends and it welcomed alliance with the rising capitalism which it so effectively promoted. If it tended to foster secularism and to create predominantly material interests, it could still be argued that it was in essential harmony with traditional morals and religion. But there were lacking the conditions which are indispensable to the serious application of scientific method in reconstruction of fundamental beliefs and attitudes. In addition, the development of the new science was attended with so many internal difficulties that energy had to go to perfecting the instrument just as an instrument. Because of all these circumstances the fact that science was used in behalf of old interests is nothing to be wondered at.

The conditions have now changed, radically so. The claims of natural science in the physical field are undisputed. Indeed, its prestige is so great that an almost superstitious aura gathers about its name and work. Its progress is no longer dependent upon the adventurous inquiry of a few untrammeled souls. Not only are universities organized to promote scientific research and learning, but one may almost imagine the university laboratories abolished and still feel confident of the continued advance of science. The development of industry has compelled the inclusion of scientific inquiry within the processes of production and distribution. We find in the public prints as many demonstrations of the benefits of science from a business point of view as there are proofs of its harmony with religion.

It is not possible that, under such conditions, the subordination of scientific techniques to purposes and institutions that flourished before its rise can indefinitely continue. In all affairs there comes a time when a cycle of growth reaches maturity. When this stage is reached, the period of protective nursing comes to an end. The problem of securing proper use succeeds to that of securing conditions of growth. Now that science has established itself and has created a new social environment, it has (if I may for the moment personify it) to face the issue of its social responsibilities. Speaking without personification, we who have a powerful and perfected instrument in our hands, one which is determining the quality of social changes, must ask what changes we want to see achieved and what we want to see averted. We must, in short, plan its social effects with the same care with which in the past we have planned its physical operation and consequences. Till now we have employed science absent-mindedly as far as its effects upon human beings are concerned. The present situation with its extraordinary control of natural energies and its totally unplanned and haphazard social economy is a dire demonstration of the folly of continuing this course.

The social effects of the application of science have been accidental, even though they are intrinsic to the private and unorganized motives which we have permitted to control that application. It would be hard to find a better proof that such is the fact than the vogue of the theory that such unregulated use of science is in accord with "natural law," and that all effort at planned control of its social effects is an interference with nature. The use which has been made of a peculiar idea of personal liberty to justify the dominion of accident in social affairs is another convincing proof. The doctrine that the most potent instrument of widespread, enduring, and objective social changes must be left at the mercy of purely private desires for purely personal gain is a doctrine of anarchy. Our present insecurity of life is the fruit of the adoption in practice of this anarchic doctrine.

The technologies of industry have flowed from the intrinsic nature of science. For that is itself essentially a technology of apparatus, materials and numbers. But the pecuniary aims which have decided the social results of the use of these technologies have not flowed from the inherent nature of science. They have been derived from institutions and attendant mental and moral habits which were entrenched before there was any such thing as science and the machine. In consequence, science has operated as a means for extending the influence of the institution of private property and connected legal relations far beyond their former limits. It has operated as a device to carry an enormous load of stocks and bonds and to make the reward of investment in the way of profit and power one out of all proportion to that accruing from actual work and service.

Here lies the heart of our present social problem. Science has hardly been used to modify men's fundamental acts and attitudes in social matters. It has been used to extend enormously the scope and power of interests and values which anteceded its rise. Here is the contradiction in our civilization. The potentiality of science as the most powerful instrument of control which has ever existed puts to mankind its one outstanding present challenge.

There is one field in which science has been somewhat systematically employed as an agent of social control. Condorcet, writing during the French Revolution in the prison from which he went to the guillotine, hailed the invention of the calculus of probabilities as the opening of a new era. He saw in this new mathematical technique the promise of methods of insurance which should distribute evenly and widely the impact of the disasters to which humanity is subject. Insurance against death, fire, hurricanes and so on have in a measure confirmed his prediction. Nevertheless, in large and important social areas, we have only made the merest beginning of the method of insurance against the hazards of life and death. Insurance against the risks of maternity, of sickness, old age, unemployment, is still rudimentary; its idea is fought by all reactionary forces. Witness the obstacles against which social insurance with respect to accidents incurred in industrial employment had to contend. The anarchy called natural law and personal liberty still operates with success against a planned social use of the resources of scientific knowledge.

Yet insurance against perils and hazards is the place where the application of science has gone the furthest, not the least, distance in present society. The fact that motor cars kill and maim more persons yearly than all factories, shops, and farms is a fair symbol of how backward we are in that province where we have done most. Here, however, is one field in which at least the idea of planned use of scientific knowledge for social welfare has received recognition. We no longer regard plagues, famine and disease as visitations of necessary "natural law" or of a power beyond nature. By preventive means of medicine and public hygiene as well as by various remedial measures we have in idea, if not in fact, placed technique in the stead of magic and chance and uncontrollable necessity in this one area of life. And yet, as I have said, here is where the socially planned use of science has made the most, not least, progress. Were it not for the youth of science and the historically demonstrated slowness of all basic mental and moral change, we could hardly find language to express astonishment at the situation in which we have an extensive and precise control of physical energies and conditions, and in which we leave the social consequences of their operation to chance, *laissez-faire*, privileged pecuniary status, and the inertia of tradition and old institutions.

Condorcet thought and worked in the Baconian strain. But the Baconian ideal of the systematic organization of all knowledge, the planned control of discovery and invention, for the relief and advancement of the human estate, remains almost as purely an ideal as when Francis Bacon put it forward centuries ago. And this is true in spite of the fact that the physical and mathematical technique upon which a planned control of social results depends has made in the meantime incalculable progress. The conclusion is inevitable. The outer arena of life has been transformed by science. The effectively working mind and character of man have hardly been touched.

Consider that phase of social action where science might theoretically be supposed to have taken effect most rapidly, namely, education. In dealing with the young, it would seem as if scientific methods might at once take effect in transformation of mental attitudes, without meeting the obstacles which have to be overcome in dealing with adults. In higher education, in universities and technical schools, a great amount of research is done and much scientific knowledge is imparted. But it is a principle of modern psychology that the basic attitudes of mind are formed in the earlier years. And I venture the assertion that for the most part the formation of intellectual habits in elementary education, in the home and school, is hardly affected by scientific method. Even in our so-called progressive schools, science is usually treated as a side line, an ornamental extra, not as the chief means of developing the right mental attitudes. It is treated generally as one more body of ready-made information to be acquired by traditional methods, or else as an occasional diversion. That it is the method of all effective mental approach and attack in all subjects has not gained even a foothold. Yet if scientific method is not something esoteric but is a realization of the most effective operation of intelligence, it should be axiomatic that the development of scientific attitudes of thought, observation, and inquiry is the chief business of study and learning.

Two phases of the contradiction inhering in our civilization may be especially mentioned. We have long been committed in theory and words to the principle of democracy. But criticism of democracy, assertions that it is failing to work and even to exist are everywhere rife. In the last few months we have become accustomed to similar assertions regarding our economic and industrial system. Mr. Ivy Lee, for example, in a recent commencement address, entitled "This Hour of Bewilderment," quoted from a representative clergyman, a railway president, and a publicist, to the effect that our capitalistic system is on trial. And yet the statements had to do with only one feature of that system: the prevalence of unemployment and attendant insecurity. It is not necessary for me to invade the territory of economics and politics. The essential fact is that if both democracy and capitalism are on trial, it is in reality our collective intelligence which is on trial. We have displayed enough intelligence in the physical field to create the new and powerful instrument of science and technology. We have not as yet had enough intelligence to use this instrument deliberately and systematically to control its social operations and consequences.

The first lesson which the use of scientific method teaches is that control is coordinate with knowledge and understanding. Where there is technique there is the possibility of administering forces and conditions in the region where the technique applies. Our lack of control in the sphere of human relations, national, domestic, international, requires no emphasis of notice. It is proof that we have not begun to operate scientifically in such matters. The public press is full of discussion of the five-year plan and the ten-year plan in Russia. But the fact that the plan is being tried by a country which has a dictatorship foreign to all our beliefs tends to divert attention from the fundamental consideration. The point for us is not this political setting nor its communistic context. It is that by the use of all available resources of knowledge and experts an attempt is being made at organized social planning and control. Were we to forget for the moment the special Russian political setting, we should see here an effort to use coordinated knowledge and technical skill to direct economic resources toward social order and stability.

To hold that such organized planning is possible only in a communistic society is to surrender the case to communism. Upon any other basis, the effort of Russia is a challenge and a warning to those who live under another political and economic regime. It is a call to use our more advanced knowledge and technology in scientific thinking about our own needs, problems, evils, and possibilities so as to achieve some degree of control of the social consequences which the application of science is, willy-nilly, bringing about. What stands in the way is a lot of outworn traditions, moth-eaten slogans and catchwords, that do substitute duty for thought, as well as our entrenched predatory self-interest. We shall only make a real beginning in intelligent thought when we cease mouthing platitudes; stop confining our idea to antitheses of individualism and socialism, capitalism and communism, and realize that the issue is between chaos and order, chance and control: the haphazard use and the planned use of scientific techniques.

Thus the statement with which we began, namely, that we are living in a world of change extraordinary in range and speed, is only half true. It holds of the outward applications of science. It does not hold of our intellectual and moral attitudes. About physical conditions and energies we think scientifically; at least, some men do, and the results of their thinking enter into the experiences of all of us. But the entrenched and stubborn institutions of the past stand in the way of our thinking scientifically about human relations and social issues. Our mental habits in these respects are dominated by institutions of family, state, church, and business that were formed long before men had an effective technique of inquiry and validation. It is this contradiction from which we suffer to-day.

Disaster follows in its wake. It is impossible to overstate the mental confusion and the practical disorder which are bound to result when external and physical effects are planned and regulated, while the attitudes of mind upon which the direction of external results depends are left to the medley of chance, tradition, and dogma. It is a common saying that our physical science has far outrun our social knowledge; that our physical skill has become exact and comprehensive while our humane arts are vague, opinionated, and narrow. The fundamental trouble, however, is not lack of sufficient information about social facts, but unwillingness to adopt the scientific attitude in what we do know. Men floundered in a morass of opinion about physical matters for thousands of years. It was when they began to use their ideas experimentally and to create a technique or direction of experimentation that physical science advanced with system and surety. No amount of mere fact-finding develops science nor the scientific attitude in either physics or social affairs. Facts merely amassed and piled up are dead; a burden which only adds to confusion. When ideas, hypotheses, begin to play upon facts, when they are methods for experimental use in action, then light dawns; then it becomes possible to discriminate significant from trivial facts, and relations take the place of isolated scraps. Just as soon as we begin to use the knowledge and skills we have to control social consequences in the interest of shared abundant and secured life, we shall cease to complain of the backwardness of our social knowledge. We shall take the road which leads to the assured building up of social science just as men built up physical science when they actively used the techniques of tools and numbers in physical experimentation.

In spite, then, of all the record of the past, the great scientific revolution is still to come. It will ensue when men collectively and cooperatively organize their knowledge for application to achieve and make secure social values; when they systematically use scientific procedures for the control of human relationships and the direction of the social effects of our vast technological machinery. Great as have been the social changes of the last century, they are not to be compared with those which will emerge when our faith in scientific method is made manifest in social works. We are living in a period of depression. The intellectual function of trouble is to lead men to think. The depression is a small price to pay if it induces us to think about the cause of the disorder, confusion, and insecurity which are the outstanding traits of our social life. If we do not go back to their cause, namely our half-way and accidental use of science, mankind will pass through depressions, for they are the graphic record of our unplanned social life. The story of the achievement of science in physical control is evidence of the possibility of control in social affairs. It is our human intelligence and human courage which are on trial; it is incredible that men who have brought the technique of physical discovery, invention, and use to such a pitch of perfection will abdicate in the face of the infinitely more important human problem.

Social Science and Social Control

It would require a technical survey, which would be out of place here, to prove that the existing limitations of "social science" are due mainly to unreasoning devotion to physical science as a model, and to a misconception of physical science at that. Without making any such survey, attention may be directly called to one outstanding difference between physical and social facts. The ideal of the knowledge dealing with the former is the elimination of all factors dependent upon distinctively human response. "Fact," physically speaking, is the ultimate residue after human purposes, desires, emotions, ideas and ideals have been systematically excluded. A social "fact," on the other hand, is a concretion in external form of precisely these human factors.

An occurrence is a physical fact only when its constituents and their relations remain the same, irrespective of the human attitude toward them. A species of mosquitoes is the carrier of the germs of malaria, whether we like or dislike malaria. Drainage and oil-spraying to destroy mosquitoes are a social fact because their use depends upon human purpose and desire. A steam locomotive or a dynamo is a physical fact in its structure; it is a social fact when its existence depends upon the desire for rapid and cheap transportation and communication. The machine itself may be understood physically without reference to human aim and motive. But the railway or public-utility system cannot be understood without reference to human purposes and human consequences.

I may illustrate the present practice of slavishly following the technique of physical science and the uselessness of its results by the present zeal for "fact finding." Of course, one cannot think, understand and plan without a basis of fact, and since facts do

[First published in *New Republic* 67 (29 July 1931): 276–77.]

not lie around in plain view, they have to be discovered. But for the most part, the data which now are so carefully sought and so elaborately scheduled are not social facts at all. For their connection with any system of human purposes and consequences, their bearing as means and as results upon human action, are left out of the picture. At best they are mere physical and external facts. They are unlike the facts of physical science, because the latter are found by methods which make their interrelations and their laws apparent, while the facts of social "fact finding" remain a miscellaneous pile of meaningless items. Since their connections with human wants and their effect on human values are neglected, there is nothing which binds them together into an intelligible whole.

It may be retorted that to connect facts with human desires and their effect upon human values is subjective and moral, and to an extent that makes it impossible to establish any conclusions upon an objective basis: that to attempt inference on this point would land us in a morass of speculative opinion. Suppose, for example, all the facts about the working of the prohibition law and its enforcement were much more completely known than they are; even so, to establish a connection between these facts and the human attitudes lying back of them would be a matter of guess work. As things stand, there is much force in the objection. But if made universal, it would overlook the possibility of another kind of situation.

Wherever purposes are employed deliberately and systematically for the sake of certain desired social results, there it is possible, within limits, to determine the connection between the human factor and the actual occurrence, and thus to get a complete social fact, namely, the actual external occurrence in its human relationships. Prohibition, whether noble or not, is not an experiment in any intelligent scientific sense of the term. For it was undertaken without the effort to obtain the conditions of control which are essential to any experimental determination of fact. The Five Year Plan of Russia, on the other hand, whether noble or the reverse, has many of the traits of a social experiment, for it is an attempt to obtain certain specified social results by the use of specified definite measures, exercised under conditions of considerable, if not complete, control.

The point I am making may be summed up by saying that it is

a complete error to suppose that efforts at social control depend upon the prior existence of a social science. The reverse is the case. The building up of social science, that is, of a body of knowledge in which facts are ascertained in their significant relations, is dependent upon putting social planning into effect. It is at this point that the misconception about physical science, when it is taken as a model for social knowledge, is important. Physical science did not develop because inquirers piled up a mass of facts about observed phenomena. It came into being when men intentionally experimented, on the basis of ideas and hypotheses, with observed phenomena to modify them and disclose new observations. This process is self-corrective and self-developing. Imperfect and even wrong hypotheses, when *acted upon*, brought to light significant phenomena which made improved ideas and improved experimentations possible. The change from a passive and accumulative attitude into an active and productive one is the secret revealed by the progress of physical inquiry. Men obtained knowledge of natural energies by trying deliberately to control the conditions of their operation. The result was knowledge, and then control on a larger scale by the application of what was learned.

It is a commonplace of logical theory that laws are of the "if-then" type. *If* something occurs, *then* something else happens; if certain conditions exist, they are accompanied by certain other conditions. Such knowledge alone is knowledge of a fact in any intelligible sense of the word. Although we have to act in order to discover the conditions underlying the "if" in physical matters, yet the material constituting the "if" is there apart from our action; like the movements of sun and earth in an eclipse. But in social phenomena the relation is: "If we *do* something, something else will happen." The objective material constituting the "if" belongs to us, not to something wholly independent of us. We are concerned, not with a bare relation of cause and effect, but with one of means and consequences, that is, of causes deliberately used for the sake of producing certain effects. As far as we intentionally do and make, we shall know; as far as we "know" without making, our so-called knowledge is a miscellany, or at most antiquarian, and hence without relevance to future planning. Only the knowledge which is itself the fruit of a technology can breed further technology.

I want to make the same point with reference to social prediction. Here, too, the assumption is generally made that we must be able to predict before we can plan and control. Here again the reverse is the case. We can predict the occurrence of an eclipse precisely because we cannot control it. If we could control it, we could not predict, except contingently; just as we can predict a collision when we see two trains approaching on the same track—provided that a human being does not foresee the possibility and take measures to avert its happening. The other day I ran across a remark of Alexander Hamilton's to the effect that instead of awaiting an event to know what measures to take, we should take measures to bring the event to pass. And I would add that only then can we genuinely forecast the future in the world of social matters.

Empirical rule-of-thumb practices were the mothers of the arts. But the practices of the arts were in turn the source of science, when once the empirical methods were freed in imagination and used with some degree of freedom of experimentation. There cannot be a science of an art until the art has itself made some advance, and the significant development occurs when men intentionally try to use such art as they have already achieved in order to obtain results which they conceive to be desirable. If we have no social technique at all, it is impossible to bring planning and control into being. If we do have at hand a reasonable amount of technique, then it is by deliberately using what we have that we shall in the end develop a dependable body of social knowledge. If we want foresight, we shall not obtain it by any amount of fact finding so long as we disregard the human aims and desires producing the facts which we find. But if we decide upon what we want socially, what sort of social consequences we wish to occur, and then use whatever means we possess to effect these intended consequences, we shall find the road that leads to foresight. Forethought and planning must come before foresight.

I am not arguing here for the desirability of social planning and control. That is another question. Those who are satisfied with present conditions and who are hopeful of turning them to account for personal profit and power will answer it in the negative. What I am saying is that if we want something to which the name "social science" may be given, there is only one way to go about it, namely, by entering upon the path of social planning and control. Observing, collecting, recording and filing tomes of social phenomena without deliberately trying to do something to bring a desired state of society into existence only encourages a conflict of opinion and dogma in their interpretation. If the social situation out of which these facts emerge is itself confused and chaotic because it expresses socially unregulated purpose and haphazard private intent, the facts themselves will be confused, and we shall add only intellectual confusion to practical disorder. When we deliberately employ whatever skill we possess in order to serve the ends which we desire, we shall begin to attain a measure of at least intellectual order and understanding. And if past history teaches anything, it is that with intellectual order we have the surest possible promise of advancement to practical order.

The Collapse of a Romance

Carlyle, who was a romantic, called political economy the dismal science. And it is true that the roseate hopes of the earlier economists had well nigh disappeared by his day. Ricardo had indicated that there was not enough land to go around and Malthus that there were altogether too many people. Natural laws seemed to doôm many to live on the edge of the subsistence line. In the United States, however, for fairly obvious reasons the earlier glow revived and business was ordained as the great romantic adventure.

Although the rebirth of glamor was dependent upon local American conditions, there was a genuinely romantic factor in economic theory; we did not create the romanticism, we only gave it the chance to flourish. Strange as it sounds, the economic man was himself a hero of romance. Of course another branch of the romantic tradition did not consider him as such; he figures there as withdrawing from the realm of romance into the counting room, there to engage in a prosaic grubbing into musty ledgers. But different romanticists rarely understand one another, and while the earlier tradition tended to prevail in the books, the new romantic spirit took possession of the scene of action.

The new hero of romance did not seek justification for himself in theory; the adventure was its own justification. But if he had turned to economic theory he would have found written warrant. For, in that theory, wants and desires were glorified power; at their magic touch the world was to be transformed; they were, when unshackled from legal artifice and political despotism, the sure source of prosperity and continual progress; the earthly savior of mankind. Wants stirred man to energy, rendered him

[First published in *New Republic* 70 (27 April 1932): 292–94.]

creative, moved him to thrift and produced the embellishment of the world, urged him to exchange and so made man, apart from his will, the mutual servant of his fellows. The romance of business did not stop there. Economic man had another asset beside his desires; he had an unfailing intelligence which showed him just how to direct the energy, thrift, exchange, by which in satisfying his wants he made the world over. To the eye of the romantic who lived in the genteel literary tradition, this ascription of self-sufficient rationality seemed the negation of romance. How could adventure be cool, calculating, concerned with debtor and creditor accounts, and still be romantic?

But it was just at this point that the new romanticism of business so cleverly came in. Human imagination had never before conceived anything so fantastic as the idea that every individual is actuated in all his desires by an insight into just what is good for him, and that he is equipped with the sure foresight which will enable him to calculate ahead and get just what he is after. Nor did the imaginative flight pause with this conclusion. All the work of the world, from the most ordinary to the most extraordinary, is presided over by this omnipresent deity of calculating reason, who through his uniform presence in each separate individual is summed up by integral calculus into a virtually omniscient mind. Through its beneficent and overruling power, self-interest becomes a social lubricant instead of a cause of friction, and the zeal of each one to get ahead of everybody else promotes the general welfare. If there are those who seem to be left out of its distribution, there is always the assurance that the ways of Providence are proverbially mysterious.

It is characteristic of romance, of the glamorous and imaginative projection of excited emotion, to remain outside the sphere of argument. One is either inside the romance or outside it. It is true and is the standard of truth, if you are inside; it is silly or insane, if you are outside. Thus, when one says that the present world crisis is merely the consequence of the general acceptance of the particular romance which has gone by the name of business, one speaks from the outside. It is commonly assumed that the explanation of the economic crisis must be itself economic. So it must—if one stays inside the business dream. Since it is part of the dream that cool, far-sighted intelligence controls the operation of the energies and instruments by which desires are satisfied, one within the dream must seek for a rational explanation. From outside the romance, that fact itself gives the key to the explanation; we cannot call gambling an exercise of cool and calm rationality without sooner or later tripping up.

The dictionary defines gambling as staking money on some fortuitous event. Since business is in the condition it is, since it has brought about a state of universal insecurity, it is fairly evident that the bets have gone wrong. But more fundamental still is the fact to which the present insecurity testifies. As the function of intelligent control is to achieve order, stability, security, the whole theory of the relation between business and calculating intelligence is evidently sheer fiction. Business postulates insecurity and uncertainty. It thrives on it and increasingly creates it, in order that more business may be done.

If the existing insecurity were localized in one country or restricted to one class, some explanation of it might be found or invented which would be consistent with a definition of the economic process as a rationally guided process of satisfying wants. There would also then be some sense in blaming financiers and industrial leaders for their stupidity in bringing us to this pass. But since the essence of the whole thing is the romance of adventuring on the sea of uncertainty, one might as well subject Don Quixote to criticism on the basis of reason. Because wagering on uncertainty is the heart of the whole process, the banker, as insecure as the debtor, has ceased to function; the manufacturer is as doubtful of a market for his goods as the worker is of a market for his labor and the farmer for his products. That "securities" are now so largely insecurities is typical of the whole affair.

The present scene is only an exhibition of what is inherent in business all the time, but it now happens on such a scale that the uncertainty always characteristic of it has become too overt to be ignored. The only thing abnormal about it is that the normal insecurity has got out of hand to the extent that it cannot be concealed from general recognition. In other words, the essentially romantic nature of the idea that business is a rational way of expending energy for the satisfaction of human wants becomes apparent to those who have eyes to see. There are various "rational" explanations of the present breakdown. Each has its measure of truth, but all they explain is some aspect of the irrationality, the trading on uncertainty, which is business itself.

It is interesting to note the ways in which a recognition of the identity of business with betting on an uncertain event all but explicitly comes through. We hear every day and many times a day that everything would be all right if we only had "confidence." Undoubtedly. But confidence in what or in whom? The industrialist would be pleased if the banker had enough confidence to lend him money; the banker would be pleased if someone else had sufficient confidence to buy his frozen assets at a good price; the farmer would love to have confidence that if he plants a lot of grain and cotton he will get a good price next summer; the laborer would like to have confidence that he is going to get a job, and the depositor that he is going to get his money from the bank when he wants it. Meantime, the appeal to confidence sounds like a confidence game. Can anyone imagine anything more humorous—if it were not terribly tragic—than the appeal to put confidence in a situation of complete insecurity? Again we are constantly told that the whole basis of modern business is credit. What does that signify when credit tends automatically toward inflation and the only way to deflate is to withhold credit, except that the whole business of business is to trade on insecurity, concealing the insecurity as long as possible by an ingenious pyramiding of it?

The psychology and morale of business are based on trading in insecurity. They are criticized by serious moralists as if the animating spirit were that of acquisition. These accusations do not reach the mark. Business is a game which cannot be carried on without acquisition, any more than poker can be played without chips. But it is the excitement of the game which counts; acquisition is important because it enables the game to go on at a more furious pitch. We hunt the dollar, but hunting is hunting, not dollars. It is said that love of power over others is the dominant thing. But if you have a game which cannot be played except when power over others is a condition of success, love of power grows up as a secondary and derived fact, not as an original and animating force. I see no reason to believe that the majority of important and "successful" business men are sadistic, and love the cruelty arising from power over others for its own sake. I can see how zest for the game may cause even cruelty to take on a romantic visage and render it tolerable in contemplation.

In saying that business is intrinsically a gamble in uncertainties, it is not said that manufacture or transportation of goods is a gamble. They are technological operations, based on physical knowledge of physical materials and energies. The locomotive runs on coal and steam, not on psychical acts of "confidence." But for this reason production and distribution of goods are not themselves business. In business they become instruments of a game in which trumps are possession of capital as a temporary insurance against insecurity. But the game has such a wide reach that there comes a time when the insecurity of the masses spells insecurity for the one holding trumps. The essence of business, as distinct from the techniques of production and distribution, is of course profits. But why profits? Anyone can give the answer. There must be profits in order to induce persons to "take the risks"; it is only fair that those who assume the risks should get paid for doing it. Since there is no explanation of profits which does not come down to this fact, what other evidence is needed of the intrinsic connection of business with insecurity?

Living is attended with risks; there will always be an element of uncertainty in it. One cannot object to business for taking account of this fact. But anyone whom the crisis has awakened from a romantic dream will object to any procedure which systematically sets out to glorify the process of trading in insecurity on the ground that this is the road to profits. We should at least get rid of the vast load of nonsense which now adds to our depression if we were coolly to take business for just what it is, *i.e.*, the pursuit of profit, and cease glorifying it for what it is not. Personally, I believe there would be a great rise in the so-called native I.Q. of the average American if we would get rid of this one source of mental confusion and paralysis. But what is more objectionable is the piling up of insecurity. There is enough risk in living anyway without deliberately increasing it. Take money, for example. We are told that it is a medium of exchange. Well, if it were, it would of course add to the security of existence. As a matter of fact, it is something else. It is a medium for *controlling* exchange. Hence the concentrated possession of money is a means of intensifying insecurity. The ability to control exchange is the ability to stop it, to tax it, to deflect it. To create a risk and then make a profit by assuming it, is a good rule—for those who control money.

The breakdown in which we are living is the breakdown of the particular romance known as business. It is the revelation that the elated excitement of the romantic adventure has to be paid for with an equal depression. If one knew where the glamor of imagination would next find its outlet, one could predict the future. But the reason why no one has had any success in foretelling the great turns of history is precisely because they come from the imagination and its enthusiasms and not from logic and reason. I do not think the next voyage of imagination is immediately imminent. There is one stage of the present romance not yet exhausted. We are now being captured by the romance of introduction of planning into business. What could be more romantic than the idea of retaining business, which is the process of placing wagers on uncertainties for the sake of profit, and at the same time introducing stability and security into it? So that last act of the present drama will presumably be undertaken before the imagination takes its flight to a new field.

The Way Out of Educational Confusion

It is unnecessary to say that we are in the midst of great educational uncertainty, one probably unparalleled at any past time. There is nothing accepted as axiomatic, nothing beyond the possibility of questioning, and few things that are not actually attacked. Conservatives who urge return to former standards and practices and radicals who criticize present conditions agree at least in one point: neither party is satisfied with things as they are. It is not merely this or that method for securing educational results that is attacked, but ideals and aims are under fire. Anyone can bring forward a definition of education, but there are few who would not admit that the definitions when brought face to face with actual conditions are likely to be hollow and empty.

As far as the uncertainty about standards, purposes, tendencies, and methods leads to discussion, there is something healthy about it. Doubt and questioning, no matter how far they go, are not in themselves an occasion for pessimism. But mere confusion is not a good thing. There is a confusion due to the smoke of battle obscuring the scene from the onlooker; and there is a different confusion due to combatants losing sight of what they are doing and where they are going, a chaos of uncoordinated movements and actions. Confusion tends toward obscuration of mind and ideas that leads to futility in action. Cross currents may be directed and produce an ultimate increase of energy; or they may render the waters turbid while currents neutralize each other. Perception of conflict, of what it is and why it is, may, on the contrary, conduce to clarification of confusion, and in the end contribute to harmony, and to unified energy. I propose, then, to

[First published as The Inglis Lecture, 1931 (Cambridge: Harvard University Press, 1931), 41 pp., from the Inglis Lecture on Secondary Education at Harvard University on 11 March 1931.]

consider some of the main conflicts in present educational tendencies, hoping that that course may at least clarify vision, although I recognize that I may only add to the confusion.

One must plunge in at some point since there is no general agreement even as to what conflict is most important, what is most the key to the whole battle ground, and since, anyway, all of the conflicts are more or less bound up together, I do not think it makes very much difference where the plunge is taken. I shall accordingly begin with a question which probably is not often brought into the open but which seems to me to lie at the base of disagreements on those other points, where dissension is, as the behaviorists say, verbalized.

Owing perhaps to the fact that the question is not often explicitly discussed, I find some difficulty in stating it in words which will not give rise to misunderstanding. But I shall put it in this form: What is the value of the accepted and generally current classification of subjects—meaning by "subjects" such titles as appear in any program of studies in any high school and in any college catalogue? I am inclined to think that this question concerns the ultimate divergence between those who may be conveniently called, respectively, traditionalists and modernists in education, although there are few, perhaps none, who go to the limit in either direction. And I believe, in addition, that failure to raise the question explicitly is one cause why the more radical school is at a disadvantage in discussion and in action. That is, in the degree in which the current divisions and classifications of knowledge and skill, of sciences and arts, are accepted as the basis for determining a curriculum, whether secondary-school or college, the question comes to be one concerning selection, rejection, and arrangement among these subjects, already admitted to be, in the general scheme of selection and arrangement, the proper and indeed necessary "studies" involved in learning.

I have, for convenience, described subjects by reference to titles in a program. But the question does not concern labels. Some kind of tag is necessary for purposes of identification. The question, educationally, concerns what lies back of the tag, the name. Even as things stand now, the titles, Ancient or Modern History, Physics, Botany, English Literature, do not convey much about the actual subject-matter dealt with in a course, and of themselves nothing about the method of pursuing it. They say nothing as to where emphasis will fall; courses with the same name will differ with the personality and training of the teacher and with his implicit though perhaps unconscious philosophy of education. The teacher taught by James Harvey Robinson, Beard, Breasted, or Turner will give preference to other topics in history and use a different system of weights than a teacher who has been taught by teachers with other conceptions of the nature of historical subject-matter. The same will be true in classics and in English or American literature. Standardization of the subject-matter that actually comes under a given title-subject is now confined almost wholly to mathematics, and even here there is more variation than there used to be.

I do not mean to imply that this loosening and variation within recognized subjects is intrinsically bad. It is in fact a necessity which may be taken cognizance of for good or for harm. It is a necessity because of the vast extension of knowledge. Anatole France remarked that the writing of the history of certain periods is comparatively easy; we know exactly what happened because we have only one or two accounts to rely upon. For other periods, we have so many accounts and such conflicting accounts that we cannot tell what really took place. His irony may be applied in other directions. When little was known in a given field, it was comparatively easy to standardize the material of physics, chemistry, botany, zoology, and so on. Now we know so much in any one of the fields that selection must be resorted to. And wherever choice enters, points of view, predominant interest, differences of opinion as to value, enter by the same door. It is easy to say that for an elementary course fundamentals should be selected and emphasized. But the moment the question is raised as to *what are* fundamentals, all the differences that have been alluded to begin to operate. And in many cases, fundamentals in the strictly scientific sense are just what a beginning student cannot grasp. The fundamental principles of physics, for example, are not what they were when classical mechanics had full sway; they are to some extent just the things most in dispute; and for the things which are not in dispute—as well as for ability to understand the nature of the disputes—much knowledge in command of advanced mathematics is necessary.

We are not much better off when we shift to another field. I heard a teacher of college economics say that teachers in that field are almost in despair as to how to introduce that subject to college students. Probably most instructors stick to such old divisions as production, exchange, and distribution; but many of them do so only because they do not see their road clear in other directions and not because they are inherently satisfied. And one already introduces the subject with consideration of the business cycle and another with taxation, and so on. In many subjects it is convention rather than conviction which enforces whatever degree of uniformity or homogeneity exists—including, of course, the conventions which stem from the assiduous skill of textbook publishers.

Another aspect of educational confusion is found in multiplication of courses and of subdivisions of groups. Compare a program of studies of an elementary, secondary school, or college of thirty years ago with that of the same institution to-day and you will find that the offerings have been greatly enriched; there is no need for me to go into detail. But whether the education of the young has been enriched in any corresponding ratio is matter of grave doubt. Students in high schools find that instead of having one line of study opened to them (one which from the predominance of Latin and Greek was called classical, or two lines through being offered a choice between this line and another one, which from the omission of ancient languages is termed English) they have three or four or five—scientific, industrial, etc. In the larger cities there are also high schools of differentiated types. But there is now general complaint of congestion of courses and of narrowness in the fields occupied by groups. The affair is spoken of sometimes as constituting specialization. But it is far removed as a rule from that specialization which gives the expert a measure of mastery in his field. The tendency is rather toward thinness, superficiality, and a sprawling miscellany. In the so-called "practical" lines, courses are given vocational names when they have little to do with procedures actually current in industry and where there is often much frittering away of time.

I started out with the question of the educational value of adopting current and largely traditional classifications of knowledge and the arts as the basis of courses in instruction. The connection between this question and what has just been said may not be readily apparent; what has been said may seem irrelevant to that matter. But there is in my judgment the closest kind of connection between that topic and the variability of content obtaining in courses that have identical titles, and with, also, the multiplication of courses. The cause of the two latter phenomena resides, unless I greatly err, precisely in adherence to the conventionalized division of branches of learning.

I said earlier that this way of determining studies is pretty much taken for granted by all parties to educational conflicts. I may now be asked if there is any choice, any alternative? Is there any possible conflict concerning this point? Is not, by its very nature, any subject, history, a modern language, physics, algebra just what we mean by a "study"? Conventionally and traditionally it is. But study and *a* study are different things. A study has come to signify just a definitely aggregated body of subject-matter isolated from others and treated as a unit by itself. But study is study*ing*. The physician may study "medicine" in the medical school, but in practice he studies many other things, such as his patient and how to succeed. The practitioner of law has to study a good many other things than law in order to make his former study effective. A parent studies psychology, social relations, etc., not as studies but as they apply in his responsibilities as parent. A similar duplicity is found in the word "learning." It signifies an accumulated and transmitted body of knowledge, and it also signifies the acts of apprehending, understanding, and retaining in and for subsequent use.

In this difference of meanings within the terms "study" and "learning" is implicit the point I wish to make. The titles we find in a school program, such as history, geography, algebra, botany, assume that learning is already at hand, set in proper summaries and needing only to be divided up into proper doses. They assume that this material which is unified through its isolation from other things is the natural occasion for the act of studying. This assumption has broken down through the expansion of knowledge and modes of expert skill; this breakdown has caused the immense variation in actual subject-matter which has come about even when the nominal titles remain the same. The content changes; titles persist. The persistence of names is of little account. What is important is that segregation also persists.

The name is a tag but it operates as though there were something definitely fixed underneath it. The same adherence to an outworn idea explains the multiplication of subjects. When there is too much material to be "covered" in one course, the logical thing, given the premiss, is to break the unwieldy material into pieces. This fractionizing is inevitable as long as the educational mind is dominated by the notion that studies are identical with traditional divisions of subject-matter. The fragments become first smaller cabins and then hardly more than pigeon-holes for odds and ends.

In the actual advance of knowledge and the arts, there is much more than mere extension of facts and principles. It has been attended by constant development of cross references, of interdependencies and interrelations. When we compare the actual situation with the scholastic, we find growing divergence, till now there is a split. The extension of knowledge in scope has had an effect of multiplication of courses; its movement in complex intricacy of relationships has had little effect. The scholastic and the actual now sustain an almost inverse ratio to each other. If we take a glance at only the titles of the latter we come upon many which are designated with hyphens: astro-physics, bio-chemistry, and so on. And there are many more where an adjective is prefixed to the noun that names the old subject-matter, such as physiological chemistry, physiological psychology, physical chemistry, etc. These names also testify to the breaking down of dividing walls between subjects. And quite apart from the emergence of these connecting links, every subject now borrows from others; it can be pursued only by using material drawn from other subjects in order to throw light, and by using methods developed in other subjects as tools of inquiry. The connection between physics and mathematics is very old; in spite of this fact in schools the two are taken up independently, and too often the student of physics does not see the bearing of what he has learned—that is to say, memorized—in a subject labelled mathematics; while his mathematics remains a vexing set of operations and of merely symbolic formulae apparently devised *ad hoc*. It is no wonder under such circumstances—and physics and mathematics is the field in which interdependence is best, not least, recognized—that subjects grow superficial and barren, and that their multiplication brings weariness to the spirit and the flesh.

What has been said about interdependence in branches of knowledge holds equally well in those technical activities of use of knowledge that we call industrial or practical arts. In operation they are often immensely specialized in detail. But back of the operations there lies a concentration of knowledge derived from many sources, an integration of many processes which originated in separate arts. Consider the multiplicity of problems that have to be met by a city architect, problems not just of building, but of lighting, heating, plumbing, ventilation, elevator service, perhaps electric power, decoration, and so on. The individual architect may not be master of them all but he has to know enough to coordinate the activities of specialists in these departments. The illustration is typical of what goes on in every modern factory.

I hope my point has become reasonably clear. In a situation where the skills or arts and the subject-matter of knowledge have become interwoven and interdependent, adherence to the policy forming the studies of secondary and collegiate instruction on the basis of many isolated and independent subjects is bound to result in precisely the kind of confusion we have at present.

In view of recent strictures passed upon universities—strictures many of which apply as well to secondary education—it is worth while to devote special attention to the practical turn which American education is taking, and to the resultant conflict between the operations of the "practical" aim and the liberal, cultural, and humanistic ideal. The multiplication of faculties, schools and institutes of a professional and semi-professional character, characteristic of higher education, is paralleled in secondary education. In the former, in addition to the three traditional learned professions, theology, law, medicine, we now have schools of journalism, commerce, engineering, teaching, dentistry, pharmacy, agriculture, forestry, library service, domestic and household arts. Their multiplication has certainly not lessened educational confusion. Their existence is challenged on two different grounds, which concern also the multiplication of courses and types of schools in secondary education. One concerns actual methods employed and the content offered. The other has to do with the legitimacy of their existence as parts of a general educational scheme. As the latter question is evidently more fundamental I shall begin with it, with the proviso that its consideration will lead in the end, in my judgment, solely to the question of actual content and method of instruction.

Is there any intrinsic difference between the callings to which new courses and faculties are devoted and the sacred traditional trinity of learned vocations? Historically, there is of course a decided difference; the learned professions have a background of centuries of development. But they too were once essentially trade schools, designed to give expertness in practice, a condition from which they have not yet wholly emerged. They had and still have an economic as well as a humane aspect; they prepare students for making a living in a competitive society where values are measured in terms of money. Subjects taught as liberal and humane have had and still have their professional aspect. Not the least conspicuous of their functions has been the preparation of teachers. Moreover, there was a time when the learned professions had no background. When they were taken within the precincts of academies and universities they too had no educational history behind them. They were, in their early stages, in the same position in which non-learned vocations are at present. And if I may plagiarize freely from a scholar and colleague who is himself a distinguished representative of an English university that wins the approval of those who criticize the practical tendencies of American education, the criticism is largely conventional. If you go into a laboratory and see a student devoting himself to a section of a worm, you do not, probably, object. That is of course zoology; it has its recognized place in the educational scheme. But if you find a course listed appertaining to laundry work, your susceptibilities are offended. The latter may indeed be narrow and confining. But so may the former. Either one may be so utilized as to give understanding and illumination—one of natural life, the other of social facts and relationships.

I am not, however, saying these things in order to support present practical tendencies in secondary and university education, but to introduce the question of *Why*. Why have vocational and semi-vocational courses multiplied and gained momentum? In general, the answer is clear. The arts and technologies by which the life of society is maintained are now so affected by and saturated with applied science that the routine apprenticeship methods of the past no longer serve. Somehow and somewhere there must be organized instruction concerning them. It is probably true that the chief immediate motive for giving this instruction is the belief that such instruction will better enable individuals to get on; I have no great quarrel with those who insist that as actually given this supposed value is often largely fictitious, especially in secondary schools. But the ultimate point is that instruction of this kind, but of a better type, is *socially* necessary, and that until it is properly given in educational institutions, the practical activities carried on in society will not be liberalized and humanized, to say nothing of being most efficiently conducted.

The question of where this instruction shall be given is not a matter of purely administrative detail. There is well-grounded fear that schools and courses devoted to the vocational subjects are side-shows which will ultimately obscure the show carried on in the main tent. They divert, it is said, attention, money, and energy from scholarship and humane learning. And while the fact that the record of liberal schools is not wholly one of glorious and unwearied exclusive devotion to truth and learning for their own sakes is pertinent to the issue, it does not settle it.

The real issue lies deeper. Can a culture which is divorced from the main directions and interests of modern life survive? Or, as far as it does survive, will it be, in its divorce, solid or attenuated, robust or feeble, a luxury for the few or a vital constituent of the life of the many? It is because there is a genuine possibility of development of culture, of humane, liberal, outlook in intimate connection with the practical activities of life, and because only in that connection can culture be truly vital for the many, that I conclude that the real problem is not one of the legitimate existence of professional and semi-professional schools and courses as parts of the general education system, but of what these schools and courses are to include and of how they are to teach: in short, of their content and method.

At this point, we come in sight of the connection of the conflict between practical and liberal studies with the other question that has been raised. I pointed out that the cause of the confusion resulting from multiplication of studies and variation in the subject-matter of every single study, is adherence to a traditional classification and division of isolated subjects; to lack of taking account of correlations and interdependencies which actually exist among them. The same remark applied to the defects in the newer "practical" subjects. They have not followed traditional divisions, because these did not exist aforetime in the educational plan. But they too have attempted an unreal division which has led to splitting up and multiplication, with the result of thinness, superficiality, and the impracticable character of much of the work done in secondary schools and of that done in universities, under the caption of the practical. In the degree in which this defect is remedied, there will be an approximation to the cultural and liberal. For the moment a larger and more connected view is taken, that moment genuine and vital knowledge of related sciences and a wide outlook upon history and society become necessary.

Conflict between the cultural, or liberal, and the practical will continue with result of confusion as long as both of them are narrowly conceived. I can hardly go into the philosophy of American life, but I do not see how anyone can doubt that as long as the humanistic is set off as something by itself, apart from the interests and activities in which the mass of men and women must perforce engage, it will grow thinner, more and more merely reminiscent, a struggling survival of what Santayana calls the "genteel tradition." It is equally true that as long as the actual occupations of men, with the exception of a few professions labelled "learned," are not affected by the larger outlook and the fuller background presented by the ideal for which the liberal in education stands they will be narrow and hard, tending not merely to the "utilitarian" in its restricted sense, but even toward the brutal and inhuman.

I can hardly do better than quote the words of President Morgan. "In so far as the liberal arts college stands for a perpetuation of the traditional conflict between vocation and culture, it seems doomed to play a constantly decreasing role in education. In a day when most of the occupations of men involved little more than manual skill and the repeated application of a few rule-of-thumb formulae, the concept of vocational as illiberal may have had some basis. With the modern applications of all the sciences and arts to vocations, and the successful scientific search for principles within the operations and purposes of the vocations themselves, it is no longer true. It is rapidly becoming a fact that study within one's vocational preparation is an important means of freeing and liberalizing the mind. This being true, the inevitable trend in education is toward the rapid thinning of the traditional educational wall between vocational and cultural. The liberal arts college will survive and render service in proportion as it recognizes this fact and brings its course of study and administrative set-up into effective conformity with it."

The sentences quoted explicitly refer to the college rather than to the secondary school. But the principle applies to the latter, although of course its execution demands great modification. It will not be easy to develop secondary education so that the practical and semi-vocational courses will absorb within themselves the liberal training and the social and scientific outlook which is needed. The great difficulties in the way account for their present existence in a form open to severe criticism. It is not easy to find teachers having this point of view, while the problem of selecting and arranging subject-matter and activities which will accomplish the end desired requires patient, thorough inquiry and careful testing. There is, then, nothing in what I have said that is an apologia for courses "as are." The easiest course along the line of least resistance is what always happens in the beginning of any new movement. The easiest course with the introduction of practical courses was to take certain occupations current in contemporary society, and then introduce courses having through their titles an external and nominal connection with these callings. But criticism based on the assumption that the state of affairs is one that must indefinitely endure gets us nowhere. It is helpful only when it points the way toward materials and methods that will link a liberalizing quality to the quasi-vocational. When courses in secondary schools—and in colleges, for that matter—give up the idea that they can really give adequate technical preparation, and hence make it their business to open to students the scientific and social potentialities of important occupations of society, they will become more genuinely practical as well as more liberal.

I recur now to the main theme of which this particular problem supplies one instance. It is fair for an objector to ask what is the substitute, the alternative, to organization of courses on the basis of adherence to traditional divisions and classifications of knowledge. The reply which goes furthest to the left is found in reference to the so-called "project," "problem," or "situation" method, now adopted for trial in many elementary schools. I shall indicate later that I do not believe that this is the only alternative. But the method has certain characteristics which are significant for any plan for change that may be adopted, and ac-

cordingly I shall call attention to these features. The method
mentioned is called a method; it might be taken, therefore, to be
only a method. In fact, like anything that *is* a method other than
in name, it has definite implications for subject-matter. There
cannot be a problem that is not a problem of *something*, nor a
project that does not involve doing something in a way which
demands inquiry into fresh fields of subject-matter. Many so-
called projects are of such a short time-span and are entered
upon for such casual reasons, that extension of acquaintance
with facts and principles is at a minimum. In short, they are too
trivial to be educative. But the defect is not inherent. It only indicates the need that educators should assume their educational responsibility. It is possible to find problems and projects that
come within the scope and capacities of the experience of the
learner and which have a sufficiently long span so that they raise
new questions, introduce new and related undertakings, and
create a demand for fresh knowledge. The difference between
this procedure and the traditional one is not that the latter involves acquisition of new knowledge and the former does not. It
is that in one a relatively fixed and isolated body of knowledge is
assumed in advance; while in the other, material is drawn from
any field as it is needed to carry on an intellectual enterprise.

Nor is the difference that in one procedure organization exists
and in the other it does not. It is a difference in the type of organization effected. Material may be drawn from a variety of fields,
number and measure from mathematics when they are needed,
from historical, geographical, biological facts when they carry
forward the undertaking, and so on. But the central question
acts as a magnet to draw them together. Organization in one
case consists in formal relations within a particular field as they
present themselves to an expert who has mastered the subject.
In the other case, it consists in noting the bearing and function
of things acquired. The latter course has at least the advantage of
being of the kind followed in study and learning outside of
school walls, where data and principles do not offer themselves
in isolated segments with labels already affixed.

Another feature of the problem method is that activity is ex-
acted. I suppose that if there is one principle which is not a monopoly of any school of educational thought, it is the need of
intellectual activity on the part of teacher and student, the con-

demnation of passive receptivity. But in practice there persist methods in which the pupil is a recording phonograph, or one who stands at the end of a pipe line receiving material conducted from a distant reservoir of learning. How is this split between theory and practice to be explained? Does not the presentation in doses and chunks of a ready-made subject-matter inevitably conduce to passivity? The mentally active scholar will acknowledge, I think, that his mind roams far and wide. All is grist that comes to his mill, and he does not limit his supply of grain to any one fenced-off field. Yet the mind does not merely roam abroad. It returns with what is found, and there is constant exercise of judgment to detect relations, relevancies, bearings upon the central theme. The outcome is a continuously growing intellectual integration. There is absorption; but it is eager and willing, not reluctant and forced. There is digestion, assimilation, not merely the carrying of a load by memory, a load to be cast off as soon as the day comes when it is safe to throw it off. Within the limits set by capacity and experience this kind of seeking and using, of amassing and organizing, is the process of learning everywhere and at any age.

In the third place, while the student with a proper "project" is intellectually active, he is also overtly active; he applies, he constructs, he expresses himself in new ways. He puts his knowledge to the test of operation. Naturally, he does something with what he learns. Because of this feature the separation between the practical and the liberal does not even arise. It does not have to be done away with, because it is not there. In practical subjects, this doing exists in laboratories and shops. But too often it is of a merely technical sort, not a genuine carrying forward of theoretical knowledge. It aims at mere manual facility, at an immediate external product, or a driving home into memory of something already learned as a matter of mere information.

I have referred, as already indicated, to the "project" method because of these traits, which seem to me proper and indispensable aims in all study by whatever name it be called, not because this method seems to be the only alternative to that usually followed. I do not urge it as the sole way out of educational confusion, not even in the elementary school, though I think experimentation with it is desirable in college and secondary school. But it is possible to retain traditional titles and still reorganize the subject-matter under them, so as to take account of interdependencies of knowledge and connection of knowledge with use and application. As the time grows to a close let me mention one illustration, Julian Huxley's and H. G. Wells' recent volumes on Life. They cut across all conventional divisions in the field: yet not at the expense of scientific accuracy but in a way which increases both intellectual curiosity and understanding, while disclosing the world about us as a perennial source of esthetic delight.

I have referred to intellectual interest. It is only too common to hear students (in name) say in reference to some subject that they "have *had* it." The use of the past tense is only too significant. The subject is over and done with; it is very much in the past. Every intelligent observer of the subsequent career of those who come from our schools deplores the fact that they do not carry away from school into later life abiding intellectual interests in what they have studied. After all, the period from, say, fourteen to twenty-two is a comparatively short portion of a normal life time. The best that education can do during these years is to arouse intellectual interests which carry over and onwards. The worst condemnation that can be passed is that these years are an interlude, a passing interval. If a student does not take into subsequent life an enduring concern for some field of knowledge and art, lying outside his immediate profession preoccupations, schooling for him has been a failure, no matter how good a "student" he was.

The failure is again due, I believe, to segregation of subjects. A pupil can say he has "had" a subject, because the subject has been treated as if it were complete in itself, beginning and terminating within limits fixed in advance. A reorganization of subject-matter which takes account of out-leadings into the wide world of nature and man, of knowledge and of social interests and uses, cannot fail save in the most callous and intellectually obdurate to awaken some permanent interest and curiosity. Theoretical subjects will become more practical, because more related to the scope of life; practical subjects will become more charged with theory and intelligent insight. Both will be vitally and not just formally unified.

I see no other way out of our educational confusion. The obvious objection is that this way takes too abrupt a turn. But what alternative is there save a further cluttering up of the curriculum and a steeper dividing wall between the cultural and liberal? The change is in many respects revolutionary. Yet the intelligence needed to bring it about is not lacking, but rather a long-time patience and a will to cooperation and coordination. I can see schools of education leading in the movement. They will hardly do much to reduce the existing confusion if they merely move in the direction of refining existing practices, striving to bring them under the protective shield of "scientific method." That course is more likely to increase confusion. But they can undertake consecutive study of the interrelation of subjects with one another and with social bearing and application; they can contribute to a reorganization that will give direction to an aimless and divided situation.

For confusion is due ultimately to aimlessness, as much of the conflict is due to the attempt to follow tradition and yet introduce radically new material and interests into it—the attempt to superimpose the new on the old. The simile of new wines in old bottles is trite. Yet no other is so apt. We use leathern bottles in an age of steel and glass. The bottles leak and sag. The new wine spills and sours. No prohibitory holds against the attempt to make a new wine of culture and to provide new containers. Only new aims can inspire educational effort for clarity and unity. They alone can reduce confusion; if they do not terminate conflict they will at least render it intelligent and profitable.

American Education Past and Future

The largest single army in the world, a legion of hope, industry, peace, and intelligence, began about six weeks ago to mobilize its units for this year's campaign. Tots of four and five sought the kindergarten; boys and girls of from six years to the early teens thronged the elementary school; their older brothers and sisters went to the high school, the college, the technical and professional school.

This army forms a mighty host. There are thirty million children and youth in its ranks—as many as made up the entire population of this country within the lifetime of the oldest in my unseen audience. Two-thirds of the number are in the elementary schools; four million lads and lassies are in high schools; colleges and other higher institutions take care of almost a million. This vast army is staffed and serviced by a corps of about a million administrators and teachers. More than a quarter of a million of young men and women are recruiting for future service in normal schools and teacher-training classes. The financial outlay is in proportion to the size of the task. We spend on education about three billion dollars annually, drawn from taxes and the endowments due to private beneficence. The budgets of our municipalities devote, upon the whole, about one-third of their total sum to the schools.

This is but the outside of the educational picture. In their work and achievements the schools represent the most important as well as the largest undertaking of the American nation. And their scope is constantly growing. Their rate of growth has been enormously speeded up since the World War. It used to be said

[First published as a pamphlet by the National Advisory Council on Radio in Education (Chicago: University of Chicago Press, 1931), 16 pp., from the 25 October 1931 broadcast of the second address in the "Men of America" series of radio lectures.]

that only one child in twenty succeeded in passing from the elementary school into the secondary, and only one in a hundred of the former number ever found his way to college. In the last few decades the absolute number has increased some sevenfold and the relative number, in comparison with increase in population, at least fivefold. We can search the history of the world in vain for any similar occurrence. For the first time in recorded history there is a promise that universal education will become a fact, and not a dream on paper.

Growth in the number of those who get beyond the merest elements of an education is more than matched by expansion of educational facilities. The colleges have ceased to exist simply for the children of parents who had had themselves a classic training. Their scope is now as broad as all the activities of our modern complex society: schools of agriculture, all the branches of engineering, pharmacy, dentistry, business and commerce, journalism, etc. University extension reaches out to include the public that has been deprived of higher education. The high school was once mainly a preparatory school for those going to college; it is now itself a college for the people. In our larger cities, school buildings are often better and better equipped than were the universities of a generation ago.

If the older among you will think back to the elementary school of your childhood, you will recall a series of rooms whose sole equipment was rows of benches screwed to the floor, forbidding blackboards, and thumbed textbooks. These dreary structures are now being replaced with buildings in which there are gymnasia, libraries, pictures, statuary, assembly halls for music and dramatics, shops for wood work, rooms for cooking and sewing, often dental clinics, and offices for medical inspection. In spite of cries of "fads and frills," the old curriculum of the "three R's" with a sparse smattering of history and geography, taught by rote from a single textbook, has given way to an enriched program. The ideal is that the whole boy and whole girl shall go to school and shall find there opportunities for the development of all the potentialities of a many-sided nature. Drill halls are becoming places in which children may live happily and may grow as they live. Let me cite one fact as typical of the situation. Investigations undertaken thirty years ago have been repeated lately, and have shown that the amount of reading matter covered by a pupil in a good elementary school is now eight or nine times as much as it used to be.

In addition to this internal enrichment there has been a great expansion outward. There is not a large city in which adult education is not being carried on; in some of the more progressive places, this work is as well organized as that for children and youth. Nursery schools are springing up at one end of the scale, balanced by parental education at the other. Handicapped, neglected, and delinquent children are receiving systematic attention. Schools for the deaf and blind have been greatly increased; those for the crippled and the subnormal are largely a product of the last twenty years. There is a constantly growing number of towns and cities which have community centres which provide health and recreational facilities. It is noteworthy that about one-fourth of the aims listed in the Children's Charter of the White House Conference have to do with safeguarding the physical development of the young. Recent developments in hygiene and medicine are making us realize that sound health is the basis of individual and national well-being, and the connections between schools and public-health agencies are drawing closer.

It would be foolish to assert that our educational expansion has always been well directed. On the contrary, it has frequently been attended with aimless dispersion and has led to superficiality. But when all allowances are made for mistakes and eccentricities, it still remains true that we now have for the first time in history the physical and administrative basis for a truly universal education. For a universal education means not only one that extends its advantages to all, but one which meets the immense variety of social needs and of individual capacities and wants. Much remains to do even in the way of extension. Preschool education, parental education, adult education generally are only in their early infancy. Much has been said and written about a plan of vocational guidance which will help individuals find the callings in which they can be of use to others while finding happiness in their work for themselves, but as yet the schools have actually accomplished almost nothing. The trend toward high school and college still leaves two-thirds of our future citizenship with only the bare elements of intellectual preparation. Think of your own children of from twelve to fourteen, the degree of maturity they have reached, and call to mind the complex and difficult conditions of life and of making a living, and you will realize how far even in education we still come short of realizing the ideal of an equal start and an equal chance for all. Ignorance, lack of trained skill, are handicaps imposed on two boys and girls out of three. The evil is increased by the amount of child labor, even of a seasonal migratory sort, which our laws still permit.

Nevertheless, whatever our shortcomings, it is in education more than anywhere else that we have sincerely striven to carry into execution what James Truslow Adams has recently called "the Great American Dream": the vision of a larger and fuller life for the ordinary man, a life of widened freedom, of equal opportunity for each to make out of himself all that he is capable of becoming. Some have ridiculed the American faith in education; they have called it, derisively, a religion, and a religion which is a superstition. At bottom, however, there is no difference between faith in education and a generous faith in human nature. If the whole democratic enterprise to which our fathers committed the American people is a delusion, then—but then only—is our trust in education a superstitious mistake.

For a great idea lies behind the mobilization of this army of thirty million children and youth; a great ideal is at stake in the remarkable expansion our schools are undergoing. A hundred years ago, in the thirties and forties of the last century, the wiser of our ancestors began to realize that the democratic experiment was not one which was sure, automatically, to succeed. With one voice they cried that the enduring existence of republican institutions was dependent upon the spread of popular enlightenment, that popular education was the corner stone of the Republic. As this idea was originally at the basis of the creation of the public-school system, so it has continued to be the fountainhead and inspiration of the expansion of the public-school system and its services.

The movement is an endless one; the need for expansion and alteration in education can never be ended, because the need can never be fully satisfied. It is the need of a human nature and of a society that are themselves in process of constant change. The most universal ambition of the average American parent, man and woman, has been that his boy and girl should have a better chance in life than the father and mother had. This desire, which has been the source of infinite self-sacrifice, inheres in our social system with its belief in the possibilities of the common man. It can only be carried into effect through ever renewed improvement of our educational system.

Consequently I am here this evening to say that great as have been the changes in our educational system in the last hundred years, and especially in the last thirty, they are nevertheless slight in comparison with those which must be undertaken in the next generation. How can education stand still when society itself is rapidly changing under our very eyes? The sense of unsolved social problems is all about us. There are problems of crime, of regard for law, of capital, of labor, of unemployment, of stability and security, of family life, of war and peace, of international relations and cooperation—all on a larger scale than the world has ever seen before. Anticipation of continued and large-scale changes in education is, then, not so much a prophecy as it is a warning. Unless education prepares future citizens to deal effectively with these great questions, our civilization may collapse. It cannot give this preparation unless it itself undergoes great transformations. H. G. Wells said, soon after the close of the war, that we were engaged in a race between education and catastrophe. Here in America, it might be truer to say that we are engaged in a race between a *mis*education which will bear no vital relation to the needs and conditions of the modern world and a possible education which will face the future and which will defer to the past and its traditions only as far as the past gives us aid in effectively facing the future.

The necessity of great educational change may be indicated by sketching the changes which life has undergone in the United States.

First, one hundred years ago, our life was agrarian and rural. Agrarian civilization has always when left to itself moved at such a slow pace that, to those who lived in it, it did not seem to change in any fundamental way. It is static, based on the traditions of the past, and accommodated to the course of nature. During the nineties of the last century, our society became definitely urban and industrial. It moves neither at the tempo of the ox-cart nor of the horse, but at that of electricity, the motor car, and the airplane. Life has to adapt itself to the mechanical inventions which control the processes of nature rather than to the cycle of nature itself. Invention rather than routine and custom determines the course of events, and no one can say what further inventions are going to modify the course of living in the years that are before us. We do know that the railway, telegraph, telephone, electric light, power, transportation, automobile, radio, airplane, and their multitude of accessories have revolutionized our habits of work, of amusement, of communication and intercourse. Schools which have looked upon their task as that of preserving and transmitting the classic cultures of the past have fought shy of adopting into their own aims and methods enough of the new forces, the forces which determine our life, to fit individuals to cope with them. They may wreck us unless they are intelligently regulated and employed. Our mechanical devices and processes have got far ahead of our capacity to plan and to enjoy—ahead of our minds in short. The gaps between our machines and our ability to control them for human ends is widened because education has clung to old traditions and aims of culture in the face of the new industrial situation.

Secondly, there has been a revolution in the methods by which things get done. Our fathers worked by custom and the models laid down in the past. These models and procedures have been thrown into the scrap heap, not intentionally and deliberately, but none the less effectually. For science has dictated to men new ways of doing things based upon understanding of natural energy and the relations of cause and effect. Because of scientific advance, because of the methods it puts at our disposal, a single great industrial company creates devices by which the work can be done which would occupy our entire population, men, women, children, and babes, if the work had to be done with the instruments and processes of even sixty years ago. It cannot be said that our schools have begun to introduce scientific method into their teaching to anything approaching the part which it plays in shaping our actual lives.

Thirdly, we have altered from a population with simple political problems to one with extremely difficult and complex issues. When the outlines of our school system were formed there was no great separation into rich and poor; there was free land; there were abundant unused and unappropriated natural resources. There was work and opportunity to get on for all. Then the aims of political democracy were easily understood, since they were in harmony with the conditions of soil and occupation. Now there are vast and concentrated aggregations of wealth; there are monopolies of power; great unemployment; a shutting down of doors of opportunity, a gulf between rich and poor, and no frontier to which the hard put can migrate. In consequence, the problem of democracy is no longer chiefly governmental and political. It is industrial and financial—economic. It is infinitely ramified and the threads which bind the social structure together are subtle and invisible. It would be absurd to hold educators responsible for our present depression, a depression which is obviously mental and moral as well as financial. But the depression is a warning that we live in an age in which education must take on new responsibilities and come to grips with realities which it has passed by as outside its province.

Fourthly, control of natural forces by means of machinery has brought to humanity the possibility of an amount of leisure from which the mass of men and women in the past were hopelessly shut out. At the same time, popular amusements and recreation have been seized upon as means of financial profit. The combination of these two facts has created what may be truly called a crisis in our national moral life. A new conception of the uses of leisure has to be created; boys and girls need to be instructed so that they can discriminate between the enjoyments that enrich and enlarge their lives and those which degrade and dissipate. The possibilities of artistic production and appreciation can no longer remain the privilege of a select class, but must become a universal possession. Otherwise the increase of leisure time may become a demoralizing agent on a vast scale.

Not all the social changes which are going on are good and beneficial. But it is claimed that these changes are here and must be faced, not ignored; education has the responsibility of developing types of mind and character that can direct these new forces toward good, and that otherwise they will surely become forces of destruction and disintegration.

The sum of the matter is that at the present time education has no great directive aim. It grows, but it grows from specific pressure exerted here and there, not because of any large and inspiring social policy. It expands by piecemeal additions, not by the movement of a vital force within. The schools, like the nation, are in need of a central purpose which will create a new enthusiasm and devotion, and which will unify and guide all intellectual plans.

In earlier days there was an aim which worked throughout the whole system. Education was the key to individual success, to making one's way in life, to getting on and getting ahead. The aim corresponded with the realities of social life, for the national need was the material subjugation of a continent, the conquest of a wilderness. There was always a frontier just beyond and the pioneer advanced to take possession of it. It was enough for the school to equip the individual with the tools of learning and to fire him with ambition and zeal to get on. His real education came in contact with others and in struggles with the forces of nature. The aim was individualistic, but it was also in harmony with the needs of the nation.

This earlier purpose has lost its vitality and its meaning. It survives, but operates as an oppressive handicap. As President Hoover said some time ago: "We are passing from a period of extremely individualistic action to one of associational activity." Except for a favored few, there is no longer any unbounded opportunity for advancement open to individuals. We live in an epoch of combination, consolidation, concentration. Unless these combinations are used democratically for the common good, the result will be an increasing insecurity and oppression for the mass of men and women. Education must cultivate the social spirit and the power to act socially even more assiduously than it cultivated individual ambition for material success in the past. Competitive motives and methods must be abandoned for cooperative. Desire to work with others, for mutual advantage, must be made the controlling force in school administration and instruction. Instead of imbuing individuals with the idea that the goal is to sharpen their powers so they can get on personally, they must be trained in capacity for intelligent organization so that they can unite with others in a common struggle against poverty, disease, ignorance, credulity, low standards of appreciation and enjoyment. There must be a purpose and methods which will carry over the earlier ideals of political democracy into industry and finance.

Only in respect to methods of thought and judgment should the earlier individualistic aim be retained; *there* it should be intensified. Democracy will be a farce unless individuals are trained to think for themselves, to judge independently, to be critical, to be able to detect subtle propaganda and the motives which inspire it. Mass production and uniform regimentation have been growing in the degree in which individual opportunity has waned. The current must be reversed. The motto must be: "Learn to *act* with and for others while you learn to *think* and to judge for yourself."

The problem of educational reorganization is not one which it is easy to solve. But we are discovering that the problem of maintaining the democratic ideals of our founding fathers is not easy, either. The only way to attain the latter is by giving a social direction to our educational system. If the good will, the loyalty, the political faith and hope of the American people can be united with the affection which parents have for their children, and the union can be directed by the spirit of free scientific inquiry, there is no ground for fear of failure. When the ideals of democracy are made real in our entire educational system, they will be a reality once more in our national life.

Monastery, Bargain Counter, or Laboratory in Education?

Some years ago when I was in the Adirondacks, I climbed Mt. Marcy, the highest peak of those mountains. There, near the top, is a marshy space with a little brook trickling down, apparently insignificant. A few rods away, after a slight rise of land, there is a second little brook, likewise apparently insignificant. I was told that the first one I speak of is the headwaters of the Hudson River; that the waters a short way off, separated by a watershed only a few feet higher than this swampy land, finally empty into the St. Lawrence. These little streams, that are hardly to be called streams but rather rivulets, at their source are only a few yards apart, but traversing very different lands and seeing very different scenes they finally reach the Atlantic Ocean hundreds of miles away from each other. This metaphor for purposes of comparison is trite, yet it seems to me that in its way it is representative of what happens historically. Great movements are not often great in their beginnings. Taken in themselves their inception is as seemingly insignificant and trivial as the little trickles of water near the top of that mountain. It is only when after long periods of time we look back to see what has come out of these little beginnings, that they appear important; just as it is when we see the Hudson River after it has become a majestic stream that the small rivulet at the top of Mt. Marcy gains importance.

You remember Emerson spoke about men who build better than they know. It seems to me that all great historic movements may be said to build either much better or much worse than those who started them knew or intended. This is true in the history of the founding of our own country. You will recall that

[First published in *Barnwell Bulletin* 9 (February 1932): 51–62, from the Barnwell Address delivered at Central High School, Philadelphia, on 4 February 1932.]

most of the leaders in the Revolution, George Washington himself included, hoped that there would not be a complete break with Great Britain. They had certain objects which they wanted to gain, but they did not contemplate a really new political world. They felt rather that they were protesting against abuses of the liberties which belonged to British subjects, and just as their English forefathers had protested against the tyranny of the Stuarts, so they, in protesting against the despotism of the Georges in their own day, were walking in the footsteps of their ancestors.

Certainly those who started the educational system in America had no idea and no intention of founding a new educational system. Indeed, they looked backward rather than forward. Some of them looked back to Holland, others to England; and their highest ambition was to imitate or, if possible, to reproduce those schools in which they themselves had been trained. They were in a new country, the greater part still a wilderness, and naturally their highest ambition was to come as near as possible to recreating on American soil the kind of school which they themselves had known when they were children. This attempt to continue the educational system of the Old World persisted for a long time. Upon the whole it continued in this country until—we can only speak roughly—until, say, some time after the Civil War. Up to that time our education in the main was still a perpetuator; an effort to maintain the higher culture of our European source.

That type of education had certain quite definite features. In the earlier period of the elementary school the instruction was essentially an education in the three R's, reading, 'riting and 'rithmetic, with a little history of our own country and geography of the world, but more especially the geography of our country, superadded. There was a tendency to divide the subjects and methods of instruction. The mass of pupils who had received a training in the rudiments of learning did not go on with their education in higher schools. When they left the elementary school, their education was continued mainly through serving apprenticeships in trades and callings of various kinds, entered into either by formal indenture or in an informal way. In the service of a master and from the contact arising from this relation, the apprentice acquired skill in a trade. A small number of pupils, however, continued with higher education. For them the backbone of advanced education was the ancient languages, Greek and Latin, for those going into the learned professions of law and medicine, with the addition of Hebrew for those entering the ministry. Some history was also added, but classic history, the history of Greece and Rome with the literatures of those ancient countries. In those days there was no English literature in the higher courses, and there were no modern languages. The education, as you see, for the most part was in the symbols of knowledge and in the written and printed expression, especially in the languages and literatures of antiquity. It almost seems as if it was supposed that the material was better and more precious, the further away from the present it was both in space and in time.

This type of education I have taken the liberty of calling that of the monastery. This is a metaphor which is not to be taken too literally. But it was an education intended for the few rather than for the mass of the people. It was derived from the European tradition in which it was expected that only a few would continue beyond the mere rudiments of learning into what would be really an education. And the material of it, as I have just said, was largely the symbol of learning. Mathematics was the symbol of numbers, and the written and printed word that of grammar and literature, and so on. There was an aloofness from ordinary every-day living, which perhaps does not make the term "monastery education" entirely inappropriate.

Now this type of education, derived essentially from European sources though modified in some details (since after all there was the ocean between it and its source), persisted longer than we might have expected. There were probably two main causes for the long persistence of this older education on the new soil, which in the meantime had developed a new political and to a considerable extent a new social system. One cause was that in the first decades of our Republic the practical education of the great majority of people was still obtained out of school. In the main we were still a rural and agrarian people. We were still in an age in which industry was chiefly carried on in the home and in the neighborhood by means of handicraft. If there was machinery, it was comparatively simple. There were local shops in the villages, country communities and towns to which everyone had comparatively easy access. I remember the village in which stood my grandfather's house, where in my childhood I went to spend the summer vacation. There in the village was the old-fashioned sawmill, the old-fashioned gristmill, the old-fashioned tannery; and in my grandfather's house there were still the candles and the soap which had been made in the home itself. At certain times the cobbler would come around to spend a few days in the neighborhood, making and repairing the shoes of the people. Through the very conditions of living, everybody had a pretty direct contact with nature and with the simpler forms of industry. As there were no great accumulations of wealth, the great majority of young people got a very genuine education through a kind of informal apprenticeship. They took part in the home-made duties of the household and farm and activities of the neighborhood. They saw with their eyes, and followed with their imaginations, the very real activities about them. The amount of genuine education, and of training in good habits that were obtained in this way under our earlier pioneer conditions, is not easy to overestimate. There was a real education through real contact with actual materials and important social occupations.

On the other hand, knowledge in the form of the written and printed word then had what economists call a "scarcity value." Books, newspapers, periodicals, in a word reading matter of all kinds, were much rarer and more expensive than they are today. Libraries were comparatively few. Learning, or rather the mastery of the tools of learning, the ability to read and to write and to figure, had a high value, because the school was the one place where these tools of learning could be mastered. We all have heard the story of Abraham Lincoln and other backwoodsmen and of their devotion to learning, of the great difficulties they had to contend with, of their going barefooted for miles to school, of their sitting up at night to master by candle light the rudiments of learning. For in those days, the monastery education was the only avenue to the larger world of the culture of the past. And that is why, I think, this older type of education, that seems to us today rather barren and meagre, persisted so long and relatively was so effective in achieving important results.

Gradually, with the change of those social conditions, there was brought about a very great change, a change so great as to be called a revolution in our whole educational system. I think of

the old gristmill of my boyhood days in contrast with the great
flour manufactories of today as symbolical. Then we could go
into the mill, we could see the grain, we could watch it being
ground in those great stone hoppers; we could see it passing
through the pipes, and we could follow it with our eyes until it
was turned into bran, flour and the rest of it. Today if we go into
one of these big flour mills, we would not even see the grain
going into the hopper! We may follow the whole process and see
practically nothing, not even the finished flour as it is automatically put into barrels. The youth of today have no access to the
basic realities of living, social, material, economic, at all to the
extent to which the youth of a few generations ago had. This is
what I mean by the illustration of the mills, if we take it sym-
bolically. That fact has made it necessary for the schools to
branch out in their instruction and to take up many things which
used to be taken care of in the life of the boys and girls, of the
young men and young women, out of school. In addition the
situation is reversed in reference to language and books. Printed
matter is almost a drug; it is cheap, accessible, voluminous. It
would require considerable ingenuity for one growing up in the
city to escape it. Machines take over the work of calculation and
penmanship. On the other hand, however, opportunities have
vanished for the learning and for the practical discipline which
used to be had in open fields under the skies, and in shops where
a few persons worked in close contact with one another, using
their own judgment and receiving recognition for their personal
achievements. They are now fenced-in roads where there used to
be open fields inviting the inventive to take short cuts to their
goals. The roads, moreover, are crowded and there is much
standing in line; individual pace is regulated by the movement of
the mass.

There are two outstanding facts which have changed the
course of our inherited education in schools. To maintain the
idea of democratic equality, schooling was made universal and
compulsory. In the last thirty years we have done something to
make this ideal a fact. The number of boys and girls who go to
high school and college is five or six times greater, in proportion
to the population, than it was even thirty or forty years ago. And
then the change in the character of life, the change from the
agrarian to the industrial, compelled a shift of emphasis in the

material of instruction. At first there was merely the attempt to give to the many the education which had in the old country been intended for the few. But as time went on, the very fact that it was the many who were to be schooled compelled a vast change; a change, which has been called a revolution, in things taught, in the ends for which they were taught, and in the methods by which they were taught.

The nature of this revolutionary change was determined largely by the economic factor of life. The great change which goes by the name of the industrial revolution, that is to say, the substitution of mechanical power for the muscular power of animals and man, began, of course, in England, not in the United States. But the relatively sparse population in our country together with the abundance of natural resources, including unused and unappropriated land, the great distances which had to be knit together in transportation and communication, stimulated and almost compelled in this country the rapid and unhindered growth of the new methods of production and distribution. Moreover there was another factor of great importance. In England and in Europe generally, the new industry not only developed more slowly, but also in and against a background of traditions and institutions which were long centuries old. The latter did more than check its rapid growth; they formed the banks within which the economic and industrial movement was confined. In the United States there were no such counterbalancing forces. The industrial conquest of a continent became almost by sheer force of circumstances the dominant occupation of the American people. Physical mastery tended to absorb, almost to monopolize, the energies which in Europe were expended in a variety of channels. It was impossible, humanly speaking, that this engrossing interest should not leave its deep impress upon education in the schools and in the interplay of forces outside of the school which shape disposition and form habits.

Moreover, the development of the arts and industries was more and more dependent upon techniques which ultimately rest upon scientific knowledge; chemistry and physics were making discoveries which displaced the routine, rule of thumb methods which earlier generations had acquired through imitation and apprenticeship. Many lines of activity which were not themselves of a high order from the intellectual point of view felt the infection. They had to seem to adopt a scientific technique whether they actually rose above the level of empirical routines or not. Science obtained such a high prestige value that every conceivable human activity now has its corresponding "science"—writing advertisements, doing laundry work, keeping accounts, cooking meals, stenography and type-writing, and so on through the whole inventory.

While many, perhaps most people, regard the broadening of education to meet the needs of the greater number, and especially the inclusion of a larger amount of the vocational element, as an enrichment of education, there are others who hold a contrary view. And this brings me to the second catchword in the caption of my remarks. The persons in the hostile group say that our education has deteriorated through catering to the needs of larger numbers; that what we now have is a bargain counter education; that the older kind of education relied upon the wisdom and the culture of the past to determine what was good for young people, inexperienced and unwise, to study; that the present theory and practice of education is rather to spread everything out on the educational counter, to provide some study and some course for every taste, so that the buyer, not the person who provides the education but the immature person who is to get the education, determines what kind it will be. Hence they say that the school is now a store where the storekeeper spreads out all kinds of goods in the hope that, by so doing, some one thing which catches the eye will appeal to the taste of one person, while some other thing will gratify the wants of another. And so they say that our education has become a scattered education; that it has been diluted and attenuated; that the elements of the earlier education, which made for discipline and culture, have been more and more eliminated; that the principle on which the schools are now conducted is simply that of giving young people what they want or what they think they want. They claim that education in meeting these demands has become utilitarian, "practical" rather than cultural; that its aim is simply to help an individual make his way industrially, so that he can earn money more easily, or get a better job than he could if he did not have this training. Accordingly, our universities and colleges, and also our high schools, and to some extent even our elementary schools, have been under attack on the grounds that this broad-

ening out instead of being an enrichment is a thinning, while dilution and attenuation have made a course of study congested.
The training which the youth now gets lacks depth—it is something merely on the surface.

While I do not wholly agree with these criticisms, I have
nevertheless ventured to take the title "bargain counter education," as a characterization of certain phases of the present education. It is hardly possible to discuss how far these criticisms are
really justified. The reason is that different people have such very
different standards. If one person thinks that closer connection
with life is an advance in education, and another thinks that it is
a term of condemnation since the essence of culture is that it
shall not be too closely related to the practical needs of everyday
life, there is clearly no point of contact between them. They will
judge what is going on very differently because they have different standards. Thus if Mr. and Mrs. Smith think it is a fine thing
for education to become more vocational, since it then takes into
account the fact that the majority of people have got to make
their living; while on the other hand their neighbors, Mr. and
Mrs. Jones, believe that this kind of education is a step backward, obviously they will appraise the present system quite differently. But this is too large a question to go into here. Some of
these criticisms, I may say, seem to be justified. In several respects our present education is spread out too thin, is too scattered; it lacks definiteness of aim. Very often the courses which
are called practical are not really practical except in their label.
Some of these courses try to teach things which can only be
learned in the actual business or calling itself, while they do not
take sufficient account of the rapid changes that are going on,
since the teachers are out of contact with industry and teach the
way things were done five or ten years ago rather than the way
they are done now in the actual callings of life. And they are still
less in contact with the way things are going to be done five years
from now. In consequence, even the so-called practical courses in
the long run are often not very practical.

We may make all these admissions about certain tendencies in
our present system of education, and may yet say that we have
accomplished one very important thing; we have at least broken
down the obstacles and barriers which in the traditional education, the so-called cultural education, stood between the mass of

the people and the possibility of their receiving anything worthy of the name of education. We have at least taken the first step in making education universally accessible, so that there is more reality than there used to be in the ideal of equality of opportunity for all. We have also at least broken down the wall that used to exist between what was called culture and vocation; for in fact the older type, that which I have called the "education of the monastery," (or which I might have called that of the pulpit, if I had another social class as a type), assumed that the people who were to acquire culture were people of leisure. Only those who had a substantial economic background which rendered it unnecessary for them to engage in any calling or business received education. On the other hand it was assumed that people who went into the active callings of life, especially those which in any way involved the use of the body and the hands, were people who were, of necessity, shut out from any high culture, being condemned to a life of contact with physical, material things, so that in their callings there was no avenue to things of value intellectually and artistically. This bargain counter education, therefore, even taking it at its lowest level, has got rid of this dividing line, this complete separation between vocation and culture; or, in other terms, between theoretical things and practical things; between action and doing on the one hand, and knowledge and understanding on the other.

The bargain counter education has then at least prepared the way for another type of education, to which, also somewhat metaphorically, I have given the name of the "laboratory." For as the very word laboratory suggests, there is action, there is work, there is labor involved in it. The term is of course usually confined to the scientific laboratory, that of physics, chemistry or biology. But the idea inherent in the word extends further than this restriction. The first great characteristic of a laboratory is that in it there is carried on an activity, an activity which involves contact with technical equipment, as tools, instruments and other apparatus, and machinery which require the use of the hands and the body. There is dealing with real materials and not merely, as in the old, traditional education, with the symbols of learning.

There is no reason why the idea of the laboratory should not be extended to include also the workshop. There is no reason why the kitchens, if you please, where the girls learn cooking, or the rooms where they have contact with textiles, and the manual training shops where boys learn something of the arts while using their hands, eyes and bodies, should not embody the principle of learning through action by dealing with realities. There is no reason why there should not be extended to them the kind of learning which goes on in the physics laboratory or in the chemical laboratory. There is no reason why the workshop, whether in the upper grammar school or in the high school or in the college, should be confined merely to imparting manual skill and to giving an external ability to carry on a particular trade or calling. Through active contact with a wide range of materials, an opportunity is offered for an introduction into all the resources of science. Indeed, I often think that probably for the majority of young people the shops would make a better avenue of initiation into the elements of scientific knowledge than do our laboratories. For the concepts of physics and chemistry when approached directly, as in the study of the molecule, the atom or the electron, are technical, difficult and abstract, often quite as abstract and certainly as far removed from sense-perception as anything found in the older type of education. Through the medium of such things as the automobile, the airplane and the radio, there is a direct avenue to the principles of physics, chemistry, the structure of materials, which is on the line of least resistance, and yet which is capable of giving young people a personal and intelligent grasp of scientific principles. Such knowledge then comes to them in terms and through means which are associated with their daily experience; it means something to them in terms of their life instead of in abstruse and remote technical symbols.

Through the workshop when conducted as a laboratory, that is, as a means of learning and discovery, there is also the opportunity of arousing the curiosity of pupils and of equipping them with the methods for finding out things. The laboratory education also offers a means of access to an understanding of society. For after all, our society is largely what it is today because of the scientifically controlled occupations which are carried on in it. It may not be advisable to subordinate or limit our education to the making of farmers, engineers and merchants, but since the very large majority of the young people who come to our schools go into these various callings, it does seem desirable that they who are to be farmers shall be intelligent farmers, capable of intellectual invention, having initiative and mental control of their materials; and similarly, that the persons who are to enter the other callings shall have an education which will equip them to be flexible and independent in their judgments and original in their outlook. This is the education I would call the laboratory type. Beginning with activity, it would through that activity bring the student into actual contact with real things, and would then use this contact with objects for intellectual training and for arousing a thirst to understand, and not merely to fit pupils into some narrow groove of later trade and business life.

There is one other characteristic of what I call the laboratory education. The older traditional education was based on the thought that the teacher or the textbook knew in advance what the young ought to learn. The teacher or the textbook told the student what was so. The student's effort was largely confined to passive absorption and reproduction—a process which we might call a pipeline education; the teacher and the textbook, pouring the information into the student, who was supposed to be a reservoir which received the knowledge and which on suitable occasions (chiefly those of the examination period), gave out what it had received. This method of education might also be called a phonographic education. For the mind of the student was regarded as a phonographic disc upon which certain impressions were made by the teacher, so that when the disc was put on the machine and the movement started (which, again, would be during the examination period), it might reveal what had been inscribed upon it. The laboratory education, however, to which the bargain counter type is at least a transitional stage, puts much more responsibility upon students themselves. The method of the laboratory is an experimental one. It is a method of discovery through search, through inquiry, through testing, through observation and reflection—all processes requiring *activity* of mind rather than merely powers of absorption and reproduction.

To go back now to my original metaphor. At first at the original water shed were the elementary district schools, started by parents in localities who wanted their children to have some of the opportunities which the Old World afforded, but which could not be had in the New World unless the parents themselves started the school. Then there were the universities, intended very largely as you will remember to train the clergy. Our ancestors were for the most part a pious folk who wanted pastors, and educated pastors to conduct the services in the churches. Within the past one hundred and fifty years, but more especially and with increasing acceleration during the last thirty or forty years, the streams originating in the traditions and conditions of past times, have been growing into a broad current. This current is often meandering, dividing up, getting thin and superficial. But still it has potentially the energy to create a new and significant kind of education; an education which will be universal not merely in the fact that everybody will have the chance of going to school, but universal in the sense that it will be adapted to all varieties of individual needs and abilities. Society, instead of having simply the benefit of the training of a limited class, then will be able, through the development of every individual composing it, to get the benefit of the vast resources of all its members, resources which in the past have been latent because so few people have had the opportunity of realizing their full capacities. Public education will then also be public not merely in the sense that it is conducted by the State at public expense through taxation, but in the sense that it really trains all individuals for some kind of social service. After all, it is through vocations of one sort or another that society is ultimately served, and not by those individuals who, however cultivated they may be, regard their culture as so personal and private a matter that it is not put into vital and organic connection with the work of the world. When these capacities and potentialities are fully brought out by our education, we shall have in this country a genuinely new type of education. This new education will also give the promise and potentiality of a new type of culture, one in which old barriers will be broken down, and in which learning and the pursuit of knowledge will be regarded as public trusts exercised for the benefit of society.

But as yet our education has not found itself; the stream has not reached port and the ocean. It has left behind traditional education; it can never return to its source. It has to meet the problems of today, and of the future, not of the past. The stream just now has gathered up a good deal of debris from the shores which it has flooded; it tends to divide and lose itself in a number of streams. It is still dammed at spots by barriers erected in past generations. But it has within itself the power of creating a free experimental intelligence that will do the necessary work of this complex and distracted world in which we and every other modern people have to live.

Appreciation and Cultivation

A great deal has been said of late of the importance of appreciation in education and of its neglect. Much of the discussion turns about the growing significance of leisure in American life and the need that education should prepare for proper use of leisure, as well as for vocations. The revolt against domination by the "business mind," whether in life or in the schools, is all to the good. But I think I see signs that appreciation is taken too narrowly—that its universal scope as a function of all normal experience is not sufficiently perceived. Consequently, as my mind has been occupied with a similar theme in connection with lectures given here at Harvard University, I have thought to submit to you today a few remarks on the theme of appreciation— remarks, I hope, not too formal for the occasion.

The narrow tendency to which I just referred concerns the limitation of appreciation to a few subjects, studies like literature and the fine arts. Now I do not wish to inflict anything upon you about the old topic of interest. But the presence here of my colleague, Mr. Perry, may, I hope, serve to remind you of the intimate connection of interest and value. Without attempting an accurate definition of appreciation, we can at least say that it is a sense, a personal realization, of value. One conclusion seems inevitable. If there is value in any subject, a value which is actual to students and teachers and not merely nominal and external, then the place and the role of appreciation cannot be restricted to any particular list of studies.

If there is not appreciation in geography, history, yes, in arithmetic and algebra, we are forced to the conclusion that although there may be value somehow in those subjects, the students do

[First published in *Harvard Teachers Record* 1 (April 1931): 73–76, from an address to the Harvard Teachers Association, 21 March 1931.]

not personally come into possession of it. What then is appreciation? What is its nature that it may extend to all subjects and themes? Literature and the fine arts may give us the key to the answer. For while not having a monopoly of power to arouse appreciation, they exemplify it in a conspicuous way.

I suppose that all would agree without labored argument that capacity to arouse emotion and imagination is a distinctive feature of poetry, novels, the drama, music, painting, and other arts. If this be admitted, then we have the clue to two marked traits of appreciation. It involves a stirring of emotion and an immediate development of imagination. If certain school subjects do not offer material which is appreciated, it must then be because of lack of emotional and imaginative power as these subjects are taught and learned.

The psychology of emotion is a somewhat obscure matter. But some characteristics of it are evident to ordinary inspection. It involves at least personal participation. The things that leave us cold are things indifferent to us. They may be so and so, but they make no difference to *us*.

> Be she fairer than the day
> Or the flowery meads in May,
> If she be not so to me,
> What care I how fair she be?

To be emotionally stirred is to care, to be concerned. It is to be *in* a scene or subject not outside of it. A slight and passing emotional stir occurs when something at least touches us. A deep emotion is more than tangency; it is secancy. The more anything, whether an object, scene, idea, fact, or study, cuts into and across our experience, the more it stirs and arouses. An emotion is the register of the extent and way in which we are personally implicated, involved, in anything, no matter how external it is to us physically.

Some emotions are gross. They manifest themselves in direct unmistakable, observable, changes of the face, the hands, and the postures of the body. Rage, extreme grief and elation, fear when it reaches the point of terror, are examples. In such cases, there is no manner of doubt as to the degree in which some physically external event comes home to one. The event so enters into us, is so experienced as a part of our own very selfhood, that we are lifted up, cast down, attracted so that we want to make it more fully our own, or repelled so that we want to cast it out and destroy it. But emotions exist on the most extensive scale from the coarse to the refined and subtle. We are elated by a victory of *our* side in a football game, a political election; by an access of sudden fortune, by the recovery of a critically ill friend. But we also may be elated, set up, by a sunset, a picture, by a new idea that has dawned on us, by the perception of a relevancy of a fact to some problem that has been occupying us. Then we relish the object; we are drawn to appropriate, possess, and linger with affection. In short, we appreciate.

Transformation of the coarser, instinctively organic emotions into subtler and more delicate forms, of the glaring hues of black and white, red and green, into variegated tints and shades, is a large part of the process of refinement of personality. Aristotle said that anybody could get angry, but to get angry at the right time, place, object and in the right degree is the mark of a moralized human being. The principle of the saying applies to all the emotions; as they are nicely and justly adapted to conditions, they are shaded and refined. While refinement and cultivation are not wholly synonymous in all respects, they are identical in some of their phases. No amount of possession of facts and ideas, no matter how accurate the facts in themselves and no matter what the sweep of the ideas—no one of these in themselves secures culture. They have to take effect in modifying emotional susceptibility and response before they constitute cultivation.

I am not concerned to make a too explicit and literal application to the matter of instruction and learning. But it should be clear that while certain subjects, like the fine arts, may be more easily employed than some others to secure emotional appropriation of material and thereby effect a transformation of native crude emotions, it is fatal to confine appreciation to them. Unless pupils, for example, acquire a certain fastidiousness of taste in the use of words in all classes, a sensitiveness to shades of meaning, the lack cannot be made up by set subjects of composition and literature. Unless a fact or piece of information in geography, history or botany is emotionally responded to, and in a way which makes emotional disposition more graded and delicate, we cannot safely depend upon music and poetry to perform the task.

I think one could go through the defects and mistakes of teaching and learning generally and find that they are associated with failure to secure emotional participation. Take two of the universally deplored features. Mere receptive passivity on the part of a pupil and mere pouring in by textbook and teacher, are themselves proof of absence of that personal participation which we call emotion. The schooling that puts chief stress upon mere memorizing, upon committing to heart, is an instance of the same failure. The trouble is that material is not committed to *heart*; it is only entrusted to some portion of the cerebrum. In consequence, personal cultivation is not attained.

Unless there is emotional sensitiveness to facts and ideas, to problems and solutions, wherever they present themselves, there is great likelihood that the attempt to secure genuine appreciation through the means of specially selected subjects will fail and go wrong. It is one thing for a child, youth, or adult to *feel* a sunset, and another thing for him to learn that certain rhapsodic utterances are conventionally expected of him. There is a like danger in the educational use of music, poetry, and the drama. Unless the pupil comes to these subjects with a background of experience in which prior perceptions of meanings and relationships of form are configured, his emotional response is bound to be one in which the cruder emotions are dominant, or else one that is factitious because irrelevant to actual subject matter. Limitation of appreciation makes some subjects dull and dead while it renders others the occasion of temporary excitation, amusement, and escape into the realm of reverie.

With respect to imagination I should approach its definition, educationally, through the spontaneous carrying power which information and ideas sometimes possess. There is a kind of study and learning in which what is acquired falls with a dead weight. It stops short with itself. It has no propulsive charge. Such knowledge, if we dignify it by that name, points, by contrast, to the nature of imagination. The connection of emotion and imagination is not accidental. Emotion provides the carrying impetus. Imagination denotes that to which we are carried when the emotion is not so coarsely organic as to lead to direct overt action. A man in a rage may smash and tear about. If his emotion is refined and controlled by thought of objects, it leads to consequences in imagination. The resentful man may fancy his foe placed in all sorts of predicaments in which he suffers dire distress, or he may project himself, taking sweet revenge in some public humiliation of the object of his wrath. A more refined indignation may set to work to explore imaginatively the source of a public wrong and to construct measures of remedy. Or a Dickens may be led to an imagination which discloses the situation to others through the medium of a novel.

Such instances should not obscure the educational bearings of the power of emotion to awaken and direct imagination in all sorts of situations. A fact of natural science or a principle in mathematics, if it does not drop dead with a thud into mind, will suggest other facts and ideas; it will propel the mind forward. Suggestion is a simple case of imagination; apt and vivid metaphors are the work of that carrying power named imagination. An obverse example is the irrelevant play of fancy so common among pupils. Attention can be held only as it is carried forward. Absence of power to stir in subject-matter presented has its counterpart in mind-wandering; the mind lets itself go into all kinds of scenes and situations which do afford congenial imaginative exercise.

None of these illustrations is very fundamental compared with that absorption in a subject, problem, or undertaking which of itself carries one forward to all sorts of relations and consequences which have the tang of novelty and surprise. Imagination is nought but a free play of mind, a play which, if it is really of the mind, does a work which no reluctant and enforced toil can accomplish. The caricature of interest and attention which disfigures the schoolroom is due to acting as if a closed object or situation had interest and intellectual possibilities. Degradation of interest into amusement results when it is forgotten that only expanding movement, intrinsic development of subject-matter can sustain interest; nothing is more boring or exhausting than momentary excitation; and that is all any situation or activity that is closed, that ends with itself, can provide. These statements do not signify that interest or imagination should be conscious or be consciously appealed to. They mean that wherever there are freely moving ideas, wherever information is fruitful in suggesting other meanings than those contained in what is immediately at hand, there is of necessity imagination and intellectual interest.

Appreciation, in short, is more than immediate and transient emotional stir and turmoil. It shapes things that come home to us, that we deeply realize have possibilities, entail consequences. To appreciate is to trace mentally these out-leadings, to place the possibilities before the mind so that they have felt significance and value. There is no fact and no idea or principle that is not pregnant, that does not lead out into other things. The greatest and the commonest defect in teaching lies in presenting material in such fashion that it does not arouse a sense of these leadings and a desire to follow them. There is then no appreciation, no personally experienced value, because what is presented is presented as if it had its meaning complete in itself, as if it were closed and shut. Think over the teachers that you would call inspiring and you will find that they were the teachers who made you aware of possibilities in the things which they taught and who bred in you desire to realize those possibilities for yourself. I can give no better exemplification of the true nature of appreciation nor of its capacity to attend all subjects of instruction.

Political Interference in
Higher Education and Research[1]

It is not easy to define political interference in higher education. It may cover anything from meddling with a particular appointment, so as to do a favor to a friend, to a deliberate attempt to control the personnel and educational policies of an institution in the interest of a party or a faction. It is not easy to draw the line between interference for economic and other social reasons and political interference.

The alleged reason for dismissal of Professor Miller at Ohio State University was a supposed indiscreet remark made in India, tending to cast discredit on Great Britain. This certainly was not a case of domestic politics. Since the British Government made no diplomatic representations it was hardly a case of foreign politics. What was it? Or if, as was indicated by some evidence, domestic prejudice about race and color entered in, under what heading does that come?

The activities of the "Power Trust" in subsidizing a certain number of college instructors by a variety of means were primarily economic in nature; they did not proceed from any political office, but their intention was admittedly to discourage consideration of public ownership of utilities and to secure a public opinion favorable to legislation in behalf of private ownership and management. Economic in origin, it was political in effect.

Under a somewhat similar heading would come the organized efforts of persons connected with the War Department to prevent speakers suspected of pacifism from getting a hearing by students, and similar efforts by persons influential in the commu-

1. Presented as a part of the symposium program under the Committee of One Hundred on Scientific Research at the New Orleans meeting of the American Association for the Advancement of Science [28 December 1931–2 January 1932].

[First published in *School and Society* 35 (20 February 1932): 243–46.]

nity to prevent socialists or others holding radical economic views from being heard. For while these latter moves do not concern regular classroom instruction, they do affect students' access to ideas and information having a bearing upon legislation and political administration.

If I mention these cases which seem to lie upon periphery, it is for two reasons. One is that direct interference from state officers, from those clothed with evident political authority, and having an evident political aim in view, is universally reprehended, and is for the most part confined to those parts of the country which are admittedly backward. On the other hand, the cases of mixed origin and motive are much more common; they are found in states which pride themselves upon their educational and cultural advancement, and in institutions of high academic status. Because they operate indirectly, employing relatively subtle means, they are much more dangerous in the long run than direct attacks upon educational integrity undertaken for obvious political reasons. They are, moreover, often condoned by university instructors and by the educated public who would be indignant at interference proceeding from a governor of a state or some political board responsible to the governor.

In political matters, even of the narrower sort, indirect interference is much commoner, more insidious and more injurious than the overt cases which attract public attention. The Board of Regents of one state university adopted the following by-law: "If any professor or teacher of the University shall become a candidate for any public office or for a nomination thereto, or be a delegate to any political convention, or openly seek a nomination thereto, he should be taken and considered as having resigned his position." Inquiry has not disclosed that any other state has a similar regulation on the books. But pressure accomplishes the same result in other cases. A professor of one of the largest and most populous states in the union is on record to the following effect:

> There is not an institution of higher learning in the state supported by the taxes of the people where any member of the faculty from the president to the humblest instructor would be permitted to engage in any kind of political activity, at least of such a character that it would be pro-

nounced or conspicuous. . . . If a professor has political convictions that he wishes to express in an effective manner there is only one course open to him, and that is to give up his job. . . . Institutions of learning under the auspices of religious groups have their shortcomings and disadvantages, but in this state their presidents and faculty members take a much more active part in public affairs, especially where the question of politics may be involved, than is the case in state institutions.[2]

That cases of direct political interference are more readily and effectively dealt with than the covert and indirect cases is seen in the instance of the educational institutions of the state of Mississippi. During June and July, 1930, wholesale dismissals and demotions were made at the four chief state-supported educational institutions. This action, instigated from political sources, stirred up an immediate reaction of the public. Various professional bodies of educators took action. The Southern Association of Colleges and Secondary Schools suspended the four state institutions from membership as a manifestation of "disapproval of political interference with state-owned schools"—a courageous action which was much resented locally, but which, coming from the neighboring states, had great influence. The American Society of Civil Engineers took similar action as far as engineering schools were concerned. The Association of American Medical Colleges placed the School of Medicine of Mississippi on probation for one year. Such organizations as the American Chemical Society, the Association of American Universities, the Association of University Professors, passed resolutions of condemnation.

The case of Mississippi is especially cited because it demonstrates so clearly that obvious overt political interference will call out wide-spread protests which are pretty sure in the end to be effective. Professor Bates, chairman of the committee on academic freedom of the Association of University Professors, states in the report for 1923, that cases of "open and clear interference with freedom of speech will be few. The more baffling cases are those in which a steady and powerful, but almost invisible and impalpable pressure of an academic hierarchy suppresses, dis-

2. *Bulletin of the American Association of University Professors*, for 1931, pp. 572–3.

courages and seriously interferes with the usefulness and development of the independent and original thinker."

We might add to the list of cases in which the political activities of teachers are curtailed, the cases of suppression of liberal clubs among students and of extreme censorship of college publications when their utterances seemed to have a radical tinge, economic or political. Such instances do not directly affect instruction in the classroom. Many persons, including some university teachers who strongly resent interference with their freedom of research in their own special lines, are not sensitive to interference with activity outside the classroom. Permission of such outside activity involves, as does all free action in any line, some risk. But its denial, whether by direct action, as in the case of the by-law cited above or by indirect pressure, sterilizes thinking on the part of a class to whom, by reason of their especial education, a democratic community might be supposed to look for guidance; it lowers the whole tone of political opinion and action; it reacts unfavorably in classroom instruction by producing a type of teachers who have the habit of suppressing their real views and who finally cease, in consequence, to have any significant convictions.

Teachers and investigators in the more developed and exact branches of science are sometimes so aware of the relative crudity of the state of the social and political subjects that, because of personal economic and political conservatism, they tend to condone restrictions placed on outside activities of teachers in other branches. But they should recall the struggle their own sciences once underwent in order to get a hearing, and be convinced that the social subjects can not attain a more scientific status so long as those who teach them suffer from suppression.

Upon the whole, direct political interferences will, with growth of popular enlightenment in the backward states, tend to become fewer. Local sentiment always resents outside criticism and yet almost always modifies local action because of such criticism when it is fair. At the same time, I do not think the time has come when scientific men through their organizations can afford to be quiescent. If our different professional organizations are alert for infractions upon the integrity of inquiry and teaching of a direct sort, they may profitably extend their activity to take more cognizance than they have done in the past of indirect infractions. Public opinion among educators is tending, as far as I have been able to observe, in the following direction. Let the American Association of University Professors institute a list of accredited colleges and universities. Membership in the association should be confined to those teaching in the accredited institutions. Violation on the part of any institution of the principles of freedom of inquiry and expression should, when proved after investigation, be sufficient cause for removing the institution in question from the accredited list; this would automatically carry with it the dropping from the rolls of the association of members from that institution. All the more special organizations, having scientific and professional aims, should adopt the same course. Both the professors and the scientific associations should have suitable and stringent rules regarding the conditions under which an institution once dropped could be restored to the list.

If the public opinion of the profession could be organized first for its own enlightenment and then for express action along the lines indicated, there would be every prospect, I believe, that cases of infringement of freedom of investigation, speech and writing, including those of political interference, would be reduced to a minimum.

The Economic Situation: A Challenge to Education [1]

Since the present economic collapse is a challenge to every institution in our present civilization, it surely is also a challenge to our schools. This fact is so evident that it is useless to dwell upon it. The important thing is to know how the schools might and should meet this challenge. But, when statesmen falter, industrial chieftains are bewildered, and economists hesitate to express a judgment regarding either causes or remedies, those of us who approach the matter from the educational side may well be at a loss. I am so far from knowing what the schools can actually do to prevent the recurrence of a similar breakdown in the future that I shall have to confine myself to one aspect of the problem. I believe that if we, in common with others, can honestly and courageously face the situation, our combined wisdom, if it holds the problem steadily in view over a long time, can accomplish what overwhelms the mind of any one individual.

In the first place, let me say that the words I have just used, "honest and courageous facing of the elements in the problem," suggest the main thing of which I wish to speak. It takes a good deal of courage for educators to face the situation, and it requires an unusual amount of mental energy to be honest in fact and not merely in intention. One of the functions of education is to equip individuals to see the moral defects of existing social arrangements and to take an active concern in bettering conditions. Our schools have failed notably and lamentably in that regard. We are depressed just now, and trouble makes persons more willing to think and certainly more willing to criticize and to listen to criticism. But foresight and prevention are better than after-

1. A paper read at the general session of the Department of Supervisors and Teachers of Home Economics of the National Education Association in Washington, D.C., February 22, 1932.

[First published in *Journal of Home Economics* 24 (June 1932): 495–501.]

thought and cure, socially as well as medically. The atmosphere in our period of seeming economic prosperity tended to suppress serious thought on fundamental social matters and to encourage a complacent emotional acquiesence in and laudation of things as they are, or were.

One illustration will indicate what I mean. I heard a debate the other evening on military preparedness. A speaker, who held that this preparedness tended to provoke war, cited the fact that Holland held Java, perhaps the richest colonial possession in the world, and yet was free from all danger of attack although having no army and navy to speak of. He said that during most of the nineteenth century the United States with negligible military forces was secure, and that only after adoption of an imperialistic policy, which had made us feared and disliked, did the cry for a big army and navy arise. I am not concerned here to consider the justice of these remarks, although to me personally they seem sound. My point concerns the reception they received. General Fries, speaking for military preparedness, said that if the speaker and others like him thought so highly of Holland while he criticized the United States, why didn't they go to Holland to live and leave the country they thought so poorly of. There was great applause from a certain part of the audience, and members of so-called patriotic societies rose to their feet to lead the cheering.

The episode in itself is trivial or even childish. But as an illustration it has tremendous significance. It is typical of an attitude which has too nearly dominated teachers, and increasingly so, ever since the outbreak of the World War at least. It is "unpatriotic" to point out or even to admit that there are any weak spots in our institutions and habits and to suggest that there are matters in which we might learn from other countries. There has been a heavy pall of "hush-hush" imposed upon teachers, and the easy way for them, the way of inertia, has been to become "yes" men and women.

I do not know how it is today, but only a few years ago the names of some of the leaders of thought in this country were on the black books of departments in Washington as dangerous characters, potentially seditious because they had indulged in criticism of our tendencies in industry and were not afraid to put their fingers on sore spots like suppression of free speech. The branch of the War Department which is responsible for military training in colleges in one of its published statements for use in stimulating military spirit in the colleges called Jane Addams, whom most Americans call the best beloved woman in America, the recent recipient of the Nobel prize, the "most dangerous woman in America."

Again, such an instance, taken by itself, seems silly to the point of childishness. Miss Addams has obviously come to no harm. But for the few who by temperament and fortunate circumstances can rise above such attacks there are scores and scores who are induced to keep quiet, to gloss over social ills, and to accustom students to believe that all is for the best in this best of all possible countries. The representatives of large economic interests have been especially sensitive to anything approaching criticism of the existing economic régime and have pretty well succeeded in attaching to critics of it the epithet of "red" or "Bolshevist"; so much so that the publicity agent of the power interests is on public record as advising that all teachers who discuss public ownership favorably should be branded Bolshevists.

Now, when such a spirit prevails through the schools, it is impossible that education should accomplish its social function. For the primary social duty of education is not to perpetuate the existing social order—economic, legal, and political—but to contribute to its betterment. This work is constructive and positive, but it cannot be effected by indiscriminate laudation of the *status quo* any more than a physician can better the health of a patient by carefully averting attention from everything which ails the latter. And the doing of the work depends on the courage and energy of teachers.

The result is that the great majority of the students in our schools go forth unprepared to meet the realities of the world in which they live. They have been filled with highly idealized pictures of the actual state of things, idealizations created in part by omission of any reference to ills and unsolved problems, partly by excessive glorification of whatever good things exist. Then the graduates find themselves in a very different kind of a world. The split between their generous beliefs and liberal hopes and what they get into is often tragic; for the sensitive and thoughtful it requires a painful readjustment to find the gap which exists between what they had been taught to believe and things as they are. But even if they succumb without a struggle and accommodate themselves to the *status quo* in the hope of getting ahead individually, they are not qualified to cope with the causes which produce such catastrophes as our present economic breakdown. They are rather positively disqualified. Consequently, we all stand aghast and impotent, while some resort to measures of desperation like pumping oxygen into a sinking patient.

This actual incapacitation, much worse than mere failure to prepare, comes from the fact that the policy of concealment and laudation which is so strongly encouraged by the ruling economic elements gives students the impression that they live in a static world where pretty much everything has been fixed and settled and where all that is necessary is for individuals to take personal advantage of what is provided for them. I remember the experience of those of us who almost fifty years ago went to take graduate work in Johns Hopkins University. The previous schooling of most, if not all of us, had been conducted as if the book of knowledge had already been written full to the last page and that all we as students had to do was to absorb something from its finished pages. But there we found ourselves breathing a new atmosphere. Everywhere was the feeling that what was known was little in comparison with what remains to be found out and that it was possible for us to contribute; that we could and should transform ourselves from mere absorbing sponges of what was already known into active creators of new knowledge.

In this instance, the sudden change was salutary and inspiring. For the readjustment was only intellectual. But the change from the fixed and finished world of an idealized social *status quo* to the moving, dynamic, changing world of actual existence demands a practical readjustment which most persons fail to make because they are not equipped to meet it. In reading lately Merriam's book on *The Making of Citizens*, I was much struck by the testimony of this scholar of politics. He says,

> . . . the state must make its case not once and for all, but continuously for each new generation and each new period. . . . Plans of civic training that do not reckon with the social background of political power are defective. . . . The appearances of power are deceiving. . . . Facing the stern lines of authority with its steel and stone, and looking per-

haps into haughty faces equally steely and stony, it is difficult to realize the poverty of power.

He speaks also of the "false front of omnipotence and unassailability."

Dr. Merriam is speaking of political institutions and power. If their fixity is so illusory, what shall we say of the stability of other social forms and arrangements, the everyday and secular affairs of men in industry, business, and finance, affected by almost every new scientific invention and changing with every change in the desires and plans of human beings? Over against this scene of constant change we have our schools, of which it is not too much to say that they engage in eulogistic contemplation of the false front of an unassailable stability.

The point which I am making may seem remote from the question of just what education can do about such things as the present economic depression. But it is my conviction that it cannot do anything important until there is a change in that underlying intangible thing which we call atmosphere and spirit. The change from acquiescent complacency to honest critical intelligence, from the fiction of a static and finished political and industrial society to the reality of a constantly shifting, altering, unstable society will not of itself enable those who go forth from our schools to forestall and prevent such crises as the present nor to cope with them when they come. But I believe that the detailed ideas and plans, which are indispensable if these results are to be brought about, cannot get a hearing, much less be adopted, unless there is a prior change in the prevailing tone and spirit of educational undertakings.

Accordingly, I shall make no apology for speaking of another general consideration that at first sight is also remote from the immediate emergency. Critics of American life have said a great deal of late about the standardization of opinion and regimentation of belief in American life. There is, I think, a much more deliberate attempt to produce this uniformity than there used to be. But it is my observation, growing out of an experience covering a good many years, that among cultivated people there were never as many truly free minds as there are now. I do not recall a time when one met so many persons mentally alert, forming their conclusions after informed inquiry and not on the basis of prejudice. There are, I feel, many more persons than there used to be emancipated from stereotyped ideas; fewer who are content to give utterance to what they regard as wise ideas or sayings merely because they have become stale with time. In my opinion, this country has never seen a time when so many persons took delight in ideas and in finding out things.

But, on the other hand, I cannot remember a time when collective thinking—the ideas that are organic to large numbers—was so stupid, so incredibly incompetent as it is today. It is a common remark that we have a surprising absence of effective leadership in this crisis, domestic and international, economic and political. Now leadership, like a bargain, has two sides. There can be leadership as there can be following only when human beings think together about a common theme with a shared purpose to a common result. Leadership is absent because this power of collective thinking in connection with solidarity of emotion and desire is lacking today. We have in its stead attempts to whip up a seeming unity of idea and sentiment by means of catch-words, slogans, and advertising devices. Few persons, however, are fooled by them except possibly those engaged in promulgating them.

Now this contrast between the alert state of the minds of cultivated individuals and the dead and impotent condition of collective thought is so paradoxical that it, too, issues a challenge to education. Why does this contrast exist? How did it come about?

One thing seems quite certain. Traditions form our collective beliefs; they are the intellectual cement of a society. Certain traditions in religion, morals, economics, and politics are still nominally held by the mass of adults, men and women. They are taught in schools. But the actual movements of social life are contrary to these traditions. They contradict and undermine them. We believe one thing in words and, to a considerable extent, in sentiment. We believe another thing in our deeds. The split prevents the older traditions from giving us real guidance, while they retain enough hold on people's minds so that they are not replaced by other collective ideas.

For example, our tradition in economics and industry is that of rugged individualism. We are taught to believe that all start equal in the economic race without any external handicaps being imposed on any persons and that reward and victory go to those of superior personal energy, ability, industry, and thrift, while, barring the exceptional cases of physical disease and accident, those who fall behind do so because of individual defects. We are taught that in this equal struggle between individuals all the great virtues of initiative, self-respect, self-help, standing on one's own feet, moral independence, and the rest are acquired.

Now these things may have been true once. They are not true now. Industry is mainly collective and corporate today, and economic opportunities are dependent upon collective conditions, as the condition of hundreds of unemployed men and women, graduates of colleges and technical schools, testifies at this moment. The concentrated control of finance and business is the basic and conditioning fact of industry today. But recognition of the fact goes contrary to our cherished tradition of equality of opportunity and of advancement solely through individual merit. The public clings for the most part to the nominal acceptance of the tradition, and the schools are forced to cling to it still more closely. Under these circumstances, it is practically impossible that there should be effective collective thinking regarding our economic situation in general and the depression in particular. Thinking could become effective only by being relevant to realities; in order to be related to the realities of the situation it would have to recognize that collective conditions call for collective control by the public in its own interest.

I think that teachers who led students to observe this state of things would find themselves called opprobrious names, and would be lucky if nothing worse happened to them. But unless and until we permit or rather encourage the schools to abandon the following of traditions—that is of collective ideas—which have no relation to existing social realities, our thinking in matters of the greatest public concern, including peace and war as well as industrial prosperity and depression, will continue to be thoroughly stupid and our leaders will be such only in the sense in which the blind lead the blind.

Since the schools are subject to pressure exercised by powerful forces outside the school, the challenge issuing from the present economic situation cannot be said to be primarily directed to educators. There is one aspect, however, of the challenge which comes home directly to teachers. They have been too passive, too submissive, to the dictation of these outside powers. It is our part to maintain the intellectual independence of the educative process and to strive for the right to present the defects as well as the excellencies of the existing economic order, even if by so doing some interests are offended. It is our duty as well as our right to show present society as dynamic, undergoing continuous change. To accomplish these things is the least we can do in faithfulness to the work of education itself. If we can make clear that otherwise we are failing in the operation of education, we shall also at least prepare the type of mind that can deal more effectively with economic conditions and crises than they are dealt with at present. This may not seem a very high ideal at which to aim compared with ambitious schemes which might be proposed. But those who realize the difficulties which stand in the way of securing for teachers the right to a critical and realistic consideration of existing economic realities will not despise the suggestion that the schools be emancipated from the clutches of those economic interests with their allied military and political auxiliaries which have done so much to bring the world to its present pass.

A group of educators, speaking from the standpoint of history, has recently put forth a manifesto in which they say that textbooks used in our schools still reflect more or less "the distortions of war-time propaganda" and fail to reveal that "millions of citizens in all nations were moved again and again to acts of supreme idealism and unselfishness by propaganda of interested groups controlling national interests."

Those would be naïve who assumed that the principle here stated is confined to war and the story of wars. It operates constantly in peace time and with reference to economic matters; and until schools escape its influence through a declaration of independence by teachers, it will prevent the schools' meeting the challenge made by economic crises. The first challenge, accordingly, is to teachers to unite to inform themselves more adequately about economic and social realities and then to combine to impress upon public opinion the right and duty of intellectual freedom to deal with these realities in their teaching.

The Schools and the White House Conference

The discussions of the White House Conference on Child Health and Protection were wisely limited. They touched upon the school child, but not upon the child *in* school; they did not consider distinctively educational problems. They left that aspect of the question, I take it, to the educators themselves. The men and women who met to carry on the work of the conference dealt with school conditions as far as they affect the general health of pupils; they called for a health program; they demanded adequate recreational facilities; they pointed out the need of special classes for defectives and for the subnormal; for training to guard against delinquency and to give sympathetic and curative treatment to those unfortunate boys and girls who had already come under the arm of the law; they emphasized the need for adequate vocational guidance. They did not raise the question of the relation of the regular school curriculum and the daily administrative work to these great ends. They left, I repeat, this task to the educators themselves.

This fact constitutes, to my mind, a challenge to teachers and to school administrators. It is a challenge, moreover, which will not be met even if all the specific recommendations of the conference which have to do with school work are actually carried out. For there would still be left the question of the contribution of the general work of the school, in its studies, its methods of teaching and of discipline, to that wholesome development of child life which is the end sought in all the special recommendations.

This is far from being the first time that those in charge of schools have had challenges put up to them from the outside. Those on the inside have improved the techniques of their work and perfected its details. Great educational changes have usually

[First published in *American Teacher* 16 (February–March 1932): 3–4.]

been effected by social demands from without. There is now an opportunity for educators to reverse the process and, instead of waiting until society has spoken with an imperative voice, to take the lead. For the aims set forth in the Children's Charter cannot be realized by independent and isolated special institutions, classes and agencies. The need is that the entire school in all its methods and processes day by day be so organized as to promote child welfare.

Take the matter of vocational guidance for example. How can the ideal set forth be realized without a greater change in traditional subject-matter than has yet taken effect in most schools? It is absurd to suppose that a curriculum based on traditional academic subjects will reveal the vocational tastes and abilities of pupils. It is equally absurd, though not quite so obviously so, to suppose that the lack can be made up by adding on a special advisor, no matter how expert, or by tacking on a special course. The pupils must be brought in their regular work in contact with a sufficient variety of materials to disclose aptitudes, and the material must be taught by methods which manifest the students' own ideas, capacities, weaknesses—an end that will never be realized as long as the main object is to test how much information he or she has stowed away.

Article Ten of the Charter reads: "For every child an education, which through the discovery and development of his individual abilities prepares him for life; and through training and vocational guidance prepares him for a living which will yield him the maximum of satisfaction." Fine, I say, and fine you all will say. But what is stated here is nothing less than the supreme problem and the supreme test of life itself. The ideal cannot be realized by instituting special devices. The whole work of the school must be coordinated and brought to bear upon its execution. The demand of the next article that every child shall have such teaching and training as will prepare him for successful parenthood, home-making and rights of citizenship is also fundamental. But it is so fundamental and so difficult that it can be met only by the organization of the entire educational system, which means practically, in probably the majority of American schools, their reorganization.

Consider, moreover, the health aims which at first sight are more attainable by special means. A very little reflection shows that health is anything but a special matter to be cared for by special means. Without doubt things can be specified on the negative side. We must get rid of foul air, of bad lighting, of seating that almost forces bad posture; positive means can be specified, ample play grounds as well as good ventilation and so on. But health signifies wholeness, and it can be made secure only by conditions and activities which operate all the time.

A physician, concerned with the mental hygiene movement, once told me that he was convinced that there was a close connection between the level of the general health tone and the interest which a student of college years took in his work. And the connection was independent of the question of definite overwork or strain, and much subtler than causes of that fairly evident sort. The connection of mind and body is so intimate that mental indifference, even if far short of actual repulsion, will not only dull the mind but depress bodily vigor, even though there is nothing which can be called illness which calls for the attention of a doctor. There is a great deal of what traditional education would call learning and getting knowledge in which mind and body are both cramped and made more wooden, less flexible. A pupil may acquire a special skill but at the expense of poise and adaptability to new conditions.

Health, it is hardly needful to say, includes mental well being. I have long thought that there is no greater challenge to education than the fact that persons suffering from mental disorders of some sort require as many beds in institutions as those suffering from all other diseases whatever. If normality can be calculated on a statistical basis, it looks as if, in case mental disorder keeps on increasing at the past rate, the abnormal people will be the normal ones. Now I do not wish to suggest that the schools are in any large measure the cause of these breakdowns; they grow to a much greater extent out of maladjustments in the home and family relations. But is it not the province of education to develop more positive immunity against these mental and moral failures? Is it not part of its function to develop some prophylactic?

I do not see how special measures, however desirable in themselves, can accomplish this result. The activities of the school as a whole in play and work ought to be of an all-around sort which will develop stability of mind and character. In connection with both physical and mental health, nothing can be more important than the role of the emotions. If the schools have not done what they might do in protecting from future mental and moral instability, it is, I think, largely because of neglect of the emotional factors in the human make-up. We are still under the dominion of ideas which grew up when learning was remote and difficult, and when there were few avenues of access to it. Under such conditions, there naturally grew up a great reverence for knowledge just as knowledge, for learning as acquisition of facts. In spite of the broadening of the educational scheme, this ideal, with its neglect of the life of desire and affection, persists. Even when the arts are introduced, they are often so dominated by the intellectualistic aim borrowed from the older studies that they fail to give emotional enrichment. It is possible to teach music, drawing or any one of the industrial arts by set models and rules, and by analysis of a vital whole into mechanical elements.

Let me give one more instance of the impossibility of meeting a particular recommendation of the White House Conference by anything except the general organization of the whole school system. The conference emphasized, and properly, the significance of the life of youth and children outside the home and school: their relation to church, special agencies for organizing the leisure time of boys and girls, recreational facilities, moving pictures and the theater, radio, libraries, camping, commercialized amusements including those which verge on vice, etc. The report on this phase of child welfare concludes by saying that since 40 per cent of the lives of most of the children and youth is spent in spare-time activities and since leisure-time activities exert an important influence in character formation, homes and communities should focus attention upon this phase of child welfare.

Since streams cannot rise higher than their source, is it not clear that this problem cannot be safely set off from the problem of education in the school? Youth will take to their clubs, recreation fields, amusements, camps and so on, the attitudes which are formed in the schools. It makes an immense difference whether these agencies are looked upon simply as supplements to the educational work of the school, making good their deficiencies, struggling to correct their faults, or whether the ideas and ideals of life in and outside the school harmonize and work together all the way through. That it is necessary to raise this question is indicated by two sentences from the report of the committee dealing with Youth Outside of Home and School. The passage reads: "Our system of education in general does not stimulate inventiveness, imagination or initiative. Comparatively little has been done by the school to train esthetic taste which could be a guide to selection of activities in leisure time." It is clear that in the measure in which these statements are true, all the outside work recommended will be more or less crippled and perverted. There is a wide gap between spare time activity which supplements in the sense of extending and expanding and that which supplements merely by counteracting what the schools are doing.

I hope that my main point has not been concealed from view by the various instances I have cited. I wish to lay down the proposition that the fine purposes set forth in the Child Welfare Conference cannot be realized by breaking up the influences which operate to shape the life and character of youth into separate and independent fractions. This is one of our American weaknesses. We add on more easily than we reconstruct from the centre. The great lesson which educators can learn from the conference is that if its inspiring aims are to be realized, the whole work of the school, in its courses of study and its methods, must be organized with those ends in view. They cannot be adequately served by a variety, however great, of separate agencies and tacked-on courses. Education is not the place where the motto of "divide and conquer" holds good. Every boy and girl is an individual, an undivided unity. This unity cannot be reached by treating the boys and girls as if they were a bundle of independent elements, each one of which can be reached by a separate agency of development. If the school is the central educational agency, then what it does and does not do determines ultimately the efficiency of every other agency.

As the various reports of the conference close with definite recommendations, let me end with two items of counsel:

First, educators should study carefully the reports and recommendations of the various committees of the Child Welfare Conference with a view to asking themselves how they can and should cooperate in carrying them out.

Secondly—and in my judgment even more important—they should consider how far the schools can become the central and unified agency for realizing the aims set forth, and should especially consider what internal changes should be made in the schools in order to prevent the dispersion of what needs to be done throughout a multitude of separate agencies, each operating with an unreal fraction of a whole child. It will require a good deal of reorganization to bring about this result. But it is in line with what the more forward-looking schools are trying to do anyway.

The fundamental need in fact is change in the attitude of the educators themselves. It is surprising and sometimes appalling to see how much of the efforts of those who train teachers and of those who direct their work has been devoted to improving the special techniques used and setting up highly specific objectives. In this process the directive and inspiring ends for the sake of which techniques exist get lost from sight, and the school goes on its way with little sense of its social responsibility. In my judgment, the great lesson which educators have to learn from the work of the White House Conference is an enlarged sense of social responsibility, so that the challenge for unification of the ordinary day-by-day program of the schools will be met. Otherwise, leadership will pass from the schools to a variety of special organizations. Only through integration of child and social welfare into the regular work of the school can the schools be maintained as the central agency in promotion of child welfare.

Dewey Describes Child's New World

Explicit acknowledgment of the importance for society of the physical, intellectual and moral development of every child born into the world seems to come late in human history. But the delay is not due to absence of affection and sympathy in former days. The present recognition springs from two great causes. One is the existence of social relations so complex, so intertwined, that the family alone cannot secure to children all the conditions that are required to insure their best growth. The other cause is the development of knowledge which has put in the hands of society scientific resources which did not formerly exist.

A treatise on sociology would be required to state the social changes which in the last century have affected the life of the child, and these words are not a sociological treatise.

But it is matter of common knowledge that the walls which formerly surrounded the individual family have broken down. Mothers as well as fathers are in industry. American life has changed from rural to urban. The family home with its environing land for free play and work has disappeared for millions of children. The city apartment and tenement, with no outlet save the congested and perilous streets, has taken its place.

The industries of the household and the neighborhood, open to view, offering opportunity for instruction and for gradual sharing in intimate responsibilities, have well nigh disappeared. The substitute is the factory with its machinery and mechanical operations. The systems of apprenticeship by which the young were once prepared for adult duties have gone.

The home and household are no longer the centres of recreation and amusement. They are found outside, on the street, in

[First published in *New York Times*, 10 April 1932, sec. 3, p. 7.]

the movie house, the automobile. At the same time that the social horizon has immensely widened, so that the future citizen
will find himself living in a wide world, affected by complex and
remote conditions, the homes of most children are less able than
ever before to prepare for any worthy citizenship on even a narrow scale.

It is not the children of the poor alone who suffer from these
changed conditions, but those of the well-to-do as well. For opportunities for natural participation in the activities of an intimate group are vanishing. Everywhere we look, the older means
for securing the well-being of children are relaxing.

On the other hand, the development of medicine and hygiene
have made us aware that many evils once regarded as inevitable
are within human control. It has been discovered that, with
present knowledge, a high death rate among infants is wholly unnecessary. Contagion and infection can be enormously reduced,
and in principle at least eliminated. Various devices have made it
possible to secure practical immunity against such a scourge as
diphtheria. Although the mortality of mothers at child birth has
been on the increase, the need and the possibility of prenatal care
of mothers is becoming generally acknowledged.

On the physical side, the question is no longer whether resources are at hand for an indefinitely better nurture of children
than existed at any previous time in the history of the world, but
whether society is ready to acknowledge its responsibility for the
extensive use of the resources it possesses.

The sphere of preventive and remedial care has been extended
to include unfortunate children—the crippled, blind, deaf, subnormal. In these matters, as in proper medical care of illness,
hundreds of thousands of families are in no condition, whether
from ignorance or from economic incapacity, to give the attention which is needed.

Closely bordering on these cases are those of children who are
orphans, or who are deserted by one or more parents. When left
to unorganized individual care, these children largely drift into
lives of little social usefulness or into positive crime. When systematically cared for, experience has already demonstrated that
the great majority, even with apparently bad heredity, become
self-respecting and useful members of the community.

While scientific knowledge and methods in psychology and

psychiatry are relatively not as advanced as the physical and biological, there has already taken place an intellectual revolution.
We know almost infinitely more than we formerly did about the
processes of mental development and the conditions which are
favorable and unfavorable than did our grandparents. Those
who deal with mental instability in adult life are convinced that
in a large number of instances the causes are found in emotional
and social maladjustments of childhood. In matters of moral and
intellectual health the principle that prevention is better than
cure applies in an intense degree.

With the increase in mental disorders characteristic of our
civilization, the duty of society to check and reduce the great
number of sufferers is clear. When one recalls that the number of
beds in institutions for the mentally ill is equal to those for all
other forms of disease, and that society has to provide this care,
merely selfish economic reasons dictate the unremitting use in
childhood of all available scientific resources.

This then is the situation. There is a junction of a new social
necessity and a new ability, due to knowledge and skill. It is this
situation which makes the problem of childhood an urgent one
and which inspires the remarkable cooperative efforts recorded
in the proceedings of the White House Conference.

It is the simplest and most familiar of all facts that all who
have matured to adult life die. The fact is familiar, but its full
import is often overlooked. Civilization is not transmitted by
physical means, but by care, nurture and education. It would die
out in two short generations if it were not renewed by the newly
born. The kind of training the latter receive determines the future of society itself. There have been simple and relatively static
civilizations in which family and friends sufficed to insure that
reproduction of the culture of the community which would
maintain its continued existence. The fact that every civilized
country has found it necessary to adopt systems of public education proves that we are no longer living in that period.

But what is characteristic of our own day is the recognition
that mere schooling is not enough to achieve the renewal of civilization. Prospective parents must be educated. The mother must
have adequate prenatal, natal and post-natal care. If the future
citizen is to contribute to the advancement of society, instead of
being a drag upon it, his health must be looked to by all possible

measures of prevention, including regular examinations by competent persons. The sources of infection must be guarded against. There must be a proper environment, including not merely protection against foul air, milk and water, bad and inadequate food, but through supply of the positive conditions of a proper home and facilities for recreation. The body is maimed by accident and weakened by lack of nourishment and by illness. But it is also such a delicate mechanism that it is warped, and sanity of mind and body injured, whenever the home and neighborhood environment is defective.

It is impossible to separate care of the body from other means of nurture. The brain and nervous system are part of the body, but they develop properly only when an adequate mental and moral education is secured.

It is hardly necessary to say today that such an education includes more than mere absence of illiteracy, more than mere book learning. It is a social as well as individual necessity that each child be prepared to do his part in the industrial organization of society. He must be so educated that he can contribute through his work to serving others and to making secure his own happiness in his work.

The resources of scientific knowledge must be used to discover his strong and weak points, uncover his tastes and talents, and insure both him and society against the unhappiness and the loss that come from the square peg in the round hole. When there were but few callings, and those few were simple, organized attention to development for the selection of the right calling and for proficiency in it were not necessary. Today they are necessary.

And so one might go through the whole circle of relationships and responsibilities incumbent upon the future citizen and show the necessity of that systematic development which only organized social action can secure. Unless the family and civic life, from the local community to the Federal State and the community of nations, are to disintegrate and be wracked by disorder and war, there must be the devoted and unremitting devotion of society to serve the needs of the young who are component members of future adult society.

The problem is an extraordinarily difficult one, the hardest in many respects that the world has ever faced. But we have at command, as has been stated, new resources of knowledge and skill.

If the problem is once recognized as a general social responsibility, these new energies will not be dissipated and directed to lesser and technical ends, but will be directed to meeting the need.

Fortunately, there is a strong sentimental reservoir which can be drawn upon. Affection for children is one of the strongest traits of human nature. And in our country, as perhaps never before in the world, there is the widespread desire on the part of parents that their children shall have better and fairer opportunities in the world than they themselves ever had, and not merely economic opportunities but as well those for a richer and fuller share in all the things that make life lovely, significant, worth while.

The reservoir of energy with which to meet the problem is, however, much more than that of affection of parents for children. There is involved the entire concern of thoughtful persons for the future well-being of society itself. Personal affection is reinforced by all patriotic and humane considerations.

The Children's Charter adopted by the White House Conference touches every side of the life of the child that affects the welfare of society itself. In recognizing "the rights of the child as the first rights of citizenship," it adopts the most fundamental philosophy of social order and progress which can be formulated. As far as the citizens of the nation carry out in action the philosophy which the charter sets forth we may face the future with confidence.

Discussion of "Freedom, in Relation to Culture, Social Planning, and Leadership"

There are a number of traditions in this country. These different traditions interfere with one another; they often conflict. The result of this divergence and mutual hostility is undoubtedly a condition of drift and relative aimlessness. Doubtless freedom and power would result from identification of the school teacher and student with some one of those competing traditions provided it were sufficiently in harmony with the general movement of the larger economic, political, and intellectual movements of society. But here is where the rub comes in. One dominant tradition, with which I am no more in sympathy than is Dr. Counts, is for example that of getting ahead in a competitive struggle for pecuniary gain. Those who identify themselves with it successfully doubtless achieve a certain kind of freedom and power.

But this fact only emphasizes the relativity of freedom: freedom in what and for what? And the same question must be asked regarding power. In other words, the question of value and quality comes in as to both freedom and power. Since there is competition and conflict, we must choose. On what basis shall our choice be decided?

Now both the Bolshevist and the Fascist schemes, which represent the most definite alternatives to a policy of drift and conflict, make that decision in advance of the process of education, a fact which signifies that those educated do not have an opportunity to make the choice or to share in making it. It is made for them, and they have merely to accept and adopt the con-

[First published in *Theses on Freedom* (Washington, D.C.: National Council of Education of the National Education Association, 1932), pp. 13–15, from Dewey's contribution to the National Council of Education discussion on 20 February 1932. For George S. Counts's theses, see this volume, Appendix 1.]

sequences of the choice. This fact seems to me the essence of indoctrination.

Before deciding then that in order to escape aimlessness and a suffocating absence of freedom and power, we have to move in the direction of either the Russian or the Italian solution, I should like to ask whether there is not another alternative and possibility.

Besides the aspect of tradition in culture, Dr. Counts speaks of that other aspect which consists in tools, inventions, practises, institutions, customs, etc. I do not think that the two aspects can be sharply marked off from each other, but there is an undoubted difference according as one or the other is emphasized. I suggest that the alternative not definitely considered in Dr. Counts' paper is the possibility of bringing students face to face with the aspect which is relatively non-traditional. Here the question is not one of adoption and identification, but of facing the situation intellectually and critically, in its various phases and the consequences of the different strands in it.

For example, one fact of actual life is the rapidity of social change and shifting of aims and methods in society. Upon the alternative I have in mind students would be familiarized with this fact, not in the abstract way in which it has just been alluded to but as a concrete phenomenon in its various manifestations. Since our education now predominantly assumes a static situation, one to be accepted in the main because it is presented in an idealized and eulogistic fashion, we should have a definite plan departing from present educational procedure very widely. In fact there would be, I think, an educational revolution if the schools from top to bottom took account of the constantly re-adjusting mobile phases of contemporary culture.

Yet facing this fact would not involve a prior identification with any particular tradition. It would not for example demand a choice such as would have to be made between the conservative and the liberal, progressive, tradition. For example, there is city planning at the present time, not because a deliberate choice has been made between these two traditions, but because new conditions like street cars, automobiles, skyscrapers create new needs. Using this case to generalize from, the student would not be asked to identify himself with any tradition pre-selected by others, but to observe and reflect upon the situation as presented, including the various methods urged for dealing with it and the various traditions related to it.

The students would presumably in the end, most of them at least, arrive at the adoption of some tradition. But it would be from each one's own choice and through his own participation in the processes which lead up to choice and not because of inculcation of a choice made by others. And as a rule I do not think his choice would be sheer identification with a pre-existing tradition. It would rather be a process like that which Dr. Counts calls fashioning or refashioning a tradition.

The objection which is usually urged against what I have said is that it also involves a prior judgment of value and choice of an end and hence a process of indoctrination. This reply seems to me purely dialectical, due to taking a concept formally without regard for its content. The value which is prized is that of permitting and encouraging each student to do his own observing and reflecting and arrive in the end at his own scheme of valuations. If the result is called indoctrination it is at least a self-correcting indoctrination, not one which demands the subordination of critical discrimination and comparison. For the unified end is based on method, not on pre-established conclusions to be arrived at.

This alternative seems to me more in consonance with the conditions of American life than either the Russian or Italian systems. It is therefore more practical. However it involves such a departure from the existing scheme of education and would involve so much, and probably such adverse, criticism of many of our existing habits of life, political and economic, that it would also arouse much opposition. One can hardly imagine so-called patriotic societies and chambers of commerce taking it any more enthusiastically than they would the Russian scheme. For as I have already said the present system is predicated for the most part upon a static conception involving glorification of the *status quo*.

Aside from a preference for an aim and plan which does not limit the field of inquiry in advance and load the intellectual processes in favor of a pre-arranged conclusion, this alternative has in my judgment an advantage from the side of continuity of development over a longer time. No one knows how many mistakes will have to be dealt with later that, at present, are being made in Russia and Italy because of suppression of criticism outside of fixed limits. The tangible results of one decade or generation are rarely those of succeeding periods. I think we must beware of overlooking the time element, and be aware of the danger of judgments based on too short periods, and of impatience for too immediate results. I think dissatisfaction with the type of educational effort I am suggesting (among others than reactionaries) is due mainly to the slowness of the method. But it may make up in sureness what it lacks in speed.

Education and Birth Control

The opposition to the birth-control movement is not a unique or isolated fact. It is an expression of an ever-recurring struggle between darkness and knowledge. We are given to thinking that science has overthrown all enemies to its advance. This may be true of the technical aspects of science, those which have no clear social bearings. It is not true when newly discovered knowledge has important bearings upon the conduct of life. There is always a rearguard of ignorance, prejudice, dogma, routine, tradition, which fights against the spread of new ideas that entail new practices. It has been so in astronomy, physics, biology. It is not surprising that it is so in the case of medicine.

The line of battle changes. The particular ideas that are resisted change. But relatively the fight is constant. Men do not any longer, except a few cranks, strive against the Copernican astronomy. But some conflict between new truth and what is old and intrenched goes on, and probably will go on as long as man lives with a past behind him and a future ahead of him.

We forget how comparatively recent is any scientific knowledge concerning the processes of procreation and conception. It was only late in intellectual history that they were discovered to be chemical in nature, and that something of their mechanism was learned. Now, new knowledge always means the possibility of new control. With this particular scientific discovery there arose the possibility of intelligent control of blind natural processes. This is the logic of the birth-control movement. Just as expanding knowledge of electricity brought with it the electric light, telegraph, telephone, dynamo, so scientific knowledge of the transmission of life enables mankind to bring that process

[First published in *Nation* 134 (27 January 1932): 112.]

under human direction. Because knowledge always means increased control, there can be no doubt of where ultimate victory will lie in this particular conflict. The conflict between ignorance and knowledge becomes one between chance and control.

Meantime, however, individuals are prevented by law and by public sentiment from access to the knowledge which would give them more complete control of their conduct—laws and public sentiment that were formed when adequate scientific knowledge was lacking. How can anyone who believes in education and in enlightenment of the public through education fail to be opposed to this restriction on the flow of intelligence? The opposition to it should be all the stronger because what is proposed is only a legislation which places the source of this flow in the hands of scientists and physicians. There is always wholesome sanitation wherever there is free circulation of intelligence. We need light and circulation of air in intellectual and moral matters as in physical. Suppression and secrecy breed unfairness, mental and moral disorder. Our plea, from the side of education, is that there be removed arbitrary restrictions to that movement of knowledge and understanding which brings the action of the blind forces of nature under the control of intelligence.

The other point I wish to make is just as simple. All educators today attach great importance to the development of individual capacities. They are all opposed to merely mass education, to regimentation, the lock step, to uniformity imposed upon boys and girls, no two of whom are alike. But as long as multitudes of families have too many children and those children badly spaced, it is not possible for each child to have proper individual attention—physical, intellectual, moral. I have no hesitation in saying that no matter what educators may say and do in behalf of better development of individuals as individuals, their ideals cannot be realized unless there is intelligent control of the size of families. Mere mass and number will stand in the way with the great majority of families.

I can think of no change which would be more beneficial than one which would make us prize quality more and quantity less. Our American zeal for size is one thing that stands in the way of our giving proper attention to higher values. The exaggerated importance attached to size has affected our schools and the instruction they give. It stands in the way of a multitude of desirable improvements. If parents were in a position to make quality of life supreme in their own households, the larger problem of the schools would be taken care of.

"The Irrepressible Conflict"

Our League was formed because of a realization that our existing political parties in the conduct of government are more concerned to serve the selfish and financial interests of the few than the human needs of the many. A day or two ago Senator Borah felt called upon to comment upon the letter we recently addressed to Senator Norris. He said among other things, "It takes some single dominating issue, accompanied by a dramatic crisis, to swing people from their old moorings into new positions." I agree with the distinguished senator. But I differ from him because I think that a dominant issue is already here; where our League splits off from him and other insurgent senators is that we, in company with a multitude of others, see the issue, while they are blind to it.

The dominant issue is bigger than tariff; bigger than public control or ownership of the great modern utilities; bigger than any phase of the traction, transit and transportation question; bigger than the problem of just taxation. It is bigger, because all of these questions grow out of a deep fundamental issue. The dominant issue is whether the people of the United States are to control our government, federal, state and municipal, and to use it in behalf of the peace and welfare of society or whether control is to go on passing into the hands of small powerful economic groups who use all the machinery of administration and legislation to serve their own ends. This is the one dominant issue of which all special issues are parts.

It is the misfortune of Senator Borah and his insurgent colleagues in both parties that they cannot see this fact. They can continue to snipe, and occasionally to bring down some game

[First published in *News Bulletin of the League for Independent Political Action* 1 (January 1931): 4–5, from an address delivered before the New History Society, 30 December 1930.]

that needed, heaven knows, to be got out of the way. But it is they, not we, who in the long run are unpractical, if they think they are ever going to accomplish anything important without facing the basic issue of which I have spoken. Some think they can make Big Power the issue in 1932. I am no politician, but I am willing to go on record with the prophecy that unless this power issue is linked up in the minds of the people with the deeper issue as to whether special interests or the people are to control government, it will be as great a flop as was the attempt of the Democrats to come into power in 1924 on the issue of the damnable corruption of the oil scandal of the Harding administration.

The instincts of the people will not be aroused until the political questions presented to them get down to bedrock. I repeat that I am sorry for the insurgent senators in both parties who are afraid to get down to this bedrock. They may get by in their local elections, and they may continue to keep their own parties stirred up and in a mess—which is well enough as far as it goes. But they themselves have no hope of reforming their own parties from within; they are not so silly as that. They know who rules their parties better than we do. What they are waiting and hoping for is that dramatic, or melodramatic, crisis of which Senator Borah speaks, that will create a tide on which they can ride, without having to take risks. It is too bad they lack courage. But it's their own loss in the long run. When the movement gains the headway it is bound to get, it will move so fast that these men who are waiting to take advantage of its momentum will be left stranded on the shore.

There has been some misunderstanding of our letter to Senator Norris. The leadership we wanted him to take was primarily that of breaking with the old party and openly recognizing the need of a new political line-up based on the facts of 1930 instead of those of 1820 and 1860. Such a movement on his part would be like the opening of a crevasse in a dam; it would precipitate a flood. The further leadership we should have liked from him would have been in the direction indicated in our letter—building frankly, openly and continuously in the direction of what was called in our letter to him "social planning and social control." Senator Norris like everybody else is influenced by his environment and his associates; it is greatly to his honor that he has been as independent and fearless in spite of these things as he has been. But we thought that if he would completely break with the things that have hampered him and hold him back, he would under new associations move forward rapidly; he wouldn't have to waste his time in guerilla warfare and sham battles. He could get down to the basic question of whether there is to be social use and social control of the agencies of government or whether, under the guise of rugged individualism at the top and ragged individualism at the bottom, agglomerations of great wealth are to make our democracy a farce and stench.

Well, they say we aren't practical; I have a number of editorials telling me how impractical I am. I am not, thank God, what is called a practical politician. But I am practical enough in my mind to see that there is an irrepressible conflict coming as real and as deep as that to which Lincoln called attention. In the face of such a conflict I think the practical thing is not to shut one's eyes, or to shilly-shally and postpone, hoping some run of the tide will make it safe to come out on the side of the people and against the big business interests. I am willing to leave a monopoly of that kind of practicality to the insurgent senators and their timid friends. Nor have we been so unpractical as to launch a new party. If you will read the literature which has been provided you will see that we are attempting to do the educational work which is a necessary preparation for the formation of a solid and enduring new party movement.

A party formed on the basis of a temporary crisis however dramatic will not outlast the emergency which produced it. An effective party cannot be built for example out of the discontents of the present depression. It might be possible to capitalize them but the party would fade away with the return of prosperity. The depression however should induce persons to think much more than they have been doing for ten years past, and if people do some thinking there will be the vital seeds of an enduring political movement.

For their thinking will lead them to one conclusion. The existing parties are the servants of those economic interests which use the government and which debauch governmental agencies to do their will at the expense of society. This explains why there are no real differences between the two parties, and why their conflicts are staged battles. It explains the apathy of the people who realize they make very little difference for which party they vote. A new movement can be started only on the basis of an issue which goes down to the roots of social life. There are too many obstacles in the way of a party formed on any basis except the most fundamental issue. The life of today is economic, industrial. All significant political issues grow out of this fact. The old parties dodge it, except as they can turn it to advantage in getting campaign funds or votes in return for special favors. Just as the Republican party was born in the irrepressible conflict against extension of chattel slavery, so the next party will be born to liberate men, women and children from the enslavement of governmental agencies to selfish and predatory economic interests. That is an issue which people can understand. But it takes organization, sacrifice, cooperation of all persons of good will, to get it presented to the people and to create in them the will to put into effect their vision of a new society and a new history. We ask your help; we have a right to ask it because we are not working for ourselves, not to gain something selfish by means of deluding voters, but as forerunners in helping usher in that new day which you too see about to dawn.

The Jobless—A Job for All of Us

It is no longer necessary to convince sensible persons that lack of employment is not a sign of laziness, shiftlessness or unreliable character. There is probably no one at the present time who does not have the knowledge of persons out of work who are industrious, faithful and competent; persons who want work above all else and yet cannot get it.

It is adding insult to injury to hold these persons, thousands, millions, of them, responsible for their inability to work. They are victims of the economic system. They are victims just as a man who suffers a physical accident when a railway train is thrown off the track is a victim. Something goes wrong in the running of our industrial train, and uncounted numbers suffer.

There is not a civilized country which does not recognize in some way its responsibility for those who cannot support themselves and those who are dependent upon their labors. Poor houses, poor relief, organized charity are indirect acknowledgments of social responsibility. Every humane person takes shame to himself and to the society in which he lives when he hears that one of his fellow creatures has starved to death. The right to life is the fundamental right which society has to secure to its members. When murder is rife and life is generally insecure, we know that the social system is at fault, not the men who are murdered. The right to life is invaded when men and women desirous of doing an honest day's work find themselves thrown out and left stranded. The social responsibility is the same as when because of general social lawlessness these men are directly and physically attacked.

Although public charity is a recognition of social responsibility it is a belated recognition. It comes after the catastrophe. Pre-

[First published in *Unemployed*, February 1931, pp. 3–4.]

vention is always better than cure, and charity is rarely even a cure. It is at best a temporary stopgap. And when the suffering and the catastrophe are constantly recurring, the recourse to charity, as an afterthought, is criminal. If a railway system had a continuous succession of derailments in which many persons were injured, every one would recognize the absence of competence and of foresight in the system itself.

Unemployment is not only recurrent but chronic. There exists all the time what is known as "normal" unemployment. Our industrial system is speeded up beyond its power to stand the wracking that comes from its own movement. Such a crisis as the present calls attention in a dramatic, even a sensational, way to something that exists all the time, but which under ordinary circumstances most men are too blind to observe. At such a time as the present, private committees raise large funds, private organizations open soup kitchens, and make provision for bread lines. Legislatures make special appropriations out of public funds raised by taxation. These are tacit and half-hearted recognitions of social responsibility, which are forced upon us by the stress of tragic circumstance.

They are necessary, and in the midst of an emergency, no one can say a word against such methods. Common humanity demands them. But they touch symptoms and effects, not causes. I said that civilized peoples show indirect recognition of social responsibility for unemployment. But I ought to have said that as long as this recognition operates only after the evil has shown itself and millions are suffering from no fault of their own (except too great patience with a bad system), the nations are only half-civilized.

Social responsibility, through charity, for unemployment is a back-handed, clumsy, inhuman, way of admitting society's responsibility for furnishing men and women security through steady employment at a living wage. The industrial system which cannot do this thing has written its own indictment and predicted its own down-fall. That men should starve because there is no bread in time of famine is a tragedy. But that men should lack bread because there is too much wheat, because farmers cannot sell although they have a superabundance and others cannot buy because they have no work and nothing to buy with, is no tragedy of nature's making. It is man's doing, and men, especially the men who manage and men who support the present economic system, are responsible.

To split hairs about over-production and under-consumption is like two men quarrelling when scales do not balance, one man saying it is because one pan is too heavy and the other man insisting the other is too light. The fact is the whole thing is out of balance.

When the present crisis is over in its outward sensational features, when things have returned to a comparatively more comfortable state called "normalcy," will they forget? Will they even complacently congratulate themselves upon the generosity with which society relieved distress? Or will they locate the causes of the distress of unemployment and modify the social system? If they do the former, the time of depression will recur sooner or later with renewed violence until the social system is changed by force. The alternative is such a recognition of society's responsibility for the evil as will by planned foresight and deliberate choice change the economic and financial structure of society itself.

Only a change in the system will ensure the right of every person to work and enable every one to live in security.

The Need for a New Party

I. The Present Crisis

At the present time it seems almost silly to advance an argument for the formation of a new party. In a general way the need for one speaks for itself, and clamorously. Of the first ten persons you meet who have no definite connection with one of the old parties, either officially or through some form of self-interest, at least seven or eight will not question the fact that a new party is needed. What they will question is the practicability of trying to form one. For the old parties are so firmly entrenched throughout the nation, and the organizations are so closely bound to the business system, that unorganized individuals feel themselves helpless. Nevertheless, a statement of the nature of the need and an account of why it is so generally felt are necessary preliminaries to any discussion of how a new party may grow up and what its program will be. For it is the pressure of necessity which creates and directs all political changes.

There has long been an indifference to political parties. Masses of voters have been more than apathetic; they have been jaded. They have lost all confidence that politics can accomplish anything significant. They have even accepted the cynical belief that the parties are dominated by big business. But the present revulsion against parties has two striking characteristics which make it unique. Every depression has produced a certain amount of revulsion, but usually it has assumed the form of a repudiation of the party in power and a general support of the other. In the next campaign this sentiment may be sufficiently strong to elect a Democratic President, but the sentiment will not be accom-

[First published in four parts in *New Republic* 66 (18 March, 25 March, 1 April, 8 April 1931): 115–17, 150–52, 177–79, 202–5.]

panied by any hope or expectation. On the contrary, it is generally believed that organized finance and industry have already taken this possibility into account and are casting about for a candidate who will be "reasonable"—a practical synonym for subservient.

The second difference is even more important. In the past, the dissatisfied masses have been stirred by one particular measure. Cheap money, free silver, trust-busting, have been proposed and accepted as panaceas. There is no cure-all in sight now, and people show no disposition to seek for one. The industrial crisis is so severe that even dull eyes can see the foolishness of adopting any measure which leaves the underlying structure just as it was. To offer a panacea now would be to open oneself to ridicule. Dissatisfaction thus proves to be much deeper than it ever was during former depressions. In fact it amounts to unrest. And though it may assume the form of resentment rather than of thought, the tendency among most people is to think much more deeply than before and to go farther into action.

There is a deep-seated reason why the common man is convinced that neither the Democratic nor the Republican party represents him or his interests. The Republican party has played the role of Providence. It has told the people that its leaders in alliance with big business are the guardians of that general prosperity which is attained under the direction of organized capital. It has declared that when big capitalists were made prosperous, a general state of welfare would seep down and be enjoyed by the masses. It was not for the masses to do anything; they had only to wait, hold out their hands and receive what the gods above would give them. The masses did not exactly believe this gospel, but they saw nothing that they could do—and so they waited. The conviction that prosperity begins above and then descends below has been the underlying doctrine of every Republican policy since the War. It is typified in every utterance and every act of that representative of the Messiahship of big business—Secretary Mellon.

President Hoover is a willing and to all appearances a sincere believer in the gospel. There were those who thought the "engineering mind" would effect some healthful regeneration. They forgot that the engineer at present looks two ways. On the one hand, he looks to the efficient use of materials and processes: he is the servant of technological progress. But on the other hand, he is the servant of capital employed for private profit. He is used to thinking in the same terms and speaking the same language as his masters. And when his engineering ability has been employed, not in actual engineering enterprises, but in some eminently profitable undertaking, he is completely identified with the gospel current among men of large business and wealth, who have to rationalize their behavior by making themselves believe that it is in the interest of general welfare. However, this gospel begins to be questioned when the income of the majority of the people falls below a decent subsistence level, as it has during the present depression. Providence can maintain itself securely only when it provides. A self-professed Providence which not only does not provide, but shakes the very structure of economic society and endangers the elementary securities of life, is a self-confessed fraud.

Unfortunately for the permanent prospects of the Democratic party, its leaders prematurely accepted the gospel truth of the doctrine that prosperity descends from above. For the Democrats during the process of assuring the people that they would be just as "safe" as the Republicans, and in assuring big business—and asking for campaign contributions on that basis—that they would be as good and obedient boys as the Republican leaders, not only habituated themselves to the Republican mode of thought, but committed themselves to the policy of alliance with big business. Many independents who voted for Smith in the last presidential campaign did so under mental protest. They disliked the leadership of Raskob and the campaign of "hush-hush" on the economic issues which he fostered. Their fears of what would happen under this overt committal, which was the culmination of the covert committals practised for some time, were borne out by the feeble action of the Democratic party in the new tariff legislation, and in the subservience of the leaders to the demands of finance in connection with drought relief and unemployment. The generally acknowledged absence of genuine leadership in the Democratic party is a necessary by-product. No carbon copy of an original can pretend to leadership or force.

There is no hope that either of the old main parties is going to change. The reason lies even deeper than the self-interest which binds leaders and office holders so closely to "business" that they can be freed only by acts of treachery. Their mental habits are formed in the pattern of this alliance. Conservatism tends to come with age, and the two parties are old. It comes the more surely and exercises its reactionary effect the more disastrously when professed leaders have based the very structure of their beliefs on the doctrine of popular salvation by means of dependence on property interests. Whatever may be the convictions of individuals within the parties, the parties themselves are property-minded. In the clash between property interests and human interests, all their habits of thought and action fatally impel them to side with the former. They make concessions, but do not change the direction of their belief or behavior.

I do not mean that the whole alliance of the parties with organized business is consciously sinister and corrupt, though it is easily demonstrable that this is somewhat true. I mean rather that both old parties represent that stage of American life when the American people as a whole felt that society was to advance by means of industrial inventions and their application; by the development of manufacturing, of railways and commerce. It was that stage of American life when all but a few took for granted the natural control of industry and trade by the profit motive and the necessity of accumulating money capital.

This idea may once have played a part in the development of the country. It has now ceased to be anything but an obstruction. But the two old parties are so wedded to this belief, both by mental habit and by external alliance with organized industry and finance, that there is no hope of their ever cutting loose. They mouth the watchwords of bygone generations, they appeal to Jefferson and Lincoln, because they are themselves anachronisms. Quite apart from a deliberate and sinister connection with malefactors of great wealth, the parties are out of touch with present needs and realities. They perpetuate and cling to ideas and ideals of a past that has forever departed. The realization of this fact is the cause of the present fundamental discontent with both old parties. These are so out of vital contact with the times, that the people are out of touch with them.

I should like to make the point definite. The needs and the troubles of the people are connected with problems of consumption, with problems of the maintenance of a reasonably decent and secure standard of living. Our political life, proceeding under whichever of the old parties happens to be in power, deals with production. The tariffs have not only established certain producing interests as economic power, but they are based upon a consistent disregard of the consumer. Special privilege entrenches itself at the cost of consumption. Transportation and the mechanism of distribution are connected with production and they have been constantly fostered with no regard for the consumer or his standard of living. Our land system, our mines, our forests and now our water power have, when politics has touched them, fallen under control of ownership by the "producer." Our taxation system is controlled by the same interest. Mr. Mellon's solicitude for the incomes of those in the higher brackets was openly an anxiety concerning the forces of production.

The statement that our politics has been controlled for production purposes at the cost of consumption cannot be overemphasized, nor can it be too sweeping. Let anyone consider the history of politics for the last fifty years and he will find no policy which does not come under this generalization. Exceptions are mere passing episodes. The latest proof of it is the controversy regarding relief for those suffering from drought and unemployment. There is no great difficulty in getting help from Congress to promote processes of production, such as loans for tools and seed, for animals and other productive instrumentalities. But there is the greatest difficulty in getting help for living beings to maintain themselves even at the lowest standard of living. The veterans get attention on the express ground that their relief will stimulate buying and thus help business. Even with a powerful organization behind them they might have pled in vain if the plea were decided wholly on the human grounds of subsistence. Complete failure to provide legislation to stabilize employment is glaring evidence of the general subordination of consumption to immediate production.

The problems and needs of life for the masses have to do with consumption. Even business men have learned that overproduction and cycles of depression are closely connected with underconsumption, and hence those whose consuming power is unimpaired are taking an unprecedented interest in consumption. The middle class finds its income from investments sharply impaired because of the prevailing lack of effective capacity in consumption. And the unemployed—the five to nine millions who face starvation, or live on charity, and who are losing courage, hope and self-respect—do not need to have the problem of consumption brought to their attention.

Here again we have the reason why the present political unrest is so unlike any in the previous history of our country. The needs, experienced where men live, concern the standards of living for themselves and their families. They find themselves in a political situation where no provision is made for this necessity, where interest is centered almost wholly upon stimulating production and distribution without any reference to the way they impinge upon consumption. I do not say the contradiction has been thought out or formulated. But it is *felt*, and political discontent and immense resentment is the consequence. Here is the need for something radically new in our political life which only a new party can promulgate and execute.

It demands a new party to meet a new social situation. I shall not repeat what I have said about the old parties. But this fact explains why fundamental needs cannot be met by the insurgents in the old parties or by a coalition of those elements. They can serve a useful purpose in obstructing the worst measure of predatory greed; they are useful brakes. But it is utopian to expect that they can recreate the parties under whose standards they eke out their precarious existence; for these parties are too committed and too habituated to purposes and policies diametrically at war with their intentions. The dough is too extensive and too sodden for the leaven to take effect. They might form, conceivably, the nucleus of a new party. But their own ideas will remain truncated and half-formed until they break loose and associate themselves openly with new interests, needs and companions. A Lucas, representing a Hoover, will always get the better of a Norris within the party, no matter how personally independent the latter may be; and a Raskob will dominate a Wheeler or a Walsh.

II. The Breakdown of the Old Order

I said in my previous article, published last week in the *New Republic*, that present politics is wholly out of line and out of touch with the realities of American life, that it is bound up with the interests of production, of industry, transportation and finance, in separation from the needs and problems of consumption and the standard of living. As I am writing, I find a vivid picture in the Sunday magazine section of the *New York Times* of the state of affairs in Washington, painted by an unusually keen and shrewd observer, Anne O'Hare McCormick. She finds the prevailing physical fog there to be symbolic of a mental and moral fog that obscures from the denizens of the Capitol and the White House all vision of the realities of the country. "An economic earthquake has struck the world. . . . Changes of the most baffling character are taking place in the structure of society, and more than anywhere else in the structure of American society. . . . And so far as you can see and hear, no real sense of these events has penetrated the capital. . . . It is the sense of reality that is missing from this scene, the sense of participation in human experience. It is a place where everything is expressed and nothing is felt, a place where all the emotions are vicarious emotions, a place where all thoughts are clichés.

"The whole effect is histrionic, shoddy, empty of life. . . . The world of politics is lost in the fog it creates. . . . The old iron dome is a kind of last refuge from reality, but the refugees have a growing fear that they are missing something big." While the "world is turning somersaults, the politicians are living in the future, in the next campaign; and at the same time living in the past." It is no wonder that everything is confused and complicated. "What appears on the surface is too trivial or too intricate for warfare on the epic scale. . . . Nobody remembers when so many conflicts broke at once and when the sides were so tangled up and so indistinct. . . . All the deadlocks, mergers, sub-mergers, strategies, party slogans, interchangeable Lefts and Rights, sound hollow because they are hollow; there is no body to them, certainly no soul." The only remaining reality is the next election, and consistent thought is given only to trying to guess the effect of this and that measure and strategy upon the voter. It is, if I may paraphrase, a struggle for immediate power with no one having any idea of what is to be done with the power if it is gained—except to use it again in the next election.

I have ventured to quote scattered statements at considerable length because the picture of the immediate situation in Wash-

ington is typical. The condition at Washington reflects accurately
the condition of politics throughout the country. The former has
nothing to do with the realities of American life because the latter is completely out of connection. The situation explains the
discontent and disgust of the people with the old parties and it
constitutes the opportunity for a new party. We have long been
told that politics is unimportant, that government is merely a
drag and an interference; that the captains of industry and finance are the wise ones, the leaders in whose hands the fortunes
of the country are safely entrusted.

The persons who keep reiterating such sayings forget, or they
try to conceal from view, that the confusion, the perplexity, the
triviality, the irrelevance, of politics at Washington merely reflect
the bankruptcy of industrial "leadership," just as politics in general is an echo, except when it is an accomplice, of the interests
of big business. The deadlocks and the impotence of Congress
are definitely the mirror of the demonstrated incapacity of the
captains of industry and finance to conduct the affairs of the
country prosperously as an incident to the process of feathering
their own nests. It would be ludicrous, were it not tragic, to believe that an appeal to the unregulated activities of those who
have got us into the present crisis will get us out of it, provided
they are relieved from the incubus of political action. The magic
of eating a hair of the dog which bit you in order to cure hydro-
phobia is as nothing to the magic involved in the belief that those
who have privilege and power will remedy the breakdown they
have created. As long as politics is the shadow cast on society by
big business, the attenuation of the shadow will not change the
substance. The only remedy is new political action based on social interests and realities.

When the country was enjoying what was called prosperity,
the doctrine that big industrialists are the true guardians of the
welfare of society in general had a temporary appeal. It is hard to
imagine any doctrine more inept than this is now, when such
"leadership" has brought the country to the present impasse,
marked by widespread human woe. The wise and powerful leaders are still disputing among themselves how the present crisis
came about; they assign this and that cause. They have no idea
how long it will last or how we shall get out of it. They are gambling with chance; they put their faith in the blind goddess of

luck. They could not, most of them, even guess right on their own specialty, the stock market. Their pretension to social leadership has been exploded. The bursting of the loaded shell has left loss and ruin behind it.

American memory is notoriously short; we go from incident to episode in the briefest moment. But it is possible to recall the time when we were told that delay in passing the tariff bill was the major obstruction to the revival of business and prosperity; the day when the organs of big industry were holding up recalcitrant Senators as the only significant obstacle. Well, the tariff bill was passed, raising our tariff walls still higher. The Democratic party, having decided that the way to win power was to wear the Republican uniform, made no effective opposition; it was, on the whole, an accomplice to the passage of the bill, passive and even active. The result was just what impartial economists predicted. It was a challenge to the world to engage in economic war. The response was prompt. Imports were curtailed and production at home was lessened because the access to the market was hindered. Exports fell off. The consumer paid a higher price for what he was still able to buy, but the manufacturing interest lost rather than gained, because the margin supplied by export trade was cut down.

The tariff situation is significant far beyond itself. It exemplifies the bankruptcy of archaic political ideas and policies. It demonstrates the bankruptcy of industry as now conducted in conserving even its own economic interests. There were indeed some industrialists, drawn chiefly from the new, expanding lines of manufacture, who had no sympathy with making tariff walls higher and more obstructive. But they made no active and aggressive campaign in opposition; they were afraid to do so, because the whole economic system was so interwoven with the political policy of favoring production at the expense of consumption. They disliked particular instances of the policy, but they endured them rather than do anything which might alter the system itself.

There can be little doubt, I think, that the new tariff was unpopular with people in general. But they were unable to make an effective protest; they were too bewildered to attempt to protest. They had no organ of opposition, because both old parties were tied to the system of fostering the immediate short-time interests of production without reference to its effect on the consumer and the standard of living. It has seemed over and over again as if the limit had been reached in the way of high tariffs; there are many who predict that the last tariff is the expiring move of the ultra-protectionists. But I should hesitate to join these prophets. For the tariff policy is not an isolated thing. It has been the mistake of those in favor of lower tariffs to treat the matter as if it were isolated and could be treated by itself. A general reversal of the trend of political life can alone emancipate the tariff from the clutches of parties which are themselves in the hands of the dominant economic interests.

What has been said about the tariff applies also to the other economic questions which are already in politics—transportation (the railways), power and the allied public utilities, finance, banking, credit and the control of the issuance of securities. Neither of the old parties is prepared to do more than make concessions to the interest of the public; nothing fundamental can be expected from them. They are hindered both by their dependence upon those who control these interests and by their own habits of mind. The things which have been mentioned are interlocked. The proposed railway mergers cannot go into effect in any case for several years; the public endorsement of the plan by President Hoover (so direct that it had to be toned down and more or less explained away) had an eye to the stock market and to speeding up business rather than to the issue itself. As the *New Republic* has pointed out, the St. Paul decision makes it doubtful whether the mergers are to be managed in the interests of the general public or even the shippers, or in those of the bankers who handle the reorganizations.

With the growing domination of industry by finance, a domination which is now all but an accomplished fact, any attempt at regulation of electrical power is met, and will be met more and more, by a concentrated money power operated through the big bankers who finance the power companies and public utilities. The connection is so close that some of the big companies producing electric power are hardly more than branches of big financial houses. The latter are in turn locked into the big industrial companies which produce the equipment and apparatus employed in the production and use of power and light and radio communication. The acme of reckless inflation in the late stock market of malodorous memory was reached in the power companies and their allies. Mergers nominally undertaken in the interest of increased economy and efficiency were floated for stock-jobbing purposes. The union of power-production companies, banking and manufacturing will be hard to buck; their combined influence radiates in every direction, including the well known attempt, in considerable measure successful, to control the public press by purchase and by pressure of advertising.

I agree with those who believe that the power issue is the most weighty single issue in the political field. The question is whether the public will lose the opportunity it has, as it did when the great development of railways was the uppermost factor in American life. But, as I have been saying, the power issue is not in fact single. On the contrary, it is a phase of the immense complex of production and finance which rules, but does not govern, industry and society. For governing implies the maintenance of an order and stability (to say nothing of welfare) which the present regime fails to obtain—as is evident in the present breakdown. Because the power issue is only a part of the economic situation, it cannot be successfully tackled as an isolated affair. And this is the only way in which the old parties will tackle it at the very best; they are more likely to attempt only feeble and half-hearted gestures.

The entire situation makes it imperative that there be fundamental thinking and action along new social lines. The chaos and confusion at Washington are the mark and proof of the total inability of the old parties even to be aware of the condition of affairs which so stirs society. It is unrealistic in the highest degree to suppose that they can or will do anything about it. Though Lincoln and Jefferson should rise from the dead, they would not be persuaded. Their organizations from top to bottom are bound up with the very things that need to be attacked. And, as I have said, even if this external connection did not tie their hands, their habits of mind, their ideas and thoughts, are tied to the old order. A Saul here and there may see the new light, but the parties will go on thinking only of what concessions at this minor point and that may help them win the next election. What is needed is a party that will go to the legislators not as suppliants but as masters, a party that will command the doing of the fundamental things that need to be done.

III. Who Might Make a New Party?

Discontent with the two old parties does not of itself compel the formation of a new one. The realization that both are alike because both are servants of big business is a step toward the creation of a new alignment of political forces. However, it is a step which does not necessarily lead to organized action. For, one might ask, why cannot and should not a new alignment grow out of or within one of the old parties? This question is asked by those who are thoroughly dissatisfied with the old parties as they stand; who want to see radical changes in their conduct; who believe, to state it briefly, in new purposes, new policies and new methods in politics.

The question deserves an answer. On the one hand, it implies the possibility and the desirability of boring from within by methods which will eventually produce a complete face-about and reorganization. And on the other hand, it implies the organization of independent progressive voters so that they will hold the balance of power and be able to throw their weight in every election on the side of candidates who stand for progressive measures. One or the other of these tactics is usually urged by persons having a practical experience with politics, a practical experience which the present writer lacks. Moreover, they consider any other strategy utopian and doomed to failure.

Let us take, for example, a Democrat in one of the Northeastern states, in New York or Massachusetts. He will point to the progressive leaders in his party and to the great measure of popular response they evoke. Why not, he will ask, utilize the liberal leaders and elements in the Democratic party as the basis for new methods and goals? Though he will admit that the present difference between express policies of the two parties is slight, he will go on to point out that, historically and temperamentally, the Democratic party is the party of the common people, of the industrial laborers and the relatively poor, and that its tradition commits it to opposition to the privileged, and to support of the masses, in distinction from the "aristocratic affiliations" of the Republican party. On the other hand, if we take a Republican from the Middle West, we will get an opposite reaction. He will point to the insurgency within the Republican party of the West; to the fact that historically the Republican party originated in support of liberty. In brief, he will invoke Lincoln, as the Eastern Democrat invokes the Jeffersonian tradition. Furthermore, he will point out that the Democratic party in the East is the party of Tammany Hall and of corrupt city machines; that the Southern wing is the very stronghold of conservatism, and that its historical conservatism is reinforced at present by an industrial development. And anyway, he will conclude, the Northern and Southern wings of the Democratic party have nothing in common save the desire for party victory. But to all these accusations the Eastern progressive Democrat will reply: And what is there in common between the Eastern reactionary and the Western insurgent wing of the Republican party, and which wing dictates national policies and candidates?

To my mind, the two sets of statements are facts which completely neutralize each other. Taken in conjunction they give the answer to the question: Why not bore from within and reform one of the old parties? I speak as one who as far back as 1912 hoped for a resurrection of the Republican party, as one who has at times in national elections hoped for a revival within the Democratic party. But at last I am disillusioned; I am humiliated at the recollection of the length of time it has taken me to pass to something like political maturity. For, I submit, it is an infantile cherishing of illusions, a withdrawal from the realities of economic and political facts, to pin one's hopes and put one's trust on the possibilities of organic change in either of the old major parties.

Winning the balance of power is a scheme which has its attraction for some. To my mind, its attractiveness is sentimental, although it is presented in the guise of superior practicality. The labor required to weld independents into a group effective in action is as great as that required for creating a new party. The idea of bringing it to pass is even more utopian. It may prove effective here and there, in scattered localities, but not on any national scale. It can lead only to guerilla warfare; with the occasional support of a progressive candidate or measure. But it contains within itself no promise of continuous and systematic effort; it contains within itself no promise of steady *direction* of political action. And directed action is the one great lack and need in American public life.

At present there are insurgents in Congress belonging to both parties. If there were anything solid in the idea of influencing political policies in a constructive way through the use of a balance of power, these men would long ago have gathered together, agreed upon positive measures and appealed to voters, irrespective of party, to support these measures. They have done nothing of the sort.[1] Search where you will and you will find no more conclusive proof of the impracticability of the idea of an independent balance of power. I will venture the prediction that the next Congress, which will afford an unparalleled opportunity for the manifestation of this balance of power, will be marked by confusion, uncertainty, recrimination and deadlocks.

Finally, if there is anything in either of these two ideas or in both of them combined, the creation of a new party is the surest and readiest way of putting into effective force whatever elements of strength they may possess. If we are to have government by blocs, or if we are to have a revival of progressivism within either of the old parties, definite action in behalf of constructive policies will depend upon the creation of an aggressive third party, which, even if it remains a minority opposition, will justify itself by the pressure it will exert upon the action of the old parties. It alone can force their hands and compel some manifestation of positive leadership within them.

Then there are the Socialist and Communist parties. Why should not political discontent and unrest express itself through them? Not much need be said about joining the Communists. As a party, they are directly governed from Moscow, and foreign control is simply out of the question for any party in the United States that means to be a going concern. And, aside from the fact that the Communist party does not speak the American idiom or think in terms relevant to the American situation, it is identified with a fanatical and doctrinaire inflexibility.

The Socialist party, on the other hand, has lost much of its alien atmosphere—once mainly German as the Communist is

1. This was written before the call for the recent progressive conference. How far the conference will affect the truth of the statements made is a matter of the future. My guess is not far, unless it marks the beginning of a new party.

Russian. It has freed itself to a large extent from doctrinaire dogmas, though internal division within the party on this score has still to be taken into account. Let me anticipate my later discussion by saying that I think a new party will have to adopt many measures which are now labeled socialistic—measures which are discounted and condemned because of that tag. But while support for such measures in the concrete, when they are adapted to actual situations, will win support from American people, I cannot imagine the American people supporting them on the ground of Socialism, or any other sweeping ism, laid down in advance. The greatest handicap from which special measures favored by the Socialists suffer is that they are advanced by the Socialist party as Socialism. The prejudice against the name may be a regrettable prejudice, but its influence is so powerful that it is much more reasonable to imagine all but the most dogmatic Socialists joining a new party than to imagine any considerable part of the American people going over to them.

Sentiment is more than sentiment; it is a force. I recognize that there is a large amount of routine attachment to parties from mere force of custom, a kind of hereditary Republican and Democratic affiliation, and that there is also an emotional attachment. But very large numbers have already been weaned, and engage in at least sporadic manifestations of independence. The immediate problem in tactics is to consolidate this element and to expand its size. It is the natural nucleus of a new party. Aside from the gradual weaning process which has now been going on for a long time, and which was accelerated by giving women the suffrage, an emergency like the present gives an immense jolt to great numbers, a jolt which shakes them loose from old ties. Now is the psychological time for launching a new political party devoted to well defined and new political issues.

Since it is the failure of the old parties to deal with the realities of our economic life which is the source of the present discontent, the appeal and the strategy of a new movement must be founded on these realities. I do not mean that they should try merely to utilize immediate economic self-interest; in spite of any temporary adherence such a movement might gain, I doubt its permanent success. It would be likely to go to pieces as soon as conditions change. There has been the appeal to idealism in the initiation of every significant American political movement, as well as to direct self-interest. The plight of the liberals in recent years has been caused largely by the absence of any defined social philosophy which would give direction to this latent idealism. I do not see how you can get a popular social idea and ideal merely by funding the discontents of economic distress. These afford an opportunity, but not an aim.

For these reasons, the first appeal of a new party must be to what is called the middle class: to professional people, including, of course, teachers, the average retail merchant, the fairly well-to-do householder, the struggling white-collar worker, including his feminine counterpart, and the farmer—even the farmer who has not as yet reached the ragged edge of despair. In spite of the disparaging tone in which "bourgeois" is spoken, this is a bourgeois country; and an American appeal couched in the language which the American people understand must start from this fact. Equality of opportunity is still an American ideal. The middle class is now concerned as to whether it will be able to maintain this ideal for itself, and it believes in a realization of the ideal for those less fortunately situated. A new political movement should aim to protect and render secure the standard of living enjoyed by the middle class and to extend the advantages of this standard, in both its cultural and economic aspects, to those who do not enjoy it. This should be attended with whatever leveling down of the idle, luxurious and predatory group such a goal necessitates.

I have argued that neglect of the consumer and his standard of living at the expense of fostering production is the ultimate cause of much of our present distress. This middle portion of the community represents most adequately the interests of the consumer. Moreover, in spite of what is said by theorists about the rigid division of classes and the necessary class conflict, this class is still fairly fluid. It reaches in both directions. It is the repository of sympathy for the under-dog. It is possible to mobilize this feeling in effective ways, and the attempt to do so is in line with whatever remains of the characteristically American tradition. This sentiment was the backbone of the Progressive movement of 1912 and of the La Follette insurgency of 1924. It cannot be argued that the abortiveness of those movements proves the futility of depending upon the middle class to form the backbone of a new political movement. The causes of their failure are extraneous to the point. It is true that the chief obstacle to a development of an organized liberal party in this country has been the hope and ambition of members of this class—and indeed of the laboring class—to rise to the higher capitalistic level. But aside from rude frustration of this expectant desire, it is this class which is most amenable to direct social appeal in the general social interest.

Although I have included the farmer who is not completely bankrupt, because of failure of banks and crops, in this middle class, it is true that the farmers occupy a peculiarly important position at present. In the North and West they have almost systematically voted the Republican ticket, in spite of the domination of that party by the interests of finance, manufacturing and transportation. This cleavage of interests is apparent enough to produce the insurgency of Western Republicans. It remains to drive home to the farmer the depth and width of this cleft. Take one example: the tariff. The farmer is beginning to realize that the price of most of what he has for sale is fixed in a world market uninfluenced by our domestic tariff, while the prices of what he buys and consumes are greatly controlled by a tariff which merely puts money into the pockets of the manufacturer. Farmers as a class have always been sensitive with respect to the politics of money, and the control of credit, and to the way in which their interests are affected by railway rates. In respect to all three things, tariff, transportation and finance, the farmers' interest coincides with the general social interest. Awaken them to this fact, and a new political party is on the way.

I hope that the fact that I have not so far mentioned the industrial wage earner will not be taken as a sign that I do not consider him and his interests of fundamental importance. No movement can ultimately succeed that has not enlisted the hearty support of labor. But in initiating the movement, we should not be misled by a supposed analogy with British conditions. There are three factors in the growth of the British Labor party which do not exist here. The racial homogeneity of Great Britain is lacking here; the new party in Great Britain had the aggressive support of organized trade unions. The American Federation of Labor is officially no more than lukewarm to political action. And the British Labor party had an organized cooperative movement of producers and consumers to rely upon. There is no corresponding body in this country. It is not, then, because I happen to belong to the middle class that I have emphasized the need for appealing to it as of initial importance.

Appeal must be simultaneously made to labor. There are enough lines of approach and methods of contact. There are the yellow-dog contracts, the abuse of the injunction power by courts; there is unemployment, the general absence of stability and security and the failure of both old parties to do anything except make a few temporary concessions in times of a critical emergency; there are old-age pensions and guaranteed adequate aid in times of illness and incapacitation; there is the whole question of inequity in the distribution of national income. Running through all of these is the fundamental question of obtaining and maintaining a reasonable standard of living, including the present underconsumption of cultural as well as of material goods. The appeals are numerous and the causes they embody are so urgent as to be heart-rending.

The elements of the population which are the potential constituents of a new party are numerous enough to justify the enterprise of launching one. The needs of these elements and their troubles call aloud for political action. The difficulty and doubt do not lie on that side. They concern the energy, the willingness for sacrifice and power of cooperation on the part of those who have vision and sympathy.

IV. Policies for a New Party

Insurgents of both parties in the Senate have united in calling a conference to consider some "economic and political problems affecting the welfare of every citizen, which must be solved if this Republic is to endure." The conference will have been held before this article is published, but its opening statement will become historic. "In the midst of depression this country is without effective political or economic leadership." These words are an authoritative statement of the fact upon which this series of articles is based. The further fact that the call for the conference emphasizes its non-partisan character is a reenforcement of the claim that the old parties and the party system operated by them have broken down.

It is significant also that throughout the call the words economic and political are everywhere conjoined. Four of the five problems chosen for discussion are economic: the fifth, "return to representative government," is political. And the political issue only states the conclusion that follows from the economic issues. Why does there have to be a "return"? What has caused the departure from representative government which makes a return necessary? Everybody knows the implication of the political demand. Economic privilege has taken possession of government.

It is because of this fact that the real issues of the day cannot be considered and solved separately. The whole is greater than the mere sum of its parts. I stated publicly some time ago that "the dominant issue is bigger than the tariff, public ownership of modern utilities, transportation and just taxation combined." The people must be persuaded to see these questions in relation to one another, as aspects of one inclusive and overshadowing issue: Are the people of the United States to control the government and to use it in behalf of the peace and welfare of society; or is control to continue to pass into the hands of small, powerful economic groups which use the machinery of administration and legislation for their own purposes?

Were it only a matter of using legislation to get this or that remedial measure passed, I should be willing to believe that a union of progressives from both parties might be effective. But to get one measure enacted requires the cumulative force of a people aroused to an underlying and inclusive issue. For many years, taxation on land values has been urged; it has the weight of the best economic opinion behind it—not indeed in the form of the "single tax," but as a taxation of socially created values. Its justice and its importance are evident to any clear-thinking person who is not swayed by self-interest. Why has it made so little progress? I think it is because as an isolated issue it is impotent against the entrenched economic forces of privilege which would suffer if it were made a law. Only when it unites with other issues in one overpowering fundamental issue can it gain the power needed to sweep away the forces that obstruct it. The enemy is one, for its elements are combined to maintain economic privilege in control of government.

I see no difference between this case and that of the tariff, the power issue, insecurity of unemployment and basic relief of the farmer. Divide and conquer is a good policy for the opposition;

it is fatal for the progressive human cause to believe that it can divide itself into partial issues and win any significant victory. Unite the different streams and you will have a flood that will sweep away every obstruction. Division, however, will only continue the past futility of progressivism.

Even if remedial action is successfully taken on some one point, it will not amount to much in the end unless it is an integral part of a larger movement. Organized business is elastic and adaptable. It gives way in one place only to bulge out in another. How many "reform" causes have been adopted in the past only to become relatively impotent in the end? Industrial and financial interests have fought them, or circumvented them, or even used them for their own purposes. Though many a reform is denounced as "anarchistic," or fatal to a republican form of government, in a few years it becomes part and parcel of the accepted and unchanged business regime. It is no wonder the people have grown weary and cynical about the value of such reforms.

Again, no movement gets far on a purely intellectual basis. It has to be emotionalized; it must appeal to the social imagination. A certain number of persons can get excited about Muscle Shoals, or about the attempts to grab a monopoly of water power in Montana or Virginia. Pool these problems together under the title of "superpower" and to most people it is a relatively technical issue with details too numerous to remember for any length of time. How many persons now recall what the issue was in Montana, or why some employees of the Power Commission at Washington were dismissed?

Everything points to a single conclusion. The only way to achieve any lasting reform is to find the one great issue on which all others converge. You can then show how special issues are parts of it, and can make your more intellectual appeals. Flags and flag waving *are* necessary, not because, as Carlyle said, people are mostly fools, but because man is so constituted that every great movement in history has owed its force to the stirring of emotion.

Democracy was once such a cause. Equal opportunity for everyone to better his condition and that of his children brought hundreds of thousands to this country and led them to give it their devoted allegiance. Though the words have lost their magic, their fundamental meaning remains, and the problem is to translate them into terms that signify something vital in the present complex situation. All great powers of the past, political and ecclesiastic, have had their day and then fallen into complete or partial obscurity. For their power was not inherent, but was derived from the passivity and submission of the elements over which they exercised dominion. So it is today with dominant economic power, in spite of all its ramifications and its subtle methods of control. It endures not of its own might but by grace of those who do not care, or who hope to draw profit from it themselves. A political change cannot be produced offhand. But there are times when a large number of social tendencies previously more or less separated draw together, and masses of people feel, even if they do not clearly see, their unity. Such a time is here.

In order to be workable, the policies of a new political movement must be elastic and must have unified appeal. Recovery of the agencies of the government by the national community for the service of the nation meets both conditions. It is neither rigid and doctrinaire nor so vague that it cannot be translated into definite legislative measures. It is not committed to any dogma about ultimate ideals, nor to any preordained theoretical scheme as to the way in which desirable social changes must be brought about. Negatively, there is a foe that can be located and identified. The usurpation of functions of government by an economic group in its own interests gives the opportunity for aggressive attack; and a sense of conflict and battle is a necessary part of any movement which enlists the imagination and the emotions. Much of the confusion and fatigue of tired liberals has been due to the fact that they felt the situation to be so complicated that they could not focus their attack. The present depression has made clear the incapacity of captains of industry and finance to lead the social host into anything but chaos, suffering and insecurity.

Mere attack without a constructive counterpart is always futile in the long run. The recovery of the agencies of legislation, administration and judicial decision to serve social ends, which the Preamble to the Constitution declares to be the object of government, translates itself almost automatically into terms of a flexible political program. No commitment to dogma or fixed doctrine is necessary. The program can be defined in terms of direct social needs and can develop as these change. While opportunistic in application, it will be definite and concentrated in purpose. It will not get lost in a dispersed inventory of scattered items of reform so long as it sticks to the unifying principle of the use of government to effect the subordination of economic forces to the maintenance of human justice and happiness. The unregulated play of these forces has brought us to our present condition. Even if the leaders of finance and industry were so frightened by the work they have accomplished as to make an effort at coordination and stabilization, governmental action must come into play. President Hoover's constant appeal to self-reliance, enterprise, private initiative, is simply puerile; it is a voice from the grave in which human hopes and happiness are buried. Not that these words do not represent excellent qualities, but that their exercise *under existing conditions* is just what has brought society to its present catastrophe. Governmental action is necessary to change these conditions and give them a new direction; only then can the honored qualities have a chance for expression.

Since the specifications of the general program must develop immediately out of the needs and troubles of society, they will be elastic and growing. But the needs and troubles are now sufficiently evident so that some of the specifications are clearly indicated. Big power occupies the same strategic position today that the railways did fifty years ago. The whole industrial development of the future (as well as a multitude of domestic amenities and comforts) is bound up with the question of whether the generation and distribution of power is to be in the hands of finance or is to be controlled, and, if ownership is necessary to ensure adequate control, owned by society organized to protect itself. President Hoover has denied that he is acting in behalf of the power interest. His personal intent is of no importance in comparison with the fact that his entire belated philosophy leads his *actions* to the support of that interest.

It is impossible to think of power and its relation to public utilities without thinking of how largely the orgy of the stock market of defunct "prosperity" was turned into a funeral wake by the stock jobbing connected with the power interests. Stock holding, with its attendant buying and selling, is, I am competently informed, the greatest single industry in these United States. The issuance of securities needs regulation. It would be a good deal to expect that those who profit by manipulation will undertake this regulation. In default of such action, the millions who are now the victims of this lack of regulation cry out for governmental control. Only those expert in economics can work out the means of such regulation. But adequate publicity, "cards on the table" as Robert Hallowell said, is clearly one factor in the program.

Since private control of natural resources, of the land with its mines, mineral deposits, water power, oil, natural gas, is the stronghold of monopolistic privilege, it must be attacked in its fortress. Society always controls the agency of taxation; taxation of land values, which are due to the requirements of society, is the only adequate method. Since industry under present conditions is dependent upon transportation and communication, since the consumer as well is at the mercy of the same agencies, and since these agencies tend automatically to become monopolistic, they must, by municipal, state and federal action, pass into the hands of the public.

Control of opinion is the greatest weapon of anti-social forces. We are ruled by headlines, publicity agents and "counsellors of public relations." Propaganda can be attacked and its force weakened only by one agency—informed publicity. The steady encroachment by organized capital upon guaranteed civil liberties can be met only by organized vigilance in behalf of free speech, free press and peaceable assembly. The forces which are undermining these instrumentalities, upon which all other forms of freedom depend, are so subtle and efficient that there is no hope of recovering these fundamental rights, unless they are made an open issue. A free circulation of the pure air of intelligence is a prerequisite in any attempt to cleanse society of its corruptions and enable it to lift its load of oppression.

We have long been without leadership in international affairs. Some progress has been made in the interests of peace, and our relations with the countries to the south of us have undergone a degree of improvement. But the absence of war and military intervention is not the equivalent of genuine peace. The source of our imperialism, at best only transferred from armed intervention into more subtle channels, lies, as everybody knows, in industry and finance moved by desire for personal gain. The interest of normal industry is in the direction of friendly and cooperative relations with other countries. But this general interest is constantly interfered with and deflected by special interests of finance and by monopolists of natural resources who call upon the government to protect them by diplomacy or force. Every imperialistic adventure on our part produces resentment in other countries; it degrades their standard of living and operates to reduce the market for foreign consumption of goods produced by normal industry in this country—and all to enrich a few already endowed beyond the limits of rational use, and to feed their fever for inordinate power. Our mad rush for economic hegemony is retarding the normal growth of industry in Great Britain and Germany; in the end, if continued, it is bound not only to destroy our foreign market, but to throw Europe into a condition ripe for revolution. The question of reparations to Germany and debts owed us by our late allies is allowed to drift. A new party must have a sincere and clear-cut policy as to our international relations.

There are many matters not mentioned which are incidents of general policy. They will almost take care of themselves as the general movement gains momentum. The question of proper surtaxes on the higher brackets of income is an instance of what I mean, and so are death duties on vast fortunes. Action in behalf of social well-being requires money. Recognition of this fact by the wealthy is one of the chief causes of opposition to the extension of public responsibilities and to a decent relief of suffering. A public awake to the control of government in behalf of social needs will recognize this fact as surely as does Mr. Mellon. The unemployment issue is another instance. Something will be done in any case. But the thoroughness with which anything is done will depend upon whether the measures are a sop, or are part of a general policy. The ultimate problem is not one of unemployment, but of opportunities for stable and secure employment. The national income of some ninety billions is adequate to take care of the situation. Measures which actually effect its equitable distribution will give work to those willing and able to work; and only such measures will bring about this result.

I am under no illusion as to the obstacles to be overcome in creating a new party to undertake the task that has been sketched. The task goes down to the fundamentals of social life. But in that fact lies the hope for its success. A movement cannot be created; it has to create itself. The issue is too grave and the consequences at stake too momentous to permit half-measures. Those who suppose that with a little patching up here and there things can go on as they have been going are under an illusion greater than that of those who believe in the possibility of a new political formation. If they cannot see the signs of the times, if they carry their resistance too far, their illusion will be rudely and violently shattered. No power endures forever—that is the one thing which history teaches.

When economic power is social and political power on a large scale and yet is irresponsible, a change from chaos and anarchy to order is inevitable. Civilizations have gone down because of eruptions from without or exhaustion from within. But a society possessed of science and technological equipment will not commit voluntary suicide. The alternative is planned economy. At present there are no signs that "business adrift" has the will or the intelligence to coordinate itself in the social interest. Politics on the other hand cannot do everything. Even if the Russian experiment succeeds in accomplishing economic planning by political means, Russia is Russia, and the United States is the United States. Starting from scratch, industrially speaking, with a people which lacks the individualistic tradition psychologically as well as economically and politically is a very different thing from reorganizing advanced industrialism saturated with traditions of liberty and self-help.

But a planned economy cannot come into existence without political action. George Soule has recently indicated in these columns some definite ways in which the government can intervene through boards of control. Industry self-regulating in behalf of social interest is a remote ideal. Even if the more intelligent among industrial captains were desirous of effecting a movement in this direction, they cannot accomplish much unless organized society lays down general conditions and provides a mechanism. The people's recovery of the control of government from the usurpation by interests which, as I have said, reign but do not govern, is not an end in itself; it is a precondition for the adoption of measures and policies which will make economic power responsible.

A planned economy will reverse the direction of our economic movement. Instead of throwing the whole weight of legislation and administration upon the promotion of production, at the expense of consumption and the standard of living, it will regulate production in the interest of consumption. Though we can repeat indefinitely the fact that our national income and technological resources are adequate to ensure a decent and secure living for all, we will not get anywhere until we are prepared to use politics as an agency for obtaining a distribution of wealth which will maintain a high standard of living. A planned economy, and industry and finance administered in the interest of consumption, are synonymous terms. This is the goal of a new political movement, as the need for it is found in the present disordered condition. The measures I have indicated are steps toward that goal.

Is There Hope for Politics?

The most marked trait of our recent political life is the growing disregard of politics. The disregard is shown in apathy, cynicism, and contempt. Indifference is proved by the difficulty that is experienced in getting voters to the polls. One out of two possible voters exercises the right of franchise. Even the last presidential election, which drew upon the outside interests of religion and personal tastes in drink, did not increase the ratio very much. There is no other country in which anything like so much money is spent in political campaigns, and there is none in which citizens are so apathetic about taking part in an election. To this indifference is added cynical contempt. There is apathy because the potential electorate feels that nothing in especial is gained by voting; nothing happens of public significance in consequence of approval of one party rather than another. But joined to this feeling is one of positive disrespect for politicians which reacts to create the belief that politics itself is an unworthy and low affair. "Politician" has always conveyed a sense of depreciation in this country. In latter years the feeling has deepened into a conviction that they are chiefly occupied with promoting their own private interests. Holding down the job is the main thing, and the public is thought lucky when the job is not also made the source of personal profits outside the official scope of the job. Politics is assumed to be so much of a racket that it is extremely difficult to arouse public indignation even when corruption comes to light. "What did you expect, anyway?" is the comment, voiced or silent, of multitudes of citizens.

The rapid growth of competing interests is one great cause of apathy. Interest in government has declined from the same causes which have brought about decline of interest in the church.

[First published in *Scribner's Magazine* 89 (May 1931): 483–87.]

There are too many other interesting things to do and to enjoy. When men gather together there is likely to be one conversation about the affairs of government to a hundred about automobiles and trips. Politics may appear on the first page and on the editorial page of newspapers, but the sport pages occupy more space, and the average reader turns to these pages with an eagerness which contrasts with the languid way in which he reads the political news and skips the editorials. At election time political speeches get the attention of thousands or millions on the radio; but dance music and Amos 'n Andy continue the year around. I should venture to say that there is more conversation in the homes of the nation about the fortunes of Amos 'n Andy than there is on any one political theme. And all this ignores the preoccupation of men and women with their own business and domestic affairs, which are more complicated and more absorbing than ever before.

By the side of the fact that competing interests are more numerous and more attractive than in previous times stands the fact that real governmental affairs are more technical than they used to be. They are problems for the expert, and experts are few. The raiser of sheep pays attention to the wool schedule in the tariff bill, and the manufacturer of dyes to the chemical schedule. But the tariff as a whole is so complex and its impact on the average citizen is effected in such roundabout ways that he gives up the whole matter in despair. This fact is symbolic of about every issue and problem that concerns the governments of the nation, of states, and of municipalities. Even the cities have grown so big and their public interests so multifarious and complicated that the average citizen does not know how to take an intelligent interest in them even if he wants to. The situation makes the opportunity for special interests to have their way, since they know what they want and how to get it, and the result only increases the distrust and disgust of private citizens with the whole business of politics.

And then there is the whole inescapable affair of prohibition. About that topic there is plenty of conversation wherever men and women gather together. It is both a political and a non-political matter. It is non-political in that it primarily concerns personal tastes and moral principles. It is non-political in the party sense, since up to the present both parties have either officially dodged it, or have given the prohibitory amendment and the Volstead Act their nominal indorsement. It is in politics because it demands action on the part of legislators and administrators. It is getting more and more in politics as it becomes not only a theme of eternal discussion, but also raises the question of whether a candidate is wet or dry.

The net effect is to obscure and deflect *general* political interest. The question of prohibition lies across all other issues and covers them from view. It does not line itself definitely and emphatically with any consistent set of principles and policies on other matters. The Democratic party in the South is dry; in the North and West, where it is concentrated in big cities and industrial centres, it tends to be wet. The Republican party on the whole is dry in the West and wet in the East. If there were a movement in the insurgent elements of the two parties, say in the Senate and the House, to unite in a declaration of common positive principles and in appeal to the public for support of them irrespective of party affiliations, the movement would be faced by the differences of opinion among the progressives on the subject of prohibition. And these differences would probably check organized union in behalf of progressive principles. There are those whose political history is distinctly conservative and reactionary who arrogate to themselves the title of liberals on the ground of opposition to interference by the government with personal taste in food and drink. These would identify liberalism with the political policies of old-fashioned "individualism" and thus use their "liberalism" to support and extend the *laissez-faire* policy of allowing big business to go its own way, unregulated by law and administration. Those who have been most active in promoting liberal principles in that loose sense attached to the word "progressive" are largely dry in *personnelle*. Prohibition thus cuts across definitely political issues so that there is little hope of interest in it arousing a wider and more intelligent interest in political life in general. In fact, I think it makes in the other direction.

Is there any hope in politics? Is there any hope *for* politics as a serious concern of the masses who are not interested in governmental jobs? These questions are not academic. Much less are they arbitrary and forced. They are, for example, definitely connected with the decline of democracy and the growing despair of its efficiency. For the theory of political democracy was predicated upon the assumption that with the widening of the franchise there would also go a wholesome widening and deepening of watchfulness, concern, and activity in the points and places where government in any of its aspects touches the life of the people. The contrary has largely been the case. The more extensive the influence of government, the more indirect and concealed do its ramifications become. That individual to whom I have made frequent reference, the average citizen, gives up the problem, much as he gives up the prospect of understanding the theory of Einstein about the universe in which also he lives. And as in the case of Einstein, attention to ideas and principles gets transferred into an exaggerated and irrelevant interest in personalities. Even were the level of intelligence of the general population as low as those assume who talk glibly about morons, boobs, and persons with eleven-year-old mentality, that level might work effectively enough when conditions are fairly simple. But now even superior minds are distracted and appalled by the intricacy and extent of the problems which confront society.

Is there hope to be had from the formation of a new party? The question is pertinent. A very considerable part of the apathy to which I have alluded is due to the feeling that there is no important difference between the two old parties and that accordingly a vote for one or the other signifies little. Shrewd observers tell us that a large part of the half of the electorate that does still vote is voting against something or somebody rather than from positive belief and expectation. Ten years ago the assertion of the basic similarity of the two major parties was a novelty. To-day it is almost a platitude, an accepted commonplace. Acceptance of the idea will be found in the most unexpected places, including partisans who vote the regular ticket from force of inertial habit. In spite of the stable hold of the Republican party on the national government, independence has grown to a point where it is the despair of old-line politicians. I cite three facts in evidence. One is the insurgency of individuals nominally committed to a party. Effective opposition to the policies of Harding, Coolidge, and Hoover has come largely from within the Republican party. The most important measures of the latter two Presidents have been shot to pieces from within the party; opposite policies have been kept from the statute-book only by presidential veto. The second fact is the election of Democratic governors in states in which the other party triumphs in national elections. The third consideration is the kind of treatment now given by the large newspapers, both in news and editorial columns, to political matters. Partisanship has not disappeared, but desire to hold the reading constituencies has compelled an impartiality not found twenty years ago.

Growing independence, hastened undoubtedly in many places (though not everywhere) by the enfranchisement of women, does not, however, guarantee either the development of a new interest in politics, or the development of a new party. There are many and long steps to be taken before the disgust of scattered and unorganized persons will be crystallized. The situation does, however, indicate that with success in the creation of a new party is bound up such success as may be achieved in renewal of trust in political action and in renewal of hope of something significant coming out of political life. To put the matter baldly and briefly, indifference to politics is the product of unbelief in the sincerity of the old parties. Nothing is hoped from them because it is felt that they are both the servants of the same dominant railway, banking, and corporate industrial forces. Disgust with politics, cynical acquiescence in corruption, is due to the fact that this covert, this unavowed, alliance of government in cities, states, and the nation with "big business" is known to be the chief cause of graft and loot in politics. There was a general resentment directed against corrupt politicians in the nineties and early years of the present century. The indignation which was aroused led to a series of political house-cleanings, more or less successful for the movement. Now there is wide-spread recognition of the fact that the guilty politicians are not the ultimately guilty parties. The political racket is a symptom of an underlying economic racket. Seeing no way to deal with the latter, it seems a saving of time and energy not to get too excited about the former.

This situation, however, does not make it any easier to bring a new party to birth. Indeed, it indicates the difficulty in the way of it. The radiations and ramifications of the economic régime under which we live are so subtle and wide that they create a feeling of general helplessness and timidity about the possibility of any significant change. The open flouting by Mencken and his followers of the idea of any real improvement in public and social affairs finds a feebler echo in the minds of "tired liberals." They would like to do something, but they do not know how to go to work nor where to begin. The whole situation is out of hand.

I am not content, however, to stop without pointing out that the revival of intelligent hope for and from political life is identical with the cause of creating a new political party. There are certain practical conclusions which follow from this unity. One is the fundamental character of the principles upon which a new party must be built. It must start from the fact that all vital political questions of the day have an economic origin, and have their impact where men live, industrially and financially, in the shop, home, and office. The principles and policies of new political thought and interest must not be afraid to borrow and to develop many measures which have been stigmatized as socialistic and which have been allowed, in their political bearing, to become too much a monopoly of a practically ineffective socialistic party. It is not enough to make the masses aware of the extent to which government has become an instrument of economic privilege, and to urge abolition of this control exercised by a small class in behalf of their own advantage. Negations and oppositions sometimes arouse temporary sentiment of great immediate force. But they are transient in themselves and in their effects.

I shall not try to write a platform which will fulfil the condition of basing political action upon industrial, commercial, and financial realities, instead of upon sham issues long dead historically. But certain matters may be pointed out to illustrate and give body to the idea. Modern business is carried on by money and especially credit. Those who control the giving and withholding of credit govern the country, whoever controls government in name. The government must resume in fact control of credit. Private, unregulated ownership of natural resources in land, which signifies mines, oil, timber, and water-power— which means, also, to-day, electrical power—must yield to drastic taxation of the land values created by the community and necessary to the healthy development of the community. Operations which tend to be become natural monopolies, like railway transportation, public utilities, means of communication, must come under a governmental regulation so complete as not to be distinguished from public ownership. It must be realized that civil rights, liberty of speech, assembly, publication, are not merely individual rights, but are essential to the welfare, the healthy growth, of society. Such points as these at least illustrate the nature of the principles upon which alone a new party can be built, while they demonstrate the fundamental and radical character of the political thinking which must be done.

The situation also discloses a fact important for the tactics to be pursued. They must be long-time, and at first primarily educational, tactics. I should have little faith in what a new party could accomplish if it came into power in 1932 or 1936. Past third-party movements have been ineffectual because they aimed too much at immediate success, and because these had done little preliminary work in thought, study, and the preparation of men able to carry new ideas into effect in legislation and administration. My statements may suggest to some persons a continuation of the tactics which rendered liberalism ineffectual in the fact. By "educational activities" may be understood a cloistered withdrawal from the scene of action, an idea that "appeal to reason" is enough. But such procedure is not education; it is at best a preparation for education, and is likely to be something much more futile. There is no education when ideas and knowledge are not translated into emotion, interest, and volition. There must be constant accompanying organization and direction of organized action into practical work. "Ideas" must be linked to the practical situation, however hurly-burly that is.

The thing which gives me least fear and discouragement is the statement, no matter how often it is reiterated, that such a movement can appeal only to a minority, and at the outset a comparatively small minority. In the first place, there is already political discontent and unrest among the masses. These need direction and organization, but there is something there to direct and to organize. Apathy is in large measure due to the fact that nothing fundamental, nothing sufficiently radical in the way of principles, has been offered. And in the second place, every movement of any account in the history has been the work of minorities. I do not agree with the statements which are freely propagated in the interest of reactionary policies about the low mentality of the masses. The adult is more apt to learn than youth. But the courage and conviction which instruct them must first proceed from the few. The question of whether there is hope in and for politics is finally a question whether there is a minority having the requisite courage, conviction, and readiness for sacrificial work.

Peace—by Pact or Covenant?

As I write at the close of the first week of March, a very different outcome for the Shanghai fighting may be envisaged. The talk about a truce and peace may come true. But it may also be true that Japan is repeating her previous tactics, and is drugging world sentiment into temporary quietude while preparing aggressive measures in the Yangtse basin. But whatever is going to be the outcome, there is great need that pacifists take stock of their attitude and come to a reasoned position toward their future action.

One reason why Japan has kept the world confused as much as it has succeeded in doing is because the very rapidity of her moves has kept public sentiment busily engaged with speculating about the meaning of each one separately, and has thereby prevented the formation of any settled unity of judgment about the course that best leads to lasting peace. Moreover, as I shall indicate later, this confusion (which has been such an asset to Japan) has been increased because of conflicting cross-currents in the means appealed to in behalf of peace.

Since I am writing from the standpoint of the Pact of Paris, I may properly preface my remarks by saying that I feared from the start that the Pact was prematurely adopted. For its power lies wholly in the moral force of the peoples behind it, and there was no adequate evidence that the education of the peoples regarding its meaning had been anything like adequately completed when the Pact was officially signed. The Pact should have been the conclusion of an irresistible public demand; to a considerable extent it was the termination of the maneuvers of diplomats. There has, therefore, always been the danger that official

[First published in *New Republic* 70 (23 March 1932): 145–47.]

adoption of the outlawry idea would turn out to be an embalming of the idea rather than an embodiment of it.

No matter whether the Japanese have reached the end of their campaign or are just beginning to do for the whole Yangtse Valley what they have already done for Manchuria, the need is great to centralize public sentiment about the principle of outlawry. Prevailing feeling is fairly well represented by the saying that the Paris Pact did not prevent war; it only prevented a declaration of war. This seeming relegation of the Pact to the realm of dishonored scraps of paper presents, however, material for serious consideration. It cannot be repeated too often that outlawry signifies the withdrawal of juridical status from the war *system*, not the outlawry of a nation which goes to war, whether with or, as has been the habit of Japan, without a declaration of war. The acceptance of outlawry in the Peace Pact of Paris thus gives an entirely novel status to her adventures in Manchuria and the Yangtse Valley. If there had been a state of war under the old regime, Japan's action would have been legally regularized. Even if she had been subjected to moral condemnation by some or many persons, her activities would have been in accord with the principle that war is the ultimate arbiter of legal international justice, the last court of juridical resort in the settlement of disputes.

Under the regime that preceded the Paris Pact, other nations would have been obliged to take official cognizance of the state of war. They would undoubtedly have done so by proclamations of neutrality. But popular sentiment of the different nations would have taken sides; commercial and financial interests would have moved in one direction or the other; the anti-Chinese antipathies of British Tories and the pro-Japanese sympathies of French diplomatists would have had surer occasion to express themselves, and, presumably, there would have been contrary movements in this country.

The history of the World War shows how precarious is the preservation of neutrality under modern conditions of intercourse. We can at least say that the juridical nonexistence of war has helped save other nations from the strain which would have occurred without the existence of the Peace Pact. Nor has the general absence of the war spirit in other countries and the failure so far to inoculate the peoples with war fever been due

wholly to the memory of the last War. The Paris Pact has operated as a constant reminder that we have at least committed ourselves nominally to living in a different sort of a world. And there
is some gain in the fact that Japan, instead of being engaged in
sending abroad idealistic reasons as to why she is at war, has to
content herself with explaining that she is not at war at all. Spontaneous ridicule is not the least effective among the moral forces
of the world.

I have not yielded in what I have just said to the temptation,
natural to one who believes strongly in the outlawry idea, to indulge in a Pollyanna justification of it. One may point to certain
gains without holding that the Paris Pact has emerged with complete glory. Some months ago, Salmon O. Levinson, the original
instigator of the outlawry movement, proposed what he termed
a "peace sanction" in lieu of the sanctions of force. He proposed
that the nations signing the Paris Pact should follow up their signature with an express declaration that all "exactions, territorial
acquisitions or rights obtained by occupation or seizure by war,
or under the menace of war, or in the presence of armed force,
are null and void under the pact of Paris." No general and concerted action in this direction has taken place. But a significant
step has been taken. Secretary Stimson in his note of January 7 of
this year (repeated in his letter to Senator Borah of February 24)
said that our "government would not recognize any situation,
treaty or agreement entered into in violation" of the Nine Power
Pact and the Paris Pact, and went on to indicate (and virtually to
invite other nations to say) that similar action by other nations
would effectively bar any title obtained by pressure and treaty
violation.

There is another passage in Secretary Stimson's letter which
does not appear to have received the attention it merits. Speaking of the Far Eastern situation as it now exists, he says:

> It is not necessary in that connection to inquire into the
> causes of the controversy or attempt to apportion the blame
> between the two nations which are unhappily involved; for,
> regardless of cause or responsibility, it is clear beyond per-
> adventure of a doubt that a situation has developed which
> cannot, under any circumstances, be reconciled with the obli-
> gations of the covenants of these two treaties.

Under the international law which obtained prior to the signing of the Paris Pact, diplomats and public opinion would have had no other alternative save to consider causes and to apportion blame. There has been, of course, considerable discussion attempting to perform these two tasks. But under the Pact of Paris it is irrelevant and immaterial. Every article discussing the illegal acts of China which gave provocation to Japan has only distracted attention from the one important fact, namely, that Japan was seeking redress by means which she in common with other nations had solemnly disavowed. There is nothing surprising in the fact that Japan has tried to fix the attention of the world on these matters of antecedent provocation. The fact that so many publicists have been misled into playing Japan's game only shows that the public's grasp on and belief in the Kellogg-Briand Pact is still lamentably superficial.

Still more lamentable, and for the reason that it indicates neglect of and lack of understanding of the Pact, is the fact that public sentiment on the whole has been more stirred by danger to American national life and property than it has been by Japan's flouting of the pledged word upon which the peace of the world must rest. To vast numbers there is something more dramatic, more appealing, in a threat of danger to an American life than there is in a threat to the solemn engagements into which the nations of the world have entered. The old ethic of national honor and defense of prestige still bulks largest in public imagination. There has developed as yet no dramatic identification between national honor and the international agreement to abandon all but pacific means of settling disputes. The fact that Secretary Stimson in the letter to Senator Borah resorted to an implicit threat of building a big navy and of fortifying Far Eastern possessions is something which weakens the other appeal which has just been mentioned. It mixes an appeal to force with an appeal to observe the pledge to employ only pacific means.

The only conclusion to be drawn from the facts of the situation, both those indicative of the value of the Pact in an emergency and those unfavorable to its constructive power, is plain. Lovers of peace should concentrate attention upon the Peace Pact; they should deny themselves the use of all methods of agitation and appeal which are contrary to its letter and spirit. If this were done, the work of public education which was interrupted by the more or less premature official adoption of the Pact would be reundertaken and carried on more vigorously than before. In this case, the Far Eastern embroilment will strengthen the force of the Pact instead of weakening or perhaps destroying it. For the point to be kept steadily in mind is the permanent bearing of the Far Eastern conflict upon the peace machinery of the world. This effect is more important than any other phase of the present armed struggle. I would not yield to any one in sympathetic appreciation of the human tragedy enacted in and around Shanghai. But if we get so stirred up by the scene of death and destruction that we lose sight of its basic cause, the war system, we shall in the end only confer added force upon this system.

A further point is that effective action for peace has been confused and hampered because of diverse currents among the advocates of peace. The simple fact is that different machines in the world's peace machinery have got in one another's way and have thereby slowed down if not stalled the operation of the machinery. I would not be guilty of using the present situation to discredit the League of Nations. I believe that some of its inefficacy is due to the failure of our own government to cooperate heartily in the early stages of the Manchurian invasion. The appointment of General Dawes turned out to be an empty gesture and his conduct gave Japan an early understanding of its emptiness, upon which she at once acted. On the other hand, some American devotees of the League have used the present crisis to advance the cause of the League rather than to serve directly the cause of peace. Article Sixteen of the Covenant is, together with the connection of the League with the Versailles Treaty, the great obstacle to the adherence of the United States. But it is more than that; it is also a great cause of the failure of the moral judgment of the world to base its condemnation of Japan wholly upon her violation of the Paris Peace Pact. MacDonald called the punitive clauses of the Covenant "dead wood." They are worse; they are foci of infection with that dependence upon force which is the essence of the war system. That they are ineffective because they will not be set in motion, I do not doubt. But, alas, they are effective in another respect. They prevent the resolute and unanimous dependence of the nations of the world upon enlightened public judgment. That in the end is the strongest force there is; all

treaties, including pledges to use the sanction of force and to resort to so-called international war, themselves depend finally
upon nothing but the moral force of sentiment and opinion.

I plead then for three things: First, that the basic idea of the
Paris Pact be put to the front and be kept there, and that all judgments and policies relating to the Far Eastern situation be based
upon it, and upon it alone. Second, that the Pact be carried to its
logical conclusion in a common statement of all nations signing
the Pact that all demands, acquisitions, pretended rights, obtained in violation of it, are null and void. Third, that the force
clauses of the League of Nations Covenant be abrogated so as to
bring the Covenant into agreement with the Pact which was
signed later, in order that the League influence reenforce that of
the Peace Pact instead of working against it.

Are Sanctions Necessary
to International Organization? No

The problem of the use of sanctions to achieve a peaceful international organization involves many questions. But two great principles run through the complexity of details and reduce them to clarity and order. The first of these principles is that the use of sanctions is impracticable, so much so that any attempt in that direction is sure to make international relations worse instead of better. Even the attempt to push it to the front in discussion is ill-advised, for it distracts attention from the measures likely to be of efficacy in improving the relations among nations. The second principle is that even if the use of coercive force by joint agreement were possible it would be undesirable, since resort to force fastens upon us the war system as the ultimate means of settling international controversies. "Enforcement of peace" is a phrase which combines two contradictory ideas.

I

In spite of Articles X and XVI in the Covenant of the League, the latter has consistently refused to invoke the use of sanctions. Its record in this respect is without a flaw. This fact is of itself evidence that the notion of applying sanctions is utopian. If the idea is capable of practicable application, how is the policy of the League to be accounted for? If the blame is put on the nations outside the League, it only becomes the clearer that nations are still so divided among themselves that the idea of combined joint action is utopian. If the claim is simply that the Council of the League has failed in its duty, this alternative only

[First published in *Are Sanctions Necessary to International Organization?* Foreign Policy Association Pamphlet no. 82–83 (New York: Foreign Policy Association, 1932), pp. 23–39. For Raymond Leslie Buell's affirmative statement, see this volume, Appendix 2.]

proves that even those nations which are most united among themselves are incapable of uniting to employ coercive force.

The statement that the failure of the League is due to the non-adherence of the United States deserves, however, particular attention. As I see the matter, the actual case stands almost at the opposite pole. As a matter of fact it is Americans, those advocating that we join the League, who are most active in urging the policy of sanctions. France is committed to the use of sanctions under especial conditions connected with maintaining the sanctity of the Versailles treaty, and with the added qualification of either an international force with its own staff, or military and naval guarantees from Great Britain and the United States. Some of the smaller nations that are satisfied with the *status quo* think sanctions would strengthen their security against the imperialistic tendencies of the greater powers. But in general the great powers are so much opposed to the invocation of sanctions that their attitude is represented by the statement of MacDonald that reference to them in Article XVI is "dead wood" and should be cut out of the Covenant.

The evidence of the steadfast refusal of the powers to resort to sanctions is found in the history of the League at every emergency which has arisen. Sober students and historians who believe thoroughly in the League have praised it on the special ground that it has resorted only to publicity, to conciliation, to the building up of harmonious public opinion and sentiment. Strangely enough it is only advocates of the League on this side of the ocean who criticize the League for failing to use coercive measures:—possibly because of their remoteness from the factors which actually control European action in international matters. I can think of nothing more unrealistic than urging the impossible—in spite of the appearance of realism which is said to attend the "implementing" by force of the conduct of the League.

Since I cannot go over the whole history of the League, I shall select one case which to me is typical. In connection with Locarno, Great Britain agreed to guarantee the Franco-German frontier, while refusing to guarantee the Polish-German settlement. It was everywhere admitted that Great Britain's attitude was dictated in part by the realization that in the latter case she could not carry the other members of the British Commonwealth of Nations with her. What then is the prospect of Britain's signing a blank check in favor of forcible guarantees to be applied all over the world?

And of course there are other causes for the abstinence of Great Britain. Europe is not a united happy family. Even the nations which were allies in the World War have opposed interests. It would be impossible for Great Britain to surrender her traditional foreign policy to the extent of actually promoting France's hegemony on the continent, such as would be effected if Great Britain cordially assented to sanctions in order to guarantee the war settlements in Eastern Europe. The rivalries of nationalistic interests, the sore spots, the resentments, suspicions, and jealousies which exist among the great powers make the execution of united coercive measures impossible; to try to use them would only increase existing antagonisms and fan a dormant flame into a blaze.

The particular point which has been mentioned is of course but one aspect of France's unceasing demand for a guaranteed security of the perpetual force of the Versailles treaties. As Walter Lippmann wrote in the *New York World* in 1927: "Substitute the word 'revision' for the word 'aggression' and the words 'maintenance of the Paris treaties' for the word 'security' and you have the real meaning of this interminable debate." Aside from the question of right and justice, conflict of interests will continue to forbid that effective unanimity which is required for the use of sanctions. So far as Great Britain and France especially are concerned, the situation was well stated by a writer in the *Round Table* for June 1928: "When the English-speaking world uses the word peace it thinks of a state of things in which not only there is no war, but in which the political structure is the result of general acceptance and is not merely acquiesced in because there is *force majeure* behind it. When France talks about *la paix*, she means rather the political situation created by the treaties of peace. It is a legal rather than a moral situation."

Suppose a case, apart from any reference to the peace treaties, in which Great Britain, France or the United States was pronounced in such default in meeting an international obligation as to justify, under the terms of the Covenant, an appeal to sanctions. Does anybody believe that they would be put into operation? And what would be the effect upon public sentiment in this country if an effort were made to set them in motion? Would the effect be favorable to the promotion of international organization for peace? If one will face in his thought the picture of the reaction that would occur here, the inevitable inflammation of nationalistic sentiment, he will appreciate the effect on any other strong nation of the invocation of sanctions against it. And why limit the scope of the nations which might be affected by it? In the minds of American advocates of sanctions there seems to exist always an unexpressed premise as to just what nation is to be the guilty party.

Let us take a less hypothetical case. Suppose that in 1929 Russia in her dispute with China in Manchuria had gone as far as Japan went in the same province in 1931–32. The feeling against Russia was, on grounds quite aside from her supposed action in Manchuria, such that sanctions might possibly have been invoked against her. But would it have been possible to convince Soviet Russia or her sympathizers in the rest of the world that the real ground for action was the alleged one? And how could the sanctions have been executed? How could they have been made effective? Is it not obvious that nothing but an old-fashioned bigger and better war would have served that purpose? And is it not highly probable, practically certain, that there would have been enough domestic opposition in various nations to prevent punitive action? Could labor in Great Britain have been brought to the use of sanctions?

For we are not on speculative grounds in dealing with the case of Russia. There was an economic "quarantine" of Russia attempted at the height of the hostility to and fear of her communism. Russia suffered undoubtedly; many persons were added to the roll of those who starved to death. But in the end it was unsuccessful except in embittering all Russians, independent of their economic philosophy, against the rest of the world. Even nations much weaker than Russia have the power of withdrawing into themselves and enduring until the storm is spent. During the storm, however, old resentments are renewed and the temper which makes for future war is fostered.

I can only conclude that those who mourn and who rebuke the League because it has not chosen to employ the sanctions provided for on paper assume a decadence of nationalistic rivalries and ambitions which does not accord with facts. They assume a harmony in the various Chancellories of the world which is non-existent. If the assumption of the existence of this harmony were acted upon, the action would merely accentuate the disagreements which already exist. There may not be the most elevated diplomacy in Europe which is conceivable. But its foreign offices are at least wise enough to realize the danger attending an appeal to sanctions, and hence agree to allow the clauses relating to it in the Covenant to become a dead letter. I can but believe then that the League has been well advised in putting up with rebuffs rather than to adopt the sensational and striking course of resort to coercive measures. That which is academic in American discussions would be fatal in Europe. Nor is the matter wholly academic here. Appeal to sanctions keeps alive and invigorates all the attitudes and convictions which have caused us to remain outside the League. Worse than that, it stimulates the activities of the extreme isolationists; it provides them with ammunition, and all in a cause which is hopelessly utopian.

II

In what I have thus far said I have ignored the distinction drawn by Mr. Buell between economic and military sanctions, in behalf of the former and against the latter. Is this distinction practicable in fact? Certainly it is not authorized by anything in the Covenant of the League. Article X declares that nations agree not only to respect but to "*preserve*" territorial integrity. There is no limit set to the means to be employed; to "preserve" means to preserve. Article XVI states the means to be used. Section one specifies economic and financial measures. But the impression that this section stands complete in itself so that invocation of economic sanctions may or may *not* be followed up by military measures has no warrant in the document. It is opposed to its express terms. The two following sections are integral with the first. For the second section begins, "It shall be the duty of the Council in *such* case to recommend to the several Governments concerned what *effective military, naval and air forces*," etc., while the third section obligates member-states to permit passage of troops. From the standpoint of the Covenant, economic sanctions are not a possible substitute for war; they are one of the instruments of war.

Those who make the distinction between economic and military sanctions may at least have something in common with the opponents of sanctions: They should strive to modify radically Articles X and XVI of the Covenant. Even then the question remains how far the separation is practicable, and whether the framers of the League were not sufficiently realistic in combining the two so that if reference to military sanctions is eliminated, economic sanctions should go too.

First let me say something about the prevailing use of the term "boycott" by the adherents of economic sanctions. Its use is not only loose but is actually misleading. A boycott is a private individual or group affair, non-political in nature:—a refusal to give economic patronage either to a particular firm or corporation or to business representatives of a particular nation. Its nature is indicated by the conditions of its origin in Ireland, and by Indian and Chinese boycotts. Neither the word nor the idea has any application in international affairs. *There* we can have only embargoes and blockades. In the Covenant there is of course no such loose and irrelevant term as boycott. There is "*severance* of all trade or financial relations"; "*prohibition*" of intercourse among nationals, and "*prevention*" of all intercourse between nationals, financial, commercial and even personal. The terms are sweeping enough to remind one of a medieval interdict. In any case, severance and prohibition mean embargoes, while prevention is meaningless without a blockade.

The question then comes up whether economic sanctions can be *successfully* applied without a blockade by land or sea: a recourse to war measures. I doubt if an answer can be given applicable to all cases. In the case of sanctions applied to a weak nation with the practically unanimous and earnest support of all other nations the threat of them might operate. But it seems to me clear that even with a nation which is weak (the case of Russia has already been mentioned) there is no assurance that the threat would be successful unless followed by war-measures, while it seems quite certain that the effect upon public sentiment would be to create great resentment and to foster militarism. The nation against which sanctions are used would feel that it had yielded not to the claims of justice but to superior force, quite as much as if it had been defeated in war.

In many cases, all the precedents go to show that a purely economic boycott would not be successful even against weak nations. I think of Turkey in its war of liberation with Greece. Turkey had constant clandestine French support against the help given by Great Britain to Greece; both the French and Italians joined in smuggling arms and munitions through even a blockade for the sake of profit. I can think of but few cases in which desire for profit and political rivalries would not go far to render a so-called economic boycott ineffective. Even in the World War, with all the military and naval resources of the Allies, the blockade of Germany, openly an act of war, was not completely successful.

There is a great deal of talk of a rather irresponsible sort, intellectually speaking, about putting "teeth" into the League and into the Paris Pact. Everything goes to show that *merely* economic sanctions would be a set of poorly made, easily broken, crockery teeth. Teeth in international affairs mean *teeth*—blockades and other war measures. Mr. Buell is quite right I think in taking the case of Japan as crucial. It is argued that if the League and the United States had made an early demonstration of the intention to apply economic sanctions in case China and Japan did not submit their dispute to some kind of adjudication, the Mukden incident would probably have been quickly settled and the Shanghai campaign prevented. It is of course extremely difficult to deal with historic cases in which it is alleged that if something had happened which did not happen, something else would have or would not have happened. The speculative character of the proposition is not reduced when Mr. Buell urges that the peaceful settlement would have been brought about not only by economic sanctions alone, but that a blockade would not have been necessary for the successful operation of the economic sanction. All that was required, according to him, was legislation prohibiting the clearance of exports to the "aggressor" state and the entrance of imports from it.

Speculative hypothesis for speculation, mere "prohibition" without "prevention" would not have been successful in deterring Japan from her course, while it would have created resentments most detrimental to the development of a world order and would have played into the hands of the military. We can be pretty sure that Japan would have withdrawn from the League; that, since the United States is the chief importer of her goods,

she would have laid up a resentment against us highly provoca-
tive of war, ulterior if not immediate, and that the outcome
would have strengthened the powerful party in Japan which desires Japan definitely "to go Asiatic."

A realistic appraisal of the probable action of Japan will have
to take into account her peculiar position and traditions. Westerners are likely to forget that Japan is not only an island separated from America and Europe but also from Asia, and that for
centuries she pursued a deliberate policy of seclusion and exclusion. It is impossible to exaggerate the effect of these conditions
upon Japanese mentality. The late war taught us how comparatively easy it is in any case for a government to control public
opinion by propaganda and by shutting out all news and information contrary to its case. The task is immensely easier to accomplish in Japan. Since the Japanese public believed with intensity of ardor that its cause against China was just and a matter of
national self-preservation, it is unrealistic to suppose that merely
passing laws, without a blockade and other show of force, would
have altered the policy of Japan, or that its effect would have
been other than to increase resentment and add to the prestige of
the military party.

The belief that this would have been the case is not a mere
matter of speculation. One hundred and thirty-five American
missionaries on the ground in Japan signed, without trying to excuse the action of Japan, a statement in which the following sentence is included: "Without necessarily renouncing the use of
economic pressure by all the nations against an aggressor as provided in the Covenant of the League we believe in the present
circumstances that the threat of an embargo against Japan only
serves more fully to unify Japanese public opinion in support of
the military policies"—a statement whose moderation makes it
the more worthy of credence.

The conception that fear of economic loss will deter any nation whose emotions are inflamed from conducting warfare is
disproved by all recent history. Japan is probably the only country in the whole world on whom such fear would have the least
deterrent effect. The dread of economic sanctions may be expected to have the most force in those countries in which industrial interests are paramount and in which they have the most
weight in civilian government. In Japan the situation is reversed.

Prestige lies with the military because of the strength of the feudal tradition, and the military elements are superior to the civilian in the cabinet. All facts go contrary to the belief that a mere legalistic gesture would suffice to swerve the policy of a country where the military have taken the bit in their teeth in a runaway race and have the support of public opinion. To argue for sanctions and "teeth" and then to stop short in their use is as impossible in fact as it is inconsistent in logic.

By retracing what actually did happen in Manchuria one can reconstruct what probably would have happened if there had been the threat by all the powers of economic coercion of Japan—supposing, that is for the moment, that all the powers had had sufficient unanimity of opinion and policy to make the threat. Day after day there were inquiries and protests. Day after day, the civil authorities made explanations, and gave certain conditional assurances about future actions. Day after day the military went ahead with their foreordained plan of campaign, leaving the civilian authorities blandly to explain that the conditions upon which their promises had been based had not been fulfilled. Events moved rapidly. There is no reason to suppose that Japan would not have followed the same course with a threat of economic sanctions impending until she confronted the world with her *fait accompli* in Manchuria. It is not a pleasant spectacle but nothing is gained by concealing from ourselves that this is the kind of world in which we live.

The retort that all this could not happen if the Paris Pact were implemented with force, or if the teeth in the Covenant were used, merely sets before us the original dilemma. Teeth that are not mere false teeth, only paper teeth, signify a blockade and a readiness to go as far as events make necessary in further use of armed force. If successful, it is the kind of "success" which any war brings with it, a success which events have demonstrated is *not* conducive to an organized world order, and which in the case of Japan would have left intense resentment behind and strengthened the supremacy of the military. Without the use of armed force, the show of economic teeth would have produced resentment without any practical effect in Manchuria, and would have left recourse to purely pacific measures in a position more ridiculous than at present. There is one fact that is now assured and not merely speculative. Japan is actually withdrawing her forces from Shanghai, and an official spokesman admits this is done because Japan incurred the "odium" of the rest of the world. Even if she had withdrawn under a threat of coercion (which with a proud nation like Japan is hardly likely), I submit that the after effect in Japan would have been a much sorer and more bellicose attitude than now exists.

It should be added that if international economic sanctions had been adopted, China could not have held aloof; she would have been compelled by forces within and without, to be a party to them. Japan has claimed that the non-official boycott in China was sufficient justification for her Shanghai adventure. Obviously if China joined in an official boycott, the alleged excuse of Japan would have been greatly reinforced. Her intensified sense of provocation would have been the basis for carrying her campaign against China as far as she wished. In all probability, her campaign would have extended up the Yangtse valley to Hankow; to Tientsin and Peiping, possibly to Amoy and Canton. All that China gained by refraining from a declaration of war would have been lost.

III

I turn from the point that economic sanctions cannot be severed from military and still be successful, to another point which bears upon their practicability. Before economic sanctions can be put in operation there must be a determination of the state against which they are to be employed. The term "aggressor nation" is currently employed to describe this state, and it is employed as if it had a recognized standing in the Covenant. In fact it does not appear there, the nearest approach being "covenant-breaking State." But whatever the term, the guilty nation must be settled upon. What is the basis upon which it is assumed that Japan could have been held guilty in time to arrest the Manchurian expedition and prevent the one in Shanghai, even if the rest of the argument for the efficacy of economic sanctions be accepted? The investigating commission to determine the facts of the case has only just arrived in Shanghai—in April, 1932. This fact is a sufficient commentary on the assumption that it is a simple and easy matter to determine the nature and residence of the guilt which justifies the use of sanctions. Doubtless the inquiry might have been expedited; that it could have moved as rapidly as the Japanese army moved, I take the liberty of doubting. And it would have been faced at every step by Japan's claim that the Chinese were the real aggressors, and by the claim that since Japan was being attacked she could not postpone positive action.

There is another special feature complicating the determination of the covenant-breaking state. In its exact form it belongs only to the Sino-Japanese situation, but something corresponding would be found in every complicated dispute between important nations. Japan's claim that China was the real "aggressor" is bound up with the Chinese claim that the treaties ensuing upon the Twenty-One Demands are not valid, because they were secured under duress—and also, as Chinese civilians unanimously believe, by bribery of Chinese officials. Anyway China served notice as soon as she could that she did not regard them as binding. What a fine situation in which to determine which nation is responsible! Imagine the enthusiasm with which France would greet a decision that treaties obtained under duress are invalid! Even as it is, the international commission will, I imagine, skirt this question, contenting itself with scolding China for neglect in observing her treaty duties. What it would have done if the imposition of economic sanctions and the outbreak of a general war had been dependent upon its decision, I will leave the believers in sanctions to pass upon.

IV

It is asserted that the failure to check Japan in her course has strengthened the idea that reliance must be placed on armed force, has weakened the peace movement and the desire for disarmament, and has set back the prospects of world organization. Specifically, it is urged that non-resistance by force has intensified Japan's faith in armed force as an instrument of national policy; has furthered the belief in China that international agencies cannot be depended upon; has aroused fear in Russia which finds outlet in increased dependence upon armed force, and has created unrest and fear of the consequences of disarmament all over the world.

There is sufficient truth in these statements so that I have no desire to deny them. I agree fully with the statement that "had the League and the United States successfully curbed Japanese militarism and secured a peaceful settlement of the difficulties between China and Japan, the international consciousness of the great powers, especially, would have been immeasurably strengthened, a fact which would have greatly facilitated the solution of other pressing international problems." But what does such a statement signify in and of itself save that *if* peaceful measures had achieved a peaceful solution, the state of the world would now be much more pacific than it actually is? So far as it is implied that appeal to sanctions would have "curbed" Japanese militarism (even if we go so far as to hold that the military would have been scared off from their adventure), or more generally still would have secured a peaceful settlement, the statement is either a *non sequitur* or a begging of the question at issue.

It is quite true that pacific means have not up to date been highly successful in restraining Japanese militarism,—although it is probable that there has been an arrest, since it is likely that original plans went much further than Shanghai. But the assumption that threats of coercive force would have really restrained her militarism sound to me much like the pleas we gave way to during the World War, that militaristic opposition to and conquest of German militarism would sound the death knell of all militarism. Instead we have a world more completely armed than in 1914. I submit that by this time we ought to have got beyond the notion that resort to coercive force is going to weaken the tendency to resort to coercive force; it only shifts its focus.

Of course the answer which is constantly made to this point is that there is a great difference between national and international force, between war as an instrument of national policy and international war; that what is now argued for is "international defense and international sanctions." I do not see that the analogy with the World War is at all weakened by this retort. Nations from the five continents outside of Europe were in arms against the Central powers. That seems to mark a fair approach to international war and international sanctions. In retrospect, however, matters look very much like an old-fashioned alliance for various ends of nationalistic defense and nationalistic aggrandizement. Although there was a "sacred union," the Allied nations do not seem now united even secularly, to say nothing of sacredly. The world has had its lesson as to the power of a union for the exercise of coercive force to create a real harmony of interest and purpose. A coercive combination against Japan might accomplish a decisive victory more quickly than did the combination against the Germanic powers, and with less suffering and destruction. That it would promote genuine world organization for peace seems to me as illusory in one case as in the other.

Since personally I do not think the argument that economic sanctions would cause suffering to the innocent is at all a conclusive argument against employing sanctions (provided there were assurance that they would really be successful in creating an international order of and for peaceful international relations), I shall only make one remark on that phase of Mr. Buell's argument. There are plenty of innocent people in the world suffering at the present time. There can be no justification for adding to their number unless it is clear beyond all reasonable doubt that the addition will really be a factor in promoting a genuine harmony of interests among the nations of the world. And that is just the point to be proved and which has not been proved.

There are certain other points in Mr. Buell's paper which seem to be irrelevant to the main issue, but which I shall touch upon for the sake of completeness. I do not agree with those who urge that resort at present to sanctions is a European idea and opposition to it is an American idea. As I have already said, it seems to me that at present Europeans are altogether too realistic to believe in invocation of sanctions, while it is American advocates of the League who urge their use and who urge us to join with Europe in imposing them. In this attitude these Americans are faithful to the role of Wilson in insisting that this factor be made a part of the Covenant. But it can be said with truth that American opposition to the idea of sanctions was a chief factor in keeping the United States out of the League, and that opposition on *principle* as well as on grounds of practicability was a decided factor in generating the American idea of outlawry of the institution of war—that is of war as a juridical means of settling international disputes. In so far, opposition is an American idea.

It is argued that it is inconsistent for those who oppose international sanctions to join in a *private* boycott of Japanese goods. On the contrary, except for those extreme pacifists who believe that any overt act which may inflict suffering on any one else is wrong, such a boycott is the only form that economic action against Japan can consistently take. It *is* a boycott, not a blockade. It does not involve even a suggestion of political force. It expresses moral disapproval in a way which it is hoped will arouse attention. The assertion that a private boycott runs on all fours with a political, financial and commercial interdict logically implies that Japan is correct in her contention that a Chinese boycott of Japanese goods is justification for armed retaliation on the part of Japan, and that Gandhi's boycott of British goods justifies armed retaliation on the part of Great Britain—a position which even the British party of coercive force has not taken in defence of its action.

My discussion would not be wholly ingenuous if I passed in silence over a phase of the argument which holds that as matter of fact the great nations did not hesitate to send military and naval forces to Japan in defence of their own national interests. Probably there are some who, independently of their views on the topic of sanctions, would deny this statement. I am not among them. Persons who support the intervention of the United States in Latin America have frequently justified our nationalistic action there on the ground that under the Monroe Doctrine we are really acting as a kind of trustee for European powers. There is another possibility: abstinence from *all* armed intervention. The same is true as to China. The sole alternative to conjoint coercive action is *not* individualistic national action; it is cessation of the policy of protecting, by means of armed force, persons and property voluntarily placed within a jurisdiction where they are endangered. If two great European powers were at war, the United States would not regard it as a hostile act if American property were destroyed when it happened to be located on a field of battle. The same principle can be applied in "backward" countries. All nations might suitably have joined in sending ships to evacuate all nationals endangered by local warfare, but such action as that, while appropriate and desirable, has nothing to do with imposition of sanctions; it is not "defensive" war, national *or* international.

V

The main positive contention for the use of sanctions is that the creation of a "successful international organization" is dependent upon assurance that there is a force at the disposal of cooperative action which can bring the peace-breaker to terms, and that nations will not disarm nor trust themselves to the adoption of exclusively peaceful measures unless there is assurance that an international force will undertake their defense. Short of an international force devoted to keeping the peace it is said that nations will rely upon their own force.

The argument appears to surrender the restriction to economic sanctions. But much more important than this fact is that in as far as it is admitted to have weight, it points straight to the French proposal for an international army and navy under the control of a general staff, while it rests upon the French premise that security is the all important thing, and that security can be guaranteed only by force. If security is the main thing, and if an international army will achieve it and if nothing else will, the conclusion seems to be the necessity of an international army. All the arguments which can be brought against the latter weigh against the premises from which it follows. The argument that international order and a coercive force to enforce peace are so nearly synonymous that we cannot have one without the other proves, if it proves anything, the necessity for a superstate with its own army and navy.

But even so, the argument that the use of sanctions under conditions which now exist is a prerequisite for the creation of an international order puts the cart before the horse. *If* there existed a general concert of interests and harmony of purposes, a specific international organization would at least be practicable of attainment, whether or not it were desirable; and its force might be directed against a recalcitrant nation. But to suppose that the use of combined coercive force is a means of promoting the formation of such an organization—to say nothing of it being the best or only means—is like supposing that individuals can be clubbed into loving each other. It reminds one of the statement given out by the Japanese that they were fighting the Chinese at Shanghai in order to promote the friendly relations of the two nations.

In connection with the argument that organization for coercive purposes (that is, the use of sanctions) is a necessary precondition of an internal order, Mr. Buell assumes that the opponents of sanctions believe that "good faith" will *suffice* to create such an order. I do not know who these optimists are, and I regret that I cannot share their optimism.

It is well-known that conditions can be indispensable without being sufficient. I do not see how world organization of and for peace can be brought into existence without the growth of harmony of interests and community of values along many different lines. I do not know of any single device which will bring it automatically into being. But I can think of no one thing more hostile to the development of this needed harmony and community than the overhanging menace of coercive force. All who oppose the invocation of sanctions in international affairs believe that reliance on informed public opinion and good faith is a *sine qua non*. They also believe that it is a power favorable to the growth of stable peace, while the use of force is by its very consequences hostile to such a growth. This brings us to the other basic principle: the undesirability of recourse to coercive force in order to accomplish international ends, of peace, even if it were practicable.

VI

While I sympathize heartily with criticisms of the dangerously exaggerated nationalism which afflicts the world today and agree with those who hold that it constitutes a situation close to international anarchy, I get the feeling in reading some proposals for remedying the situation that the attributes and activities of national states have been merely transferred over to some bigger substitute organization. It is extremely difficult to get away from concepts and modes of thinking which are sanctified by long tradition. It is much easier to seek improvement by

setting up some rearrangement of them in a new pattern than it
is to develop new concepts and to think in terms of them.

So in reading about "international war," "international defense," and an international order equipped with coercive powers
I cannot escape the impression that policies are being framed and
plans formed on the basis of an imagination still in thrall to nationalism, at least to that aspect of nationalism which enthrones
force as the ultimate arbiter. I realize that this feeling or impression is no argument, but I record it for what it is worth. In grandiose plans for the world-state, it is certainly clear that the start
is made with the idea of the state as at present organized, which
is then magnified till all states are absorbed into one. I cannot
think that emancipation from the evils of nationalism will be obtained by any manipulation of the elements which constitute the
nationalistic state, but only by development of that sort of interaction between social units and groupings that is exemplified in
the intellectual, industrial, commercial relations of the states of
the Union with one another. It is these interactions operating to
effect reciprocal advantage for all concerned that holds the states
together in unity, not any political entity superimposed upon
them and exercising coercive force upon them.

I do not claim the analogy is perfect, but I think no reasonable
person will hold that the coercive force of the federal government is chiefly or in any large degree that which keeps the various states together; or that it is a factor of any great importance
as compared with the bonds of common tradition, habits of
mind, beliefs, information, intercommunication, commerce, etc.,
which tie the people of the states together. Nor can I imagine any
sensible person today who, when he looks at rivalries of interest
and latent frictions between sections which still exist, would
urge as a remedy the strengthening of coercive force exercised
from above upon them. (We tried "force bills" after the Civil
War.) I cannot imagine such a person proposing anything but
means which will positively intensify the bonds of common interest and purpose which exist among sections. If civil war were
finally resorted to it certainly would not be as a desirable remedial measure but as an awful evil which had to be endured.

Coming to definite arguments, that in regard to the analogy of
international coercive power with domestic police power in the
enforcement of law seems to have reached a deadlock; the rea-

sons put forth by each side do not seem to have much effect on the other. I cannot refrain however from summarizing the reasons which actuate those which deny the justice of the analogy, since they bear directly upon the fact that international coercive force is a form of war—something admitted by both sides to be undesirable.

The most obvious, but at the same time the least fundamental, reason why the proposed analogy breaks down is that, with respect to the internal affairs of the state, there already exists a body of laws (common and statute) which determines both the material and the manner of the use of force; which decides, that is, both the objects for which public force shall be employed and the exact ways in which it shall be used. There is no provision that force may be used for any purpose which a court at any particular time thinks desirable. There is a large body of regulations and precedents which determine as narrowly as possible the circumstances in which and the ends for which public authority will employ force for purposes of execution and restraint. Police, sheriffs, and so forth, are so far from being allowed to employ any kind of force which they judge may be effective that they themselves act under laws which prescribe and limit their use of force. All of these precedent conditions are notoriously lacking in the case of the so-called police application of international sanctions.

I remarked that this particular defective analogy was not so fundamental as others. It points, however, to one which is fundamental. The reason why there are laws regulating both substance and procedure in the use of police force is because, within each state where the laws run, there is substantial agreement as to important social interests and values. In other words, the laws do not exist because there is the possibility of the use of coercion for their enforcement, but force can be used because the "laws" apart from coercion are the customs, the agreed upon modes of life, of the community; or else they are declarations of the recognized will of the community by *methods* which in the main are self-enforcing in the life of the community. Laws that are enforced are enforced because there is a community consensus behind them. The threat of force does not bring about the consensus. So at this point the analogy between the domestic police force and the use of sanctions as an agency for promoting the formation of a stable and peaceful international order breaks down completely.

The considerations just adduced bring us to the third element of difference. How can the employment of police force against individuals or at most small gangs be thought to have any similarity to the use of force against an entire nation? Not only would the domestic criminal, if known, be reprehended by all about him, but he is, if the force against him is successful, only an insignificant fraction of the population. If the population of New York State were practically unanimous in refusing to obey a federal law, it would not be police which would be called out if it were decided to use coercion, but the army and navy. The result would be civil war, not the ordinary processes of courts and sheriffs. There may be circumstances in which civil war is practically unavoidable. But I cannot imagine any one saying that it is intrinsically desirable or that it should be provided for in advance because such provision is a necessary means of promoting a peaceful order.

Although I am compelled to believe that the use of police force in executing decisions of courts and other legal bodies is necessary in every stage of human civilization so far attained, I confess I cannot understand the satisfaction which upholders of sanctions find in seeking justification for international force in the fact of police force. I am not such an extreme non-resistant that I believe we can dispense with coercion in domestic matters. But that the use of coercive force in domestic matters does an immense amount of harm, that at times it is doubtful whether it accomplishes enough good to offset the evil it does, seems to me clear. Ex-Justice Holmes is on record, if I recall correctly, in expressing a doubt on this very point. Doubtless there are still some persons who cling to the abstract notion of vindictive justice. But most civilized persons today are convinced that coercive and punitive forces are last resorts; that the necessity for appealing to them is itself proof that something is wrong in normal social processes, and that the social ideal is to find the measures which will change the causes which make the invocation of force necessary in particular cases. It is a strange thing to me that in the very country and at the very time when it is so tragically apparent that reliance upon coercive force in domestic matters is a broken reed, there should be an active agitation for treating appeal to coercion as the important and necessary condition of good international relations.

The arguments against the practicability of using sanctions overlap the question of desirability. To a considerable degree their use is impractical because the best judgment of the world instinctively realizes its undesirability. What was said about the practical impossibility of invoking sanctions against Great Britain or the United States may also be cited as evidence of its undesirability. But we may use another illustration. South American countries have not all of them as yet reached a condition of stability in their relations to one another. Disputes between them are unfortunately relatively frequent. How many persons even among those who theoretically give assent to the principle of sanctions would think it desirable that the United States engage in a boycott in every dispute which threatens peace between nations there? Is it desirable that the people of the United States should be so stirred up about the Chaco treaty that they would be ready to impose a boycott on either Paraguay or Bolivia, having first juridically determined just which one is at fault? Where is the thing going to stop if it is once adopted as a principle? And if it is not a principle, then it is merely a convenient dodge or mask for getting us involved in an old-fashioned alliance or war. I do not for a moment believe that it is intended to be the latter; I am speaking only of the logic of the thing. But I do believe that some of those who are ardent supporters of sanctions are still so much influenced by sympathies which grow out of the last war, that they, like the French, can imagine only one particular nation or set of nations as the "aggressor" and hence have never generalized the operation of their principle.

To the opponents of sanctions the points which have been made seem sun-clear. The upholders of sanctions claim, on the other hand, that there is such a real likeness of police force and international sanctions that the latter is as necessary as the former and of the same kind. It is claimed that sanctions and war are radically different. I believe that, however, the world will act upon the honored logic that if the animal looks like a frog, jumps like a frog and croaks like a frog, it *is* a frog. The definition of war is not determined by intellectual pigeon holes nor legalistic distinctions, but by the test of behavior. That which involves general interdictions and blockades, backed with threat of guns and explosives and poison gases, is none the less war because called by another name.

I believe that it is a tragic illusion to think that a sharp line of difference can be drawn between "international war" and other wars. The idea of war itself perpetuates that interpretation and treatment of international relations in terms of force which is the stronghold of the war-system. The custom of curing the bite of a mad dog by swallowing one of his hairs is innocent in comparison with the idea of getting rid of coercive force by the use of coercive force.

When the talk of sanctions is directed against a particular nation, it necessarily stimulates the war spirit in it and in the countries which contemplate the use of sanctions. The case of Japan affords a good illustration. The demands for invoking sanctions against her were, in the American populace at large, directly proportional to the animosity aroused against her. In order to have brought American public opinion to the point where it would have been willing to resort to sanctions, it would have been necessary to dwell upon the wrongs committed by Japan, cruelties, reputed atrocities, until a veritable war spirit had been created. The technique required would have been not unlike that used to create willingness to go to war against Germany, the technique which operated in the case of millions of peace-loving Americans. I am confident that there are many of our citizens, who a few weeks ago would have said they were in favor of a boycott, who are now glad the matter went no further than it did. The difference is that their emotional resentments have cooled off. I do not imply that emotion rather than reason operates in the case of those who argue on principle for the use of sanctions. But I do mean that the general population would sanction sanctions against a particular nation only in the case of long standing animosity, or else an immediate intense emotional outburst, against her. The idea that this state of things would be merely transitory, and that finally a remote impersonal machinery would set sanctions in operation without an emotional flutter in the breasts of citizens of the nations using sanctions does not agree with human nature as I am acquainted with it. One does not set out on a course of coercion to inflict suffering unless one is emotionally excited.

I stated earlier that I had no doubt that the course of Japan had for the time being at least strengthened militaristic influences in the world, although I held that the attempt to coerce Japan into another course would have only made matters worse. There is no inconsistency between admitting the harm done the peace of the world by Japan's course and at the same time holding that in the larger sense Japan's course has not been a striking success. There is probably no case on record in modern times when moral sentiment, public sentiment, has been so nearly unanimous and so spontaneously expressed. The sentiment and its peaceful expression did not cause Japan to desist. But the position of Japan today is not an enviable one, and while a sensible person hesitates to predict the future, there is good ground for thinking that her position in China for the future has been rendered less tenable than it would have been had coercion been resorted to. Japan is all but completely on the defensive in the court of public opinion. She has experienced a moral defeat. It is hard to believe that she can live it down without a change in her policies. Appeal to coercion would have convinced her that she had justice on her side; it would have solidified her intransigeant attitude. Now she will have the opportunity to stand all the hard consequences of her conduct as the consequences of her own conduct, and not as something forced upon her, in spite of her righteous conduct, by the jealousy and ignorance of a hostile world. And if we go outside Japan, I doubt if any nation on earth has had the desire to strengthen, to imitate the conduct which has brought such general condemnation upon Japan. As one who would like to see the real power of the League for peace grow, I believe that her failure to invoke sanctions, even if Japan did not desist (which she probably would not have done anyway) is a real contribution to the cause of world peace, since her action did something to solidify and express the moral judgment of the world. The settlement of disputes by peaceful measures, provided for by the Paris Pact, is recent; its significance is still far from having penetrated adequately into the public consciousness. For example, apologists for Japan as regards Manchuria still think to exculpate her from blame by making known the provocations she received from the Chinese. Admit for the moment that the case stands just as these apologists claim, and their argument totally ignores the fact that Japan has been arraigned because of failure to use the peaceful measures provided for in the Nine-Power Pact and the Pact of Paris in order to remedy her wrongs. In the degree in which attention is centred on this matter and is not dissipated in the consideration of previous rights and wrongs, we have a new situation in the world and one whose efficacy for peace is immeasurable.

VII

We come now to comparison of the value of sanctions with that of other measures which may be used. First, and with respect to the Paris Pact, I want to say a few words about the subject of "defensive" war. I quite agree with those who hold that "defensive" war logically implies "aggressive" warfare, and the need for some criterion for distinguishing between them. The original idea of the outlawry of war was to outlaw the institution of war and not just some special brand of war. It was pointed out that nothing could destroy the right of self-defense—the same right that an individual has, when violently assailed, to protect himself. This latter right does not depend upon making a distinction between offensive and defensive assault and battery; this is completely outlawed. So with war.

Unfortunately, however, there was not an adequate education of the public in the meaning of the idea of outlawry before its official adoption. Still more unfortunately, there were believers in the necessity of military force among the politicians of the world who strove to give the idea an innocuous meaning, and who tried to turn the fact of self-defense, which is neither a product of law nor capable of being abrogated by law, into the concept of the legality of defensive war. Influential statesmen anxious for the speedy adoption of the Pact indulged in ambiguities. Either M. Briand himself never fully grasped the idea or he was interested in mitigating its force. For in his speech of August 27, 1928, he limited the idea of renunciation of war in a way which left room for introducing the idea of two kinds of war, one of which was not outlawed. He said that it was "war as a means of arbitrary and selfish action" which was outlawed. And several times, as if for the sake of emphasis, he limited the significance of the Pact to "selfish and wilful" war, thus giving ground to those persons who claim that even under the Pact there is a place for a kind of war which is noble and disinterested. Moreover, a number of Americans who had previously ridiculed and opposed the idea of outlawry, and who were devoted to the idea of sanctions, seized upon this loophole; and, making it central in their interpretation of the Pact, brought forward the notion of "international" defensive war.

Consequently there is still an ambiguity in the Pact which can be taken advantage of to sustain the contention that the Pact itself demands international sanctions and war, unless the "defensive war" it permits is to become purely nationalistic. However, there is another and better alternative. That is to clarify international law so that the distinction between the right of self-defense and the concept of "defensive war" is made clear. Had this been done before Japan's incursion into Manchuria, every pretence on her part that she was fighting a defensive war and therefore had not broken the Pact would have been swept away.

The argument is made that the refusal of other nations to admit the legality of accessions of territory, or other gains, resulting from violation of the Paris Pact will not be adequate; that it is a half-way sanction, but *only* a half-way one. The argument is supported on the ground that past non-recognitions have not operated to prevent nations from enjoying the fruits of their aggression. The argument from precedents overlooks one important difference. The cases cited are refusals of recognition by *particular* nations, as of Great Britain's seizure of Egypt by France, of various undertakings of the United States with respect to Latin American countries. The refusal which is contemplated by the "peace-sanction" (originally suggested by Mr. S. O. Levinson, the author of the Outlawry idea) is one to be exercised by all nations in common, and one which, through the influence of Secretary Stimson, has been officially acted upon by the Assembly of the League. If there is no difference in results to be expected from isolated national action and organized international action, what becomes of the argument regarding the difference between national and international defense, national and international war? The logic of the argument from the failure of national non-recognition to the necessary failure of present and future international non-recognition compels us to conclude that the *only* merit of international sanctions is that it represents a stronger economic and military coercive force.

The argument that non-recognition of say Japan's position in Manchuria will not lessen the ability of Japan to establish herself there so solidly that non-recognition will mean nothing raises hypothetical questions. It ignores to my mind the slow but effective operation of imponderables. But speculative matters aside, it raises the question: Upon what shall those who desire a world organized for peace depend: upon force and the threat of force, or upon peaceful measures in the development of common interests and purposes?

"Peace-sanctions" are not "half-way" sanctions because they are not sanctions at all in the sense of those who argue for economic and military sanctions. For they do not involve the application of coercive force. They are sanctions simply in the sense in which undesirable consequences which flow intrinsically from the performance of an act are sanctions. If a nation obtains territory by means which are juridically banned, then juridically those gains are null and void. To some it will seem unrealistic to put faith upon strictly moral agencies and influences. But it would seem as if the history of war, the history of the consequences of the use of physical and coercive force, were enough to convince reasonable persons who want peace of the unrealistic character of any other means.

We do not insist that good faith and moral pressure are *sure* to operate, that they are bound to be sufficient. But we do say that the measures which can be taken in their name are more promising roads to stable and enduring peace than is recourse to coercion, actual or veiled. It is not now necessary to argue that the possibility of using the latter rests back upon the former, since the pledge to use coercive force depends for fulfilment upon the good faith of the nationals making it. You cannot employ coercion in an endless regress against those who do not observe good faith. Mr. Buell admits the point. "Admittedly all international obligations in the last resort must rest upon good faith and the force of public opinion." Since this is fact and since it must be the fact, we hold that consistent action upon the basis of the fact is the best way to promote the positive influence of good faith and public opinion, while the habit of continuing to think and act in terms of coercion perpetuates the ideas and emotions which sustain the institution of war. It correspondingly weakens the operation of the good faith and public opinion which are admitted to be the ultimate reliance.

Any one of us can sympathize with those who are impatient with the present relations of nations and who are indignant with those nations that, after professing a love of peace and promising to forego the use of warlike measures to settle their disputes, fail to live up to their good word. Their breach of good faith has the psychological effect of causing us to doubt the efficacy of all good faith and to imagine that the use of coercion is the only thing which nations will respect. But in spite of a reaction in this direction that is natural because of desire for speedy results, all history and understanding of human nature tells us, I believe, that the view is short-sighted and in the end defeats its own purpose. I am not convinced beyond every peradventure of a doubt that the Outlawry of War will rid the world finally of the war system. If nations insist upon fighting they will do so, just as individuals commit suicide.

But I am sure of two things: First, that if the peoples of nations *want* to have done with war, the Outlawry idea is the best method for giving expression to that desire which has yet been discovered, and, Secondly, that it is fatal for those who welcome the Outlawry idea and who believe in it to play, even in thought, with the idea of sanctions or coercive force. In so doing they, however, unintentionally, reinstate the idea of war and undermine their own position. Devotion to sanctions comes naturally and logically only from those who believe that wars are the inevitable way of settling disputes between nations, and who do not believe that the traditional policies of balance of power and alliances can be done away with. For, in effect, the enforcement of sanctions signifies only that at a given time and for the time being there is an alliance of nations which thinks itself sufficiently strong to restrain by coercion some nation from going to war or else to conquer and penalize that nation if it does go to war. Were it not for the fear that some one would think that I was recommending the idea, I would say that the conception of a *Pax Romana* can be realized more readily by a thorough-going alliance, economic, financial, military and naval, of the British Commonwealth of Nations and the United States than by any scheme of "international defense and war" yet devised.

VIII

In the long run, the efficacy of the Paris Pact, of the Outlawry idea in general, depends upon the growth of community of interests and purposes among the nations of the world. The Outlawry agreement, like any jural arrangement, is protective of interests that exist; it reinforces them with the power of pledged good faith. But there are definite measures which can be adopted that will add to the efficacy of dependence upon good faith and public opinion as expressed in the Paris Pact. I believe that if the energies of those who want peace were united to promote these measures, immensely more would be accomplished for peace than will be effected by keeping discussion and thought fastened upon the use of coercion.

1. The Covenant of the League, by modification of Articles X, XV and XVI, can be brought into harmony with the Pact of Paris. Unless this is done, opposition to the adherence of the United States will continue. The one thing most certain in our foreign policy is that we shall not assign to any group of foreign powers a disposition of our own decision as to our future course of action in matters involving war and the threat of war. Quite aside from the attitude of the United States, such action will prevent different methods and measures from assuring peace from interfering with each other and virtually encouraging war-like action—an interference which unfortunately took place in the Sino-Japanese embroglio.

2. There can be formally adopted as a part of international law the principle that all occupations, privileges, possessions that are effected in violation of the Peace Pact, that is by acts which are not consonant with the pledge to use only peaceful measures in settlement of disputes, shall be juridically null and void. The principle has been endorsed by the Assembly of the League and can and should be officially incorporated into international law.

3. There should be adopted into international law the principle that any dispute or controversy not brought to settlement

by the ordinary processes of diplomacy, or by mediation, conciliation, arbitration, etc., shall remain in *status quo*.[1] Doubtless this idea is implied in the Paris Pact but if it were made explicit and nations were to pledge themselves to it, a given violation of the Pact would stand out more clearly and the response of public opinion would be quicker and more pronounced.

4. The fundamental distinction between the right of self-defense and the concept of defensive war should be established in international law.

5. The United States should adhere promptly to the World Court to which should be referred, with a view to the enlightenment of public opinion and the unification of the moral judgment of the world, any and every case in which there is a claim that the terms of the Pact have been violated, when the question is not settled by the ordinary means of negotiation among nations.

Finally, it should go without saying that these measures are additional to and not substitutes for the increased use of all possible means of consultation, conference, mediation, arbitration, and all other possible agencies of peaceful settlement. Let us throw our energies into strengthening them and not, because they and the Pact have not as yet been completely successful, fall back upon the continued use of coercive force.

1. This suggestion like the one in the preceding paragraph is due to Mr. S. O. Levinson and was first made public in the *Christian Century* for February 3, 1932.

Address to the National Association for the Advancement of Colored People

I cannot come to you with the encouraging and optimistic word about the present depression that some persons in high places seem to be willing to offer. I do not believe, for example, that the children of the country were made better off by the depression because their parents cannot get work and so are compelled to stay at home—unless they are walking the streets. There are other features of it which do not seem to me as encouraging as some people in high places appear to think. I do think, however, that the depression marks the end of the period of illusions and hallucinations. There is a collapse which has demonstrated the falsity of the political and economic philosophy upon which we have been feeding. The paradise of folly in which we have been living has broken down. That at least is some gain. It is something to become aware of the need for new ideas, new measures, new policies, new leaders, to bring about a great social reconstruction. More specifically, I think our depression has compelled us to think more fundamentally on social matters, economic matters, political matters, than we have been thinking for many years. I met an engineer, a leader in his profession, a few weeks ago and he said, "Do you know I have only begun to think since 1932." I would not take his remark too literally because I knew he had thought very effectively; but I knew he meant he had not had to consider the relation of his work, that of the engineering profession, to the whole social and economic construction before that collapse of 1929 in the way he has to do now.

Now, this compulsion to think more fundamentally has also

[Address delivered at the Twenty-third Annual Conference of the National Association for the Advancement of Colored People, Washington, D.C., 19 May 1932. From an unpublished typescript in Group I, Series B, Box 8, NAACP Records, Manuscript Division, Library of Congress, Washington, D.C.]

the advantage of bringing with it a greater freedom not merely of thought but of expression. In that way it gives the minority, the oppressed, groups of this country a better opportunity to express themselves, their needs, their wrongs, their demands for greater freedom, a larger opportunity and a wider field than they have done in the past.

The conservative people, people who were in positions of power and influence, are many of them saying things today, saying them in public places as well as in private, that would have been regarded as highly subversive and dangerous if they had come from radicals a few years ago. There is not merely this increased opportunity for thinking and for expression of the result of thinking, even when it is critical of the economic and political order in which we live, but the depression has also disclosed a community of interest among all the minority, repressed and oppressed groups of the country. It has made clear that all of these groups that are suffering, while they are not suffering in exactly the same way, are after all fundamentally the victims of the same causes. I do not mean that I think this lesson of the community of interest among all these different groups of whatever race or color has been very fully learned as yet or that the consciousness of it has sunk very deep or spread very wide. But I think that, the fact that all of them are suffering in greater or less degree from the same causes has been made clear and that the recognition of that fact is going to grow with increased rapidity, sink deeper from now on.

Doubtless the group which you represent has suffered more than any other, more keenly, more intensely. Doubtless you are the first, on the whole, to lose employment and the last to be taken on. You are quite likely the last to get an equal opportunity to share in whatever measures of relief or constructive public work, to tide over the depression, undertaken. But none the less, the causes from which all are suffering are the same.

It may be said truly that all the laboring groups of the United States with respect to their power and ability to control economic conditions are in the same boat; while members of your group have been discriminated against more than others they are only experiencing in a more intense degree what all the labor groups, especially the unorganized ones, are passing through. So it seems to me that the lesson for one of these groups is the same that it is for the others. And so the things that I should like to say to you tonight are the same sort of things that I would say to representatives of any white group that is also at a disadvantage economically, industrially, financially, and at a disadvantage politically in comparison with the privileged few.

And while I am going to try to draw a few further conclusions regarding the political situation, I would like to say that I am very glad to have had the privilege of listening to the previous remarks (of George S. Schuyler) and quite agree with the speaker in thinking that economic organization which will bring men together for initiation, for organization, for self-management of their own affairs in industry, is more important at the present time than the political angle. Nevertheless, it seems to me that something needs to be said about the importance of political organization and activity if only as a tail to the structure of the economic kite.

The community of interest between the different groups that are under-privileged, in the struggle for life is indicated in our political system. In many parts of the country your particular group is more definitely disfranchised than other groups. But if you stop to look over the field you will realize that there are large numbers of white groups that are voluntarily un-enfranchised if not disfranchised. The average vote in our national elections is about one-half, fifty per cent, of those who might go to the polls and vote. That seems to me a very significant fact. Practically one-half the people who might vote voluntarily decline to do it; they disfranchise, un-enfranchise themselves. Why?

I know there is a great deal of preaching and urging and raising of campaign funds in every town and district and precinct. Yet with all that effort every other person does not go to the polls and vote who might go. Why? Because they are practically not represented, or worse than that, they are misrepresented by the major political parties of this country; and while they may be foolish, misled, there is an underlying instinct that under the existing conditions it is just the difference between tweedle-dee and tweedle-dum which of the two old parties gets into power. You may or may not have heard the story of the Englishman who wanted to know the difference between the Democratic and the Republican parties. An American gentleman said, "I will tell you. You see here two bottles, exactly the same size, the same make, with the same contents; but they have different labels pasted on them."

Under those circumstances I am not inclined to join in the complaints and charges against the intelligence of the group that stays away from the polls, if their only opportunity is to vote one of the two old parties. I do think there is a charge which might be brought against them, for not using their energy and influence to find a new political outlet, a different one, which would give them some kind of actual representation. It is sometimes said we need a third party; but as many others before me have pointed out, it should be said we ought to have a second party, for we only have one now in national politics operating under two different names. If you look at the vote which has been taken here in Washington, in the Senate and in the House, during the last session, you will find all the proof of that statement that is needed. There was, for instance, the Costigan-La Follette Bill, the first serious effort to give some federal help to those who are suffering from causes of unemployment, insecurity, that are nation wide, not merely local. The vote in favor of that bill was practically evenly divided between the two parties, and the majority vote against it was practically evenly divided between the two parties. There was the measure of Senator Couzens to make the rich, those who have enough income, pay income taxes, and bear a greater part of the burden of the country. It was voted down; but the votes in favor of it were again practically evenly divided between the two old parties and the votes against were also evenly distributed between the two parties. It was leaders of both groups that joined in the House a few weeks ago to add to the burdens of the poor men and the consumer by putting a sales tax on everything he buys, and it was the vote of members of both parties that put down that measure.

In other words, the elements that really have some regard politically for the interests of the masses of the people are not found exclusively in one party or the other. They are found in both while the machines which control both parties are equally united against all measures that would really help the common man of the country.

Under these circumstances, what is it that the two old parties offer for the minorities, the under-privileged groups of this country? In the first place, they offer a past history and name. The

Republican party has the advantage of the great name of Lincoln. An emancipation policy is the significance of that name for the colored group of the country. But we are living, my friends, as certainly all of us know, not in 1863 but in 1932, and the names and movements of the past while they deserve the admiration and respect and honor that we give to all great men and great movements, have no leadership, no reality in our present lives. They are used simply as a bait with which to delude the voter.

Then we have the idea, which is somewhat better than this attempt to stampede a particular group because of their loyalty to a great man of the past, that in the northern and border states where the colored population in many cases has actually or very nearly a balance of power in voting, that they should distribute favors, giving them to that particular party which in the particular locality puts the most colored candidates on the ticket or gives out the most jobs after election to colored men. I think that is a little better than simply holding out something that happened seventy-five years ago as a sufficient reason for voting for a particular party. But I also think it is a beggarly pittance when the only thing that really binds the members of the two parties together is to see which one will get to the trough first and closest to it and stay there the longest. It is not a very agreeable invitation to political action to be told that if you vote with this particular party you will be given a back seat somewhere near the trough, a little nearer than the other party would let you have.

What is needed is some more fundamental reorganization of political lines, some remedy for conditions that control economic welfare more fundamental than giving a certain number of leaders jobs; and, as we know, because of the refusal of the white labor group to go into politics through belief that they can get what they want by distributing their votes between the old parties, they are continually sold out by the political parties. In many of our great cities labor groups themselves have developed leaders that are expert in manipulating their followers in order to get money and power and influence for themselves.

Then there is another group that says, "Well, of course, our party has not done just all it ought in the past, but now we have a new man, a great man, and the party is going to change. This new leader is a real Moses who is going to take us into the Promised Land." The American people seem to have a wonderful fondness for being fooled in that particular way, thinking that some day, some time, a new man, as particular leader with better character, more honest, and more human and sympathetic, is going really to change the character of the whole party. I think the American people have been fooled that way almost often enough. There was Theodore Roosevelt who was powerful in the Republican party. No sooner was he dead than the very men he had been fighting capitalized his name, and influence to put over the very policies he had been fighting. If anybody can point to any permanent things Theodore Roosevelt or the Republican party has done he has better political insight than I have. Where is any impress he left on the permanent policies of the Republican party? And what goes for Theodore Roosevelt goes also for any other Roosevelt.

In short, the real political issues of the day are economic, industrial and financial, and both of the old parties are engaged in the game of hide-and-seek, hiding their own attitude from the masses of the people; and seeking constantly favors and campaign contributions and the backing of the business and financial institutions that really control our public life. Certainly, if any group of people should know that the economic, industrial issue is the dominant one in politics it is the colored people. Why were you kept in slavery except for economic reasons? What was slavery except a manifestation of the motive for private gain? Why is it that the denial of civil liberty, of cultural equality still continues, except as an aftermath of that economic oppression from which you once suffered? And this is not simply a question of the past and what holds over from the past. What is the economic order in which we live today excepting one of competition? Fundamentally, the disadvantages, or the inequalities— civil, political and cultural,—of the colored group, of every under-privileged group of this country, exist because we are living in a competitive order which, because it is competitive, has to set man against man, brother against brother, group against group. Not only that, but as the whole state of the world at the present time shows, it sets nation against nation—if not in active war then in that economic war of the tariff and of all the other influences that divide nation from nation.

Now, I submit to you the thing I would submit to any white

group that is also at a disadvantage, since your fundamental difficulties do not come through color or any other one thing. They come from the fact that in a society which is economically and industrially organized as ours is, those who want the greatest profits and those who want the monopoly, power, influence, that money gives, can get it only by creating suspicion, dislike and division among the mass of the people. A cooperative economic and social order is the only kind of order in which there will be a genuine possibility for equality among human beings irrespective of race, color and creed, and of the other things which are now played upon to divide people in order that a few may have a monopoly of privilege, power and influence.

Certainly, under these circumstances it seems to me the least that any group can do is cry, and act upon the cry "Bunk" when they are appealed to simply in the name of past history or when they are appealed to merely in the name of handing out certain special prerogatives or particular jobs to particular leaders if the vote goes in one direction rather than another.

In what I have said I have not, I hope, been unmindful at all of the special disabilities which the colored group suffers. I know how great they are, how serious they are, how they are intensified at a period like the present. But I also know that those who wish to keep power, political and economic, in their hands—political power that follows from the possession of economic power—believe in the principle of dividing so as to conquer. I think the leaders of the two old parties will be perfectly satisfied, I believe the big business which control the two old parties would be perfectly satisfied, if they can keep the different minority groups divided. They are perfectly willing that this group should support the Republican party and that group the Democratic party provided they can play them against each other and keep them divided, while the leaders of the two old parties agree in everything excepting in who is going to hold the offices the next few years. As long as they can keep the groups divided they can maintain control. In the degree in which all the minority groups cut loose completely from both of the old parties and join in some new party which will help bring about a social and economic reconstruction in the interest of a society which is cooperative and human, in that degree the day of economic slavery for the masses in this country will come to an end.

The Place of Minor Parties in the American Scene and Their Relation to the Present Situation

The first part of what I have to say is historical. It has to do with the part played during the last sixty years by minor parties in this country. The other part concerns the present day and the reasons which exist for believing that we are on the eve of political changes which will bring about a new political alignment.

Since the Republican party, although still a minority party, achieved victory in 1860, no party beginning as a small third party, as the Republican party did with the Free Soilers, has (with the exception of the Socialists and Prohibitionists) succeeded even in maintaining a continuous existence through a number of campaigns.

Nevertheless, the notion that the minor parties accomplished nothing of importance, and that they were led by cranks, fanatics, and wild men, is far from the mark. These political manifestations have undoubtedly attracted more than their fair share of what Theodore Roosevelt called the "lunatic fringe." But it was said with some truth that Theodore himself stole the political clothes of Bryan while the latter was in swimming, just as the latter had taken over the ideas of the Populist party, so that a common name for the Democrats during the time of Bryan's supremacy was "Popocrats." The minor parties have performed first the function of protest, of serving notice that there is something wrong in the social order; that there is a demand for more justice in social arrangements. And, second, in most cases, they have been influential in introducing new ideas and demands in one or the other of the old parties. They have left a decided impression on both legislation and subsequent party platforms.

[First published as Government Series Lecture No. 13 (Chicago: University of Chicago Press, 1932), 9 pp., from a 28 June 1932 radio address in the "You and Your Government" series sponsored by the National Advisory Council on Radio in Education.]

One of the most careful and thorough of the historians of American political life, Dr. Fred E. Haynes, says with great justice:

> Often short-sighted and visionary in their specific remedies, the leaders of the Greenback, Granger, Free Silver, and Populist parties were fundamentally sound in their opposition to the growing power of wealth. Their instincts opened their eyes to features in contemporary developments that were not discovered for many years by the people in the older parts of the country. It is only necessary to read the platforms of the minor organizations to find the origin of many of the planks that are later prominent in the proposals of the Democratic and Republican parties. For the most part these short-lived parties represent forward movements in the development of government of the people, by the people and for the people, rather than outbursts of fanatical reformers based upon the imaginings of poorly balanced minds.

An account of the vagaries of minor parties might be amusing. But the instructive thing is to give, as far as time permits, an idea of the social causes that were back of the parties which failed and to indicate some of the points where they left a permanent impress on subsequent political action.

Aside from the Socialist movement, which stands for various reasons somewhat by itself, there have been at least six minor movements since about 1870 which deserve mention, though most of them overlapped, merged, divided, and fused again both with one another and with other lesser political insurgencies.

The first was the liberal Republican and "mugwump" revolt. It began as a revolt against the corruption which followed the Civil War and as a protest against the policies of force and animosity employed against the seceding southern states after their return into the Union. By 1880, the end of the Hayes administration, their work had borne fruit. The "bloody shirt" ceased to be waved in order to insure Republican votes in the North; wholesale corruption was checked; measures for civil service reform arrested, if they did not wholly abolish, the prostitution of federal office-holding, especially in post offices, to partisan ends.

This movement was concerned with the machinery of government rather than with the social ends which government should serve. Not so with the other movements to be listed. The second began with the western farmers. Its first expression was non-partisan, the Granger movement which made a great stir during the early seventies. The farmers of the great wheat- and maize-growing states found their sale of surplus crops in the East and in Europe checked by high freight rates. They went into state politics under various names, as the Independent, Reform, Anti-Monopoly parties. They did not succeed in socializing the means of transportation in this country. They were themselves still too much under the influence of individualistic political philosophy even to aim at that result. But they did establish the right of states to control rate-making and to abolish discriminatory favoritism toward a few shippers.

This revolt overlapped the third movement, that of the Green-backers, and in 1877 made common cause with it. The farmer suffered from the reflex effects of the industrial depression and financial panic as well as from high railway rates. It was a time of industrial unrest, of strikes, especially on railways. The resumption of specie payments and return to a metallic standard bore heavily on the debtors. Westerners believed, and with good logic, that the legal-tender quality of greenbacks was a distinctly Republican party invention, and with poorer logic associated the high prices of the war with the use of unredeemable paper money. There was a cry for paper money to decrease the stringency and raise commodity prices. In the elections of 1878 the Greenback party polled a million votes. It brought the question of social control of money and credit permanently into the field of political thought and contributed definitely to the Populist agitation of the nineties.

It is significant that this and other minor-party agitations of the same period brought forward incidentally many issues which later assumed great prominence. Among them were prohibition, political equality of men and women, abolition of child labor, creation of postal savings banks, a parcel post, reform of education in an industrial direction, etc. On the side of political machinery, movements for the direct primary, for the referendum and the initiative, for popular election of senators, and even for the abolition of the electoral college were offshoots of the minor-party movements of the seventies and eighties.

The fourth movement to be mentioned was essentially a broadening out of the second and third to include an assemblage of economic issues, all growing out of the troubles of the farmers and the growing disparity between the rich and the poor. It raised for the first time on a large scale the cry of the privileged class set over against the unprivileged mass. Its chief political representative was the People's party. While dominantly agrarian, it marked the first significant attempt to bring together in political action dissatisfied wage-earners and discontented farmers. The preamble of the platform of 1892 declared that the convention consummated "the union of the labor forces of the United States." The climax of Populism came in 1894 when, during the depression, its congressional candidates reached a total of a million and a half votes.

The real victory of Populism, however, consisted in its virtual capture of the Democratic party in the South and West. The candidacy of Bryan in 1896 was associated with adoption of a large part of the Populist platform. His further nomination in 1900 and in 1908 continued, under changed and changing conditions, its essential philosophy, and consequently weakened, beyond the possibility of forceful independent activity, the Populist party as such. The eclipse of the more conservative wing of the Democratic party is seen in the fact that its candidate, Parker, received in 1904 a million less votes than Bryan got in 1900.

The Progressive or "Bull Moose" revolt of 1912 was the counterpart in the Republican party of the Populist amalgamation in the Democratic party. Personal elements entered in, but inherently the popularity of Theodore Roosevelt was associated with a belief that he would give a squarer deal to the mass of the underprivileged population. The demand for "social justice" was abroad in the land. For the time being it appeared as if there might be a logical redistribution of the voters of the country into a liberal party on one hand and a conservative on the other. Actually nothing came of it immediately save the election of Wilson on the Democratic ticket. In substance, however, the La Follette candidacy of 1924 may be classed with the Progressivism of 1912 as constituting the fifth minor-party movement. The fact that La Follette, with practically no preliminary organization and small campaign funds as compared with the old parties, obtained almost five million votes is proof that there is a large electorate awaiting a party whose economic views are believed to be more in the interest of the masses than are those of the old parties. But subsequent events showed that the time had not arrived for the permanent organization of such a party.

The various attempts which were made to unite the farmers of rural districts and the factory workers of the cities were continued in the formation of the Farmer-Labor party, the sixth of the independent movements to be mentioned. It was formed in 1920, when it captured the Chicago convention from the Committee of Forty-eight, which was a continuation of the Progressive movement of 1912. The party obtained only about a quarter of a million votes in that presidential election. It maintained itself, however, in the Northwest, where it has secured a very considerable number of local victories and elected the only minor-party representative in the present Congress.

The Socialist Labor party was formed in 1876, mainly through the influence of the educated element among the German immigrant workers. There were a number of alliances between it and the more radical portion of the labor-farmer organizations. One wing of this party was in pretty constant conflict with the trade unions because of their refusal to go into politics. The result was finally the formation of the present Socialist party with Debs at its head and Berger and Hillquit as chief leaders. This party had its first national convention in 1900. From 1910 to 1912 the party gained many victories. In some fifteen cities the Socialists polled about one-fifth of the total vote. In the national election of 1912 Debs received almost a million votes for President. The World War gave the rapidly growing party a backset, since there was a division between those who opposed the war and those who wished Germany to be decisively defeated. The systematic persecution of individuals which resulted from the war, typified by the imprisonment of Debs and the suppression of newspapers and public assemblies, had an even greater destructive effect. The success of the Bolshevist revolution in Russia also divided the party, the more radical wing becoming the Communist party.

Certain facts stand out in any survey of minor political parties in the United States. One is that they are perennial; if they go, they also come afresh. Another is that the voters, unlike those of Continental Europe, refuse to divide on specific grounds into a large number of parties each of which represents a definite point of view and political philosophy. The nearest approach to this division is the formation of blocs within parties. A group of senators working within the Republican party, coming mostly from the western states, has frequently offered more energetic opposition to the policies of the official Republican administration than has the Democratic opposition. Still more significant, perhaps, is the existence of blocs outside Congress which do not become parties but which bring pressure to bear upon representatives of both major parties. The American Federation of Labor, for example, has refused steadily to join in creating a Labor party, thinking it better policy to influence candidates in both parties. The Anti-Saloon League, the American Legion, the Farmers' Union are similar blocs, which in Europe would probably themselves become minor parties.

Another feature of the political life of the last fifty years is the increase of the independent voter. As a rule the Democratic party in national elections does not command more than 40 per cent of the vote, but it often elects governors and other local officials in states that vote for the Republican presidential candidate. Another trait of American life is the conservatism of the average voter in his loyalty to the party to which his parents belong. Another fact is the great cost of effective party organization. Many states have also passed laws which make it extremely difficult for a minor party to get a place on the ticket.

There are, however, those who hold that in spite of all difficulties in the way, the creation of a strong mass party, having socialistic ideals in a form adapted to American conditions, is inevitable. They point to the fact that new social conditions always demand new political organs and agencies, that American economic and social life has been revolutionized since the Civil War, and that as yet no corresponding political change has come about. We have passed from a condition in which individual choice and initiative leading to individual success was the rule to a situation of vast organizations of capital and concentration of power. The average individual, it is asserted, is very much at the mercy of impersonal economic forces over which he has no control. The present crisis has emphasized the fact that in millions of cases individual industry and ability are no guaranty against tragic loss. We cannot continue to do political business in the age of the radio, airplane, and electric motor with the political methods which have come down to us from the era of the stagecoach and tallow dip.

The believers in a new political movement in harmony with existing conditions in industry profess themselves not at all discouraged at the failure of previous third-party movements. Aside from the fact that the two movements which polled the largest popular vote were the shortest-lived of any of them because they were built around personalities, they have expressed temporary and local discontents rather than an appreciation of the fundamental change going on in society. They reacted to special symptoms rather than to fundamental causes. Events moved so rapidly that there was not time enough for the average voter to realize that we had passed from an age of individualism to one of collective action. The Socialists, who pointed out that fact, spoke until recently too much of a foreign language to make themselves understood. The continuation of the depression has made millions conscious of economic realities in a way in which they were not before.

Those who assert that the time is at hand for a third-party movement on a mass scale claim that there is not the slightest evidence that either of the major parties can meet the new conditions. There is no longer any essential difference between them, it is asserted. The tariff on oil, coal, lumber, and copper was voted into the revenue bill, for example, by a majority vote which included one-third of the Democratic senators, in spite of the fact that the old party was opposed to a high protective tariff. While the present Congress has had an unusually large number of issues to deal with, there is not one case in which a measure has been carried or defeated on party lines. The meaninglessness of present party divisions is made evident, it is urged, by the fact that voters are so disgusted with their unreality that only one out of two of the potential voters goes to the polls in a national election. The difference between the two wings within each party is much greater than the difference between corresponding wings in the two old parties.

The conclusion is drawn that events are rapidly educating the voters to realize the flabbiness and futility of the old parties, along with the fact that neither of them has either the desire or the ability to deal in any fundamental way with the causes of our industrial and financial collapse. The new party of protest will differ from those of the last fifty years in an attempt to go to the roots of our social evils instead of urging some special measure as a panacea. Whatever its name, its platform will contain social-istic planks in the sense that it will demand that our enormous natural resources, our vast machinery of production and distri-bution, and the wonderful technical skill the country possesses shall no longer be used to enrich a privileged few but be directed to serve the well-being of all men and women of good will. Its aim will be to put an end once for all to the scandal and the trag-edy of want in the midst of plenty, of inability to buy and con-sume in the midst of abundant production, and to make liberty and equality a reality by bringing about a cooperative industrial society.

Democracy Joins the Unemployed

The political conventions of the two old parties have just been held under appropriate conditions. They did their stuff in a gang-ridden, boss controlled city, where both parties have worked for years in combination with tax-evaders, corporations seeking favors, and racketeering law-breakers. Teachers, policemen and municipal servants are unpaid because of a tax-system so confused and dishonest that the city is in a complete financial mess. Twenty and more banks were failing at just about the time the conventions met. More and bigger ones were trembling on the edge, held back from bankruptcy by aid from a federal government which can find help for corporations weakened by participation in gigantic stock-jobbing schemes of public utility mergers, but which grudges assistance to the common man and woman who have lost their jobs.

In saying this I am not throwing mud at Chicago. On the contrary the situation there is typical, differing only in degree from that of most of our large cities. In this crisis, which is political, industrial, financial, the only topic on which either of the two old parties could stir excitement and rouse enthusiasm was the question of alcoholic liquors. In one semi-hysterical period we adopted prohibition in order to win the war; in another time of hysteria, we are going to abolish it in order to restore prosperity! All other subjects receive perfunctory attention. This one alone creates real feeling and a real debate. Yet we are in a crisis the greatest any one living in this generation has seen, a crisis of the world and this nation, which demands the most serious thought and the creation of the most thorough-going and constructive policies.

[First published as a leaflet (New York: League for Independent Political Action, 1932), 4 pp., from an address delivered at the third annual conference of the LIPA in Cleveland on 9 July 1932.]

It is easy, only too easy, therefore to criticize the old parties. They are so feeble, so futile, so fraudulent, so lacking in courage and in ideas that they are hardly worth the breath it takes to condemn them. We cannot refrain from pointing out their evasions, their cowardice and their total lack of constructive action. But our positive task is infinitely greater and more difficult. It is to show the American people the causes which lie back of the bankruptcy of political leadership and to point out the path of the redemption of our country.

Our nation has had no pretence of leadership since the war. We have been politically bankrupt for a long time. The foreclosure proceedings began in 1929. But the bankruptcy goes back much further. It was covered up by fraudulent political bookkeeping and the issuing of false political balance sheets. We had the orgy of political corruption following the war. The stench of oil is still in the air. It was fitting that this corruption should be accompanied by wholesale suppressions of civil liberties in which both parties engaged. Then we had the do-nothing regime of Calvin Coolidge. Because the Administration was committed to complete passivity, the country was turned over, bound hand and foot and almost gagged, to the mercies of unregulated predatory business. The orgy of blind speculation which followed was labelled Prosperity, spelled with capital letters. It was announced to be the beginnings of a new economic era. Under the blessing of the Republican party and the Great Engineer, who between them took over the work of divine Providence, poverty was to be abolished. The loudspeaker in every home, the chicken in every pot and the two-car garage were to be the outward and visible signs of the inward spiritual grace and supreme reign of social justice which resulted from devotion to rugged individualism.

Actually, the industrial, financial and social condition of the country was all this time getting internally more and more rotten. The collapse of 1929 was the advance notification of the inevitable breakdown of political leadership which followed when the country was turned over to business and financial interests concerned only with the maximum of private profits in the shortest possible time. The three years since the notice of bankruptcy was served are the liquidation which is the essence of every collapse.

Publicists and economists may dispute as to the cause of this or that detail of our tragic situation. But in general the cause is as plain, as easy to see, as is the effect. In the face of all law, natural and moral, we have supposed that social harmony could be secured by the competitive efforts of individuals, each to promote his own personal advantage; that men could become the keepers of their brothers' welfare by pursuing them with weapons of destruction on battlefields of war and of industry; that the planning of privileged individuals for their own private gain was an effective substitute for social planning; that society could deliberately cripple its only agent of self-control, popular government, and yet maintain its order and health; not only that the American nation could serve both God and Mammon, but that material success is the surest proof possible that divine favor rests upon us as a nation.

We are reaping what we sowed. After the war to end war, every nation, though in a time of universal depression, is spending more on armies and navies than it spent when times were, by comparison, good. Every nation has raised its tariff walls against every other nation, this nation striking the key-note for economic war. Every nation has used its ingenuity to find means of economic attack and retaliation. The war on both the military and the industrial field is the direct effect of an economic regime which seeks for profit at any cost, by special command of raw materials, special access to markets; by surrender of the government's right to tax to special privileged parties to use in their own private behalf. It is an old maxim that the right to tax is the right to destroy. Greedy manufacturing interests which have used the right to tax conferred upon them by the special privilege of the tariff have demonstrated the truth of this maxim in their all but complete destruction of foreign trade, the consequent shutting down of American factories, and the loss of foreign markets by the farmer. Indirectly our international situation of fear, jealousy, suspicion, in short of suppressed warfare is the effect of the habit of mind bred by a ruthlessly competitive, socially unplanned and unregulated, economic system. The effect is before us; the cause is equally plain to anyone willing to open his eyes and see.

Every sermon, every newspaper, every honest public man proclaims that we are in an era of unparalleled lawlessness; of unchecked crime carried on by organized groups which not only defy the law but which often control city lawmakers, and city police. Racketeering is a profession, and breaking laws is so remunerative that the only way to punish big men in it is to detect them in evading payment of taxes on their swollen incomes. Crimes of violence undertaken for the sake of money are committed by persons of a constantly decreasing age. This fact is so general and so striking that some experts who correlate this fact of increased juvenile crime with the extension of school education, make it the basis of a general attack on our school system. These men however do not look far enough in their search for causes. They forget that our economic system of individual material success, with the devil of loss and suffering taking the hindmost, is so tremendous and so constant an educational force that the schools cannot offset its force.

Human beings, especially the young, have greater and greater difficulty in detecting where business leaves off and racketeering begins. Is not profit the measure of both according to our economic system? There is not a single city in the land where organized crime is rife in which the political forces that control that city are not allied on one hand—the left hand—with criminal elements, getting support from them. On the other hand, the right hand, the same political forces are allied with big business interests. These business interests on account of franchises granted, assessments reduced, legal infractions winked at, profitable advance information and other favors received, keep the corrupt political elements in power and are responsible for the unchecked license of the elements which engage in avowedly criminal activities.

Then there is the immediate industrial breakdown, whose effect is so overpowering that the thought of it is ever with us:— Banks failed, building and loan societies gone down in ruin, savings that were invested in bonds, domestic and foreign, wiped out; factories shut down, millions of men and women wholly out of work, millions more working for reduced wages and salaries and on part time; mortgages foreclosed; homes lost; farms taken for taxes or for security on money loaned; mutual confidence gone; everywhere insecurity, fear, black depression.

The effect is too evident to need description. And the cause? Is it, do you suppose, our fertile fields, our unmatched natural resources, our rich mines, our glutted granaries and warehouses, our numerous factories, our marvellous means of transportation with their machinery of wonderful inventiveness and mechanical efficiency? Is it our remarkable technical and engineering ability and training? Is it our native ability, character and education which are the cause at fault? Is it some visitation of a diabolic power? Before we answer in the affirmative, let us note two facts. One is that industry and commerce are carried on by means of credit, and that we, the American people, have abdicated from any social control of credit. We have turned over this economic force, which in no metaphorical sense is the life blood of industrial life, to private individuals and groups to be managed by them for their own enrichment. Their use of the means we so casually entrusted to them is a matter of record. Billions were put into pieces of paper ironically called securities, floated through control of all the machinery, legal and extra-legal, of corporations, mergers, issuing of stocks. Billions were poured into stock-speculation which inflated things which ironically were called values into a bursting balloon. Billions were loaned, almost forced, upon European and South American countries, so that bankers might have commissions on the tokens of credit they passed on to their customers in a criminally irresponsible fashion. These loans were then used to inflate business in foreign countries. Their deflation reacted to start our own industrial and financial crisis. Let experts quarrel, if they will, about the details of the causation of our economic collapse. But in the large, one cause is so stamped upon it that anyone who wishes can read. Credit which is absolutely the sole indispensable vital agent of modern economic life has been made a football of private gain by private individuals. This has been made possible because society has not attempted control of money and credit.

The other fact at which I ask you to look is the dependence of the crisis upon the enormous inequity in the distribution of the national income. When a small part of the population, a very small part, has an income far beyond any possible extension of consumption of goods and services, it must invest the surplus in plants which increase production still further, thus creating more goods to be consumed—provided there exists purchasing power to buy them as a preliminary of consumption. But meanwhile the mass of the population are not receiving, because of private control of the sources of production and exchange, the means which will enable them to buy what the plants are producing. Finally, some crisis, in connection with credit, forces this disparity to the foreground. Goods are not sold; factories shut down; men and women are thrown out of work and can buy still less; more factories close; shops close because they are losing money; banks fail, and so on, in the vicious circle in which we are now enclosed. Society has used no means for control of the delicate mechanism of production and distribution in relation to consumption and purchasing power. It has not in this country the constitutional means which it can use to effect control. Thus our crisis is not an accident, nor our unemployment a visitation from heaven or hell—except the hell of our own making. Under modern conditions of mass production, it is impossible to leave the balance of production and consumption to a group of men whose interest is only the monthly profit and loss balance sheet of their own private ledgers. They can't have the wisdom even if they had the character to do the work. A private profit system is necessarily one in which secrecy and the taking of risks rule. A system of complete publicity and of elimination of risk for the sake of competitive profit would be the end of the profit system.

It is because the cause of our present collapse lies so deep in our social system and because we are all of us so involved in the creation and toleration of this system, that I shall not here take time to blame the old parties. In their inefficiency and their false pretenses, their pitiful evasions and their ridiculous circuses, they are only running true to form. Without an understanding of the causes of the present plight and without the will to deal with these causes, they grasp at the liquor question or some other superficial symptom because that is the only thing of which they understand the political meaning. If we who are gathered here had the winning of office as our chief purpose we should doubtless act in the same way.

We are told that democracy has failed. It has certainly joined the unemployed. There are those who even after the spectacle of the Kreuger and the Insull failures, have the nerve to claim that any government except a dictatorship will be so inefficient or so corrupt that popular social control of economic forces is out of the question. The lesson that we have to learn, and that we have to tell to our fellow citizens, is that political democracy is bound to be a failure when it permits economic autocracy to grow up.

We have permitted business and financial autocracy to reach such a point that its logical political counterpart is a Mussolini unless a violent revolution shall bring forth a Lenin. The business of forming a new party is the business of educating the people until the dullest and the most partisan see the connection between economic life and politics. Its business is to make the connection between political democracy and industrial democracy as clear as the noon-day sun.

The task is not an easy one. The full development of democracy will not be secured in a day. We must enlist for life, for our own lives and for the sake of the lives of our children. We do not wish to build a party on temporary discontent nor on trumpery remedies and patchwork measures. Those who wish to arrest the course of inevitable change can get behind the elephant; those who wish the appearance of progress without its reality can train with those who hold a few carrots before the nose of the donkey. It is the task of the League to educate the American public to fundamental economic realities and the necessity of a new political order so that the spirit of democracy may have a re-birth. To that task we pledge our devotion.

Prospects for a Third Party

The League for Independent Political Action is the out-growth of discussions carried on by a relatively small group after the election of Herbert Hoover to the presidency in 1928. (Since I have often been wrongly given credit for initiating the League, I wish to take this opportunity to say that while I gladly responded to the invitation to attend these discussions, I was not one of the originating group.) There was no optimism with respect to speedy results among those who took part in the conversations. There was no expectation of immediate success in forming a united mass party, much less of its victory in any proximate presidential election. I recall frequent reference to the early history and slow progress of the British Labor party. There was repeated mention of enlistment for at least a thirty years' war. There was, however, a positive conviction that American political life could not continue indefinitely without squaring itself with economic conditions.

In discussing the future there was agreement on the unreality of the prosperity boom the country was "enjoying." There were no believers in the arrival of a new economic era. All who enlisted were convinced that the bursting of the bubble was sure, even though they would not venture to set the date of the collapse. It was felt that when the inevitable reaction came there would be a change in the political atmosphere toward one much more favorable to the propagation of political ideas based on economic conditions. The stock-market crash of 1929 came even sooner than was anticipated, and there is no need to say that it has been followed by a revival of political doubts and questionings on a large scale.

We were and still are amateurs in what is called "practical

[First published in *New Republic* 71 (27 July 1932): 278–80.]

politics." But we can console ourselves with the assurance that we were at least realists. There was no mere sentimental ardor, as there were no false hopes. There was no discussion of utopias and millennia. No time was given to remote goals and abstract ideals. There was not even the emotional aura which usually attends the efforts of "reformers." There was rather a sense of necessity; first of the necessity of economic change and then of the necessity of corresponding political change.

I engage in this brief reminiscence because it seems an appropriate introduction to saying something about the impressions left in my mind by the recent annual conference of the League in Cleveland. In our original meetings, when the prospect of a future industrial overturn was mentioned, it was stated that our movement must not be based upon the temporary discontents which every depression brings with it. We recalled that all prior political revolts which built upon contemporary depression had been short lived, melting away before the rising sun of returning prosperity. It was decided, accordingly, that the League's educational work should go deeper than an attempt to pool discontents, and would not surrender to temporary expediency for the sake of attaining a quick mushroom growth.

What happened in the Cleveland meetings was wholly in line with these earlier convictions. There are probably at least twenty different political revolts in the country at this particular time, each one based on discontent, and each one seeking a cure-all through some particular measure. There is no doubt that the disgust with the Republican and Democratic parties is enormous. The Cleveland conference was successful beyond our most sanguine expectations in demonstrating that the revolt is beginning to have teeth, and also that the public mind is not now looking for special panaceas and vote-catching devices, but is searching for fundamental causes and fundamental remedies.

The extent of the interest in the kind of a new party alignment was made evident by the attendance of delegates and members who came from far and near; by the large local audience of representative men and women who crowded the hall and who sat with serious attention through sweltering hours. It was shown by the change in the character of newspaper publicity, in quality as well as quantity. Before, during and after the meetings, the conference "made" the front page, and it even received serious and friendly attention on the editorial pages of the old-line party newspapers. In spite of the radicalism of the platform adopted, it was welcomed as likely to have a future influence on the old parties, even though a new party was denied all chance of success. Yet it was only a short time ago that the League received either perfunctory or else contemptuous notice. There can be no doubt of the change in the tone of public political sentiment, nor of the great revival of interest in the economic aspect of our politics.

All intelligent observers have been aware for a long time of the growing indifference of voters to the old parties as parties. The heavy vote for Hoover in 1928 was, if the managers of the machines had only known it, a sign of this indifference and even disgust. Only the most indurated partisans have claimed in the last few years that there is any significant difference between the Republican and Democratic parties. The Democratic Convention at Chicago went through some of the motions of trying to convince the people that there was to be a difference in the future. There were at the conference signs of a disposition on the part of disgruntled agricultural elements to support Roosevelt for the sake of expressing their intense resentment against Hoover, but even from these sources came also reports of their intention to steer clear of the Democratic party. The earlier passive conviction of the essential similarity of the two parties is turning into something like a positive hatred of them, if indications at the conference are to be trusted. They are not held directly responsible for the depression. But they are held responsible for dodging the issues which it has raised and for their desire to carry the election by diverting attention from actual issues.

One rather curious cause of the great change is worth mentioning, for while trivial in itself it is important as a sign. The radio brought with it political enlightenment in an unexpected form. If party managers had wished to take the voters of the country into their confidence as to the irrelevance and trickiness of the methods by which they select candidates and form their platforms, they could not have devised a method equal to putting on the air the proceedings of the last two national conventions. They disclosed in an effective way the dearth of ideas, the total unconsciousness of even the need for any ideas, and the deliberate dependence upon the silliest and most stereotyped emotional appeals. Even the newspaper organs of the old parties were compelled to join to some extent in exposure of the ways by which these parties have managed to influence public opinion in the past. The episode was of tremendous influence in converting passive indifference into active indignation.

The conference bore out our earlier belief that the inevitable economic reaction would create a political change. But it also bore out the conviction that there would be demand for political measures which were neither panaceas nor quack remedies. The discussions and the platform stuck resolutely to consideration of basic economic causes and remedies. More than one promising new movement in politics in the past has been blighted by having its deliberations captured by extremists who were more emotionally hot against abuses than intellectually informed and balanced. This element was not wholly lacking at the conference, and Mr. Devere Allen, the presiding officer, did not employ a steam roller to run over them. But while its representatives succeeded at times in prolonging discussion, they left no permanent impression on the deliberations. If anything, the conference leaned over backwards in omitting all appeal to temporary expediencies. There was, for example, universal discontent with the way in which the banking, money and credit problems have been handled by the administration, but a resolution in favor of inflation was voted down, not because the need for controlled inflation was not felt, but lest it give encouragement to the fiat-money party. There was general agreement also that the debtor class, especially the farmers, were suffering unjustly from the maintenance of fixed charges while the price level was lowered, but the resolution on this point was carefully safeguarded. These actions would be misinterpreted if they were taken to mean that the conference did not believe in radical measures; it only wanted to be sure that measures adopted were sound and not transitory vote-catching devices. And if I can interpret its sentiment correctly, this attitude was definitely political in nature. It was felt that the prospects of an enduring third party would be favored only by dealing with causes rather than with symptoms. This feeling was, I should say, the thing which most marked the meetings in distinction from abortive new-party movements in the past.

Nothing won more spontaneous or greater applause in the

conference than the condemnation of the two old parties for "subordination of urgent economic issues to the liquor question." This fact does not mean that the delegates were predominantly Drys; many of them will vote personally for repeal of the Eighteenth Amendment. But it does mean in my opinion that from now on there will be increasing resentment of the tactics of the managers of the old-party conventions in trying to put the liquor question ahead of industrial and financial questions, and in giving the impression that the repeal of the Eighteenth Amendment is to occur soon and will, by some miracle, restore prosperity. There are many who are Wet on prohibition as a separate issue who are still sober in judgment, many more than formed the booing galleries of the Chicago conventions.

The directly practical deliberations of the conference gathered about what is to be done in bringing a united third party into existence. There has been pressure within the League for action in the presidential campaign of 1932. There were those who felt the time had come for immediate action and that failure to take it would lead many to turn away from the League with the feeling that it does not mean business. But the opinion prevailed that the groundwork of such action had not as yet been laid, and that in the coming presidential election the Socialist platform and the Socialist candidates, Thomas and Maurer (the latter having been a vice-chairman of the League since its inception), came sufficiently near to representing the aims of the League to justify urging its members to work and vote in this campaign for the Socialist ticket. A resolution was unanimously adopted asking that a call be issued early in 1933 for a joint congress of all independent groups to bring the united party into positive existence. The executive and national committees of the League were instructed to make out a list of candidates for Congress outside the Republican and Democratic parties who should be aggressively supported by the League. There was a general belief that if a nucleus of such persons could be sent to the next Congress, there would be a definite stimulus given to insurgents within the old parties to withdraw nominal allegiance and come out openly for the new party.

In the past the greatest strength of the League has been in the professional and white-collar classes—which, as Paul Douglas pointed out at the conference, are essentially identical. It has consisted of teachers, clergymen, social workers, physicians, engineers, newspaper men, office workers, to a greater extent than manual workers. There were encouraging signs at the conference of a broadening of its scope. The limitation was never intentional, but came about because those who initiated the movement had their contacts more particularly in this field. No speeches had a warmer reception than those of A. J. Muste of the Conference for Progressive Labor Action and Mr. James Dick, an eloquent and militant textile worker from Connecticut. There were many reports of the increasing tendency of local unions to break away from the official policy of the A.F. of L., in order to undertake independent political action. Many labor people are coming to believe that aggressive political activity is the only assurance against disintegration of organized labor in the industrial field.

The one discouraging aspect of the outlook has already been referred to. Some of the important leaders in the Farmer-Labor party are about to come out in support of Roosevelt for President. There is a tepid belief in his liberalism, an intense belief in the desirability of beating Hoover and a willingness to adopt almost any course which promises that result. One of the practical tasks of the League in the coming campaign will be to convince the agrarian element of the suicidal character of such a policy. I think the members of the League yield to none in distrust of President Hoover and his policies. But the idea of supporting Roosevelt and yet not adding to the strength of the Democratic party is a hopeless one. The hope for the future is such a demonstration of the weakness of the Democratic party and the strength of the liberal element as will send conservative Democrats into the Republican party where they belong, and will bring progressive Democrats into a new party which will undertake a genuine attack on special privilege and a genuine defense of the common people by means that are adapted to present economic realities.

I have often been discouraged at the prospects of successful political action through a new party based on recognition of economic realities and devoted to social control of rugged, that is, brutal, economic individualism. I conclude by saying that I came away from the Cleveland conference more encouraged than at any time in the past. The constituency is waiting; the response is waiting. Work and organization are the agencies needed to effect the creation of a strong new party which will, moreover, quickly become more than a party of mere protest.

After the Election—What?

Our League set out after the overwhelming victory for Hoover four years ago to work for a new political alignment. We are continuing to work for that end after the present overwhelming victory for Roosevelt. A shift of a six million popular plurality from one side to the other confirms our belief that faith in and loyalty to the old parties are disappearing. Their stability is undermined. Independent voters already have a good deal more than the balance of power. More than a quarter of those who voted the Republican ticket four years ago swung loose this year. And they intended their swing to be to the left. They may be still ignorant and misled as to the way to move to the left, but Mr. Roosevelt and his advisors are even more ignorant and deluded if they think voters have committed themselves to the Democratic party. The voters wanted a New Deal. There was a large grudge vote. But the change of voters was more than a spite vote. It was more even than a protest vote. It was in large measure a vote for a new alignment in political measures if not for it in political parties. The Democratic press is mostly as conservative as the Republican press. It joins with the latter in talking as if the last election were only a swing from one party to another. It wants to cover up the fact that the change in vote was the expression of an enormous discontent and of hope for a radical change in the forces which control our government—a change from reactionary standpattism in support of big business to support of the common people who are suffering.

We in the League for Independent Political Action, have long believed that our real test and our real opportunity was going to come after the election. We believed and still believe that the

[First published in *News Bulletin of the League for Independent Political Action* 1 (November–December 1932): 1–2, from an address to the L.I.P.A. on 21 November 1932 in New York City.]

greater Governor Roosevelt's vote, the bigger would be the mass of voters doomed to sure disappointment. It is part of our job to catch these citizens on their rebound and make them see that a New Deal means a New Deal and can be carried out only through a new party. A big vote won't resurrect the Democratic party from its grave. Its majority will only demonstrate how far the corpse has disintegrated.

In going on with our educational work, we have a wonderful foundation upon which to build in the great educational campaign carried on by the candidate for president whom the League supported, Norman Thomas. The fruit of his educational work is not measured in the least by the disappointingly small total vote he received. Everyone has knowledge of persons who are profoundly convinced of the necessity of radical social and economic changes of the kind advocated by the Socialists in the campaign, but who nevertheless failed to vote for Thomas and Maurer.

There are millions of these persons in the country. They are the ones among whom the League must carry on an aggressive work. First and foremost stand the farmers. The five Congressmen elected by the Farmer-Labor Party from the state of Minnesota are a beacon which lights up the future. A Democrat elected to the United States Senate said the other day that the western farmers had turned down one party for its failure to meet the needs of the country and they stood ready to turn down the other party if it also failed. It will fail. Somebody must see to it that four years from now they do not simply swing back in to the Republican party which will then be the "promising" party. The League for Independent Political Action has a definite call to extend the support we gave the Farmer-Labor Party in this campaign into other states so that that movement may be the agricultural nucleus of the new alignment.

The labor vote in the industrial centres is the most discouraging part of the situation. The comparatively slight support it gives to the only candidates and only measures which stand for its interests are a sad commentary on the leadership of organized labor. It is also a sufficient condemnation of that small group of doctrinaire Socialists who think that the only hope of a radical party in the United States is a proletariat, which politically speaking is non-existent.

We know, however, that there are rising labor groups all over the country which are disgusted with the do-nothing policies of their superiors who have got out of touch with the working people. This discontent is going to grow in the long days ahead. They are ready and waiting if we do our part.

The third field of labor is that which responded most directly to the radical appeal of the last campaign. It is symbolized by the enormous response of college students in the last campaign to the inspiring leadership of Norman Thomas. Professional classes, teachers, engineers, social workers, clergymen, in very large numbers are already with us even if many of them under the stress of what seemed to them immediate need, failed to vote with us this year. I recognize the limitation in numbers as well as in other respects of this group. But I also believe that what the intelligent and most impartial group of citizens believe today is the best material for predicting what will happen in the future.

In 1934 a new House of Representatives will be elected. The depression, I venture to predict (no economist denies it) will still be with us. The problems of unemployment, of taxation, of peace and war, of the farmer, of the laboring men threatened with ever greater growing insecurity; the problems of the skilled intellectual workers, engineers, architects, writers, teachers, bewildered by a society which needs their services but is too chaotic to use them, will be with us. The goal we set for the League is the tenfold multiplication of our local branches, a tenfold multiplication of aggressive organization and educational work that we may be ready for 1934. We must begin now, not next year nor two years from now. At the last dinner meeting which I addressed I invited you to engage in a new thirty years' war. That invitation I now repeat, to join in the battle for a new society in which cooperation for public good will take the place of competition for private gain, and peace in an organized world will take the place of hostility in our present international disorder of economic war.

Reviews

College Sons—and Parents

Life in College, by Christian Gauss.
New York: Charles Scribner's Sons, 1931.

Good sense is rare enough to be called, for reasons that psychologists can explain, common sense. In the case of Dean Gauss—perhaps always when it exists in abundant measure—it is accompanied by humor and by so much experience that it has been funded into instinct. The humor, moreover, is not simply that good humor which is so near to sentimentality in its cheerful refusal to note facts; it is the humor that penetrates, often mordantly, into the incongruities and contradictions of our civilization. The strain of hopefulness that tempers the account rendered of the modern undergraduate boy is therefore the more significant.

The book is not an apologia for contemporary youth, nor a defence of the American college against its many critics. Indeed, the author admits to "a guilty feeling that in one respect it is almost unique. As a book dealing with an educational subject, it lacks something. It offers no cure for the many ills of our institutions of higher learning." And he adds "if this volume seeks to reform anything or anybody, it is the American parent." This sentence tempts me to make a generalization which the author was too wise to make explicit. The things that are wrong with the American college—which he admits are many—are the things, fundamentally, which are wrong with American life in general.

It manifests the lack of a sense of perspective—and of a sense of humor—to criticize our higher institutions of learning as if they did not of necessity reflect, for evil as well as for good, the conditions of American life. Dean Gauss's book is addressed even more to the parents of students than to the students themselves: its burden, upon the whole, is that the larger part of the

[First published in *New Republic* 66 (4 February 1931): 332–33.]

disciplinary cases, the misfits, the failures of boys in college go back to the home. Students are overmothered, and under-fathered. Parents do not take the time nor the pains to understand their offspring; they coddle too much, and they indulge in spasms of excessive harshness; misguided ambition leads them to send those to college who should never go (perhaps a third of the college population, he thinks, should never have gone); they are both too lavish and too stingy with money.

The book closes, naturally and properly with an examination to be taken by parents. Its thirteen questions are searching. One can only hope that they will be pondered by fathers and mothers having children in college and by those thinking of sending them. They sum up in concentrated form the possible "reform" of parents which Dean Gauss would like to see effected. The points made are illuminated throughout the book by the method of cases drawn from the Dean's own experience. Without this context of illustrative material a reviewer's summary would be dry and preachy—which the text never is. The Dean's examples enforce in one way and another the statement that "it is probable that because of the rapid changes which have come over the manners of youth, there are fewer fathers who are thoroughly comfortable in the presence of their sons and their sons' friends than there were twenty years ago. . . . Complete and sympathetic intelligence between them does not now seem to be the usual situation." This leads to the moral that "in general, the advances should come from the father."

There is a quality about the book which lifts it above the level of even sound advice and counsel to youth and parents. Dean Gauss sees that the troubles and ills of youth in college have their source, generally speaking, in conditions outside of college walls:—first in the home, and then in the larger setting of American life that affects the home. In effect, this mode of treatment, even though it appears as an undercurrent, makes the book a critique of contemporary American society as it is revealed in the cross-section of college life.

This phase of the book, although it is only implied and not too explicitly insisted upon, lends itself to comment better than does the shrewd and informed advice which the book abundantly supplies. I cannot refrain from quoting at length the closing sentences of the author's Introduction. "In some respects, therefore,

I feel that the college student has been maligned. His critics urge that conditions on the campus should be made to conform more nearly to conditions in the world outside, that he should be 'educated for life,' by which they mean usually for business life. Instead of attempting to force the college more narrowly into line with our social and economic system, I am compelled to wonder whether it would not be wiser, for a little while, to have such reformers direct their attention to a study of our somewhat hugger mugger world outside with a view to bringing it a little more closely into accord with some of those finer aspects of human nature so frequently illustrated in the conduct of the average undergraduate."

Chapter Five is entitled "The New World and the Undergraduate." It is in this chapter together with that on "Troubles at Home—Divorce" that Dean Gauss deals most explicitly with the connection between changes in the undergraduate situation and those in the world outside. There is the decay of romance. The literature which is read "appeals not to sentiment, but to the simpler, often more brutal, instincts, and to the intelligence." Again, "the barriers between the university and society have broken down. The undergraduate of to-day, far more generally than his predecessors, talks like a young worldling."

The cause for these and many other differences between the society and youth of to-day and those of a generation or two ago is that the new world is forced upon us by scientists and inventors. The automobile alone has broken down the isolation of the college from the world that was once outside. Add the long-distance telephone and the radio, and it is no cause for wonder that life, especially for the young, has become mobile and fluid. "It is much less centred in the home and much less centred in the college; it is much less localized and much less easily supervised."

These are simple words and words about a matter that is sufficiently obvious. Yet they go to the root of the problems of higher education in a way which many elaborate discussions of university questions fail to do. Dean Gauss has deliberately abstained from touching the issues of college curricula and college methods of instruction save as they incidentally affect the life of the undergraduate who comes for discipline or advice into a dean's office. But, he suggests, I think, the only promising and intelligent approach to these larger problems. He has made it clear that the life of the college as lived from day to day cannot be isolated from that of the home and its social setting. I believe that no great light will dawn on the educational problems of the college until they too are considered, fully and frankly, in the context of American life.

"Surpassing America"

The Challenge of Russia, by Sherwood Eddy.
New York: Farrar and Rinehart, 1931.

The Soviet Challenge to America, by George S.
Counts. New York: John Day Co., 1931.

These Russians, by William C. White. New
York: Charles Scribner's Sons, 1931.

Ten years ago, publishers and readers alike were so indifferent to Soviet Russia, or so actively hostile even to hearing about it, that it was hard for a manuscript to find a printer or a public. The enormous change which has taken place in the position of Russia in the world is nowhere better shown than in the present eagerness to learn what is going on in the vast territories of the U.S.S.R., and to hear report, surmise and speculation about its consequences for Russia and even more for the rest of the world. The first two books listed above add to the number of writings concerned with the Russian situation in its bearings on the rest of us: Mr. Eddy wishes to aid in the understanding of Russia as a challenge and as a menace; Mr. Counts is concerned especially with the challenge to the economic and cultural system of the United States.

The two books complement each other. That of Eddy is a summary of pretty much all sides of Russian life. That of Counts centres about one thing, the scope, development and prospects of planned and coordinated industry. What is incidental in one is prominent in the other. Communism is the basic theme of the first named, with its application through the fields of agriculture, industry and labor, political organization, education and culture, morals and marriage, law and justice, and religion. Mr. Counts begins with a brief account of the Communistic philosophy, party organization and educational system, and then devotes the major part of the book to a consideration of the State Planning Commission and its Five Year Plan of construction. While some

[First published in *New Republic* 66 (15 April 1931): 241–43.]

of the same material is found in both books, it is presented in a different perspective, so that the reading of both is an aid to a binocular vision of the Soviet Republics. Eddy's book is more descriptive and covers a wider field; Counts's is the more analytic and concentrated.

One who wishes a bird's-eye view of present Russia, enlivened by particular episodes and made definite by judiciously chosen and wisely scattered statistics, will find an excellent introduction in Mr. Eddy's book. And, speaking of statistics, both authors make the point that while errors are inevitable, it is silly to suppose that they are cooked. The whole development of the Russian scheme depends so intimately upon the approximate accuracy of the figures given that the statistical bureaus of the various branches of Russian government and industry cannot afford to take chances with them. Moreover, the recent but already inveterate habit of dependence upon "science" has resulted in the gathering of rather too much bulk in the way of figures. But the various reports and estimates can be checked one by another, and they are all subject to the acute devotion of present Russia to "self-criticism."

I have already mentioned the various themes covered in Mr. Eddy's book, and must refer to the book itself for their adequate exposition. He emphasizes the many contradictions of the system as it now exists: the union of high humanitarian aims with ruthlessness of means employed in their realization; of the goal of complete emancipation of individuals with drastic suppression of individuals when they come into conflict with the "cause"; of doctrinaire rigidity with flexible opportunistic adaptation to changing conditions; of the abolition of individual competition with adoption of "socialized" competition, and of the theoretical condemnation of money with its free use in the way of prizes. Of course, the Bolsheviks explain all these contradictions on the basis of the "transitional" state of present economy. Mr. Eddy quotes from Lenin the saying, "the kernel of the situation is that one must find a means of directing the evolution of capitalism in the bed of state capitalism so as to insure the transition of state capitalism into Socialism." These words give the theoretical key to the quick changes of Bolshevist policy. There has never been on earth a government that was so much all things to all men, while keeping a single end in view.

On the positive side, the two things that impressed me most in Mr. Eddy's account are the agricultural revolution and the cooperative development. He says, "The present agrarian revolution may have a significance and magnitude second only to the great industrial revolution of the eighteenth century." The rural character of Russian life, and the obstinately individualistic bias of the Russian peasant, have united to make it necessary for a government which rests upon the industrialized proletariat to attempt the most thoroughgoing alteration known to history of the habits, the technique, the morale, the general culture, of workers of the land. The success or failure of the communistic attempt depends upon whether or not the agricultural revolution goes through. One cannot read the account in the third chapter, dealing with agriculture, without wondering how much of the plan could be utilized in American farming communities without a political and economic revolution. Perhaps the cultural as well as the economic future of the American farmer depends upon whether, by voluntary cooperation, he can do some of the things for himself which a dictatorship is doing for farmers in Russia. The account of the cooperatives reveals not only their rapid extension, but their internal democracy, subject, of course, to governmental control of prices and allocation of materials and machinery.

Mr. Eddy closes with an indictment of Communist policy on three counts: first, the dictatorship (in dealing with which he shows how it automatically extends itself through the details of life); second, the zeal for world revolution; and third, the bigotry of attitude toward religion. His general point of view is that of the liberal, reforming socialist. His general conclusion is that while the capitalist world moves gradually toward socialism, Russia should move toward Western democracy.

Mr. Counts's book is on the whole more sympathetic with the Russian point of view. His account, for example, of the indoctrination practised in Russia is the most powerful exposition of its grounds that I have seen anywhere. He does not fear the indefinite perpetuation of the dictatorship when conditions have changed, relying on the constant control exercised by minor groups and organizations upon Moscow. He gives a fuller account of the ways in which this pressure is exerted than I have seen elsewhere. But it is good Marxian doctrine that those who have power never surrender it save when compelled by violent revolution. The outstanding trait and merit of his book is its concentration on the theme of planning. Russia is a challenge to America, not because of this or that characteristic, but because we have no social machinery for controlling the technological machinery to which we have committed our fortunes, while Russia assumes that "social phenomena are capable of being controlled so that the development of human society can be made subject to the human will"—a striking commentary on the frequently expressed notion that Marxianism is fatalistic in its subjection of human ideas and effort to necessary economic laws of history.

The entire account of the Five Year Plan is made to centre about this point; the result is a unity often missing in discussions of it. The book differs also from most other reports of the Five Year Plan in giving weight to its cultural and educational aspects. I know of nothing more exciting than Dr. Counts's report of the way in which schools and all agencies of education, theatre, cinema, clubs, trade-union activities, organizations of children and youth, etc., are made to contribute to the plan and its execution. I would call especial attention to the statement of the definite responsibilities assumed by the Pioneers, as an illustration of the effective thoroughness with which all forces are made to contribute. And it is only one example among very many cases related by Dr. Counts.

The temper of the book may perhaps be conveyed by the following quotation:

> Industrial society in its present form is a monster possessing neither soul nor inner significance. It has succeeded in destroying the simpler cultures of the past, but has failed to produce a culture of its own worthy of the name. . . . Whether this state of moral chaos is the temporary maladjustment of a transition epoch or the inevitable product of a society organized for private gain is one of the most crucial questions of our time.

Whether one agrees (as does the present writer) or disagrees, Mr. Counts's book is an unsurpassed statement of the whole, and not merely of the economic, challenge of Russia to America. It will be a long, long time, I think, before it is a serious industrial challenge. In some respects, it is already a searching spiritual challenge, as it is an economic challenge to coordinate and to plan. Mr. White's book differs from both of the others. We find in it a vivid picture of the impact of the Communist theory and practice upon the lives of individuals. It deals, as he says in his preface, not with Russia as an entity, but with individuals. Conversations with housewife, professor, student, merchant, engineer, worker, priest, typist, tutor, soldier, village doctor, shoemaker, miller, etc., are related in ways which give, as far as they go, a cross section of Russian life as it is affected by the working out of the Communist way of life. There is obvious room for selection; only one thoroughly familiar with Russian conditions can decide how fair Mr. White's selection is. But it is only just to say that all the reports have an authentic ring. They include all shades, the disaffected and "deprived," the would-be neutral, the one who vacillates, the sympathizer who is not a party member, the party member. Only the farmer is lacking—perhaps because there are so many of him. Incidentally, the stories are charged with Russian humor, especially of the grim, ironic type.

Upon the whole, it is interesting to see how the personal reports dovetail with the general statements. For example, the general expositions emphasize the great subordination of "light" industry to "heavy," that is, of articles of consumption to equipment designed to speed up production: the development of mines, electrification, oil, new machinery, plants, motor cars and tractors. The stories show how this subordination affects the people; it makes vivid the great sacrifices entailed in industrializing Russia. Naturally the personal reaction varies with the status of the individual. The sacrifice entailed makes clearer the account given by Mr. Counts of the multiple and intense campaign of the rulers to keep up the morale of the people. If the first two books complement each other, that of Mr. White supplements them both. I think Mr. White would be among the first, however, to admit that the universal habit of grumbling is especially chronic among Russians, and that this fact must be borne in mind in assessing the final worth of the individual stories.

Corporate Personality: A Study in Jurisprudence, by Frederick Hallis. London: Oxford University Press, 1930.

The work of Mr. Hallis is definitely a study in philosophical jurisprudence; it is a study of the concept of personality in its juridical application rather than an analysis of legal practice. He holds, however, that the result of the study must be of value in practice or otherwise the study is not juridical. In consequence, Mr. Hallis is engaged in striving to maintain an equilibrium which, as I shall indicate later, seems to me rather unstable; at all events, his endeavor to maintain the position of philosophical analysis on one side and of practical application on the other, makes it somewhat difficult to ascertain just what, finally, is his own position.

On one side he holds that the value of the concept of personality in jurisprudence is "essentially practical in the sense that it consists in enabling us to do something with the fact of social life. In itself, therefore, the juristic concept has no value. Its value consists in the extent to which it ministers to the practical end which the law has in view." One would accordingly expect his treatment to consist in showing the practical ends which the concept of corporate personality serves in law, and to rest a justification of it on the ground that there are important ends subserved by this concept which cannot be met by any other legal device.

But this mode of treatment appears to him too pragmatic and empirical. For some reason (which I confess he does not make clear to my mind) he thinks that this interpretation leads logically to the fiction and concession theories, which he criticizes adversely, and with much force. Against this view, he holds that it is necessary to maintain that the legal concept of personality really has something in common with the philosophical concept in its non-legal sense.

[First published in Yale Law Journal 40 (June 1931): 1338–40.]

As a logical result of Mr. Hallis' attempt to find a *via media*, he is led to an examination of existing theories of jurisprudence concerning corporate personality. He first takes up the rationalistic theories which he dismisses as too formal and abstract, and then the sociological theories which he finds unsatisfactory because in emphasizing social facts they neglect the peculiar character of juristic concepts. Under the first head, he engages in a careful analysis of the Neo-Kantian and Neo-Hegelian philosophies of law, taking Stammler as typical of the former. Under the second caption, he discusses Duguit particularly, following his criticism with a sketchy account of modern sociology. The criticism of the rationalist philosophy is based on the ground that they exclude social facts from their conception of morality, and thus leave us with a legal system which, while it is connected with morals, has no intrinsic social basis and function. Against jurisprudence of the type of Duguit, Hallis brings the opposite objection. It bases law so exclusively upon social facts that it has no room for the special function of law—"the very soul of juristic thought"—in providing a *rational* coordination of social life. Duguit, according to our author, leaves out "will" and hence "drops out of account the element of personality, which is the essential differentia of the social." We may remark incidentally that Mr. Hallis employs empiricism, positivism and pragmatism as synonymous terms, and that in many instances he seems to base his criticism on his opposition to these philosophies rather than upon Duguit's own doctrines.

In the third part of his work, Mr. Hallis takes up von Gierke, Korkunov, Jellinek, Krabbe, and Hauriou, displaying upon the whole the greatest degree of sympathy with the views of the latter. He groups them together because they all realize the close connection of jurisprudence with sociology without falling into the error he imputes to Duguit of confusing them. Von Gierke is right in dwelling upon the reality of the corporate groups which law recognizes as juridical personalities. But he errs in overlooking the fact that this personality is conferred upon social groups from the standpoint of the ideal aim of law itself; he treats as a social fact that which is a juristic rational construction. Somewhat surprisingly Mr. Hallis criticizes Ihering for being too formal and rationalistic—which is also his criticism of Austin's theory of sovereignty and law. Korkunov advances upon Ihering in considering rights as legally *delimited* interests, instead of legally *protected* interests—a distinction which seems to Mr. Hallis to give greater recognition to the independent existence of interests in society itself. But like Ihering he fails to notice the source in personal will of the interests which law defines.

Jellinek was interested in showing that the state as a corporate personality is itself subject to law, holding that sovereignty is a historical rather than intrinsic attribute. But while he gives will and thus personality to the state, he fails to state the ends and interests which will must serve, and thus finally makes the rights of subordinate social groups a matter of virtual concession. Krabbe carries even further opposition to the idea that law is an arbitrary creation of power, but only succeeds in substituting an abstract moral will for the Austinian power, and thus ends also in a concession theory, although a concession from a moral being. Hauriou is praised for seeing that legal personality has a social sub-stratum, but is condemned for not seeing that the reality of the former is a conceptual or rational construction of law, in which an ideal aim is combined with scientific observation of social realities.

It will be noted that the method of our author is to play one school of thought against the other. One school in emphasizing social facts fails to take account of the rational and ideal purpose of law, and attributes to the former what comes from the latter. The other school so emphasizes the rational purpose of law that it loses sight of the social realities to which it refers. "Juristic problems always have both a real or *de facto* aspect and an ideal or normative one." In his eclectic desire to combine, Mr. Hallis shows himself a true disciple of Vinogradoff to whose memory he dedicates the book. He believes that he has made a synthesis of the true elements in both. But I fear that he has been more successful in using each to condemn the other than in reaching a solid synthesis. His own "solutions" when stated positively seem to be hardly more than verbal assertions that both the rational and the empirical factors *must* be united in a valid theory. But no reader can fail to obtain valuable instruction from his careful analyses of the theories of the most important modern continental theorists in jurisprudence.

The Autobiography of a Philosopher, by
George Herbert Palmer. Boston and New York:
Houghton Mifflin Co., 1931.

A Defence of Philosophy, by Ralph Barton
Perry. Cambridge: Harvard University Press,
1931.

The Genteel Tradition at Bay, by George
Santayana. New York: Charles Scribner's Sons,
1931.

Professor Palmer's too brief account of a long, active,
and serene life is more than a personal record. On its personal
side it is a report of a long-continued struggle against years of ill
health and such mediocre opportunities for education in philosophy as our country provided for the first half of his life. It
includes a succinct statement of his own conclusions in the fields
of morals and religion—an original evangelical Puritanism soft-
ened and liberalized by interest in art and literature, and broad-
ened by philosophic study. Reading between the lines, one finds
also a record of the development of higher education in the
United States, and an appreciation of the enormous reconstruction of university education stimulated and effected by President
Eliot. It is almost impossible for one to-day to appreciate the low
tone of collegiate instruction, apart from an inspiring personality
here and there, a half-century ago. It is worthy of note that Professor Palmer gave the first constructive course in philosophy at
Harvard as late as 1889. Others than the many students drawn
to philosophy by Professor Palmer and stimulated by his rare
gifts in teaching—gifts which were constantly cultivated with
great care—will be glad of this gracious record of a significant
life.

Mr. Perry's little book is enlivened with humor. He does much
to accomplish the task which he says is needed: relieving the philosopher of his reputation for edification and omniscience. The

[First published in *New England Quarterly* 4 (July 1931): 529–31.]

brochure is particularly successful in indicating how and why philosophy is an "affront to common sense"—how it is bound to turn current beliefs inside out and upside down, since philosophy begins with distinctions familiar to common-sense, but presses the distinctions far beyond the point where popular belief is willing to follow. The habits of doubt instilled by philosophic study are invigorating glands of secretion in the body politic. Like American pioneer life, philosophy is a pushing out of the frontiers. For this reason, it need not fear being accused of speculative tendencies, or going beyond the bounds of scientific evidence.

Mr. Santayana's volume is an urbane and ironical contribution to the discussion raised by the new humanistic movement. It is quite definitely written from "above the mêlée," and as the patriotic Frenchman said about Romain Rolland's book during the world war, it has something of the attitude of *le bon Dieu* surveying the over-excited and vain struggles of mankind. After the author's recent excursions into metaphysics, many a reader will welcome this volume as a return, with ripened insight, to the manner of the earlier *Life of Reason*. The "Analysis of Modernity" with which the book opens is so devastating that it does not leave much of value to the credit of modern life. The three Rs, the Renaissance, the Reformation, and the Revolution, are all assessed and found wanting. The first, the true Humanism, emancipated the passions; the second reduced the spirit to an instrument of material welfare and progress; the third has brought industrialism and material comfort. All have operated under high-sounding names irrelevant to their actual consequences. Against these is set a fourth R, to which Santayana, to the surprise perhaps of the reader, is much more sympathetic, namely, the spirit of Romance. Moved perhaps by the exaggerated assault upon Romanticism made by the new "humanists," Mr. Santayana says, "I confess that I can hardly imagine in the near future any poetry, morality, or religion not deeply romantic." The second essay is a statement of the theoretical arguments for, and the actual facts against, supernaturalism, which, it is intimated, is the proper haven of the "humanistic" position. The concluding essay on the moral adequacy of naturalism is the most constructive of the series, closing with the statement that "only a morality frankly relative to man's nature is worthy of man." And there is an intimation that such a morality is alone genuinely humane.

Charles Sanders Peirce

Collected Papers of Charles Sanders Peirce,
edited by Charles Hartshorne and Paul Weiss.
Vol. 1, *Principles of Philosophy.* Cambridge:
Harvard University Press, 1931.

The first word of a reviewer of these papers must be in
acknowledgment of the patient devotion of the editors, Doctors
Hartshorne and Weiss, and of the service rendered by the department of Philosophy in Harvard University and the Harvard Press.
No outsider can begin to appreciate the difficulties experienced in
editing the manuscripts which are to appear in the series of ten
volumes. Unpublished papers, the introduction tells us, number
several hundreds, and exist in all stages of incompleteness; there
are beginnings without endings, conclusions without record of
what led to them, hiatuses, repetitions. The material covers a
vast range of subjects, yet none of it falls readily, because of the
originality of Peirce's mind, into conventional divisions.

Nevertheless, judging from this first volume, the work of editing has succeeded to a degree which one would hardly have
thought possible, in arranging the material in orderly fashion.
When the first six volumes have appeared, the public will be in
possession of the contributions made by the most original philosophical mind this country has produced to general philosophy;
to logical theory, both in the traditional form, as a theory of scientific method and a modern symbolic logic; to metaphysics, to
pragmatism, to mathematics. The remaining four volumes will
contain his writings on physics and psychology, his book reviews, correspondence, etc.

It is not at all likely that Peirce will ever become popular even
in that highly limited sense in which the adjective "popular" ever
applies to a philosopher. He is a philosopher's philosopher, and
in an unusual degree. The fragmentary condition in which he left
his writings is one reason. As the editors say, he possessed the
system-making mind. In one of his fragments, printed as a pref-

[First published in *New Republic* 68 (6 January 1932): 220–21.]

ace, he confesses to the ambition of setting forth a philosophy as deep and massive in its foundations as that of Aristotle. He wanted to outline, in terms of modern knowledge, a theory so comprehensive that the findings of thought in all fields, for a long time, would be used only as illustrative detail. The scheme was too grandiose to be carried out; it agreed neither with Peirce's own habits nor with his relations to other thinkers, to universities or publishers. He was, as the editors all say, not "a leader of movements," but "an originator of ideas." The ideas are seminal ideas, often left, even those which he wrote out most fully, as undeveloped germs, still needing to be planted, cultivated and brought to harvest.

The contrast between Peirce's intent and the conditions of executing it, both personal and environmental, resulted in an intellectual tragedy. There is no adequate presentation of his thought as a well developed whole. In consequence, thinkers will go to him to find novel suggestions, fresh points of view, fertilizing ideas often thrown out almost arbitrarily and at random, "flashes of brilliant light," as James called them, extraordinary emancipations from tradition on themes seemingly grown so commonplace as to be subjected only to conventional treatment. They will find eccentric, almost fantastic, notions, explained, I think, by the isolation from other minds in which he worked. Even so, however, I would not count too confidently upon the entirely erratic character of these notions. His flat denial of some of the principles of the physics of his day is, for example, wholly in line with recent discoveries. It is possible that if a sterner discipline of himself had given the presentation of his thought greater completeness and consecutiveness, it would have been at the expense of a regimentation which would have lessened his freshness and originality. He was a meteor—one of those meteors whose appearance is unpredictable and whose course is unchartable.

In consequence, no two persons would probably select the same ideas as those most truly characteristic of Peirce's thought, and most significant for present philosophizing. One, for example, might select his emphasis upon the reality of final causes and the efficiency of objective thought. Another might be interested in assembling ideas that seem, in spite of a radically different terminology, to anticipate some of the principles Whitehead has been setting forth. The fact is that he not only throws out ideas without developing them, but sometimes sets forth ideas which in their older historic setting have been employed to contradict one another. His intuition of the connecting links which would bring these ideas into harmony is not elaborated. Consequently, in what follows I shall doubtless put the selective emphasis on points which appeal most to me.

I am reasonably sure, however, of being on safe ground when I say that what Peirce called "fallibilism" is central in his thinking. There is nothing extraordinary in the assertion that it is human to err. Skeptics, as well as Peirce, have held that nothing in human belief is exempt from this liability. But the peculiarity of Peirce is that in his thought the idea is not connected with skepticism, and proneness to err is itself taken to be a reliable indication of the state of the universe, instead of being a *merely* human trait. Peirce is not a skeptic, for he has an intense faith in the possibility of finding out, of learning—if only we will inquire and observe. The assertion of certainty is harmful precisely because it blocks the road to the inquiry by which things are found out. It is a fallacy, he says, to suppose that science signifies knowledge. It is rather "the pursuit of those devoured by a desire to find things out." It is in a state of constant "metabolism and growth." Established truths are so far from defining science that they are things "labelled and put on the shelves of the scientist's mind, arranged to suit his convenience, while science, the living process, is busied only with conjectures which are either getting framed or getting tested."

Fallibilism is also more than a necessary postulate of method. It has definite philosophical implications. It points to the continuity of all things in nature. "The principle of continuity is the principle of fallibilism objectified." It signifies that as our knowledge swims in a continuum of indeterminacy, so things themselves swim in continua; there are no exact breaks and divisions such as would make exact knowledge possible. Only the idea of fallibilism opens the mind to observation of the merging edges, the fluidity of all things. To Peirce the idea of evolution is one form of the principle of continuity. The scientific dogmatist (or mechanist, since the two are synonymous for Peirce) holds to uniformity, repetition; his mind is closed to all evidence for variety, novelty, spontaneity. Continuity points to the conclusion that all things can be explained only on the basis that they *grow*. Even laws themselves are evolutionary growths. Wherever there is genuine diversification, there must be spontaneity and contingency.

Peirce had an excellent knowledge of the past history of thought, especially of Aristotle, the scholastics and Kant— whose *Critique of Pure Reason* he says he knew practically by heart. Like all independent minds, however, he took great liberties in interpreting historic views, and often gives their authors the benefit of his own greater insight. A striking case is seen in his adoption of logical realism in opposition to the fashionable nominalism of his day. Peirce believed thoroughly in the objective reality of the general. But he understands it in a way which would have been abhorrent to Aristotle and the scholastics, and to some at least of the contemporary philosophers who appeal to Peirce as if he confirmed their views. For Peirce understands by the reality of a "general" the reality of a way, habit, disposition, of behavior; and he dwells upon the fact that the habits of things are acquired and modifiable. Indeed, he virtually reverses Aristotle in holding that the universal always has an admixture of potentiality in it.

There is one aspect of Peirce's thought which comes out most clearly, I think, in his conception of philosophy itself, a conception which in my judgment is likely to be revived in the future and to dominate thought for a period at least. He holds that philosophy is that kind of common sense which has become critically aware of itself. It is based upon observations which are within the range of every man's normal experience; it does *not* include matters which are more conveniently studied by students of the special sciences. To my mind this statement is the more weighty because it comes from a man who was so devoted to the sciences and so learned in them. What makes me believe that this notion of philosophy will dominate thought in some future time is perhaps its similarity to my own conception that the starting point and the ultimate test of philosophy is what I have called gross or macroscopic experience. Philosophy leans on science not for its subject matter, but for its attitude of experimentation (what Peirce calls the laboratory mind, as distinct from the seminary mind), and draws from science the apparatus by which common experience is critically viewed. What will cause the movement in the direction of Peirce's conception is, I imagine, the increasing remoteness of physical science from everyday experience and its increasing involvement in paradoxes. I do not mean, any more than Peirce meant, that the results of the sciences are negligible, much less erroneous, but that philosophy is concerned with the outgrowth of the sciences from everyday experience and their reabsorption back into it. Much of present-day philosophy that claims to be ultra-scientific seems to be wandering in a wilderness because, instead of taking this point of view, it tries to build upon the results of the special sciences in independence of, and in opposition to, coarse everyday experience.

In what I have said I have only touched upon the larger points in which Peirce connects with the tendencies of present-day thought. I have passed over the things which are, technically speaking, of greatest importance to philosophers. But professional philosophers will, it is to be hoped, betake themselves in any case to the volumes of which this is the first. What professional philosophy most needs at the present time is new and fresh imagination. Only new imagination is capable of getting away from traditional positions and schools   realism, idealism, pragmatism, empiricism and the rest of them. Nothing much will happen in philosophy as long as a main object among philosophers is defense of some formulated historic position. I do not know of any other thinker more calculated than Peirce to give emancipation from the intellectual fortifications of the past and to arouse a fresh imagination.

Marx Inverted

The Emergence of Man, by Gerald Heard.
New York: Harcourt, Brace and Co., 1931.

Mr. Heard has written a book which will be regarded by
some as a revelation; if it had more backbone and structure it
might even mark the beginning of an intellectual cult. To the
present reviewer, it seems an elaborate phantasy, suggested, I
should venture to guess, by brooding on Egyptian history until a
series of episodes translated themselves into pictorial symbols of
the history of mankind. Historians and anthropologists, especially the latter, will have the ultimate decision between these
two views. Mr. Heard, however, will have a retort satisfactory to
himself if these authorities decide against him. His own logic will
compel him to say that they have not risen as yet to that psychological interpretation of history which distinguishes his book.

The main points in Mr. Heard's philosophy of history are as
follows: All history is a drama with a single protagonist, Man—
not men or a plurality of events and actions. Man, whose development, whose emergence constitutes history, is Mind. This fact
could not be grasped until the science of mind, psychology, had
reached its present development. History is evolution transferred
from external nature and animals into mind. All human acts and
achievements "can be co-ordinated and understood if we realise
that they are shadows cast on the outer world by the changing
shape of his spirit, projections and symptoms of a slow inner
evolution of the mind." *This* evolution, internal and self-impelled,
comes first; what is ordinarily called "history," the story of events
and acts, is but an externalization of mental changes. Hence if
we begin, as historians have done up to this time, with acts and
events, we lose the key to history. "Society is the outward physical symptom of an evolution of mental co-ordinations and associations." This evolution is essentially identical and uniform in

[First published in *New Republic* 70 (24 February 1932): 52.]

all the groups and peoples among whom progress has occurred. In all of them, there are "similar thresholds of advance . . . every important step in the advance of civilisation is repeated in all the world-wide variants of man's common fundamental culture." This statement sufficiently dates Mr. Heard in respect to contemporary anthropology. It is, however, a perfectly logical conclusion from the thesis that history is the evolution of a single mind. Consequently the worth of the premise may be judged from the conclusion it necessitates.

The great bulk of Mr. Heard's book is an outline of the various stages which the evolving consciousness of mankind has traversed, outward events and institutional changes being interpreted as fossils from which to read the growth of mind. Mr. Heard has a nice gift of pictorial description, so that incidentally he makes a number of suggestive remarks. I do not intend to be ironical when I say that by his picture of the apelike man as he developed through life in trees, caves, the stone age, etc., children might be led to an intelligent interest in prehistory—provided they took the account imaginatively and not for what it is given out to be.

Mr. Heard's method may be fairly described as a complete inversion of the popular interpretation of the Marxian philosophy of history. Changes in consciousness precede, instead of following, changes in natural and social conditions. For example, kingship did not arise from conquest, but arose because consciousness had developed to a stage at which it was aware of the continuity of the group and needed an external symbol for that fact. The invention and increased use of money were the effect and not the cause of the growth of individualism in the eastern Mediterranean, etc. These cases are typical of the book's theory of social causation. One does not have to be an adherent of the popular interpretation of Marx to believe that Mr. Heard has indulged in a phantasy. Mr. Julian Huxley's seeming approval is interesting—especially for the student of Mr. Huxley's literary career.

Self-Saver or Frankenstein?

Man and Technics, by Oswald Spengler.
New York: Alfred A. Knopf, 1932.

It is a familiar saying that the great intellectual work of the nineteenth century was the discovery of history. The idea of evolution was an extension of its discovery of history, evolution but stretching history to its limit of elasticity. As we notice the shift of emphasis and interest which is now going on we may question, however, whether the familiar saying is more than a half-truth. Would it not be nearer to the truth to say that the nineteenth century discovered *past* history? Since what is characteristic of the present time is speculation about the future, perhaps it will be the task of the twentieth century to discover *future* history. Even more significant than our anxious preoccupation with the question of "Whither Mankind?", is the fact that so early in the century the idea of planning has taken possession of the imagination. There are many points of view from which the Victorian age may be regarded, and as many corresponding definitions of its essence. One of these definitions, at least as true as the others, is that it regarded the present as the culmination, the apogee, of the past. Hence its complacency. Today we think of the present as the preparation for a future; hence our disturbed uncertainty.

The contrast between history which is past and history which is future, together with the reaction upon present mood and attitude of the sense of this contrast, might be carried, without forcing, to the interpretation of many characteristic movements. "Evolution" has ceased to be the unwinding of what is already rolled up on the reel of destiny, an unfolding of the leaves of a scroll, and the rendering visible of passages inscribed at the beginning in a secret indelible ink. The introduction of the idea of mutation marks nothing less than a revolution in our entire

[First published in *Saturday Review of Literature* 8 (12 March 1932): 581–82.]

scheme of interpretation. What also is the notion of emergent evolution save recognition of the novel, unexpected, unpredictable? Nor do I think it fanciful to say that the domination of social thought in the nineteenth century by the idea of *laissez-faire* was a practical tribute to the sway exercised by history as past, just as the importance of the idea of planning is our tribute to history as future. Instead of thinking of ourselves, of our institutions and laws, as effects, we are beginning to think of ourselves and of them as potential causes.

The preoccupation of so much of contemporary thought with the machine and its technology finds its place in the problem of the relation of past and future history. It also gives striking evidence that the force of nineteenth century thought is still with us; that we are still far removed from any universally shared apprehension of the machine in terms of what we can do with it. The more vocal contemporary part of thought still thinks of the machine as something outside of human purpose, as a force proceeding from the past and bound to sweep on and carry us whither it will. As yet, the most obvious sign of change from the nineteenth century temper is the transformation of paeans into lamentations. Instead of jubilation because the machine is sure to usher us automatically into a promised land, we now have the jeremiad that it is sure to land us in waste lands.

But even with respect to the machine, to technology, and the industrial operations which have accompanied the machine, there are signs of a change of attitude. There are an increasing number who remind us that after all the machine was invented and constructed by man, that it is used by man, and that man will be its creature instead of its creator only just as long as he chooses that role for himself. There was no trait of our late prosperity and the "new economic era" more amusing, except that it was alarming, than the assumption so loudly trumpeted by those accepted as leaders that at last we had attained a constantly expanding régime of production equated to consumption which was automatically guaranteed to continue by some inherent process. The tragic collapse of the fact has reacted somewhat— though not as much as one would expect—against the theory. But one may fairly say that at least the problem is now raised. Must man helplessly abdicate before his own production? Can human beings check the tendencies of industrialization which have swept us along for a generation? Can we arrest machine industry at the point of reasonable subordination to other interests, and then turn it to account as a servant of other values? Or are we enslaved by some necessary inescapable cosmic force?

Spengler's little book, *Man and Technics*, both belongs and does not belong to the class of books in which is raised this fundamental issue. He has a vivid sense of the importance of "technics"; he has a much clearer grasp on their nature than most writers. He heartily accepts the idea of mutation; everything decisive in world history has happened suddenly, without warning. He is temperamentally against evolution by gradual cumulative changes; they are too tame and domesticated for him; he demands something dramatic in the way of change. He also sees how fully the issue of our present culture is bound up with what happens to our machine technology. But his analysis and his prophecy are couched wholly in terms of something called destiny. He sees life and history as an inspired oracle of old might have conceived a Greek tragedy of fate, if the oracle had also been gifted with the potentially vast audience of that modern oracle, the publicity agent. For Spengler fairly press-agents Doom, and in the end his technic becomes a mere puppet playing the part assigned to it in the tragedy of destiny.

The volume was originally conceived as an account of prehistoric times; as a story of origins told after the method and manner of *The Decline of the West*. The canvas has been reduced in order to be accommodated to the vision of the reader who is unfitted to grasp the whole scene in the total grandiose pictorial form in which it appears in the *Decline*. Reference to early epochs coming before the age of "High Cultures" remains, but it is now set forth as the first act of the drama which fate is playing with mankind.

A few ideas, strikingly stated, dominate the volume. Technics is not to be identified with the machine or even with the implement and tool. It covers all the ways in which a fighting animal contends with its environment striving to get the better of it as an adversary. It is exemplified equally when the word is used as a weapon (as by the diplomat) and when stalking is employed by the lion. In every technique, things are subordinated to purposive activity, to an idea. Machines are no part of mere economics because they are simply means in the universal conflict of man with nature. The importance of technics in culture was totally overlooked until the nineteenth century. Culture has been supposed in the entire literary and philosophic tradition to be something elevated far above the machine; this tradition measured culture in terms of books, pictures by idealists and ideologues.

The utilitarian, materialistic, socialist movement of the nineteenth century corrected this error but only to fall into a more shallow one. It thought of the machine as the means by which the ease and comfort of humanity were surely to be achieved; its ideal was a devastating state of tranquillity which Spengler describes in terms which remind one of William James's account of the tedium of the eternal tea-party with which the millennium has been identified. Man being a beast of prey, his technics, including the machine, is the armory from which are drawn the weapons with which man fights nature. Since every work of man is artificial, the machine is unnatural, an act of rebellion, of intentional matricide. The higher a culture, the greater is the rift between man and nature, and the more must man become the bitter enemy of nature. Since nature is the stronger, every culture is a defeat: the destiny of tragic doom is within it.

The machine is simply the most powerful of the weapons of man in his combat with nature. But it has created a whole series of tensions in the life of man; tensions between the few leaders and the mass which is led; between the processes of work and its results; between the industrialized nations and the rest of the world; between life and organization, since vital things are dying in the grip of mechanical organization. The machine is failing even from the standpoint of economy or production. In consequence, man is in revolt against the machine which has enslaved him. The knell of this machine culture is sounded, and with its doom there is enacted another act in the tragic destiny of mankind. But to this doom we were born. It is as cowardly as it is futile to strive to resist it and to divert the course of history. What we can do is to perish heroically; or, as a correspondent of mine has put it, we can "wade in chin high" to meet the destroying flood.

I am quite aware that a summary like the one which I have just given may appear like a parody, although it is as faithful an epitome as space permits. But this book indicates what many readers of Spengler's earlier book must have suspected, that the real significance of his work does not lie at all where he himself conceives it to lie but somewhere else. In other words, Mr. Spengler's vast generalizations have a fustian quality. They are rhetorical rather than eloquent; they are tags pasted on, rather than convictions growing directly from the material dealt with. Mr. Spengler has real strength. But it lies in swift, penetrating, incidental remarks. There are a dozen insights in this little volume which are rare and precious. But they have almost nothing to do with the march of any argument; they do not support his final conclusions; they can be converted to many another intellectual use than that which their author makes of them.

It is a pity that Spengler's passion for sparks and glitter is so great. He raises a real problem; he says many things which will have to be taken into account in its solution. But it is extremely doubtful whether many readers will carry from the book the intellectual provocation which a less partisan book might have given. He is committed in advance to write history as a high tragedy, moving from catastrophe to catastrophe on an ever vaster scale. He is committed to looking at all attempts to plan for the future so as to divert forces now operating into more humane channels, with contemptuous indifference. He is a learned German Mencken, but with an obsession that he was born to write high tragedy instead of to be amused at the spectacle of human folly and stupidity. Hence it is that he belongs and does not belong among the thinkers who realize that the most important problem of the present is what we are to do with the new techniques which have come with the advent of the machine. He perceives that the present age is what it is because of the new technology, but his discussion is completely controlled by his concern with destiny and doom. It is, of course, conceivable that the present culture is to collapse; in its present economic form it surely will in time—and probably with only a few to mourn it. But the total destruction because of machine technology of all factors in civilization will occur only if all the rest of us—from levity and routine rather than from a sense of tragedy—agree with Spengler that human desire and thought are impotent. It does not help to say that we are completely in the grip of an over-whelming cosmic force, when in reality we are faced with the problem of what we are to do with a tool we have ourselves created.

Bending the Twig

The Theory of Education in the United States,
by Albert Jay Nock. New York: Harcourt,
Brace and Co., 1932.

This volume contains the trenchant lectures given by
Mr. Nock at the University of Virginia in 1931. Mr. Nock always
knows his own mind and conveys it to the reader with a clarity
of expression equal to its vigor. He has convictions about the
past, present and future of education in the United States; beliefs
that are clear-cut and assured beyond any shadow of doubt or
blurring of edges. Some who are not gifted in generalizing on
a priori grounds will, indeed, wonder if there is anything human
about which one can be as certain as Mr. Nock is about American education.

Behind us in the past was the Great Tradition. It committed
the student in his early years to the acquisition of the three R's;
after that time, the staples were Latin, Greek and mathematics.
The study of the elements of the two languages was begun early;
it went on along with arithmetic and algebra nearly all the way
through the primary school, and all the way through the secondary; when a student arrived at the college doors, he could read
anything in either language and could write in both. Henceforth
he dealt with the languages from the literary point of view, and
he went on to cover practically the whole range of Greek and
Latin literature in the four years of college, where he also mastered mathematics as far as the differential calculus.

The result was disciplinary and formative, the disciplinary
effect having never been seriously disputed, at least so far as Mr.
Nock knows. The formative influence was such that a man who
had had this education instinctively viewed "any contemporary
phenomenon from the vantage-point of an immensely long perspective attained through this profound and weighty experience
of the human spirit"—a statement which is at least an inspiring

[First published in *New Republic* 70 (13 April 1932): 242–44.]

summary of what education should be and do, whether or not it has much relevancy as a record of the usual outcome of the type of education described.

As far as colleges and universities are concerned, the Great Tradition (Mr. Nock never forgets the capitalization) lasted till about thirty-five years ago. Now it is dead in this country. In the old education (the word "old" is superfluous, since, according to Mr. Nock, the old type alone *is* education), each educational unit kept absolutely in its own bailiwick; there was no overlapping, no going back to previous units to patch up deficiencies, and no reaching ahead to anticipate later developments. Moreover, the curricula at each level were invariable in content and uniform for all students. All knowledge was treated as formative, and not as a means to doing something or getting somewhere. There was a sharp division between training and education, for the whole system was selective; it enforced the rejection of all pupils but those with minds that were educable. (This statement provides, by the way, a satisfactory criterion for Mr. Nock's purposes. If a skeptic were to point out that the benefits which Mr. Nock claims for the three R's, Latin, Greek and mathematics system were confined, at a liberal estimate, to one student out of fifty, there is a final answer: The forty-nine others were the uneducable minds, the chaff that the system automatically winnowed out.)

It is hardly necessary, says Mr. Nock, to point out how different is the present situation. The modern American college and university are entirely different in structure, function and intention from the institutions historically entitled to the name. They are not associations of scholars, but associations, more or less sprawling, of pedagogues, upon whom the whole burden of learning has been shifted from the students, who formerly had to assume it. The repertory reaches back into secondary schools and ahead into professional schools. The subject matter is mainly "practical"; the institutions are "vocationalized"—Mr. Flexner's recent book being cited for evidence—the universities give drug-store education. The only educated persons in this country are either over sixty years of age or else were educated in Europe. Moreover, the non-professional scholar has disappeared. We have perhaps some persons who are eminent in science, and more who are conspicuous because of ballyhoo. But we have no ingrained respect for science and, in any case, science is out of account, not being included within the Great Tradition.

The theory underlying our present system of education had its origin in a sentiment which was engaging and honorable—the desire of our forefathers that their children should have a better chance at the humane and good life than they themselves. But the theory has led to unfortunate results, since it is based on three false conceptions—of equality, of democracy, and of the relation of literacy to public order and good government. Equality has been perverted into the notion that everybody is educable and that no person should aspire to anything which is not within the reach of all. Democracy has come to be regarded as our political system, but this, in reality, is only republican or non-monarchical, while democracy is economic in nature, being a doctrine of public property, of diffusion of ownership, which does not obtain in many republican countries. Because of the perversions of equality and democracy, we have the belief that democracy "must regulate itself by the lowest common denominator of intelligence, taste and character," and that the schools should give people "what they want." The third element in the theory results in an absurd and fantastic exaggeration of the political value of literacy.

For a time we endeavored to maintain the Great Tradition along with an attempt, based on our underlying theory, to educate everybody. Since only a few are educable, the two purposes could not be harmonized. Consequently training was substituted for education, for all persons *are* capable of being trained. The outcome is our system of "practical," vocational schools, with their dilutions of knowledge and their substitution of instrumental for formative and cultural knowledge. Training is worth while for the mass and should be encouraged; but the schools which give it have no title to the name of colleges and universities.

Probably many persons will need no more than the summary just given, largely in Mr. Nock's own language, to turn away from the book. It contains at least as much fantastic exaggeration as is attributed to the American faith in literacy. Since I was educated (or at least trained) in the period which antedates Mr. Nock's revolution, and since I have been meeting teachers and students in the long intervening years, I may put on record my own conviction that the number of scholarly teachers and of students who conform to Mr. Nock's conception of education has increased in that period. Since the total number of attendants at college has enormously increased, the number of idlers and of those who attend for purely "social" reasons, in the conventional sense, has also grown. So has the number who go to college for technical and professional reasons. But I doubt if the ratio of the latter has increased. Whatever the Great Tradition was in theory, it was, as a matter of cold fact, largely a vocational preparation for the ministry and for teaching. What has happened is that the number of callings for which schools prepare has greatly multiplied. And, apart from vocational ends, the great mass got only "training" from their Latin, Greek and mathematics.

Since there is no arguing about facts, I merely record these opinions in distinction from the equally dogmatic opinions set forth by Mr. Nock. Since anything Mr. Nock writes is worth pondering both for its style (though in the present work his literary manner is often more reminiscent of Matthew Arnold's than of his own) and for substance, it is to be hoped that the extreme exaggeration of his book will not repel educators and trainers from giving it serious consideration. Although Mr. Nock does not appear aware of the fact, it raises, or should be used to raise, vital questions. Mr. Nock is under no illusions as to the country's economic system. He suggests, accordingly, although he does not expressly discuss, the question whether the narrow pecuniary utilitarianism which affects much of our so-called vocational training is inherent in vocations or is the reflex effect of our economic system. Do the schools give what the people actually "want," or what economic overlords think it best for them to have? If we had a democratic system—which, as Mr. Nock sees and says, is an economic affair—would the divorce between liberal cultivation and preparation for a calling that would bring contentment to the individual and use to others, be what it now is? Since return to the so-called narrow classical system is wholly out of question, and since it never was what it has come to be in Mr. Nock's idealizing nostalgia, these are indications of vital questions which are suggested by this book. Its author has positive notions about the number of human beings who are educable. I do not believe that we shall know the number, nor shall we be able to select those who are educable, whatever their number, until the cultural environment is different. For, while educability is a matter of native endowment, it is also a matter of the prevailing social state of culture. Since the cultural environment is, in turn, profoundly affected by economic factors, why not try democracy, in the sense of Mr. Nock, before dogmatizing upon who is educable and what are the sole means by which an education can be had?

Making Soviet Citizens

New Minds: New Men? by Thomas Woody.
New York: Macmillan Co., 1932.

History of Russian Educational Policy, by
Nicholas Hans. London: P. S. King and Son,
1931.

In 1930 Dr. Hans, in collaboration with another political emigré, Dr. Hessen, who had been a professor of Education
in the University of Leningrad (while it was still St.
Petersburg), published an account of *Educational Policy in Soviet Russia.*
While the authors did not conceal their anti-Bolshevist sympathies, the book was upon the whole an objective statement—giving, however, the outward facts rather than the inner life. It was
especially valuable because it contained a statement of these later
developments, initiated with the dismissal of Lunacharsky, which
moved definitely away from the cultural in the direction of the
technical, and which substituted a "unification" policy for the
educational autonomy previously permitted the various states in
Federal Soviet Russia. It thus supplied a needed addition to and
correction of accounts (including my own) written a few years
earlier. In the present volume Dr. Hans gives a similarly factual,
rather dry account of the history of the development (and lack of
development) of public education in Russia under the old regime. It is a story of the victory of a "class" over a democratic
system, mitigated only by insincere and futile concessions, and
by the genuinely liberal efforts of two progressive ministers of
education. Dr. Hans concludes that the class character of Russian education was a definite factor in generating the violent
revolution. While he himself does not draw the moral, what he
says points to the conclusion that some features of the Soviet administration may be explained as a continuation of the old policy, with reversal of classes, and of class privileges. So far as this
is a just conclusion, it confirms the belief that the Revolution and

[First published in *New Republic* 71 (8 June 1932): 104.]

present-day Bolshevism are much more definitely Russian phenomena than either the extreme partisans or the extreme opponents of the system are willing to admit.

Dr. Woody's book is written not from the outside, but as the
result of many months' direct contact with hundreds of Russian
schools scattered all over the country, and of acquaintance, often
intimate, with scores and scores of Russian educators. Its general
tone is, I think, indicated by the presence of the mark of inter-
rogation in the title. The author speaks somewhere in his pages
of a "kindly skepticism." He is not referring to himself, but the
phrase describes better than any other that occurs to me his own
attitude. "Skepticism," however, is to be taken in its literal sense.
It signifies the doubting that is equivalent to questioning and sus-
pension of judgment, not that which is identical with denial.
Much that is in the book will come like a dash of cold water to
the ultra-enthusiasts; and partisanship aside, it contains much
material which may be used to support the belief of those who
hold that the Soviet rulers are doing their cause an eventual
disservice by excess of dogma and indoctrination. Dr. Woody
brings out clearly enough the access of energy which can come to
an educational system when it is linked up with a social ideal.
But he also gives much evidence, and in concrete detail, that
constant and uniform social propaganda can become as formal
and wooden as any other mechanized system, while it ends, in
many cases, by producing tough callousness and a perfunctory
adherence.

Dr. Woody makes no attempt to cover the entire scheme of Soviet education, although one chapter is given to a general sketch
of the system, including some sample curricula. What he deals
with is the attempt by means of the schools to produce a new
type of mentality, favorable to the collectivist economy and political order which the Communist party is striving to create.
Every phase of the undertaking, as far as it affects school life and
teaching, is dealt with by the author. Moreover, it is dealt with
not in generalities, but in concrete detail, often in verbal extracts
from extensive notes made on the spot. The report on schools
opens with a picture of Shatsky's educational colony—the school
which I imagine best embodies the intrinsic spirit of the new
education with the least admixture of routine, conventional
and mechanical letter. Then there are chapters devoted to chil-

dren's literature; Octobrists and Pioneers; the Komsomols, or Communist Youth organization for party apprenticeship; self-organization and self-government; the anti-religious campaign; internationalism; collectivism; feminism, and finally a chapter on physical education.

The unifying thread which binds the chapters together, as well as the various topics considered in each chapter, is the character of the new mind which it is hoped to form. Dr. Woody sums up the desired qualities of this mind under twelve heads. At the risk of undue formalism I will cite them. The new mind is to believe in the dictatorship of the Communist party, which it is to be able to justify by Marxian dialectic; it is to be militant, activist, class-conscious; secular (or atheistic), political, collectivistic (cooperative with groups), anti-nationalistic and international; based on physical health, and making no distinctions on the ground of sex. And finally it is to glorify labor and the laborer.

There is so much detail in Dr. Woody's book that for many persons it will serve as a book of reference rather than as material for consecutive reading. For general reading, it is rather over-documented. Dr. Woody has too conscientiously abstained from generalization. But, nevertheless, it is a mine of information; those who prefer concrete facts to large and loose generalizations will find it indispensable. Certainly no teacher interested in what is going on in Russia can afford to be ignorant of it. Those whose interest in the Soviet experiment is political and economic can gain from the book a better picture of the difficulties in the way of its success, and of the immense amount of hard work that has to be done, than from many a book dealing directly with the Soviet system. It breathes the spirit of suspended judgment, of toleration, of human sympathy; it will not satisfy partisans on either side. For this very reason, it will perhaps command the confidence of those of us who have a genuine interest in the Russian undertaking, who would like to see it succeed in its ultimate aims, but retain enough of democratic faith to be skeptical about the ruthlessness of its intellectual as well as of its political measures. I wish especially that all our recent literary converts to Communism would study the book until they have definitely made up their minds on the subject of dictatorship and all it implies—for, if they want communism without dictatorship, then the most essential thinking, that which concerns the road to be taken to the ultimate goal, still remains to be done. If it should be decided that democracy is the only alternative road to dictatorship, there will, I think, ensue a great clarification of turbid radical thought—equally so, if the decision is in favor of recourse to dictatorship.

The Meiklejohn Experiment

The Experimental College, by Alexander
Meiklejohn. New York: Harper and Bros.,
1932.

In reflecting upon this book after an absorbed reading
of it, I seem to see three points of view from which it might be
reviewed. In the first place, it gives an account of a particular experiment undertaken in a particular American college. During
its course, this experiment attracted great attention, not to say
controversy, in other colleges as well as in the University of
Wisconsin. It excited enthusiasm and animosities; it was a standing subject of rumor and gossip in university circles. Like every
large educational innovation it involved a clash of persons as
well as of educational principles and practical policies. It engaged the emotions quite as much as the intellect.

The strictly local features of the experiment appear in the author's account only between the lines. The personal factors are
passed by without notice; and the theme is discussed with can-
dor and calm objectivity. Only by indirection would one gather
from the book that an educational tempest had raged. The difficulties arising from internal faculty opposition are left to be
guessed at. No extreme claims are made for the success of the
experiment. "Our report is not that we have a scheme of teaching whose merits have been demonstrated, but that we have a
plan which seems worthy of consideration by an American college of liberal arts." The problems which are intrinsic to every
such experiment are frankly dealt with—such as the possibility
of granting students fresh from the regime of the high school as
much freedom and self-direction as they were given under Mr.
Meiklejohn. On this point the author speaks with positiveness.
Since the lesson of self-direction is one to be learned some time
by every self-respecting person, he believes the experiment demonstrated that American youths between the ages of eighteen
and twenty showed themselves capable of learning it.

[First published in *New Republic* 72 (17 August 1932): 23–24.]

Another aspect of the book is its contribution to the art of teaching—its discussion of what goes on, or may be induced to go on, in the contact of mind with mind. To the teacher, the chapters devoted to this topic are most enlightening. No teacher can fail to recognize, in all that is said about the intellectual discipline and instruction of young men—about the values and limitations of lectures, conferences, individual and group, about the conditions under which mental self-activity is stirred, about differing types of students—all the marks of the born and trained artist in conduct of that intercourse which excites and guides the thought of others. Whatever may be the judgment of the teacher about the worth of the purpose and plan of the experiment, whatever the doubt about the value of the attempt to communicate intellectual excitement to the young, there will be none as to the ability with which the work was carried on from the teaching side.

I think, however, that the larger aspect of the report is the one which will command the most enduring attention. The book is fundamentally a discussion of the place and function of the college of liberal arts in the entire scheme of American education. If I may say so without frightening anyone away from an extremely lucid and readable book, it is a contribution to the philosophy of American education; the liberal college, the first two years of our traditional college course, is discussed in relation to what precedes and what comes after that period. The discussion of the theory is, of course, the more pointed and the more significant because, unlike most such discussions, it comes to us as the philosophy of an actual undertaking, not as a full bolt from the blue of abstraction. Moreover, the educational ideas presented are tied up with a clearly thought-out conception of the nature, the defects and promise, of American culture and life.

I cite a few sentences which at least suggest the character of this conception. "There is no hope that in such a society as ours, young people will find a peaceful, a non-intellectual adjustment in the world which we have made for them." "The essential incoherence of a social order [like that of our own country] can bring into confusion and bewilderment the activities of its teachers." The teachers in the experiment were concerned not only with "what young men are and may be," but with what "America is and may become." "The essential difficulty with which the education of young Americans has to deal is that they do not *think* about the information which they already have." With such an outlook it is not surprising that Mr. Meiklejohn made the dominant aim of the experimental college the development of intelligence, the assumption of intellectual responsibility; nor that the function of intelligence was conceived to be "service of men in the creation of and maintenance of a social order, a scheme of individual and group living, which will meet the human demands for beauty, strength, justice, generosity."

The experiment was conceived in terms so remote from the complacency and aimless drift of much of our social life, it was such a challenge to the accidental empiricism which so controls our college studies and teaching methods, that it is not surprising that it evoked bitter opposition or that it failed of achieving its supreme purpose. For it faced frankly that which is the great difficulty in the American college because it is the greatest defect in American life outside the college. Anyone who claimed that the problem could be solved in any term of five years, or of double or treble that time, would be a quack—and Mr. Meiklejohn is no quack. No one can read the book with mental honesty and not see that the experiment was something quite other than that manipulation of minor details which constitutes the ordinary process of educational innovation. Whether or not the right procedure was undertaken is a minor matter compared with the complete openness with which the problem was attacked. The time at disposal did not allow even a test of the ultimate value of the methods followed, beyond the fact that further trial is well worth while.

The book ought to accomplish something in transferring discussion and controversy from the fitness of the study of Athenian culture and American life (through the medium, largely, of Plato's writings and *The Education of Henry Adams*) to the deeper question of the end which these studies were intended to serve. In the author's words, these instrumentalities were "a device for stirring a young man to see that with which he is already acquainted, to think about that which he already knows." And again, "to understand a civilization is nothing else than to face and to solve, as far as one can, the questions with which its intelligence is dealing."

I probably should not be alone in wondering whether the

methods actually pursued did not involve an overestimate of the function of books in developing intelligence. On the other hand, I recognize that a person who like myself is habituated to the use of books may, because of familiarity, underrate the part they can play in development of a self-directed responsible intelligence. And there can be no doubt that special emphasis should be laid upon the use of books of the first rank, because the average student "has been formed and shaped by a society which does not regard living in the companionship of books as constituting great success or high achievement"; and because, again, "the American home, the American school, the American social order do not, at present, create acceptance of the value of liberal understanding."

Were I to go further into the characteristics of the experiment, there are two points I should want to emphasize. One is its adherence to the conviction that integration is indispensable. The time will come, I imagine, when there will be surprise that such a miscellaneous, scattered body of studies as our college students now deal with, does not fail even worse than it does in the fostering of intelligence. The other point is that a genuinely integrated learning and discipline cannot be attained without an integrated relationship of teacher and student. One conclusion is "the conviction that educational planning and teaching should be done not by large faculties, but by small and independent groups of teachers," and that "all the members of the teaching force shall have genuine and intimate intellectual acquaintance with one another."

At every point, the experiment at Madison ran counter to the weight of precedent and tradition. There is little cause for wonder that it aroused an opposition which renders its continuation doubtful. The report ends with a suggestion that teaching should be a self-criticizing activity, continued experimentation being a contribution to that end. Is there an American college which is willing and able to carry its self-criticism to the point demanded by the Meiklejohn experiment? I doubt it.

A Philosophy of Scientific Method

Reason and Nature: An Essay on the Meaning of Scientific Method, by Morris R. Cohen. New York: Harcourt, Brace and Co., 1931.

The subtitle of Professor Cohen's book best describes its content and value. I know of no recent work, save that of Meyerson, which unites such command of scientific material, ranging from mathematics and physics through biology and psychology to the social sciences, with both insight and the power of lucid exposition. The fullness of material and breadth of topics compel a reviewer to resort to the time-honored device of sending a reader to the book itself.

The main title describes the book from the author's own angle of philosophical interpretation. The first part in particular contains less discussion of actual science and a fuller statement of Mr. Cohen's own standpoint than most of what follows. The epilogue of the book is "in dispraise of life, experience, and reality." The first part is in eulogy of reason—a word which Mr. Cohen employs to cover honorifically everything from apprehension of universals or invariants to reasoning and thoughtfulness. In consequence, the "nature" of which his book treats is not so much nature as it confronts and intercepts man in life; still less is it Nature as celebrated by poets: it is nature distilled through the alembic of science and logic. Mr. Cohen's nature is *the* nature, the character, of things, their universals. This, to my mind, is both the strength and the weakness of the book. Not that a thinker is unjustified in selecting for discussion that aspect or property of the world which most attracts his intellectual interest; he is not only justified but compelled so to do, unless he is to treat vaguely and miscellaneously of all things. It is rather that by implication and often explicitly, Mr. Cohen employs the object of his particular regard to cast discredit on that to which he is not personally drawn.

[First published in *New Republic* 66 (29 April 1931): 306–7. For Cohen's reply, see this volume, Appendix 4, and for Dewey's rejoinder, see this volume, p. 304.]

Thus, the strength of the book is its exposition of what science actually does and how it does it, irrespective of philosophical interpretation. Anyone who wants to know about this matter, and who is willing to see popular myths exploded which perhaps he has shared, has a rich treat awaiting him. The book is extraordinary in its comprehensive and accurate learning, and remarkable for clearness of exposition, whenever it deals with the actual subject matter and methods of the exact sciences. If these qualities are less marked when the author is dealing with psychology and the social sciences, the fault lies probably with the present status of those subjects rather than with Mr. Cohen. But philosophically the work suffers, in my estimation, from failure clearly to define issues—a strange defect to impute to a logician. The blurring is apparently due to the author's aversion to certain views opposed to his own, and to a somewhat intense moral conviction of the harm these views work. The aversion is so strong that he cannot endure to dwell upon them long enough to see just what they are, as long as they can be labeled with depreciatory tags.

An instance trifling enough in itself is found in the fact that he introduces his dispraise of life with a quotation from William James about the philosophic movement of the early part of this century. Of it, James said, "It lacks logical rigour, but it has the tang of life." The remark was an innocent comment; taken in its own perspective the historian of philosophical thought will find it just. But in Mr. Cohen's unsympathetic hands, it becomes a text from which is derived opposition to logic and reasonable thought and regard for mere life irrespective of its quality. He imputes to James in another passage an "unavowed definition of experience as immediate and vivid sensations," and a dependence upon British sensationalistic empiricism. In fact, James brought against this type of empiricism the most devastating criticism to which it has ever been subjected on psychological grounds, and insisted upon the importance of experience of objective relations.

These matters are relevant to Mr. Cohen's failure definitely to state the fundamental issue with which he is concerned—that between rationalism and empiricism. By identifying empiricism with a sensationalistic particularism he wins an easy victory for his rationalism. The problem of whether and how actual experience can explain the existence and role of rational thought is therefore never faced. In consequence, the doctrine that reason is something over and beyond experience is not rationally supported with convincing evidence; the position is rather begged.

Since most philosophers, however, are better acquainted with other philosophers than with science, it is well occasionally to have the roles reversed. And in any case it is a pleasure to turn from criticizing the book to describing its more positive content. It would require too much space to deal with his treatment of psychology and the social sciences, in discussing the latter of which Cohen's knowledge of law comes into effective play; so I shall speak mainly of his significant treatment of mathematics and physical science.

The book will give little satisfaction to the old-fashioned rationalist, the one who would either deduce the whole complex of the universe from reason or gather all its manifestations under the guardian wings of rationality. That procedure the author designates as pseudo-rationalism; in the traditional sense of the word, his book is much less rationalistic than is, for example, Whitehead's *Process and Reality*. Mr. Cohen's fundamental metaphysics is contained in the principle of polarity, the strife and balance of opposites, such as universal and particular, form and matter, the necessary and the contingent. I know of no better exposition of the irreducible character of the contingent than that offered on pages 151 and 152 of the present work. Science is bound to assume, no matter how far back it goes, a given distribution of material particles for which no reason can be assigned; these are just brutely so and so; moreover, all scientific explanation is selective; laws must limit themselves to a small number of variables; and this fact is identical with recognition that for law (and the sum of laws) facts excluded as irrelevant are contingent. Finally, laws themselves have contingency. We can carry back laws to a more general law, but that more general law has undemonstrable terms. In fact, the more general the law, the less deducible, by truism, are its terms. Contingency is final because things in the universe have individuality, as well as having relations which are necessary, universal and invariant.

But having once recognized contingency as an ultimate category, Mr. Cohen is not interested in its interplay with law—that is, with nature as it actually presents itself to us—perhaps because that would take him too close to dispraised "experience." Except when he refers to the fact of contingency as a weapon of criticism of other theories, nature remains for him the character of things as determined in universal relations.

Given the author's standpoint, nothing could be more satisfactory than the treatment of Chapter III of the first book, which deals with the gathering of facts, the ideal of science, induction and deduction, the logic of probability, and the *a priori*. The criticism of current views about induction and deduction is particularly trenchant and effective. One phase of it is well expressed in the statement that the actual growth of knowledge is not from the particular to the universal, but from the vague to the definite. There are no rules by which this growth can be determined; progress into the unknown is always a leap into the dark. "Methods," whether inductive or deductive, are the ways in which we safeguard this leap as best we may: this statement is not made by Mr. Cohen, but it seems to be a fair interpretation. The chapter is especially successful in showing how deduction actually leads to discovery of new truths and facts, and is not *merely* a method of arranging and expounding what is already known.

For the rest, I can only refer to some points which have especially impressed me, selecting them somewhat arbitrarily. Mathematics is identified with logic, while the latter is taken to be, not the science of thought, but the science of invariant orders among all possible entities. It is applied, as in physics, when an order is employed to isolate an object for study and to determine or formulate it in such a way that further significant relations can be computed. As a description of all invariant relations, it is perforce a description also of those which are found in the comparatively small number of possibilities that are actualized. There are several points in Mr. Cohen's treatment of this and related matters not wholly clear to me. He speaks of mathematics as having the character of "rules or formulae of procedure." There are some who would derive the invariant forms of mathematics and logic precisely from this methodological character, rather than from their being characters as such of existence, whether possible or actual. Mr. Cohen justly criticized those who would regard forms in their character of methods as purely arbitrary, but he nowhere discusses the view that while they are *conditioned* by actual existence (and would not otherwise be applicable to it), they are not in themselves characters of existence. Yet this is the crucial issue.

The chapter on mechanism and causality in physics, and the related chapter on vitalism and mechanism in biology, I found particularly noteworthy. They make clear the difference between the earlier notion of mechanics as an assumption that all physical phenomena are to be deduced from the special properties of masses—including of course motion as displacement—and the methodological hypothesis that all phenomena are to be *physically* explained. The actual development of science has compelled a surrender of the former assumption, but leaves the latter intact—a consideration which disposes equally of dogmatic metaphysical mechanism and of the notion entertained by some popular writers on religion and science, that its breakdown opens the way for "spiritual" causation.

I have barely touched on a few of the more important themes which Mr. Cohen discusses with well grounded knowledge and in ways which never fail to illuminate the topic with which he is dealing. I can only hope that my somewhat random sampling will send readers who have a serious interest in the methods and procedures of science to this book, for which the intelligent public is indebted to Morris Cohen.

Reply to Cohen's "Reason, Nature and Professor Dewey"

Sir: I could not and did not expect that Professor Cohen would accept the validity of my moderate criticism of his *Reason and Nature*. I did not anticipate, however, that in replying he would provide such an excellent example of the trait chiefly criticized, namely, unwillingness to conceive of "experience" except in traditional, sensational and mental terms. For he explains that I differ from him because I am "primarily interested in the human world and in the psychologic growth of our ideas about things." This is a good instance of a failure to define a crucial issue because of misconception of alternatives. Until it is recognized that the newer conception of experience is precisely one which is concerned to break down the traditional isolation of the human from the "natural," of "ideas" from "things," by placing the human and mental in continuity with natural processes, the blurring of issues will persist.

[First published in *New Republic* 67 (17 June 1931): 127. For Cohen's article to which this is a reply, see this volume, Appendix 4, and for Dewey's review, see this volume, pp. 299–303.]

Miscellany

Prefatory Remarks in
The Philosophy of the Present

The difficult task of drawing for the reader a map in which the main features of George Mead's thought are set before us (as is the business of a good map), in their proper relations to one another has been performed by Dr. Murphy in his Introduction. It would be of little or no assistance to the reader were I to go over the ground which he has traversed. There is, however, a trait of Mr. Mead's mind which when it is recognized will help protect the reader from some of the pitfalls into which one is likely to fall in dealing with an original thinker. While Mr. Mead was an original thinker, he had no sense of being original. Or if he had such a feeling he kept it under. Instead of bringing to the front as novelties the problems which were occupying his own mind (which they were even as problems), he chose to link them to ideas and movements already current. An excellent instance of this trait is found in the pragmatic theory of knowledge to which Professor Murphy refers. Mr. Mead does not seem to have had any consciousness of the way and the degree in which his own conception was a novel contribution; he preferred to treat it as if it were a natural outgrowth with at most some change of emphasis in statement.

When I first came to know Mr. Mead, well over forty years ago, the dominant problem in his mind concerned the nature of consciousness as personal and private. In the 'eighties and 'nineties, idealism prevailed in Anglo-American thought. It had a solution of the problem of consciousness ready to offer. Mind as consciousness was at once the very stuff of the universe and the structural forms of this stuff; human consciousness in its intimate and seemingly exclusively personal aspect was at most but a variant, faithful or errant, of the universal mind. I almost never

[First published in George Herbert Mead, *The Philosophy of the Present*, ed. Arthur Edward Murphy (Chicago: Open Court Publishing Co., 1932), pp. xxvi–xl.]

heard Mr. Mead argue directly against this view. I suppose that it never seemed real to him in spite of the fact that it was the official doctrine of most of his own teachers and was, in some form or other, the philosophic conception most generally put forward in the philosophical writings of the period. When, however, it was urged upon him, instead of combating it, he took the ground that it did not touch the problem in which he was interested. Even if it were true and were accepted as such, it did not explain how states of mind peculiar to an individual, like the first hypotheses of a discoverer which throw into doubt beliefs previously entertained and which deny objectivity to things that have been universally accepted as real objects, can function as the sources of objects which instead of being private and personal, instead of being merely "subjective," belong to the common and objective universe.

As I look back I can see that a great deal of the seeming obscurity of Mr. Mead's expression was due to the fact that he saw something as a problem which had not presented itself at all to the other minds. There was no common language because there was no common object of reference. His problem did not fall into the categories and classifications of either idealism or realism. He was talking about something which the rest of us did not see. It lay outside of what used to be called "apperceptive masses." I fancy that if one had a sufficiently consecutive knowledge of Mr. Mead's intellectual biography during the intervening years, one could discover how practically all his inquiries and problems developed out of his original haunting question. His sense of the role of subjective consciousness in the reconstruction of objects as experienced and in the production of new customs and institutions was surely the thing which led him to his extraordinarily broad and accurate knowledge of the historical development of the sciences—a knowledge which did not stop with details of discoveries but which included changes of underlying attitudes toward nature. His interest in the problem of self led in one direction to the study of the organism as the biological unit corresponding to the self. In the other direction it necessitated that study of the self in its social relations which carried him into social psychology—the field in which, I suppose, he had the greatest immediate influence through the effect of his teaching upon his students. The nature of his problem was such, as

one can readily see, to make him acutely sensitive to the doctrines of Whitehead, especially the effort to include matters usually relegated to an exclusively subjective realm within the constitution of nature itself. Since his problem was (and that long
before the words "emergent evolution" were heard), essentially
that of the emergence of the new and its ultimate incorporation
in a recognized and now old world, one can appreciate how
much more fundamentally he took the doctrine of emergence
than have most of those who have played with the idea. Against
this background, his generalization of the idea of "sociality" and
his interpretation of emergence in evolution take on a meaning
which they do not otherwise have.

There is a passage to be found in the recently published first
volume of Peirce's work which explains to me the kind of originality which marked Mr. Mead. "It is," Peirce said, "extremely
difficult to bring our attention to elements of experience which
are continually present. For we have nothing in experience with
which to contrast them; and without contrast, they cannot excite
our attention. . . . The result is that round-about devices have to
be resorted to in order to enable us to perceive what stares us in
the face with a glare that, once noticed, becomes almost oppressive with its insistency." The power of observing common
elements, which are ignored just because they are common,
characterized the mind of George Mead. It accounts for the difficulty which he had in conveying what he observed to others.
Most philosophical thinking is done by means of following out
the logical implications of concepts which seem central to a particular thinker, the deductions being reinforced by suitable concrete data. Mr. Mead's philosophical thinking often, perhaps
usually, reverses the process. It springs from his own intimate experiences, from things deeply felt, rather than from things merely
thought out by him, which then seek substantiation in accepted
facts and current concepts. His interest in the concept of emergence is, for example, a reflex of that factor of his own intellectual experience by which new insights were constantly budding
and having then to be joined to what he had thought previously,
instead of merely displacing old ideas. He *felt* within himself
both the emergence of the new and the inevitable continuity of
the new with the old. So too he experienced within himself the
struggle of ideas, hypotheses, presentiments, at first wholly pri-

vate, a matter of intimate personal selfhood, to find and take their place in an objective, shared, public world. His sense of "sociality" as simultaneous existence in two different orders seems to me to have something in common with the combination of great originality and unusual deference to others which marked his own personality.

In contrast with the kind of originality which marked his thinking I realize that much which passes for original thinking is a reworking, in the light of some new perspective, of intellectual attitudes already pretty well conventionalized; the working of a vein of ore previously uncovered but not adequately exploited by others. I realize also that in much of what seems like clearness of literary expression, the clearness is but another name for familiarity rather than something intrinsic to the thought. The loss which American philosophy has suffered by Mr. Mead's untimely death is increased by the fact that there is every reason to think that he was beginning to get a command of his ideas which made communication to others easier and more effective. The manuscript of his Carus lectures—for whose careful editing we owe so much to Dr. Murphy—gives hardly more than hurriedly prepared notes of extreme condensation. He was planning to expand them to three or four times their present length, an expansion which would have clarified the thought and not merely swelled the number of words. But in spite of all limitations, I believe that a widening public will increasingly find in his writings what personal students have found for many, many years: a seminal mind of the very first order.

Introduction to *Studies in Philosophy*

I had occasion recently in writing a few words about Mr. Mead's forthcoming volume of Carus Lectures to speak of a certain trait of his mind or rather of his personality which in his case was identified in an unusual way with mind.[1] The characteristic in question was a union of remarkable originality with deference to the position of others,—a deference which apparently obscured his consciousness of his own originality. I cited in this connection the fact that he regarded his own work mainly as an extension of pragmatism. While Mr. Mead was in sympathy with the pragmatic position, at least in one of its many forms, his essential contribution goes far beyond anything found in any pragmatic writing before his own thought received expression. Even the problem with which he was most deeply and uniquely concerned was not one which had found any especial recognition among the pragmatist writers, any more than it had among thinkers of other groups. It was, if I may state it too briefly for adequate expression, the problem of the place of consciousness, that is, of the *objects* of consciousness, in the total frame of things. The problem came home to Mr. Mead from many sides and in many ways. The way which is grasped most readily (because of its connection with the historic tradition of modern philosophy) is well indicated in Dr. Lafferty's article. Physical science had excluded from the realm of its objects all purposes and values, the things which are precious and prized in life-experience. Hence, following Descartes, philosophy had created

1. I may remark that I think that Dr. Van Meter Ames was the actual author of the saying which Mr. Lafferty attributes to me. But I so heartily endorse it that I am glad to be associated with the sentiment. [For Dewey's remarks regarding Mead's book, see this volume, pp. 307–10.]

[First published in Theodore T. Lafferty, *Studies in Philosophy*, Lehigh University Publication, vol. 6, no. 7 (Bethlehem, Pa.: Lehigh University, 1932), i–ii.]

a realm of consciousness which these values and purposes might inhabit—a realm, in Mr. Mead's striking phrase, of the "rejects" of physical science. This consideration, in connection with the allied fact (which Mr. Mead felt more deeply, I think, than any other contemporary philosopher) that the world of objects of physical science is general and public, while the objects of "consciousness," in the modern tradition, constituted the personal individual mind as such, determined the general course of Mr. Mead's thought. His attitude toward it, the objective and metaphysical solution he had to offer, was one with his conception of the significance of the *social*. It was worked out in main outline before the change took place from Newtonian physics to those of relativity and related themes. But Mr. Mead, with originality equal to that of his earlier thought, saw that the change could and must be interpreted in a way which gave the social interpretation of consciousness, of mind as individual, a place in the new and enlarged universe which physical science itself was compelled to set up. In his later writings he used largely the terminology of Mr. Whitehead's interpretation of the new physics as a medium for expressing the conception which he had earlier arrived at. The papers of Mr. Lafferty's are a true and yet fresh and independent version of the problem which occupied Mr. Mead's mind, and are faithful to the spirit of his solution. Consequently, while I do not feel that his papers are in need of any introduction from any outside source, my constantly growing sense of the importance of Mead's philosophical contribution has caused me gladly to accede to the request for a few words by way of an introduction.

Foreword to
The Coming of a New Party

There exist books giving a history of political parties in
the United States; describing the rise and fall of new parties; giving an analysis of political tactics; diagnosing our present political ills; picturing our economic situation in its social effects; and
arguing for a new party. Mr. Douglas has taken essential elements from all these fields, and has put them together in a single
book. He has not laid them side by side in a mechanical way; he
has combined them in a vital union. There are so few who have
mastered the variety of facts which Mr. Douglas presents in this
book that to most of its readers it will bring a genuine political
education—and this quite independently of whether or no they
agree with his conclusion about the necessity of a new party. The
spirit, the ardor, the hope, which permeate the book make it an
inspiration as well as an educative force.

We have here no remote academic argument for the coming of
a new political movement. We have a vivid and authoritative picture of the existing American scene—documented, concrete,
moving. The reader feels that he is not dealing with the opinions
of the author as to why there should be a new party, but with the
factors in our industrial and social life which are bound to bring
one into existence. Mr. Douglas has so marshalled the material
that we see political forces on the march. The difficulties in the
way of creating a new party are not evaded; they receive full consideration. But as one reads one is made to see forces at work
which will overcome these difficulties. The picture of the forces
shaping the life of the average man and woman in the United
States is so clear, so authenticated, that even those persons who
do not believe in a third party and even those who fancy they are
not interested in politics will derive from the book a realistic

[First published in Paul H. Douglas, *The Coming of a New Party* (New York:
McGraw-Hill Book Co., Whittlesey House, 1932), pp. vii–viii.]

understanding of our conditions and our problems. There is nothing doctrinaire about the book; there is a convincing statement of the material out of which our future policies must be formed.

If I knew any way to make this book compulsory reading for all citizens, especially for all young men and women, whose political minds are not closed to facts and ideas, I would gladly do so. And my desire for this end is not actuated just by the hope that they would be converted thereby to the idea of a new party. No matter what their final conclusion, those who read the book will be more intelligent, more alert and energetic citizens of whatever parties they choose to join.

Introduction to *The Use of the Self*

In writing some introductory words to Mr. Alexander's previous book, *Constructive Conscious Control of the Individual*, I stated that his procedure and conclusions meet all the requirements of the strictest scientific method, and that he has applied the method in a field in which it had never been used before—that of our judgments and beliefs concerning ourselves and our activities. In so doing, he has, I said in effect, rounded out the results of the sciences in the physical field, accomplishing this end in such a way that they become capable of use for human benefit. It is a commonplace that scientific technique has for its consequence control of the energies to which it refers. Physical science has for its fruit an astounding degree of new command of physical energies. Yet we are faced with a situation which is serious, perhaps tragically so. There is everywhere increasing doubt as to whether this physical mastery of physical energies is going to further human welfare, or whether human happiness is going to be wrecked by it. Ultimately there is but one sure way of answering this question in the hopeful and constructive sense. If there can be developed a technique which will enable individuals really to secure the right use of themselves, then the factor upon which depends the final use of all other forms of energy will be brought under control. Mr. Alexander has evolved this technique.

In repeating these statements, I do so fully aware of their sweeping nature. Were not our eyes and ears so accustomed to irresponsible statements that we cease to ask for either meaning or proof, they might well raise a question as to the complete in-

[First published in F. Matthias Alexander, *The Use of the Self: Its Conscious Direction in Relation to Diagnosis, Functioning and the Control of Reaction* (New York: E. P. Dutton and Co., 1932), pp. xiii–xix.]

tellectual responsibility and competency of their author. In repeating them after the lapse of intervening years, I appeal to the
account which Mr. Alexander has given of the origin of his discovery of the principle of central and conscious control. Those
who do not identify science with a parade of technical vocabulary will find in this account the essentials of scientific method in
any field of inquiry. They will find a record of long continued,
patient, unwearied experimentation and observation in which
every inference is extended, tested, corrected by further more
searching experiments; they will find a series of such observations in which the mind is carried from observation of comparatively coarse, gross, superficial connections of causes and
effect to those causal conditions which are fundamental and central in the use which we make of ourselves.

Personally, I cannot speak with too much admiration—in the
original sense of wonder as well as the sense of respect—of the
persistence and thoroughness with which these extremely difficult observations and experiments were carried out. In consequence, Mr. Alexander created what may be truly called a physiology of the *living* organism. His observations and experiments
have to do with the actual functioning of the body, with the organism in operation, and in operation under the ordinary conditions of living—rising, sitting, walking, standing, using arms,
hands, voice, tools, instruments of all kinds. The contrast between sustained and accurate observations of the living and the
usual activities of man and those made upon dead things under
unusual and artificial conditions marks the difference between
true and pseudo-science. And yet so used have we become to as-
sociating "science" with the latter sort of thing that its contrast
with the genuinely scientific character of Mr. Alexander's observations has been one great reason for the failure of many to appreciate his technique and conclusions.

As might be anticipated, the conclusions of Mr. Alexander's
experimental inquiries are in harmony with what physiologists
know about the muscular and nervous structure. But they give a
new significance to that knowledge; indeed, they make evident
what knowledge itself really is. The anatomist may "know" the
exact function of each muscle, and conversely know what muscles
come into play in the execution of any specified act. But if he is

himself unable to coordinate all the muscular structures involved in, say, sitting down or in rising from a sitting position in a way which achieves the optimum and efficient performance of that act; if, in other words, he misuses himself in what he does, how can he be said to *know* in the full and vital sense of that word? Magnus proved by means of what may be called *external* evidence the existence of a central control in the organism. But Mr. Alexander's technique gave a direct and intimate confirmation in personal experience of the fact of central control long before Magnus carried on his investigations. And one who has had experience of the technique *knows* it through the series of experiences which he himself has. The genuinely scientific character of Mr. Alexander's teaching and discoveries can be safely rested upon this fact alone.

The vitality of a scientific discovery is revealed and tested in its power to project and direct new further operations which not only harmonize with prior results but which lead on to new observed materials, suggesting in turn further experimentally controlled acts, and so on in a continued series of new developments. Speaking as a pupil, it was because of this fact as demonstrated in personal experience that I first became convinced of the scientific quality of Mr. Alexander's work. Each lesson was a laboratory experimental demonstration. Statements made in advance of consequences to follow and the means by which they would be reached were met with implicit scepticism—a fact which is practically inevitable, since, as Mr. Alexander points out, one uses the very conditions that need re-education as one's standard of judgment. Each lesson carries the process somewhat further and confirms in the most intimate and convincing fashion the claims that are made. As one goes on, new areas are opened, new possibilities are seen and then realized; one finds himself continually growing, and realizes that there is an endless process of growth initiated.

From one standpoint, I had an unusual opportunity for making an intellectual study of the technique and its results. I was, from the practical standpoint, an inept, awkward and slow pupil. There were no speedy and seemingly miraculous changes to evoke gratitude emotionally, while they misled me intellectually. I was forced to observe carefully at every step of the process, and to interest myself in the theory of the operations. I did this partly from my previous interest in psychology and philosophy, and partly as a compensation for my practical backwardness. In bringing to bear whatever knowledge I already possessed—or thought, I did—and whatever powers of discipline in mental application I had acquired in the pursuit of these studies, I had the most humiliating experience of my life, intellectually speaking. For to find that one is unable to execute directions, including inhibitory ones, in doing such a seemingly simple act as to sit down, when one is using all the mental capacity which one prides himself upon possessing, is not an experience congenial to one's vanity. But it may be conducive to analytic study of causal conditions, obstructive and positive. And so I verified in personal experience all that Mr. Alexander says about the unity of the physical and psychical in the psycho-physical; about our habitually wrong use of ourselves and the part this wrong use plays in generating all kinds of unnecessary tensions and wastes of energy; about the vitiation of our sensory appreciations which form the material of our judgments of ourselves; about the unconditional necessity of inhibition of customary acts, and the tremendous mental difficulty found in not "doing" something as soon as an habitual act is suggested, together with the great change in moral and mental attitude that takes place as proper coordinations are established. In re-affirming my conviction as to the scientific character of Mr. Alexander's discoveries and technique, I do so then not as one who has experienced a "cure," but as one who has brought whatever intellectual capacity he has to the study of a problem. In the study, I found the things which I had "known"—in the sense of theoretical belief—in philosophy and psychology, changed into vital experiences which gave a new meaning to knowledge of them.

In the present state of the world, it is evident that the control we have gained of physical energies, heat, light, electricity, etc., without having first secured control of our use of ourselves is a perilous affair. Without control of our use of ourselves, our use of other things is blind; it may lead to anything.

Moreover, if our habitual judgments of ourselves are warped because they are based on vitiated sense material—as they must be if our habits of managing ourselves are already wrong—then the more complex the social conditions under which we live, the more disastrous must be the outcome. Every additional complication of outward instrumentalities is likely to be a step nearer destruction: a fact which the present state of the world tragically exemplifies.

The school of Pavlov has made current the idea of conditioned reflexes. Mr. Alexander's work extends and corrects the idea. It proves that there are certain basic, central organic habits and attitudes which condition *every* act we perform, every use we make of ourselves. Hence a conditioned reflex is not just a matter of an arbitrarily established connection, such as that between the sound of a bell and the eating-reaction in a dog, but goes back to central conditions within the organism itself. This discovery corrects the ordinary conception of the conditioned reflex. The latter as usually understood renders an individual a passive puppet to be played upon by external manipulations. The discovery of a central control which conditions all other reactions brings the conditioning factor under conscious direction and enables the individual through his own coordinated activities to take possession of his own potentialities. It converts the fact of conditioned reflexes from a principle of external enslavement into a means of vital freedom.

Education is the only sure method which mankind possesses for directing its own course. But we have been involved in a vicious circle. Without knowledge of what constitutes a truly normal and healthy psycho-physical life, our professed education is likely to be mis-education. Every serious student of the formation of disposition and character which takes place in the family and school knows—speaking without the slightest exaggeration—how often and how deplorably this possibility is realized. The technique of Mr. Alexander gives to the educator a standard of psycho-physical health—in which what we call morality is included. It supplies also the "means whereby" this standard may be progressively and endlessly achieved, becoming a conscious possession of the one educated. It provides therefore the conditions for the central direction of all special educational processes. It bears the same relation to education that education itself bears to all other human activities.

I cannot therefore state too strongly the hopes that are aroused in me by the information contained in the Appendix that Mr. Alexander has, with his coadjutors, opened a training class, nor my sense of the importance that this work secures adequate support. It contains in my judgment the promise and potentiality of the new direction that is needed in all education.

Introduction to *India's Outlook on Life*

It would be difficult to find one less fitted by previous study and knowledge to write an introduction to an account of Vedic philosophy than the present writer. But, with the increasing intellectual contact of the East and West, it is obviously of importance that we of the Western world should have authentic information regarding the culture of India. The philosophy associated with Brahmanism is an essential part of that culture. In some respects knowledge of it is a key to the historic thought of India. Not only all scholars, therefore, but all interested in promoting spiritual exchange between the East and the West will welcome the series of publications of which this is the initial number.

Even one who, like myself, is not expert in Vedic philosophy will recognize the system, thoroughness, and lucidity with which Pandit Chatterji has presented that philosophy. It may safely be said that nowhere will the reader and student find available such a comprehensive and clear account set forth by a competent authority. It is not necessary to say to the Western reader that the foundations and the method of this Oriental system of thought are far removed from those current with us; it is not easy to translate from one system into the other. This very fact increases the value of the complete and clear statement which is set before us. It gives a much needed chart of bearings.

[First published in Jagadish Chandra Chatterji, *India's Outlook on Life: The Wisdom of the Vedas* (New York: Kailas Press, 1931), p. 7.]

The People's Lobby

Sir: There has been considerable misunderstanding in the press as to the nature of a special committee of one hundred now in process of formation by the People's Lobby. The primary purpose of this committee is to offset as far as possible the effect of the hysterical propaganda being carried on against the Russian Soviet Union, particularly by Mr. Matthew Woll and his recently announced Committee of One Hundred. Our committee is of the opinion that Mr. Woll's campaign is sowing the seeds of international hatred and war. In contradistinction we advocate a fair and friendly policy toward Soviet Russia, both as the proper attitude toward a great social and economic experiment and as a means of furthering international understanding and peace.

A secondary object of our committee is to call attention to those wretched social and economic conditions in this country which are the basic cause of the present widespread misery, unrest and violence. We believe that Mr. Woll and his associates would be better advised to agitate for the cure of these conditions than to issue polemics against Russia and stimulate the persecution of American radicals.

JOHN DEWEY,
President, People's Lobby

New York City

[First published in *New Republic* 68 (26 August 1931): 48.]

To Replace Judge Cardozo

Sir: I am informed that Governor Roosevelt is considering Mr. Walter Pollak to fill the vacancy left by the promotion of Judge Cardozo to the Supreme Court of the United States. The news is most encouraging, and those who have greeted the latter appointment with such hearty approval will realize the peculiar appropriateness of the appointment of Mr. Pollak to serve in the New York court. The following proportion comes naturally and inevitably to mind: As Judge Cardozo is to Justice Holmes in the Supreme Court, so is Mr. Pollak to Judge Cardozo on the New York bench. Mr. Pollak was long the personal assistant of Judge Cardozo when the latter was engaged in private practice; his clear penetrating mind is like Cardozo's, and he is recognized as one of the ablest men in the legal profession. Moreover, he is a true liberal in the same sense in which the term is applied to Justice Holmes and Judge Cardozo. The popular applause which followed President Hoover's appointment will greet Governor Roosevelt's action if he maintains the high traditions of New York's high court through the appointment of Walter Pollak.

JOHN DEWEY

New York City

[First published in *New Republic* 70 (9 March 1932): 102.]

A Third Party Program

Sir: In behalf of the League for Independent Political Action I thank you for the generous amount of space you accorded its recently published program. I note that you regret that the program "was not built around a central, unifying idea." The reason for the absence of any attempt at a unifying philosophy might perhaps have been made clear to your readers if you had noted that the program is entitled "A Four Year Presidential Plan: 1932–36." The League has a long-time educational program. But the present document is deliberately confined to a short-span statement. Liberals and radicals are perhaps too much given to putting forth "central" ideas in large forms and remote from application. In any event, our aim was to indicate things which needed to be done in the next presidential term of office and which might be done if a genuinely progressive party were in power.

You also indicate that in your judgment the central idea should be a "planned national economy." Speaking for myself rather than officially for the League, I would say that in my judgment, a planned economy is a matter of a general educational policy and is supra-political (or infra-political), not a matter for a political campaign. I fear that the attempt to present it as political matter will be confusing, and if indulged in will play into the hands of the upholders of the present system. After the depression has lasted a year or two more and the inefficacy of the palliative measures now being taken is evident, I expect to see representatives of this system themselves put forward definite stabilization plans for congressional action. But that is, quite literally, their funeral. I do not see why radicals should help them. If, however, the latter

[First published in *New Republic* 70 (24 February 1932): 48–49.]

have urged a planned economy as a present *political* policy, they will find it difficult to enlighten the public mind when they are forced to begin opposing Fascist schemes for stabilizing the speculative-profit system.

JOHN DEWEY

New York City

Vladeck and Laidler

To the *New York Herald Tribune*:

The ballyhoo of the presidential campaign is in danger of so deafening the ears and disgusting the minds of intelligent citizens that they will overlook the importance of Congressional elections and candidates. President Hoover is balancing his promises of prosperity of four years ago with threats of ruin if he is not reelected. Governor Roosevelt is smiling amiably at all and sundry, men and measures alike. Citizens who do not think a national election should be conducted as if it were a census of morons have fortunately the opportunity to vote for the Socialist candidates who have a constructive program and who have been able to carry on an intelligent campaign.

Even if Thomas and Maurer cannot be elected in 1932, a number of intelligent, independent, informed members of Congress can perform a much needed service in the troubled years ahead. Messrs. Vladeck and Laidler, who are running for Congress in the 8th and 6th Districts, are most distinctly men of this type. I wish I could reach every voter in these Brooklyn districts with a personal appeal. These men stand head and shoulders not only above their competitors in this election but above most members of the House. They will bring wide and trained knowledge, sound judgment and humane sympathy and thought to the performance of their duties. Voters in these Brooklyn districts have an extraordinary opportunity to do a patriotic service to the nation in electing these men.

JOHN DEWEY

New York, Nov. 1, 1932

[First published in *New York Herald Tribune*, 3 November 1932, p. 22.]

Funds for Brookwood Labor College

Sir: An educational institution which is doing pioneer work in new lines is likely to be one which has a peculiarly close relation to contemporary conditions and needs. It is also likely to lack the endowment and financial support possessed by institutions that operate along more traditional lines. Both of these probabilities meet in the case of Brookwood, the representative school for training of men and women from the ranks of labor to work in the field of labor. It is the unfortunate lot of these institutions to suffer most at the very time when their services are most needed. Accordingly it is society which suffers from any threat to the continued efficiency of such institutions. We cannot believe that a public which recognizes the important service rendered by Brookwood Labor College and the pressing need which there is for extension rather than for contraction of its services will permit Brookwood to be crippled. As one of a large number of educators, religious leaders, publicists, economists, social workers and labor leaders, I am making an appeal for contribution of funds. Ten thousand dollars is imperatively needed in a short time. Pledges may be sent direct to A. J. Muste at Katonah, New York.

Attention is also called to the Brookwood Bazaar given at the Irving Plaza on December 2–4. This Bazaar is conducted by Brookwood graduates. The loyal devotion of Brookwood graduates is one of the best evidences of the success of the Labor College in carrying out its aims.

JOHN DEWEY

New York City

[First published in *New Republic* 73 (7 December 1932): 101.]

Help for Brookwood

To the editor of the *Nation*:

Sir: The undersigned urgently appeal to all friends of workers' education to come to the aid of Brookwood Labor College. Brookwood must raise not less than $10,000 in the next two months if this outstanding educational project is to carry on through this, its twelfth school year.

Food for the mentally and spiritually starved American workers is as necessary in this crisis as food for the physically starved. Appeals are constantly being made for generous contributions to social agencies which are engaged in "character-building" or "faith-restoring" activities. We submit that no activity can be more important than that of a labor college giving to workers themselves the vision of a new world and some comprehension of the means by which it may be achieved.

Since its founding in 1921 Brookwood has made an outstanding contribution. In every section of the country its graduates are giving creditable, in some instances noteworthy, service to labor, progressive, and radical movements—in unions, labor colleges, cooperatives, labor political organizations, unemployed leagues. It has given inspiration and help, has been a rallying centre, for other workers' education enterprises, such as summer schools and local labor colleges and classes. The members of its staff have written books and pamphlets which are used throughout the workers' education movement. The need for more such material is keenly felt. Through extension classes and lecture services the school reaches each year thousands of workers who cannot take a residential course.

Brookwood now faces a formidable task in raising the budget required to enable it to keep its doors open for this year. The size

[First published in *Nation* 135 (14 December 1932): 592.]

of the student body has been reduced. Drastic cuts have been made in the budget. Students and faculty are prepared to make still further cuts to the absolute limit, if the minimum required to keep the enterprise going can but be raised. For the most part, however, workers and workers' organizations cannot give now, though in the past they have contributed to Brookwood sums aggregating many thousand dollars. We therefore call upon all friends of education, all who believe in the crucial importance of developing an effective and intelligent labor movement in this country, to respond—immediately, enthusiastically, generously—to Brookwood's present appeal for funds. Contributions should be sent to A. J. Muste, Brookwood Labor College, Katonah, N.Y.

> JOHN DEWEY, EDUARD C. LINDEMAN, OSWALD GARRISON VILLARD, SINCLAIR LEWIS, STUART CHASE, and the other members of a sponsoring committee of about eighty educators, labor officials, editors, authors, and publicists.

New York, November 21

What Is It All About?

The first reading of Mr. Tate's article left me dazed. I not only could not understand why Mr. Tate attributes to me the ideas he does, but I could not understand the ideas themselves. They seem to be a sorry mess, intellectually and practically. I feel quite sure that if I thought any living being held them, I could, provided I understood them, say worse things about them than does Mr. Tate. After several more readings I formed a hypothesis which, since I do not profess to understand the workings of Tate's mind, I put forward with diffidence. It is to this effect: Mr. Tate thinks that philosophers have but one string to their harp; he conceives me to be always harping on the one string of my intellectual instrument, no matter what topic I write on; and, unfortunately, he has very hazy and quite inexact notions of the sounds this instrument gives forth when it *is* played upon. This hypothesis may be quite wrong. I put it forth to explain the course I shall follow in my reply, that of restating the ideas actually set forth in the article of mine against which Mr. Tate issues his animadversions. For the ideas imputed to me are so irrelevant and so alien to those which I entertain that any other course would reduce me to the necessity of quoting a series of sentences from Mr. Tate and contradicting them one by one.

The essay, "Affective Thought," on which Mr. Tate bases his article is a piece of psychological analysis; whether good or bad analysis, it is conceived in terms of the psychology of human experience and not in those of any species of social theory or social propaganda. Its point of departure is not pragmatic nor instrumental philosophy but Rignano's account of the nature and process of thinking, an account made from the standpoint of a psy-

[From an unpublished typescript in the Allen Tate Papers, Princeton University Library, Princeton, N.J. For Tate's article, to which this is a reply, see this volume, Appendix 5.]

chology having an organic biological basis. Rignano claims that thinking arises and develops within the matrix of affective, or emotional, experience. Acceptance of this view cancels the warrant usually assumed to be given by psychology for separation between the intellectual and the affective, a separation which relegates their respective typical products to isolated, non-communicating, compartments of experience. The division between the two, with a separate compartment of voluntary action, received the sanction of Kant and has had an enormous influence on esthetic criticism and theory ever since his day. It is reflected in the prevailing notion that fine art, science, and action, especially moral action, are wholly independent of one another so that they constitute isolated realms of human experience. I pointed out that if the sounder psychology of Rignano were accepted, the warrant for this division alleged to be supplied by scientific psychology, would disappear. It would then be recognized "that the differences between coherent logical schemes and artistic structures in poetry, music and the plastic arts are technical and specialized rather than deepseated."

In consequence, in words quoted by Mr. Tate, "it *then* becomes possible to break down the traditional separation between scientific and intellectual systems and those of art, and also to *further the application* of the principle of integration to the relationship of those elements of culture which are so segregated in our present life—to science, art in its variety of forms, industry and business, religion, sport and morals" (italics not in the original text). In getting rid, in other words, of the false alleged scientific warrant for a division of our experience into segregated and unintegrated departments; in substituting the fact of an underlying psychological unity of experience in science, art and activity, we can, at least—notice the modesty of the claim made—"further the application" of the principle of integration in actual life. This is the context in which reference to action and social life comes in. It is not a premiss or foundation for any theory of art, nor a plea for any kind of regulation of art in the interest of supposed social utility. It is simply a statement that a better psychological analysis than the current one gives us an intellectual instrumentality for attacking the segregations which afflict contemporary life. That these segregations *are* a fundamental affliction was certainly implied, and Mr. Tate's article confirms my conviction to that effect. But I fail to see how the idea that a correction of a false theory (which has been used to give intellectual support to these segregations) might operate as an intellectual weapon "to further the application of the principle of integration" among interests now split up can be tortured into any such doctrine as Mr. Tate imputes to me. The wonders of Biblical exegesis pale beside his method.

The essay on Affective Thought is a pendant to an article on Qualitative Thought. The latter article is both much more extended and more carefully and thoroughly reasoned out in its analyses. It reaches from the standpoint of logical analysis the same conclusion that the one on Affective Thought reaches from a psychological standpoint. The start made is not in the least from or with any theory of social action but with the fact that qualitative situations, coming to us as wholes, because they are qualitative, are the background and the eventual terminus of all thought, of all science; that intellectual operations and their results are "instrumental" to the enrichment and control of these qualitative wholes. (The idea that "instrumentalism" means instrumental to *action*, an idea which Mr. Tate seems to have swallowed whole, is an idea fostered by critics who have more zeal in writing than intelligence or care in reading.) The conclusion—stated with explicitness in other writings of mine—is the opposite of what Mr. Tate attributes to me, namely, that "art is another kind of science." It is that science is a kind of art. I think the general realization and acceptance of that idea would help destroy the influences which segregate science and which make it a kind of False Messiah. They would, in my opinion, further an integration in which the values represented by science would serve as method and instrument, and those of art as *end and consummation.*

Because I find "unity-in-variety" to represent the living thing in art and to be a standard for integration in any field, Mr. Tate assumes that I have inconsistently adopted idealism for the nonce. A sophomore who has studied philosophy could tell Mr. Tate that the idealist conceives of unity-in-variety as wholly the work and mark of *thought*. I find unity-in-variety in the very stuff of experience in its qualitative character, and to be *affectively* appreciated. Thinking, according to the logical theory which I tried to set forth, begins from and finally terminates in precisely these immediate harmonies. Then Mr. Tate, apparently puzzled by the fact that I do after all give art a certain value, concludes that I think of art only as a means of creating harmony in society. Well, taking art in the sense in which it includes science and ordered political and economic action, I should trust art rather than any other device or method to create social harmony. But my point was a more modest one; that art, especially fine art, produces a standard, a frame of reference in the mind, which is favorable to integration of experience in all fields.

I hope the above re-interpretation of my essays renders it unnecessary to engage in the tedious task of going through Mr. Tate's statements seriatim to show how irrelevant they are to my position. I confine myself to two points. The imputation to Dr. Barnes, on the basis of a quotation from me, of a "utilitarian" theory of art carries Mr. Tate's misconception of my ideas to the point of an even worse misconstruction of the analysis of plastic art given by Dr. Barnes. It carries irrelevant and foreign attributions to the nth degree since the point of Dr. Barnes' method is analysis of pictures in strictly pictorial terms. Speaking in terms of Shelley—who of course in his defense of poetry is much closer to my theory as to the potential social function of the arts than he is to the tenor of Mr. Tate's criticism—what I have written does not subordinate "conception" to "calculation." On the other hand, using "conception" as a short term for the immediately or intuitively experienced grasp of qualitative wholes, and "calculation" for those scientific operations in which number and measure play a dominant part, I have pointed out that calculation is subordinate to conception, since it arises from the latter and terminates in another richer and more fully ordered qualitative situation. There is nowhere a claim, however, that science has as matter of fact adequately performed this function, nor that art has realized its possibilities of instituting a vital sense of the ends, the consequences, to which all experience should contribute, and providing a standard of reference in criticism and construction. On the contrary, I have pointed out that both science and art are hampered in the execution of these functions by their prevailing segregation from each other. The reference to social action comes in, I repeat, at this point. It is not the premiss nor philosophical foundation. It is the final *practical* conclusion of appeal to institute a type of social action which would help break down these compartmental divisions in life. Mr. Tate may be satisfied with things as they are, or he may be opposed to undertaking any such social action. That is quite within his own right. It does not justify him, however, in attributing to me the idea that "art and science are merely conventionally different modes of social adaptation." I do not know whether there is any benighted soul who entertains such a view. If there is, I modestly suggest that he read some of the things I have written in order to learn better.

People's Lobby

Urges Tax on Rich to Meet Debts Cut

Declaring that most thoughtful Americans favored canceling or reducing of war-time debts of foreign nations to this country if German reparations also were canceled, the People's Lobby in a letter to Dr. Nicholas Murray Butler of Columbia University, asserted, however, that this would not be done until taxes on large incomes were greatly increased in this country.

The letter of the lobby, of which Professor John Dewey is president, was made public here today in reply to an address made by Dr. Butler on Friday before the League of Nations Association at Chicago, in which he advocated cancellation.

The letter read:

"With the general purpose of your recent speech in favor of canceling at least part of the government debts the nations with which we were associated in the World War owe our government, most thoughtful Americans are, we believe, in agreement, provided these nations cancel their claims for German reparations and stop getting ready for another war.

"As a practical matter, however, we shall not cancel these debts until there is a heavy and progressive increase in surtaxes upon income over $50,000 and particularly over $1,000,000.

"Under our present tax systems, Federal, State and local, the major part of all government revenue is paid by the masses, whose income is not sufficient to enable them to maintain a decent healthful standard of living, as the present depression shows, nor to consume a reasonable proportion of the goods they produce, when they have the opportunity to work. The poorest pay infinitely heavier taxes than the favored five hundred odd with incomes over $1,000,000.

"The unemployed and partly employed—at least one-fifth of

[First published in *New York Times*, 26 January 1931, p. 13.]

the potential wage earners of the nation—continue to pay taxes until they are forced to poorhouses, missions and bread lines.

"Can you think of a single person in public life who would suggest increasing taxes on such unemployed of whom there will be at least 3,000,000 for probably a year or two to come?

"The only alternative for the Federal Government is to increase surtaxes on large incomes and from 75 per cent to 98 per cent of such incomes is derived from ownership or control of property.

"In 1928 the aggregate net income of the 511 persons having incomes over $1,000,000 was $1,108,863,041 and they paid in Federal income and surtaxes only $185,140,211, or about one-sixth of their unearned income.

"That same year the aggregate net income of the 15,977 persons who had incomes over $100,000 was $4,451,207,685 and their total income was $4,997,683,014—nearly one-eighteenth of the national income.

"They paid in Federal income and surtaxes only $714,183,379, or less than one-sixth of their income from property.

"The foreign investments of American citizens now amount to about $14,000,000,000 and are increasing. As recently shown by the Department of Commerce, our leading manufacturers, while getting high protective tariffs to keep labor employed at high wages here, have been busily exporting jobs by starting branch factories or moving their plants abroad.

"Will you cooperate to secure an increased Federal surtax equal to the British on incomes over $100,000, so as to make practical such cancellation of foreign governments to the United States, as you so eloquently advocate?"

Urges State-Aid Plan for Work Insurance

In a letter to Senator Hebert, Republican, of Rhode Island, chairman of the special Senate committee which will open hearings on unemployment insurance here Tuesday, the People's Lobby today asserted that "the principle of Federal subvention of State unemployment insurance systems, provided in the bill introduced last session by Senator Wagner, is the immediately practical one, although the Federal Government may have to pay up to $500,000,000 a year for a time."

Quoting Senator Watson of Indiana, Republican floor leader, as having said that "every man under the flag is entitled to a job," and that "government fails and falls unless all men have an equal opportunity to work," the lobby added it was obvious that the Federal Government had failed in this duty.

"Whether it is to fail depends largely upon what the next Congress does to provide aid for Federal unemployment insurance, that is for maintenance of the unemployed until the government provides them work when industries fail to do so," the letter said.

"The immediate problem before your committee, as we understand it, is how large a part of the total cost of unemployment benefits should be paid by the Federal Government, since the constitutionality of a direct system of Federal unemployment insurance is questioned; but there is no respectable doubt as to the right of Congress to pay any or most of unemployment benefits under State systems."

Holding to the view of the Federal responsibility for domestic economic trends, including taxes and tariffs, and for international policies, the letter concluded:

"The Federal Government can no longer enjoy the perquisites

[First published in *New York Times*, 30 March 1931, p. 2.]

without paying the price of governing. It must provide work or wages for the workless until American industry comes of age, abolishes the crushing taxes upon legitimate industry and works out intelligent plans for production and distribution so 12,000,000 of our people will no longer live in dire poverty."

Full Warehouses and Empty Stomachs

In April Prof. John Dewey gave the following talk over a coast to coast hook-up, through the courtesy of the National Broadcasting Company.

Wheat is lower in price than for many years; elevators are crammed with grain; the government has millions of bushels on hand, and thousands of persons are starving and being fed from soup kitchens in the midst of plenty. Coal mines shut down because they can't sell coal, and thousands have shivered through the winter for lack of heat. Warehouses are stuffed with shoes and cloth, and men and women are going ragged and out at the toes and heels. Money is loaning on call in New York City for one and a half per cent; commercial rates are lower than for years, and there are people without a cent in their pockets, while industries have difficulty in getting credit. Banks congested on one hand, empty pockets and idle factories on the other.

Everywhere there is complaint of excess production. Too many plants producing goods; too many farms producing grain; too many plantations producing too much sugar, coffee, cotton, and rubber. Too many security factories turning out stocks, and so along all the line. Then there are the multitudes of people who can't get these things when they want them, and who cannot get work. Poverty, destitution, suffering also, all along the line. Six million men who want work, out of employment, at the conservative government estimate. Suppose that each one has a family of three more persons dependent upon them, and there are one-sixth of the entire population of the richest and most advanced industrial nation on earth crippled in their homes or entirely out of any home. And I suppose the estimate of unemployed does not

[First published in *People's Lobby Bulletin* 1 (May 1931): 1–3, from a radio broadcast on 13 April 1931.]

count the thousands and thousands of farmers who are suffering from drought, inability to pay interest on their mortgages, etc.

I shall not insult your intelligence by saying there is something wrong. Even the captains of industry are admitting that the economic system has broken down, and that capitalism is on trial, and that something must be done. But who is going to do it and how is it to be done? We are informed on the authority of Republican leaders that "politics are adjourned," and that Congress will not meet to do anything about it. They fear that discussion would make business worse, they say. In other words, they admit that the political system has also broken down. If both the economic and the political system have broken down, it is up to the common people to do something. There must be a public opinion which will compel industrial and political "leaders" to do something. Else they should get out of the way and allow others to do something.

Why go on prating about over-production when poverty and unemployment make it clear that under-consumption is what ails us? The loss of wages from unemployment in the city of New York alone for the month of February was eighty million dollars—at the rate of almost a billion a year in one city. Competent statisticians have estimated the loss for the whole country for last year at nine billion six hundred million dollars. Of course, warehouses are glutted and mills shut down when the workers have nine billion less with which to buy. Take one item—milk. The American Association of University Women, after carrying on investigation into the proper diet of children, reports that "if economic depression lasts for another thirty months, as economists predict, the children of the country may suffer and perhaps be handicapped for life." Anybody who saw the generation of children that grew up in Europe during the World War knows what that means. An investigation carried on by the Children's Bureau of the Federal Government shows that four-fifths of the families investigated, were already in debt for food, fuel, rent and medical service, and that unemployment was having a "direct and disastrous effect upon the welfare of children." The staple food of children is milk. Ask the dairy farmers whether, while millions of children are having too little milk to nourish them, their business is prospering! The advice of our benevolent administration at Washington to the farmers is doubtless to cut down production still more. Why don't they do something to bring up consumption of a necessity of life? The People's Lobby urged an appropriation of one hundred millions, to be spent under direction of the public health authorities, for the benefit of suffering children. The appeal was not heeded. It might lead to increase of taxation on the higher brackets of swollen wealth.

If national resources and wealth were inadequate, the situation would be necessary and we should have to stand it as best we can. But, although the national net income has sunk from ninety-three billion dollars to about eighty, there is still enough to give every family of five an annual income of over three thousand dollars per year. This is enough, according to the National Bureau of Economic Research, to enable every family to live comfortably.

The simple fact is that income is not distributed justly enough for consumption to keep up with our productive resources. Meanwhile, government does everything for the big men in production; little for the employees who produce, and next to nothing for the consumer except to load him with indirect taxes, including that which he pays without knowing it, when he pays rent.

Statistics are not very interesting. But the figures given by the Government at Washington are exciting enough if they are understood, to arouse the distressed millions in the United States. Not one person out of fifty in the United States had enough net income in 1929 to pay any Federal income tax at all; three-fourths of the reported incomes were under five thousand dollars. Moreover, of the total income paid upon, only 55% came from salaries and business gains; the other 45% came from rent, royalties, interest and dividends—almost one-half is what the Government itself classes as "unearned income." But there were nearly 39,000 in the millionaire class, nearly 500 in the class between twenty million and one hundred million, and 36 in the class with one hundred million, and over. The 500 persons with an average income of over a million dollars a year had between them fifty million dollars more income than the whole group of 201,000 whose net income for the year was between five and six thousand dollars. How they compared with the hundred and twenty million whose income didn't call for any Federal income tax at all, you can judge for yourselves. Over ninety percent of the income of the richest class came from the unearned classification, less than two percent from salaries, in spite of the size of individual salaries some of these men get; while sixty-one percent of reported incomes under five thousand dollars came from actual work done. But why continue? The gist of the whole matter is that according to the most reliable estimates, 4 percent of the population control 80% of the wealth of the country.

The amount of goods, even of luxuries, which the 4% can consume is limited; their excess fortune must go into investments further to swell production. A large portion of the 80 percent haven't the means to buy what they need and can consume. That is the story in a nutshell. The consequences are things that don't appear in statistics: Distress, bodily and mental; insecurity and despair, men and women begging desperately for work and refused a chance. Equalization upwards from the low and downwards from the high incomes is the sole means which will fill empty stomachs and put the stores of goods that have been piled up, into circulation, so that men can then get work to keep up the outflow.

We are supposed to be glad because it is officially announced there will be no increase of income tax in spite of the deficit. Congratulations to the over one hundred and twenty millions who don't pay any income tax anyway! Congratulations to the million and a half in the lowest bracket whose taxes would not be raised anyway. And pity the sorrows of the 40,000 who had one-sixth of the total taxable income of the country, and especially of the few billionaires. Why not relieve them of part of their burden by increased taxation of the higher brackets, the money to go to give proper nourishment to underfed children, and to relieve the starving, and to give as many as possible work upon public enterprises, and thus stimulate consumption to catch up with production?

The People's Lobby stands for these things; it stands for an extra session of Congress to bring them about. Write your United States Senators and Congressmen, demanding the extra session, to be limited to these purposes. Help the People's Lobby, which began the agitation last August when high officials were still saying that the depression was about at its end. Join it, and add to its force.

The President and
the Special Session

"We cannot hope to legislate ourselves out of a world economic depression." These words purport to state President Hoover's reason for declining to call an extra session to deal with the problem of unemployment. Since no one has ever claimed that we can legislate ourselves out of our present mess, President Hoover's words either lack sincerity, or they are a confession of political bankruptcy—or both. He places the lawmakers at Washington side by side with industrialists and financiers. Having done what they could for years to bring on the crisis, they now want to wash their hands of the affair and appeal to chance.

Legislation can do something. It can help unload the burdens that politicians subservient to great wealth have piled on the backs of the helpless consumer; it can assist the return of employment by taking away some of the favors that have been given to the privileged class. It can save millions from the dire suffering which is bound to come in greater measure next winter than last, by assisting state systems of insurance for the jobless and by providing public works. It can help the children of the unemployed from conditions that permanently impose a stunted life. Why does not President Hoover face the real issue instead of distracting attention to an unreal one? Is it because measures of relief would impose heavier surtaxes on the favored few and lessen contributions to campaign funds?

[First published in *People's Lobby Bulletin* 1 (June 1931): 1.]

Secretary Klein Asked
Basis for Optimism

Prof. Dewey, on behalf of the People's Lobby, has sent the following request for information to Dr. Julius Klein, Assistant Secretary of Commerce, whose frequent outbursts of concocted cheer, stamp him the official hard-times-optimism announcer for the Administration.

Your speech to the Radio Manufacturers' Association in Chicago, June 9th, raises questions which are of nation-wide import.

You say that according to "five of the leading indices," (not mentioned in the press report) "the bottom of the depression was hit in January. Since then we have been bumping along the bottom and leveling out. We are in a valley. But the depression has ended. The valley usually runs across six or seven months. If history repeats itself this means that in July up we go."

You are a trained economist, and not uninformed as to the actual conditions and the operating forces not only in the United States but throughout the world.

Your recent extended foreign trip afforded you opportunity to learn world currents such as no member of the Cabinet, nor the President himself has had, recently.

That you sensed the situation a year ago, is evidenced by your statement in a letter you wrote May 19, 1930, to Senator Barkley of Kentucky replying to his request for information regarding the establishment of American branch factories abroad. You said:

As regards the reasons for the establishment of branch factories, while, of course, it would be impossible to check up the intended purpose of every such factory, it is believed from our personal contact with industries most active in the branch factory movement, that in practically every case the

[First published in *People's Lobby Bulletin* 1 (June 1931): 3–4. For Klein's reply, see this volume, Appendix 3, and for Dewey's rejoinder see pp. 351–54.]

primary reason was to overcome the high duties levied by foreign governments. In some particular cases, of course, transportation is also a very important factor, and in the case of products requiring a good deal of servicing, an assembling plant enables the American manufacturer to maintain an adequate technical staff available for service.

Nearly a year earlier on June 29, 1929, you wrote Senator Nye of North Dakota:

It is possible to furnish collateral data which make it clear that you are correct that the difficulty with regard to markets for agricultural products is not so much over production in the world as a whole as underconsumption.

You quoted figures showing that in 1927, on the basis of United States consumption or use, the deficiency in the consumption of wheat and rye was 1,505,000,000 bushels or about one-fourth, of wheat alone 2,911,000,000 or nearly three-quarters, of sugar 79,714,000 tons or nearly three times the actual consumption. Of cotton the deficiency in consumption you reported was 44,100,000,000 pounds or four times world consumption, of wool 6,138,000,000 pounds or about twice the world production, of silk 1,298,000,000 pounds or twelve times the world use, and of rubber 6,014,436 long tons or nearly ten times the world use.

Of pig iron the deficiency, you reported, was 512,210,000 long tons, or nearly six times the production, of copper 10,026,000 short tons or about six times the actual production or use.

For all major minerals you reported a similar deficiency in world consumption, which for petroleum was about nine times the actual consumption.

Because of your intimate knowledge of economics and of economic conditions, will you let us know how you think it is possible to keep climbing out of the valley as you phrase the present status, until there is a different distribution of our national income, or as long as Americans have about two-fifths of the world's wealth, and of the world's income, and control about two-fifths of the world's mineral production?

Perhaps reducing the margin requirements for stock may give a short fillip to the stock market, which does not necessarily indicate anything except the desire of holders of stocks to unload upon the investing public.

Even the national income last year, estimated at about $78,000,-000,000 as compared with such income of $93,400,000,000 in 1929, was adequate to afford a fair standard of living for everyone in the United States, with the admitted lower costs of living, and still permit of capital savings to invest in new plants, although as you have frankly stated, we are now suffering from underconsumption.

Underconsumption is chiefly due in the United States, to maldistribution of the national income as between property and labor, and as between different classes of producers.

It is generally admitted that the estimate of Standard Statistics Company that wages and salaries paid in 1930 were about $9,500,000,000 less than in 1929, is accurate, and that the reduction from 1929 will be as large this year.

You will doubtless admit that wages and salaries even in 1929 were not adequate to permit a current domestic consumption of goods produced here out of current earnings or income, to maintain production, since recourse was had to installment buying to the extent of between four and five billions of dollars. Exports seldom exceed one-tenth of production.

Last year and this, millions of the unemployed used part or all of their savings.

That these will not last long is evident, since on June 30, 1928, the total savings in all banks was only $28,413,000,000—an average of $1,533 for each of the 16,181,000 depositors.

Postal savings on the same date were only $152,143,000, while the total assets of nearly 12,000,000 members of Building and Loan Associations were only a little over $8,000,000,000.

On the other hand the Commissioner of Internal Revenue reports that on December 31, 1928, the surplus and undivided profits of corporations, less deficit, were $47,156,183,422, of which 1,258 corporations, out of 237,491, had $23,606,761,000, or nearly one-half.

For the same year, 1928, these 1,258 corporations, had a net income of $5,930,285,000, or about one-half of the net income of 268,783 corporations reporting such net income.

The Commissioner also reports that the aggregate of cash and stock dividends paid by corporations in 1928 was $7,623,851,877, of which the 1,010,887 persons reporting net incomes over $5,000 received $4,009,914,502, or nearly four-sevenths, and the 511 persons with incomes over $1,000,000 received $316,130,826 or slightly over one twenty-fifth.

A very small per cent of the families of the nation will get most of the surplus and undivided profits of corporations.

The National Bureau of Economic Research reported that in 1928 wages paid in the United States were $32,235,000,000 and salaries $17,823,000,000—a total of $50,058,000,000, while the Commissioner of Internal Revenue reports that the 1,010,887 persons receiving net incomes over $5,000 got in salaries and wages $5,008,286,141. That left for the approximately 45,500,000 others gainfully occupied in 1928, with incomes of less than $5,000, only $45,050,000,000. This class chiefly, is hit by unemployment, and in 1930 they lost over one-fifth of their earned income during 1929, and will lose about as much this year.

This may appear to you a valley, but government employees are the only ones who have not been compelled (through wage or salary reductions) to pass through this valley of the shadow, if not the reality of debt.

The National Bureau of Economic Research also reports that of the national income which it estimates for 1928 at $89,419,000,000, the labor return to 47,100,000 employees was $51,123,000,000 as salaries, wages and pensions, or a little over five-ninths of the national income, while the share of entrepreneurs and other property owners in money and commodity income was $32,996,000,000, and in imputed income (a 6% return on investment in homes, etc.) $5,300,000,000—a total of $38,296,000,000, or nearly four-ninths of the national income.

The Commissioner of Internal Revenue reports that in 1929, the 969,001 persons reporting net incomes over $5,000 had an aggregate income of $16,237,296,000 or over one-sixteenth of the total income of the twenty-five or twenty-six million families in the United States, and of this income nearly three-quarters was from ownership or control of property.

The deflation of the past two years has increased the value of the public and private debt amounting to about $140,000,000,000, by at least one-sixth, and increased the burden on debtors by the same proportion.

No informed person denies that about 4% of the population owns nearly four-fifths of the national wealth.

How can you expect any marked improvement in economic conditions, with the existing inequitable distribution of the national income, wh:ch our tariff, taxation, banking and currency systems tend to aggravate instead of remedy?

That there is adequate capital is evidenced by the fact that the recent $800,000,000 issue of Treasury notes was more than seven times over-subscribed.

With a fifth of the nation's population seriously affected by the present unemployment, and cumulatively impoverished, and kept out of the consuming class except for bare necessities of existence, is it not essential to increase public works very largely by government credit, since no expansion of any plants for production is needed?

Since the initiating of such a policy rests with the Government how can it consistently criticize industrial leaders for failure to employ men to produce what cannot be sold, until it does its share to begin such a redistribution of the national income as will start up employment?

Has not the cataclysmic economic aftermath of the reduction of taxes on large incomes chiefly derived from property, made it clear that a reversal of policy is essential to attain even a modicum of national well being and safety?

Hasn't the boomerang of the unprotective tariff demonstrated sufficiently the futility of attempting to ring off America from the rest of the interdependent world?

Rejoinder to Secretary Klein

Thank you for your letter of June 22nd answering mine of June 11th.

I fear you misunderstood part of my letter.

We do not, of course, deplore the fact there are so many and so valuable natural resources in the United States, but rather the fact that these natural resources are so largely monopolized by a few, many of whom have obtained them for an inadequate compensation to the public, and that their development has been attended with reckless waste because of their socially unplanned use. Coal and oil seem to us, adequate illustrations of this fact.

It is not the possession of natural resources of itself, but their efficient production and use for the common good which enriches and benefits a nation.

Your reference to our high standard of living seems to indicate failure to appreciate not only the present situation, but the condition of millions of families in our own country during the so-called prosperous years 1928 and 1929.

Not one major industry paid on the average then to all its workers, a sufficient wage to maintain a family of two adults and three minors, on the minimum standard of the United States Department of Labor. Only a few of these industries paid enough to maintain the wage earner alone on such a basis.

Was not the system of installment buying rapidly extended partly to enable people to discount their future earnings, and so help consumption keep pace with production?

What is your authority for the statement—"Real wages have been multiplied many times during the past five or six decades"?

[First published in *People's Lobby Bulletin* 1 (August 1931): 4–5. For Klein's letter to which this is a rejoinder, see this volume, Appendix 3, and for Dewey's first letter to Klein see pp. 346–50.]

Do you hold this is true for all wages paid in the United States, and from what basis or standard was such increase made?

Prof. Paul Nystrom of Columbia University estimates recently that we have now 40,000,000 poor, of whom 8,000,000 are in dire poverty, 12,000,000 have a bare subsistence, and 20,000,000 have a fair subsistence.

The President in his speech at the White House Conference on Child Welfare last fall quoted one of the Committees of that Conference that of 45,000,000 children in this country, 6,000,000 are improperly nourished.

The Committee on Dependency and Neglect of that Conference stated:

> Studies of the distribution of income in the United States show that the majority of families in this country are living close to the margin of economic want. The experience of social agencies shows that there is a group living below this margin. . . . minimum comfort budgets and data as to distribution of income in the U.S. . . . throw considerable doubt upon the ability of large numbers of male wage-earners to earn enough to support a family at current wages even if steadily employed . . .
>
> There is no certainty then that many wage-earners will earn enough to support a normal family even when steadily employed. When the hazards of unemployment, illness and accident are taken into account, in many cases all hope of his doing so vanishes. . . . We have now reached the point where those interested in child welfare must advance through the medium of greater economic protection of parents . . .

Do you mean to impeach the veracity or the accuracy of the 1,200 preachers, rabbis, priests, Community Chest, Red Cross and other Social Workers, and economists who have urged the President to call a Special session on unemployment stating— "Regardless of any change that may occur in the business outlook, millions of our fellow citizens face a winter of acute poverty and distress, nor can there be any marked improvement in business conditions, till there is a marked increase in the purchasing power of the American people"?

It is true that the capital savings of the United States range from $6,000,000,000 to $8,000,000,000 a year, while we have

8,000,000 in dire poverty, and some of these billions are exported. England has had a similar situation for generations, but India, China and Egypt can hardly be cited as proving the success of that system.

For years, as Chief of the Bureau of Domestic and Foreign Commerce, you worked with great ability, to increase our foreign trade. You are in a strategic position to know that the tariff walls we have built up preclude a proportionate payment in goods by foreign nations for the goods we send them. We feel poor unless we have a large "favorable" trade balance. As a result, we have piled up gold, and debts to us owed by nearly every advanced nation. Americans own or control the major part of the external funded debt of ten Latin American countries.

You are well aware of the poverty in other nations much of whose natural resources Americans have secured, or whose bankers they are, or whose industries they are seeking to control.

Eight years ago when you had charge of the investigation ordered by Congress, and for which an appropriation of $500,000 was made, of the foreign markets for American products you were asked to make a study of what goods should be consumed in each country to maintain a healthy standard of living, and what increase would be required. You declined, on the ground that it would not be considered friendly for us to point out the disparity between what the people of those countries should consume and what they could afford to consume. Have those conditions changed materially anywhere?

Of course there is a potential market in this country for all the goods you mention, as well as for food, clothes, shoes, and houses, and it will stay potential, until there is the different distribution of the national income between property and producers which we urge.

You may have a quarrel with some who urge foolish public construction, but we have not done so. There are still hundreds of thousands of miles of wasteful dirt roads, thousands of miles of too narrow roads, and millions of people living in disease breeding tenements and hovels.

It seems obvious that a system which does not permit the masses of the people to enjoy a standard of living commensurate with the wealth, production and income of that country, and obviously ours does not—is doomed.

You advocate another expansive and unplanned production to overcome the devastating results of such an era through which we have just passed. That does not seem to us logical.

Why do you favor an industrial expansion to supply goods which you say are now "beyond the reach of even the wealthiest people"—instead of such production as will meet the real needs of the masses of the American people?

Challenge to Progressive Senators to Act for Relief

Prof. Dewey as President of the People's Lobby, last April challenged the five Senators who called the Conference of Progressives in Washington—Norris, La Follette, Cutting, Wheeler and Costigan to join with the Lobby in working for a special session of Congress on unemployment.

The letter follows:

You gentlemen called the conference of progressives in March, at which the Administration, and the President, were severely denounced for failure to meet the national crisis, and for permitting Congress to adjourn in such a crisis.

Senator Costigan was not a member of the past Congress, but chief responsibility for not having a special session of Congress and for failure of the past Congress to act, rests upon the other four of you, and upon the other Senators in the past Congress who claim to be progressives—including Senators Borah, Couzens, Frazier, Nye, Brookhart, Shipstead and Dill.

You could have blocked the enactment of essential appropriation bills, and forced this session, and the economic conditions in our nation, in a description of which several of you have indulged, not only justified such procedure but made it imperative, to prove your good faith. The chief real fight made in the past Congress was on behalf of the independent oil operators by Senator Thomas of Oklahoma, who made his speech an aggressive war upon special privilege, and not merely an oratorical gesture of impotence.

Your Conference after denouncing the Administration for adjourning Congress appointed a Committee to investigate whether a special session of Congress were justified, which has not yet reported,—though the answer is obvious from your denunciation of the Administration.

[First published in *People's Lobby Bulletin* 1 (June 1931): 5.]

What has paralysed Progressive Senators into acquiescence in the plan of exploiting interests to reduce the American people to a state of industrial feudalism and serfdom?

What influence has dragged you down from loyalty to the program upon which the late Senator La Follette, in 1924, had counted for him, 5,000,000 votes?

The program definitely pledged:

> The use of the power of the Federal Government to crush private monopoly.
>
> Unqualified enforcement of the constitutional guarantees of freedom of speech, press and assemblage.
>
> Public ownership of the nation's waterpower and creation of a public superpower system.
>
> Retention of surtaxes on swollen incomes, restoration of the tax on excess profits and rapidly progressive taxes on large estates and inheritances.
>
> Reconstruction of the Federal Reserve, and Federal farm loan systems.
>
> Public ownership of railroads with democratic operation.
>
> Abolition of the tyranny and usurpation of the courts.
>
> Common international action to effect the economic recovery of the world from the effects of the World War.
>
> Repeal of excessive tariff duties and of nuisance taxes on consumption.

The creation of a super economic council you have considered, however desirable, is probably the last phase of an advanced socialized economy, nor would the benefits of such an agency reach consumers appreciably unless special privileges were first eliminated, as pledged in this militant program of 1924.

You gentlemen, (excluding Senator Costigan) who gave the Administration the sinews of war to continue the rule of special privilege by permitting appropriations to be voted, cannot escape responsibility for the suffering this summer and fall and the far worse suffering inevitable next winter, unless Congress legislates by early fall at latest.

Will you drop your vacations and join us in a nation-wide campaign for a special session to face and end America's serious and increasingly desperate economic chaos?

The Key to Hoover's Keynote Speech

On June 26 President Dewey wrote President Hoover a letter regarding his Indianapolis speech, which we summarize. It is of great significance, with the present dangerous crisis in Europe.

In your final paragraph of your Indianapolis speech you said: "In conclusion, whatever the immediate difficulties may be, we know they are transitory in our lives, and in the life of the nation."

I wish you had been more explicit as to whose lives you refer to. Is it the lives of the ten million unemployed—and only partially employed, the millions more suffering from wage and salary cuts in one form or another, or is it the lives of the few hundred thousand whose investments are not bringing in the usual return? I wish too you had been more definite about the amount of time it will take to make the present state of affairs "transitory," for we are told, that given time enough, all things will change somehow.

Your tragic failure to appreciate the situation as millions of your fellow countrymen are forced to do, doubtless accounts for your opposition to summoning Congress to deal with the crisis. It throws light on your equally determined opposition to moderate help for the unemployed by the Federal Government. Although as Federal official you exercised dictatorial powers in controlling consumption of food during the world war, you seem to be unaware that for millions of men, women and children today, the crisis is as grave as that of the world war.

In any case, Mr. President, the weight of expert opinion is against you.

Prof. John R. Commons, the well known economist of Wis-

[First published in *People's Lobby Bulletin* 1 (July 1931): 3–6.]

consin University, we believe, voiced the view of most economists in his statement: "We may expect that history is repeating itself, and that the world is in for perhaps another 40 or 50 years of revolutions, dictatorships, economic depression and unemployment, following the world war of 1914."

In the same speech you made another statement which is equally disheartening that because "we are economically more self-contained than any other nation this degree of independence gives assurance that with the passing of the temporary dislocation and shocks, we can and will make a large measure of recovery, irrespective of the rest of the world. We did so with even worse foreign conditions in 1921."

Most informed persons will rather agree with the statement of the eminent German banker, Mendelssohn, at the Congress of the International Chamber of Commerce here in May: "There is no method by which economic well being can be permanently isolated in one country." He remarked that there are now twenty million unemployed in the world.

How do you reconcile your statement that our economic independence of the rest of the world is going to promote our rapid recovery, with your other statement that we are suffering because the depression is world-wide? And when you hurried home from your speech making to urge a moratorium for Germany, was your action wholly altruistic, or did your information lead you to believe that a crash in the German mark would have frightful economic consequences all over the world, including finance and business in this country?

You can, of course, continue to refuse to call Congress together until the statutory time next December. In that respect your powers are as autocratic as that of any former Russian Czar. You can veto remedial legislation if it should be passed. You cannot so easily postpone starvation till December, nor so effectively veto the advance of mechanical mass production.

You evidently hold that standardization, efficiency in production and distribution, and science, can so reduce the costs of production, as to increase consumption, keep our people employed, and at the same time permit the paying of a tribute of at least twenty billion dollars a year of unearned income to land owners, controllers of credit, stockholders, owners of natural resources, and controllers of patents.

Your main hope for better times, as you make clear in your speech, is to set idle capital at work to produce more goods.

You refer to increased savings in savings banks. You have access to data not available to ordinary citizens—but banking officials admitted even last winter that half of the savings bank accounts have a balance of less than $100.00.

Of what avail, however, is it to increase savings at the cost of health and comfort and needed present consumption, to provide against poverty in old age?

You are probably aware also that most of the added savings is a desperate move on the part of those who are looking to the future with fear of losing their jobs or having to stand further reductions in salary. To say they are saving is not true; they are merely not spending.

America is prostrated now, because of the concentration of capital and of income, and as President you have aggravated this concentration.

Your proposed "American plan" to extend over twenty years entirely ignores the basic cause of our hard times, and can neither deceive the unemployed and oppressed, nor end our economic evils.

In 1928 the last year of alleged "normalcy," the retail value of manufactures, (exclusive of exports) was about $55,000,000,000, while the total value of manufactures sold at retail here, was only about $50,000,000,000.

The total money income of families with incomes under $5,000—numbering about 24,000,000—was around $65,350,-000,000.

Allowing a minimum outlay for living expenses, exclusive of manufactured goods, such as housing, interest, taxes, insurance, medical care, fresh fruits, and vegetables, milk and other unprocessed foods,—the maximum these families could spend for manufactures was about $38,000,000,000.

The 936,470 persons with incomes over $5,000 in 1928, even with their aggregate income of $19,423,000,000—over one-fifth of the national income—could not have purchased $27,000,-000,000 of manufactured goods, while the total value of all manufactured and semi-manufactured goods exported in 1928, was only $3,714,000,000.

The preliminary tabulation of data collected in the 1930 "Census of Manufactures," places the total value (at f.o.b. factory prices) of all products reported for 1929 at $68,453,486,518.

It is true that the cost of living has been reduced since 1928.

Dr. Benjamin M. Anderson, Economist of the Chase National Bank, in their Economic Bulletin for June, gives the cost of living index as 162.1 in December 1928, and 142.0 in March this year. The index of Real Wages for All Wages was for the respective dates 139 and 154, for Industrial Wages 143 and 165, for Railroad Wages 130 and 139, and for Agricultural Wages 99 and 89 (April 1, 1931).

The year 1914 is taken as the base 100.

Superficially the increase in real wages of industrial and railroad wages particularly, and of all wages, indicates prospective prosperity for the nation.

Reflection, however, convinces that this increase is little cause for gratification under an economic system geared up to high production, unless it applies to a sufficient number of workers to maintain general employment, and to permit current consumption out of current income.

You stated in Indianapolis: "Over 95 per cent of our families have either an income or a breadwinner employed."

The National Bureau of Economic Research estimates that on July 1, 1928, out of the 83,600,000 persons over 15 years of age 46,580,000 were gainfully employed.

That was slightly over 1.8 persons per family for 25,000,000 families.

The total earnings of all those wage earners, an average of about one and four-fifths per family, was at least ten billion dollars short of the amount needed to purchase the output of American factories,—for which no foreign market could be found.

It is clear that if only one person is working per family, those families, even with the real wages of the worker about one-ninth higher than in 1928, can barely exist. They certainly cannot purchase their quota of general manufactures.

If even about one-twentieth of the families as you intimate, are without a bread or income winner, that fact alone would continue the depression.

It should be noted, moreover, that the increase in "real wages," does not cover increases in taxes, nor the heavier burden of debt, with a deflated dollar, and most wage earners carry mortgages or have other debts contracted in inflated dollars. Neither were real wages in 1914 adequate.

Statisticians estimate that within forty years our population will be about 170,000,000, an increase of some 46,000,000, and remain there.

The United States Department of Agriculture eight years ago reported that farm acreage in the United States would maintain a population of nearly 300,000,000 or more than twice the present population, and with little increase over the number then engaged in agriculture, and Dr. O. E. Baker of that Department recently stated he thinks the domestic demand for crops will never be more than twenty-five or thirty per cent greater than today.

Every line of essential production has an enormous surplus productive capacity now, and for some years it will probably not be possible to increase the sale abroad of our products, manufactured or raw, very materially, either in value or volume.

Your suggested twenty-year plan smacks more of political desperation than of practical application, unless the Federal Government promptly reverses its major policies.

Our standing army of 10,000,000 unemployed and part time employed, cannot pay rent for new and better homes, hardly for existing disease breeders.

It cannot eat beautiful public buildings.

We have too many factories now, with the present income distribution, without your proposed thousands of new ones.

The railroads now are bewailing the lack of traffic so your suggestion to increase their capacity and the mileage of new roads and construct new waterways would most seriously cripple them if operated independently of truck lines and inland waterways.

Mr. President, regardless of politics you will have to face the fact that our economic system has broken down past the possibility of patching.

Failure to recognize that fact very soon, may result in serious disorders in our nation.

You have always been concerned with property rights, and refused to recognize the prior claims of workers.

There is no possibility of more than brief recovery from the present depression as every disinterested and courageous economist will agree, as long as we have the present uneconomic and unethical distribution of the national income, and as long as Government is chiefly concerned with property rights.

Discussing public unemployment insurance you stated: "The net results of governmental doles are to lower wages toward the bare subsistence level and to endow the slacker."

We have not any "dole" in the sense in which you use that word to describe unemployment insurance, and yet we have nearly six million people without any means of subsistence except what you designate "charity," and probably five million people approaching "the bare subsistence level."

The contradiction between your usual insistence that the American people are rugged individualists and your apprehension that if they can't live that way, they will degenerate into slackers, must be disconcerting to you, yourself.

How many years longer do you expect the American people to uphold the system of undetermined existence you advocate under which, as you stated in this speech "We have passed through no less than fifteen major depressions in the last century"? That is an average of one major depression about every six and a half years.

The key to your keynote speech, Mr. President, appears to be your blind devotion to the system of special privilege, through which you have accumulated your adequate fortune here and abroad, and your ingrained contempt for labor, as such.

You said: "The remedy to (for) economic depression is not waste, but the creation and distribution of wealth."

We have a superabundance of wealth, not in any chief measure created through our business or financial systems, but primarily through the gifts of nature.

The concentration of most wealth and much income in a few hands with the commensurate control of economic and hence political power, has brought us to our present condition.

Nearly every large fortune in America is chiefly due to some "dole" in the form of special privilege granted by government.

You are committed to the continuance of that system from which the progressive thinkers of every nation in industry, commerce and finance, are turning.

The outcome of next year's election is of course in doubt, but the necessary impermanence of the system you advocate under which in our nation nearly four-fifths of the national income goes to property and a million people get nearly two-fifths of that property income, is doomed.

Government chiefly caused that inequitable distribution and government must end it.

The question to be answered within the next very few years is, whether the present controllers will yield, or whether our people will be driven to the more drastic methods which have been forced in other nations.

Lobby Challenges Senator Borah's Opposition to Reconsideration of Interallied Debts

In the following letter to Senator Wm. E. Borah, Prof. Dewey, as President of the People's Lobby, challenges Senator Borah's opposition to reconsideration of interallied debts:

In your article in the current *Collier's* on reconsideration of interallied debts, you say:

"Economic health is essential to disarmament and peace."

It is precisely that viewpoint which leads us to favor complete readjustment of interallied debts, with actual outlawry of war, and of the instruments thereof.

You also state "There can be no permanent or durable peace that does not have its foundation in economic justice."

That fact is appreciated as well by the nations with which we were associated in the World War.

They know that although we took no territory and accepted no mandate as a result of the war, our advocacy of the rights of small nations to self determination did not lead us to abandon our conception of the Monroe Doctrine as giving us priority in profitable ways in Central and South American nations.

They know, too, that Americans control about two-fifths of the world's mineral production and have about two-fifths of the world's wealth and of the world's income.

Fifteen thousand Americans receive approximately one-fortieth of the income of the more than one and a half billion people in the world.

You suggest that Americans who have made privately investments and advances abroad to the amount you say, of $17,000,-000,000 should with equal fairness scale down their credits.

The case is not completely parallel.

As Chairman of the Senate Committee on Foreign Relations,

[First published in *People's Lobby Bulletin* 1 (July 1931): 7–8.]

you know that we are now committed definitely officially to the position that neither diplomatic pressure, nor force will be applied by our Government to the collection of private loans made by American citizens abroad, and that Americans may no longer look to intervention nor interposition by their government on behalf of property to which they hold title, abroad, other than is sanctioned by international law.

Furthermore, as you know, there has been for years before your Committee on Foreign Relations, a resolution introduced by Senator Wheeler calling for a complete official investigation and a public record of concessions, Americans have obtained abroad, for development of natural resources, construction, etc., as to methods by which they were obtained, and the equities of such procedure. Could you not have at least reported that Resolution out of your Committee?

Still further, foreign nations have the full authority of international law to prescribe the conditions under which investments of Americans in their nations may be operated, to determine working conditions of those engaged in connection therewith, and to tax the profits directly, or to demand and collect heavy royalties upon natural resources extracted from their soil, by Americans, or any foreigners.

Americans who have made private investments abroad have adequate reason to realize that they are not apt to continue to be the bonanzas they have been in the past.

Congress has full power also to tax income derived by its citizens from their foreign investments at a rapidly progressive rate, as well as to surtax progressively and heavily income from property located in the United States.

No American justifies the heavy expenditures of foreign governments for war purposes, and no informed American can doubt that the nations of the world fear that the United States seeks World domination—while millions of Americans vainly seek a chance to earn an honest living at home.

Secretary of War Hurley, Chairman of the Cabinet Congressional Commission investigating War Policies, stated to a witness before that Commission in March this year, "You may know where it is going to be necessary to defend yourself, but we have not that power of prophecy."

In view of the fact that we, separated by oceans from any nation strong enough to fight us, are spending several hundred million dollars a year more for war purposes than before the world war, do you not think we should pluck the beam of military aggression out of our own eye, before we use the mote of military protection or even aggression, of our neighbors as an excuse for refusing to consider the readjustment of the financial hangover of four years of international stupidity?

You ask what reason there is to doubt that if the American taxpayer should decide to let up on poorer taxpayers in other nations, "the advantage derived from such action would go to swell the budgets for more armaments."

One reason is that such action would be evidence to other nations that America is beginning to realize that "live and let live" is a sound economic principle for international relations as well as for domestic tranquility.

You assert there can be "no tariff disarmament, without which we cannot hope for prosperity, nor, consequently, for social, political and moral calm"—without disarmament.

The Congress, of which you are a dominant member voted more tariff and more armament. Which was designed to justify the other?

It appears to us that you have the logical procedure reversed, and that tariffs should be first reduced to give that feeling of economic security which experience shows armaments never afford.

We deplore your advocacy of an export bounty on farm products which will help to keep our unprotecting and war breeding tariff policy in force, because we agree so heartily with your statement, "Neither leagues, nor pacts, nor international courts can maintain peace when economic justice is absent."

It is of course the purpose of these agencies to bring about economic justice.

One final consideration highly pertinent at this time when the peace of the world hangs in the balance—because we have not achieved international economic justice.

On December 31, 1928, the latest date for which the figures are available, the surplus and undivided profits, less deficit of some 174,000 corporations here, was $47,156,000,000—or about four times the total net debt owed our Government by foreign governments. Two hundred and twenty-six corporations had surplus and undivided profits of $15,426,557,384, or nearly one and a third times governmental indebtedness to our government.

In 1929 the income from property of 63,404 Americans was almost as great as this governmental debt to our government.

Today the wealth of the hundred richest persons in America is considerably greater than that governmental debt to us.

Our gross national debt is an insignificant percentage of our national wealth, while the national debt is a devastating proportion of the national wealth of most of the nations whose governments are in debt to ours.

It will probably be necessary to have a capital levy here to clear off the war debt and such a levy would doubtless be an adequate preventive of our participation in any future war—be it ever so defensive.

We do well to remember that we are the only nation in the world in which involuntary unemployment and poverty is completely preventable, and to end such unemployment and poverty—but today any nation which essays to live unto itself alone, is doomed to die by itself.

President Dewey Opposes
Blanket Freight Increase

On behalf of the People's Lobby President Dewey wrote the Interstate Commerce Commission opposing the flat increase in freight rates sought by the railroads:

The extremely tense economic situation prevalent throughout the world threatens the existing economic order. As the distinguished economist, Dr. John R. Commons, recently stated: "We may expect that history is repeating itself, and that the world is in for perhaps another 40 or 50 years of revolutions, dictatorships, economic depression and unemployment, following the world war of 1914."

The suggestion of a moratorium for Germany—however inadequate such action may be with respect to international debts, trade and reparations, is of great significance as showing that all governments recognize early changes are essential.

A chief issue is the relative rights of property and of labor to the national income of every nation, as well as the external relations of nations.

That issue—to what return is property entitled and what property is so entitled is presented to you in the application of the railroads for permission to increase freight rates 15% on all commodities with adjustments "in the case of coke, coal and certain other commodities."

The representatives of the three groups of railroads—Eastern, Western and Mountain Pacific, and Southern in their application for permission to adopt a blanket freight increase say: "The actual return has been during the years 1921 to 1930 inclusive for Class I carriers of the United States, an amount of net railway operating income about $2,579,000,000 less than the amount

[First published in *People's Lobby Bulletin* 1 (August 1931): 6–8.]

which would have been obtained, had the rate of return on the capital employed prescribed by the law been realized."

This is an average of nearly $258,000,000 for the ten years.

You state in your reports that the ratio of dividends declared to all stock of steam railways was as follows: 1921, 5.13 per cent; 1922, 3.78 per cent; 1923, 4.53 per cent; 1924, 4.14 per cent; 1925, 4.35 per cent; 1926, 5.06 per cent; 1927, 5.95 per cent; 1928, 5.25 per cent, 1929, 5.70 per cent, and 1930 (for Class I Railways) 6.1 per cent.

The application of these representatives for permission to increase freight rates, an average of over one-seventh, while the prices of nearly all commodities and many services is being reduced, indicates their desire to start further speculation in stocks of railroads. They state:

"The return on the value of the railway property of the Class I carriers of the United States, as that value was tentatively found by the commission in 1920, with the addition of the cost of subsequent improvements, was diminished until it reached for the year 1930 3.54 per cent.

"The market price of railway stocks began to undergo further decline and railway bonds began to be affected by the approach of railway earnings toward the point where the available income of the corporations would fail to meet the relationship to fixed charges necessary to render them marketable to insurance companies, savings banks, and trusts—a relationship which has become an investment standard by which the value of railway bonds in all markets is affected."

You state in your "Statistics of Railways for 1929"—"For 1929 the net income of steam railways of Classes I, II, and III, and their nonoperating subsidiaries was 9.92 per cent of their capital stock. The dividend-yielding stock was 76.23 per cent of the total, the highest percentage in the history of the railways. The average rate declared on dividend-yielding stock was 7.47 per cent, and the ratio of dividends declared to all stock was 5.90 per cent."

The representatives of the Railroads asking to increase freight rates upon prostrate agriculture, prostrate mining and prostrate manufacturing one-seventh, quote the President's slur (as Secretary of Commerce) upon Government control of Railroads during the war period. They know the railroads under private control had broken down and were utterly inadequate and only government control made it possible for them to function during and after the war. The representatives of the Railroads state in their application: "The theory of the law is that railway property is private property affected with a public use; that in being devoted to such use it foregoes exceptional opportunity for the assurance of fair return. If the sacrifice already made under conditions of prosperity is to be greatly enlarged because of conditions of adversity, the result is that railway property has become public property affected with a private obligation to maintain it. It cannot be expected that investors in railway securities will assume and perform such an obligation."

The more correct statement is that unless the railroads can operate more efficiently public ownership and operation will be demanded.

Your Commission will recall that the Cummins-Esch Railroad Act was opposed by progressive organizations of every sort, most vigorously by all the Standard Railway Employees, partly because of the extravagant valuation put upon the roads.

Your Commission has been working for many years to ascertain the true value of the railroads. You have found that records were destroyed, and have been blocked.

The Bureau of Railway Economics attempting in a recent publication to belittle the value of the 155,000,000 acres of land granted the railroads, assumes the value of this land was 94c an acre and puts the total value at $125,243,000.

It is not conceivable that the Cummins-Esch Act was intended to validate for purposes of rate making and dividend payments the billions of dollars increase in the selling price of land given the railroads or the increase over the price they paid therefor.

Section 15 of the Interstate Commerce Act seems to confer upon your body the power to determine what are just and reasonable rates, and we respectfully submit that in the present emergency no increase in freight rates should be granted till the Railroads can present such a bill of particulars with respect to the values upon which they claim the right to earn a stated dividend, as any business man would require, precedent to any business transaction.

The late Franklin K. Lane as a member of the Interstate Commerce Commission, in the Western Rate Advance Case estimated the increase in the value of land owned by the Chicago, Burlington and Quincy Railroad over the price (if any), paid therefor at about $150,000,000 and said:—"We may agree with the contention of the Burlington that it is no concern of ours, as to whether these lands were obtained by private or public donation in whole or in part, but a larger question of public concern is involved—the legal right of a carrier to continuously increase rates, because of the growth of the community which gives the added value to the land over which the railroad runs."

It was clearly not the intent of the Cummins-Esch Railroad Act to authorize such freight rates as would defeat the avowed intent to yield a certain revenue, nor to cripple the industry of the nation—for transportation is a distributive function and not basic, and competitive methods of transporting commodities are easily provided over a period of a few years.

The Supreme Court of the United States in its decision in "Ann Arbor Railroad Co. et al. *v.* United States et al.," involving the Hoch-Smith Resolution directing your Commission to adjust rates on agricultural products affected by the depression, stated that the words in the Resolution "should not lightly be disregarded," but that if they were intended to change the existing law they "give rise to a serious question respecting the constitutional validity of the paragraph of which they are a part."

Similarly if the strict interpretation of the Cummins-Esch Act results in serious injury to the nation, it is not reasonable to suppose such to have been the intent of Congress.

Greater efficiency on the part of the Railroads, lower salaries to official employees, effecting economics through consolidation should be tried before any general increase in freight rates is granted. If then the railroads need larger revenues for efficient operation, then we believe such revenue should be voted as a dole to stockholders to be obtained by increasing surtaxes, rather than by increasing freight rates upon necessities of life.

President Dewey Calls on Hoover to Recognize Government Responsibility for Unemployment

President Dewey, who has just returned from several weeks in Europe, has written President Hoover the following letter urging his recognition of Government responsibility for unemployment:

It is a misfortune when a person in high and responsible office is committed to ideas and policies which are absolutely contrary to the actual and inevitable course of events. It is not only a misfortune for his own political career, but a calamity for the nation, and even for humanity. You have had the sad experience of proclaiming the economic independence and isolation of the United States just at the time when events were demonstrating to the dullest eye the economic and financial interdependence of all countries. You have applied your philosophy of isolation to the questions of debts and reparations until the financial breakdown of Germany and Great Britain has made it an established fact that neither debts nor reparations will be paid. You no longer have that problem to meet; your only problem now is to break the news to the American people as gently as possible, and to find the phrases which will conceal if possible how completely actual conditions have compelled a reversal of the policy to which you so futilely clung.

Why repeat the sad mistake in the matter of care of the unemployed? You have stubbornly committed yourself to the principle of the ineffective and humiliating care of the suffering by the dole of private alms. But facts which are even more stubborn, are daily demonstrating that this method is as much a relic surviving from bygone conditions as that of national economic and financial isolation.

Why not do the gracious act? A voluntary statement on your

[First published in *People's Lobby Bulletin* 1 (September 1931): 1.]

part of recognition of the responsibility of the public, of organized society, for the proper care of men, women and children suffering in mind and heart as well as in body would bring relief and cheer to hundreds of thousands of your and my, fellow-citizens. It would change the whole atmosphere of American life. It might well change it to such an extent that it would be the beginning of a real and wide-spread economic improvement.

Mr. President, is it not possible for you to realize that we are living under new conditions which demand new ideas and new measures on the part of those in public life? On behalf of our suffering fellow-citizens.

President Dewey Opposes Community Chest Drives for Unemployed

President Dewey in the following statement which received wide publicity in the press, urged limiting contributions to local community chests to usual local needs and an adequate government program:

The program devised by the Administration to localize efforts for relief of the unemployed and their dependents, and to throw responsibility upon private charity to meet a national crisis must give way to an inclusive government program.

It is probable that cutting of wages will spread rapidly, since major corporations having a large part of the accumulated surplus and undivided profits of all corporations, and hence best able to maintain the level of wages, have started the practice.

The cutting of wages at this time is even more serious than in time of prosperity because an overwhelming proportion of wage earners and salaried people employed are not only obliged to care for their own immediate dependents, but are constrained by both pride and affection to help care for relatives out of work and with savings exhausted, and even for friends similarly situated.

The whole force of the concentrated wealth of America is being exerted to prevent additional taxes upon large incomes.

This appears to be the real purpose in the creating of the President's Organization on Unemployment Relief, as it was obviously the purpose of its predecessor, the Emergency Committee for Employment. That Emergency Committee delegated to the National Association of Community Chests and Councils the nation-wide mobilization of local welfare and relief resources.

That Emergency Committee issued a report showing that in 244 of the 376 cities of 25,000 or more population, the work is

[First published in *People's Lobby Bulletin* 1 (September 1931): 1–2.]

to be carried out by Community Chests, and in the remaining 132 cities by special committees.

As is well known, Community Chests and special committees rely for a large part of their collections for relief upon wage earners and others with small and equally precarious incomes, that is through the pressure of publicity and sometimes semi-official sanction, the semi-destitute are levied upon to care for the impoverished.

It would have been no more inappropriate to finance the war by passing the hat, than is the proposed method of raising funds to care for an army of 10,000,000 unemployed or part-time employed and their dependents, the adequate care of whom would involve nearly as large a sum as was spent on our armed forces during the World War.

The wage earners and small salaried people who have already paid their tithe to stockholders by the reduction in wages, should not be compelled to contribute further to care for the victims of Government policies.

It is not merely the right but the duty of every American man and woman to limit his contributions to local Community Chests to such local needs as are usual, and to demand that the Federal Government in connection with State Governments assume the burden of caring for the extraordinary emergency in which the country is plunged. Great pressure will be brought upon those of you who are of moderate means to support the Hoover policy, conceived in the interests of the wealthy, and to substitute private charity for public taxation. You will render a patriotic service if you resist this pressure, and cooperate with the forces which are bringing pressure upon the Government to perform its duty.

We urge that in every city a committee be created to wait upon the Mayor and communicate with the Governor, to insist that they demand that the President call Congress in special session to act on unemployment and that they instruct their United States Senators and members of the House of Representatives to refuse to vote for any other measures till Congress enacts adequate legislation on unemployment, including relief, insurance, municipal housing, and public works, and until the President signs such legislation so that wealth and not want shall care for misery.

We appreciate the fact that the organized force of big finance, backed by the administration is behind the proposal to make the moderately well to do carry the burden of caring for unemployment so as to relieve organized business from paying its just share for the relief of the suffering which its callous and grasping methods have so largely produced. We appeal to you to prove that the capacity of the American people to govern themselves has not been destroyed. Use your political power to get action from your political representatives. Do not be stampeded nor coerced into allowing the Government to shirk its just duty because a small band of the highly wealthy exercise more power over it than do the mass of the people.

The Federal Government and Unemployment

This Government represents the people of the Nation as a whole. It is the organization, and the only organization, of the whole people, established to promote the general welfare and to secure the blessings of liberty. It cannot delegate its responsibilities to private individuals nor agencies however worthy they are. We are in a crisis which mirrors the condition of the whole nation and which affects every citizen in every part of the nation. It knows no bounds of city, county or state. Farmer, manufacturer, railwayman, employee, retailer, teacher, doctor, and lawyer, social worker, father and mother concerned for bringing up their children, in short, all persons in all callings and classes, are touched by the common economic catastrophe. And yet up to the present when asked for bread, it has given only words—with which it has been most generous. And to all appearances, if its inaction drives men in despair to violence, it is getting ready to give them bullets, instead of forestalling violence by constructive aid.

But there are definite causes why the Federal Government is responsible. Its acts of omission and commission have helped bring on the present crisis. It has a definite liability to those who are starving, to those who are pinching to the point of family distress, to those who are living in humiliating dependence upon the meagre dole of private alms, because of its past course. The Federal Government has permitted, it has encouraged, by its legislation and its methods of taxation, an economic system to develop in which thirteen million wage earners received in 1929, (the year of the height of the boom) only three per cent more wages than in 1923, eight millions on farms six per cent less, while the richest one hundred thousand persons,—say one-tenth

[First published in *People's Lobby Bulletin* 1 (December 1931): 5.]

of one percent of the population,—had their incomes more than doubled. It is responsible for maintaining a system in which productive plant is encouraged to increase, simply in order that surplus wealth may find investment, while it loads burdens on consuming power till it cannot begin to purchase what is produced in food, clothing, shelter, capacity for transportation, and so on. In order to avoid recognizing the responsibility of our national policies for the creation of the present situation, its spokesmen put the responsibility for present conditions on what they call natural economic laws, instead of placing it where it belongs, on the use of governmental power, to further the greed of those who by favor of government have been given economic privilege. Having undermined the spirit of neighborliness by fostering inequality, having adopted policies that make many the victims of exploitation by the few, they now appeal to brotherly love and neighborly kindness to help relieve the suffering which has been created, and to avoid recognition of their own responsibility. It is usually considered cowardly for a strong man to hide behind the skirts of a woman and to use a child as a shield. What shall be said of the conduct of those who having fattened on privilege would now pass the responsibility for relief to private charity and to the impoverished who have been fortunate enough to retain some sort of a job?

The Only Way to Stop Hoarding

The Administration has formed a committee to discourage hoarding. President Hoover is authority for the statement that at least one million three hundred thousand dollars was hidden away, a sum which limits the granting of credit to perhaps ten times that amount. Why not go to the root of the matter and instead of preaching to people to use their funds, DO something which will put money in circulation by increasing the power to the unemployed to buy?

The scale on which hoarding exists is equivalent to a vote by the American people, of Lack of Confidence in the present rulers of the country, economic and political. The men who according to former Ambassador James W. Gerard were the real rulers of this country, and who would have saved Great Britain if they had lived in England, have fallen down on their job, although Mr. Gerard has not as yet called public attention to that fact. In countries which have parliamentary government, a vote of lack of confidence compels resignation of the men in power, and a change of policies. The American people has voted by its hoarding, a complete lack of confidence in those now in power in our own country.

Our political machinery makes no provision for their resignation and the calling of others to power:—the more is the pity. But a modicum of political sense dictates that as a matter of self-interest the party in power should at least reverse its policies, in view of the big vote of lack of confidence passed by American citizens of all classes. The first step is positive action in favor of the Costigan-La Follette Bill. The next step is adoption of the policy of large appropriations for public works, with reduction of the number of working hours per week without reduction of

[First published in *People's Lobby Bulletin* 1 (March 1932): 1.]

wages. Give to the unemployed funds with which to buy, and in addition to relief of their suffering, the wheels of industry, now idle, will begin to spin, because buying will begin, and with the resumption of manufacturing and commerce, even the bankers will cease hoarding.

The idea of our present rulers that the depression can be cured without dealing with the problem of unemployment is the most absurd and suicidal idea ever entertained by any Bourbon class.

Gentlemen in power: Will you heed the vote of lack of confidence which the American people has passed upon your policies? Or will you await the still more emphatic vote of no confidence which is surely coming if you continue your present policies?

Church Leaders Ask Church Act on Unemployment

The following letter, signed by John Dewey, Rabbis Edward L. Israel and Stephen S. Wise, Bishop Francis J. McConnell and Rev. Dr. John A. Ryan, has been sent to rabbis, priests and preachers throughout the nation:

We are sure that you agree that the organized religious bodies of America have a solemn obligation in the present economic situation.

We therefore ask your active cooperation in securing the enactment by Congress of the bill introduced by Senators Costigan and La Follette, and Representative Lewis of Maryland, appropriating $375,000,000 to supplement relief given the unemployed and their families, by states and local governments, and $375,000,000 for the construction and reconstruction of highways.

The month's hearings on this bill before the Senate Committee on Manufactures and the House Committee on Labor, and the three weeks' debate in the Senate on this bill proved the need for it.

While larger cities can care for their unemployed, as can some of the wealthier states, the only way to compel the wealth of the nation to pay fairly for the care of the unemployed, is through progressive Federal taxation of large incomes and estates.

Will you request the preachers, priests and rabbis of your city to join you in organizing at once a public meeting, with the cooperation of leaders of your local labor, civic, social work, and women's organizations, to voice the demand of your city that both your United States Senators, and your Congressman actively support this Federal Relief Bill?

Will you also request that your representatives in Congress op-

[First published in *People's Lobby Bulletin* 1 (March 1932): 2.]

pose every proposed increase in taxes on the masses of the people, such as sales taxes, and increase surtaxes on large incomes, and estate taxes, instead?

Have your meeting adopt resolutions on these two measures and send them to your local press, your United States Senators, and your member of the House of Representatives.

It would also be very helpful if you could get all the rabbis, priests and preachers in your city to discuss these two bills, and request their audiences to write personally to their Senators and Representatives.

While the Costigan-La Follette-Lewis Relief Bill was not adopted in the first vote in the Senate, it will be forced to another vote soon, and we have every hope that it will pass the Senate, as well as the House.

Prosperity Dependent on Building from Bottom Up

The People's Lobby has held from the beginning of the depression that an increase in the purchasing power of the masses was indispensable to recovery. That has been one reason for support of federal relief, of unemployment insurance, and of large federal appropriations for public works. We have held from the start that the policies of the Administration were an attempt to solve the depression from the top by assisting the small class of investors instead of by helping the large class of wage earners and salaried persons. The following from the *New York Times* shows that it has come at least half way to our position. When will the *Times* take the other and positive step?

The upturn expected to follow operation of the various credit relief measures recently adopted has failed so far to materialize in the shape of expanded industrial or trade operations.

The basic industries still wait upon expanded automobile output. The *Times* weekly index has eased further, with only the power production series showing an increase. Similarly, commodity prices have weakened, and last week Dun's list reversed its former favorable showing by recording nineteen advances as against twenty-seven declines.

In all the reconstruction measures so far undertaken the country has been witnessing an effort along traditional lines to make business good by helping out major industries. The railroads, banks and large enterprises have been assisted directly in the hope that they may extend the benefits to all the lesser fry. This plan has failed before, as in the tariff, and the country may be nearing a point, in the opinion of some observers, where the all-essential buying power of the rank and file will have to be improved in some manner.

[First published in *People's Lobby Bulletin* 1 (April 1932): 1.]

Calls Wagner "Keyman" on Unemployment Aid

Senator Wagner, by his sponsorship of the labor exchange bill, of Federal aid in unemployment insurance and particularly by his construction bill, has made himself "the keyman on unemployment in the present Congress," according to the People's Lobby, of which Professor John Dewey of Columbia University is president. Failure of Congress to adopt the Wagner construction bill would be a "dastardly betrayal of the unemployed," it was declared in a statement issued at the Lobby's headquarters here today.

"Senator Wagner's aggressiveness in fighting and exposing the opposition of brutal reactionists in both parties to these first-step measures to abate the scandal of unemployment will be a real test of the genuineness of his interest and the interest of Tammany Hall in facing the issue of unemployment," the statement said.

"The Wagner relief bill squarely placed the responsibility for seeking Federal loans for relief upon the Governors of States, who will be held accountable by their citizens for their prompt action. All the objections of Democratic Senators whose votes in favor would have passed the Costigan-La Follette bill have been met. There is no excuse for a Democratic vote against it. Die-hard Republican Senators from New England and others mentally rock-ribbed will consistently advocate higher protective tariffs and vote against loans relief for the victims of present skyscraper protective duties for workers and farmers.

"Failure of Congress to adopt substantially the Wagner construction bill, authorizing Federal credit of $1,100,000,000 chiefly for forest service, public roads, flood control, rivers and

[First published in *New York Times*, 18 April 1932, p. 2.]

harbors projects already authorized by Congress, would be a dastardly betrayal of the unemployed.

"The action of party leaders on these unemployment measures and the revenue bill will largely determine this year's election."

You Must Act to Get Congress to Act

Congress has marked time on unemployment.

The President's program on unemployment—the Reconstruction Finance Corporation, the Glass-Steagall Banking Bill, the increase in the capital of the Farm Land Bank, and the recent Glass Banking Bill, have failed to create that general sense of security in employment and income, which is necessary to stop hoarding, and to start employment.

Wide readjustments in occupation, a shorter week in nearly every occupation, a drastic redistribution of the national income between property and workers, and between different income classes are inevitable—before America can get out of the present depression.

Some of these changes will take at least many months, and probably several years.

There cannot be permanent improvement in economic conditions, until these changes take place.

Our entire history and experience proves that the financial and industrial leaders of the nation will not make these changes voluntarily—they will not, except under compulsion, surrender their most profitable share of a system which has concentrated four-fifths of the nation's wealth in the hands of one twenty-fifth of the people.

The Federal Government alone, has the power to force the wealthy owners of the nation to surrender their control over the lives and destinies of the overwhelming majority of the American people, and the first step is to compel them to pay taxes commensurate in sacrifice, with that of people with very small incomes.

[First published in *People's Lobby Bulletin* 2 (May 1932): 1.]

The *People's Lobby Bulletin* readers live in about 3,200 cities, towns, and villages.

Every reader is a leader in his, and her community. You can organize the existing, though perhaps dormant, sentiment, for the minimum program on unemployment which Congress should enact before adjournment for the two conventions:

The Wagner Relief Bill (S3696) appropriating $375,000,000 as loan relief to states, to be spent before June 30th, 1933, and the same amount for construction, or the Costigan Bill (S4592) appropriating $500,000,000.

The Wagner Construction Bill (S4076) appropriating $1,100,-000,000 for the construction of public works already authorized by Congress.

A Revenue Bill which increases surtaxes and estate taxes to the war level, and taxes the huge corporation surplusses and the income from tax exempt securities, and does not tax any sales—even as an excise tax.

The Senate Birth Control Bill

To my mind the most striking feature of the Senate Bill 4436, regarding the giving of information about contraceptives, is its genuine conservatism. It is conservative in its limitation of those authorized to give out the information. It is incredibly absurd that at present the Government itself, medical societies, schools and journals cannot give out scientific information without being guilty of a crime. The time will come when such a state of affairs will be classed with belief in witches and persecution of them. The so-called "dark" ages know nothing darker than such restriction. One would judge from the statements of some opponents of the modernization of the statute book, that there was a move on foot to compel the information to be given out, instead of simply permitting distribution of scientific information by those competent to give, and desirous of giving it.

The measure is conservative in another sense. It is aimed at reinforcing all the factors which conserve human life and well-being, that of mothers, of children, of families. It is aimed at the prevention of abortion which takes such toll of human life in this country. It aims at substituting the administrations of competent physicians for the activities of unscrupulous quacks. Can anything more absurd be imagined, than that clinics should be established for the care of women, and that a reputable physician should be guilty of a crime if he gives information as to the location of these clinics, to a woman needing care?

The measure is conservative because it substitutes light for secrecy, knowledge for ignorance, science for quackery.

Organized groups have a right to attempt to dissuade their own members from resorting to contraceptive measures if they

[First published in *People's Lobby Bulletin* 2 (May 1932): 1–2.]

are willing to take that responsibility on their conscience. But it is un-American, undemocratic, and despotic, for those groups to attempt to use legislation to create crimes, in order to impose their special moral views upon others.

Joint Committee on Unemployment Demands Congress Act

The morning papers carry a report of the speech of Secretary Mills. He says that the only way to bring "adequate relief to the people of the United States is to set in motion forces which will make economic recovery possible." Why then does not the administration of which Secretary Mills is an important part, do something positive and constructive to set these forces in motion? Why not give the federal relief which, while it keeps men and women alive, will also increase their purchasing power? Why not start a program of public works which will actually move the forces of production as well as set men at work?

He says that "credit and confidence" are the magicians upon which we must depend. Does Secretary Mills not know that millions and millions have no chance at getting credit; that the savings of their friends and relatives are exhausted, and that many cities and states have no credit upon which they can any longer borrow to provide work and relief? How can millions and millions have "confidence" when they have neither work nor security? Why mock these millions of men and women, Mr. Secretary? Why add that mocking to their already exasperated situation? Why not give up reliance on magic and depend upon something real like relief and the provision of useful work?

There are millions of homes in which budgets will not balance or in which they are being balanced only by extreme privation and starvation. Do you, Mr. Secretary, and your Administration and the members of Congress believe that the suffering millions are forever going to swallow words about the importance of balancing the national budget and keep it balanced, till something is

[First published in *People's Lobby Bulletin* 2 (May 1932): 3–4, from a statement at the conference of the Joint Committee on Unemployment in Washington, D.C., on 30 April 1932.]

done to give work and security so that the plain men and women of the country can balance their personal and family budgets? It is not merely justice and humanity which speak. It is necessity. If its voice is not listened to—well, next winter is coming.

Voters Must Demand Congress Tax Wealth Instead of Want

The brutality of the twenty-eight Republican Senators and the twenty-four Democratic Senators who voted against the Couzens Amendment to the Revenue Bill, restoring the 1918 income tax rates and surtax rates, is almost incomprehensible. Everyone of them knows the situation. Most of them have been in Washington several years. All of them understand perfectly, that our present depression is primarily due to the concentration of wealth and income, resulting chiefly from Federal policies dictated by selfish and irresponsible financial and commercial interests.

These Senators know that the alternative to taxation of wealth through high surtaxes, estate taxes, taxation of income from Government securities, and taxation of land values and of corporate surpluses—is to tax those with small incomes. They know that the major part of large incomes is derived from ownership and control of property, and that only by increasing surtaxes, as the Couzens Amendment provides, can the Federal Government equalize even approximately, the sacrifice of the tax payers.

They know too, that before we can begin to renew prosperity there must be a drastic redistribution of the national income through taxation. Private industry cannot do this satisfactorily, and private industry does not propose to do it, as shown by the wage-cutting campaign.

Write your United States Senators to back the whole program of the progressives on the Revenue Bill, and on unemployment, and let them know that you will not condone their failure to do this.

[First published in *People's Lobby Bulletin* 2 (June 1932): 1.]

President Dewey Asks Senators
to Stay on Guard

Sensing the tense situation developing from widespread continued suffering and deprivation, Prof. Dewey as President of the People's Lobby has written the following letter to a group of progressive Senators, asking some of them to "standby" in Washington, while Congress is not in session.

The deliberate drive of newspapers and interests that represent concentrated wealth and privilege to discredit the law-making body of the United States cannot have escaped your attention. The so-called financial and industrial leaders led the country into its present impasse; they did their best to impose their special policies on the country. They are now using attacks upon Congress to divert attention from their own failure and to provide an alibi for themselves. Every day a smoke screen of poisonous gas issues from them.

The attempt to discredit the legislative branch of the Government is connected with an attempt to exalt the Executive even to the point of permitting the Executive to usurp the function of initiating Federal legislation vested under the Constitution, in the Congress of the United States. We regard this as the first step toward the establishment of some form of fascism or extra legal control, in view of the widespread distress and consequent unrest.

The recent suggestion for the resurrection of the Council of National Defense and for a bipartisan Administration, are equally significant, and dangerous. We have criticized certain actions of members of Congress, but they at least are responsible for their action to their constituents, whereas the substitution of war-time powers of autocracy in times of peace, for the give and take and discussion which are inherent in coordinated Legislative and Executive functions of Government, is a standing menace to civil

[First published in *People's Lobby Bulletin* 2 (June 1932): 2–3.]

liberties, as well as to economic justice. It may be that Congress will adjourn before the Convention, or in any case recess for several weeks. We feel that it is of vital importance that there should be present in Washington whenever Congress is not in session, two or three Senators who can call attention to any overt act on the part of the Chief Executive of the Nation, subversive of popular rights. We are writing the following Senators, Blaine, Borah, Brookhart, Costigan, Dill, Frazier, Howell, La Follette, Long, Norbeck, Norris, Nye, Sheppard, Schall, Shipstead, Thomas (Okla.), and Wheeler, to ask if you will not get together, and arrange to have two or three of your members present in Washington whenever Congress is not in session, to meet such a situation as we have described above, which may so quickly arise.

Roosevelt Scored on Relief Policy

Governor Roosevelt was tonight criticized for his attitude on unemployment relief by the People's Lobby, of which Professor John Dewey is president, who in a statement issued here declared that this is the paramount issue of the campaign.

"Governor Roosevelt holds the same position as predatory wealth, that the poor throughout America shall be forced into abject poverty to care for the unemployed locally, before the wealthy of New York, the cream of the beneficiaries of the Democrat's World War, are taxed a penny," Professor Dewey said in his statement. "Governor Roosevelt is speaking for the class he trains with.

"For the year 1929, $6,253,465,699 income was reported to the Federal government by New Yorkers, over one-fourth of the total reported income in America.

"In 1929, 513 net incomes of over $1,000,000 were reported in America, of which 276, considerably over half, were reported by New Yorkers, whose aggregate net income was about $644,000,000, an average net income of about $2,340,000, of which about nine-tenths was from ownership or control of property. Their income was also over half that of all those with million dollar incomes.

"For 1929 corporations in New York paid cash dividends of $2,777,527,000 out of total payments of $7,841,802,000 in the United States—almost one-third.

"A major part of the surplus and undivided profits of large corporations, which amounted at the close of 1929 to $29,383,-000,000, were in the tin boxes of New York corporations.

"Governor Roosevelt's understanding heart leads him to tell the millions of semi-employed and half-paid workers of America

[First published in *New York Times*, 24 October 1932, p. 7.]

that he prefers to have them taxed to care for the unemployed, rather than to tax incomes of $2,340,000 to do this. He also brags to the social workers that he increased the income tax rate on incomes of $2,000 in New York as much as he did on incomes of $2,340,000.

"Governor Roosevelt tells the social workers he would hold public works down to what the rich taxpayers will let government do, a tragic admission that he prefers to leave feeding the unemployed to the 'actual love of their neighbor,' most of whom are desperately in debt."

Get Mayor and Governor to Demand Relief

Of the $300,000,000 made available by the "Emergency Relief and Construction Act of 1932" for loans to States and political sub-divisions thereof for direct relief and work relief, only about $65,000,000, or a little over one-fifth has been allotted by the Reconstruction Finance Corporation.

Of the $1,500,000,000 credit made available by Congress for self-liquidating projects, only $135,000,000 has been authorized by the Reconstruction Finance Corporation, and none has been disbursed.

The letters from Governors and their representatives printed in a following article, show the desperately and dangerously low standards of both direct relief, and work relief.

Part of the failure of the Reconstruction Finance Corporation to grant adequate funds for relief, and to grant credit for self-liquidating projects, is due to the failure of Mayors, Governors, and organizations, to ask for sufficient amounts.

Responsibility for such failure rests in part upon citizens throughout the nation.

Only 33 Governors have even made application for relief loans, while only about 20 applications for credit for self-liquidating projects have been granted.

A group of citizens should ascertain what amount should be spent by each city for relief till next spring, to maintain a decent standard, and how much the city and State can pay, and insist that the Mayor ask for the difference from the Reconstruction Finance Corporation.

Mayors must be induced to act promptly. Their request will be expedited, if backed by Governors.

Needed projects which can be made self-liquidating, should be

[First published in *People's Lobby Bulletin* 2 (November 1932): 1.]

urged upon Mayors and Governors, as well as upon others (including non-commercial-profit making organizations) who can initiate them. Application for funds for such projects should be made to the Reconstruction Finance Corporation.

Won't you organize a group in your city or town to get action?

Introduction [Unemployment Insurance]

The question of unemployment is to the fore; it is the chief issue of the day. Although itself a symptom, an effect, it dramatizes in a vivid human way the breakdown of our economic and political system. Poverty, distress, suffering are always tragic; when they affect persons able and willing to work, when they affect millions whose greatest desire is to do some form of useful labor in order to support their families and themselves, the situation is socially disgraceful, as well as tragic to individuals. The evils which unemployment entails cannot be measured by malnutrition, by tendency to starvation, by exposure to illness due to lack of sufficient food. Nothing is so completely disheartening and so demoralizing; it takes away nerve and eats into moral fibre. Nor are the evils confined to those actually unemployed. The fear of being thrown out of a job haunts millions more. The average worker to-day is living in a state of mental and moral insecurity. His whole family shares the moral disturbance.

Human sympathy and a sense of justice demand that something be done. It will doubtless be a long time before the fundamental causes of unemployment are removed. No one can tell how far economic changes must go, how far the capitalistic system must be changed, in order to ensure work for all who are capable of useful service to society. But there are two principles that cannot be denied. Organized society is responsible for alleviating the distress due to unemployment; any social order has an obligation to take care of the wreckage caused by its operations. In addition, society has the responsibility to do what it can to relieve its members from the fear of impending loss of work. Aside from the immediate effect of unemployment insurance in

[From an unpublished typescript in the Benjamin C. Marsh Papers, Manuscripts Division, Library of Congress, Washington, D.C.]

helping families whose breadwinner has not work, a system of insurance would do much to lessen dread for the future. This very fact would do more than can be told to stimulate consumption, and hence trade and production, and thus help stabilize industry.

Carlyle once remarked on the spread of contagious disease from slums to the homes of the well to do. He said that it was one way of proving that all men are brothers, and are their brothers' keepers. That the effects of unemployment spread through modern industrial society and have disastrous consequences for the manufacturer, the store-keeper and the farmer, the present situation demonstrates. Some kind of systematic action is more than a measure of benevolence and even of justice to the worker. It is a measure of self-protection for all engaged in production and distribution of goods and services.

This little book by Mr. Marsh contains an impressive statement of the facts of the case, and makes a powerful plea for ample federal aid to state systems of unemployment insurance. The plan leaves the states free to adopt whatever system each local unit judges best. But it emphasizes the national aspect of the situation and the consequent need for national action. The moral effect of federal action would be as significant as its direct financial aid. As Executive Secretary of the People's Lobby and by long residence in Washington, Mr. Marsh has had access to the facts as far as anyone can get at them in our haphazard system, and is in constant contact with the play of political forces. His presentation of the situation has a claim upon the most serious attention. Not all will accept the remedy he urges, and to which the People's Lobby is committed. But even such persons cannot fail to be impressed by his facts and figures. They cannot fail to see that there is something basically in need of remedy. The less they accept the proposed plan, the greater is the obligation upon them to come forward with some workable and efficient remedial plan.

Interviews and Reports of Statements and Addresses

Setting New Goals at Seventy

This was no setting for drama. Thin, autumn sunlight picked out John Dewey's spare figure in the chair by the drawing-room table and showed him pensive, looking a little tired. It was quiet, decorous, here, the humdrum of East 72nd St. seeping only faintly through the windows.

But this was drama. It was if patriarchal John Brown's "Forward!" was in 1859 at Harpers Ferry, or if young Bryan's "You shall not crucify mankind upon a cross of gold!" was in 1896 at the Chicago convention.

For, at 72, as calmly as if he had been thinking aloud, Dr. Dewey, the foremost philosopher of America, gave a voice to revolution. His words suddenly were battle drums beating; suddenly they were an army with banners.

"We've been living on hypocrisy and bunk and catchwords ever since the war! The result is disgust with politics and a good deal of loss of faith in democratic principles!"

Sounds Clarion Call

"A new party is needed! It must be a party with a definite, constructive, social program based on economic realities. It is needed not merely to support certain measures but to give a new tone to American political life!"

This was not new in Dr. Dewey's mind. It has been alive there a long time. But it was ringing proof in the East 72nd St. drawing room of a goal ahead, at 72—and the burden of the years forgotten in the struggle for social reform.

[First published in *New York World-Telegram*, 4 November 1931, p. 23, from an interview by William Engle.]

The crusade is on, he said. A quiet, gentle philosopher will lead the way. In a young man's world a professor emeritus, mild-mannered and diffident, will preach a doctrine to lead the oppressed—the dark-fated thousands caught in the wheels of the present's politico-economic system—out of capitalistic bondage.

This, as the years crowd fast, is his burning interest now—the third party, to be exact, the League for Independent Political Action, precursor of the party in actuality, of which he is head.

Objectives Many

A federation of liberal groups of the country, under the banners of the league—that is the mighty goal of Dr. Dewey, mild in the drawing-room, militant along the world's avenues of constructive thought.

But it is only one of a vast number of goals. John Dewey, a fortnight past 72, in this young man's world, seemed today as his unimpassioned voice hesitated for precise meanings a shining sword of justice. Age fell away from him. The shadows of the drawing room dissolved. He was not a gray, calm-talking man; he was a vital, impersonal force for liberal thought.

It is as this that he means to live out his time; he pays a way, not exorbitant, in a tall co-operative apartment house in East 72nd St. and his mind dwells in the living rooms of the lowly everywhere.

He smites Matthew Woll's committee of 100 for "Red-baiting." He proposes an international conference not merely of statesmen but of economists. He heads the Rollins Conference which issues an epochal manifesto of rational higher learning. He appeals to the country to nullify the aims of President Hoover's unemployment relief organization "conceived in the interests of the wealthy." He offers an emergency relief plan of his own, supported by 100 economists, social workers and clergymen; he urges $5,000,000,000 for federal public works, $250,000,000 for family relief, $250,000,000 for unemployment insurance reserves.

And as head of the People's Lobby his voice is sharp thunder along the Washington horizon.

Voice of Inarticulate

The voice, unhurried and low—drum beating, thunder rolling—went on today in the drawing room; it told why he has not had time yet to think at all of retiring from the American economic scene; it explained why, after a half-century given to philosophy and economics, he today fathers the League for Independent Political Action, with units coming into being up and down the country.

"I am an independent," he said. "For many years I voted for the most progressive candidates. But finally I became convinced of the futility of that course.

"The parties are much more influential than any so-called leader could be. Even Roosevelt didn't succeed in changing the direction of the Republican party.

"I saw the need of a new party not hampered by the conditions and tie-ups which prevented the progressive elements in the old parties from accomplishing anything."

He chose the words carefully. He let them take on significance without benefit of vehemence.

"I feel there are hundreds of thousands in the old parties who are fairly liberal at heart but who haven't waked up to realize that party control is of a nature completely to nullify their progressive aspirations.

"Consequently I see no hope for sanity and reality in American political life except through the agency of a new party!

"The persons who argue that progressives should aim at getting a balance of power and getting through certain special measures misconceive, I think, the whole situation.

"The result is disgust with politics and a good deal of loss of faith in democratic principles. While the country needs certain definite policies carried through, it needs still more a new atmosphere of political life."

It was then, in that same monotone, that he derided bunk and catchwords and advocated a new party to prick their balloons.

"Just now we are trying to bring about a federation of liberal groups."

He meant that the League for Independent Political Action is establishing branches from Broadway to Michigan Blvd. and Market St.

Five classes he hopes to rally to the banners—the professional labor group; retail merchants; the white collar proletariat, male and female; farmers; laborers.

Inured to Opposition

But that, he conceded readily, will be a miracle not expeditiously wrought. All these classes, he feels certain, stand to gain by establishment of such an order as he advocates. Yet to win their united and vigorous support is something to dream about largely and to speak about with an optimism that is tempered by hard logic.

He is quite undaunted, though, by opposition. In the half century during which his ideas have profoundly affected every phase of American thought he has grown used to opposition.

So pronged words of his drift down the wind to Washington.

"The administration's program to localize efforts for relief of the unemployed and to throw responsibility upon private charity to meet a national crisis must give way to an inclusive governmental program.

"Community chests and special committees rely for a large part of their collections for relief upon wage earners and others with small and equally precarious incomes; that is, through the pressure of publicity, and sometimes semi-official sanction, the semi-destitute are levied upon to care for the impoverished."

Interests Broaden

"It would have been no more inappropriate to finance the war by passing the hat than it is to propose methods of raising funds to care for an army of 10,000,000 unemployed or part-time employed and their dependents, the adequate care of whom would involve nearly as large a sum as was spent on our armed forces during the World War."

The years gather. Dr. Dewey's interests broaden. Decades have passed since he was known only as a pragmatic philosopher or as the leader who freed the American school system from the sing-song method and substituted the principle that the student should learn to accomplish rather than pack his mind with facts, since mere knowledge is not power unless it is applied.

Now the whole field of economic thought is his. At 72 he is out of the schoolroom, the people's champion.

His clans rally, not to a man, but to an idea. Progress seems slow, but certain, too. The challenge is down.

"A new party is needed."

John Dewey Surveys the Nation's Ills

A Philosopher Sees the Time Ripe for Radical Changes in Our Fundamental Ideas on Both Education and Politics

While the outbursts of convention oratory were still re-echoing through the air, a retiring, slow-spoken, silver-haired college professor sat in his library and discussed political theories. No flood of imagery swept away the simplicity of his words, nor did eloquence or emotion enter into his arguments. Quietly and almost haltingly John Dewey enunciated theories that might be the planks of a third party platform. A hesitancy of manner, by its very contrast, added weight to the arguments of a philosopher who has always preferred to deal with the actualities of life rather than to search for the reality back of the material changes in the universe.

John Dewey, above all else, is essentially American. New England has left its horny thumb mark indelibly upon him. Neither the breezy Middle West, where he was professor at the universities of Michigan, Minnesota and Chicago, nor the East in the shape of Columbia has spoiled his simplicity or dulled his quaint humor. His soft brown eyes which for so many years have pored over the written words of thousands of philosophical treatises, still twinkle merrily behind their large rimless spectacles.

The twinkle was there as he told me that four years ago, when a scrubwoman had asked for whom he was going to vote and he had answered Smith, she said to him: "Oh, professor, you surely do not believe that such an uneducated man should be in the White House."

[First published in *New York Times Magazine*, 10 July 1932, pp. 9, 16, from an interview by S. J. Woolf.]

There is an intense practicality about John Dewey, a quality inherited from his Vermont ancestors, which has prevented him from being lost in the wilderness on a vain search for the Absolute. To his mind the greatest harm has come from dissociating thinking from acting and regarding it as something, for that reason, more desirable. He believes that feelings, habits and volitions are as important and as worthy of study as so-called pure reason.

These being his ideas, it follows that this Yankee philosopher has not shut himself up in his library, allowing the world to pass by unheeded. Causes of all kinds have found in him a stanch champion. More than forty years ago, while still a Professor of Pedagogy, he published *School and Society*. Edison was then perfecting his electric light, the Wright brothers were attempting to solve the problem of flying. Westinghouse and a host of others were working on their epoch-making machines. Bland and Bryan were preaching the spirit of unrest that was shaking the country.

It was then that this professor of education in the University of Chicago saw students throughout the country, in classrooms in which shades were drawn and windows closed to keep out both sights and sounds, bending over old-fashioned readers and reciting fixed formula by rote. Neither their teachers nor their books opened the eyes and minds of students to what was going on about them. To John Dewey this all seemed ridiculous. Why not connect learning with life and make education a helper in the problems of life? He proclaimed this doctrine and it helped to bring about a revolution in the science of teaching. He has carried out his theories in his own career, maintaining a vital touch with the world about him.

It was therefore natural that the first topic of conversation should be the college man in public life.

"For the last twenty years or so," said Professor Dewey, "teachers and students have been called in to solve our national economic problems. This was more or less of an innovation here, notwithstanding that in Europe men of learning have long taken a part in governmental affairs. But economics has not been the only subject in which expert advice has been sought. Throughout the country there has been a distinct trend toward employing experts in working for a solution of other questions. There have been all sorts of commissions whose members included college professors.

"The country has need of expert service of this kind, but there is one objection to it. In economic questions, in municipal problems and in State problems one is likely to find that most of the work is in the nature of compiling statistics. Statistics are all right in themselves, but unless the man of learning is competent to apply statistics to the questions at hand, they will not help matters. What is necessary is an interpretation of them. Changes are going on rapidly all about us and we must be able to interpret them.

"I do not blame the experts for this. Lack of ability to apply to conditions the information which they have gained from their investigations is not their fault. The blame lies in the training which they received in their schools and colleges. Social science at the present time has collected too many facts upon which it has not worked. It has gone about matters in the wrong way. Facts after all are not physical objects which can be caught, labeled and put in glass cases. The greatest collection of them so displayed will get us nowhere. Theories must evolve from them, otherwise there is no use in bringing them together. They must lead to control and action.

"At the present time higher teaching is beginning to broaden and to pass from intense specialization to a more direct dealing with fundamental issues. There is a distinct tendency now to connect in more ways than ever what is taught in the classroom with the problems of life.

"The present economic crisis will assist in this movement. For during the last two years our colleges have been graduating thousands of young men and women who suddenly have been brought to the realization that most of what they have learned will not help them to gain their livelihood. They are beginning to think for themselves and to appreciate the fact that they must do something to bring about a change in present-day affairs. At last they have come to the realization that they must use their efforts to alter a system which affords them no opportunities.

"This is a mighty good thing," he continued, "for the average college graduate displays a lack of interest in public affairs. Of course, when I say this I mean those in this country. But I am not surprised at this, for college still tends to an academic aloofness which has become almost a tradition. The student gets the idea that he should not pay much attention to such sordid things as business unemployment or present-day politics.

"Our higher education apparently evades serious consideration of the deeper issues of our social life. Our young people
emerge from these homes of academic tradition and find that we
are governed by one of two parties controlled by vast political
machines in which there is a varying amount of corruption. The
futility of opposing these great parties is apparent. Moreover, in
all of us there is a strange feeling of wanting to vote for some one
who has a chance of election; the result is that many who do not
believe in either party vote under the banner of one or the other
rather than, as they imagine, throw their votes away.

"How many of these new voters realize that a great modern
industrial country is now being run on pre-Civil War methods?
Or, if they do realize it, how many make any efforts to change it?
The present division of parties is based on what happened in
the days of Thomas Jefferson and Abraham Lincoln and has little
to do with American life except to dodge the vital issues that
beset us."

As he continued he ruffled his gray hair until it shot out in all
directions. "The most important and most dangerous question
in our present-day life is economic insecurity. Millions of men
anxious to work are recurrently out of employment, and apart
from those unemployed by reason of the depression is a standing
army which at no time has regular employment. While we hardly
know the number of these, we know still less of the psychological and moral consequences of the precarious conditions in which
this vast multitude lives.

"Insecurity is worse than unemployment. It is the most pressing problem before us today, yet both of the great parties more
or less gloss this over in their platforms and raise the question of
prohibition above it in importance. I am not minimizing the importance of the latter, but I feel that our economic problems are
those which require our most concentrated efforts."

"How would you solve them?" I asked.

"That is not an easy question to answer," he replied as he
settled back in a carved Chippendale chair. For a moment his
eyes rested on an old Chinese painting on the wall opposite. Behind his head was a bookcase in which volumes of Shakespeare's
plays, bound in red, were most prominent.

"The first work must be educational," he went on. "People are
beginning to seek some direction. They want to learn with what

kind of policies they can successfully face the present issues of life. They are becoming desirous of finding out how they can bring about some political action that will have an effect upon their work and life. They regard the future with dread; they require reinforcement and courage that come from a sense of union with others in their position. One can almost sense this groping in the very air.

"I am not saying that popular thinking has reached a point of great clearness. It is confused and attended with less light than heat, less understanding than emotion. Nevertheless, I believe that the fundamental point is better understood than ever before. It is known that politics is a farce unless it deals openly and bravely with questions of work, commerce and finance, with things which affect men where they live. Both of the great political parties are intellectually and morally bankrupt on this question. The reason for this bankruptcy is beginning to be understood. They are both so tied up with interests that they literally cannot afford to have any ideas or policies on these questions."

Professor Dewey does not believe that the desired changes in our government could be brought by either the Republicans or the Democrats. I mentioned the so-called insurgents.

"Most of them are followers rather than leaders," he said. "They wait for enough people to create a tide in favor of a certain measure and then, and not until then, do they espouse it.

"If this were not the case you would find that they would come forward with definite plans; instead of which they primarily obstruct what has been proposed. I do believe that if their policy were constructive, instead of destructive, the result would be that men and women of this country would recognize the need of a new party."

"Do you believe that the average worker, whether he works by hand or brain, is getting a fair share of the national income?"

"I do not think that many people feel that the great mass of the American people has been getting a square deal. The great American principle of equality has become a myth.

"This is apparent more and more to the rank and file of our citizens. The depression has impressed the fact upon them to a greater degree. I can see a great party rising from all these classes, a genuine political party of opposition, based upon principles and not upon power and pelf resulting from doing errands for organized business.

"But," he continued, "even if a new party should come into power the necessary economic changes would not occur immediately. There must be something more than political action. There must be vital changes in education as well as in the attitude of men in responsible places in industry. The immediate and central issue, however, is of a definite political nature. Before desired legislative, administrative and judicial changes can be brought about, control of government must be redeemed from special interests, which have usurped it, and restored to the people. If this does not happen then political democracy is doomed."

"You then still believe in democracy?" I asked.

"I do," he answered, "provided that all those critics who claim that democratic government is a failure get down to business and, instead of finding fault with it, endeavor to direct attention to the economic forces which seriously threaten it.

"And this threat is a serious one. We are faced with a situation in which there is a conflict as great as that between the North and South seventy-five years ago. Either the economically privileged groups are going to seize the reins of government and drive wherever they will, or else the people in general, the masses of hard-working, peaceably inclined men and women, are going to take hold and run things to promote general welfare."

Statements to the Conference on Curriculum for the College of Liberal Arts

[At the 19 January 1931 morning session of the Curriculum Conference, Dr. James Harvey Robinson suggested that a "number of us report on processes we estimated by which we got such education as we admit ourselves that we have." He said that the "so-called college years have to be brought into relation with the whole process of life," and that "education has come to be . . . an excessively individual enterprise, and it mainly evolves on us." He advocated that "we ought to participate in our own education. I think that is coming to be recognized now and I do not know of anything that would make the situation more vivid, and probably at the same time more confusing, than the confession on Dr. Dewey's part as to how he got that way" ("Proceedings" 1:15). Robinson was the first participant to relate his educative experiences, followed by Dewey, who chaired the conference.]

CHAIRMAN DEWEY: I am going to take advantage, or, from your point of view, perhaps disadvantage, of being Chairman and be the next, as Dr. Robinson made a sort of challenge to tell how I got that way. I do not know what way I am, so I do not know just how I got that way, but I realize I never really made a survey of my own education and lack of it. I want to go back to public school education, common school education.

The impression I got, and as with all children, those impressions are largely unconscious or unformulated at the time, was of pretty continuous boredom and lack of any definite intellectual interest, and consequent waste of time. I was fortunate in one respect. I got to high school and continued in college. I had certain outside interests, not very wise, perhaps, too much reading, and high school and college work interrupted that more or less,

[From the unpublished typed transcript in the Rollins Archives, "Proceedings, Curriculum Conference," 3 vols. Rollins College, Winter Park, Florida, January 19–24, 1931, 1:49–54, 203–5; 2:420–27.]

and it had the advantage of stimulating a fairly intense study when I studied, so I could get it out of the way and get at things I was more interested in. The fact that somewhat unconsciously I did not like to study out of school and take my books home made me work harder in school.

Then when I had children of my own, quite a number and no two alike, I remembered this boredom, this intellectual boredom, mental boredom of early school days, and it made me feel, and I still feel, that the college problem is primarily not a college problem, but it is in what we call the grades and the high school, and that the habits of wasting time, of puttering along, of not going at things in any wholehearted way, are habits that are formed in the earlier days. It is hard to estimate the bad habits that are formed, to my mind, under these earlier conditions.

Along with that I got the idea and I did come to reflect upon it and formulate it, of the very great importance of interest, which my friend, James Harvey Robinson, has already spoken of. I did not get my conception of the importance of interest from theory, but rather as a deposit of my own experience as a student, watching other students, fellow students, and then when I came to teach, noticing my own students.

Of course, it is a word that means many different things to many people. Some people think it means amusing students, but I think it means having a kind of internal hunger and thirst which leads students on to do something for themselves, and it seems to me that which goes with this curiosity that Dr. Robinson spoke of, is a normal, human attribute and that natural curiosity and natural interest in something or other get destroyed and killed out, and if we could find out what destroys them, we would take the first step toward fundamental improvement in our whole educational scheme.

Then I got to be a graduate student in philosophy, which my friend doesn't have much use for, though he admits he is attracted toward it, curiosity of the human mind. Certain wheels go around in your head or else they don't. The wheels in my head took this particular form. Then I found out that I could not follow readily a consecutive line of thinking. I don't like the word "concentration," because it suggests a kind of tense rigidity of mind and really what you want is a play and movement of mind, but it has to have continuity and consecutiveness. The hardest thing I have ever done in my life was to develop out of the bad habits I formed earlier, in the early years, some power of continuous, consecutive, coherent mental operation, and that gives in brief perhaps my two fundamental points: First, the importance of discovering (for I think it is always there although it has got very much concealed and overlaid) some line, native or acquired, of definite intellectual hunger and thirst, curiosity, that will move from within and move of itself; second, the conditions that will develop this element of persistence, continuity in following out some line of study which will lead to learning, and keep the mind alive and after it.

That suggests, of course, the question of specialization. There are all kinds of specialization. There is interest in specialized topics like the manor or Latin epigraphy, which are narrowing, perhaps, and I think often are artificial, as in the cases illustrated. It isn't that kind of specialization so much as this native line of interest or interest which will keep a person moving of himself.

When my own children came to go to college, they had a very bad system, six or seven different studies, two hours each, in the freshman year, a deadly scheme in my opinion, and I told my children (I don't suppose they paid any attention to it, but I remember telling them, although they probably do not remember being told) I didn't care about their slighting some courses or making snap courses of them, but I did hope they would find some one thing they were interested in to which they could really devote their thoughts and mental operations.

All my recent years have been given to graduate teaching. I have had practically no college teaching, and I have the degree of ignorance necessary to make me a suitable Chairman of this meeting. I don't think my ignorance is systematized. It is highly chaotic. In graduate work I have somewhat deliberately slighted college problems. They seem to me so difficult and so complex. My own tendency, since this is a confessional meeting, has been to go into a hole and pull the hole in after me along the line of my own interest.

I do think this problem of college study, direction and weighting of interest of people of college period is about the most difficult out of a whole series of educational problems and, therefore, I welcome the opportunity of being present and listening to these discussions.

There is only one thing more. I mentioned two points that seemed to me to stand out, the discovery and reawakening, I think I have said, of what I think I have said is there underneath, some line of direct and genuine intellectual interest and curiosity, and the ability to pursue some line of study in a consecutive way. The other side I alluded to is the very obvious disadvantages, dangers, of overspecialization. There must be a variety of interests, of course, or else one loses the open mind and one becomes narrowed, even in his own speciality, if he does not have a varied outlook upon the world.

I have been impressed with the desirability of taking an interest in some unpopular cause or subject of interest, unpopular at that particular time. I think it is something to be recommended to the young people, not to fall in line too much; not necessarily to become a crank, but not conform too much to the more obvious tendencies of the day.

Another thing in connection with this, though it may not seem to be closely associated, is the fact that the parts of college life that seem to be most actively engaged in by a great many of the students, are the so-called student activities, which have nothing to do with the activities of the student, in the ordinary sense of the word; and that question of taking advantage of these outside (in most colleges they are outside) activities and of getting the advantage of momentum and independent organization on the part of the students themselves, is bringing that into more organic relations with college life itself, seems to me a very important thing. ["Proceedings" 1:49–54.]

[The participants in the Tuesday morning session on 20 January discussed general and special interests of students and "what science may mean in the enrichment and enjoyment of daily life." Dewey commented on James Harvey Robinson's statement on physical sciences.]

CHAIRMAN DEWEY: There is one point on which I feel like taking issue, or at least adding something. I cannot see why it should be said that we have to leave the world around us and go into a laboratory to get the study of physics and chemistry. I think that we have had a very good statement of the whole point of view from which the biological sciences should be approached, in their unity, instead of in their classified and analytic subdivisions, which are useful for special investigations and in their connection in life with the world of matter itself, but, as Dr. Robinson illustrated, we inevitably get into processes of physics and chemistry in the study of living processes themselves; but then this point that I wanted chiefly to make is that I believe Dr. Robinson came down here parked away in a motor car. I take it that he has electric lights, probably, in his apartment, and he eats food, presumably, several times a day, and in this whole world of human activities we come quite as close in direct contact with physical and chemical processes as we do with living things when we walk around outdoors, and, therefore, there is something wrong, I think, in the conception that physical and chemical sciences are something which have their locus only in the laboratory.

We certainly have in our daily contacts a very genuine place and operation in all the more significant activities of society about us, and it seems to me there is an opportunity there. In other words, the two modes are approached which ought to meet, dovetail into each other from the standpoint of living things on the one hand, and from the standpoint of all of the mechanical, technical apparatus, tools, and machinery of modern life, electric light, heating apparatus, motor car, all of these things which touch us daily. They are all illustrations of what I mean, and they are not living things, but they are things that determine very largely our modern ways of living, and they go out into an understanding, or have the possibility of leading out in an understanding of social institutions and even of political conditions.

Anyone who could tell just what the machine has done in modern life in the last one hundred or one hundred and fifty years, would certainly have not merely a very specialized body of information, but also a wide and broad outlook on life. We have not merely life in the biological sense, but also life in the social and political sense.

I wonder if we could find any better approach to that than through a study of the actual locus and operations of all of these devices and means of modern life and the changes that they have made in the ways of living.

But, as I say, we are getting away perhaps somewhat from the more direct topic of interest into the question of actual subject matter. However, I would like to make a suggestion at this point that there are two modes of approach which inevitably interweave with each other; each one leads into the other, but that we can't get a spherical view of the whole question unless we somewhere approach the subject of the world in which we live from these two different points of view.

There are other questions about interest that might be raised. There is the question of intellectual interests, and I don't suppose even Dr. Robinson has completely discussed it with history. There is a question of what is our interest in our own derivation, in our historical background. What is the interest of students in the whole subject of method of operation of their own minds? I don't mean logic or much less formal logic, but the securing of an effective way of thinking, seeing things, the method side of science. ["Proceedings" 1:203–5.]

[At the Wednesday morning session on 21 January, Dean Max McConn, of Lehigh University, stated that the Steering Committee had asked Dr. Dewey to sum up the essence of what the conference had so far explored and to "contribute to it from his own philosophy in general and philosophy of education" ("Proceedings" 2:319). McConn reported that Dewey agreed that he would "do something of that sort or try to do something of the sort, probably not at this morning's conference certainly, nor probably today . . ." ("Proceedings" 2:319). Dewey made the following statement at the evening session on 21 January.]

CHAIRMAN DEWEY: The Chairman was asked to make some kind of statement. He doesn't know exactly what sort of statement was wanted of him.

President Morgan [Arthur E. Morgan, president, Antioch College] said this morning (I will have occasion to refer to that later) that any education of which we have spoken was in a dilemma. As I say, I want to refer to that point later, but first I want to say that the Chairman is in a dilemma, or a dilemma is in him, and, in fact, as he is a Chairman, he is a dilemma.

I suppose being Chairman something is expected of me in the way of assisting the progress of discussions, some kind of conclusion; that while our discussions are theoretical in nature, they are supposed to end up in something which is at least capable of practical application, and I fancy and I fear that if we do not reach some kind of conclusion of some fairly definitive sort, the responsibility and the blame will either be the Chairman's or he will be a convenient goat for the failure of the Commission to reach some definite conclusion.

That is one horn of the dilemma. On the other hand, this is, after all, the Conference's own meeting, and I am sure that no one of you, if you were in my Chairman's place, would desire in any way to try to lead the discussion in any direction or, for the sake of getting some definitive opinion, suppress discussion or turn it too much in any one direction. So much for my personal dilemma.

Now, as a point of text to my remarks, I want to take two statements that have been made here, both of them, I think, this morning. To one I have already referred. The other, I think was a question asked by Dr. Hart [Joseph K. Hart, Vanderbilt University], Why is this Commission here? or, amplifying it a little, as he did, Why is it that the curriculum has become a problem?

Of course, college faculties have been tinkering with curricula for a very long time. It is a continual process, but I don't know of many discussions, in fact I don't know of any just like this, where people were brought together at the invitation of a hospitable institution and a very broadminded president, to discuss the principles or criteria which should govern the determination of a curriculum with all barriers down and the ground thrown freely open. I think the question, then, that was asked this morning as to why that has taken place now, when such a thing would have been almost inconceivable a few years ago, is a very pertinent question and a question which has certain bearing upon the tenor of our deliberations.

It would take a very long time to answer that question, but I should like to suggest that one reason is that the conditions of American life have changed very rapidly in the last generation and have changed so rapidly that the changes in life in general have outstripped the educational principles, philosophy, and practices of the college. Our pioneer period is long passed, of course, and if one were to try to put a date upon the general change of conditions in this life from rural and agrarian to urban, semi-urban, and industrial, I suppose we would fix the date somewhere roughly in the nineties, or say a generation ago.

It seems to me this change, which was barely hinted at in that remark, is one reason for the feeling which has crystallized in this meeting that there is a need of a new independent consideration of this whole question and one which through this intellectual as well as other generosity of the President and Rollins College, has not any fixed limits to it, so that we are free to consider any possibility and explore any and every aspect of the field.

In conversation with Dr. Hart my attention was recalled to an article by Professor Mead, of Chicago University, which presents another aspect perhaps of the same general question, namely, the divorce and the somewhat increasing divorce between what we call culture, for lack of a better name, and the more indigenous and spontaneous movements of American life.

There seems to be a split somewhat similar to that which Mr. Santayana some years ago called the split between the drawing-room in the home and the kitchen and the dining room, the somewhat exotic nature of those higher interests that we call culture as compared with the actual, dominating interests and activities of the great mass of the American people, and I think if I might indulge in a perhaps too philosophical presentation of the situation, one reason we have to discuss such questions as we are discussing here is that there is felt, if not consciously formulated, the need of making a closer connection between all those interests that go by the name of culture and the dominant interests and activities of the great body of the American people.

It would take too much time to go into detail about these points and to add others which I think will naturally occur to you, but if one were to attempt to translate these general remarks over into more definite and refined terms, it might seem to me to at least express some of the main problems and issues, and movement underlying the issues, questions which come before us. How shall we readapt or readjust the general movement of college life in the college of arts that will have it take into greater, more intimate account in some way or other, and how, is one of the problems we have to determine with the great change that is taking place in American life within the last generation; and the other is how shall we make the colleges count in developing a culture which is more truly indigenous. It is not imported or exotic; it grows out of American life and still more reacts into our American life to refine and elevate it in all of its different phases.

The other text I was going to take is this remark of President

Morgan which is: at best, under any circumstances, education is a dilemma. We cannot (if I am not misinterpreting him) set up any absolute goal or ideal of perfection. We have to choose, if not between the better and the worse, at least between the better and the good, and the good in contrast with the better would then be the worse. They have to make, in other words, adjustments or even, if you please, compromises between various competing interests, interests that compete in colleges because they compete not harmoniously in life itself.

That suggested to me one point which perhaps is a little nearer the practical issue than the general remark that I have already made. If we cannot conclude satisfactorily with any program, not of curricula, but of criteria, meaning ideas on which we unanimously agree, it would be at least a step forward if we could define the dilemma, if we could determine more definitely what the alternatives are that have to be met, for even that, I think, would give genuine guidance. It would tend to put some limits to flux and introduce more of definite aim and purpose or goal, or might be made to contribute to that end in American life.

So, I suggest that at least so far as there are differences of opinion among us, as there certainly must be in a group like this, we do not regard ourselves as defenders of any particular, irreducible dogma, but rather that we use our differences of opinion to help define and describe this dilemma of college in such a way that we might at least suggest some alternative school.

I was reading in the *New York Times* the report from an educational discussion of a somewhat different sort, being held in New York City, in which one educator in that city is quoted as saying that it is desirable that all American colleges should have the same curricula. I rubbed my spectacles and my eyes. I thought I had read it wrong, but of course what he said was that it was not desirable that all American colleges should have the same curricula, but there it was, at all events, "It is desirable that all American colleges have the same curricula."

If we believe there is room and desirability for different curricula in different liberal arts colleges of the United States, then I think we would, as I have said before, at least help contribute to the guidance of different institutions in defining the dilemma so that various alternatives, various alternative types of curricula, different lines of experimentation, might be laid down.

I have just used the word "experimentation" and that suggests my final point. All education is experimental, whether we call it that or not. We simply can't help that and we are experimenting with very precious and valuable material in the lives of these young people. We may think or try to convince ourselves that there is no experimental element in the situation, but practically everything we do, every course we lay out, and every class we meet, is in its effects an experiment for good or for bad, and if we can help so much more to define alternative modes of experimentation and make the situation more clear in that way, perhaps we will be enabled to capitalize the difference of opinion that must exist among us, rather than have it bring us to an unfortunate deadlock in reaching a conclusion.

I thank the Conference for their kind attention. I don't know that I thank them for asking me to do this, but that concludes my remarks. ["Proceedings" 2 : 420–27.]

A Résumé of Four Lectures on Common Sense, Science and Philosophy

Lecture I—Common Sense

There are two different meanings of the words "common sense." Two philosophies have claimed to be founded on common sense. Berkeley had said that matter did not exist. Hume had said the self did not exist. The Scotch philosophers, at a loss to meet these views, fell back on common sense, which assures us of the existence of matter and of self. To them common sense was the power which conceives truth and wins assurance by instinctive belief. This process was too simple in its way of getting rid of problems, and could not last. Spontaneous belief is poor evidence of reality. According to common sense the sun runs about a stationary earth. All general conceptions, scientific or religious, seem to be based on common sense. Both science and philosophy question this conception of common sense. Science has questioned a stationary earth and also the fixity of species, which seemed to rest on common sense. Philosophy similarly questions many seemingly common sense beliefs.

But there is another way of looking at common sense. This is to consider it as consisting of sound practical judgments, general sagacity. Both science and philosophy have a more practical, less hostile relation to common sense considered in this particular way.

The philosophy which interests me most results from observations anyone can make every hour of his daily life, and not on those technicalities which can only be considered by specialists furnished with technical devices. Certain judgments are forced

[First published in *Bulletin of the Wagner Free Institute of Science of Philadelphia* 7 (May 1932): 12–16, from four lectures delivered under the Richard B. Westbrook Free Lectureship Foundation at the Wagner Free Institute of Science on 1, 2, 8, and 9 April 1932.]

on man by the situation in which he finds himself. The present tendency is to feel that philosophy should be based on scientific observations.

Where does philosophy start? Whence does it get its data? Bertrand Russell says mathematics furnishes the only proper material on which to base philosophy. Charles Peirce, a well-trained laboratory worker, started with evident facts as the most certain basis and went last to mathematics. Shall philosophy start with the common materials near at hand or with the more abstract intellectual results of thinking? I think that philosophy should start with the common experiences. But here there is a difficulty. The commoner and more familiar things are, the harder they are to deal with philosophically. We lose consciousness of things that are quite familiar. We do not hear the loud clock to which we are used, but we notice the instant it stops.

It is not aspersion to say that the philosopher turns things upside down to look at them. He must see them from an unusual viewpoint.

Another difficulty is that each of us comes to an object with ready formed judgments that we think are common sense when they are only early acquired and long held ideas. The wearer of blue glasses does not know what things are really blue. A large part of philosophy consists in getting rid of these presuppositions. The painter talks of recovering the innocence of the eye. The philosopher must recover the innocence of the mind. What are some of the most common traits of our world of common sense? This world of common objects is not one in which the intellectual element is important, but is one to be used and enjoyed. The philosopher is concerned with looking at things from the intellectual side and not for their enjoyment or use. In this he differs from the ordinary man.

The present general interest in science is very late. Every new scientific inquirer naturally meets hostility and often persecution, because he seems to get so far away from the common way of using and enjoying.

Language began not for its usefulness but as an overflow of joy and hilarity, somewhat in the nature of song. It was not invented to convey thought. This is probably also true of all early activities.

Classic philosophy was based on this point of view. In the

twelfth century Aristotle's philosophy was taken up by the church and is still widely taught by the Catholic Church. It looks on the world as to be used and enjoyed, and on thinking as a joy of the mind. It seeks the purpose of everything. Hence final causes were sought for rather than generative causes. It was a philosophy of qualities. Things were used in accordance with their qualities: hard and soft, light and heavy, wet and dry, hot and cold, were such qualities. Combinations of these made up the four elements. For two thousand years this mode of thinking prevailed and formed the backbone of religious beliefs. For only the last two hundred years has there been a real scientific attitude of thought.

Lecture II—Science

Up to the seventeenth century there was little recognized difference between philosophy and science, and both of them were nearer the ordinary thinking. Modern science deals with sizes and velocities which are quite beyond ordinary perception.

The Greeks are unjustly spoken of as not being observers. Their art and their architecture show this to be a mistake. Truly they were too closely tied to observation and did not go to indirect observation or into calculation. They had only the unaided eye. Their discoveries were simple additions of the old kind of materials. There seemed to them no place for progress in a finished world. This state of mind lasted until modern times.

Roger Bacon made question of all this, as later did Francis Bacon. The latter proposed a new kind of science, with a new method, leading to the relief and perfecting of the human estate. With prophetic vision the Bacons both anticipated many modern inventions.

Modern science is the product of observation as aided with modern inventions and methods of calculation. The growth of the crafts and the collection of materials for medicines contributed much. So also did the search for the elixir of life and the transmutation of the base metals into noble. The exploration of new worlds in the sixteenth and seventeenth centuries contributed much to the new method of science. So also did the taking up from other countries of paper making and of printing from movable type. Gunpowder had come through the Moslems from the Chinese as also had the compass. The lens and the pendulum were also new tools. Astronomy took a new turn with the lens. The pendulum gave new accuracy to measurements of time.

The newly borrowed Arabic numerals made calculation far easier. Algebra, again borrowed from the Arabs, gave added capacity for calculation. Then the invention of analytical geometry and of the calculus made possible more complex mathematical calculations. The science of today owes far more to our instruments, physical and mathematical, than to any supposed higher brain power.

Greek philosophers lacked manual dexterity because manual work was delegated to slaves. Mechanical inventions, if made, seemed to them rather in the nature of toys.

Modern science is experimental because of new tools borrowed from the craftsman. Only then did ability to know prove related to ability to make. When men manufactured and analyzed water they first knew what it was. The Greek philosophers looked for the purpose, the end, as explanation of the thing— the final cause. Modern science cares for the generating causes— how things are made—how they happen. This begins to lead to control. When you know how a thing happens you are in the way of finding how to make it happen.

A less obvious consequence follows. What are the objects studied by physical science? For example, is color in the object or in the eye? The Greeks never doubted that any quality belonged to the object. Science now knows that color is due to certain wave lengths of light. Thus taste, temperature, and so forth, are not inherent in the object. Do we know the thing in itself, the reality?

What we ask of science is not so much knowledge of the inner nature of things as power of prediction and of control. You look at a barometer to foretell coming weather, but you do not think of the weather as originating in the barometer.

The scientific world is not a rival of our commonly perceived world, but it gives us control or prediction of phenomena, to which we then adjust ourselves.

We need not fear that science will take away our enjoyment of the world as it is, but it gives the intellectual tools for reshaping this world.

Lecture III—Philosophy

Philosophy is concerned with beliefs. They are the raw material of Philosophy. Philosophy has been defined as premature science. We overlook the fact that hypotheses are the forerunners of all science. Science insists that speculations be confirmed. No great scientific work has been done by merely collecting facts. Newton got his idea of the formula for gravitation by a guess and then collected facts to substantiate the guess. Darwin's theory was founded in the same way. There is, however, another function of philosophy. This aspect is suggested in the original Greek meaning of the word—love of wisdom. Wisdom means knowledge plus. Some people accumulate knowledge but are not wise. Philosophy once expressed a certain way of living in Greece two thousand years ago, in the banding together into schools. This old stoic idea of the philosopher still survives to a certain extent.

A philosophy is a certain way of adjusting one's self to the world in which we live—making an adjustment through ideas. If any philosophy is genuine it will give one a certain intellectual balance. In one sense, philosophy is an intellectual recipe for being at home in the world. More fundamental beliefs are the direct object of philosophy. What do we mean by belief? By etymology, "belief" is "beloved." Belief is that which we would rather have so and is connected with our English word "love." Belief means trust or confidence in something or somebody. Belief means a kind of going out of our emotions or will to the object, so that we commit ourselves to it. One kind of judgment is intellectual. Other judgments are concerned not simply with facts but with values. Strictly scientific judgments have nothing to do with the value of objects with which they deal. The immediate object of philosophy lies in our fundamental judgment of values. Philosophy should be based on science. Bertrand Russell holds that mathematics is the most perfect kind of science. Philosophy should be lined up then conclusively with mathematics. Therefore, philosophy has nothing to do with social affairs. Herbert Spencer said philosophy is completely unified knowledge, while science is only partially unified. Philosophers have to accept the findings of scientists on the nature of the world and then to frame the judgments of value and to determine what we are to do in the world.

There is a real division of labor between the philosopher and the scientist. Philosophy tells us what these scientific facts mean, and what course of action we should pursue. When philosophy is thought of as a kind of science, it has misled many. In the first place, philosophy is not a form of knowledge in the sense that science is. Again, philosophy depends on science. Objection has been brought against philosophy that it does not go ahead like science and that philosophers do not agree among themselves. Men may agree about facts, but they cannot agree about the values of life. Men see life from different angles. Philosophy tries to make differences of education and of experience more clear so that men may be conscious of just the angle from which they are seeing life. Study of the history of philosophy has value because it broadens the intellectual and moral outlook of the student. I do not think it possible to exclude the element of choice. We have to make a choice and act upon it. While philosophy is not a kind of science it must depend on science to get its picture on which to act. Science is very modern and is still a very thin crust which overlaps traditions which have come down from the past. The older views still persist in a certain amount of debris which civilization keeps in its garret. Science itself means the adoption of a certain attitude, the experimental attitude, of a searching, inquiring mind which accepts conclusions only on the basis of evidence. This experimental attitude of mind has not made much of a dent in modern culture, political views or moral conceptions. The older, prescientific attitude of mind prevails.

In the third place, there are leading concepts of science. Older science taught that rest was more important than change; that change was in itself an evidence of a lack of full realization of reality. Modern science has taught us that we live in a world in which change is inevitable. If modern minds would completely accept this idea of change and if we would trust ourselves, we might be better able to direct the change.

Lecture IV—The Return to Common Sense

You will remember that common sense has a double significance. It may mean belief in ideas that have come down so long and are so widespread that we are apt to think that no one of common sense can doubt them. To this philosophy has a negative if not a destructive attitude. The other meaning—judgments about the common things of life—seems to be just horse sense, good judgment, appreciation of real values. With reference to these values philosophy is a critic and a guide. It is not a dictator, but it helps us to judge discriminatingly. It gives us a more intelligent attitude.

Scientific observations are of great assistance to philosophy in forming these judgments.

Common sense is concerned with the qualities of things which give us the use, enjoyment, purposes for which we employ them. But attitude to things is commonly practical rather than intellectual. This is natural. We have bodies which we must adjust to our surroundings if we are to have intellectual enjoyment.

If we accept evolution we know our brains and nervous systems did not originate for intellectual purposes, but simply to make adjustment to our environment. In contrast with this, the whole development of physical science tended to eliminate these qualities and give us a world of electrons, of energy, while what we call qualities depend really on the effect of these motions on our bodies. Science now gives quantities and measures and deals much less in the qualities which make the world enjoyable to us.

This gives us a mechanistic idea of the world, which seems to rob us of our well-known universe. It makes the world seem hard and cold, even hostile. But science interests us in the aspects of things which help us to predict and to control. Science, which seemed at first to destroy values, makes them in reality more secure. In the old view Nature seemed closer than it does today, because it seemed purposeful. It seemed as if there was an inner vitality always striving to reach its destined end, which was perfection. But there was a distinct limitation in this old view. Man could not help the process; he must simply accept these inherent ends. When science removed the idea of these ends the world became more serviceable to us. The purposive activities were taken out of the world, which yielded to the purposes of man. Man changed animals and plants nearer to his needs. This is just as true of inventions, as they relate to metals and the forces of nature, which can be controlled to man's ends. This process is still only partial in the short portion of human existence during which there has been any real science. The future possible advances in this line may well be believed to be enormous. Discovery is still rather haphazard and accidental.

Let us apply these ideas to human freedom. The old idea was that human freedom depended on understanding and on insight. The Greeks thought of a few of themselves as having this freedom beyond all others. These others were creatures of appetite and impulse. Plato described a slave as one who was not capable of framing an end which could control his own life. Hence only the intellectual aristocrat was fit to rule.

There are doubtless differences in intellectual capacity, but not such differences as the Greeks imagined. Everyone not an imbecile or a moron is sufficiently intelligent to bring certain conditions under control. Such is also the case in social life. If democracy is possible it is because every individual has a degree of power to govern himself and be free in the ordinary concerns of life. If not, there must be either anarchy or dictatorship.

Through increase of knowledge and of science we should be able to work out a technique, effective to develop this power in man.

The older philosophy considered thought as a thing in itself, the product of pure reason. We still have "pure" science as different and higher than applied science. This view prevails in wide circles. But the pure scientist is not pure. He must find actual facts to corroborate his pure conceptions. In this he is like the painter and the poet. Not all applications are such as may be financially profitable. Philosophy is a mode of thought and it too must find embodiment and application. It cannot rival science in its application to railways and radios. It applies more fully to human life, especially to social life. Education is either by routine, descended from the past, or it receives intellectual guidance from philosophy.

It is not the part of philosophy, as past thinkers held, to solve the problem of evil and to justify the ways of God to man. The real problem of evil is not to account for evil but to show how to control and lessen it.

Philosophy may be conceived as a process of devising methods and hypotheses for the improvement of human life. It will not stop with analyzing and classifying as science does, but must devise ends worth striving for, and must find what resources we have for accomplishing these ends.

Historic idealism has been the attempt to prove that the world already is spiritual and measures up to our highest ideals. Now we practically consider one an idealist who sets to work to find the methods and resources by which life may be improved. The real demand of philosophy should be for idealism of this latter sort, which, through legislation, education, economics, devotes itself to discovering how ideas of betterment may be carried out.

This seems to some a derogation for philosophy, but I think this change will take place in philosophy just as it did in science. Application tests and confirms philosophy.

Teachers as Citizens

John Dewey, eminent professor of education and honored member of the American Federation of Teachers, was presented by the education committee of Local 195 in a lecture entitled "Teachers as Citizens" on April 9. The audience filled the largest hall obtainable, and included the Cambridge Superintendent of Schools, a number of members of the School Board, members of teachers' clubs in neighboring cities, professors and students in near-by colleges, as well as Cambridge teachers.

Besides stressing the need of giving the teacher more freedom in school and out, and the importance of training pupils to meet the demands of life as individuals and citizens, Mr. Dewey spoke feelingly of the work the American Federation of Teachers is prepared to do in the community and the nation.

He passed very lightly over the question of a teacher's political right as a citizen, considering that right too obvious to be discussed.

Dr. Dewey said in part: All other reforms in education depend on those who are engaged in the teaching profession. If any scheme could be devised to secure teachers of character and initiative who are fond of children, little more would be desired.

Unfortunately the organization of many schools may be compared to that of the army or factory in which those who are regarded as being in the lower ranks receive orders from those considered above them, and dividing walls are almost universal between administrative and teaching forces. Hence there is too little initiative on the part of teachers. There will not be individual responsibility unless there is freedom. When responsibility is concentrated in a few, it is taken from others who would assume it of their own accord.

[First published in *American Teacher* 16 (October 1931): 7, from a report by Anna L. P. Collins.]

When programs are laid out and methods of teaching prescribed it marks destruction of teaching ability. No one can
throw his whole heart and energy into prescribed tasks. If teaching by phonograph is bad, it is equally bad for teachers to be
phonographs.

All citizens of the country are citizens in some other aspect as
well. Failure to acquire the proper training in home and school
leads to failure in meeting responsibility in larger circles. The
corruption in high places of government shows the need of the
school's fulfilling better its duty in forming citizens for the city,
the state and the nation.

If students do not hear public issues discussed in a frank, open
way, how are they going to have adequate preparation for citizenship? Is knowledge to be picked up by chance in a partisan
spirit, or should it be presented in an open impartial manner?
Schools must not take part in propaganda, but there has been
too much dodging of the vital issues of the day. In trying to be
impartial we have become futile. Of course we must consider
that we are dealing with immature minds, yet in the upper grades
pupils do live pretty much in the world. They know what their
parents are talking about and what is in the newspapers. In the
school there should be more complete discussion of the difficulties and evils in political life.

If any study was ever denatured before it reached the student,
it is civics. Its anatomy is taught but practically nothing of the
way it is worked out in life.

The type of teacher in the American Federation of Teachers is
the most socially progressive, fearless and farseeing in our school
system. They are always to be found in the front ranks fighting
any corruption or injustice in the schools of which they are a
part. The enemies the Federation has made in Chicago, New
York and Seattle are a compliment to the organization.

There certainly should be no objection on the part of officials
or teachers to affiliation with Labor. Such objections as have
arisen have been due to snobbery or cowardice. Since the greater
mass of pupils in the public schools is drawn from the workers of
the country, teachers should be in a position to act as interpreters between Labor and the community. In order to develop
Labor's children, one must understand the problems of Labor.

In prefacing his remarks on the American Federation of Teachers, Mr. Dewey said that he was proud of his long years of membership in the organization and in the American Federation of Labor, and that he always carried his "Union card" with him.

A Statement by the Executive Committee

The League for Independent Political Action desires to correct some misunderstandings which have arisen through various erroneous interpretations of Professor Dewey's recent correspondence with Senator Norris. It therefore wishes at this time to reaffirm its allegiance to the fundamental principle that a new party must be the expression of workers of hand and brain who seek political control to promote security and abundant life for the many. It will not be satisfied with a political realignment which has no profounder purpose than the elimination of dishonesty in public office. It believes that the government is dominated at present by the powerful industrial and commercial classes. Whether they conduct the government according to, or in defiance of the accepted canons of honesty, they use the power of the government for the perpetuation of the privileges of these classes.

The League believes that the hold of these groups on the government can be destroyed only by a political movement which has a sound economic basis and which will draw its chief support from the farmers and workers. These classes even in times of plenty were refused admittance into the charmed circle of prosperity and are now bearing an undue portion of the burden of depression. Millions of workers are forced to beg the bitter bread of charity because they lack the protection of unemployment insurance. This essential minimum of social legislation long since accepted in all other industrial nations is still stubbornly opposed by the dominant classes here. Even if a measure of prosperity returns the lack of income among workers and farmers will continue the evil of technological unemployment.

[First published in *News Bulletin of the League for Independent Political Action* 1 (February 1931): 1.]

All relief measures offered to the impoverished farmer by the old parties have been proved to be bogus.

At the same time the League believes that large numbers in the middle classes are ready to support such a political movement. Some will do so because they have discovered that the increasing centralization of control and wealth in the hands of the few is actually destroying their economic security, as for instance the annihilation of the small merchant through chain store developments. Others will support such a party even though not immediately affected because they recognize that the general welfare of society demands that centralized economic power be brought under the control of the whole of society.

The League is not anxious to see a new party rush into the presidential campaign without a political philosophy adequate to the needs of an industrial society. It believes that any political movement will be premature and futile, which is not based upon a recognition on the part of the underprivileged groups of the necessity of militant political action, and upon the realization of citizens of all groups of the necessity of the social control of economic power. The League, therefore, regards it as its chief function to bring together farmer, labor and other groups for counsel and common action, to support and stimulate third party movements which represent the principles of the League and to initiate various forms of political education which will make American citizens aware of the political needs of our generation.

Prof. Dewey Is Impressed by Discontent

Declares Dissatisfaction with Capitalist Parties Widespread
Discussion at Friday Dinner

Declaring that he had never in fifty years seen so much and such deeply rooted political unrest in the United States, John Dewey returned Tuesday from a month's trip that took him west to California and south to Florida.

His statement, issued by the League for Independent Political Action, follows:

"At no time in the last fifty years have I seen so much political unrest as confronted me on my trip through the country, extending west to California and south to Florida.

"I was tremendously impressed with the amount of discontent expressed about both old parties, even by those who have been in the past hard-boiled partisans. I met with but few who still believe there is any significant difference between the two. Disappointment with the Hoover administration is such a matter of common knowledge that it requires no comment. Those who are turning to the Democratic party are doing so without much hope, but as a measure of desperation. Even in California I found but few who felt that Hoover measured up to what had been expected from him.

"It is not dissatisfaction with particular leaders or party methods so much as it is a feeling that a thorough overhauling of basic principles and policies is needed. The political unrest is still confused and comparatively unorganized. It is awaiting a chance for eager inquiries about the development of independent political

[First published in *New Leader* 8 (7 February 1931): 6.]

action, looking forward to a new party. There was much inquiry as to the stand taken by the liberal blocs in Congress and much surprise at their failure to take a positive stand in behalf of a definite realignment of political parties. I met a growing disappointment at the prevailingly negative character of their activities and a belief that if they would get together to formulate and put openly before the people a definite body of positive principles and measures there would be an immediate and powerful response from the voters of the country."

Dr. Dewey will be the principal speaker at a dinner given by the League for Independent Political Action at the Hotel Woodstock, Friday evening. There will be a symposium on "A New Party" with the following editors participating: Bruce Bliven, editor of the *New Republic*; Mauritz A. Hallgren, associate editor, the *Nation*; Reinhold Niebuhr, editor, the *World Tomorrow*.

Dewey Raps Progressives on Parley Eve

Liberal Leader Finds Old Party Legislators
Ineffective on Unemployment

Prof. Dewey, president of the People's Lobby, indicts the Senate and House progressives for their failure to conduct the filibuster necessary to force a special session of the new Congress, in a statement issued as a preliminary to his taking part in the conference called for Mar. 11–12 by Senators Norris, La Follette, Cutting, Wheeler and Costigan. His frank criticism of the progressives who were members of the 71st Congress is indicative of the tone that may be anticipated of discussion when the conference begins to formulate a program of legislative action. One group demands that efforts to compel President Hoover to call the new Congress to Washington to deal with the nationwide misery of the unemployed be seriously made.

"Nearly every income in the United States under $5,000, except the income of government employes, is in jeopardy," Dewey said. "Hardly a farmer knows from one year to another whether the return from his crops will pay his rent or interest on the mortgage on his farm, taxes and expenses of production. . . . Less than one-tenth of the wage-earners of the nation, not in government employ, have any assurance of permanency of tenure. The nearly 3,600,000 small business men on their own, small tradesmen, etc., exist by sufferance, pending threatened absorption by larger concerns or mergers. The rights of these producers of wealth should be the first responsibility and concern of government."

[First published in *New Leader* 12 (14 March 1931): 2.]

SUGGESTS KINDERGARTEN

"While the present depression has been acute for a year, it has been impending for three years. In spite of this fact, the progressives of both branches of Congress have in every session of Congress, by voting appropriation bills apart from needed legislation, lost the opportunity to get even fair consideration for the measures of general welfare they were assumed to sponsor. They have been urged at the beginning of every session to make the passage of appropriation bills contingent upon at least a record vote upon the measures they were elected to put through.

"An aggressive fight by the progressives in the Senate in the past session would have insured the enactment of legislation to meet the unemployment crisis, and other constructive measures sponsored by these progressives in the non-partisan elections of 1922 and 1924. After appropriation bills are voted to pay interest to the rich on government bonds issued because the government refused to tax wealth to pay for wars and their aftermath, and to get ready for more wars, and to maintain an army of spies, and only a pittance for education and health—all hope of getting legislation for the common people is gone.

"The progressives have repeatedly as in the past session played into the hands of the reactionists and exploiters who control the present administration, and voted the government the wherewithal to continue its protection of wealth, and its punishment of involuntary poverty. Do progressives need a kindergarten course in the development of popular rights?"

Appendixes

Appendix 1
Freedom, in Relation to Culture, Social Planning, and Leadership
By George S. Counts

Theses proposed by George S. Counts for discussion by the National Council of Education, Saturday morning, February 20, 1932.

Theses

I. FREEDOM AND CULTURE

1. Freedom cannot be absolute and primal. All genuine freedom is relative and derivative. Freedom is an achievement rather than a gift or a condition. The freedom of mankind has come thru the development of culture; the freedom of the individual comes thru the mastery of culture. Only thru culture does man, either individually or collectively, achieve control over his destiny. Any form of freedom that does not give control and power is deceptive and futile.

2. From the standpoint of education, culture presents two aspects. On the one hand, culture is instrumental and practical—a body of tools, inventions, practises, folkways, customs, institutions, knowledges, and ideas on which the survival and perpetuation of society is dependent. The transmission from generation to generation of this stock of spiritual possessions has always been and must always be the major responsibility of education.

3. To the extent that this aspect of culture is free from error and is adapted to the conditions of life, its mastery leads to power over the environment and to freedom. Only thru it does

[First published in *Theses on Freedom* (Washington, D.C.: National Council of Education of the National Education Association, 1932), pp. 3–6. For Dewey's contribution to the discussion, see this volume, pp. 142–45.]

the individual gain that development of his powers and that disciplining of his energies which distinguish man from the brute.

4. On the other hand, culture is an expression and the repository of the hopes, the aspirations, the values, the soul of a people. To this aspect of culture, which is integrative, directive, dynamic, and qualitative, the term tradition is sometimes applied. Thus we speak of the Christian, the Mohammedan, the democratic, the communistic, the artistic, or the scientific tradition. It is here that the most severe educational controversies arise. It is here that the question of imposition and indoctrination assumes its most acute form.

5. The thesis advanced in the present outline is that tradition gives meaning not only to the life of a people but also to the life of the individual and to the educative process. Human energy is consequently released, not by freeing the individual from tradition, but rather by inducing him to identify himself most completely with a vital and growing tradition and to find the fulfillment of his life in that tradition. Only as he is influenced by and nurtured upon some particular tradition can his life become integrated and effective.

6. The real question, therefore, is not whether some tradition will be imposed by intent or circumstance upon the coming generation (we may rest assured that this will be done), but rather what particular tradition will be imposed. To refuse to face the task of the selection or the fashioning of this tradition is to evade the most crucial, difficult, and important educational responsibility.

7. Traditions are born, grow to maturity, and then decay. As a consequence, traditions once vital may become rigid, formal, and sterile and paralyze the creative energies of a people. Our present educational difficulty lies not in the fact that tradition is being imposed upon the coming generation but rather in the fact that the tradition which we impose, whether in the sphere of politics, religion, morals, or art, has lost its vitality. In many areas our tradition is out-of-joint with the times.

8. Our first concern should be not to follow the interests of children, for in that direction lies futility and dissipation of energy, but rather to bring to the younger generation a vision which will call forth their active loyalties and challenge them to

creative and arduous labors. A generation without such a vision is destined to a life of absorption in self, inferiority complexes, and frustration.

9. This means that the first and major task of American education is to create a tradition which has roots in American soil, which is in harmony with the spirit of the age, which recognizes the facts of industrialism, and which will appeal to the most profound impulses of our people. Communism and Fascism constitute the only realistic efforts on the part of Western peoples to meet the general situation which we all face. It seems quite possible that these two developments, in varied form, represent the only alternatives with respect to the future. If there is to be another possibility, its outlines should be sketched without delay.

II. FREEDOM AND SOCIAL PLANNING

1. Freedom is a product of cooperative endeavor rather than a condition to be maintained or recovered. The savage is perhaps the least free of men. Freedom, individual freedom, is primarily a positive *social* achievement rather than a throwing off of restraints.

2. This dependence of freedom on cooperative endeavor is due partly to the fact that freedom comes thru the growth of culture and that culture is a group product. But it is also due in part to the fact that power is a cooperative achievement. Strength lies in the union, specialization, and integration of numbers. Without power there can be only the freedom of quiescence, resignation, and death.

3. The social foundations of freedom are becoming increasingly apparent at the present time. The situation, however, is somewhat confused by the changed conditions of freedom which have come with the industrial order. As a consequence in the name of an archaic and illusory form or conception of freedom, essentially aristocratic in origin and predatory in spirit, we are being asked to reject the one road which will lead to freedom for the masses.

4. Thru the advances of science and technology an economic system of extraordinary power has been developed. If this power would be fully utilized, the economic question could be disposed

of and poverty abolished forever. The foundation would then be laid for a measure of freedom that mankind has never known in the past.

5. The complete and uninterrupted functioning of our economic system, however, because of its complexity and intricacy, requires careful and comprehensive planning of economic processes. But the objection is raised that the adoption of a general economic plan would result in the reduction of the liberty of individuals.

6. The extent to which planning the economic order would curtail the freedom of the individual is largely a question of the methods employed. However, even if the methods were crude and "undemocratic," the gains in freedom for the masses would far outweigh the losses. A planned economy should give economic security to all. And without economic security freedom can have but little meaning. In place of the somewhat questionable freedom to acquire a fortune by means of speculation, manipulation, and exploitation, the ordinary man would gain release from economic worries.

7. Thru social planning, moreover, man places himself on the road to an ever increasing measure of freedom. The development of a social science which can give man control over his destiny would seem to be dependent on the inauguration of a system of planning. Until man seeks to use knowledge for purposes of control, social science will probably remain what it is today— merely a record of events.

III. FREEDOM AND LEADERSHIP

1. Freedom is also dependent upon leadership. Culture and social planning are not enough. No society without gifted and courageous leaders can be said to be free in the fullest sense of the word.

2. The development of social and economic planning in a highly integrated industrial society will require new forms and new types of leadership. The arrangements suited to the needs of the simpler societies of the past are no longer adequate.

3. At present, altho our society requires leadership as it has seldom required it before, leadership is lacking. This is one of the most discouraging features of the present situation and is un-

doubtedly due, not to the lack of talent among our people, but rather to the failure of the traditional methods of choosing leaders.

4. Our methods of choosing leaders are derived from a time when society was very simple in organization and when the political state was relatively distinct from the economic state. At any rate the economic order lacked integration and was capable of independent operation.

5. In this simple society in which the police function was the chief responsibility of government and the general welfare was but slightly dependent upon the operations of the state, a simple form of political democracy was possible and adequate. Even in this society, however, it was clearly the intention of the fathers that the people should rule indirectly thru their representatives.

6. That leadership in the complex society of the future, in which the economic and political functions will be closely interwoven, can be chosen by the crude methods of popular suffrage evolved under simple agrarian conditions is scarcely tenable. Rather will leadership emerge as a natural product of the various functional groups of which society will be composed. Individuals will not be torn from their occupations and laden with responsibilities about which they know nothing. Neither will leadership be entrusted to a race of professional politicians. Rather will men of energy and capacity be advanced from level to level in the fields of their special knowledge. Eventually the most capable will find themselves in the highest positions of leadership.

7. The function of leadership will then be to lead rather than to follow. Genuine leadership involves a certain measure of moral or intellectual ascendancy over the masses which is traceable to some real superiority. While the highest type of leadership neither bamboozles nor coerces, it also never truckles or flatters. It leads because it can challenge, inspire, and point the way. Such leadership is required today in every department of life.

Appendix 2
Are Sanctions Necessary to International Organization? Yes
By Raymond Leslie Buell

Part I. Force as a Necessary Corollary of Law

As a result of six months' fighting, in which thousands of lives have been lost and vast amounts of property destroyed, Japan, in violation of its obligations under the League Covenant and the Anti-War Pact, has succeeded in separating from China its northernmost provinces and in securing the establishment of an "independent" state in Manchuria under Japanese control. While the world attempted to restrain Japan by "moral pressure," League members did not apply to Japan the provisions of Article 16 of the Covenant for the imposition of economic and military sanctions against a state which illegally goes to war.

Would not the Mukden incident, out of which the Sino-Japanese fighting arose, have been quickly settled had League members promptly applied all the provisions of the Covenant to Japan and China? Would not Manchuria be part of China today, and would not the Shanghai episode have been prevented altogether had League members, in cooperation with the United States, early demonstrated their intention of applying economic sanctions unless the parties to the dispute submitted it to some form of adjudication? Has not the failure of the League and the United States in the recent Sino-Japanese crisis been due partly to unwillingness to apply sanctions, and has not this failure greatly weakened confidence in existing international organization? Will not this failure impede the movement for the reduction of armaments and international economic cooperation? In short, if we are to bring a successful international organization into exis-

[First published in *Are Sanctions Necessary to International Organization?* Foreign Policy Association Pamphlet no. 82–83 (New York: Foreign Policy Association, 1932), pp. 3–22. For Dewey's opposing statement, see this volume, pp. 196–223.]

tence, must we not make some provision for the use of coercion in support of law?

THE ROLE OF FORCE TODAY

This question can be answered first by inquiring into the place coercion now holds within the state as well as in international relations. Except for the rapidly disappearing philosophical anarchists and a few religious sects such as the Mennonites and Shakers,[1] all schools of political and ethical thought recognize that within the state force is a necessary corollary of law. The very meaning of the word government implies power to command. Although a state is based on the community of interests of its members, it cannot rest on this principle alone. The state must hold a police power in reserve; otherwise it will dissolve into anarchy.

As the maintenance of large armies and navies shows, force also plays an important rôle in relations among states. Unlike the use of force within the state, however, force in international relations has not been a corollary of international law or of an international organization which composes differences between states, as differences between individuals within a state are composed. Force in international relations has been an instrument of national policy; it has been used by one state to prosecute its national objectives when they came into conflict with those of another state. The result of this system of force was the World War. Force harnessed to law means order; force exercised in the absence of law means anarchy. It is from this latter condition that the world has attempted to emerge during the past decade.

ARTICLE 16 OF THE COVENANT

The first attempt to organize the world upon a basis of law and order was made in the League Covenant. The authors of the Covenant did not believe it possible to eliminate conflicts among nations or to base international relationships purely on good faith, any more than they believed it possible to eliminate

1. Clarence Marsh Case, *Non-Violent Coercion* (New York, Century, 1923), p. 63, 110.

conflicts between individual interests and settle individual disputes purely on a basis of reason. The authors of the Covenant did believe it possible, however, to establish pacific means for the reconciliation of conflicting national interests. They consequently provided that states should submit their disputes to arbitration or investigation, and in case a state defied this injunction and embarked on illegal war—i.e., became an aggressor—the other members of the League would subject such a state to severance of all financial and economic relations with the outside world. Such is the provision for economic sanctions contained in the famous Article 16.

Under the war system, both parties embarking upon hostilities would claim to be acting in "self-defense," and each would charge the other with being the "aggressor." Under existing international organization, however, any state which refuses to place its dispute before an arbitration court or the League Council should be *ipso facto* presumed to be the aggressor if it resorts to armed force or war. According to this test, there is no doubt that Japan, whatever its grievances against China in the recent dispute, was the "aggressor" state, for Japan would not allow the League of Nations or the World Court to take jurisdiction over its differences with China. Whenever any state insists upon being judge and party to the same cause the world is justified in deeming it to be the aggressor.

THE LIMITED SCOPE OF ARTICLE 16

In considering the nature of international sanctions, it is necessary to make a distinction between two types of international obligations. The first type—a negative obligation embodied in the Anti-War Pact and in certain Articles of the League Covenant—consists of an undertaking not to embark on illegal war, not to invade a neighbor's territory. The second is more positive in nature. It is embodied in many treaties and represents an obligation on the part of a state to perform or to refrain from performing within its jurisdiction acts for the benefit of other states, usually in return for the performance or non-performance of similar acts by other states. Such examples may be found in treaties by which states promise to extend commercial privileges to aliens, to protect minorities, or not to fortify certain colonial areas. Obviously it is difficult to coerce a state failing to live up to this second type of obligation. As the French intervention in the Ruhr demonstrated, it would be extremely difficult for an inter-Allied army forcibly to collect reparation in Germany, even if an international tribunal had adjudged Germany to be in default on reparation payments. In such a case, coercion involves an attempt to induce a state to perform within its own territory acts which are repugnant to it.

The opponents of international sanctions usually ignore the fact that the League Covenant makes no provision for sanctions in the case of a state which does not live up to its positive obligations.[2] The function of international sanctions is not to compel Japan to pay its dues to the League of Nations in case of default, or even to prevent Japan from illegally fortifying its Pacific Mandates. In such a case, the difficulties of imposing sanctions are admittedly great; and since failure to live up to this type of obligation does not result in any immediate damage to other states, as would be the case in the event of war, the League is content for the present to rely on the intangible force of public opinion. Consequently the analogy of attempting to enforce an unpopular law on a community does not hold. In case Japan invades a neighboring state, however, the League Covenant rests on the belief that the imposition of sanctions is just and practicable. In such a case the injury done is far greater than when a government merely fails to perform a discretionary act within its own territory; and it is far easier, from the practical point of view, for a combination of states acting under League authority to prevent a state from invading its neighbor than to compel it, say, to pay a sum of money. All that at present the League sanctions aim to do is to organize the force of a group of states in accordance with the principle of cooperative defense to neutralize the illegal use of force by the aggressor.[3] In other words, sanctions do not create war; they come into existence only after war has broken out; they are for the purpose of repressing war. When international organization becomes more firmly established, it may be-

2. It is true that the Council (Art. 13, par. 4) "shall propose what steps should be taken to give effect" to a judicial decision which is not observed, but this article does not have the obligatory effect of Articles 15 or 16.
3. Cf. W. E. Hocking, *Man and the State* (New Haven, Yale University Press, 1926), p. 59.

come necessary to apply sanctions in support of both types of obligations. For the time being at least, sanctions are obligatory only to repress illegal war; the remaining relations among states are allowed to rest upon the basis of "good faith."

PEACE MORE IMPORTANT THAN JUSTICE

Realistic students of international affairs will declare, however, that any system of sanctions is unjust which compels State A not to attack State B, without in turn compelling State B to live up to its obligations to State A. They insist that it is unjust for the League to attempt to prevent Japan from invading Manchuria without at the same time obliging China to live up to its treaty obligations, on the fulfillment of which the welfare of the Japanese people may depend. The weakness of this argument in the recent Manchurian controversy is that Japan refused to give the League an opportunity to decide whether China had violated its obligations to Japan. It is essential for the League to support every kind of international obligation and to secure a peaceful revision of the *status quo* when the legitimate interests of certain nations require such a change. Nevertheless if one goes so far as to insist that any effort to abolish war as an instrument of national policy should be postponed until after the machinery for peacefully changing the *status quo* is perfected, one is arguing not against sanctions, but against the very principle on which the League Covenant and the Anti-War Pact are based: namely, that there is no grievance which justifies a state in embarking on war, at least without first submitting this grievance to an international tribunal. Within the state the law protects swollen fortunes at times when thousands are in want; the state may allow these people to seek a peaceful redress of their grievances at the polls, but the state cannot allow the poor to take the law into their own hands. Similarly, no international community can be developed which permits each state to retain the right of war until the injustices in the *status quo* are removed. No one who believes in the Anti-War Pact can oppose sanctions because they would prevent a state from going to war to correct an "injustice." That right is already voided by the Anti-War Pact.

"MORAL PRESSURE" STRENGTHENED BY SANCTIONS

It cannot be denied that in the past governments have, in violation of their promises, invaded neighboring territory. In view of the rapidly broadening scope of treaty obligations, it is probable that similar violations will be frequent in the future unless adequate sanctions against such violations are provided. Just as within the state the police are needed to enforce law, so in international relations, sanctions are needed to make effective the protest of world opinion against an aggressor. Public opinion may complain against the evils of unemployment, but it achieves results only when it proposes a definite cure. Similarly, in international relations public opinion is likely to prove diffuse and ineffective in stopping war unless it supports some concrete means for this purpose, such as a system of international sanctions. The existence of such a system gives public opinion a concrete focus for its energies.

Moreover, the application of international sanctions to an aggressor would indicate the extent to which the ideal of international cooperation had gripped the world, and would strengthen that ideal in the future. When public opinion, however, applies only "moral suasion" to an aggressor and fails to check the aggression, as in the case of Japan, then the idea of international cooperation and of "moral suasion" is inevitably weakened, while nationalism and the trend toward higher armaments are increased.

SANCTIONS AS A PREVENTIVE OF AGGRESSION

International sanctions are much more than a repressive measure employed to stop fighting after war has illegally broken out; the mere knowledge that sanctions may be imposed will prove a deterrent to, if not a preventive of aggression. Undoubtedly the Japanese military staff, before starting its Manchurian campaign, had reached the conclusion that no government would interpret its obligations under Article 16 of the Covenant in a literal sense. In this particular instance such a conclusion was accurate. Had the Japanese government, however, been given concrete evidence that sanctions would be applied, there is little doubt that the Mukden incident would have been quickly settled, and the Japanese liberals and industrialists could have held their own against the militarists.[4] It is impossible to believe that had economic sanctions been applied to Japan in the early stage of its dispute with China, the militarist group would have gone to the extreme which ultimately resulted in the shocking assassination of Prime Minister Inukai. Had Germany in 1914 known that England and the United States would enter the World War, it is probable that Germany would have induced Austria to localize the Sarajevo incident, and thus maintained peace. So long as governments refuse to commit themselves in advance, some state may risk war on the assumption that governments removed from the immediate dispute will remain aloof. A system of sanctions in which governments loyally undertake to act against an aggressor would destroy this assumption, and thus serve as an important preventive of hostilities.

As to the general preventive value of international sanctions, a recent study states:

> General knowledge, in any country considering aggressive action, that world-wide economic sanctions might be invoked against it, would certainly call into action the fears of all business and industrial interests in that country; and their influence, exercised entirely directly and within the country, would in many cases suffice to turn the scale against the contemplated aggression.
>
> Influences of that sort become more and more powerful as a country becomes more and more completely industrialized; and they would weigh more heavily in the greater industrial States than in the backward nations. And since it is clear that only these great industrial States can seriously contemplate embarking in a war of modern type, the psychologic effects of economic sanctions—when employed merely as threats—are strongest in just the areas where deterrents are most needed.[5]

4. The Tokyo correspondent of the *New York Herald Tribune* wrote on March 1 that the "foremost" reason why the Japanese Cabinet decided to make a peace proposal in the case of Shanghai "was the fear that an economic boycott of Japan might result from the meeting of the League of Nations [on March 3]."
5. Committee on Economic Sanctions, *Reports of Research Findings*, 1931, p. 222.

Thus sanctions are a preventive measure of great importance; they are concrete means by which public opinion may be mobilized against a potential aggressor.

THE DANGERS OF NATIONAL SANCTIONS

Although the provisions for international sanctions in the Covenant remain so far a dead letter, the leading powers still support huge military establishments. Under the present veneer of internationalism, stark nationalism still dominates the world— a nationalism represented by glowering armaments. Governments profess an abhorrence at using force to uphold international objectives but they cling to force in pursuance of national objectives, couched under the phrase of "security" and "self-defense." Unless this deadlock is soon broken, it can result only in strengthening the war system.

In the recent crisis in the Orient, we may find a vivid example of the contradictory position in which the world lives today. China vainly called to the League for help in accordance with the principle laid down in Article 16. International aid failing to materialize, China employed its own forces to resist Japan.

Moreover, although the various governments declined to admit China's appeal for international sanctions, the leading powers did invoke national sanctions. Thus the United States, Great Britain, France and Italy dispatched military and naval forces to Shanghai following the Japanese bombardment. The American government, in addition to sending vigorous protests to Japan, concentrated its entire fleet of 202 vessels in the Pacific and even intimated that it would increase the size of its navy unless Japan respected the Nine-Power Treaty. In other words, it supported its "moral protests" by a show of naval force. Under such delicate circumstances, war might easily have occurred.

Unless one believes in complete non-resistance, no one can condemn China for having employed force in "self-defense" against Japan. Even the supporters of the outlawry of war movement accept this right of self-defense.[6] If the doctrine of "self-defense" is sound, the doctrine of cooperative defense is even

6. C. C. Morrison, *The Outlawry of War* (Chicago, Willett, Clark & Colby, 1927), p. 50, 209.

more sound.[7] If it is logical for one nation to rely on its own army and navy for protection, why is it illogical for nations to rely on the combined forces of the world community? Able to rely for its defense on the principles of "cooperative defense" and "international sanctions," a state can afford to reduce its armaments, while if it is obliged to rely on its own resources, it cannot reduce armaments without fear of being exposed to attack. Disillusioned concerning the guarantees contained in the Covenant and the Anti-War Pact, millions of Chinese, as a result of the recent "war" with Japan, have come to believe that the return of Manchuria can be secured only by force. China has been given every incentive to become a militarized nation. In other words, the inevitable result of the failure to apply international sanctions is to induce a state threatened by a stronger neighbor to expand its own armaments—and thus increase the tension out of which wars arise.

INCREASING TENSION

The failure of the League and the United States to prevent Japanese aggression in Manchuria also has led Russia to become apprehensive concerning the designs of Japan and to increase its military establishment in Siberia. Japan, for its part, has met unexpected resistance at the hands of Chinese troops; it fears a clash with Russia, and must suppress revolts in the new state of Manchoukuo. Consequently Japan has an added incentive to arm. Finally, the United States, alarmed at Japan's aggression, has threatened to increase its fleet. On May 6 the Senate overwhelmingly voted in favor of building up our navy to the London "treaty" level, at a cost of $786,000,000. If the United States, which is in less danger of attack than any other great power, increases its military establishment following this dispute in the Orient, all other powers will be encouraged to do likewise. Thus the application in the recent Sino-Japanese dispute of the doctrine of "self-defense" and "national sanctions," instead of "cooperative defense"and "international sanctions," has strained relations among a dozen powers and inevitably weakened inter-

7. R. L. Buell, "The Next Ten Years of the League," *World Tomorrow*, June 1930; Luigi Sturzo, *The International Community and the Right of War* (New York, R. R. Smith, 1930), p. 243.

national peace machinery. Had the doctrine of "cooperative defense" and "international sanctions" been applied, there can be no doubt that China would have been better protected from Japan than it has been by the force of its own arms. There can also be little doubt that the application of economic sanctions would have restricted the extent of Japan's aggressions, if indeed the threat of such sanctions would not have prevented such aggressions. It is even probable that the threat of sanctions would have prevented the military extremists in Japan from seizing power. Had the League and the United States successfully curbed Japanese militarism and secured a peaceful settlement of the difficulties between China and Japan, the international consciousness of the great powers would have been immeasurably strengthened, a fact which would have greatly facilitated the solution of other pressing international problems.

DISARMAMENT IMPOSSIBLE WITHOUT SANCTIONS

The fact that the League members and the United States failed adequately to support the principle that war should not be used as an instrument of national policy has made it extremely difficult to secure any degree of disarmament; on the contrary, it has set in motion forces working in exactly the opposite direction. The American frontiersman did not throw away his rifle until a system of courts and police had been established in which he had confidence. Similarly, nations are unlikely to disarm until a world organization is created which embodies an effective system of cooperative defense. Thus the whole question of disarmament and security is inseparably linked to the question of international sanctions.

To escape from this conclusion, one might insist that states could disarm by agreement, leaving the comparative security of each state unimpaired. For example, if State A and State B each maintained an army of 100,000 men, their relative security would be the same if they agreed to reduce their armies to 50,000 men. Why cannot the powers, therefore, agree to a 50 per cent cut in armaments, without regard to the question of sanctions and the settlement of political differences? The reason is two-fold. First, the powers are unwilling to freeze the *status quo* in comparative armament strengths. The adoption of this relative reduction principle in 1914 would have perpetuated the supremacy of the British navy, which Germany would not accept. The adoption of that principle today would mean the supremacy of the French army in Continental Europe, and the Japanese army in Asia. Some governments insist on freedom of action to overcome present French or Japanese superiority. France and Japan are unwilling, for their part, to reduce their armies in greater proportion than other powers because this implies the renunciation of interests each deems vital. Until the League can guarantee that neither Germany nor China will use force in tearing up treaties—a principle which the Anti-War Pact lays down, neither France nor Japan will renounce its present military power. In other words, a basis for the reduction of armaments and for wiping out present military differences can be found only when an international organization is established which will secure the pacific settlement of disputes and provide security against attack by a system of international sanctions. After the recent events in the Orient, it would be folly to ask either Japan or China to disarm.

In the second place, the powers are unwilling to disarm by agreement because of the difficulty of framing a reduction treaty to cover every phase of armament strength, to prevent evasion and to guarantee that a state will not violate a disarmament agreement. For example, today at the Geneva Disarmament Conference Germany is demanding equality in armaments with France. France declares, however, that even if equality in effectives were admitted, Germany would still maintain a superior "war potential" by virtue of its resources and industrial organization. Germany has the strongest chemical and aviation industries in Europe, and although it is forbidden by treaty to manufacture poison gas and military planes, it is almost impossible to devise any agreement which would prevent Germany, in the event of hostilities, from utilizing such industries for the production of poison gas and military planes which might eventually overwhelm France. Consequently, in the absence of a system of international sanctions, France insists on maintaining a larger army than Germany in order to achieve an initial victory on the outbreak of war, which would prevent Germany from utilizing its war potential. Only the establishment of a system of sanctions offsetting Germany's advantage in war potential would permit France to surrender its present military superiority.[8]

Even though every government in the world entered into a disarmament agreement, the possibility of evading that agreement, especially in view of the multiplicity of means by which wars may now be fought, will remain. Until a system of international sanctions is erected against the possibility of evasion, states now having large military establishments will be loath to trust to paper guarantees. It may be possible to secure a small measure of armament reduction without touching the security question; but it is highly improbable that a real attack on this problem can be made without some provisions for sanctions.

TREATY REVISION AND SANCTIONS

Critics will argue that the solution of the difficulties between France and Germany, on the one hand, and China and Japan, on the other, lies not in the development of a system of sanctions but in removing the underlying causes of dispute. They urge France and Japan to surrender interests which are responsible for the maintenance of large military establishments. In other words, France should allow Germany to take the Corridor from Poland, and Italy to absorb territory in the Balkans. Japan, on the other hand, should renounce all its rights in Manchuria. Any such reasoning assumes that the claims of Germany, Italy and China are "defensible," while the claims of France and Japan are "indefensible." When one examines the substance of these disputes, he will find that the right is by no means all on one side. According to nationalist standards, Poland can make as strong a case for the Corridor as Germany; while if Japan should surrender its economic interests in Manchuria, it is probable that many Japanese would starve. Admittedly every effort toward compromising national interests should be made. But in view of the complicated nature of these disputes and the conflict of in-

8. It may be pointed out that France should be satisfied with the Locarno security agreement, but this agreement does not apply to the frontiers of Eastern Europe, and it is largely a dead letter so long as the attitude of the United States toward an embargo against an aggressor remains unknown.

terests which are virtually insoluble under existing nationalist tenseness, there is no possibility, within the next few years at least, that a solution satisfactory to every party will be found.

As long as the fear remains that a government harbors the desire to impose a solution by force, a feeling of insecurity will persist, perpetuating large armaments together with an atmosphere which makes the peaceful settlement of these problems well-nigh impossible. For example, as long as France feels that Germany intends to recover the Polish Corridor by force of arms, it will refuse to consider the merits of the Corridor question, while neither France, Germany nor Poland will consider internationalization or any other forms of compromise as a solution. If the leading parties to the Anti-War Pact, however, should undertake to support a system of sanctions effectively preventing the outbreak of war from any cause whatsoever, France and other interested states might be induced to disarm, and at the same time to consider the revision of "unjust" treaties in accordance with Article 19 of the Covenant. In fact, it is only through the establishment of a security system that it will be possible for the forces of reasoned opinion, by which Professor Dewey sets such store, to operate effectively. The removal of the causes of war is of course fundamental; but in the case of two states whose difficulties are of long standing, it is doubtful whether this end can be achieved without an international organization which will guarantee that these states will keep their word.

FEDERATIONS AND SANCTIONS

To reinforce what has been said as to the necessity for coercion against a state which defies the world community, we shall point to the history of a number of lesser groupings of states. There seems to be no instance in the history of the world, from the city states of Greece, through the Papacy, the Holy Roman Empire, and the city states of Italy to the federations of modern times, where an effective political grouping of independent states has been held together purely on a basis of "good faith," "the force of public opinion," and "community of interests." The separatist instinct which leads a group to subordinate an ultimate good to immediate interests is the strongest of all political instincts. Consequently, in an effort to control separatism, nearly every federal state in existence today makes provision for sanctions. The Swiss constitution provides that in case of "trouble" between the cantons, the federal government may, at the request of one of the parties, call out troops and summon the other cantons to assist in the maintenance of order.[9]

In the case of the German federation, the power to coerce a state is even more precise. Article 48 of the Weimar constitution declares:

> If a state fails to carry out the duties imposed upon it by the national constitution or national laws, the President of the Reich may compel performance with the aid of armed force.

Finally, the history of the United States, beginning with the Revolution of the thirteen colonies and the Civil War of 1861, demonstrates that reason and good faith are not enough to bring into existence and maintain a federal union. Since the Revolution and the Civil War were extra-legal in character, they will not be regarded as examples of a legal coercive power. Nevertheless, in 1777 the thirteen independent states came together in the Articles of Confederation which established what amounted to a League of Nations. These articles made provision for compulsory arbitration of all disputes among the thirteen states, and for cooperative defense.[10] The reasons why the Articles of Confederation did not establish a permanent form of government are well-known. Localism was too strong to enable the states to cooperate on a basis of independence for a common purpose. Consequently the Constitution of 1787 established a federal government in which the states definitely surrendered many of their former powers to a government at Washington. This government was given authority to coerce individuals, including state officials, to prevent the violation of federal law. In addition, the Supreme Court definitely decided in 1918 that the federal gov-

9. Article 16, Constitution of 1874. Dareste, *Les Constitutions Modernes*, II, p. 546.
10. For an interesting comparison between the Articles of Confederation and the present League, cf. Oscar Newfang, *The United States of the World* (New York, Putnam, 1930); also Charles Warren, *The Supreme Court and Sovereign States* (Princeton, 1924), Chapter I.

ernment had the power to compel one state to pay its debts to another state.[11]

While the American Union rests on "good faith," it also relies on the power of coercion, whether of individuals or states. The history of the United States has been an evolution from a loose form of association, embodied in the Articles of Confederation, to the establishment of a superstate having definite powers of coercion. Had the authors of the American Constitution adopted the argument of "good faith" as an adequate basis for association, there can be no question that the thirteen states would have recovered their independence and soon become engaged in a series of wars.

The League of Nations today is for the world what the Articles of Confederation were for the thirteen American states. The same defects may be found in the League which were present in the Articles. In view of the present strength of the nation-state, and the traditional hostility which exists among nations, it is difficult to believe that the League is moving at the moment toward a closer international unity. Nevertheless the door to such a development, however remote, should not be closed. There is grave danger, however, that just as the "no-sanctions" doctrine, had it been accepted by the authors of the American Constitution in 1787, would have led to the disruption of the American continent, so the acceptance of the "no-sanctions" doctrine today will prevent the growth of a world community and therefore strengthen nationalism and armaments.

SUMMARY:

Thus we are led to the following conclusions:

1. Just as force is a necessary corollary to law in domestic society, so force must become a necessary part of any inter-

---

11. *Virginia v. West Virginia,* 246 U.S. 565. As we have seen, this type of coercive power is not vested in the League of Nations, which has power to repress aggression only. By virtue of its guarantee to each state of a republican form of government—a guarantee which in certain respects resembles Article X of the League Covenant—there can be little doubt that the Federal Government of the United States could use force to overthrow the establishment in any state of a Communist or Fascist form of government.

national machinery for the prevention of war, if this machinery is to achieve its end.

2. It is necessary to choose between national sanctions employed to support national objectives, and international sanctions employed to support international objectives.

3. The continuance of the present system of national sanctions means the perpetuation of large armament and a feeling of insecurity.

4. It is possible to attain real security, the reduction of armaments, and an objective attitude toward treaty revision and other political problems only with the establishment of an international organization, in which international sanctions play a fundamental part. If the governments fail to establish a system of international sanctions—if, as Professor Dewey argues, such a system is "impracticable"—then the world is doomed to a continuance of the war system.

5. A system of international sanctions is especially important as a preventive of illegal war.

6. All successful federations of states, including the United States, provide for coercion against a state or individual violating the federal law.

Part II. The Inadequacy of "Moral Pressure" and "Non-Recognition"

Although opponents of sanctions declare that "good faith" is an adequate guarantee of peace, many of them contradict themselves by declaring that "moral pressure"—as contrasted with economic sanctions—should be employed to restrain states threatening to go to war. They support the recent strictures of the League Council and the United States against Japan, but would abstain from reinforcing such strictures by concerted economic measures. While "moral pressure" is undoubtedly of great importance, it nevertheless constitutes an effort on the part of the outside world to induce a state to do something against its original wishes, and hence is in itself a "sanction." Since moral pressure is a type of sanction, the real question is whether it is adequate to achieve its ends. The recent failure to check Japanese aggression in China by "moral pressure" would indicate that by itself this sanction is inadequate. Supporters of the "moral pressure" school nevertheless insist that the various governments did not fully apply this pressure during the recent crisis, and that once the League of Nations is reorganized, and the general world situation improves, "moral pressure" will prove adequate to meet every emergency. During the recent Sino-Japanese controversy, the League members did not even declare Japan formally guilty of having violated its obligations partly because they would have been obliged to impose an economic boycott against Japan under Article 16 of the Covenant. As they were unwilling to apply this economic pressure, they refrained from exercising moral pressure.

Possibly the failure of the League Council to act may be attributed to the existence of Article 16. A more valid explanation, however, is that the great powers represented on the Council were conscious of the fact that in the past they had engaged in interventions similar to that undertaken by Japan and might wish to engage in similar interventions in the future. It seems obvious, moreover, that if the great powers should pronounce drastic judgment against an aggressor, having first made it clear that they would not support such a judgment by sanctions, the aggressor state would pay no more heed to such an injunction than Japan has recently paid to the world's representations concerning its action in Manchuria.

Representatives of the "moral pressure" school assert, nevertheless, that our judgments are too hasty and that despite failure to check Japanese aggression, Japan will ultimately suffer from its present venture, and China will ultimately triumph. This romantic theory that good always conquers evil finds little support from history. Such a theory could be used to justify the World War and, if sound, would make all peace machinery unnecessary. What this theory overlooks, among other things, is the tremendous amount of suffering and irremediable damage caused by the process of war. Ultimately China may succeed in reestablishing its control over Manchuria, which is now in the hands of Japan. But if this end is secured only by keeping the Orient in a state of recurrent war and economic disorder during the next century, and if it involves the militarization of the Chinese and Japanese people, then the cause of world peace and human cooperation will have been inevitably defeated, even should Manchuria be restored eventually to China.

Those who believe in moral pressure explain the recent failure to stop Japan on the ground that the moral forces of the world have not been active because of the grave internal problems caused by the depression and the persistence of international disputes originating in the World War. Once prosperity returns and a better feeling is restored among the great powers, then "moral pressure" will be more effective. The difficulty with this reasoning is that it conditions success on the establishment of a millennium which never arrives. The world will always be confronted with problems; what is important is that more enlightened methods for settling these problems should be adopted. When a great power like Japan is allowed to take the law in its own hands, the doctrine of nationalism is strengthened in every country, and the capacity for exerting "moral pressure" in the future in support of international standards is inevitably weakened.

THE INADEQUACY OF THE NON-RECOGNITION DOCTRINE

Reluctant to admit that the outside world failed in stopping Japan's aggressions, a number of spokesmen, official and private, assert that the "non-recognition" doctrine laid down by the United States and the League will eventually bring about the return of Manchuria to China, and will serve as a guarantee—more effective and less dangerous than the guarantee of economic sanctions—against future aggressions in any part of the world. According to this doctrine, no government should recognize any "situation" arising out of violation of the Anti-War Pact and the League Covenant. In the present instance, this doctrine aims at preventing the "recognition" of the new state of Manchuria which has come into existence as a result of Japanese military operations.

If the principle which the non-recognition doctrine embodies can be enforced—i.e., that no treaty made under duress is valid—it will mark an important change in international law. The application of this principle to Manchuria, moreover, may serve as a legal basis for the future intervention of League members and the United States. Nevertheless, to claim that this doctrine is a substitute for economic sanctions and constitutes a guarantee that will make it possible for nations to disarm is utopian, to say the least. This doctrine can not be made effective unless it is supported by measures involving something more than words.

The limitations of the non-recognition doctrine, unsupported by other acts, may be demonstrated by a few historical examples. By withholding "recognition" from Russia, the United States has hoped to induce the Soviet régime to pay the Kerensky debts. By withholding recognition from revolutionary governments, we have hoped to encourage stability in Central America. Nevertheless, despite the non-recognition policy, the Soviet debt remains unpaid, while revolutions in Central America are as numerous as ever.[12]

In 1883 the British government established control over Egypt in supposed violation of certain rights claimed by France. France declined to "recognize" the British position in Egypt until the conclusion of the Entente Cordiale of 1904. This belated recognition improved the British position, because the control which France had previously exercised over Egyptian finance was then relaxed. France's refusal to recognize British control between 1883 and 1904, however, did not prevent Great Britain from achieving its political objective.

An even closer analogy to the situation in Manchuria is the establishment of the Republic of Panama in November 1903. This republic could not have been established except for the armed intervention of the United States. The government of Colombia, on whose territory the new state was so summarily erected, was bitterly antagonized by the intervention of the United States and did not "recognize" the existence of Panama until 1921. Its refusal to do so, however, did not constitute the slightest obstacle to the construction of the Panama Canal by the United States.[13]

Now France in Egypt and Colombia in Panama had far greater material rights than has the United States in Manchuria. Despite

12. R. L. Buell, "The United States and Central American Revolutions," *Foreign Policy Reports*, Vol. VII, No. 10, July 22, 1931.
13. Mr. Frank H. Simonds reminds us that Prime Minister Asquith warned the Balkan states in 1912 that territorial gains following the pending war with Turkey would not be recognized; nevertheless the great powers acquiesced in the Treaty of Bucharest, which distributed Turkish territory among the victors of the war. *New York Herald Tribune*, May 10, 1932.

these rights, the "non-recognition" doctrine failed to obstruct the ends of imperialist powers determined to realize their objectives. It is difficult to see how the adherence of the entire world to the "non-recognition" doctrine would of itself have affected the aims of the British in Egypt or of the United States in Panama. The final result of the two incidents was that France and Colombia recognized the newly established positions of Great Britain and the United States, in return for a consideration. Is not Japan likely to win a similar victory unless the powers are prepared to go further than a mere refusal to recognize?

Should governments take this non-recognition doctrine literally, they might seriously embarrass Japan's position in Manchuria. Mr. Stimson could urge American citizens in Manchuria not to pay taxes to the new régime, and to disregard its courts. He could instruct American consular officers not to accept exequaturs from the new Manchurian government. The result of such a course would be the immediate exclusion of American commercial interests from the country and the erection of the Closed Door against the United States. "You may come and trade on a basis of equality with other nations," the Manchurian authorities would say, "but only on condition that your government accepts our jurisdiction and that you conclude with us a commercial treaty."

If seriously determined to secure its objective, the United States could next decide to embargo American loans to Manchuria. Assuming that capital is needed, the embargo might constitute a brake on Japanese development. The Soviet Union, however, has been able to carry out an imposing Five-Year Plan without the aid of long-term financial assistance from the United States. Japan could probably develop Manchuria without such aid. Should the United States and the League members boycott loans to Manchuria, Japan could increase its borrowings from abroad, thus releasing internal funds for use in Manchuria. Finally, the United States and the League members could boycott trade with Manchuria; but the consequences of this action would be to throw the new state completely into the arms of Japan, in which case Japanese ports would become the ports of entry for Manchuria. Thus there is no method of applying the "non-recognition" doctrine literally to Manchuria except by declaring an economic and financial embargo against Japan itself.

If economic sanctions are to be applied, surely they should be applied to restrain a government from causing the enormous suffering of armed intervention.

Subject to certain conditions, the incorporation into international law of the principle that an agreement made under duress is invalid would constitute an important advance. Under private law, however, this principle protects the victim of duress because the party employing duress cannot enforce the rights claimed under the contract without the support of the state. Under international law, however, an aggressor state which annexes territory as a result of a war can enjoy the benefits of *de facto* annexation, regardless of whether such annexation is "recognized" by other powers. Consequently the new doctrine of non-recognition will become important only when states agree to prevent the aggressor from enjoying the results of duress—i.e., when they are willing to apply concrete sanctions. To do nothing more than refuse to "recognize" a settlement established by war will merely encourage the defeated state to attempt the reconquest of its lost territory. The attitude of the United States and the League in the recent Sino-Japanese case is thus causing China to gird itself for a new war. Even if this war should not come in the immediate future, the fear of a new outbreak will hang over the Orient, intensifying the present unrest.[14] If governments intend to prevent war certainly the invocation of the "non-recognition" doctrine—and nothing else—is the wrong way to go about it.

Recognizing the difficulties of any effort permanently to apply the non-recognition doctrine, some of its supporters state that if non-recognition does not succeed in dislodging an aggressor from forcibly acquired territory, an international conference should be called to determine an ultimate settlement. Such a procedure could only mean that unilateral violation of the Anti-War Pact could be legalized by multilateral consent. On its face, this appears to be a questionable solution. If it is wrong for an aggressor to annex the territory of a neighboring state by force, how is this act made any less wrong by virtue of the belated consent of the "neutral" powers, which had previously promised not to recognize any situation created in violation of the Anti-War Pact? Such a solution would encourage the aggressor to cling to

14. Cf. R. L. Buell, *New York Herald Tribune*, March 27, 1932.

his spoils in the knowledge that the other powers would ultimately give way. Thus it is evident that by itself alone the non-recognition doctrine is a faulty method of preserving the territorial integrity of a state against an aggressor or of maintaining peace, and that it cannot serve as a basis for disarmament. International sanctions must be more realistic and decisive in nature.

PROGRESSIVE SANCTIONS

A number of critics declare that Article 16 of the Covenant, in providing for a complete embargo against the trade of an aggressor, is so sweeping that no government is willing to apply it. They contend that the article should be changed to give the League greater discretion. In their opinion, sanctions should be employed only against certain "key" articles of vital importance to the aggressor state, leaving the remainder of its trade unimpaired. For example, the recent proposal of the Committee on Economic Sanctions of the Twentieth Century Fund advocates a protocol in which the signatory states would pledge themselves in the event of threatened violation of the Anti-War Pact "to consult together to determine upon measures of non-intercourse appropriate to keep the peace," and the Capper resolution of April 4, 1932 merely enjoins financial assistance to an aggressor as well as the shipment of arms "or other supplies of war." [15] The criticism that Article 16 is too rigid may be sound. There may be room for difference as to what particular type of sanction would best meet a given situation and at what stage in a conflict sanctions should be applied. Once it is admitted, however, that some kind of coercion is desirable, it follows that the principle of sanctions is sound.

Part III. The Objections to Sanctions

Despite these arguments, which indicate that unless international organization provides for sanctions the war system is

---

15. Cf. an interesting address by John Foster Dulles, *Annals of the American Academy*, July, 1932. On October 4, 1921 the League Assembly adopted a resolution authorizing progressive sanctions under certain circumstances, and stating: "In cases of prolonged application of economic pressure, measures of increasing stringency may be taken. The cutting off of the food sup-

likely to be perpetuated, a number of objections are raised. Opponents of sanctions do not advance any conclusive arguments that the war system can be overthrown merely by "good will," but concentrate their efforts on demonstrating that sanctions "will not work."

Their arguments may be summarized under the following headings:

1. Sanctions are a part of the European militarist system.
2. Sanctions unjustly injure "innocent" people.
3. Sanctions mean war.
4. Sanctions are impracticable.

I. ARE SANCTIONS A EUROPEAN IDEA?

The idea that international sanctions are "un-American" was advanced by President Hoover in his Armistice Day speech of 1929, when he declared:

> The European nations have, by the Covenant of the League of Nations, agreed that if nations fail to settle their differences peaceably then force should be applied by other nations to compel them to be reasonable. We have refused to travel this road. We are confident that at least in the Western Hemisphere public opinion will suffice to check violence. This is the road we propose to travel.[16]

The implication of this contrast is that the principle of sanctions is part of the old European system of militarism and balance of power, to which the United States has been traditionally opposed.

There is little historical basis, however, for this supposed contrast. In 1910 the American Congress passed a resolution in favor of "constituting the combined navies of the world, an international force for the preservation of universal peace." At one time, Presidents Roosevelt and Taft, and Senator Henry Cabot

---

plies of the civil population of the defaulting State shall be regarded as an extremely drastic measure which shall only be applied if the other measures available are clearly inadequate." Resolutions and Recommendations adopted by the Assembly, Second Session, p. 26.
16. Cf. also President Hoover's D.A.R. address of April 14, 1930.

Lodge supported the idea of sanctions in support of international law,[17] as did the League to Enforce Peace during the World War. At the Paris Peace Conference, the American drafts of a League of Nations likewise made provision for sanctions.[18] Moreover, although professing that the force of public opinion has been sufficient to settle disputes in the Western Hemisphere, the United States has rigorously applied the principle of national sanctions in the Caribbean where it has repeatedly used marines to accomplish its ends. In fact, under the Roosevelt Corollary to the Monroe Doctrine, the United States arrogated to itself the task of acting as policeman for the outside world in this region. It is true that opposition was expressed to the sanction clauses of the League of Nations in the Senate; this opposition, however, did not proceed from the belief that the use of force is morally wrong, but from an unwillingness to pledge the use of force in advance.[19]

All extreme nationalists, whether in America or Europe, oppose the idea of international sanctions. This opposition arises out of an unwillingness to subordinate national military establishments to international control. The desire for "freedom of action" is due, not to a general pacifism, but to a latent fear that international organization will interfere with incompatible national interests. During the recent Sino-Japanese dispute, avowed nationalists as well as spokesmen of governments which have verbally accepted the doctrines of internationalism, have been quick to seize on the no-sanctions argument of one school of peace advocates to justify an unwillingness to make any sacrifice on behalf of the Anti-War Pact and international organization. In thus playing into the hands of the extreme nationalists, the no-sanctions pacifists give another example of the proverb that the best is enemy of the good.

17. Cf. R. L. Buell, *International Relations* (New York, Holt, 1929, revised edition), p. 594.
18. Cf. the House and Wilson drafts, D. H. Miller, *The Drafting of the Covenant* (New York, Putnam, 1928), Vol. II, p. 9, 14, 79, 101.
19. Professor Dewey states that the idea of international sanctions has been dropped in Europe, and is kept alive only by Americans. The recent French proposal for an international police force, the discussions at the London Naval Conference over a consultative pact, and the present deadlock of the Geneva arms conference partly over the sanctions question shows that in Europe sanctions are much alive.

2. SANCTIONS AND "INNOCENT" PEOPLE

Opponents of international sanctions deny that there is any analogy between the use of police within a state and the attempt to coerce a state. The police single out a presumably guilty individual, and operate with overpowering force against him without disturbing the general life of the community. The imposition of international sanctions against a state, however, would mean the coercion of all individuals within the state, few of whom had a consciousness of guilt, and some of whom might even be opposed to the policy of their government which the outside world was attempting to change. The punishment of crime committed by an individual may be "just," but the coercion of millions of "innocent" people is unjust.

This distinction between a municipal police force singling out only the guilty individual and international sanctions coercing "innocent" people is not so great as opponents of sanctions assert. The state does not hesitate to use force against groups, some of the members of which defy its authority. Moreover an offense committed by or punishment imposed on an individual inevitably affects "innocent" members of his family as well as the community as a whole. Society cannot be deterred from imposing punishment upon a guilty individual by the consideration that such punishment may indirectly cause suffering to others.

"Innocent" People in the Aggressor State

Even admitting this contention, some critics find it difficult to agree that a people should be held responsible for the acts of its government, especially when that government is undemocratic as in the case of Japan. The seizure of German private property in foreign countries under the Treaty of Versailles, on account of reparation for which the German government was liable, met with severe criticism. Would it not be even more unjust to boycott a people when its government, over which it might have little direct control, embarked on illegal war? Here again it is necessary to draw some distinctions. The attempt to *punish* individuals because of the acts of their government may be reprehensible; but it does not follow that international organization should not exert whatever pressure is necessary upon individuals in order to *repress* the acts of their government. It is literally impossible to separate a government from the individuals under its jurisdiction; it is from these individuals that a government secures its revenues and its man-power. Even if it were possible to make this distinction, the adoption of the principle that a people should be immunized from the consequences of administrative acts would make governments completely irresponsible.

A people can always find means of inducing its government, no matter what the form of constitution, to desist from aggressive war as soon as it is convinced that the war is inexpedient and costly. In other words, the people of a country can escape from the hardships of an international boycott by causing its government to live up to its international obligations. The fact that the attempt to blockade Germany or Russia during the World War led to injustice offers no analogy, since these blockades were part of the old war system. Under a pacific international embargo, imposed after a state has been formally adjudged guilty of having embarked on illegal war, it would be the duty of the international organization imposing the embargo to do everything in its power to convince the people of an aggressor state that the object of the embargo was not to effect the conquest of that state, but to cause it to desist from invading another country. As one of the means to achieve this end, the blockade might even exempt food ships, in accordance with President Hoover's Armistice Day speech of 1929. Such an exemption would remove the fear of starving people but could still make possible the starvation of the industrial and financial organization of an aggressor state.

"Innocent" People in an Invaded State

In considering whether an international embargo would injure "innocent" people in an aggressor state, it should not be forgotten that the invasion of foreign territory by an aggressor imposes vast suffering upon "innocent" people in that territory. When such aggression leads to a military struggle between two fairly equal powers, the injury done to "innocent" people is likely to be far greater than that done to the aggressor state by an international boycott quickly bringing the aggressor state to terms.

One possibly might contend that while the outside world is not responsible for the injury done, for example, to "innocent" Chinese by the Japanese military machine, it would be responsible for the injury done by an international boycott to "innocent" Japanese. This argument, however, overlooks the fact that if it were not for the continuance of Japan's international trade, Japanese aggression which does damage to innocent Chinese could not be successfully carried on. To oppose economic sanctions means a policy of "business as usual" with an aggressor state. A policy of "business as usual" results in underwriting aggression and making a mockery of international engagements not to go to war. The idea of neutrality and the right of belligerent trade is incompatible with the principle of the Anti-War Pact.

"Innocent" People in the Boycotting States

Finally, it is declared that the principle of international sanctions is unjust because the burden will unjustly fall upon a few exporting or importing groups within the states imposing the embargo and more heavily on some states than others. Obviously the people of a state imposing sanctions may suffer as much as the people of the state against which sanctions are imposed. To equalize this burden, it should not prove impossible to work out a plan whereby an international economic committee may temporarily purchase the exports which normally go to the aggressor, and find substitutes or new sources of supply to take the place of the embargoed imports from the aggressor state.[20] The League of Nations might develop the idea embodied in the Convention for Financial Assistance in case of Aggression, i.e., of creating an international fund which during the application of sanctions could be used to support industries adversely affected in the boycott-imposing countries.

Moreover, it is probable that when an effective system of international sanctions is established, it would not provide in the first instance at least for an absolute embargo upon all articles of import and export, but only upon those articles which are regarded as absolutely essential to the industrial existence of the aggressor state. The application of limited sanctions would reduce the injury to industrial interests in the sanctions-applying states and

20. A similar system was actually followed under the Allied blockade during the World War. Cf. Louis Guichard, *The Naval Blockade* (New York, Appleton, 1930); M. Parmelee, *Blockade and Sea Power* (New York, Crowell, 1924).

thus facilitate the success of any plan for compensating such interests.

We may conclude that the war system will do far more damage to "innocent" people and economic interests in every country than would result from the establishment of an international system of sanctions, which would tend to prevent war from coming into existence, or quickly repress such wars in case they actually occurred.

3. DO INTERNATIONAL SANCTIONS MEAN WAR?

It is contended in the third place that the imposition of international sanctions would lead to war and the revival of the nationalist emotionalism which characterized the World War. If sanctions are only another name for war and lead to all the abuses of the war system, they should of course be condemned.

The answer to this argument depends first on whether the use of international economic sanctions will lead to armed clashes between the aggressor and the sanctions-applying states, and second, on whether such clashes, if they should occur, may properly be characterized as "war."

The fear that an international boycott would lead to armed clashes is based on the assumption that to make such a boycott effective it would be necessary to establish a naval blockade of the ports of an aggressor and erect a military cordon around its territory, which might invite reprisals. Actually, however, all that should be necessary, in the beginning at least, is action by foreign governments merely prohibiting the entrance of goods from the aggressor state into their respective territories and preventing the clearance of exports to the aggressor state. A boycott is an effective method of bringing people to recognize their international obligations without necessarily resulting in loss of life. An economic boycott applied by the world community against an aggressor does not mean "war" any more than a strike of labor against capital necessarily means the shedding of blood.

It is theoretically possible that an aggressor state would resist an international embargo by force of arms—by declaring war against the entire world participating in the embargo. This contingency, however, would be extremely remote in case a boycott were really international—and only in such a case should a boycott be imposed.

Nevertheless let us admit the possibility that international economic sanctions might lead to armed clashes. Should they consequently be opposed on the ground that they might lead to "war"? Again it is important to make a distinction. There is a fundamental difference between military force used by a state for the prosecution of national objectives—which is what happens when war occurs—and the use of force by states under international organization after all efforts at peaceful settlement have failed and a state has formally been adjudged guilty of having violated its obligations and embarked on illegal war. Ethically and legally the use of force by a state to advance interests to which a legal claim has not been established is in an entirely different category from the use of coercion by the world community to protect one of its members from aggression. Even if the imposition of economic sanctions should result in armed clashes, which is unlikely, such clashes could not properly be called "war." Should such clashes occur, the aggressor would be quickly brought to terms, provided governments really believed that a war anywhere is of profound international concern. The danger that international sanctions will lead to "armed clashes" is not nearly so great as the danger that illegal war, left to run its course, may spread throughout the world. Any community which holds back from applying its law to a criminal from fear of retaliation is in a morally backward condition. No international organization can hope to come into existence if states decline to act in upholding international standards from fear of conceivable resistance on the part of a state embarking on aggression. Taken literally, such timidity would prohibit even a moral protest against aggression.

A War Psychology Necessary?

Will it nevertheless be possible to obtain popular consent to the application of sanctions against an aggressor state without stimulating a psychology which, instead of developing a genuine international consciousness, will revive the worst excesses of nationalism? If statesmen apply sanctions because of a real desire to uphold the principles of international cooperation and not because of some hidden nationalist motive, there is no reason why they should appeal to jingoism to obtain their ends. Once an effective system of sanctions is organized, Parliaments will probably enact legislation authorizing the Executive to embargo certain articles of trade with any state which illegally goes to war. Under such legislation the Executives of the boycotting countries, after consulting with each other through an international economic committee or other international organ, could impose an embargo without any more danger of stirring up animosity against the aggressor state than is stirred up today when the Executive of the United States imposes an arms embargo on Mexico or China. The fundamental issue is whether the people in the leading countries of the world can be induced to accept temporary material sacrifice for the sake of an ultimate international good. If people can act only out of consideration of immediate economic interests or blind nationalism, not only is there no hope of successfully applying international sanctions—there is no hope of developing a world community.

4. ARE SANCTIONS PRACTICABLE?

Finally, it is contended—and this is the gist of Professor Dewey's argument—that any effort at establishing a system of international sanctions is impracticable. Because of the economic sacrifice involved and the inability of leading governments to unite on a common policy, any system of international sanctions is bound to become a dead letter. It is even asserted, somewhat inconsistently, that out of fear of the imposition of such sanctions, governments will aim at complete economic independence from the outside world.[21] No system of international sanctions, moreover, could expect to be effective against the resistance of great powers.

For those who have historical perspective, the question of whether in the present stage of world politics sanctions will "work" is immaterial to the fundamental question of whether the principle of sanctions is sound. Having reached the conclusion that an international community cannot be erected and the institution of war uprooted without guarantees other than "good

21. Cf. George Soule, "The Fallacy of the Boycott," *Harper's*, May 1932.

faith," and being convinced that the establishment of an international community is essential to human welfare, we cannot be side-tracked from our goal by the objections of the "practical" man. It is true that during the past few years governments have been unwilling to apply international sanctions and that Article 16 of the Covenant has become largely a dead letter. This has been due partly to the unwillingness of the United States to renounce its right to trade with an aggressor, and partly to the fact that the obligations of Article 16 are couched in too sweeping terms. Fundamentally, however, this opposition to international sanctions is due to the persistence of unreasoning nationalism. During this period the same governments which oppose international sanctions have been unwilling to reduce tariffs and armaments, or to modify any other policy causing international friction. Governments do not hesitate to impose sacrifices upon their subjects to advance national objectives. If they are unwilling to impose any immediate sacrifices for the sake of developing an international community, then not only sanctions but any kind of real international organization is "impracticable." The consequences of the failure to establish an effective world organization, in which sanctions will play a fundamental part, means the perpetuation of the war system. The evils of the war system are far greater than any evils which opponents now conjure up against an international sanctions system. Those who believe in the development of a world community cannot accept *a priori* arguments that international sanctions "are bound to fail." They must be willing to take a risk on behalf of world peace; they must resist any of the assumptions of the no-sanctions school until experience forcibly demonstrates that sanctions are unsound.

Much the same answer may be made to the statement that sanctions will not succeed in the case of the great powers, and that such powers, to escape the danger of sanctions, will adopt a policy of complete economic independence. As we have pointed out, the great powers are highly industrialized and hence more sensitive to the preventive pressure of international sanctions than small, agricultural countries. In view of the modern interdependence of the world, an economic boycott is bound to have some effect on an aggressor state, and since such a boycott would be imposed only after moral pressure had been attempted, a boycott would have more effect than moral pressure.

If any government should build up tariff walls to escape the effects of international sanctions, it would have to confess that it contemplated aggressive war. If governments harbor such ambitions, not only will sanctions fail, but so will any form of international organization.

If governments, however, believe that the interests of every nation in the long run can best be advanced by international cooperation, then they will enter into agreements reducing tariffs and armaments, while at the same time developing an effective system of sanctions. The further this development toward economic interdependence and disarmament goes and the more closely national interests become intertwined, the less occasion will arise for the actual imposition of sanctions. If the occasion does arise under these circumstances, it is more than probable that the application of sanctions will be decisive.

Quis Custodiet Ipsos Custodes?

The final argument against the "practicability" of international sanctions is semi-legalistic in nature. It is contended that such a system adds nothing to the security of a state because the promise to coerce an aggressor is of no greater value than the promise not to go to war. If a nation fails to live up to its obligation not to go to war, there is no reason to believe that it will keep a promise to coerce an aggressor. Both promises rest on good faith. In fact, since the promise to coerce an aggressor assumes that the promise not to go to war will be violated, the existence of the first promise weakens the moral value of the second. This argument against international sanctions is summed up in the Latin maxim, *quis custodiet ipsos custodes* (who shall guard the guardians).

In support of this objection it is pointed out that while a state may enforce its laws against individuals and groups, it cannot be compelled to enforce self-imposed constitutional restrictions. If a government chooses to disregard such restrictions, there is no power in the state which can legally prevent or punish such violation.[22] It is contended that the same principle applies in the realm of law among states. If they show bad faith in violating interna-

22. Cf. Sir T. E. Holland, *Elements of Jurisprudence* (New York, Oxford University Press, 1910, 11th ed.), p. 365.

tional law, there is no higher power which can impose a legal sanction. Consequently international law should rest only on "a broad-based public opinion."[23]

The enforcement of all international obligations in the final analysis depends on the good faith of governments, on public opinion, and on a community of interests. One must be precise, however, in stipulating what is meant by public opinion and whose good faith is involved. Even more than individuals, governments are apt to act in defiance of reason. A state may believe it profitable to steal from a neighbor, when its real interest is to leave the neighbor alone.

Moreover, at the very time when the government of a single country, perhaps contrary to the wishes of important opinion within its own state, is determined to carry on war, the predominant sentiment throughout a large part of the world may be in favor of peace. This predominant sentiment can make its influence felt by demanding the imposition of sanctions. If governments are reasonably democratic, they will impose sanctions; but if public opinion is only lukewarm in its desire for peace, it is improbable that governments will take such action. Thus there is no necessary legal defect in the present structure of international organization which will prevent a group of states from acting together to coerce a single state to refrain from embarking on aggressive war. In the last analysis public opinion in the leading countries, working through an effective system of sanctions, will constitute the "guard over the guardians."

The one justification for refusing to apply sanctions to the state is that it has a higher morality than other groups—a view which facts do not support. Many students of nationalism and psychology assert that people acting in national groups will commit acts the very thought of which they would repudiate as individuals. From this point of view, there is even greater need to erect substantial barriers to the misuse of force on the part of the nation-state than on the part of individuals. To contend, as opponents of sanctions do, that the state should be exempt from the responsibility which it imposes on groups within its jurisdiction is merely to increase the excesses of nationalism.

23. R. M. MacIver, *The Modern State* (New York, Oxford University Press, 1926), p. 289.

Conclusion

To be logical, the no-sanctions school should support complete non-resistance—a doctrine which cannot possibly be made the basis of any kind of society. Far from supporting non-resistance, however, the no-sanctions school accepts the principle of self-defense which inevitably means the perpetuation of armaments and the war system. This system, we have demonstrated, will only disappear when a new system of cooperative defense and international sanctions, acting in support of international law, has been established. In asserting that sanctions will not "work," the no-sanctions school is really saying that no kind of international organization involving the sacrifice of national objectives will "work." My whole contention has been that both international organization and sanctions will "work," if people deeply and intelligently desire peace rather than war. It is well to preach the importance of "good faith"; it is well to insist "upon removing underlying causes of dispute" in international relations, just as it is important to preach the Golden Rule. But these doctrines mean little to society until institutions are established which will carry them into effect. Even among men of the highest personal character vital differences will sometimes arise which can be settled only by intervention of the state. Similarly, differences between states cannot be left to "reason" and "good faith" alone; when one state attempts to solve these differences by force, it is imperative that its aggression should be forcibly resisted by international organization.

Every effort should be made to develop "peace" sentiment throughout the world—to perfect machinery for settling disputes on the one hand, and for peacefully removing injustices in the *status quo* on the other. The success of these developments will depend, however, upon whether the principle of international sanctions is at the same time maintained and developed. It is entirely logical for those who believe in an unrestricted state sovereignty, with its corollaries of nationalism, militarism and imperialism, to oppose international sanctions; but for that very reason, this principle should be supported by those who believe in international cooperation and peace.

The unwillingness of the United States to inform the world

whether it will insist upon trading with an aggressor state is one obstacle to the development of an adequate system of sanctions by the League of Nations. To remove this obstacle the pending Capper resolution and the project of the Committee on Economic Sanctions, organized by the Twentieth Century Fund, propose that the United States undertake to consult with other powers as to measures of non-intercourse to prevent the threatened breach of the Anti-War Pact. The adoption by the United States of such a proposal would be a contribution of great importance to the development of world peace.

Appendix 3
Secretary Klein's Reply to Prof. Dewey
By Julius Klein

In our June Bulletin we published Prof. Dewey's letter asking Assistant Secretary of Commerce Klein his grounds for optimism about economic conditions here. Secretary Klein replies:

"I have read your letter of June 11 with considerable interest, and I am particularly interested in two or three of the important points which you raise.

"With respect to your comments on America's control of about two-fifths of the world's wealth, I do not see how that situation could be changed even if it were desirable to change it. It is true, I believe, that with a very small proportion of the world's population we are fortunate in possessing a very large proportion of the world's natural resources, and this in itself is probably chiefly responsible for our high standard of living. In my opinion, however, such a situation is hardly one to be deplored. It is rather one for which we can be truly grateful. Moreover, so far as the rest of the world is concerned, I do not see how our control of these resources is to their disadvantage. After all, we use them in raising the standard of living and purchasing power of our own people to the end that we purchase much larger quantities of products, we are able to manufacture goods for export at low cost, and we are able to accumulate surplus capital which is exported to the rest of the world—to the decided advantage of peoples living in areas less well endowed with natural resources.

"About the only way we could be more generous would be to open our doors to immigration from all parts of the world without any restriction. Surely you would not recommend this.

"You state again that underconsumption is chiefly due to poor

[First published in *People's Lobby Bulletin* 1 (August 1931): 3–4. For Dewey's article to which this is a reply and for Dewey's rejoinder, see this volume, pp. 346–50 and 351–54.]

distribution of income between property and wages. I am not at all sure that there is not a tendency at times for too much of the national income to go into the purchase of producers' goods for increasing output and too little into the purchase of consumers' goods, but if that is true the price deflation, which of course occurs in a major depression, helps to rectify the situation. If you will examine the record of the past depressions in the United States, you will find that although labor suffers severely during the depression itself, the relatively greater deflation in prices than in wages always results in allowing labor to come out of the depression with a substantially higher real wage than when it entered the depression. This has been so true that real wages have been multiplied many times during the past five or six decades.

"With respect to the suggestion on page 4, that it is essential for public works to be increased very largely by government credit 'since no expansion of any plants for production is needed,' I am inclined to disagree with the latter part of your premise. At the bottom of a depression like the one we are now experiencing, it always appears as if there were an overproduction of everything. That is probably true so far as the well established commodities are concerned. It is not true, however, that all or nearly all of the world's needs and wants are being satisfied, or even the needs and wants of our own population. Is it not true, for example, that there is a tremendous potential market in this country for heat and noise insulation materials, for cooling devices which will make offices, factories and homes as comfortable in summer as they have been made in winter through central heating, for more rapid means of personal transportation, for better communication, and for a host of other material commodities and services many of which are utterly unknown at the present time?

"It seems to me that out of this depression will grow many new industries which, in another ten or fifteen years, will be supplying what we shall have come to regard as necessities, but which are now regarded as luxuries and beyond the reach of even the wealthiest people. This is the sort of industrial expansion that will take place, and it seems to me that a program of public works expenditures, involving several times what is now being spent would be the most effective means of diverting capital from these new industries which so sorely need it into public construction, much of which would be unproductive in a social sense. The Federal Government and many of the States are now engaged in construction programs which, when completed, will provide for their needs for a good many years to come. It would be just as unsound to complete public works construction at the present time, which would not be used for another fifteen or twenty years, as it would be for an automobile manufacturer to build an additional plant which he did not expect to bring into production until 1950. In either case, it would mean locking up of capital in a fixed form so that it would remain unproductive for many years. It is exactly this diversion of capital into unproductive channels which in my opinion is of substantial importance in bringing about these great industrial depressions.

"Such a program of public works as has been suggested in the press lately would, in my judgment, not only impede recovery at the present time by diverting investment funds into the government bonds necessary to inaugurate any such program, but might contribute very substantially to bringing about another major depression in a few years' time."

Appendix 4
Reason, Nature and Professor Dewey
By Morris R. Cohen

Sir: Professor Dewey's review of *Reason and Nature*, in the *New Republic* of April 29, is on the whole so highly generous that it may seem ungracious for me to express anything but gratitude. And yet—if my account of scientific methods is worthy of such praise, its philosophic basis cannot be unworthy of defense against serious misapprehensions.

1. Professor Dewey charges me with failure to define philosophic issues clearly. Now, as I have in the main dealt with such issues not directly but only as they are involved in the actual methods of the sciences, it is *a priori* altogether probable that I have expressed myself inadequately in a number of places. But all that Professor Dewey says in support of his contention seems to indicate that he finds my philosophy blurred because he does not consider my problems in my own terms and assumptions, but states them in his own (from my point of view essentially obscure) concepts and theories of experience and nature. This is very much like charging Einstein with the obscurity which follows from stating his views in terms of the traditional physics. Thus, when Professor Dewey charges me with holding and failing to support the doctrine that "reason is something over and beyond experience," I cannot admit that any view of mine is thus justly characterized, and I can only suspect that his difficulty is due to the fact that he uses the word experience in an all-inclusive sense, while I restrict it to events in personal biographies. In any case, if experience, whatever it may be, follows scientific method, it must (as I try to show) assume laws or invariant relations in nature. If reason denotes this systematic phase of nature, then we must, unless we arrogate to ourselves divine om-

[First published in *New Republic* 67 (17 June 1931): 126–27. For Dewey's review to which this is a reply, see this volume, pp. 299–303, and for Dewey's rejoinder, see this volume, p. 304.]

nipresence and omniscience, regard it as often beyond what we have actually attained in our personal experience and knowledge. For obviously no finite number of past physical experiments can by themselves prove a genuine universal for all possible cases. If, on the other hand, *reason* denotes the process of reasoning (and I have taken the trouble to make the context clearly indicate which meaning of the word is intended), I explicitly contend that not only is such reason itself an experience, but that in general we ought to have more of it.

The differences between Professor Dewey and myself are not merely personal, but are indicative of two historically different approaches to philosophy. While to me the basic problems are ontologic, i.e., concerning the nature of things, Professor Dewey is primarily interested in the human world and in the psychologic growth of our ideas about things. Thus he speaks of "nature distilled through the alembic of science and logic," where I should rather say that this holds only of our idea of nature but not of the nature that existed before our birth and before our acquisition of any experience and knowledge. For I cannot believe that science creates the sun when it discovers its chemical composition.

The Lockian tradition, reënforced by Kant, has made it fashionable to hold that we can approach nature only after a prior study of our ideas. For reasons often indicated in my book, I cannot agree to this. I rather hold with the pre-Lockian Spinoza and the post-Kantian Hegel that a scientific study of mind is impossible without previous knowledge of nature, that psychology presupposes physics and physiology. This does not deny the value of psychologic contributions to philosophy. Hume, James and Dewey seem to me to have displayed real genius in this field. But their subject matter is essentially more complicated than physics and their insights are always difficult of direct verification. I often feel that they are right, but can see no scientific proof of it. For this reason they have offered little toward a scientific philosophy of nature. The more fruitful path has in fact been the one opened by the pre-Socratic philosophers and followed by modern natural science. None but an obscurantist would deny the necessity of going on to a scientific psychology. But psychology is arrogant if it claims to be the only possible philosophic method or thinks it can dispense with objective logic.

In any case, if we believe that sciences like physics and biology give us truth, then a philosophy of nature must be based on them rather than on the pre-scientific notions of nature "as it confronts and intercepts man in life." For the latter are full of practical confusion, just as the poets' views are full of esthetic illusion.

2. Professor Dewey thinks that I achieve an easy victory by beating the dead dog of sensationalistic empiricism. But due attention to current accounts of scientific method, most of which follow Mach and Pearson, shows that though the dog is sick, his bite is still dangerous.

3. Professor Dewey implies that I am somewhat deficient in knowledge of my fellow philosophers, and more especially that I am unjust to William James. It would, indeed, be strange to claim that unlike other philosophers, and human beings generally, I have succeeded in being perfectly just to those from whom I differ. Nevertheless, what Professor Dewey offers as evidence on this point is not based on what my book actually says. I was not giving an account of James's philosophy, but was concerned with the popular anti-intellectual temper of our age when I quoted his preference for the "tang of life" over rigorous logic as a characteristic of philosophy. It is not due to my lack of sympathy that popular usage has derived opposition to logic and rational thought from James's remark.

As to my imputation to James of an unavowed definition of experience as immediate and vivid sensation, the attentive reader will, I think, find my text fully borne out by James's avowed nominalism and disparagement of conceptual thoughts, as well as by his expressed sympathy with Mach and Pearson. Against this Professor Dewey brings the argument that James was a keen critic of sensationalistic empiricism. But this, every careful reader will find, is the very thing on which I insist from the very first sentence of my account of James (page 42). Only I do not take it for granted that because James says one thing in one context he cannot say something quite different elsewhere. James's was a great and generous mind, rich in insight, but hardly inclined to sacrifice variety to logical consistency. My account of him is a serious and I believe sympathetic effort to understand the reasons for his diverse positions, and in doing this I have had the benefit of frequent discussions with him. My dissent from

James's views may be due to my hardness of heart, but not to the fact, as Dewey puts it, that I cannot endure to dwell upon them long enough to see just what they are. It is precisely by dwelling upon them that I have been forced to my present position. Nor will the patient reader find that I dismiss James's views with only deprecatory tags, though I do feel that his "piecemeal supernaturalism" seriously threatens all the values of rational life and enlightened civilization. And I do believe that the latter really need and are worth defending.

Appendix 5
The Aesthetic Emotion as Useful
By Allen Tate

The belief that man is perfectible would not have arisen in a society lacking the tradition of man's depravity. The birth of the later belief depended on the existence of the earlier one. Is poetry similarly dependent on science? Anthropologists assure us that once upon a time art and science, and more particularly poetry and science, were one. Even now, so they say, science is the proper element of poetry, systematized and made predictable. Whatever that means, until the end of the seventeenth century, poetry was as much an unquestioned member of the intellectual community as philosophy and mathematics. Thereupon, however, poetry began to lose ground before the spectacular triumphs of scientific method, and it has continued to lose ground ever since. I believe, indeed, that if poetry survives to-day, although so evidently an art with which one cannot "cash in," it is thanks to the theory that poetry is not only quite different from science, but is in its essence opposed to science and so must be let go its own way.

Yet to-day that theory is no longer very assured. An apt early statement in modern language of the modern position of poetry in the community is Shelley's *Defence of Poetry*. That is a landmark of criticism. With a power of synthesis vouchsafed to few minds, Shelley put in one sentence the problem poetry had to confront, when he said, "Our calculations have outrun conception." By "calculations" he meant science as it is known to-day—ideas susceptible to measurable demonstration; by "conception" he meant what we loosely call "intuition" or the perception of the value of "calculations" as human experience. Subsequent critics have not greatly improved upon the view expressed in that sen-

[First published in *This Quarter* 5 (December 1932): 292–303. For Dewey's unpublished reply, see this volume, pp. 330–34.]

tence. It embodies what is still our way of looking at science and poetry—and, in fact, at science and the arts—respectively. But whereas Shelley deemed it the privilege of "conception" to settle the degree of value to be placed upon "calculations" *qua* human experience, we constantly warn the artist, and more particularly the poet, that he must abandon metaphysical isolation and bow down to "calculations" if he wishes to preserve a position among us. For poetry, we say, is a kind of action; like everything else, it must "make good," and it can only "make good" according to a standard of action.

The suggestion here is a difficult one to fathom. I do not pretend to be able to fathom it. Indeed, the purpose of this essay is negative. It would not be my intention to set forth any principles of art, or of science, or of social action, even if I understood them. I want simply to ask the meaning of some statements made about art by Mr. John Dewey, our leading American philosopher. They are statements contained in his recent book *Philosophy and Civilization* and in that chapter of this book called "Affective Thought" (pp. 117–125).

Mr. Dewey justly deplores in the chapter in question that the poet should be at odds with our scientific society. Seeing that the arts tend to be banished from this society the while they cling to what appear in that society's eyes to be outworn feelings and attitudes, he thinks the remedy is to restore the arts to the living current of our life by giving the "conception" of art a meaning in terms of the modern world's "calculations." And he tries to effect this remedy. The notion prompting him is, like the suggestion I mentioned above, a difficult one to grasp. It might be the notion that poetry is to dictate to society. More likely, the notion that poetry must reflect the contemporary scientific and social action. I believe that, actually, Mr. Dewey's notion of the relation of the two is a compromise in behalf of neither science nor art, but in behalf of what he conceives to be human society. The general question I have to deal with is, then, this: If, as it seems to me, Mr. Dewey wishes to bring the arts closer to life solely on his own terms, are those terms acceptable?

He considers naturally enough—or he would not take up the matter—that art should be re-endowed with its former prestige. But the desideratum raises questions. How is the prestige to be recovered? Art is now off on an unsocial tangent, but can we be certain that by providing it with a deliberate programme of socialization we shall bring it back? And, further, what is it that has to be set right? If it is society, there is surely the danger that art will be destroyed in the process. On the other hand, I do not see how, if it is art which needs to be set right, it can be society that will put it right. Anyhow, the opinion seems to be that art is not to be adjusted to modern life on terms inherent in the work of art. It is the work of art which on the contrary will have to be changed to suit the scientific method, a method which in social life means the collective, the socially workable and "good."

But, assuming that there is a social science, this observes the individual person and the individual object only in so far as both share certain constant features with other individual persons and individual objects. The aim is to have a collective person and a collectively envisaged object. Hence, before one can give the "conception" of art a meaning in terms of the modern world's "calculations," as Mr. Dewey attempts to do, one has to ascertain if art is at all concerned with the collective person and the collectively envisaged object. We must find out if art can have as its specific function to decide upon the constant features of experience and to put them into practical form.

These things Mr. Dewey does not face. I shall try to show from his own words that he has accepted the function of art in society as having been historically only one of the things it may have been. Because art is, in all its variety, the supreme expression-form of a human society, he regards the value of art as lying in its being a manifestation of the collective impulse. To my mind, his justification of art is this—and it is a kind of would-be justification that makes art seem more futile than ever—that the desire for right social action should be the exclusive motive for writing poetry, painting pictures, composing sonatas, and sculpturing. He practically pictures the artist as saying, "Society is disorganized. Lo! I will unify it with my art." But it is very easy to realize that this is nonsense. For even if one grants that art may balance our minds or unify a particular mind beyond the moment during which that mind inspects a particular work of art; even if one grants the contention of Mr. I. A. Richards that poetry has the power of "ordering" our minds; one still has nothing to lead one to the conclusion that this supposed order, or ordering power, of art is tantamount to a social order.

Mr. Dewey's attitude to art may be interpreted in two ways. One may take it as being the view that art and action are related. Or it may be taken as a view having value for approaching works of art. In the latter case, it would be the attitude that art is action, that art has some bearing on action to the extent that it is a perception of the "qualitative whole" of an event. But then it would be a view reposing on a harmless tautology. For if you say, "Art is action," your words can only mean either that art is art or that action is action. In the former case, however, the attitude would be vague and dangerous. For then we should have to recognize that Mr. Dewey was trying to identify a particular artistic intention with a general feeling for social values, and the fact is that in the work of art these values defy definition. Their practical consequences, if they have any, cannot be charted and controlled. When the scientific formula H_2O is demonstrated, nothing is involved on the part of the individual scientist who demonstrates it. But the formula, "Art is socially valuable," cannot be demonstrated in that way. Indeed, it cannot be demonstrated at all. It can only be asserted in a given particular case. For the proof that art is socially valuable has nothing to do with the actual character of all works of art or of one work of art. The proof depends on some notion of the socially good which is never to be deduced from the character of art itself or of a particular work of art. And the individual artist, or any other individual, who declares that the socially valuable is so-and-so assumes a responsibility most people would hesitate to assume. Rousseau's *Émile* had no social value when it was first published. Since, it has influenced educational theory and practice, and forms of society have arisen indirectly as the result of the book which lead us to say vaguely that *Émile* has been made pragmatically good. Thus the only fixed social value assignable to *Émile* is that it is both socially valuable and socially negligible. At one time it was useless; at another time it has been useful.

It is the conception of art as a *general* form of action, and not as a realm of specific objects—pictures, poems, sonatas, buildings—that I find at the root of Mr. Dewey's aesthetics. He says, for example:

It then becomes possible to break down the traditional separation between scientific and intellectual systems and those of art, and also *to further the application of the principle of integration* to the relationship of those elements of culture which are so segregated in our present life—to science, art in its variety of forms, industry and business, religion, sport and morals (italics mine).

For this passage to be intelligible, we must understand the nature of the "principle of integration" it mentions. For that principle to be valid in Mr. Dewey's own Instrumentalism, it must be a *concrete* principle. It must account for the definite integration of certain concrete factors of social life. If the principle is to be applied through art, we must ask how the integrating art is to do is done. Possibly Mr. Dewey would say that art must be organically, practically, functionally, rooted in the central impulse of society. But that is merely to state the condition of its integration. Apparently it not only has to be integrated, but to do some integrating as well. And what one wants to know is how it can integrate. The point may be insisted upon by referring to Mr. Dewey's "faith in intelligence," a faith he expounds in that interesting book of his, *The Quest for Certainty*. Presumably intelligence too, just like art, is expected to integrate, and we may ask how it does so. For either intelligence does integrate individually and collectively, or the word "intelligence" is only a synonym for integration. The fact is that, much to the pleasure no doubt of the shades of Michelet, Taine, and Renan, and—who knows?—to the satisfaction of the Standard Oil Company as well, Mr. Dewey argues in this chapter "Affective Thought" I am considering that art and science are merely conventionally different modes of social adaptation among several really similar modes; and we are led to suppose that art-science-religion-industry-business-sport-morals is thought by him to integrate its own vast qualitative wholeness.

Now I turn to two other passages. The first is as follows:

The fact that this more subtle and complete integration [of painting] usually involves deformation or distortion of familiar forms—that is, conflicts with associations formed outside the realm of painting—accounts for the fact that they are greeted at first with disdainful criticism.

The other runs thus:

[Art] is such a deep and abiding experience of the nature of fully harmonized experience as sets a standard or forms a habit for all other experiences.

These two passages confront one with a puzzle. Take an instance of "associations formed outside the realm of painting"—in physics, say, or in any science. Since the associations of art are here in some sense special to art, the associations of physics, or of any other science, must be, at least in relation to painting, special also. How are two such kinds of special associations related? Mr. Dewey does not tell us. Nor does he tell us if each kind is valid. Throughout his career as a philosopher Mr. Dewey has developed the idea of social action proceeding on the basis of verified knowledge, knowledge that will collectively work, and this kind of knowledge, if it exists, is science. As we have seen, for Mr. Dewey art is only another kind of science, and since its associations are apparently special to its own realm, this raises the question whether these associations can benefit by a special form of verification. For unless art is verified, or verifiable, knowledge—and then its associations must in some way be verifiable—art cannot be only another kind of science.

I am driven to hark back to the principle of integration. It really seems that, although for Mr. Dewey's views it is necessary that art and science should somehow be the same, it is also necessary that they should be different in order that art may be, as he claims it is, the integrating principle effecting "a fully harmonized experience." I shall say nothing about the presence in the argument of a Pragmatist of the Idealistic unity-in-variety notion of aesthetic effect, although, of course, I might point out the lack of "fully harmonized experience" in a work of art called *Hamlet* or raise the problem whether there is in *Lycidas* any experience whatever. It is enough that we are as much in the dark as before concerning how the harmonized experience which Mr. Dewey declares art to be can promote harmony in individual persons or in the collective person of the State.

Mr. Dewey says that art "sets a standard or forms a habit for all other experiences." But he neglects to describe the kind of standard or habit that is thus set or formed. He can scarcely contend that the habit is the habit of looking at "life" as one looks at a painting. Since the Pragmatist is so fond of Occam's razor, it seems to me that he should admit the habit formed by literature to be merely the habit of reading. For my part, I frankly do not believe that the "associations" of art, while undoubtedly they do "affect" action, do more than trickle off minutely, unpredictably, and uncontrollably, into the total quality of society. For them to be controlled socially, Mr. Dewey would have to set up a censorship capable of successfully prescribing people's aesthetic associations in advance.

In this same chapter entitled "Affective Thought," Mr. Dewey says: "Integration in the object [i.e. the art object] permits and secures a corresponding integration of organic activities." This is pure dogma. "A new line," he continues, "is built up, formed on the basis of unalloyed aesthetic experiences." This leads me to wonder whither—if the experiences are, as he says, "unalloyed," i.e. pure of action and unique—the new line leads. Is it to the Ivory Tower? I wonder too if the "corresponding integration of organic activities" is similarly "unalloyed," for in that case it would surely be socially useless. The suspicion creeps over me that Mr. Dewey is actually seeking to get out of art some fixed, objective, and authoritative standard which will provide a transcendent sanction for a world which is otherwise entirely sheer action. But one does not see how, for Pragmatism, there could be such a standard. In any case, it is not to be allowed that a habit could be a valid standard. Mr. Dewey is indeed arguing in a maze of cross-purposes. He naturally desires content for his "faith in intelligence," and seems to have picked on art to help simply because nobody knows much about art. For the habits of art to be good the art must of course be good. As I said earlier, that leaves open the question of what is good art. It remains for Mr. Dewey to shoulder the responsibility of settling what is good art. Then, by "habit" he means, needless to say, "right habit" or "good social habit." But I fear that habits of that kind will only be integrated in society after Mr. Dewey has selected them for society. This being the task his argument calls for, it begins to look as if Mr. Dewey's integrating principle must be no other than Mr. Dewey himself and his "faith in intelligence" simply faith in Mr. Dewey.

I fall into such pleasantry because I fear that the public looks on Mr. Dewey as having settled the questions of what is his integrating principle and of what he means by "faith in intelligence."

How far, however, he is from having done so, one more passage
will help to make evident:

> . . . The statement of an objective criterion of value in
> paintings *set forth for the first time by Mr. Barnes* will make
> possible in time an adequate psychological, even physio-
> logical, analysis of aesthetic responses in spectators, so that
> the appreciation of paintings will no longer be a matter of
> private, absolute tastes and ipse dixits (italics mine).

Without inquiring how a private taste can be absolute, I confidently assert that neither Mr. Barnes—whom Mr. Dewey has
obviously read—nor Mr. I. A. Richards is the first to put forward the Utilitarian theory of art. Its fathers are Bentham and
Mill. No doubt Mr. Richards, in his *Principles of Literary Criticism*, is its ablest living defender. His belief that art, more particularly the art of poetry, may be in its power of "ordering" experience the means of saving civilization is on all fours with Mr.
Dewey's view that "integration in the object permits and secures
a corresponding integration of organic activities." On the theory, art appeals to and organizes the greatest number of desires
in the individual, and thereupon passes into the greatest happiness of the greatest number of persons. Now, it seems to me
that there is a reason for this queer revival of utilitarian aestheti-
cism, according to which art is the centre of life in virtue of its
supreme utility, and the reason is, I believe, more interesting than
the theory itself.

That reason is the decline of organized religion. Of this decline
philosophers are so frightened that they readily pick up as great
a "superstition" under another name.* Mr. Dewey's theory of
the integrative power of art attributes to art all the psychological
virtue of a religion, and he welcomes it as possessing that virtue
because thereupon, lacking all dogma, it is unaffected by the disadvantages now suffered by religion proper. Art has not been
battered to a pulp by the historical method. True, it has been dis-
credited by the laboratory, with which it cannot compete; but it
has no inconvenient politics, and it is still respectable enough to

---

*I suggest for the reader's consideration the kinship I find between Mr. Dewey's
"principle of integration" and "faith in intelligence" and Mr. Walter Lippmann's "scientific disinterestedness," as developed in the latter's *A Preface to
Morals*. What new and thrilling names our age has found for Jesus Christ!

be revived, especially if the philosopher who revives it can successfully allege that it has really been useful and scientific all the time. In short, I find that Mr. Dewey's *Philosophy and Civilization* makes of art a makeshift religion and that he puts it forward as such with the purpose of destroying it itself.

That sounds pretty strong. But let me explain. I have pointed out that Mr. Dewey's aesthetics are either a tautology or an attempt to reduce art to common features of experience which may be repeated and used in collective enterprise. Mr. Dewey protests at one moment that art is "different"—for that is his foundation of an at least momentary faith—only in the next moment to withdraw his protest. He withdraws it when he identifies art, science, and religion, as "satisfying the same fundamental needs," for to do that he describes them all as action. If the arts are to maintain no specific forms which are inviolable, and if they are to be valued solely for their practical consequences, we get the formula, "All art is action," and the converse—which is astonishing—that "All action is art." It is thus that art, art itself, is destroyed, at least in the mind of our leading American philosopher. For what Mr. Dewey is asking us to practise and enjoy is not art, or science or religion, or even business, sport, and morals. He is asking us to practise simply society. I leave the analysis of this Gargantuan proposal to those whom it may entertain.

In the domain of aesthetics, the conclusion to which one is led by the Instrumental Philosophy is that we should yield to an intellectual anarchy for the sake of a kind of collective enterprise which it neglects to define. Mr. Dewey's criterion for action is right habits based on verified knowledge—perhaps, also, the verified habits of art!—and the special form of this criterion is at once art and not-art, science and not-science. No doubt it is lamentable that our culture-forms, our methods and techniques, are not organically related. There can be no surprise at such a deficiency having worried William James's best pupil, Mr. Dewey. Yet, in seeking to remedy it, he reveals himself to be but a fake mystic. He would ignore the material of life, the concrete forms of the intelligence, in his desire to seize a mystical unity underlying them. In his case, however, this mystical unity is entirely his own. It lacks all objective content. One may grant to it the subjective content of the philosopher's prejudices and desires, and of his insight into the human spirit. But its having this still leaves it quite private. As such, it is an irresponsible abstraction.

Finally, it remains that Pragmatist aesthetics can be hoisted with their own petard. They are open to this objection, that, lacking the sense of aesthetic form in one of the chief kinds of action—art—they are not "pragmatic" enough.

Notes

These notes, keyed to the page and line number of the present edition, explain references to matters not found in standard sources.

84.25   President Morgan] Arthur E. Morgan was president of Antioch College in Yellow Springs, Ohio. Although the published source of this quotation ("The Curriculum for the College of Liberal Arts," *Rollins College Bulletin* 26 [February 1931]: 9–10) lists no author, Dewey was chairman of the conference and was thus aware of Morgan's statement in the report of the committee on the "Place of the Liberal Arts College in Education, and its Function." The statement is identified in the unpublished typed transcript in the Rollins Archives, "Proceedings, Curriculum Conference," 3 vols., Rollins College, Winter Park, Florida, January 19–24, 1931, 3:777–78.

118.10   Professor Miller] Herbert A. Miller, professor of sociology at the Ohio State University, was dismissed mainly because of his allegedly political statement in Bombay, India, on 12 March 1930, at a gathering of Hindus on the eve of Gandhi's "salt march." For a report on the AAUP investigation of the dismissal of Miller see "Academic Freedom and Tenure at the Ohio State University," *Bulletin of the American Association of University Professors* 17 (October 1931): 443–73.

124.6–24   I heard . . . cheering.] Dewey is referring to a debate on "Resolved: That Continuous Preparedness is Necessary for the United States" at Carnegie Hall on 8 February 1932, sponsored by the New History Society. Dewey presided at the debate by Rear Admiral Bradley A. Fiske and General Amos Alfred Fries for the affirmative and Rabbi Stephen S. Wise and John Haynes Holmes who argued for nonresistance and peace. Holmes was the unidentified speaker to whom Dewey referred. See "Militarists Meet Pacifists in Debate," *New York Times*, 9 February 1932, p. 4, and "Pastors Clash with Militarists in Arms Debate," *New York Herald Tribune*, 9 February 1932, p. 3.

149.7   Senator Norris] As national chairman of the League for Independent Political Action, Dewey urged Norris to withdraw from the Republican party and help form a new third party. See "Dewey Asks Norris to Lead New Party," *New York Times*, 26 December 1930, p. 1 [*Later Works* 5 : 444–46].

165.27   St. Paul decision] A decision by the United States Supreme Court, which avoided Interstate Commerce Commission regulation, to permit the reorganization by bankers of the Chicago, Milwaukee and St. Paul Railway Company. See "A Bad Omen for Railroad Consolidation," *New Republic* 65 (4 February 1931): 313–14.

371.1   Western Rate Advance Case] Although the reference to this case has not been emended in the text, Lane's report states that this case is popularly known as the "Western Advanced Rate Case." The previous paragraph, ending on 370.39, was probably the end of Dewey's letter to the ICC. The information on the specific cases was most likely supplied by Benjamin C. Marsh, executive secretary of the People's Lobby. See Franklin K. Lane, "In Re Investigation of Advances in Rates by Carriers in Western Trunk Line, Trans-Missouri, and Illinois Freight Committee Territories," *Interstate Commerce Commission Reports* 20 (1911): 307–99.

416.14   manor] Prior to Dewey's statement, Dr. James Harvey Robinson had commented on a student's wish to study the mediaeval manor as an aspect of the Middle Ages. See "Proceedings," 1 : 45.

Textual Apparatus

Index

Textual Notes

The following notes, keyed to the page and line numbers of the present edition, discuss readings adopted in the critical text, whether emendation or retention of copy-text readings where emendations might have been expected.

50.39–40   age. [¶] The] The single-sentence paragraph deleted at this point is repeated at 51.1–4 (Our . . . fields.). The first rather than second instance of the sentence was deleted on the basis of the reading at 60.38–61.2 in the expanded and extensively revised essay with the same title published in *Philosophy and Civilization*, this volume, pp. 53–63.

77.5   Breasted] Dewey must be referring to James Henry Breasted, professor of Egyptology and Oriental History at the University of Chicago. Breasted was a contemporary of Dewey and the other educators mentioned. This misspelling of the name can be attributed to misinterpretation of Dewey's handwriting or inadvertent mistyping of Breasted's name.

89.21-22   No prohibitory . . . containers.] Although "There are" should precede this incomplete sentence, Dewey's meaning can be understood. The document used for typesetting was probably hastily handwritten or typed by Dewey for the Inglis Lecture, and not polished for the printed version. Dewey wrote to Albert C. Barnes the week before the lecture that he had to give an educational lecture the next week and it was only about half done. [Dewey to Barnes, 3 March 1931, Joseph Ratner/John Dewey Papers, Special Collections, Morris Library, Southern Illinois University at Carbondale.]

183.27; 186.1, 23   states] The capitalization of "States" in the copy-text is attributed to *Scribner's Magazine*. It was not Dewey's usual practice to capitalize "states" in the context discussed in this article, and the lowercase form has been restored.

220.33   nationals] Article 16 of the Covenant of the League of Nations uses the word "nationals" to designate the people of the member nations.

333.10   renders] The verb "render" has been emended to "renders" because of Dewey's incomplete alteration of this sentence. Where the typescript had read "the above re-interpretation of my essays will render it," Dewey deleted "will," without altering "render."

Textual Commentary

Volume 6 of *The Later Works of John Dewey, 1925–1953*, comprises all Dewey's known writings for the years 1931 and 1932, except for Dewey's and James H. Tufts's 1932 *Ethics*, which is republished as volume 7 of the *Later Works*. Of the eighty-six items in volume 6, twenty-nine are essays—five were published separately as books or pamphlets, one appeared in the *Encyclopaedia of the Social Sciences*, twenty-two were published in various journals or bulletins, and one, Dewey's address to the National Association for the Advancement of Colored People, has not been previously published. The additional items are eleven book reviews and a review rejoinder; twelve miscellaneous pieces; twenty-five People's Lobby items; two interviews with Dewey; and six reports of statements and addresses.

Dewey's original typescripts are extant for three previously published items—the memorial essay "George Herbert Mead as I Knew Him," the introduction to Theodore T. Lafferty's *Studies in Philosophy*, and the letter "Vladeck and Laidler"—as well as Dewey's holograph manuscript for the *New Republic* review "College Sons—and Parents." In addition, Dewey's typescripts exist for the previously unpublished reply to Allen Tate, "What Is It All About?" and the People's Lobby item "Introduction [Unemployment Insurance]." According to the editorial principles and procedures followed in this edition, these documents necessarily serve as copy-text for these items.[1]

Only nine items in the present volume were republished during Dewey's lifetime: the essay on George Herbert Mead in the *University of Chicago Record* and as a memorial booklet; "The Collapse of a Romance" in the *New Republic Anthology, 1915–*

---

1. This principle is described by Fredson Bowers in "Textual Principles and Procedures," *The Later Works of John Dewey, 1925–1953*, ed. Jo Ann Boydston (Carbondale and Edwardsville: Southern Illinois University Press, 1984), 2: 407–18.

1935 (New York: Dodge Publishing Co., 1936); *American Education Past and Future* in *School and Society* 34 (31 October 1931): 579–84; "Vladeck and Laidler" in the *New York World Telegram*, 4 November 1932; and five in collections edited by Joseph Ratner with Dewey's cooperation and approval, but without his direct intervention—"Social Science and Social Control" and "Are Sanctions Necessary to International Organization? No" in *Intelligence in the Modern World: John Dewey's Philosophy* (New York: Modern Library, 1939) and "Monastery, Bargain Counter, or Laboratory in Education?" "Political Interference in Higher Education and Research," and "The Economic Situation: A Challenge to Education" in *Education Today* (New York: G. P. Putnam's Sons, 1940).

Although the existence of a single authoritative text for most of the items in this volume eliminates copy-text problems, comment on some of these can illuminate Dewey's writing habits and activities. The depressed state of the world economy, the events in the Far East, and the political campaigns influenced much of Dewey's writing during 1931 and 1932. During these years Dewey was active in several social and political organizations and contributed articles to their publications. He was national chairman of the League for Independent Political Action, which published the *News Bulletin of the League for Independent Political Action*; a vice-president of the League for Industrial Democracy, which published the *L.I.D. Monthly* and the *Unemployed*; and president of the People's Lobby, which published the *People's Lobby Bulletin*.

Despite Dewey's intense interest in social and political events, it was in his primary role as philosopher that he delivered the George Holmes Howison Lecture at the University of California, the Inglis Lecture on Secondary Education at Harvard University, and served also at Harvard during the spring of 1931 as the first appointee of the William James Lectureship. The series of ten William James Lectures were later published as *Art as Experience* in 1934.

Context and Thought

Dewey delivered *Context and Thought*, the 1930 George Holmes Howison Lecture, on 14 January 1931 at the

University of California at Berkeley; it was published in August in the University of California Publications in Philosophy, vol. 12, no. 3 (Berkeley: University of California Press, 1931), 203–24, which serves as copy-text for this essay.

T. V. Smith commented on the importance of *Context and Thought* in his 1932 review of Dewey's *Philosophy and Civilization*. Smith said that the book's underlying theme—that "pragmatism remains as it began more hospitable to idealism than to the newer realistic tendencies"—is "generalized best perhaps in . . . *Context and Thought*."[2]

Four WS (Works Source) emendations in this essay restore the spelling and capitalization of the original readings in quoted material. In addition, omissions of "in" in the phrase "in doubt" at 14.13 and of "s" in "beliefs" at 19.9, probably made in the process of composition, have been corrected in the text.

George Herbert Mead as I Knew Him

When George Herbert Mead died on 27 April 1931, Dewey was in Cambridge, Massachusetts, as the first William James lecturer at Harvard University. Dewey was informed of Mead's death that same day and wrote a short note to Benjamin Marsh: "My friend Mead has died suddenly in Chicago & I am going out there today—back next Monday the 4th."[3]

John Dewey, Edward Scribner Ames, and James H. Tufts delivered addresses at the funeral service in the Joseph Bond Chapel in Chicago on 30 April 1931. Ames spoke of the general facts of Mead's illness and Mead's life as his neighbors and university co-workers knew him. Dewey followed with his address. Tufts then offered more personal views of Mead.[4]

Dewey returned to Harvard immediately after the service.[5] Upon his return, he found a request for his address from Wendell

2. Smith, *Journal of Philosophy* 29 (21 July 1932): 412.
3. Dewey to Marsh, 27 April 1931, Benjamin C. Marsh Papers, Library of Congress, Washington, D.C. Marsh, with whom Dewey had been corresponding regarding articles for the *People's Lobby Bulletin*, was the executive secretary of the People's Lobby.
4. Mary H. Webster, "Mr. Mead's Funeral." Typescript, George Herbert Mead Papers Addenda, University of Chicago Archives, University of Chicago.
5. Irene Tufts Mead to Anne Sharpe, 21 February 1983, Center for Dewey Studies, Southern Illinois University at Carbondale.

T. Bush, co-editor of the *Journal of Philosophy*. Dewey wrote immediately to Ames, chairman of the philosophy department at the University of Chicago: "The enclosed from Bush is self explanatory Perhaps you could send him a copy of the paper I left with you. I'll write him that he can edit it & leave out the more personal parts if he wishes."[6]

Dewey's memorial address was first published by Bush in the *Journal of Philosophy* 28 (4 June 1931): 309–14 (JP), with the title "George Herbert Mead." A footnote to the JP article indicated that "This article is the greater part of what Professor Dewey said at the funeral of Professor Mead. . . ." The entire address was first published in the *University of Chicago Record* 17 (July 1931): 173–77 (UCR), with the title "George Herbert Mead as I Knew Him" apparently supplied by Ames. The full title was not used by JP, probably because of the less personal nature of the address as printed there.

The addresses of Dewey, Ames, and Tufts, with the addition of a biographical essay by Henry Castle Mead, were published in a memorial booklet (B) during the summer of 1931. The small (5" × 6⅞"), thirty-nine-page booklet has "George Herbert Mead" stamped on the off-white, deckle-edged cover, is quarter-folded, and is bound with a white braided-cord bow.[7]

Dewey's rough typescript (TS), with many holograph revisions, had been left with Ames after Mead's funeral, as indicated in Dewey's letter. The title and author, presumably written by Ames, as the handwriting matches that on other Ames documents, appear in ink at the top of the first page of the TS.[8] TS and a retyped copy (TS²) are in the George Herbert Mead Papers Addenda, Box 1, Folder 6, University of Chicago Archives. TS, which stands in the closest relation to the author's intentions, serves as copy-text for this essay.[9] Only when evidence of the author's subsequent alterations exists can the printed version exceed the manuscript or typescript in authority. The four addi-

6. Dewey to Ames, 4 May 1931, Edward Scribner Ames Papers, Special Collections, Morris Library, Southern Illinois University at Carbondale.
7. James H. Tufts Papers, Special Collections, Morris Library, Southern Illinois University at Carbondale.
8. For example, the typescript for Ames's memorial address in the George Herbert Mead Papers Addenda, University of Chicago Archives, University of Chicago.
9. See Bowers, "Textual Principles and Procedures."

tional texts were therefore examined to determine the extent of Dewey's alteration of his original address. Collation of JP, UCR, TS², and B with TS shows clearly that Dewey himself made no further changes in this address, and that the variations among the four other extant documents result from typists', editors', or compositors' error or intervention. Thus, on the evidence described below, the publications of Dewey's address in JP, UCR, and B have no authority.

A comparison of the printed texts (JP, UCR, B) with TS suggests that JP and UCR were typeset from a retyped original and carbon copy that Ames had prepared and sent to JP and UCR after Dewey wrote to him regarding Bush's request. The nature of the agreement in several substantive readings that appear only in JP and UCR substantiates the existence of such a retyped document and its carbon, both now lost, here designated as TS¹. The possibility that such internal substantive agreement could result from UCR having been set from the printed JP copy is rejected because JP eliminated the first two paragraphs and the last half of the final paragraph (28.16–24) that do appear in TS. As the material deleted by JP appears in UCR, UCR could not have used JP as setting copy.

The hypothesis of a lost TS¹ and its carbon that served as printer's copy for both JP and UCR is further substantiated by the concurrence of JP and UCR in thirteen accidentals, all instances of punctuation, none of which appears in the extant TS. Further, at 23.17 both JP and UCR printed "or" rather than "nor" and at 24.27 both read "time" rather than "period." The readings "nor" and "period" appear in all other versions. Dewey's TS reads "Every one who knew him at all philosophically is aware . . ." at 27.8–9. In ink Dewey wrote an "s" over the "m" in "him," restored it to "him" again, and circled "philosophically," using a guideline and caret to show that it should follow "him." Both JP and UCR have "him philosophically," probably reflecting the wording of the lost TS¹.

Ames apparently also had a second typescript (TS²) made from Dewey's original TS for use as setting copy for the memorial booklet (B). TS² has the title and author's name typewritten at the top; printed in an unknown hand across the top of TS² are the words: "Printed in the Mead Memorial Service." TS² incorporates Dewey's own alterations of his TS, and corrects twenty-three typographical errors apparently overlooked by Dewey, although it repeats three TS typographical errors—"collegues" at 25.16, "encyclepedic" at 25.32, and "spontanously" at 26.26.

TS² and B concur in three substantive readings that do not appear in TS, the conjectured TS¹, JP, or UCR. At 25.15–16, TS reads "was his students"—the reading that appears in JP and UCR. Examination of TS indicates that "only" was interlined, not in Dewey's hand, resulting in the reading "was only his students" in both TS² and B. At 27.9 Dewey had made the alteration in TS that led to the reading "him philosophically" in JP and UCR, described above. In TS² it appears that the typist had some difficulty deciphering the change: the incomplete typing of "his philosophically" ("philosophic . . .") was erased and changed to "philosophy," which agrees with the typist's interpretation of the "him/his" alteration. The resulting reading of "his philosophy" in TS² is also that of B. At 27.12, TS, JP, and UCR concur in the wording "this interest"; in TS² the "t" in "this" was absent, probably a typographical error, and the reading "his interest" thus appears in B.

The punctuation in TS² and B varies from that of all the other documents at 23.22, 25.5, and 26.10. In addition, B varies from both TS and TS² in one accidental and four substantives, all of which can be attributed to the editor or compositor of B: at 22.13 a comma was added after "natures"; at 23.21 "of" was deleted in the phrase "or of the"; at 27.6 "it" was changed to "them"; at 27.12 "am" was changed to "was"; and at 27.35 "its" was changed to "their."

Variants in the hypothetical TS¹ and the extant TS² are not included in the historical collation of this essay. However, JP and UCR are credited in the Emendations List as the first appearance in print for thirty corrections in TS that would have been made editorially for this volume. Twenty-four of these emendations correct typographical errors in TS. Of the remaining six, one corrects the verb phrase at 26.8 from "has known" to "has been known"; one expands the ampersand at 26.13; three supply missing periods to the abbreviation "Mr." at 26.18, 27.20, and 27.30; and one corrects the alteration of "foregoing" to "foregoe" to "forego" at 27.8.

The present edition omits five subheads that appeared in UCR at 22.22+, 23.40+, 24.37+, 25.28+, and 27.3+.

Dewey's alterations in his typescript for this essay appear in the present volume in "Alterations in 'George Herbert Mead as I Knew Him.'"

Science and Society

Two essays by Dewey, both entitled "Science and Society," are included in this volume. On 9 June 1931 Dewey delivered the commencement address entitled "Science and Society" at Lehigh University. His address was published in the *Lehigh Alumni Bulletin* 18 (July 1931): 6–7. The following fall, a chapter with the same title was published in *Philosophy and Civilization* (New York: Minton, Balch and Co., 1931), pp. 318–30. Although *Philosophy and Civilization* republished seventeen essays written by Dewey over the years from as early as 1896, Dewey's introductory note states that "the final essay on *Science and Society* has not appeared in print before."[10]

Some points Dewey made in his commencement address are incorporated in his *Philosophy and Civilization* essay. However, the essay is expanded and rewritten to the extent that it cannot be considered a "later" version of the commencement address, and therefore appears separately in this volume.

The emendations in "Science and Society [Address]" correct "men's" at 50.24 and "régime" at 51.15, and delete a single-sentence paragraph at 50.39–40 that is repeated at 51.1–4. There were no emendations in "Science and Society [*Philosophy and Civilization*]."

Social Science and Social Control

Dewey's essay "Social Science and Social Control," *New Republic* 67 (29 July 1931): 276–77, emphasizes the need for "social planning and social control," which Dewey attributed to Senator George W. Norris in a letter published in the *New York Times*, 26 December 1930 (*Later Works* 5:444–46). Dewey also commented on this need in his speech "'The Irrepressible

10. "Introductory Note," *Philosophy and Civilization*, p. v.

Conflict'" (this volume, pp. 149–52). In August, Dewey traveled to Vienna upon learning of his granddaughter's death. After his return he received a letter of condolence from Max Otto commenting on the *New Republic* article:

> I want also to say a word, which has been on my mind since the summer, about your powerful article, "Social Science and Social Control", in the New Republic. I was much encouraged by it. The statement is splendid and I do not see how the position made so clear by you can be refuted. And you open up a fine prospect, full of suggestions for those who are puzzled about the use of experimental method in the social science field. Young men here, at work in that field, who have felt themselves hard pressed by their colleagues' insistence upon "unreasoning devotion to physical science as a model", have been much cheered by reading your paper.[11]

The article was later included in *Intelligence in the Modern World: John Dewey's Philosophy*, edited by Joseph Ratner (New York: Modern Library, 1939), pp. 949–54.

The Way Out of Educational Confusion

While Dewey was giving a series of ten lectures at Harvard University during the spring of 1931 as the first appointee of the William James Lectureship, he delivered at least four additional talks at Harvard, one being the Inglis Lecture on Secondary Education on Wednesday, 11 March 1931. A newspaper notice for the lecture listed the topic as "Educational Confusion and Conflict,"[12] but it was published as *The Way Out of Educational Confusion* (Cambridge, Mass.: Harvard University Press, 1931).

This seventh Inglis Lecture was favorably reviewed in a number of publications. Philip W. L. Cox, a professor of education at New York University, summarized educators' reception of Dewey's address: "American education stands to gain confidence

11. Otto to Dewey, 10 October 1931, Max C. Otto Papers, State Historical Society of Wisconsin, Madison, Wis.
12. "Events Tonight," *Christian Science Monitor*, 11 March 1931, p. 3.

in its emerging reorientation from just such restatements of the challenging thesis with which Dewey's name is associated. Hence, all progressives must be grateful to him and to the Inglis lectureship sponsors for this book." [13]

American Education Past and Future

The National Advisory Council on Radio in Education was organized in 1930 "to further the art of radio broadcasting in American education." [14] Dewey's address, "American Education Past and Future," the second of the "Men of America" radio lectures sponsored by the NACRE, was broadcast on Sunday, 25 October 1931, at seven o'clock over WEAF in New York City and other stations of the National Broadcasting Company. [15]
The first publication of the address as a sixteen-page pamphlet by the University of Chicago Press in October 1931 serves as copy-text for this article. The address was also published in *School and Society* 34 (31 October 1931): 579–84 (SS), with the title "Some Aspects of Modern Education." The amount of text quoted in the *New York Herald Tribune* and its publication in *School and Society* six days after Dewey's broadcast indicate that the NACRE must have distributed the printed pamphlets prior to the broadcast.
David Snedden, professor at Columbia University Teachers College, discussed at length Dewey's address as published in SS.

13. Cox, *Junior-Senior High School Clearing House* 6 (January 1932): 312. Dewey's essay was also reviewed in: *Boston Evening Transcript*, 18 July 1931, Book section; *Cambridge Review* 53 (1932): 193 (K. B.); *Educational Outlook* 6 (1932): 250; *High Points* 15 (January 1933): 86–87 (A. H. Lass); *Junior-Senior High School Clearing House* 7 (October 1932): 127 (Philip W. L. Cox); *New York Times Book Review*, 31 May 1931, p. 28; *School and Society* 34 (7 November 1931): 640–41 (William McAndrew); *School Review* 40 (January 1932): 67–68 (Henry C. Morrison); and *Virginia Teacher* 14 (1933): 62–63 (W. J. Gifford).
14. *American Education Past and Future* (Chicago: University of Chicago Press, 1931), p. 2. For more information on the NACRE see Felix Morley, ed., *Aspects of the Depression* (Chicago: University of Chicago Press, 1932).
15. Newspapers discussed the address the following day. See "Dewey Sees Need for New Education," *New York Times*, 26 October 1931, p. 19; and "Dewey Asserts Education Must Aid Social Spirit," *New York Herald Tribune*, 26 October 1931, p. 11.

He says that Dewey has "very cogently stated the conditions which give rise to large proportions of the baffling problems of present-day American public and private educations."[16]

Monastery, Bargain Counter, or Laboratory in Education?

In March 1922 a series of addresses at Central High School, Philadelphia, had been made possible by a bequest of James G. Barnwell in honor of his mother, Mary Gaston Barnwell. So that the lectures could reach all alumni, the Mary Gaston Barnwell Foundation also authorized the printing of the text in bulletin form.[17]

Dewey delivered the thirty-sixth Barnwell Address on Thursday, 4 February 1932. Dewey's "Monastery, Bargain Counter, or Laboratory in Education?" was first published in the *Barnwell Bulletin* 9 (February 1932): 51–62. It was later published in the second volume of *The Barnwell Addresses*, which contained the texts of twenty-four addresses from 1931 to 1936 (*The Barnwell Addresses*, vol. 2, 1931–1936, ed. John Louis Haney [Philadelphia: Central High School, 1937], pp. 55–66). The texts of the *Bulletin* and the *Addresses* were printed from the same plates, with only the page numbers changed for the later publication. Dewey's address was also included in the collection of essays *Education Today*, edited by Joseph Ratner (New York: G. P. Putnam's Sons, 1940): 230–43.

Dewey Describes Child's New World

President Hoover called the White House Conference on Child Health and Protection "to study the present status of the health and well-being of the children of the United States and its possessions; to report what is being done; to recommend what

16. Snedden, "Directive Aims in Education," *School and Society* 34 (5 December 1931): 745–48.
17. John Louis Haney, ed., "Introduction," *The Barnwell Addresses*, vol. 2, 1931–1936 (Philadelphia: Central High School, 1937): xi–xvi.

ought to be done and how to do it."[18] This conference in Washington, D.C., 19–22 November 1930, was attended by 3,000 leaders in the medical, educational, and social welfare fields.

Dewey's comments and concerns regarding the White House Conference were published in the February-March *American Teacher* ("The Schools and the White House Conference" [this volume, pp. 131–36]). The following month, Dewey's article "Dewey Describes Child's New World," published in the *New York Times*, 10 April 1932, Education section, served as a general introduction to five articles by other authors in succeeding weeks. An editorial headnote to Dewey's article, not included here with the essay, explains:

> Not merely has kaleidoscopic change radically altered the environment of children; so many new possibilities have opened for influencing their fortunes that many a parent feels hopelessly at sea. The White House Conference on Child Health and Protection, called by President Hoover, drew in bold outlines in the Children's Charter the nation's pledges to its youth. Some leading thinkers on the problems have now interpreted the points it made in terms of daily experience.[19]

The nineteen points of the Children's Charter embodied the main recommendations of the various conference committees.[20]

The *New York Times* appended three explanatory subtitles to Dewey's title and inserted five subheads in the text, all of which have been omitted in the present edition. The subheads omitted were "Life Outside the Home" at 137.28+; "The Intellectual Revolution" at 138.39+; "Health Becomes a Duty" at 139.34+;

18. "Foreword," *White House Conference, 1930* (New York: Century Co., 1931), p. v.
19. *New York Times*, 10 April 1932, Education section. The five additional articles and the points of the Children's Charter considered were "Safeguarding a Child's Personality" (II), by William Heard Kilpatrick, 17 April 1932; "Preparing the Child for Citizenship" (XI), by Mrs. Franklin D. Roosevelt, 24 April 1932; "New Goals in Training for Safety" (XII), by Herbert J. Stack (chairman of the secondary school committee of the National Safety Council), 8 May 1932; "When a Child Runs Afoul of the Law" (XIV), by Miriam Van Waters (referee of the Los Angeles Juvenile Court), 15 May 1932; and "The Physical Risks in Child Labor" (XVI), by Alice Hamilton (Harvard School of Public Safety), 22 May 1932.
20. For the complete charter, see "The Children's Charter," *White House Conference, 1930*, pp. 46–48.

"Guidance in a Scientific Era" at 140.21+; and "Where Sentiment Enters" at 141.4+.

League for Independent Political Action

Seven items, distributed under Essays, Miscellany, and Interviews and Reports of Statements and Addresses, stem from Dewey's affiliation with the League for Independent Political Action (LIPA), which was organized after the 1928 presidential election by a group of Progressives and Socialists, whose aim was to help build a new party on the principle of increasing social control.[21] In 1929 Dewey was elected the first chairman of the LIPA executive committee.[22] The LIPA's official publication, the *News Bulletin of the League for Independent Political Action*, was issued bi-monthly except during July and August. The first number was published in June 1930. The *News Bulletin* continued as an independent publication until it was included in the newly formed periodical *Common Sense* in April 1933.[23]

LIPA: "THE IRREPRESSIBLE CONFLICT"

Dewey's December 1930 letter to Senator George W. Norris asking him to renounce both existing political parties and help create a new party (*Later Works* 5:444–46) prompted Salmon O. Levinson to write Dewey: "I wish you would send me a copy of your remarkable letter to Sen. Norris. I admire it perhaps more than I approve it, but I enjoy literary works of art at any rate."[24] "'The Irrepressible Conflict,'" *News Bulletin of the*

21. *The American Labor Year Book, 1931* (New York: Rand School Press, 1931), pp. 156–57.
22. The 8 September 1929 announcement of the formation of the LIPA, with Dewey as chairman, was reported in "Liberals Here Plan an Opposition Party; Prof. Dewey Heads National Organizing Group," *New York Times*, 9 September 1929, p. 1.
23. *Common Sense* began publication on 5 December 1932, with Selden Rodman and Alfred M. Bingham as editors. The *News Bulletin* as published in *Common Sense*, beginning in April 1933, retained the same identifying masthead as the earlier publication.
24. Levinson to Dewey, 31 December 1930, Salmon O. Levinson Papers, Box 16, Folder 4, Department of Special Collections, University of Chicago Library, University of Chicago.

League for Independent Political Action 1 (January 1931): 4–5 (this volume, pp. 149–52), is from Dewey's address before the New History Society in New York City on 30 December 1930, which comments on his correspondence with Norris. The large audience of approximately two thousand people attests to the great interest in the development of a third party at that time.[25]

LIPA: A STATEMENT BY THE EXECUTIVE COMMITTEE

"A Statement by the Executive Committee," *News Bulletin of the League for Independent Political Action* 1 (February 1931): 1 (this volume, pp. 436–37), although not signed by Dewey, is attributed to Dewey as chairman of the committee, as its purpose was "to correct some misunderstandings which have arisen through erroneous interpretations" (p. 436) of Dewey's letter to Senator Norris.

LIPA: A THIRD PARTY

Four LIPA items in this volume are directly related to the organization's goal of developing a third party. "A Third Party Program," *New Republic* 70 (24 February 1932): 48–49 (this volume, pp. 324–25), was a letter to the editor on behalf of the LIPA, thanking the *New Republic* for its generous account of the LIPA program for the 1932 campaign.[26] *Democracy Joins the Unemployed* (this volume, pp. 239–45) was a LIPA pamphlet publishing Dewey's 9 July 1932 address at the third annual conference of the LIPA in Cleveland, Ohio. Dewey's article "Prospects for a Third Party," *New Republic* 71 (27 July 1932): 278–80 (this volume, pp. 246–52), analyzed the results of that Cleveland conference, which was given generous coverage in the press as evidenced by Dewey's letter to Howard Y. Williams, the executive secretary of the LIPA: "We certainly got fine publicity. I was glad to see it scattered so widely. . . . I hope the notices brought

---

25. "Senate Insurgents Afraid Says Dewey," *New York Times*, 31 December 1930, p. 3.
26. Dewey's letter refers to the article "A Third Party Platform," *New Republic* 69 (10 February 1932): 335–36.

you in a lot of new members."²⁷ "After the Election—What?" *News Bulletin of the League for Independent Political Action* 1 (November–December 1932): 1–2 (this volume, pp. 253–55), written after the 1932 presidential election, urged the continuation of progress toward a new political alignment.

LIPA: VLADECK AND LAIDLER

On 3 November, the Thursday before the November 1932 election, the *New York Herald Tribune* published a letter from Dewey (this volume, p. 326) endorsing the Socialist congressional candidates Baruch Charney Vladeck and Harry W. Laidler. Vladeck and Laidler were on the executive committee for the LIPA, and Laidler was also an executive director of the League for Industrial Democracy. On the next day, the letter also appeared in the *New York World Telegram* (4 November 1932) with the title "Great Opportunity for Brooklyn Voters." An editorial in the *New York Times* also commented on, and quoted from, Dewey's letter.²⁸ Dewey had sent a typescript for this letter to Howard Y. Williams with a handwritten note on the upper right corner: "send N.Y.C. and Bklyn papers."²⁹ Williams apparently retyped the letter, distributing copies to the three New York newspapers mentioned.

Copy-text for this item is Dewey's typewritten letter in the Howard Y. Williams Papers. When Williams retyped the letter, he probably expanded Dewey's "Pres." at 326.6 and "Gov." at 326.8, capitalized "Socialist" at 326.11, lowercased "districts" at 326.19, and addressed the letter to each newspaper rather than using Dewey's general "Editor &c" at 326.2. The accidentals of the typescript have been followed except for the addition of commas following "independent" at 326.15, "Laidler" at 326.17, and "Districts" at 326.18, and a period following "Messrs." at 326.17. Dewey's alterations in the typescript appear in this volume in "Alterations in 'Vladeck and Laidler.'"

---

27. Dewey to Williams, 29 July 1932, Howard Y. Williams Papers, Minnesota Historical Society, St. Paul, Minn. For reports on the conference, see *New Republic* 71 (22 June 1932): 137; and Robert Morss Lovett, "Progressives at Cleveland," *New Republic* 71 (20 July 1932): 258–59.
28. "Socialist Candidates," *New York Times*, 4 November 1932, p. 18.
29. Dewey to Williams, 1 November 1932, Williams Papers.

The Jobless—A Job for All of Us

Dewey's article "The Jobless—A Job for All of Us" appeared in February 1931 in the second issue of the *Unemployed*, a publication initiated by the League for Industrial Democracy, of which Dewey was a vice-president, to publicize the nation's alarming economic condition.[30] The *Unemployed* had a short life, from 1930 to 1932, and apparently was offered only through street sales.[31] The first issue sold over 250,000 copies and "through the generosity of contributors . . . sent free 9,000 copies of the magazine to members, professors of economics and sociology, members of Congress, ministers, college libraries, and editors of college newspapers."[32]

The Need for a New Party

A lengthy *New Republic* editorial entitled "The Need for a New Party" appeared in the 7 January 1931 issue. The author cited Dewey's December 1930 invitation to Senator Norris to leave the Republican party and help form a new party (*Later Works* 5:444–46), but reasoned that "the practical difficulties in the way of new national parties are great, and perhaps cannot be overcome at this time. Yet a historical era in our national life appears to be opening."[33]

Dewey's four-part discussion, also entitled "The Need for a New Party," appeared in four consecutive issues of volume 66 of the *New Republic*: "The Present Crisis" (18 March, pp. 115–17); "The Breakdown of the Old Order" (25 March, pp. 150–52); "Who Might Make a New Party?" (1 April, pp. 177–79);

30. Alex Baskin, "The *Unemployed* and the Great Depression: The History of an Idea and a Journal," *Unemployed* (New York: Archives of Social History, 1975), pp. 1–10. The ten-cent magazine was supplied to the unemployed vendors at five cents a copy, which covered only printing costs. A statement on the magazine's masthead explains: "All contributions, articles and drawings, as well as editorial services, have been given without charge. No profit or income accrues to any individuals or organizations, except the unemployed persons who sell the magazine."
31. Baskin, "The *Unemployed*," p. 10.
32. *The American Labor Year Book, 1931*, p. 230, and "Notes of the L.I.D. at Work," *L.I.D. Monthly* 9 (February 1931): 8, 12.
33. *New Republic* 65 (7 January 1931): 203–5.

and "Policies for a New Party" (8 April, pp. 202–5). The *New Republic* publication of these articles serves as copy-text for the present edition. Dewey's articles were introduced by an editorial in the 18 March *New Republic*, which concluded that "as yet the sentiment for a new party, however strong and significant it is, consists of little more than an undefined recognition that great changes are essential. The first task is to define the recognition, to specify the changes, to give direction to the sentiment of dissatisfaction."[34]

Following the publication of his second article in the 25 March *New Republic*, Dewey wrote to Joseph Ratner:

> What you say about thinking in terms of the political instrument is of course sound. But our industrial life is so dam complicated, its not a question of starting from scratch—but I wont repeat my next N R article. Geo Soule [*New Republic* editor] disapproved my article as I had it first written because I hadnt brought in planning for stabilization etc; so I tucked in the last paragraphs—not but what I believe them. But I think Im a better political judge than Soule is, tho he is a much better economist. You cant make planning a political issue, not yet, but you can start things politically which will require planning as the mechanism of execution.[35]

The 5 April *New York Times* commented editorially on Dewey's four *New Republic* articles: "The last article he seeks to make constructive. Against the background of the two existing parties, which he describes as broken and useless political instruments, he sets up a new party with a new issue. This is the most significant, though perhaps not the most surprising, part of what he has been writing."[36]

Peace—by Pact or Covenant?

"Peace—by Pact or Covenant?" was Dewey's first published statement on peace and war since 1928. Dewey and

34. "Program Making vs. Power Politics," *New Republic* 66 (18 March 1931): 111–13.
35. Dewey to Ratner, 27 March 1931, Joseph Ratner/John Dewey Papers, Special Collections, Morris Library, Southern Illinois University at Carbondale.
36. "Issues and Leaders," *New York Times*, 5 April 1931, sec. 3, p. 1.

Salmon O. Levinson, the author of the outlawry of war idea and a long-time friend of Dewey's, exchanged several letters discussing the ideas in this article. On 1 March 1932 Dewey wrote to Levinson:

> Ive been thinking about you a lot in connection with the Japanese invasion. I was glad to get your reprint from the Christian Century; it ought to be pushed—your plan I mean. I thought I saw signs of your influence in Stimson's letter to Borah. I suppose you saw the N R editorial on Boycott meaning War—I doubt if they are right in case of a general boycott; Japan couldnt fight the world. But they were undoubtedly right about tieing it up with article 16 of the League Covenant. What I regretted very much was that they didnt indicate the importance, as the alternative, of tieing up the present situation with the Paris Pact. I am trying to get my thoughts organized for an essay in that direction myself; if it comes off, of course Ill send you a carbon.[37]

In the same letter Dewey expressed his belief that

> at present the Peace Pact and the League business are more or less neutralizing each other as I see it. I always felt there was some danger that the Paris Pact was premature, being too much of an official diplomatic act without enough previous popular education, but now is the time probably to start something that will give a popular education and take the Pact out of the category of paper official documents.

"Peace—by Pact or Covenant?" was published in the *New Republic* 70 (23 March 1932): 145–47, quoting from both Levinson's *Christian Century* article and Henry Stimson's letter to William Borah.[38]

According to a letter from Levinson to Dewey on 5 March, Dewey was scheduled to write on "'Outlawry of War re League, the Pact of Paris, and the Far Eastern Situation,'" which Levinson got "from a letter from Bliven, received yesterday." After a lengthy

37. Dewey to Levinson, 1 March 1932, Levinson Papers, Box 16, Folder 5. See also "Can Japan Be Stopped?" *New Republic* 69 (10 February 1932): 334–35.
38. See S. O. Levinson, "Disarmament, Manchuria and the Pact," *Christian Century* 49 (3 February 1932): 149–50; "Text of Secretary Stimson's Note," *New York Times*, 8 January 1932; and "Text of Stimson's Letter on Our Policy in China," *New York Times*, 25 February 1932.

discussion of the world political situation, Levinson added, "If you have not finished your article for the N.R. I wish you would vindicate, as you may have already done, the entire philosophy of the outlawry of war school."[39] Dewey replied on 8 March that he had had

> to sandwich the N R article in between a lot of other things at odd moments and it is hastily written, and so poorly. But I felt that time was important and didnt want to hold it up too long to improve it. My object is just to focus attention again upon the Outlawry idea in this crisis.[40]

After Levinson received Dewey's published article he wrote to Dewey: "Thanks for the N.R. Your article continues to impress me as powerfully as ever, even with its changed title."[41]

Are Sanctions Necessary to International Organization? No

One of three actions urged by Dewey in "Peace—by Pact or Covenant?" was "that the force clauses of the League of Nations Covenant be abrogated so as to bring the Covenant into agreement with the Pact." Shortly after the publication of "Peace —by Pact or Covenant?" James G. McDonald, chairman of the Foreign Policy Association, asked Dewey to defend his position more fully:

> In the light of recent events in the Orient, many of us are coming to believe that the whole basis of international organization should be reconsidered. In fact, you brought out this need very clearly in your recent article in the NEW RE-PUBLIC. The Foreign Policy Association is eager to publish a discussion, particularly of the question of sanctions, representing both points of view. Mr. Buell [research director, Foreign Policy Association], who I understand has had some correspondence with you on the matter, is already preparing a paper which argues that sanctions are necessary if we are

39. Levinson to Dewey, 5 March 1932, Levinson Papers, Box 16, Folder 5.
40. Dewey to Levinson, 8 March 1932, Levinson Papers, Box 16, Folder 5.
41. Levinson to Dewey, 22 March 1932, Levinson Papers, Box 16, Folder 5.

to have a successful international organization. I am writing to inquire whether there is any possibility that you would be able to elaborate your remarks in your recent NEW RE-PUBLIC article for the purpose of answering Mr. Buell's argument.

Unfortunately, because of the critical state of our budget, we are unable to offer any stipend for such an article, but we would be able to give this discussion the widest possible publicity. If you could be induced to participate in it, we are sure you would make a notable contribution to the cause of international peace.[42]

Dewey replied that he appreciated the importance of the topic and being asked to write upon it, saying that the question of payment did not enter in. However, Dewey postponed giving a positive answer to McDonald until he could consult with Levinson:

My views on the subject are of course only a reflection of what he [Levinson] has already urged, and he has the material much more completely at command than have I. I feel therefore that he is the one to write the article and in any case I couldnt do it without having consulted him. I take it that what you want is an authoritative exposition of the non-sanctions point of view, and Mr Levinson is the person to give it.[43]

On that same day Dewey wrote to Levinson, enclosing a carbon of his letter to McDonald, and added his further reservation about writing the article:

There is one other specific point as to why I am not the person to do it. I dont keep material on hand nor references to material. I am confident that one point which should be made is the impracticability of Buell's scheme in any important matter, and that evidence can be given that the great powers, some or all as the case may have been in different matters, have consistently drawn back before the idea; only the American devotees of the League have ever taken the idea of applying sanctions seriously; the Europeans are much

---

42. McDonald to Dewey, 5 April 1932, Levinson Papers, Box 16, Folder 5.
43. Dewey to McDonald, 6 April 1932, Levinson Papers, Box 16, Folder 5.

more realistic. But I havent the actual material or references on hand to cite.[44]

But Levinson replied: "I am most anxious for you to write the article, mainly because your name carries such tremendous weight as against the others that you will be doing an enormous service." Levinson wrote that he was still recuperating from ill health and would "consider it a personal favor if you will write the article for the Foreign Policy Association."[45]

Dewey sent a short note back to Levinson saying he did not wish to add to Levinson's burdens and implied that he would write the article. He informed Levinson that "McDonald spoke of 'replying' to Raymond Leslie Buell so I am in hopes they will submit his article first."[46] During the weeks that followed, Dewey and Levinson exchanged a number of letters regarding the response to Buell—Dewey seeking information and criticism and Levinson offering suggestions and praise.

Dewey proceeded immediately to write an outline for the article. He sent Levinson a copy with a request for assistance on two points: "the cases & causes of refusal of European nations to apply sanctions and how fatal it would be to peaceful relations among them to try to do so. Im sending another copy to Buell himself. . . . We agreed to exchange documents before final versions were made."[47] Levinson replied with four pages of ideas for Dewey to consider, commenting, "There is so much meat in your three pages that I look hungrily forward to seeing it in shape."[48] Dewey sent about one-fourth of the paper in rough form to Levinson on 28 April, with the postscript: "To get the paper into this mail Im sending it without correcting the typing   Dont let that bother you."[49] Within a week's time Levinson wrote Dewey, "Your third and last batch came. . . . I immediately took it up and have just finished its reading." Levinson was delighted with the paper, but insisted on one thing: "Take plenty of time to make this what it really is, the essence of the philosophy of Outlawry and the overthrow of the doctrine of force."[50]

44. Dewey to Levinson, 6 April 1932, Levinson Papers, Box 16, Folder 5.
45. Levinson to Dewey, 11 April 1932, Levinson Papers, Box 16, Folder 5.
46. Dewey to Levinson, 13 April 1932, Levinson Papers, Box 16, Folder 5.
47. Dewey to Levinson, 21 April 1932, Levinson Papers, Box 16, Folder 5.
48. Levinson to Dewey, 26 April 1932, Levinson Papers, Box 16, Folder 5.
49. Dewey to Levinson, 28 April 1932, Levinson Papers, Box 16, Folder 5.
50. Levinson to Dewey, 3 May 1932, Levinson Papers, Box 16, Folder 5.

Levinson asked for a copy of the manuscript in its final form, but Dewey replied on 6 May, "I am sorry that I have no time to work any longer on my article; I must get it off. . . . I rewrote and expanded the last page and enclose the sheets. IF I had a secy I would make a clean copy of the whole and send to you, but as it is I hope the main points are fairly apparent."[51] Levinson again praised Dewey's article and urged Dewey to "seriously consider striking out my name and letting it stand as the work of the greatest living philosopher and educator."[52]

In a handwritten letter to Levinson on 18 May Dewey wrote:

> I understand Buells & my articles have gone to press—I will see of course that you get copies. There is one part of Buell's article which I have not dealt with adequately—a long discussion of the Constitutional relation of the American States to the Federal Govt with respect to force. I left out more than an incidental reference or two partly because his argument didn't seem too relevant anyway, & partly because it is too much out of my field—It is in the field you have gone over & perhaps sooner or later you will feel that it should have a definite reply.[53]

The statements on sanctions by Buell and Dewey were published in June 1932: *Are Sanctions Necessary to International Organization?* Foreign Policy Association Pamphlet no. 82–83 (New York: Foreign Policy Association, 1932), pp. 3–39. The pamphlet contained McDonald's foreword, Buell's nineteen-page affirmative answer to the question, and Dewey's sixteen-page negative response. After the pamphlet's publication, Levinson wrote to Dewey:

> Your article not only devastates Buell and his philosophy, but it delivers an exposition of the heart of the philosophy of the outlawry of war, at a time when it is most needed for the unison of the peace forces.[54]

Dewey's statement was republished in *Intelligence in the Modern World: John Dewey's Philosophy*, edited by Joseph Ratner (New

51. Dewey to Levinson, 6 May 1932, Levinson Papers, Box 16, Folder 5.
52. Levinson to Dewey, 9 May 1932, Levinson Papers, Box 16, Folder 5.
53. Dewey to Levinson, 18 May 1932, Levinson Papers, Box 16, Folder 5.
54. Levinson to Dewey, 14 July 1932, Levinson Papers, Box 16, Folder 5.

York: Modern Library, 1939), pp. 566–602, with the title "Sanctions and the Security of Nations."

Address to the National Association for the Advancement of Colored People

Dewey's untitled address to the Twenty-third Annual Conference of the National Association for the Advancement of Colored People, published for the first time in this volume, was given in the auditorium of the Shiloh Baptist Church in Washington, D.C., on 19 May 1932, as part of a discussion of an economic program presented by Herbert J. Seligmann of the NAACP.[55]

Copy-text for this address is a typescript, not typed by Dewey, in the NAACP Records in Washington, D.C.[56] Whether the typescript was retyped from Dewey's original typescript or manuscript for the speech or is a transcription of the speech is not known. Works emendations in this article correct five misspelled words at 225.3, 226.18, 226.29, 226.35, 226.36; correct the date at 224.23; lowercase six instances of "party"; supply two points of punctuation at 225.32 and 229.24; delete an extra word at 227.40; and change the word order at 230.30.

College Sons—and Parents

Copy-text for this review of Christian Gauss's *Life in College* is one of the few extant holograph manuscripts by Dewey. Dewey wrote his review in January 1931 while on the Santa Fe Chief enroute to Berkeley, where he was to deliver the George Holmes Howison Lecture, *Context and Thought*, discussed

55. "Slump Is Called Aid to Minority Groups," *Washington Post*, 20 May 1932, p. 7. For other reports of Dewey's speech and the conference, see "Dewey Urges Negroes to Join New Party," *New York Times*, 20 May 1932, p. 2; and "Slump Favors Negro's Status, Dewey Holds," *New York Herald Tribune*, 20 May 1932, p. 13.
56. Group I, Series B, Box 8, NAACP Records, Manuscript Division, Library of Congress, Washington, D.C.

above. In a cover letter sent with the review to Edmund Wilson at the *New Republic* Dewey apologized, "Im sorry it isn't typewritten, but as I am behind hand already with it, I thought it better not to postpone sending it till the uncertain time when I should have access to a typewriter."[57]

The small number of alterations in the manuscript as compared with most of Dewey's typescripts illustrates that Dewey was either more precise in putting his ideas on paper by hand than at the typewriter or that he composed the review hurriedly. Because of Dewey's busy schedule that January, it is unlikely that he saw printer's proof of the review before publication. He left Berkeley on 14 January, immediately after the Howison Lecture. He then presided at the curriculum conference at Rollins College in Florida (discussed below) from 19 to 24 January, arriving home in New York City on 31 January.[58] Therefore, the *New Republic* editor must have been responsible for changes in the manuscript for its publication as "College Sons—and Parents," *New Republic* 66 (4 February 1931): 332–33 (NR). Consequently, the substantives, as well as the accidentals, of the copytext have been restored with the exceptions noted in the Emendations List. The substantive variants not accepted from the *New Republic* for the present edition are listed in "Rejected Substantive Variants in 'College Sons—and Parents.'"

The revised NR word order at 259.7–8 has been accepted as it clarifies Dewey's statement. At 259.17, where Dewey probably meant to say "says that he has" rather than "says that has," the wording "admits to" has been accepted from NR. The more specific wording "The Dean's examples" has been accepted in place of "They" at 260.18. A new sentence beginning "This leads to" has been accepted rather than a clause beginning "concluding with" at 260.25, since the moral mentioned applies to more than the quotation to which the clause was appended. The NR emendations at 261.6, 261.7, 261.9, and 261.22 restore the original readings in quoted material. NR corrected four errors in the manuscript at 259.9, 260.7, 260.16, and 260.23. Dewey's holo-

57. Dewey to Wilson, 9 January 1931, John Dewey VFM 4, Special Collections, Morris Library, Southern Illinois University at Carbondale.
58. Dewey to Albert C. Barnes, 2 February 1931, Ratner/Dewey Papers.

graph changes in this manuscript are listed in "Alterations in 'College Sons—and Parents.'"

Self-Saver or Frankenstein?

In compiling materials for inclusion in this volume, a discrepancy was discovered regarding the title of Dewey's review of Oswald Spengler's *Man and Technics* in the *Saturday Review of Literature* 8 (12 March 1932): 581–82. Milton Halsey Thomas, in *John Dewey: A Centennial Bibliography*, lists Dewey's review title as "Self-Saver or Frankenstein?"[59] The photocopy of the review in the Dewey Center files is entitled "Instrument or Frankenstein?" Three additional copies of the *Saturday Review* were examined to determine which title was most likely correct. The microfilm copy of the journal at Morris Library, Southern Illinois University at Carbondale (stamped "California State Library"), concurs with the Dewey Center file copy title "Instrument or Frankenstein?" (A), while the shelf copies of the journal in the libraries at Southern Illinois University and the University of Illinois agree in the title "Self-Saver or Frankenstein?" (B).

Comparison of the two texts revealed a number of differences between the two printings, with printing B having fewer errors. In addition to the title variation, at 281.6 a broken-type word "to" in A is completely missing in B, probably an incomplete attempt to correct the fault; at 283.19 the misspelled word "martricide" in A is corrected to "matricide" in B, although at 284.20 the misspelled word "commmitted" is overlooked in both printings. Comparison of other pages of that issue of the *Saturday Review* revealed other corrections in B made from errors in A.[60] The compositional corrections made in the two printings indi-

59. Chicago: University of Chicago Press, 1962, p. 100. *The Reader's Guide to Periodical Literature* 8 (January–June 1929–32): 687, and the *Saturday Review of Literature Index, 1924–1944* (New York: R. R. Bowker Co., 1971), pp. 204, 642, also list the title as "Self-Saver or Frankenstein?"

60. In the front-page article "Cut-Throat Bandits," the closing quotation marks were backwards in A and correct in B; in the caption under a line drawing for Hilaire Belloc's "Nine Nines" on p. 586, the publisher was corrected from "Blackwood" in A to "Blackwell" in B; and in a review entitled "Body and Spirit" on p. 586 the reviewer's name was repositioned from its placement in A to the journal's correct stylistic position in B.

cate that B was the later of the two printings, and serves as copy-text for this review.

Introduction to *Studies in Philosophy*

In the spring of 1932 Dewey wrote an introduction to accompany republication of two *Journal of Philosophy* articles by Theodore T. Lafferty of Lehigh University.[61] Dewey's two-page introduction and Lafferty's two articles make up a twenty-five-page Institute of Research circular entitled *Studies in Philosophy* (Lehigh University Publication, vol. 6, no. 7 [Bethlehem, Pa.: Lehigh University, 1932]) (SP).

After the publication of Lafferty's first article in the 16 July 1931 *Journal of Philosophy*, Dewey commended Lafferty on the directness and simplicity of his approach, adding: "I do not see how it could be better."[62] Possibly because of Dewey's stated interest in the articles, Percy Hughes, then the head of the Department of Philosophy at Lehigh University, asked Dewey to write an introduction to the proposed circular publication.[63] In April 1932 Dewey wrote to Hughes that the receipt of the 14 April *Journal of Philosophy*, with Lafferty's second article, had reminded him of how delinquent he had been and that he would "try and get a few words" to Hughes soon. He added that "Lafferty has packed so much into his paper that it seems a work of supererogation to try to add anything. . . . I appreciate your asking me, and Ill do what I can, but I cant do it as well as Lafferty himself."[64]

Copy-text for Dewey's introduction is the typescript, typed and revised by Dewey, in the Theodore T. Lafferty Papers, South Caroliniana Library, University of South Carolina, Columbia. When Dewey typed his paper he omitted periods after all in-

61. "The Dualism of Means and Value," *Journal of Philosophy* 28 (16 July 1931): 393–406, and "Some Metaphysical Implications of the Pragmatic Theory of Knowledge," *Journal of Philosophy* 29 (14 April 1932): 197–207.
62. Dewey to Lafferty, 15 August 1931, Theodore T. Lafferty Papers, South Caroliniana Library, University of South Carolina, Columbia, S.C.
63. "A Note by John Dewey," in Theodore T. Lafferty, *Nature and Values: Pragmatic Essays in Metaphysics*, ed. James Willard Oliver (Columbia: University of South Carolina Press, 1976), pp. 277–79.
64. Dewey to Hughes, 18 April 1932, Lafferty Papers.

stances of "Dr." and in all but one instance of "Mr." (312.8). These were supplied when the introduction was printed and have been accepted as emendations from *Studies in Philosophy*, as well as the SP correction of "philosophy" to "philosopher" at 312.5. Also, on the basis of Dewey's lack of attention to punctuation in his TS, six clarifying commas have been accepted as SP emendations. Dewey's alterations in his typescript are listed in "Alterations in 'Introduction to *Studies in Philosophy*.'"

What Is It All About?

Dewey's essay "What Is It All About?" is a reply to Allen Tate's criticism of "Affective Thought," one of the articles republished in Dewey's 1931 *Philosophy and Civilization*. In January 1932 Tate wrote Dewey that the *New Republic* had decided not to print Tate's criticism and Dewey's reply. Tate indicated that the editors of the *Hound & Horn*, for which Tate was a contributing regional editor for the South, had expressed interest in his article if Dewey's reply would appear with it.[65] Dewey sent a note to Tate that he had asked Malcolm Cowley of the *New Republic* to forward Dewey's reply to the *Hound & Horn*.[66] That journal did not publish either essay, but Tate's article did appear in the December *This Quarter* without Dewey's response.[67]

Dewey's reply is published here for the first time, with Tate's criticism included as Appendix 5. Copy-text for this essay is the unpublished typescript in the Allen Tate Papers, Princeton University Library, Princeton University. Emendations correct the spelling of "than" at 330.7, "italics" at 331.26, "confirms" at 331.40, "thoroughly" at 332.10, "renders" at 333.10, and "soul" at 334.7. Omitted periods have been supplied in eighteen instances of "Mr." and three instances of "Dr." The "Alterations in 'What Is It All About?'" provides a record of Dewey's development of this essay.

65. Tate to Dewey, 9 January 1932, Allen Tate Papers, Princeton University Library, Princeton University, Princeton, N.J.
66. Dewey to Tate, 13 January 1932, Tate Papers.
67. Tate, "The Aesthetic Emotion as Useful," *This Quarter* 5 (December 1932): 292–303. See this volume, Appendix 5.

People's Lobby

Dewey's twenty 1931–32 contributions to the *People's Lobby Bulletin*, four People's Lobby releases to the *New York Times*, and a previously unpublished introduction to an unemployment tract are grouped in this section. Almost half the items are open letters from Dewey as president of the People's Lobby to President Hoover, Assistant Secretary of Commerce Julius Klein, Senator William E. Borah, the Progressives in Congress, the Interstate Commerce Commission, and church leaders throughout the nation.

The People's Lobby evolved from the People's Reconstruction League, which had been organized in January 1921. In 1921 Benjamin C. Marsh, the executive secretary and primary organizer, had urged the name People's Lobby, but the other organizers were afraid of the public's reaction to the word "Lobby." The People's Reconstruction League was reorganized as the Anti-Monopoly League in 1927, and the following year Marsh was delegated to ask Dewey to become president of the organization. Dewey accepted, on the condition that the organization call itself what it tried to be—the People's Lobby. By 1931 the People's Lobby had about 1,500 members.[68]

The first issue of the *People's Lobby Bulletin* as an eight-page printed document was published in May 1931. Up to that time the monthly bulletin had been stenciled. Ethel Clyde of New York City took an active interest in the People's Lobby, financing the *Bulletin* as well as paying a deficit of about $1500.[69] On 15 April Dewey had written a lengthy, enthusiastic letter to Marsh:

> The Lord Liveth—enclosed find Mrs Clyde's check for $1616. Pay yourself for God's sake; Im not a Godsaker as a rule. . . . She has another proposition, to pay for *printing* releases in an *attractive* form, with leeway enough to send

---

68. See Benjamin C. Marsh, *Lobbyist for the People: A Record of Fifty Years* (Washington, D.C.: Public Affairs Press, 1953), pp. 69–88; and U.S. Congress, Senate, Select Committee on Unemployment Insurance, *Unemployment Insurance: Hearings on S. Res. 483*, 72d Cong., 1st sess. (Washington, D.C.: Government Printing Office, 1931), pp. 208–11.
69. Marsh, *Lobbyist for the People*, p. 91.

them regularly to all college libraries and professors of economics and sociology, and to put them on news stands for sale. She wants an estimate, and will finance the undertaking. . . . Write her at once thanking her, giving her the information in print about the P L, and tell her you are at work on the sum necessary for the printing; include enough in that of course for a big enough edition, and also for extra postage.

As a postscript Dewey added:

Get estimates from a good printer and be liberal enough as to the number that you can dispose of; estimates on numbers for newsstand circulation will have to be speculative at first, but I would include two sums, one for immediate use, and another for *later* use, after you have got the thing going.[70]

Dewey corresponded with Marsh, exchanging letters, suggestions, and drafts for release to newspapers or for use in the *People's Lobby Bulletin.* Although the press releases and *Bulletin* articles appeared over Dewey's signature or under Dewey's name as president, Dewey's correspondence indicates that he and Marsh collaborated on the letters and articles. There is no evidence that Dewey saw every article that appeared in the *Bulletin,* but most issues for 1931 and 1932 had at least one letter or article signed by, or attributed to, Dewey. Some extant 1931 Dewey correspondence with Marsh sheds light on the origin and development of a number of the items during that year.

During the spring of 1931 Dewey was delivering a series of lectures at Harvard University under the newly founded William James Lectureship. However, on 13 April 1931, Dewey broadcast a speech "Full Warehouses and Empty Stomachs" over WEAF in New York City. On 21 April Dewey wrote Marsh from Cambridge:

70. Dewey to Marsh, 15 April 1931, Benjamin C. Marsh Papers, Library of Congress, Washington, D.C. Ethel Clyde, a member of the League for Industrial Democracy with Dewey, was also chairman of the American Birth Control League and probably influenced Dewey to write his article "The Senate Birth Control Bill," *People's Lobby Bulletin* 2 (May 1932): 1–2 (this volume, pp. 388–89). A letter from Mrs. Clyde supporting the birth control bill was published in the 11 May 1932 *New Republic,* p. 355.

I found a lt of letters here about the radio speech and asking
for copies. As some of them came from the N B C I take it
they dont send out copies. . . . Some of the letters inquired
specifically about the P L. . . . I forgot yesterday to speak of
the matter of newspaper releases and publicity. I suppose the
best thing would be to republish them in the next printed
Monthly.[71]

Later in the week Dewey again wrote Marsh regarding articles
for the next People's Lobby publication:

If you are publishing my radio speech—and I suppose you
will to answer the 75 or so requests—I dont believe it is
necessary to sign the "Must it be written in red?" article; just
put it in, it will be understood to come from the Lobby.
Shouldnt the [Nicaragua] article contain some reference to
the withdrawal of marines? I dont understand the situation,
but you could put in the fact that the Peoples Lobby began
urging this in (give date) and perhaps quote some of your
activities.[72]

On 18 June Dewey wrote to Eduard C. Lindeman at the New
York School of Social Work suggesting a nonpolitical appeal to
Hoover for relief, stressing the poor condition of children. On
the back of Lindeman's 23 June reply, which said that Lindeman
would discuss it with his colleagues and see what they could do,
Dewey expressed his concern to Marsh:

The situation is getting intolerable. The head of the Municipal Relief Station told a friend of mine it was a frequent occurrence for 3 or 4 inmates to die during the night. Starved.[73]

Probably included with this note, Dewey returned a letter to
Marsh in which he "changed the first part of the letter . . . I hope
you can make out the sense. For once Ive made your statements
stronger instead of toning them down." This letter must be the

71. Dewey to Marsh, 21 April 1931, Marsh Papers.
72. Dewey to Marsh, 25 April 1931, referring to "Must It Be Written in Red?"
    People's Lobby Bulletin 1 (May 1931): 3, and "What Does America Want in
    Nicaragua?" *People's Lobby Bulletin* 1 (May 1931): pp. 5–6.
73. Dewey to Marsh, 24 June 1931, Marsh Papers.

lengthy letter to Hoover, dated 26 June, "The Key to Hoover's Keynote Speech," *People's Lobby Bulletin* 1 (July 1931): 3–6.

Dewey's letters to Marsh indicate that Marsh drafted some of the letters and articles, with Dewey adding his opinions and directions. In a 17 June letter to Marsh Dewey commented: "Your letter to the Int. State Com. Commission is fine. At the hearing you might raise the question as to the effect of freight raise on motor truck competition."[74] On 3 July Dewey returned a draft or proof to Marsh with the comment: "The enclosed seems to me all right. I imagine the railway lines will say that the rise in rates is the only alternative to cutting wages, & in deference to the Presidents policy, they wish not to reduce labor wage."[75] Although the opening paragraph of "President Dewey Opposes Blanket Freight Increase," *People's Lobby Bulletin* 1 (August 1931): 6–8, states that "on behalf of the People's Lobby President Dewey wrote the Interstate Commerce Commission . . ." (this volume, p. 368), Dewey probably would not have had ready access or the time in his busy schedule to secure the facts on the previous ICC cases quoted in the letter from 370.40 to 371.34.

The *Bulletin* had published a letter to Assistant Secretary of Commerce Julius Klein seeking the basis for Klein's optimism regarding the nation's economic condition—"Secretary Klein Asked Basis for Optimism," *People's Lobby Bulletin* 1 (June 1931): 3–4. The succeeding *Bulletin* published Klein's reply and Dewey's rejoinder. Dewey's 29 June letter to Marsh illustrates Dewey's attention to the content and style of the articles and letters that were published over his signature. In that letter Dewey made suggestions for the "Rejoinder to Secretary Klein," *People's Lobby Bulletin* 1 (August 1931): 4–5: "You have the facts and figures much better than I have on Klein's statement. There are two points Id like to have in tho, besides what you write." Dewey continued:

> One concerns his first paragraph. It would be hard to find in your previous letter any suggestion that our great natural resources and high standard of living are something to be "deplored". What is to be deplored is (1) that our natural resources are so largely monopolized by a few, with atten-

74. Dewey to Marsh, 17 June 1931, Marsh Papers.
75. Dewey to Marsh, 3 July 1931, Marsh Papers.

dant reckless waste, because of their socially unplanned use—
witness the coal and oil situations; (2) that the standard of
living for millions is not "high" but reduced to the starvation
point; and that while we export capital abroad, we make tariff walls so that their goods for a large part can be paid for,
not in kind, but by increasing their load of debt to us, and by
piling up a still greater part of the world's gold here—while
millions can hardly get enough to eat both here and abroad.
These arent the exact words that need to be used, but the
general line. The second paragraph you can take care better
than I can.

In the next paragraph his admission that the world's needs
are not satisfied should get emphasis; we agree that over-
production is largely underconsumption—but why?

And in that para and the next, he shows himself wholly
committed to an unplanned and accidental repition [repeti-
tion] of an inflated boom in things which are now regarded
as luxuries, but will be necessities. In other words, the inflation of auto and radio production is to be repeated in other
things, until the next crash comes. This isnt very clearly expressed, but I think the logic is clear.[76]

Dewey added the reminder: "Be sure and make a courteous acknowledgment of his reply in some form at both opening and
closing."

Dewey also attended to some of the details of ensuring the continuation of the People's Lobby publication. During the summer
of 1931 Dewey wrote Marsh from Hubbards, Nova Scotia: "Mrs
Clyde is certainly wonderful. She has written me about an office
clerk for the P. L. next year & financing the Bulletin for a year, so
it can go on for that time. . . . I didn't have the budget with me
& was sorry I couldn't consult you about details."[77] In January
1932 Ethel Clyde sent Dewey a formal letter outlining her agreement with the People's Lobby:

I am sending you my check for $4500 (Forty-five Hundred
Dollars), dated July 1, 1932 (not numbered), drawn on the

76. Dewey to Marsh, 29 June 1931, Marsh Papers.
77. Dewey to Marsh, n.d., Marsh Papers. The exact date of the letter is not
known, but in it Dewey said he had learned that his granddaughter had died
in Vienna, and he was planning to sail for Europe on 22 August 1931.

Brooklyn Trust Company, in conformity with which the People's Lobby agrees to publish an average of 6,000 copies of the People's Lobby Bulletin for each of the six months July to December, this year, inclusive, and to pay the Secretary's salary and that of a full time clerk as stipulated in this letter.[78]

The *People's Lobby Bulletin* items and four *New York Times* articles are arranged in chronological order. Explanatory headnotes that preceded the main text have been retained and set in italic type. Several *Bulletin* articles enclosed all of Dewey's text in quotation marks, which have been deleted to distinguish Dewey's own writing from his quotations from others. In "The Key to Hoover's Keynote Speech," three short quotations that were set as separate paragraphs—at 357.7–9, 362.4–6, and 362.26–27—have been run on in the text. Most emendations in these articles correct misspellings overlooked in the first publication.

Copy-text for the last item in this section, "Introduction [Unemployment Insurance]," is Dewey's typescript in the Benjamin C. Marsh Papers, Library of Congress, Washington, D.C. This previously unpublished item may have been intended as an introduction to "Why the National Program on Unemployment," published by the People's Lobby in 1931. Dewey's changes in this typescript are listed in "Alterations in 'Introduction [Unemployment Insurance].'"

Statements to the Conference on Curriculum for the College of Liberal Arts

The Conference on Curriculum for the College of Liberal Arts convened at Rollins College in Winter Park, Florida, from 19 to 24 January 1931. The conference was called by Hamilton Holt, president of Rollins College, who explained in his opening statement:

I want to thank this group for coming here as the guests of Rollins College, to discuss what seems to me one of the most, if not *the* most, important thing now before educators,

78. Clyde to Dewey, 29 January 1932, Marsh Papers.

namely, what is the best type of curriculum for a college of
liberal arts; not a university or a school, but a college, one
that is autonomous, like Rollins, or a college within a university, like Columbia College, or Yale College, or Harvard
College.[79]

Dewey presided at the general sessions, providing comments
and continuity between speakers. Dewey's major statements
to the conference are included in this volume. Copy-text for
Dewey's statements is the unpublished typed transcript in the
Rollins Archives.[80] Introductory paragraphs have been added
editorially to clarify the context of Dewey's statements. A reference to applause at 423.18 has been omitted.

A member of the conference, Joseph K. Hart, professor of education at Vanderbilt University, reviewed the sessions for the *Survey*, saying that

the discussions and the findings gathered about five fairly
distinct aspects of the total situation, namely: the purposes of
the liberal arts college and its place in the educational organization; the interests of the students and the part these should
play in determining the program of the college; the curriculum itself; teaching methods, teachers and teacher training,
and the administration of the new college; and finally the
problem of appraisals of work done within the college years
and at the conclusion of the course.[81]

At the closing session on Saturday, 24 January, Holt told the
gathering that he had remembered how the League to Enforce
Peace had begun with a series of roundtable dinners, and that he
had "thought we could do the same thing for education, that we

79. "Proceedings, Curriculum Conference," 3 vols., Rollins College, Winter
    Park, Fla., January 19–24, 1931, 1:1.
80. "Proceedings, Curriculum Conference," 3 vols. In Holt's foreword to a re-
    port of the conference ("The Curriculum for the College of Liberal Arts,"
    Rollins College Bulletin 26 [February 1931]: 4–14) he said the tran-
    script was to be prepared for publication by James Harvey Robinson and
    John Palmer Gavit, editor of *Survey*; however, this was never done. See also
    "The True College for a Modern Age," *New York Times*, 1 February 1931,
    sec. 3.
81. Hart, "Towards a New College of Liberal Arts," *Survey* 65 (15 March 1931):
    658–59.

could get the leaders to discuss it and out of that the practical people who make curricula might get a great deal of help. I presented the idea to Dr. Dewey, and when he said he would accept, I knew the Conference was assured." [82]

A. S.

82. "Proceedings, Curriculum Conference," 3:831–32.

Emendations List

All emendations in both substantives and accidentals introduced into the copy-text are recorded in the list that follows, with the
exception of the changes in formal matters described below. No titles
appear for the twenty-seven items that had no emendations. The copy-
text for each item is identified at the beginning of the list of emendations
for that item; for the items that had a single previous printing, no abbreviation for the copy-text appears in the list itself. The page-line number
at the left is from the present edition; all lines of print except running
heads are counted. The reading to the left of the square bracket is from
the present edition; the bracket is followed by an abbreviation for the
source of the emendation's first appearance. The order of sigla following
the bracket indicates the chronological order from the first to last appearance of the emendation. A semicolon follows the last of the sigla for
emending sources. Rejected readings following the semicolon are listed
in reverse chronological order, with the earliest version, usually copy-
text, appearing last.

W means Works—the present edition—and is used for emendations
made here for the first time. The symbol WS (Works Source) is used to
indicate emendations made within Dewey's quoted material that restore
the spelling, capitalization, and some required substantives of his source
(see Substantive Variants in Quotations).

For emendations restricted to punctuation, the curved dash ~ means
the same word(s) as before the bracket; the inferior caret ∧ indicates the
absence of a punctuation mark. The abbreviation [om.] means the reading before the bracket was omitted in the editions and impressions identified; [not present] is used where appropriate to signal material not appearing in identified sources. The abbreviation [rom.] means roman
type and is used to signal the omission of italics. The asterisk before an
emendation page-line number indicates that the reading is discussed in
the Textual Notes.

A number of formal, or mechanical, changes have been made
throughout:

1. Superior numbers have been assigned consecutively to Dewey's
footnotes throughout an essay.

544   EMENDATIONS LIST

2. Book and periodical titles are in italic type; "the" appearing before periodical titles is in lowercase roman type; articles and sections of books are in quotation marks.

3. Periods and commas have been brought within quotation marks.

4. Single quotation marks have been changed to double when not inside quoted material; however, opening or closing quotation marks have been supplied where necessary and recorded. Opening and closing quotation marks around extracts have been omitted.

5. Ligatures have been separated.

The following spellings have been editorially regularized to the known Dewey usage appearing before the brackets:

centre(s)] center 38.28, 92.13, 135.20, 254.33, 262.24, 266.13, 328.21
commonplace] common place 49.7
cooperate (all forms)] coöperate 89.5, 172.38, 173.22, 179.2–3, 194.21, 265.2–3, 265.18, 265.20, 293.13–14
cooperative(ly)] co-operative 62.35, 238.10
coordinate (all forms)] coördinate 81.10, 89.5, 177.11, 180.19, 263.25, 267.2
coordinate (all forms)] co-ordinate 60.35, 61.11, 317.1, 318.24, 319.19
meagre] meager 102.36, 377.25
reenforce (all forms)] reënforce 173.34–35, 195.13
role] rôle 4.17, 112.25, 308.28
so-called] socalled 144.30
uncooperative] unco-operative 55.28–29
uncoordinated] uncoördinated 75.22
zoology] zoölogy 77.24, 82.24

Context and Thought

Copy-text is the publication in the University of California Publications in Philosophy, vol. 12, no. 3 (Berkeley: University of California Press, 1931), 203–24.

3.2   Ogden] W; Ogdens
3.8   Pilolu] WS; Bilolu
3.17   Trobrianders'] WS; Trobianders'
3.22   organisation] WS; organization
3.24–25 Ethnographic] WS; ethnographic

14.13	in doubt] W; doubt
17.27	Aristotelian] W; Aristotleian
18.38	Melchizedeks] W; Melchisedeks
19.9	beliefs] W; belief

George Herbert Mead as I Knew Him

Copy-text is the typescript (TS), typed by Dewey, from the George Herbert Mead Papers Addenda, Box 1, Folder 6, University of Chicago Archives, Chicago, Ill. The publications in *Journal of Philosophy* 28 (4 June 1931): 309–14 (JP), with the title "George Herbert Mead," and *University of Chicago Record* 17 (July 1931): 173–77 (UCR), are noted as the first appearance in print of corrections that would have been made editorially for this volume. Although the copy-text has superior authority in both substantives and accidentals, JP, UCR, and the publication in a memorial booklet (B), all in the Mead Papers Addenda, are included in this historical collation of Dewey's essay. JP omitted the first two paragraphs (22.3–22) and the last half of the final paragraph (28.16–24). Therefore no sigla appear in the entries for omitted JP material. Dewey's alterations in the typescript appear in this volume in "Alterations in 'George Herbert Mead as I Knew Him.'"

22.1–2	George Herbert Mead as I Knew Him] TS, UCR; [*not present*] B; George Herbert Mead JP
22.7	that] UCR, B; than TS
22.8	nor] TS, B; or UCR
22.13	natures₍] TS, UCR; ~, B
22.13–14	₍Aunt Helen₍] TS, B; "~" UCR
22.14	₍Uncle George.₍] TS, B; "~." UCR
22.14	century] UCR, B; cent ry TS
22.20	pouring₍forth] TS, B; ~-~ UCR
22.22+	VIGOR OUTGOING AND OUTGIVING] UCR; [*not present*] B, TS
22.26	outgoing₍] TS, JP, B; ~, UCR
23.9	undiscriminating] JP, UCR, B; undiscr-/inating TS
23.13	unified] JP, UCR, B; unfied TS
23.17	cannot] TS, UCR, B; can not JP
23.17	nor] TS, B; or UCR, JP
23.17	shillyshallying] TS, JP; shilly-/shallying B; shilly-shallying UCR
23.21	or of the] JP, UCR; or the B; or of their TS
23.22	Helen and George] TS, UCR, B; that he and Mrs. Mead JP

23.22   them; it] TS; them, it B; them. It UCR; them! It JP
23.23   tramps∧] TS, B; ~, UCR, JP
23.26   unified] JP, UCR, B; unfied TS
23.26   fullness] TS, JP, B; fulness UCR
23.28   learned,] TS, JP, B; ~∧UCR
23.30   spontaneous∧] TS, B; ~, UCR, JP
23.37   perplexities∧] TS, B; ~, UCR, JP
23.40+   THE UNITY OF HIS PHILOSOPHY AND HIS NATIVE
         BEING] UCR; [not present] B, JP, TS
24.2   philosophical] JP, UCR, B; philosohial TS
24.14   original,—] TS, B; ~∧— UCR, JP
24.15–16 generations] TS, UCR, B; generation JP
24.18   advance] JP, UCR, B; adavcne TS
24.24   never] JP, UCR, B; nerver TS
24.25   intelligible] JP, UCR, B; intelligble TS
24.27   period] TS, B; time UCR, JP
24.27   any one] TS, B; anyone UCR, JP
24.37+   CONTINUITY OF IDEAS AND CONSTANT DEVELOP-
         MENT] UCR; [not present] B, JP, TS
25.1   were] JP, UCR, B; wwere TS
25.2   any one] TS, JP, B; anyone UCR
25.5   ago,] TS, JP, UCR; ~∧ B
25.6   has always] TS, JP, B; always UCR
25.13   dissatisfied] JP, UCR, B; dissatisif/fied TS
25.15   his] JP, UCR, B; him TS
25.15   was] TS, JP, UCR; was only B
25.16   colleagues] JP, UCR, B; collegues TS
25.20   discussion] JP, UCR, B; disucssion TS
25.21   cannot] TS, UCR, B; can not JP
25.22   without] JP, UCR, B; ithout TS
25.24   hitherto∧unsuspected] TS, JP, B; ~-~ UCR
25.25   vigor∧] TS, B; ~, UCR, JP
25.27   interested,] TS, UCR, B; interested him, JP
25.28+   THE RANGE AND BREADTH OF INTELLECTUAL INTER-
         ESTS] UCR; [not present] B, JP, TS
25.32   encyclopedic] JP, UCR, B; encyclepedic TS
25.33   literature] JP, UCR, B; lieterature TS
25.40   subject-matter] TS, JP, B; ~∧~ UCR
26.5   last] TS, JP, B; past UCR
26.7   poetry∧] TS, UCR, B; ~, JP
26.7   but his] TS, JP, B; but of his UCR
26.8   has been] JP, UCR, B; has TS
26.10   Shakespeare] JP, UCR, B; Skakespeare TS

26.10   sonnets,] TS, JP, UCR; ~. B
26.12   through] JP, UCR, B; thtough TS
26.13   flagged∧] TS, B; ~, UCR, JP
26.13   and] JP, UCR, B; & TS
26.17   digests∧] TS, B; ~, UCR, JP
26.18   this] TS, UCR, B; his JP
26.18   Mr.] JP, UCR, B; ~∧ TS
26.23   him∧] TS, JP, B; ~, UCR
26.26   spontaneously] JP, UCR, B; spontanously TS
26.28   So∧] TS, B; ~, UCR, JP
26.37   can not] TS, JP; cannot B, UCR
26.40   so"; having] TS, UCR; so;" having B; so," and having JP
27.1   possibility∧] TS, JP, B; ~, UCR
27.2   extraordinary] JP, UCR, B; extrarodinary TS
27.3+   RESPONSE TO THE SURROUNDING WORLD] UCR; [not present] B, JP, TS
27.4   one∧] TS, B; ~, UCR, JP
27.5   or] TS, UCR; nor B, JP
27.6   them] B; it UCR, JP, TS
27.8   cannot] TS, UCR, B; can not JP
27.8   forego] JP, UCR, B; foregoe TS
27.8   Every one] TS, JP, B; Everyone UCR
27.9   him philosophically] TS, JP, UCR; his philosophy B
27.11   literature∧] TS, UCR, B; ~, JP
27.12   am not] TS, JP, UCR; was not B
27.12   this] TS, JP, UCR; his B
27.15   esthetics] TS, JP, B; aesthetics UCR
27.17   esthetic] TS, JP, B; aesthetic UCR
27.20   have intellectual] TS, JP, B; have had intellectual UCR
27.20   Mr.] JP, UCR, B; ~∧ TS
27.28   between] JP, UCR, B; betwen TS
27.29   reflection∧] TS, B; ~, UCR, JP
27.30   Again∧] TS, JP, B; ~, UCR
27.30   every one] TS, JP, B; everyone UCR
27.30   Mr.] JP, UCR, B; ~∧ TS
27.31   psychology] JP, UCR, B; phyccchology TS
27.34   thinking∧] TS, B; ~, UCR, JP
27.35   its] TS, JP, UCR; their B
27.38   recreate] TS, JP, B; re-create UCR
28.1   fullness] TS, JP, B; fulness UCR
28.3   is] TS, JP, B; are UCR
28.4   expression] TS, JP, B; expressions UCR
28.7   lectures] TS, JP, B; Lectures UCR

28.10   relationships,] TS, JP, B; ~‸ UCR
28.10–11   complete,] TS, B; ~‸ UCR, JP
28.12   books‸] TS, B; ~, UCR, JP
28.15   fullness] TS, JP, B; fulness UCR
28.17   indifference‸] TS, B; ~, UCR
28.17   cynicism] TS, B; from cynicism UCR
28.18   memory,] TS; ~‸ B, UCR
28.19   generous‸] TS, B; ~, UCR
28.22–23   religious] UCR, B; religions TS
28.23   himself‸] TS, B; ~, UCR

Human Nature

Copy-text is the publication in *Encyclopaedia of the Social Sciences* (New York: Macmillan Co., 1932), 7:531–37.

39.35   *Civilisation*] W; *Civilization*
39.36   179] W; 172

Politics and Culture

Copy-text is the publication in *Modern Thinker* 1 (May 1932): 168–74, 238.

43.17   attenuation] W; attentuation
44.4   opinions] W; opinion
46.30   idea] W; ideas

Science and Society [Address]

Copy-text is the publication in *Lehigh Alumni Bulletin* 18 (July 1931): 6–7.

50.24   men's] W; mens'
*50.39–40 age. [¶] The] W; age. [¶] Our almost total lack of con-
          trol in every sphere of social life, international and domes-
          tic, is proof that we have not begun to operate scientifically
          in these fields. [¶] The
51.15   régime] W; regimé

Social Science and Social Control

Copy-text is the publication in *New Republic* 67 (29 July 1931): 276–77. Emendations have been accepted from *Intelligence in the Modern World: John Dewey's Philosophy*, ed. Joseph Ratner (New York: Modern Library, 1939), pp. 949–54 (IMW).

64.18   are] IMW; is
66.23   *then*] IMW; [*rom.*]

The Collapse of a Romance

Copy-text is the publication in *New Republic* 70 (27 April 1932): 292–94. Emendations have been accepted from the republication in *New Republic Anthology, 1915–1935*, ed. Groff Conklin (New York: Dodge Publishing Co., 1936), pp. 418–23 (NRA).

69.6   that] NRA; that that
72.22–23 withhold] NRA; withold

The Way Out of Educational Confusion

Copy-text is the publication as The Inglis Lecture, 1931 (Cambridge: Harvard University Press, 1931), 41 pp.

*77.5   Breasted] W; Braistead
84.28   role] WS; rôle
86.8   short time-span] W; short-time span
88.4   Wells'] W; Well's

American Education Past and Future

Copy-text is the pamphlet *American Education Past and Future*, published by the National Advisory Council on Radio in Education (Chicago: University of Chicago Press, 1931), 16 pp. Emendations have been accepted from the publication in *School and Society* 34 (31 October 1931): 579–84 (SS), with the title "Some Aspects of Modern Education."

94.14   cooperation] SS; co-operation
97.28   cooperative] SS; co-operative

Monastery, Bargain Counter, or Laboratory in Education?

Copy-text is the publication in *Barnwell Bulletin* 9 (February 1932): 51–62.

   101.28   details∧] W; ~,
   101.29   source),] W; ~)∧
   103.40   agrarian] W; agragrian

Appreciation and Cultivation

Copy-text is the publication in *Harvard Teachers Record* 1 (April 1931): 73–76.

   112.10   sufficiently] W; sufficently

Political Interference in Higher Education and Research

Copy-text is the publication in *School and Society* 35 (20 February 1932): 243–46.

   119.26   University] WS; university

The Economic Situation: A Challenge to Education

Copy-text is the publication in *Journal of Home Economics* 24 (June 1932): 495–501.

   130.22   war-time] WS; ~∧~
   130.25   national] WS; rational

Dewey Describes Child's New World

Copy-text is the publication in *New York Times*, 10 April 1932, sec. 3, p. 7.

   138.17   principle] W; principal
   139.22   Conference] W; conference

Discussion of "Freedom, in Relation to Culture, Social Planning, and Leadership"

Copy-text is the publication in *Theses on Freedom* (Washington, D.C.: National Council of Education of the National Education Association, 1932), pp. 13–15.

142.23   decided?] W; ~∧

"The Irrepressible Conflict"

Copy-text is the publication in *News Bulletin of the League for Independent Political Action* 1 (January 1931): 4–5.

149.7   things,] W; ~∧
149.9–10   positions." ∧I] W; positions.∧ "I
150.25   it's] W; its
152.16   society] W; sociey
152.20   dawn.∧] W; ~."

The Jobless—A Job for All of Us

Copy-text is the publication in *Unemployed*, February 1931, pp. 3–4.

153.14   recognize] W; rescognize
154.32   security] W; securty
154.34   indictment] W; indictement
155.4   quarrelling] W; quarelling

The Need for a New Party

Copy-text is the publication in *New Republic* 66 (18 March, 25 March, 1 April, 8 April 1931): 115–17, 150–52, 177–79, 202–5.

162.14   capital] WS; Capitol
162.30   sub-mergers] WS; submergers
172.37   no more] W; more
175.3   will] W; wll

Is There Hope for Politics?

Copy-text is the publication in *Scribner's Magazine* 89 (May 1931): 483–87.

   *183.27; 186.1, 23   states] W; States

Peace—by Pact or Covenant?

Copy-text is the publication in *New Republic* 70 (23 March 1932): 145–47.

   192.20   pact] WS; Pact

Are Sanctions Necessary to International Organization? No

Copy-text is the publication in *Are Sanctions Necessary to International Organization?* Foreign Policy Association Pamphlet no. 82–83 (New York: Foreign Policy Association, 1932), pp. 23–39. Emendations have been accepted from the republication in *Intelligence in the Modern World: John Dewey's Philosophy*, ed. Joseph Ratner (New York: Modern Library, 1939), pp. 566–602, with the title "Sanctions and the Security of Nations" (IMW).

   198.21   treaties] WS; Treaties
   198.30   acquiesced] W; acquiesed
   199.6   affected] IMW; effected
   199.37   sanctions] W; sanction
   200.34   *forces," etc.,*ᴧ] WS; *forces,*ᴧ *etc.,"*
   205.16   Yangtse] IMW; Yangste
   205.29   State] WS; state
   213.27   reason] W; reasons
   214.26   matters] W; force
  *220.33   nationals] W; national
   223.21   because] W; bcause

Address to the National Association for the Advancement of Colored People

Copy-text is the unpublished typescript, not typed by Dewey, in Group I, Series B, Box 8, NAACP Records, Manuscript Division, Library of Congress, Washington, D.C.

224.23   1932] W; 1922
225.3   express] W; experess
225.32   depression,] W; ~∧
226.18   under-privileged] W; under-privileges
226.29   town] W; torn
226.35   tweedle-dee] W; tweedle-de-de
226.36   tweedle-dum] W; tweedle-de-dum
227.40   offer] W; are offer
228.1; 229.8,12,14; 230.30,31   party] W; Party
229.24   reasons?] W; ~∧
230.30   group the] W; the group

Democracy Joins the Unemployed

Copy-text is the leaflet *Democracy Joins the Unemployed* (New York: League for Independent Political Action, 1932), 4 pp.

241.25   privileged] W; priviliged
243.12   their] W; thier

Prospects for a Third Party

Copy-text is the publication in *New Republic* 71 (27 July 1932): 278–80.

248.19   disgruntled] W; disgrunted

College Sons—and Parents

Copy-text is Dewey's holograph manuscript in John Dewey VFM 4, Special Collections, Morris Library, Southern Illinois University at Carbondale. Emendations have been accepted from the publication in *New Republic* 66 (4 February 1931): 332–33 (NR). Substantive variants between the copy-text and NR are in the "List of Rejected Substantive Variants in 'College Sons—and Parents.'" Dewey's changes in this manuscript are listed in "Alterations in 'College Sons—and Parents.'"

259.7–8   by humor . . . instinct.] NR; by much experience that it has been funded into instinct and by humor.
259.9   so] NR; no
259.17   admits to] NR; says that has
260.7   gone);] NR; ~∧;
260.16   Dean's] NR; deans
260.18   The Dean's examples] NR; They
260.23   ago. . . .∧] NR; ~. . . . .
260.25   situation." This leads to] NR; situation" concluding with
261.6   with our] NR; without our
261.7   while,] NR; ~∧
261.9   world outside] NR; world
261.22   worldling] NR; worlding

"Surpassing America"

Copy-text is the publication in *New Republic* 66 (15 April 1931): 241–43.

264.36   insure] WS; ensure
264.37   Socialism] WS; socialism
266.15   book] W; books

Review of Hallis's *Corporate Personality*

Copy-text is the publication in *Yale Law Journal* 40 (June 1931): 1338–40.

270.29   Vinogradoff] W; Vinagradoff

Review of Palmer's *The Autobiography of a Philosopher*; Perry's *A Defence of Philosophy*; and Santayana's *The Genteel Tradition at Bay*

Copy-text is the publication in *New England Quarterly* 4 (July 1931): 529–31.

272.2   common∧sense] WS; ∼-∼
272.29   sympathetic] W; sympathic

Charles Sanders Peirce

Copy-text is the publication in *New Republic* 68 (6 January 1932): 220–21.

275.24   labelled] WS; labeled

Marx Inverted

Copy-text is the publication in *New Republic* 70 (24 February 1932): 52.

278.23   co-ordinated] WS; coordinated
278.23   realise] WS; realize
279.3   civilisation] WS; civilization

Self-Saver or Frankenstein?

Copy-text is the publication in *Saturday Review of Literature* 8 (12 March 1932): 581–82.

281.6–7   to history] W; history
284.20   committed] W; commmitted

Bending the Twig

Copy-text is the publication in *New Republic* 70 (13 April 1932): 242–44.

286.31   vantage-point] WS; ∼∧/∼
288.18   ∧democracy "must] WS; "∼ ∧∼
288.33   than] W; then
289.18   Matthew] W; Mathew

Making Soviet Citizens

Copy-text is the publication in *New Republic* 71 (8 June 1932): 104.

    291.13   inner] W; iner
    292.9   title.] W; ~∧

A Philosophy of Scientific Method

Copy-text is the publication in *New Republic* 66 (29 April 1931): 306–7.

    299.17   "in ∧dispraise] W; ∧~ "~
    299.17   experience,] W; ~∧
    300.23   rigour] WS; rigor
    302.34   formulae] WS; formulas

Prefatory Remarks in *The Philosophy of the Present*

Copy-text is the publication in George Herbert Mead, *The Philosophy of the Present*, ed. Arthur Edward Murphy (Chicago: Open Court Publishing Co., 1932), pp. xxvi–xl.

    308.30   led] W; lead

Introduction to *Studies in Philosophy*

Copy-text is the typescript, typed by Dewey, in the Theodore T. Lafferty Papers, Caroliniana Library, University of South Carolina, Columbia, S.C. The introduction was first published in Theodore T. Lafferty, *Studies in Philosophy*, Lehigh University Publication, vol. 6, no. 7 (Bethlehem, Pa.: Lehigh University, 1932), i–ii (SP).

    311.3,10,20; 311n.2; 312.2,4,13,19,21,22   Mr.] SP; ~∧
    311.23; 311n.1   Dr.] SP; ~∧
    312.3   consideration,] SP; ~∧
    312.4   deeply, I think,] SP; ~∧ ~∧
    312.5   philosopher] SP; philosophy
    312.6   public,] SP; ~∧
    312.13   Mead,] SP; ~∧
    312.14   thought,] SP; ~∧

Introduction to *The Use of the Self*

Copy-text is the publication in F. Matthias Alexander, *The Use of the Self: Its Conscious Direction in Relation to Diagnosis, Functioning and the Control of Reaction* (New York: E. P. Dutton and Co., 1932), pp. xiii–xix.

319.6   Pavlov] W; Pavloff

Vladeck and Laidler

Copy-text is the typescript, typed by Dewey, in the Howard Y. Williams Papers, Division of Archives and Manuscripts, Minnesota Historical Society, St. Paul, Minn. (TS). Emendations have been accepted from the first publication in the *New York Herald Tribune*, 3 November 1932, p. 22 (HT). The letter was also published in the *New York World Telegram*, 4 November 1932, p. 26, with the title "Great Opportunity for Brooklyn Voters" (WT). This list serves as a historical collation for the three documents. Dewey's changes in the typescript are listed in "Alterations in 'Vladeck and Laidler.'"

326.2   To the *New York Herald Tribune:*] HT; [*not present*] WT; Editor &c TS
326.3   presidential] TS; Presidential WT, HT
326.4   intelligent] TS, WT; the intelligent HT
326.6   President] HT, WT; Pres. TS
326.6   promises] TS, WT; promise HT
326.8   Governor] HT, WT; Gov. TS
326.11   Socialist] HT, WT; socialist TS
326.15   independent,] HT, WT; ~∧ TS
326.16   service] TS, WT; serive HT
326.17   Messrs.] HT, WT; ~∧ TS
326.17   Laidler,] HT, WT; ~∧ TS
326.18   8th and 6th] TS, HT; Eighth and Sixth WT
326.18   Districts,] HT; ~), WT; ~∧ TS
326.19   these] TS, WT; the HT
326.19   districts] HT, WT; Districts TS

Help for Brookwood

Copy-text is the publication in *Nation* 135 (14 December 1932): 592.

329.14   Eduard] W; Edward

What Is It All About?

Copy-text is the unpublished typescript, typed by Dewey, in the Allen Tate Papers, Princeton University Library, Princeton, N.J. Dewey's changes in the typescript are listed in "Alterations in 'What Is It All About?'"

330.2,3,8,10,18,22,23; 331.20,40; 332.5,20,24,33,35; 333.11,15,22;
      334.1   Mr.] W; ~∧
330.7   than] W; that
331.26   italics] W; Italics
331.40   confirms] W; conforms
332.10   thoroughly] W; throughly
*333.10   renders] W; render
333.13,17,18   Dr.] W; ~∧
334.7   soul] W; sould

Urges Tax on Rich to Meet Debts Cut

Copy-text is the publication in *New York Times*, 26 January 1931, p. 13.

337.22   "Under] W; ∧~
338.25   plants] W; plans

Full Warehouses and Empty Stomachs

Copy-text is the publication in *People's Lobby Bulletin* 1 (May 1931): 1–3.

344.37   to] W; it

Secretary Klein Asked Basis for Optimism

Copy-text is the publication in *People's Lobby Bulletin* 1 (June 1931): 3–4.

348.39 Commissioner] W; Comissioner
349.4 one∧twenty-fifth] W; ~-~-~
349.26–27 entrepreneurs] W; entrepeneurs

Rejoinder to Secretary Klein

Copy-text is the publication in *People's Lobby Bulletin* 1 (August 1931): 4–5.

351.12 not∧] W; ~,
351.28 decades"?] W; ~?"
352.8 Committees] W; Committee
352.38 people"?] W; ~?"
353.7 strategic] W; stragetic
353.25 consume.] W; ~?

Challenge to Progressive Senators to Act for Relief

Copy-text is the publication in *People's Lobby Bulletin* 1 (June 1931): 5.

356.1 acquiescence] W; acquiesence
356.12 waterpower] WS; water power
356.13 superpower] WS; super-power
356.17–18 farm loan] WS; Farm Loan
356.22 World War] WS; world war
356.30 gentlemen] W; gentleman

The Key to Hoover's Keynote Speech

Copy-text is the publication in *People's Lobby Bulletin* 1 (July 1931): 3–6.

358.8 self-contained] WS; ~∧~
360.21 breadwinner] WS; bread/winner
362.12 insistence] W; inssitence
362.19 century"?] W; ~?"

Lobby Challenges Senator Borah's Opposition to Reconsideration of Interallied Debts

Copy-text is the publication in *People's Lobby Bulletin* 1 (July 1931): 7–8.

364.7   *Collier's*] W; Colliers
365.36   Policies] W; Politics

President Dewey Opposes Blanket Freight Increase

Copy-text is the publication in *People's Lobby Bulletin* 1 (August 1931): 6–8.

368.6   prevalent] W; prevalant
368.10   50] W; 10
368.29   carriers] WS; Carriers
369.31   dividend-yielding] WS; ~∧~
369.37   prostrate] W; postrate
370.6   public] WS; publice
370.18   sort,] W; ~∧
370.27 $125,243,000] W; $125,243,00
371.18(2) et al.] W; ~∧
371.18   *v*.] W; vs.

President Dewey Opposes Community Chest Drives for Unemployed

Copy-text is the publication in *People's Lobby Bulletin* 1 (September 1931): 1–2.

376.3–4   unemployment] W; employment

The Only Way to Stop Hoarding

Copy-text is the publication in *People's Lobby Bulletin* 1 (March 1932): 1.

380.9   lack of confidence] W; confidence

Prosperity Dependent on Building from Bottom Up

Copy-text is the publication in *People's Lobby Bulletin* 1 (April 1932): 1.

383.3   People's] W; Peoples
383.5   one] W; on
383.22   nineteen] WS; 19
383.23   twenty-seven] WS; 27

You Must Act to Get Congress to Act

Copy-text is the publication in *People's Lobby Bulletin* 2 (May 1932): 1.

386.4   Glass-Steagall] W; ~∧~
386.6; 387.9   Bill] W; bill

The Senate Birth Control Bill

Copy-text is the publication in *People's Lobby Bulletin* 2 (May 1932): 1–2.

389.2   un-American] W; unAmerican

President Dewey Asks Senators to Stay on Guard

Copy-text is the publication in *People's Lobby Bulletin* 2 (June 1932): 2–3.

393.28   constituents] W; constitutents

Roosevelt Scored on Relief Policy

Copy-text is the publication in *New York Times*, 24 October 1932, p. 7.

396.2 $2,340,000] W; $2,340,000,000

Introduction [Unemployment Insurance]

Copy-text is the unpublished typescript, typed by Dewey, in the Benjamin C. Marsh Papers, Manuscript Division, Library of Congress, Washington, D.C. Dewey's changes in the typescript are listed in "Alterations in 'Introduction [Unemployment Insurance].'"

400.16,24   Mr.] W; ~∧
400.23,29   People's] W; Peoples

Statements to the Conference on Curriculum for the College of Liberal Arts

Copy-text is the unpublished typed transcript in the Rollins Archives, "Proceedings, Curriculum Conference," 3 vols., Rollins College, Winter Park, Florida, January 19–24, 1931, 1:49–54, 1:203–5, 2:420–27.

414.25–26   impressions] W; expressions
418.4   processes] W; process
419.10   There] W; There there
421.11,37   indigenous] W; indiginous

Teachers as Citizens

Copy-text is the publication in *American Teacher* 16 (October 1931): 7.

434.37   position] W; poistion

Prof. Dewey Is Impressed by Discontent

Copy-text is the publication in *New Leader* 8 (7 February 1931): 6.

438.8   south] W; South
439.14–15,15   editor,] W; ~∧

Dewey Raps Progressives on Parley Eve

Copy-text is the publication in *New Leader* 12 (14 March 1931): 2.

440.6   filibuster] W; fiilibuster
440.10   71st] W; 1st

List of Rejected Substantive Variants in "College Sons—and Parents"

Rejected substantive variants between the copy-text manuscript and the printed version of "College Sons—and Parents" in *New Republic* 66 (4 February 1931): 332–33 are listed below. The reading before the bracket is from the present edition. *New Republic* readings follow the bracket. *New Republic* variants accepted as emendations appear in the Emendations List.

259.9   that] the
259.10   the humor] humor
259.14–15   significant. [¶] The] significant. The
259.25   which] that
259.27   manifests the lack of a] lacks the
259.27–28   a sense of humor] humor
259.29   for good] good
259.32   upon] on
260.3   nor] or
260.15   illuminated] illustrated
260.19   statement that "it] statement: "It
260.31   larger] longer
260.34   as it is] as
260.36–37   implied . . . upon,] implied,
260.37   to comment better] better to comment
261.14   It is . . . on] It is here, and in the chapter on
261.22–23   worldling." [¶] The] worldling." The
261.27   world . . . outside.] world outside.
261.34   root] spot

Alterations in Manuscripts

In five of the six lists that follow appear Dewey's changes both at the typewriter and by hand in the typescripts for "George Herbert Mead as I Knew Him," "Introduction to *Studies in Philosophy*," the letter "Vladeck and Laidler," the unpublished "What Is It All About?" and "Introduction [Unemployment Insurance]." In the sixth list, for "College Sons—and Parents," appear Dewey's handwritten alterations made in his holograph manuscript. All Dewey's alterations made in the course of writing and revision appear here except for strengthened letters to clarify a word, irrelevant typed letters attached to a word, false starts for a word, transposition of letters in a legible word, and mendings over illegible letters. Dewey's corrections of typographical errors, whether by typing over or marking over by hand, are also not recorded as alterations, except when the possibility exists that the error might have been another word or the start of another word rather than a simple typographical mistake.

The word(s) before the bracket refers to the original manuscript; if the manuscript has been emended or the spelling regularized, a grid # before the entry means the reading of the present edition is in the Emendations List. When reference is made to one of two or more identical words in the same line of the present edition, some preceding or following word or punctuation mark is added for identification, or else the designated word is identified with a superscript [1] or [2] or [3] to indicate its occurrence in the line.

For Dewey's alterations, which appear to the right of the bracket, the abbreviation *del.* is used to show material marked out in ink except when pencil is specifically mentioned; any alteration noted as *added* is also in ink unless pencil is specified. For interlineations, use of *intrl.* alone always means a typewritten interlineation. All carets were made by hand; when a caret accompanies a typewritten interlineation, it is in ink unless pencil is noted. When carets are used with handwritten alterations, they are in the same medium as the alteration. For material deleted at the typewriter, *x'd-out* is used. The abbreviation *alt.* is used to identify material altered in some way from an earlier form of the word; if altered by hand, the medium is given; if the medium is not mentioned it is to be assumed the alteration was typewritten. The abbreviation *undrl.* applies to underlining in ink unless pencil is specified.

With respect to position, when an addition is a simple interlineation, the formula is *intrl.* or *intrl. w. caret.* When a deletion positions the interlineation, *intrl.* is dropped and the formula reads *ab. del.* 'xyz'; *w. caret ab. del.* 'xyz'; or *ab. x'd-out* 'xyz.' *Ab.* means interlined above without a caret unless a caret is specified; *bel.* means interlined below without a caret unless mentioned; *ov.* means inscribed over the original letters, not interlined. The abbreviations *bef.* (before) and *aft.* (after) signal a change made on the same line, whether the original line or interline. The abbreviated word *insrtd.* (inserted) refers to marginal additions that cannot be called interlineations but are of the same nature.

In alterations involving more than one line, the solidus / signals the end of a line. The abbreviation *inc.* describes an incomplete word. When an alteration itself has been revised the process of revision is described in square brackets. That revision is transcribed between square brackets immediately following the single word alteration to which it refers, or an asterisk * is placed before the first word to which the description in brackets applies.

Alterations in "George Herbert Mead as I Knew Him"

22.1–2	George . . . Him] *added;* 'erbert' *in ink w. caret ab. del.* 'Her' [not in Dewey's hand]
22.4	in] 'to' *intrl. in pencil w. caret aft.* 'in' [not in Dewey's hand]
22.5	precious] *bef. x'd-out* 'memories'
22.6	that] *alt. in ink fr.* 'than' [not in Dewey's hand]
22.7	nor] 'n' *intrl. in ink*
22.7	reality] *aft. del.* 'vivid'
22.9	did] *intrl. in ink w. caret*
22.10	like] *aft. del.* 'like' *and x'd-out* 'sim'
22.11	such] *aft. del. illeg. letter*
22.12	natures] 's' *added*
22.19	²of] *ab. x'd-out* 'for the'
22.20	pouring] *aft. del.* 'generous'
22.20	forth] *in ink. ov.* 'out'
22.25	everything] *bef. x'd-out* 'every'
22.25	a] *intrl. w. caret*
22.27	have] *aft. x'd-out* 'could'
22.29	hurry,] *comma added*
23.2	somehow] *intrl. in ink. w. caret*
23.3	completely] *aft. del.* 'so'

23.3   into] 'to' *intrl. in ink w. caret*
23.6   brought.] *period in ink bef. del.* 'to him.'
23.6–7 When . . . done,] *intrl. in ink w. caret*
23.7   there] 't' *alt. in ink fr.* 'T'
23.8   unimportant] *bel. intrl. and del.* 'when something needed
        to be done'
23.8   careless] *aft. x'd-out* 'not'
23.10   him,] *comma added*
23.10   important] *aft. del.* 'on that account'
23.14–15 reflection] *alt. in ink fr.* 'reflective'
23.15   to] *in ink w. caret ab. del.* 'which'
23.15   terminate] *final* 'd' *del.*
23.15   decision.] *period added*
23.17   nor] 'n' *added*
23.20   household] *aft. x'd-out* 'the'
23.21   friend,] *comma added*
#23.21 their] *alt. in ink fr.* 'the'
23.21   and . . . the] *intrl. w. caret* ['and' *in ink ov.* 'or'; 'of the' *in
        ink*]
23.22   them;] *semicolon alt. in ink fr. comma*
23.23   recreations,] *comma added; bef. del.* 'and'
23.24   there was] *in ink w. caret ab. del.* 'it'
23.27   own] *aft. x'd-out* 'nature'
23.28   original] *intrl. w. caret*
23.28   learned,] *comma added*
23.33   manifestation] *aft. del.* 'natural'
23.35   the] *alt. in ink fr.* 'they'
23.35   produce,] *comma added*
23.36   ¹the] *intrl. in ink w. caret*
23.39–40 nevertheless tranquil] *intrl. in ink w. caret aft. del* 'yet
        calm'
24.3   utterance] *in ink w. caret ab. del.* 'expression'
24.4   often] *intrl. w. caret*
24.4   his thought] *intrl. in ink*
24.6   Yet] *intrl. in ink w. caret ov. del.* 'Yet'
24.6   this] 't' *alt. in ink fr.* 'T' ['T' *alt. in ink fr.* 't']
24.6   fact] *aft. del.* 'very'
24.7   him] *alt. in ink fr.* 'his'
24.8   within,] *comma added*
24.8   than] *alt. in ink fr.* 'that'
24.8–9 in the case of] *in ink w. caret ab. del.* 'any of'
24.12   with] *aft. x'd-out* 'that'
24.12   emphasis] *bef. del. comma*
24.12   in] *in ink ov. illeg. word*

24.13   minds,] *in ink ab. del.* 'Nds,' [*comma undel. in error*]
24.14   —in] *dash added*
24.15   ¹the] *intrl. in ink w. caret*
24.15   ²the] *in ink ov.* 'his'
24.15   ²the] *in ink ov.* 'his'
24.15   last] *intrl. in ink w. caret*
24.15–16 generations] 's' *added*
24.16   we have] *in ink w. caret ab. del.* 'there is'
24.16   knowledge] *bef. del.* 'in the case'
24.16–17 concerning] *intrl. in ink ov.* 'of'
#24.18   adavcne] *ov.* 'adance'
24.18   necessity,] *comma added*
24.19   ready] *aft. x'd-out* 'aiting'
24.26   while] *intrl. in ink w. caret*
24.26   success,] *comma alt. in ink fr. period*
24.26   there] *in ink ov.* 'At'
24.27   was . . . which] *intrl. in ink w. caret aft. del.* 'all times'
24.27   not] *intrl. in ink w. caret*
24.27   any one] *intrl. in ink w. caret aft. del.* 'no man one' ['man' *x'd-out*]
24.28   it] *in ink ov.* 'him'
24.28   new] *aft. del.* 'sense of'
24.30   thought] *aft. x'd-out* 'mind'
24.33   own] *intrl. w. caret*
24.34   him.] *intrl. in ink bef. del.* 'George / Mead.'
24.35   one] *aft. x'd-out* 'in'
24.36   occurred] *aft. del.* 'even'
24.37   look.] *period added*
24.39   much] *intrl. in ink w. caret*
25.5   ago,] *comma added*
25.7   society.] *period alt. in ink fr. semicolon bef. del.* 'and'
25.7   His] 'h' *triple undrl.*
25.15   was] *bef.* 'only' *intrl. in pencil w. caret* [*not in Dewey's hand*]
#25.16   collegues] 'a' *bef.* 'u' *del.*
25.24   their] *ab.* 'uncovering'
25.24–25 Unlike,] *comma added*
25.25   however,] *intrl. in ink w. caret*
25.27   interested,] *comma added aft. x'd-out* 'in'
25.35   universally] *aft. x'd-out* 'mo'
26.2   physical] *aft. x'd-out* 'natura'
26.7   not] *aft. x'd-out* 'his'
26.10   and Keats] *aft. x'd-out* ', Keta'

26.10   the] *in ink ov.* 'his'
26.10   sonnets,] *comma added*
26.13   me] *in ink ov.* 'him'
#26.13   &] *intrl. in ink w. caret*
26.14   him] *alt. in ink fr.* 'his'
26.14   a] *in ink ov.* 'the'
26.15   with] *intrl. in ink w. caret*
26.19   his personality] *w. caret ab. x'd-out* 'he'
26.19   lend] *bef. x'd-out* 'himself'
26.19   itself to] 'self to' *intrl. in ink w. caret*
26.23   him| *bef. x'd-out* 'self'
26.24   him] *bef. del.* 'self'
26.27   spending] *aft. x'd-out* 'giving'
26.28   too,] *intrl. in ink w. caret*
26.30   His] 'H' *in ink ov.* 'h'; *aft. del.* 'To him'
26.33   problem and] *intrl. w. caret*
26.38   has told me] *in ink ab. del.* 'remarked'
26.39   most] *intrl. in ink*
26.39   associates] *alt. in ink fr.* 'associated'
26.40   is,] 'is' *in ink ov.* 'was'; *comma added*
26.40   so";] *semicolon added; bef. del.* 'and'
27.4   shall not try to] *ab. x'd-out* 'cannot'; 'not' *intrl. in ink*
          w. caret
27.4   any] *aft. x'd-out* 'at the present time'
27.5   or] *alt. in ink fr.* 'nor'
27.7   natural] *aft. x'd-out* 'philosophy'
#27.8   foregoe] 'e' *in ink ab. x'd-out* 'ing' [not in Dewey's hand]
27.9   philosophically] *moved w. caret and guideline to follow*
          'him'
27.11   literature] *aft. x'd-out* 'philosop'
27.11   took] *bef. del.* 'in him'
27.11   his] *intrl. in ink w. caret*
27.21   indirectly,] *comma added; bef. del.* 'with Mr Mead'
27.22   "complete] *quot. added*
27.22   act"] *aft. del.* 'and integral' *x'd-out* 'mind'; *quot. added*
27.23–24 integrated] *ab. del.* 'complete'
27.24   thought,] *comma added*
27.25   emotion] *aft. x'd-out* 'action'
#27.31   phycchology,] *comma added*
27.36   first] *intrl. in ink w. caret*
27.37   into] *aft. del.* 'first'
27.38   of] *aft. x'd-out* 'and'
27.40   the] *aft. x'd-out* 'his'

28.1   its] *intrl. in ink w. caret*
28.6   Mead,] *comma added*
28.10   In] *alt. fr.* 'It'
28.12   his family, his] *in ink ab. del.* 'is'
28.12   students,] *comma added*
28.12   ⁴his] *aft. x'd-out* 'and'
28.13   But] *aft. del.* 'But'
28.16   within] 'in' *intrl. in ink w. caret*
28.18   memory,] *comma added*
28.19   whatever] *aft. del.* 'be'
28.21   all] *bef. x'd-out* 'its'
28.23   and] *ab. x'd-out* 'in'
28.24   gave,] *comma added*

Alterations in "College Sons—and Parents"

259.8   is not] *aft. del.* 'isn't'
259.11   ²the] *intrl. w. caret aft. del.* 'the'
259.15   contemporary] *w. caret ab. del.* 'modern'
259.19   our] *aft. del.* 'our'
259.23   was] *aft. del.* 'has'
259.24   are] *aft. del.* 'to be'
259.25   fundamentally] *aft. del.* 'which,'
259.31   even] *aft. del.* 'for'
260.9   The] *aft. insrtd.* '¶'
260.16   own] *aft. del.* 'exp'
#260.25 situation"] *comma del. aft.* 'situation'
260.31   setting] *aft. del.* 'social'
260.33   even] *aft. del.* 'even'
260.33   appears as] *w. caret ab. del.* 'remains'
260.37   does] *intrl. w. caret*
260.38   shrewd] *aft. del.* 'wise'
261.4   mean] *aft. del.* 'usually'
261.9   a little] *aft. del.* 'into'
261.20   society] *aft. del.* 'the'
261.21   to-day] *aft. del.* 'tod today'
262.2   college] *aft. del.* 'un' *inc.* 'd'

Alterations in "Introduction to *Studies in Philosophy*"

311.4   or] *intrl. in ink w. caret aft. x'd-out* 'of'
311.5   was] *aft. x'd-out* 'with'

311.5   identified] *aft. del.* 'unusually'
311.5   in an unusual way] *intrl. in ink w. caret*
311.5   mind.] *aft. x'd-out* 'his'; *period added*
311.5   The] *alt. in ink fr.* 'This'
311.6   in question] *intrl. in ink w. caret*
311.6   union] *aft. x'd-out* 'somewhat remarkable'
311.7   position] *final* 's' *x'd-out*
311.7   a deference] *aft. x'd-out* 'which'
311.7   apparently] *aft. x'd-out* 'obscured'
311.9   mainly] *aft. x'd-out* 'merely'
311.10   was] *in ink ab. del.* 'with'
311.11   in] *ab. x'd-out* 'with'
311.13   writing] *bef. x'd-out* 'before'
311.13   before] *insrtd. w. guideline aft. del.* 'outside'
311.13   his own] *bel. del. intrl.* 'the expression of'
311.13   received expression] *intrl. in ink w. caret*
311.17   was,] *bef. x'd-out* 'the'
311.17   if] *aft. x'd-out* 'problem of the'
311.19   that is,] *intrl. w. caret and guideline*
311.19   'of] *ab. x'd-out* 'and'
311.21   way] *aft. x'd-out* 'most conspicuous way'
311.23   Physical] *w. caret ab. x'd-out* 'Modern'
311.24   all] *bef. x'd-out* 'qa'
311.25   values,] *comma added*
311.25   the things] *in ink ab.* 'which'
311.25   are] *aft. x'd-out* 'give'
311.25   life-] *intrl. in ink w. caret*
311n.2   which] *intrl.*
311n.2   it] *bef. x'd-out* 's sentiment'
311n.3   the] *in ink ov.* 'its'
312.4   (which] *paren. added*
312.5   world] *aft. x'd-out* 'physical world was'
312.6   is] *alt. in ink fr.* 'was'
312.6-7 "consciousness,"] *comma added*
312.7   in] *aft. del.* 'wa defined'
312.7   tradition,] *comma added*
312.7   constituted] *intrl. in ink w. caret and guideline*
312.7   personal] *intrl. w. caret*
312.8   mind] *intrl. in ink w. caret*
312.8   the] *aft. del.* 'I think'
312.8   Mr.] *period added*
312.9   His] *aft. x'd-out* 'It was a'
312.9   the] *intrl. w. caret aft. x'd-out* 'his'
312.12   physics] *aft. x'd-out* 'to'

312.13   originality] *aft. x'd-out* 'eual equal'
312.14   ²that] *intrl. w. caret*
312.14   change] *aft. x'd-out* 'connection'
312.15   a way] *aft. x'd-out* 'terms of'
312.16   consciousness,] *comma added*
312.16   ²of] *in ink ov.* 'and' *bef. del.* 'individual'
312.16   as individual,] *intrl. in ink w. caret*; *comma added*
312.18   he] *aft. del.* 'there are'
312.19   the new] *aft. x'd-out* 'modern'
312.20   for] *in ink ov.* 'of'
312.20   the conception] *aft. x'd-out* 'his'
312.20   earlier] *intrl. in ink w. caret*
312.21   papers] 's' *intrl. w. caret*
312.21   are a] *intrl. w. caret aft. x'd-out* 'is' ['a' *intrl. in ink*]
312.23   are] *in ink ov.* 'i'
312.25   source] *aft. x'd-out* 'force'
312.27   gladly] *aft. x'd-out* 't'

Alterations in "Vladeck and Laidler"

326.3   The ballyhoo] *solidus betw. words*
326.3   campaign] *alt. in ink fr.* 'campaigners'
326.5   will overlook] *solidus betw. words*
326.10   conducted] *aft. x'd-out* 'a census'
326.11   fortunately] *aft. x'd-out* 'the'
326.16   the] *aft. x'd-out* 'bringing'
326.18   Districts] *bef. del.* 'in Congress'
326.19   I could] 'I' *in ink ov.* 'a'
326.19   voter] *alt. in ink fr.* 'voters'
326.20   These] *alt. in ink fr.* 'They'
326.20   men] *intrl. in ink w. caret*
326.22   the House] *aft. x'd-out* 'Congre'
326.22   wide] *aft. x'd-out* 'experience'

Alterations in "What Is It All About?"

330.1   It] 'IT' *intrl. w. caret*
330.3   understand] 'under stand' *closed up w. guidelines*
330.3   why] *intrl. in ink w. caret aft. x'd-out* 'the' *and del.* 'what'
330.3   attributes] *alt. in ink fr.* 'attributed'
330.6   if] *intrl. in ink w. caret*

330.6   them,] *comma added*
330.8   a] *added*
330.10   Tate's] *aft. del.* 'Mr'
330.12   the] *intrl. in ink w. caret*
330.14   hazy] *aft. x'd-out* 'azy'
330.15   is] *undrl.*
330.15   played] *aft. del.* 'definitely'
330.16   to explain] *aft. del.* 'only'
330.18   set] *ab. del.* 'put'
330.18   of] *aft. x'd-out* 'to'
330.18   mine] *alt. in ink fr.* 'mind'
330.18   against] *intrl. in ink w. caret aft. del.* 'on'
330.18   issues] *intrl. in ink w. caret aft. del.* 'bases'
330.26   in those] *added*
330.29   thinking,] *comma added*
330.29   an account made] *intrl. in ink w. caret*
331.2   develops] *ab. x'd-out* 'originates'
331.4   usually] *intrl. w. caret*
331.4–5   separation] *aft. del.* 'a'
331.10   ever] *alt. in ink fr.* 'every'
331.10   day.] *period added*
331.10   It] *in ink aft. del.* 'and'
331.13   so that] *added*
331.13   they] *intrl. in ink w. caret aft. del.* 'and'
331.13   constitute] *alt. in ink fr.* 'constituted'
331.13   isolated] *aft. x'd-out* 'again'
331.15   accepted,] *comma added*
331.15   warrant] *aft. x'd-out* 'alleged'
331.20   In consequence,] *ab. x'd-out* 'Then,'
331.27   false] *aft. del.* 'alleged but'
331.27   alleged] *intrl. in ink w. caret*
331.29   departments;] *semicolon alt. in ink fr. comma*
331.29–30 an . . . in] *in ink ab. del.* 'a basic unity, from the side
           of feeling or the affective, of'
331.31   can,] *comma added*
331.31   modesty] 'y' *intrl. w. caret*
331.35   any] *in ink ov.* 'some'
331.35   supposed] *intrl.*
331.37   an] *aft. del.* 'at least'
331.39   are] *undrl.*
332.1   idea] *in ink ab. del.* 'notion'
332.2   (which] *paren. added*
332.2   used] *in ink ab.* 'to'

332.2   support] *in ink w. caret ab. del.* 'foundation'
332.3   these] *alt. in ink fr.* 'the'
332.3   segregations)] *paren. added*
332.3   might] *intrl. in ink w. caret aft. del.* 'would' [*alt. in ink fr.*
         'should']
332.5   now] *alt. in ink fr.* 'new'
332.8   The] *alt. in ink fr.* 'This'
332.8   an] *alt. in ink fr.* 'another'
332.12   on] *intrl. in ink w. caret*
332.12   Affective] 'A' *in ink ov.* 'a'; *triple undrl.*
332.12   Thought] 'T' *in ink ov.* 't'; *triple undrl.*
332.12   reaches from] *solidus betw. words*
332.13   standpoint] *bef. del.* 'of view'; 'stand' *intrl. in ink w. caret*
332.13   start made] *added bef. del.* 'beginnings' ['made' *aft. del.*
         'is']
332.13   is] *in ink bel.* 'not' *w. guideline*
332.15   situations,] *comma added*
332.15   coming] *alt. in ink fr.* 'comes'; *aft. del.* 'which'
332.15   as] *intrl. in ink w. caret*
332.15   wholes] *alt. in ink fr.* 'whole' [*alt. in ink fr.* 'wholes']
332.16   qualitative,] *bef. del.* 'in character'; *comma added*
332.18   the] *alt. in ink fr.* 'their'; *aft. x'd-out* 'them—'
332.18–19 of . . . wholes.] *intrl. in ink w. caret*
332.20   action,] *comma added*
332.20   an idea] *intrl. in ink w. caret*
332.21   whole,] *comma added*
332.22   The] *intrl. in ink aft. del.* 'Its virtual'
332.22   conclusion—] *dash added*
332.23   stated] *aft. del.* 'one'.
332.23   with] *aft. x'd-out* 'ver'
332.23   explicitness] *aft. del.* 'complete'
332.23   mine—] *dash added*
332.23–24 the opposite of] *in ink ab. del.* 'so far from being'
332.24   namely,] *added*
332.25   science."] *period added*
332.25   It is that] *intrl. in ink w. caret aft. del.* 'that it *claims' [*aft.*
         del. 'is']
332.25   is] *intrl. in ink w. caret and guideline aft. del.* 'to be' *and*
         intrl. del. 'is'
332.26   help] *added*
332.27   ²which] *intrl. w. caret*
332.28   Messiah.] *period alt. in ink fr. semicolon*
332.28   They] 'T' *in ink ov.* 't'

332.28 would,] *comma added*
332.28 opinion,] *comma added*
332.30 instrument,] *comma added*
332.30–31 *end and consummation*] *undrl.*
332.32 Because] *aft. insrtd.* '¶'
332.32 represent] *aft. del.* 'be'
332.33 to be] *intrl. in ink w. caret aft. del.* 'hence'
332.33 for] *aft. x'd-out* 'of'
332.34 inconsistently] *intrl. w. caret*
332.35 who . . . philosophy] *in ink w. caret ab. del.* 'in a philo-sophical class'
332.37 *thought*] *undrl.*
332.38 experience] *aft. x'd-out* 'basic and ulterior'
332.38 and to be] *intrl. in ink w. caret*
332.38–39 *affectively*] *undrl.*
332.40 finally terminates in] *in ink ab. del.* 'leads up to'
333.1 these] *intrl. in ink w. caret aft. del.* 'such' *x'd-out* 'immediate'
333.2 after all] *intrl. w. caret*
333.2 value,] *comma added*
333.3 only] *intrl. in ink w. caret*
333.4 society] *ab. x'd-out* 'the state'
333.4 includes science] *solidus betw. words*
333.6 any] *aft. x'd-out* 'to'
333.6 to] *in ink ov.* 'for'
333.6 create] *alt. in ink fr.* 'creating'
333.6 harmony.] *period added; bef. del.* 'if it were tried.'
333.7 was] *aft. x'd-out* 'is'
333.9 fields.] *period added bef. del.* 'one ['great' *intrl.*] trouble, as I have indicated / above, is that the acceptance of intellectual premisses which support / segregation prevent the adequate working out of this possibility.'
333.10 essays] *final* 's' *intrl. w. caret*
#333.10 render] *aft. del.* 'will'
333.12 seriatim] 'e' *intrl. w. caret and guideline*
333.14 "utilitarian"] *closing quot. added*
333.15 my] *alt. in ink fr.* 'me'
333.15 ideas] *intrl. in ink w. caret*
333.17 Barnes.] *period added*
333.17 It] 'I' *in ink ov.* 'i'
333.18–19 since . . . terms.] *intrl. in ink w. caret*
333.19 Speaking] 'S' *in ink ov.* 's'
333.19 in terms] *aft. x'd-out* 'of Shelley'

333.20   in his] *aft. del.* 'is'
333.20   is] *intrl. in ink*
333.22   to] *intrl. in ink w. caret*
333.23   "calculation."] *quots. added*
333.24   the] *intrl. in ink w. caret and guideline*
333.25   or intuitively] *intrl. w. caret*
333.27   a dominant] *aft. del.* 'such'
333.29   richer] *aft. del.* 'and'
333.29   and more fully ordered] *intrl. w. caret*
333.31   adequately] *intrl. w. caret*
333.32   ¹of] *in ink ov.* 'in'; *aft. x'd-out* 'as'
333.33–34   contribute,] *comma added*
333.34   providing] *in ink w. caret bef. del.* 'in operating as'
333.37   their] 'ir' *intrl. w. caret*
333.39   nor] 'n' *intrl.*
333.39   foundation.] *period alt. in ink fr. comma*
333.39   It is] *intrl. in ink w. caret aft. del.* 'but'
333.39   practical] *undrl.*
333.40   ¹of] *intrl. in ink w. caret aft. del.* 'or'

Alterations in "Introduction [Unemployment Insurance]"

399.4   human] *alt. in ink fr.* 'humane'
399.9   socially] *aft. x'd-out* 'disgraceful'
399.9   disgraceful,] *comma added*
399.9–10   individuals] *aft. x'd-out* 'th'
399.11   starvation] *aft. x'd-out* 'suff'
399.14–15   unemployed] *alt. in ink fr.* 'unemployment'
399.16   The] *aft. x'd-out* 'They'
399.21   unemployment] *aft. del.* 'the situation of'
399.22   ¹how] *intrl. in ink w. caret*
399.22   changes must] *in ink w. caret ab. del.* 'changes must'
399.22   ²how] *in ink w. caret ab. del.* 'for'
399.23   changed,] *comma added*
399.23   ensure] *alt. in ink fr.* 'insure'
399.24   useful] *aft. x'd-out* 'it'
399.26   the] *intrl. in ink w. caret*
399.26   due] *aft. del.* 'when it is'
399.27   take] *aft. x'd-out* 'relieve the suffering incident'
400.3–4   consumption,] *comma added*
400.4   production,] *comma added*
400.4   help] *intrl. w. caret*

400.8   are brothers] 'are' *alt. in ink fr.* 'were'
400.8   are their] 'are' *alt. in ink fr.* 'were'
400.11   farmer,] *comma added*
400.13   ²of] *intrl. in ink w. caret*
400.19   The] *aft. x'd-out* 'It'
400.21   consequent] *intrl. in ink w. caret*
400.23   by] *intrl. in ink w. caret*
400.24   residence] *alt. in ink fr.* 'resident'
400.26   in constant] 'in' *intrl. in ink w. caret*
400.28   urges,] *comma added*
400.28   to] *intrl. in ink w. caret*
400.29   committed] *bef. del.* 'to'
400.31   remedy] *aft. del.* 'some'
400.31   The] *alt. in ink fr.* 'They'
400.33   workable] *aft. del.* 'other'

Line-End Hyphenation

I. Copy-text list.

The following are the editorially established forms of possible compounds that were hyphenated at the ends of lines in the copy-text:

5.2–3	non-verbal	229.33	under-privileged
11.15	framework	242.1	lawmakers
36.18	non-rational	254.40	non-existent
56.7–8	standpoint	270.17	sub-stratum
77.8	subject-matter	279.4	world-wide
79.14–15	subject-matter	295.32	self-respecting
81.25	semi-professional	296.34	non-intellectual
82.33	semi-vocational	298.5	self-directed
85.7	semi-vocational	316.28	pseudo-science
89.13	reorganization	317.27	re-education
92.30–31	Preschool	319.26	psycho-physical
117.7	out-leadings	319.32	psycho-physical
119.25	by-law	337.3	war-time
159.28	bygone	348.9	underconsumption
171.10	householder	350.9	over-subscribed
171.35	backbone	379.24–25	self-interest
175.24	"superpower"	384.27	skyscraper
176.11	offhand	393.25	bipartisan
183.37–38	non-political	397.31	self-liquidating
221.16	short-sighted		

II. Critical-text list.

In transcriptions from the present edition, no line-end hyphens in ambiguously broken possible compounds are to be retained except the following:

5.2	non-verbal	219.38	non-recognition
7.12	over-arching	223.7	self-defense
15.15	subject-matter	233.1	non-partisan
15.33	subject-matter	233.3	maize-growing
16.29	subject-matter	249.32	vote-catching
45.7	money-making	261.27	long-distance
66.12	self-developing	287.35	drug-store
70.23	self-interest	288.13	non-monarchical
77.9	subject-matter	293.2	self-organization
79.14	subject-matter	293.12	class-conscious
80.19	bio-chemistry	326.7	re-elected
86.7	so-called	331.6	non-communicating
88.30	subject-matter	351.17	so-called
156.7	self-interest	379.24	self-interest
158.15	self-confessed	384.13	first-step
166.5	stock-jobbing	388.17	well-being
177.12	self-reliance	393.28	war-time
183.37	non-political	397.16	self-liquidating
197.3	non-adherence	403.3	drawing-room
199.19	old-fashioned	404.2	mild-mannered
199.40	non-existent	406.27	part-time
211.7	pre-condition	406.33	sing-song
219.14	self-defense	408.5	re-echoing

Substantive Variants in Quotations

Dewey's substantive variants in quotations have been considered important enough to warrant this special list. Dewey represented source material in varying ways, from memorial paraphrase to verbatim copy, in some places citing his source fully, in others mentioning only authors' names, and in others omitting documentation altogether. All material inside quotation marks, except that obviously being emphasized or restated, has been searched out; Dewey's citations have been verified and, when necessary, emended. All quotations have been retained as they appear in the copy-text, with the exceptions recorded in the Emendations List. Therefore, it is necessary to consult the Emendations List in conjunction with this list.

Although Dewey, like other scholars of the period, was unconcerned about precision in matters of form, many of the changes in quotations may well have occurred in the printing process. For example, comparing Dewey's quotations with the originals reveals that some editors and compositors house-styled the quoted materials as well as Dewey's own. Therefore, in the present edition, the spelling and capitalization of the source have been restored. In cases of possible compositorial or typographical errors, corrections either of substantives or accidentals, including spelling and capitalization, that restore original readings are noted as WS emendations (Works Source—the present edition, emendations derived from Dewey's source). Moreover, Dewey frequently changed or omitted punctuation in quoted material. When such changes or omissions have substantive implications, the punctuation of the source has been restored; these changes are also recorded in the Emendations List with the symbol WS.

Dewey often did not indicate that he had omitted material from his source. Omitted short phrases appear in this list; omissions of more than one line are noted by a bracketed ellipsis [. . .]. Italics in source material have been treated as substantives. Both Dewey's omitted and added italics are noted here.

Differences between Dewey's quotations and the source attributable to the context in which the quotation appears, such as changes in number or tense, are not recorded.

Notations in this section follow the formula: page-line number from the present edition, followed by the lemma, then a bracket; after the bracket, the original form appears, followed by the author's surname, shortened source-title from the Checklist of Dewey's References, and the page-line reference to the source, all in parentheses.

Context and Thought

3.6   frontwards] front-wood (Malinowski, "Problem of Meaning," 458.4)
3.8   rearward] rear-wood (Malinowski, "Problem of Meaning," 458.8)
3.14–15   feature of rivalry] last-mentioned feature (Malinowski, "Problem of Meaning," 458.24)
3.15   also explains] explains also (Malinowski, "Problem of Meaning," 458.25)
3.22   psychology,] psychology and (Malinowski, "Problem of Meaning," 459.20)
3.23   Linguistic] We see that linguistic (Malinowski, "Problem of Meaning," 459.21–22)
4.1   language] tongue (Malinowski, "Problem of Meaning," 467.21)
4.2   context of a situation] *context of situation* (Malinowski, "Problem of Meaning," 467.22–23)

The Way Out of Educational Confusion

84.31   formulae,] formulae quickly learned by the apprentice method, (Morgan, "Curriculum," 9.2.47–48)
84.35   is no] can be no (Morgan, "Curriculum," 9.2.53)
84.40   proportion] proportions (Morgan, "Curriculum," 10.1.4)

Political Interference in Higher Education and Research

120.1   a professor] one ("Restriction," 572.29)

The Economic Situation: A Challenge to Education

127.1   into] in (Merriam, *Making of Citizens*, 10.22)
130.25   interests] policies ("School Histories," 13.1.36)

The Need for a New Party

162.19–20   The world] this unreal world (McCormick, "Foggy
        Days," 2.5.103)
162.20   iron] cast iron (McCormick, "Foggy Days," 22.1.27)
162.23   world . . . living] old planet turned somersaults, but soon
        you can answer the question. They have been living (McCor-
        mick, "Foggy Days," 2.5.113–15, 22.2.1)
173.30–31   this country] the nation ("Progressives Call Parley,"
        1.5.42–43)
174.12–13   the . . . combined.] The dominant issue is bigger than
        tariff; bigger than public control or ownership of the great
        modern utilities; bigger than any phase of the traction, transit
        and transportation question; bigger than the problem of just
        taxation. (Dewey, "'Irrepressible Conflict,'" 4.21–25) [*Later
        Works* 6 : 149.15–18]

Peace—by Pact or Covenant?

192.24   government would] government formally notified Japan and
        China that it would (Stimson, "Text of Letter," 8.7.52–54)
192.25   into] into by these governments (Stimson, "Text of Letter,"
        8.7.56)
192.36–37   peradventure of a doubt] peradventure (Stimson, "Text
        of Letter," 8.7.16)

Are Sanctions Necessary to International Organization?
No

198.29   there is] is there ("Outlawry of War," 465.13)
198.30   is not] not ("Outlawry of War," 465.15)
198.31   it. When] it. It is a moral rather than a legal situation. When
        ("Outlawry of War," 465.16–17)
200.32   *such*] [*rom.*] ("Covenant of League," 8.1)
200.33–34   *effective . . . forces*] effective military, naval or air force
        ("Covenant of League," 8.2)
201.19   *severance*] [*rom.*] ("Covenant of League," 7.42)
207.9   powers, especially,] powers (Buell, "Are Sanctions Neces-
        sary?" 8.16) [*Later Works* 6 : 459.38]
220.35   Admittedly all] all (Buell, "Are Sanctions Necessary?" 21.34)
        [*Later Works* 6 : 482.4]

220.36   last resort] final analysis (Buell, "Are Sanctions Necessary?"
          21.34) [*Later Works* 6:482.4–5]
220.36   must rest upon] depends on the (Buell, "Are Sanctions
          Necessary?" 21.34–35) [*Later Works* 6:482.5]
220.36   faith] faith of governments, (Buell, "Are Sanctions Neces-
          sary?" 21.35) [*Later Works* 6:482.5]
220.36–37   and the force of] on (Buell, "Are Sanctions Necessary?"
          21.35) [*Later Works* 6:482.5]

The Place of Minor Parties in the American Scene and Their Relation to the Present Situation

232.4   the leaders] these leaders (Haynes, *Social Politics*,
          153.20–21)
232.4–5   Greenback, . . . parties] people (Haynes, *Social Politics*,
          153.21)
232.6   power] influence (Haynes, *Social Politics*, 153.22)
232.14–15   people . . . rather] people, for the people, and by the
          people, rather (Haynes, *Social Politics*, 153.31–32)
234.9   the labor] labor (McVey, "Populist Movement," 144.22)

Prospects for a Third Party

250.2   subordination of] subordinating ("Platform and Program,"
          4.2.31)

College Sons—and Parents

260.24   now seem] seem now (Gauss, *Life in College*, 22.12)
260.25   general, the] general, however, it may be said that the
          (Gauss, *Life in College*, 22.27)

"Surpassing America"

266.8   so] and (Counts, *Soviet Challenge*, 13.2)
266.8   human society] society (Counts, *Soviet Challenge*, 13.2)
266.31   produce] create (Counts, *Soviet Challenge*, 335.11)

Review of Hallis's *Corporate Personality*

268.17   fact] facts (Hallis, *Corporate Personality*, xxix.19)
268.18   value.] value or meaning. (Hallis, *Corporate Personality*, xxix.20)
270.27   always have] have always (Hallis, *Corporate Personality*, 187.30)
270.28   one] aspect (Hallis, *Corporate Personality*, 187.31)

Review of Perry's *A Defence of Philosophy*

272.2   to] upon (Perry, *Defence of Philosophy*, 21.11)

Charles Sanders Peirce

275.21   those] those who are (Peirce, *Principles of Philosophy*, x.23)
275.24   on] upon (Peirce, *Principles of Philosophy*, 105.12)
275.24   the scientist's] each scientist's (Peirce, *Principles of Philosophy*, 105.12)
275.24–25   mind, arranged] mind, where they can be at hand when there is occasion to use things—arranged, (Peirce, *Principles of Philosophy*, 105.12–13)
275.25   to] therefore, to (Peirce, *Principles of Philosophy*, 105.13–14)
275.25   convenience,] special convenience— (Peirce, *Principles of Philosophy*, 105.14)
275.25   science] science itself (Peirce, *Principles of Philosophy*, 105.14)
275.26   only] mainly (Peirce, *Principles of Philosophy*, 105.15)
275.31   principle] idea (Peirce, *Principles of Philosophy*, 70.24)

Marx Inverted

279.2   of advance] marking the entry into a new age (Heard, *Emergence of Man*, 100.25–26)
279.3   is] was (Heard, *Emergence of Man*, 101.6)

Bending the Twig

286.33   spirit] spirit's operations (Nock, *Theory of Education*, 52.20)

Making Soviet Citizens

292.10   kindly] friendly (Woody, *New Minds*, x.19)

The Meiklejohn Experiment

296.33   is] is, therefore, (Meiklejohn, *Experimental College*, 233.20)
297.2   *think*] [*rom.*] (Meiklejohn, *Experimental College*, 56.2)
297.6   service of] to serve (Meiklejohn, *Experimental College*, xvii.5)
297.7   creation of] creation (Meiklejohn, *Experimental College*, xvii.5)
297.36   that which] what (Meiklejohn, *Experimental College*, 56.24)
297.36   already knows] knows (Meiklejohn, *Experimental College*, 56.24)
297.38   as far] so far (Meiklejohn, *Experimental College*, 72.11)
298.12   value] values (Meiklejohn, *Experimental College*, 138.14)
298.24   independent] relatively independent (Meiklejohn, *Experimental College*, xiv.18–19)

Prefatory Remarks in *The Philosophy of the Present*

309.15   is,] is, on the contrary, (Peirce, *Principles of Philosophy*, 55.3)

What Is It All About?

331.20   *then*] [*rom.*] (Tate, "Aesthetic Emotion," 297.4) [*Later Works* 6:495.38]
331.22   to] [*ital.*] (Tate, "Aesthetic Emotion," 297.6) [*Later Works* 6:496.1]
331.23   of the . . . integration] [*ital.*] (Tate, "Aesthetic Emotion," 297.6–7) [*Later Works* 6:496.1–2]

Full Warehouses and Empty Stomachs

342.28   lasts] continues (Dewey, "$100,000,000 Relief," 14.2.62)
342.29   the country] this country (Dewey, "$100,000,000 Relief," 14.2.64–65)
342.36   effect upon] result on (Folks, "Socially Handicapped," 335.19)

The President and the Special Session

345.3   cannot hope to] cannot (Hoover, "Hoover Bars Extra Session," 1.4.47)

Rejoinder to Secretary Klein

352.16   is] is always (Folks, "Socially Handicapped," 336.31)
352.17−18   minimum . . . U.S.] These figures, which are presented only as illustrative material, (Folks, "Socially Handicapped," 336.32−33)
352.25−26   his doing] their doing (Folks, "Socially Handicapped," 337.7)
352.27   advance] advance on a broad program designed to safeguard children (Folks, "Socially Handicapped," 336.1−2)
352.28   of parents] for their parents (Folks, "Socially Handicapped," 336.3)

Challenge to Progressive Senators to Act for Relief

356.8   the power] power (La Follette, "Platform," 5.6.13)
356.9   monopoly.] monopoly, not to foster it. (La Follette, "Platform," 5.6.15)
356.13−14   system. [¶] Retention] system. [. . .] Retention (La Follette, "Platform," 5.6.21−27)
356.15   profits and] profits, on stock dividends, profits undistributed to evade taxes, (La Follette, "Platform," 5.6.30−31)
356.16−17   inheritances. [¶] Reconstruction] inheritances. [. . .] Reconstruction (La Follette, "Platform," 5.6.33−44)
356.18−19   systems. [¶] Public] systems [. . .] Public (La Follette, "Platform," 5.6.46−77)
356.19   operation.] operation, with definite safeguards against bureaucratic control. (La Follette, "Platform," 5.6.78−80)

Lobby Challenges Senator Borah's Opposition to Reconsideration of Interallied Debts

366.10   advantage] benefit or advantage (Borah, "Where Would the Money Go?" 12.4.21)

President Dewey Opposes Blanket Freight Increase

369.26   railway] railways ("Text of Railroads' Petition," 24.1.139)
369.34   5.90] 5.70 (ICC, *Statistics of Railways*, xv.18)
371.9–10   the added] this added (Lane, "In Re Investigation,"
343.27)

Prosperity Dependent on Building from Bottom Up

383.17–18   operations. [¶] The] operations. [. . .] The (Hughes,
"Point of View," 19.2.54–65)
383.23–24   declines. [¶] In] declines [. . .] In (Hughes, "Point of
View," 19.2.74–83)

Joint Committee on Unemployment Demands Congress Act

390.5   which] that (Mills, "Text of Address," 17.4.21)

Statements to the Conference on Curriculum for the College of Liberal Arts

422.34   desirable] most desirable ("Educators Divided," 12.2.72)
422.35   American colleges] colleges ("Educators Divided,"
12.2.72–73)
422.35   have] should have ("Educators Divided," 12.2.73)
422.35   curricula] curriculum ("Educators Divided," 12.2.73–74)

Checklist of Dewey's References

This section gives full publication information for each work cited by Dewey. Books in Dewey's personal library (John Dewey Papers, Special Collections, Morris Library, Southern Illinois University at Carbondale) have been listed whenever possible. When Dewey gave page numbers for a reference, the edition has been identified by locating the citation; for other references, the edition listed here is his most likely source by reason of place or date of publication, general accessibility during the period, or evidence from correspondence and other materials.

Adams, James Truslow. *The Epic of America*. Boston: Little, Brown and Co., 1931.

Alexander, F. Matthias. *Constructive Conscious Control of the Individual*. Introduction by John Dewey. New York: E. P. Dutton and Co., 1923.

Ann Arbor Railroad Company et al. *v.* United States et al. *United States Reports* 281 (1930): 658–99.

"A Bad Omen for Railroad Consolidation." *New Republic* 65 (4 February 1931): 313–14.

Barnes, Roswell P. *Militarizing Our Youth: The Significance of the Reserve Officers' Training Corps in Our Schools and Colleges*. New York: Committee on Militarism in Education, 1927.

Bates, Henry M. "Committee Reports: Committee A, Academic Freedom and Tenure." *Bulletin of the American Association of University Professors* 9 (February 1923): 12–13.

Bernard, Luther Lee. *Instinct: A Study in Social Psychology*. New York: Henry Holt and Co., 1924.

"Big Rise in 9 Years in National Income." *New York Times*, 16 December 1929, p. 47.

Boas, Franz. *Anthropology and Modern Life*. New York: W. W. Norton and Co., 1928.

———. *The Mind of Primitive Man*. New York: Macmillan Co., 1911.

Borah, William E. "Borah Belittles Third-Party Move." *New York Times*, 29 December 1930, pp. 1–2.

————. "Where Would the Money Go?" *Collier's* 88 (18 July 1931): 12–13, 39.

Briand, Aristide. "'Peace Is Proclaimed' in the Treaty, Briand Tells the Nations." *New York Times*, 28 August 1928, p. 5.

Buell, Raymond Leslie. "Are Sanctions Necessary to International Organization? Yes." In *Are Sanctions Necessary to International Organization?* Foreign Policy Association Pamphlet no. 82–83. New York: Foreign Policy Association, 1932. [*The Later Works of John Dewey, 1925–1953*, edited by Jo Ann Boydston, 6 : 450–84. Carbondale and Edwardsville: Southern Illinois University Press, 1985.]

Carlyle, R. W., and Carlyle, A. J. *A History of Mediaeval Political Theory in the West*. 5 vols. Edinburgh: William Blackwood and Sons, 1903–28.

"The Children's Charter." In *White House Conference on Child Health and Protection*, pp. 45–48. New York: Century Co., 1931.

Cohen, Morris R. *Reason and Nature: An Essay on the Meaning of Scientific Method*. New York: Harcourt, Brace and Co., 1931.

————. "Reason, Nature and Professor Dewey." *New Republic* 67 (17 June 1931): 126–27. [*Later Works* 6 : 488–91.]

Cooley, Charles Horton. *Human Nature and the Social Order*. Rev. ed. New York: Charles Scribner's Sons, 1922.

Counts, George S. *The Soviet Challenge to America*. New York: John Day Co., 1931.

"The Covenant of the League." *League of Nations Official Journal* 1 (February 1920): 3–12.

Dewey, John. *Experience and Nature*. Chicago: Open Court Publishing Co., 1925. [*Later Works* 1.]

————. *Human Nature and Conduct: An Introduction to Social Psychology*. New York: Henry Holt and Co., 1922. [*The Middle Works of John Dewey, 1899–1924*, edited by Jo Ann Boydston, vol. 14. Carbondale and Edwardsville: Southern Illinois University Press, 1983.]

————. "Affective Thought." In his *Philosophy and Civilization*, pp. 117–25. New York: Minton, Balch and Co., 1931. [*Later Works* 2 : 104–10.]

————. "Dewey Asks Norris to Lead New Party; Lucas Row Is Cited." *New York Times*, 26 December 1930, pp. 1–2. [*Later Works* 5 : 444–46.]

————. Introduction to *Constructive Conscious Control of the Individual*, by F. Matthias Alexander, pp. xxi–xxxiii. New York: E. P. Dutton and Co., 1923. [*Middle Works* 15 : 308–15.]

————. "'The Irrepressible Conflict.'" *News Bulletin of the League for Independent Political Action* 1 (January 1931): 4–5. [*Later Works* 6 : 149–52.]

————. "$100,000,000 Relief Urged on President." *New York Times*, 18 February 1931, p. 14.

————. "Qualitative Thought." In his *Philosophy and Civilization*, pp. 93–116. New York: Minton, Balch and Co., 1931. [*Later Works* 5:243–62.]

Eddy, Sherwood. *The Challenge of Russia*. New York: Farrar and Rinehart, 1931.

"Educators Divided on 'Real University.'" *New York Times*, 19 January 1931, p. 12.

"Factory Output Increased in 1929." *New York Times*, 8 November 1930, p. 31.

Folks, Homer. "Socially Handicapped—Dependency and Neglect." In *White House Conference on Child Health and Protection*, pp. 319–40. New York: Century Co., 1931.

Gauss, Christian. *Life in College*. New York: Charles Scribner's Sons, 1931.

Hallis, Frederick. *Corporate Personality: A Study in Jurisprudence*. London: Oxford University Press, 1930.

Hans, Nicholas, and Hessen, Sergei. *Educational Policy in Soviet Russia*. London: P. S. King and Son, 1930.

Haynes, Fred E. *Social Politics in the United States*. Boston and New York: Houghton Mifflin Co., 1924.

Heard, Gerald. *The Emergence of Man*. New York: Harcourt, Brace and Co., 1932.

Hessen, Sergei, and Hans, Nicholas. *Educational Policy in Soviet Russia*. London: P. S. King and Son, 1930.

Hocking, William Ernest. *Human Nature and Its Remaking*. 2d ed. New Haven: Yale University Press, 1923.

Hoover, Herbert. "Hoover with Vigor Bars Extra Session." *New York Times*, 23 May 1931, p. 1.

————. "Text of President Hoover's Indianapolis Address." *New York Times*, 16 June 1931, p. 2.

Hughes, C. F. "The Merchant's Point of View." *New York Times*, 20 March 1932, sec. 2, p. 19.

Huxley, Julian S.; Wells, H. G.; and Wells, G. P. *The Science of Life*. 2 vols. Garden City, N.Y.: Doubleday, Doran and Co., 1931.

Interstate Commerce Commission. *Forty-Third Annual Report of the Statistics of Railways in the United States for the Year Ended December 31, 1929*. Washington, D.C.: Government Printing Office, 1930.

Josey, Charles Conant. *The Role of Instinct in Social Philosophy*. New York: Chauncey Holt Co., 1921.

Klein, Julius. "Asks Radio to Lead Way to Prosperity." *New York Times*, 10 June 1931, p. 34.

———. "Secretary Klein's Reply to Prof. Dewey." *People's Lobby Bulletin* 1 (August 1931): 3–4. [*Later Works* 6:485–87.]

La Follette, Robert M. "La Follette's Platform." *New York Times*, 6 July 1924, p. 5.

Lane, Franklin K. "In Re Investigation of Advances in Rates by Carriers in Western Trunk Line, Trans-Missouri, and Illinois Freight Committee Territories." *Interstate Commerce Commission Reports* 20 (1911): 307–99.

Levinson, Salmon O. "Disarmament, Manchuria and the Pact." *Christian Century* 49 (February 1932): 149–50.

Lippmann, Walter. "The Search for Security." *New York World*, 3 December 1927, p. 10.

McCormick, Anne O'Hare. "Foggy Days under the Big Dome." *New York Times Magazine*, 15 February 1931, pp. 1–2, 22.

McVey, Frank L. "The Populist Movement." *Economic Studies* 1 (August 1896): 131–209.

Malinowski, Bronislaw. "The Problem of Meaning in Primitive Languages." In *The Meaning of Meaning: A Study of the Influence of Language upon Thought and of the Science of Symbolism*, by C. K. Ogden and I. A. Richards, pp. 451–510. New York: Harcourt, Brace and Co., 1923.

Meiklejohn, Alexander. *The Experimental College*. New York: Harper and Bros., 1932.

Mendelssohn, Frans von. "Mendelssohn Asks World Cooperation." *New York Times*, 10 May 1931, pp. 1, 29.

Merriam, Charles Edward. *The Making of Citizens: A Comparative Study of Methods of Civic Training*. Chicago: University of Chicago Press, 1931.

Mills, Ogden L. "Text of Mills's Address at Associated Press Luncheon." *New York Times*, 26 April 1932, p. 17.

Mitchell, Wesley C. "Human Behavior and Economics: A Survey of Recent Literature." *Quarterly Journal of Economics* 29 (1914–15): 1–47.

Morgan, Arthur Ernest. "The Curriculum for the College of Liberal Arts." *Rollins College Bulletin* 26 (February 1931): 4–14.

New York Times. "La Follette's Platform," 6 July 1924, p. 5.

———. "'Peace Is Proclaimed' in the Treaty, Briand Tells the Nations," 28 August 1928, p. 5.

———. "Big Rise in 9 Years in National Income," 16 December 1929, p. 47.

———. "Factory Output Increased in 1929," 8 November 1930, p. 31.

———. "Dewey Asks Norris to Lead New Party; Lucas Row Is Cited," 26 December 1930, pp. 1–2. [*Later Works* 5:444–46.]

———. "Borah Belittles Third-Party Move," 29 December 1930, pp. 1–2.

———. "Statistics on Income Tax Payments Made by the Nation in Record Year of 1928," 29 December 1930, p. 30.

———. "Educators Divided on 'Real University,'" 19 January 1931, p. 12.

———. "Foggy Days under the Big Dome," 15 February 1931, sec. 5, pp. 1–2, 22.

———. "$100,000,000 Relief Urged on President," 18 February 1931, p. 14.

———. "Progressives Call Parley on Program," 3 March 1931, pp. 1, 24.

———. "Mendelssohn Asks World Cooperation," 10 May 1931, pp. 1, 29.

———. "Hoover with Vigor Bars Extra Session," 23 May 1931, p. 1.

———. "Asks Radio to Lead Way to Prosperity," 10 June 1931, p. 34.

———. "Text of President Hoover's Indianapolis Address," 16 June 1931, p. 2.

———. "Text of Railroads' Petition for Freight Rate Increase," 18 June 1931, p. 24.

———. "Text of Secretary Stimson's Note," 8 January 1932, p. 1.

———. "School Histories Declared Biased," 21 February 1932, sec. 2, p. 13.

———. "Text of Stimson's Letter on Our Policy in China," 25 February 1932, p. 8.

———. "The Merchant's Point of View," 20 March 1932, sec. 2, p. 19.

———. "Text of Mills's Address at Associated Press Luncheon," 26 April 1932, p. 17.

Nock, Albert Jay. *The Theory of Education in the United States.* New York: Harcourt, Brace and Co., 1932.

Ogburn, William Fielding. *Social Change with Respect to Culture and Original Nature.* New York: B. W. Huebsch, 1922.

"$100,000,000 Relief Urged on President," *New York Times,* 18 February 1931, p. 14.

"The Outlawry of War." *Round Table* (London), no. 71 (June 1928): 455–76.

Palmer, George Herbert. *The Autobiography of a Philosopher.* Boston and New York: Houghton Mifflin Co., 1930.

Park, Robert E. "Human Nature, Attitudes, and the Mores." In L. L. Bernard et al., *Social Attitudes,* edited by Kimball Young, pp. 17–45. New York: Henry Holt and Co., 1913.

Peirce, Charles S. *Principles of Philosophy.* Vol. 1 of *Collected Papers of Charles Sanders Peirce,* edited by Charles Hartshorne and Paul Weiss. Cambridge, Mass.: Harvard University Press, 1931.

Perry, Ralph Barton. *A Defence of Philosophy*. Cambridge, Mass.: Harvard University Press, 1931.

"Platform and Program of the League for Independent Political Action." *News Bulletin of the League for Independent Political Action* 1 (September–October 1932): 4.

"Proceedings, Curriculum Conference." 3 vols. Rollins College, Winter Park, Florida, January 19–24, 1931. Rollins Archives, Rollins College, Winter Park, Fla. Photocopy.

"Progressives Call Parley on Program." *New York Times*, 3 March 1931, pp. 1, 24.

"Restriction of Political Activity of Professors." *Bulletin of the American Association of University Professors* 17 (November 1931): 572–73.

Santayana, George. *The Genteel Tradition at Bay*. New York: Charles Scribner's Sons, 1931.

"School Histories Declared Biased." *New York Times*, 21 February 1932, sec. 2, p. 13.

"Statistics on Income Tax Payments Made by the Nation in Record Year of 1928." *New York Times*, 29 December 1930, p. 30.

Stimson, Henry Lewis. "Text of Secretary Stimson's Note." *New York Times*, 8 January 1932, p. 1.

———. "Text of Stimson's Letter on Our Policy in China." *New York Times*, 25 February 1932, p. 8.

Tate, Allen. "The Aesthetic Emotion as Useful." *This Quarter* 5 (December 1932): 292–303. [*Later Works* 6: 492–501.]

Tawney, Richard Henry. *The Acquisitive Society*. New York: Harcourt, Brace and Howe, 1920.

"Text of Railroads' Petition for Freight Rate Increase." *New York Times*, 18 June 1931, p. 24.

"A Third Party Platform." *New Republic* 69 (10 February 1932): 335–36.

Thorndike, Edward Lee. *Educational Psychology*. Vol. 1, *The Original Nature of Man*. New York: Teachers College, Columbia University, 1913.

U.S. Congress. House. War Policies Commission. *Report of the War Policies Commission Created by Public Resolution No. 98, 71st Congress, Approved June 27, 1930*. 72d Cong., 1st sess., 1931. H. Doc. 163. Serial 9538.

"University of Mississippi, Tenure Conditions." *Bulletin of the American Association of University Professors* 16 (December 1930): 614–15.

Veblen, Thorstein. *The Instinct of Workmanship, and the State of the Industrial Arts*. New York: Macmillan Co., 1914.

———. "The Preconceptions of Economic Science." In his *The Place of*

Science in Modern Civilisation and Other Essays, pp. 82–179. New York: B. W. Huebsch, 1919.

Wallas, Graham. *The Great Society: A Psychological Analysis*. London: Macmillan and Co., 1914.

———. *Human Nature in Politics*. 3d ed. London: Constable and Co., 1914.

———. *Our Social Heritage*. New Haven: Yale University Press, 1921.

Ward, Lester F. *Applied Sociology: A Treatise on the Conscious Improvement of Society by Society*. Boston: Ginn and Co., 1906.

———. *Glimpses of the Cosmos*. 6 vols. New York: G. P. Putnam's Sons, 1913–18.

Wells, H. G.; Huxley, Julian S.; and Wells, G. P. *The Science of Life*. 2 vols. Garden City, N.Y.: Doubleday, Doran and Co., 1931.

West, James E. "Youth Outside of Home and School." In *White House Conference on Child Health and Protection*, pp. 247–72. New York: Century Co., 1931.

White, William Chapman. *These Russians*. New York: Charles Scribner's Sons, 1931.

Wither, George. "The Manly Heart." In *Poetry and Drama*, edited by Ernest Rhys, p. 91. New York: E. P. Dutton and Co., 1906.

Woody, Thomas. *New Minds: New Men? The Emergence of the Soviet Citizen*. New York: Macmillan Co., 1932.

Index

The Collected Works of John Dewey, 1882–1953

The Later Works, 1925–1953